THE WORLD OF RURAL DISSENTERS, 1520–1725

There has been dispute amongst social historians about whether only the more prosperous in village society were involved in religious practice. A group of historians working under Dr Spufford's direction have produced a factual solution to this dispute by examining the taxation records of large groups of dissenters and churchwardens, and have established that both late Lollard and post-Restoration dissenting belief crossed the whole taxable spectrum. We can no longer speak of religion as being the prerogative of either 'weavers and threshers' or, on the other hand, of village elites. The group also examined the idea that dissent descended in families, and concluded that this was not only true but that such families were the least mobile population group so far examined in early modern England – probably because they were closely knit and tolerated in their communities.

The cause of the apparent correlation of 'dissenting areas' and areas of early by-employment was also questioned. The group concludes that travelling merchants and carriers on the road network carried with them radical ideas and dissenting print, the content of which is examined, as well as goods. In her own substantial chapter Dr Spufford draws together the pieces of the huge mosaic constructed by her team of contributors, adds radical ideas of her own, and disagrees with much of the prevailing wisdom on the function of religion in the late seventeenth century. Professor Patrick Collinson has contributed a critical conclusion to the volume.

This is a book which breaks new ground, and which offers much original material for ecclesiastical, cultural, demographic, and economic historians of the period. As such it is without rival.

The Puritan Meeting, by Egbert van Heemskerck, painted in England, 1678

THE
WORLD OF RURAL
DISSENTERS,
1520–1725

EDITED BY
MARGARET SPUFFORD

Roehampton Institute

Published by the Press Syndicate of the University of Cambridge
The Pitt Building, Trumpington Street, Cambridge CB2 1RP
40 West 20th Street, New York, NY 10011–4211, USA
10 Stamford Road, Oakleigh, Melbourne 3166, Australia

© Cambridge University Press 1995

First published 1995

Printed in Great Britain at the University Press, Cambridge

A catalogue record for this book is available from the British Library

Library of Congress cataloguing in publication data

The world of rural dissenters, 1520–1725/edited
by Margaret Spufford.   p.   cm.
Includes bibliographical references.
ISBN 0 521 41061 4
1. Dissenters, Religious – England – History – 16th century.
2. Dissenters, Religious – England – History – 17th century.
3. Dissenters, Religious – England – History – 18th century.
4. England – Church history – 16th century.
5. England – Church history – 17th century.
6. England – Church history – 18th century.
7. England – Rural conditions. I. Spufford, Margaret.
BX5203.2.W67 1994
280.4' 0942' 091734–dc20   93–22979CIP

IBSN 0 521 41061 4 hardback

Contents

Plates

Maps

Tables

Notes on contributors

DR ERIC JOSEF CARLSON is an Associate Professor at Gustavus Adolphus College, St Peter, Minnesota. Dr Carlson works on the medieval and early modern canon law of betrothal and marriage, and its practical application in custom and reality. He has written *Marriage and the English Reformation* (Oxford, 1994).

PROFESSOR PATRICK COLLINSON, FBA, is Regius Professor of History in the University of Cambridge, and the outstanding authority on the ecclesiastical history of the period covered by this book.

MRS NESTA EVANS has taught local history in Suffolk for the Cambridge University Board of Continuing Education for nearly twenty years, and has held several research posts. She is the author of *The East Anglian Linen Industry, 1550–1850* (Aldershot, 1985). She has also edited two volumes of abstracts of Suffolk wills, and has written several articles. She is the Honorary General Editor of the British Record Society.

DR MICHAEL FREARSON has completed a thesis on 'The English Corantos of the 1620s' (Cambridge, PhD, 1994) which is to appear (Cambridge, 1995) in the History of the Book series, ed. Dr David McKitterick. He has made an extensive study of road communications.

DR CHRISTOPHER MARSH is Lecturer in Modern History, Queen's University, Belfast. Dr Marsh is the author of *The Family of Love in English Society, 1550–1630* (Cambridge, 1994).

DR DEREK PLUMB is Head of History at Brentwood School. He has published 'The Social and Economic Spread of Rural Lollardy: A Reappraisal', in W.J. Sheils and Diana Wood (eds.), *Voluntary Religion*, Studies in Church History, 23 (Oxford, 1986), and is now working on a more detailed study of the social standing of Lollards in Hughenden and its neighbouring parishes, with the help of grants from the British Academy and the Scoulardi Foundation.

PROFESSOR MARGARET SPUFFORD, Roehampton Institute, London. She was supported by a Senior Research Fellowship from the Marc Fitch Fund to work on this book, and is now Research Professor at the Roehampton Institute. She is the author of *Contrasting Communities*

(Cambridge, 1974), *Small Books and Pleasant Histories* (London, 1981, p/b Cambridge, 1985), *The Great Reclothing of Rural England* (London, 1984), and *Celebration* (London, 1989; reprinted 1991; translated as *Kostbaarder dan het Leven* (Tielt, 1994) French translation in progress) (Angel Non-Fiction prizewinner, 1989).

DR PETER SPUFFORD is Reader in Economic History, and Fellow of Queens' College, Cambridge. He works on medieval and early modern European money, banking, and trade, and also has an interest in population mobility.

DR BILL STEVENSON is Head of History at the Perse School for Boys, Cambridge. He is also Course Director in Tudor History at the Board of Continuing Education, and a Further Education Lecturer at Hitchin College. He is continuing work on post-Restoration dissenters with a view to a book.

DR TESSA WATT is the author of *Cheap Print and Popular Piety, 1550–1640* (Cambridge, 1991). She has won the Prince Consort Prize and Seeley Medal, the Royal Historical Whitfield Prize for the best first book on England and Wales by an author under the age of forty, and the Nancy Roelke Prize given by the Conference of Sixteenth Century Studies. She works for the BBC.

Preface

A preface is always, properly, a list of debts: but these are debts I am
truly grateful to acknowledge.

This will be the second time I have thanked the Trustees of the Marc
Fitch Fund for their support. This time, I would like to make the thanks
as warm as those the Fund deserves from me. It first came to my rescue
in 1978, when the Economic and Social Research Council decided that
it could not support an application for an exploration of seventeenth-
century chapbooks, on the grounds that the project was not within the
bounds of social history. I still have the letter. Thanks to the Marc Fitch
Fund, *Small Books and Pleasant Histories* was nonetheless written.

I evolved the scheme for the present book in 1985. There was an
historical debate going on over whether 'godliness' was principally the
perquisite of the prosperous in village society, the 'chiefer sort' of inhabitant. I took the view that it was not economically determined in this
way. It seemed to me, however, that we needed far more evidence from
cross-sections of different types of sectarian, and if possible, conformist,
belief to resolve the matter. We simply lacked evidence. I wanted to find
out the 'facts', if I could, whichever view they supported. I also wanted to
examine the effect cheap print and its distribution had on these religious
opinions, if any. The inquiry was far too wide for me alone, and I decided
to try and assemble a group of research students, each interested in a
different bit of the project, but working, to some extent, together. I
wanted to know if historians could work in teams a little more, somewhat
after the manner of scientists. Five doctoral theses have gone into the
making of this book and five more have contributed material. Each was,
and is, worthy to stand alone, but together they present pieces of a massive mosaic picture which I have tried to fit together to make an overall
view in the 'Introduction'. The credit of the work obviously goes to those
who did it.

It is invidious to single out the particular academic, or personal, help
of any of my research students because they have all helped. Yet special
mention should be made of Mathew Storey and Helen Weinstein, who

do not appear in the volume, but both made a substantial contribution to it, one discussing theology, the other basic education, and providing us with Plates 1 and 6. I would also like to mention especially the labour of Mrs Nesta Evans, who has been far more than a 'research assistant' on the project. Bill Sharman helped, too.

When the group was well embarked in this scheme, our daughter became very ill. The University of Cambridge was then paying an honorific sum, still basically of seven and a half guineas a term per head, rounded up on decimalization without indexing for inflation, to those who taught its research students. It has been, and is, very difficult for the University to overhaul systems embedded in historical precedent. I was not eligible for an Academy replacement salary in 1988, since I had no salary to replace. Without part-time help to nurse our daughter, I was going to have to give up supervising. In this very awkward situation, the Trustees of the Marc Fitch Fund intervened and provided me with the part-time salary I did not have, and the research assistant I needed, so that I could continue to supervise, virtually free of charge, research students at the University of Cambridge working on their theses, and also contribute my own part to the joint enterprise. This book therefore owes its whole being to the Trustees of the Marc Fitch Fund's imaginative generosity, and to its Secretary's, Roy Stephens, successful efforts to find the money. I also owe a debt of gratitude to the Pilgrim Trust, and the Twenty-Seven Foundation, which generously helped him. The Cranmer Fund also made a grant. Any thanks I can give to the Fitch Fund's Trustees are inadequate. The book has been finished under the hospitable roof of the Netherlands Institute for Advanced Studies.

I would also like to record my thanks, yet again, to Dr Dorothy Owen, who twenty years ago drew my attention to the case of the itinerant seller of 'lytle books' in Balsham in 1578. She thus started off a whole set of thought processes, which have acted like yeast, and first gave rise to *Small Books and Pleasant Histories*, then *The Great Reclothing of Rural England*. This train of thought now culminates in Helen Weinstein's, and Tessa Watt's work. The first fruits of the former are now appearing as facsimiles of *The Pepys Ballads*, the latter came out as *Cheap Print and Popular Piety, 1550–1640* (Cambridge, 1991). How can the importance of the extra care taken by really major archival scholars be better illustrated?

In this particular volume, amongst archivists we have been much helped by the staff of the Buckinghamshire Record Office and by the County Archivist, Mr Hugh Hanley, who not only assisted by answering our queries, but also provided a set of his own unpublished maps of voters from the Poll Book of 1685. Christopher Johnson at the Lincoln Record Office has also been particularly helpful. Christopher Stell of the Royal Commission on Historical Monuments has been generous with information, and his own photograph of the Friends' meeting-house in Amersham.

There are many historians whom I would like to thank for advice, time, fruitful questions or comments, and their gifts of materials. Among them are Paul Slack and Barry Reay. The latter said, ruefully, and truthfully, 'you and I will never agree' but still took time to write a long and encouraging letter of very useful comments. Keith Snell and Paul Ell produced invaluable material and advice from the Department of English Local History at Leicester. So did David Hey, and both Richard McKinley and David Postles, who gave us expert help with surnames, which were crucial evidence for us. Ted Collins, John Broad, and Richard Hoyle all made helpful suggestions at a seminar in Oxford, and Brian Outhwaite at a seminar in Cambridge. Richard Wall and Kevin Schürer of the Cambridge Group helped us with vital advice on how to compare our Lollard group in the Chilterns with a control group of the prosperous, as well as society at large. Adam Fox has made a major contribution, both from his own work and contemporary seventeenth-century sources I had not found. Dr John Craig supplied the list of places when William Tracy's will preamble was found. Michael Frearson supplied the indispensable base of the English road network c. 1600, for Map 1. At absolutely the last minute, Mrs Janet Gyford wrote to me with an inquiry about the proper interpretation of the will preambles of the Raven family of Witham. She thereby supplied me, entirely fortuitously, with another link making a chain in an early sixteenth-century Lollard family which turned to puritan church office holding by the end of the century. Mrs Jill Leech sent us the *Diary* of Elizabeth Bury, and so linked the late Familists with post-Restoration nonconformists for us. To her, too, I am deeply grateful. Serendipity is not a methodology, but is nonetheless extremely useful.

Amongst academics, above all, I would like to thank Professor Patrick Collinson and Dr Keith Wrightson. Professor Collinson has encouraged this project throughout, and commented most constructively and helpfully on the draft 'Introduction', although not necessarily associating himself with the final views, as will appear from his own critical essay (Chapter 10) which I am delighted to include in the work. I naturally dissent, myself, from some of Professor Collinson's views, especially since, as he himself points out, Buckinghamshire was so noticeably absent from the puritan manuscript collections like 'The Seconde Parte of a Register', which forcibly suggests to me that 'our' Lollards had not formed the spring from which an orthodox puritan mainstream arose. Nor do I believe 'environment, not tradition, was all'. Had it been so, what accounts for the remarkable fact that 81 per cent of those leaving Lollard surnames reoccurred as Quakers or Baptists five generations later, in the same area, while only 29 per cent of the population at large remained static in this way? All these people lived in exactly the same environment. But Professor Collinson's contribution adds immeasurably to the book, giving as it does an internal critique, handily contained within the same covers, so that students may make up their own minds. I am very grateful to him.

Dr Wrightson supported the idea for the book, although he and I differed on the initial interpretation of the partial evidence I was about to set out to discover more fully. By doing so, he set an example of generosity and integrity in scholarship which I found, and find, awe-inspiring in its approach to the ideal. Dr Margaret Aston has encouraged me in a much needed, and much appreciated way throughout, and steered me through what for me were the totally uncharted seas of later Lollardy. Professor Alan Everitt has likewise spent much time commenting on my draft, and pulling me off reefs of ignorance, as I moved dangerously towards the equally unknown waters of the eighteenth century. He has also most forcibly pointed out to me that 'the great days of dissent still lay, in numerical terms, well in the future in 1700, and no one could have predicted its expansion'. Despite his understandable 'regret that so many historians lock themselves into the seventeenth century, and do not see beyond 1700', I feel justifiably incompetent to do anything but remain safely the far side of that magic date. I should, however, emphasize that the 'Introduction' to this volume only appears to concentrate on dissenters because the conformists of conviction, as ever, remain more elusive. The William Coes of seventeenth-century England (pp. 96–7) were much more common, but much less easy to trace. I am exceedingly glad we have at least been able to find something on Calvinists of conviction amongst the 'humble sort'. We demonstrate that they, too, in the diocese of Ely, cross the whole social spectrum (Table 1). The concentration on dissent is no way intended to imply that conformists were less convinced, or, indeed, anything but very much more numerous. I agree with Professor Collinson, who wrote in the Preface to *Godly People* in 1983:

> Now at last we may discover that the bulk of our Elizabethan and Jacobean ancestors were neither spiritual supermen nor pagan folklorists but humdrum, conventional christian believers of the kind we encounter two centuries later in the novels of Eliot and Trollope: as careful in the practice of their religion as in the drafting of a will or the making of a marriage contract. I suppose that we always knew that but thirsted for a little excitement.

I very much regret that pressure of work prevented Dr Judith Maltby contributing the chapter on the social and economic spectrum of conformists in favour of the prayer book in Cheshire in the 1630s, which, in the editor's eyes, would have provided some very necessary balance; it will be found in her forthcoming volume, *Prayer Book and People: Religious Conformity before the Civil War* (Cambridge) and should be taken into account when reading this volume.

Without the patience of William Davies as my editor at the Cambridge University Press and Linda Randall as my copyeditor, it is difficult to know how such a disorganized author could survive, never mind produce anything. I have only come to value the editorial and distribution networks of the Press as fully as I should recently, after experiencing something of commercial publishing. Mrs Anne Waites, who typed my manuscript with great skill and patience, and Anne Simpson and Pilar van Breda of the Fellows Support Group at NIAS Institute, made it possible to get the work to the Press. Lady Chadwick, with the utmost generosity, read my proofs.

Since I wrote *Celebration* I have sometimes felt I was leading a double life which verged on schizophrenia. In this situation, it has given me profound and ironic pleasure to find myself reading the typescript of the *Diary* of the tormented, barely conforming cleric Isaac Archer (to appear as *Suffolk Record Society*, 36 (1994), ed. Mathew Storey), re-reading *Religion and the Decline of Magic*, and revising the third and fourth parts of the 'Introduction' to this book, all in the medieval priest's room at St Mary's Abbey, West Malling. My imagination fused in the attempt to reconstruct what the various authors of these works, and, indeed, my precursors in the room, would feel about this exercise. However, I record my deep gratitude to my Community for its continued loving hospitality with no irony at all.

I also want to thank my husband. My work would be impossible without his continuous and constant support, and the value he places on it.

Lastly, if it is permitted for an editor to dedicate a volume, I want to dedicate this one to all the members of the group who nicknamed themselves 'the Spuffordians', both those who appear here as authors, and those who do not. I have rarely had such pleasure as in teaching, and being taught by them, and watching their work develop and take off individually. I suspect that to watch research students soar away, each into a different empyrean, is the ultimate academic pleasure, along with the specific pleasure, for the historian, of finding a new and exciting document. I give them all my thanks, along with this volume, which they themselves made.

MARGARET SPUFFORD
Annunciation 1993, NIAS, Wassenaar
Epiphany 1994, The Roehampton Institute, London

Acknowledgements

The Cambridge University Press and the Editor would like to thank the National Trust for permission to reproduce *The Puritan Meeting* at Saltram Park, the Fitzwilliam Museum for *The Singing Peasants*, the Berkshire Record Office for the probate inventory of Robert and Joan Livord, and Christopher Marsh and Mr Christopher Stell for their own photographs of the Balsham grave, and Joseph Winch's cottage at Amersham. They would also like to thank Helen Weinstein for finding the hornbook in the Folger Library and the engraving of the Italian pedlar with books and hornbooks in the Houghton Library, as well as those institutions for permission to reproduce these works.

Abbreviations

Arber	Edward Arber (ed.), *A Transcript of the Registers of the Company of Stationers of London 1554–1640*, 5 vols. (London, 1875–94).
Berks. RO	Berkshire Record Office
BL	British Library
Bucks. RO	Buckinghamshire Record Office
Cambs. RO	Cambridgeshire Record Office
CUL	Cambridge University Library
DNB	*Dictionary of National Biography*
EDR	Ely Diocesan Records, CUL
Ely CC	Ely Consistory Court, Cambs. RO
EPR	Ely Probate Records, Cambs. RO
Essex RO	Essex Record Office
Eyre	G.E.B. Eyre (ed.), *A Transcript of the Registers of the Worshipful Company of Stationers 1640–1708*, 3 vols. (London, 1913–14)
FL	Friends Library
Foxe	John Foxe, *Actes and Monuments*, ed. Rev. Stephen R. Cattley, 8 vols. (London, 1837–41)
Glos. RO	Gloucestershire Record Office
GLRO	Greater London Record Office
Herts. RO	Hertfordshire Record Office
Hunts. RO	Huntingdonshire Record Office
Lincs. RO	Lincolnshire Record Office
LP	*Letters and Papers of Henry VIII*
PCC	Prerogative Court of Canterbury
PRO	Public Record Office
STC	*A Short Title Catalogue of Books Printed in England, Scotland and Ireland and of English Books Printed Abroad 1475–1640*, ed. W.A. Jackson, G.R. Redgrave, and K.F. Pantzer, 3 vols. (London, 1976–91).
Suff. RO	Suffolk Record Office

VCH	Victoria County History
WAM	Westminster Abbey Muniments
WR	Will Register

CHAPTER 1

The importance of religion in the sixteenth and seventeenth centuries

MARGARET SPUFFORD

The social and economic spectrum of religious belief

Early modern historians are deeply divided, or at least uncertain, about the importance of religion to sixteenth- and seventeenth-century society. 'It is not clear', Professor Collinson has written, 'where this crucial period of religious change stands in the supposedly secular degeneration from a high level of religious practice in the Middle Ages to the socially circum-scribed place occupied by institutionalised religion in modern society. When did traditional Christian society come to an end, or show signs of disintegration?'[1]

The sources available may not ever permit of a clear answer, but this introductory essay will try to make a contribution to the subject. First, we must investigate and discard the distinction usually made between the self-styled 'godly' and the multitude.

'The Godly and the Multitude in Stuart England' is the title of a splendid paper written in 1986 by Dr Eamon Duffy and I cannot do better than to quote part of his Introduction.

> It is well on the way to being an axiom that the poor in early modern England were hostile, or resistant, or at best indifferent to protestant Christianity. Protestantism, runs the axiom, being a religion of the book, was the preserve of the literate. It flourished amongst townsmen and prospering 'rural elites'. It was an instrument of social control, a form of moral, ideological and economic discipline. The world of minister and godly book, of Sabbath observance, sermon-gadding and repeti-tion, sobriety, chastity, respectability and thrift, stood over against the world of the alehouse and the cunning-man, of ballad and broadside, may-poles and dancing, and sunday-sports, tabling and dicing, bowling and cards, cakes and ale and getting wenches with child. This was the world of disorder and social inversion, in which magic and survivals of the old religion provided the supernatural vehicle for the repudiation

---

[1] Patrick Collinson, *The Religion of Protestants: The Church in English Society, 1559–1625* (Oxford, 1982, p/b 1984), p. 198.

of law and order and social discipline, which the middling and better
sorts sought to impose on the 'rabble that cannot read'.[2]

Historians are engaged in a lively debate, springing out of the axiom of
which Dr Duffy speaks, about whether seventeenth-century society was
increasingly polarized.[3] If the poor were indeed hostile, resistant, or indifferent to protestant Christianity, the tension between 'rural elites', 'godly'
townsmen, and the rest, cannot but have been heavily accentuated. If,
on the other hand, we can demonstrate that some knowledge of, or even
adherence to, protestant religious beliefs, whether radical or orthodox,
spread right across many layers of the better, middling and even worse
sorts of Tudor and Stuart England, we will be better able to judge the
reality of this particular tension, or whether it is mainly an historical
construct, taken wholesale from the minds and opinions of the late six-
teenth- and seventeenth-century 'godly' themselves, and extrapolated
from their mouths by contemporary historians to cover the whole of
society.

As well as Dr Duffy's paper, we also have Professor Collinson's very
balanced consideration and summary of our knowledge of 'popular and
unpopular religion'[4] which suggests, entirely rightly, that

> The absence of reliable data [on religious practice] has understandably
> resulted in historians finding what they have been disposed to find. On
> the one hand we have Peter Laslett's extraordinary statement that 'all
> our ancestors were literal christian believers all of the time', which is
> undermined by evidence cited on almost the same page of *The World
> We Have Lost*,[5] and Margaret Spufford's more cautious persuasion,

---

[2] *Seventeenth Century Journal*, 1, no. 1 (1986), pp. 31–49. I quote p. 31 here. It is a matter
of great regret to me that Dr Duffy's book on popular religion, *The Stripping of the
Altars: Traditional Religion in England, 1400–1580* (Yale, 1992), was in press while I wrote
this.

[3] A.J. Fletcher and J. Stevenson (eds.), *Order and Disorder in Early Modern England*
(Cambridge, 1985, p/b 1987), pp. 1–15; Keith Wrightson, *English Society, 1580–1680*
(London, 1982), pp. 140–8, 220–1; and Keith Wrightson and David Levine, *Poverty
and Piety in an English Village: Terling, 1525–1700* (New York and London, 1979), p. 162;
Martin Ingram, 'Ridings, Rough Music and the "Reform of Popular Culture" in Early
Modern England', *Past and Present*, 105 (Nov. 1984), pp. 79–113; *The Religion of Protestants*,
Collinson, p. 194. The point is discussed many times in Barry Reay (ed.), *Popular
Culture in Seventeenth-Century England* (London, 1985). I have not attempted to footnote
individual agreements and disagreements with this volume here. The primary disagreements are probably that I emphasize the closely intertwined nature of oral and
literate culture born of reading skills in the seventeenth century much more, pay
much more attention to the spread of orthodox and unorthodox doctrinal belief
amongst even the 'meaner' sort of people, whilst in no way dismissing folk religion,
and doubt the development of great social polarity in the seventeenth century,
except, of course, on the great chalk uplands where the 'thresher poet' Stephen
Duck recorded it so well in the early eighteenth century.

[4] Collinson, *The Religion of Protestants* chapter 5, *passim*.

[5] Peter Laslett, *The World we Have Lost* (2nd edn, London, 1971), p. 74.

derived from the study of certain Cambridgeshire village communities, that 'even the humblest members, the very poor, and the women, and those living in physical isolation, thought deeply on religious matters and were often profoundly influenced by them'.[6] Whereas Keith Thomas thinks it likely that certain sections of the population, 'below a certain social level', managed without religion altogether: 'Although complete statistics will never be obtainable, it can be confidently said that not all Tudor or Stuart Englishmen went to some kind of church, that many of those who did went with considerable reluctance, and that a certain proportion remained throughout their lives utterly ignorant of the elementary tenets of christian dogma.'[7] Peter Clark has been bold enough to put a figure on this 'certain proportion':[8] 'Probably something like a fifth of the population of Kent stayed away from church on a regular basis in the later sixteenth century.'[9]

Patrick Collinson's own main sources, which must, as he says, be used with extreme caution, are the 'pessimism of the sermons and the literature of complaint' and the 'implied complacency of the records of ecclesiastical administration and justice'.

As Professor Collinson says, I am myself an interested party, inclining towards the view that there was a deep interest in religious matters in the sixteenth and seventeenth centuries, which crossed all social divides, and which involved some of the very poor, even including, perhaps, the vagrants, on whose opinions little information can ever be obtainable.[10]

So far historians involved in this debate on the percolation of 'godly' religious belief throughout society have mainly proceeded by case-studies of particular communities. I found very different patterns of diffusion of Congregationalist adherence in two Cambridgeshire villages in the 1670s: in Orwell, the adherence was spread right through village society from top to bottom with a slight bias towards the poor; in Willingham, both Congregationalists and Quakers were normally neither drawn from the top, nor the bottom, of the social structure. They were the relatively comfortable, but not outstanding, taxpayers on two or three hearths. Further work on two more settlements only confused the picture further. In one, Congregationalists and Quakers were rather more evenly socially spread than at Willingham, but less so than at Orwell; at yet another, Quakers were only to be found amongst the poor.[11]

Since then, Dr Wrightson and Dr Levine have found a heavy concentration of 'godly' and indeed sectarian puritan beliefs amongst the 'better

---

[6] Margaret Spufford, Contrasting Communities: English Villagers in the Sixteenth and Seventeenth Centuries (Cambridge, 1974), p. 343.
[7] Keith Thomas, Religion and the Decline of Magic (Harmondsworth, 1973), p. 159.
[8] Peter Clark, English Provincial Society (Hassocks, 1977), p. 156.
[9] Collinson, The Religion of Protestants, p. 198.
[10] But see below, pp. 64–5.
[11] Contrasting Communities, pp. 300–6.

sort' at Terling in Essex[12] and Dr Wrightson has extrapolated from this
to write

> the sober piety of the Reformation ideal could appeal to people of all
> ranks, and demonstrably did so, but it found its most receptive audi-
> ence among a minority of the gentry, the yeoman and craftsman of the
> villages, and the merchants, tradesmen and artisans of the towns. It
> was they who formed the reading public for devotional works ... The
> Interregnum saw the disintegration of English puritanism into a multi-
> plicity of denominations and sects ... In the proliferation of the sects
> ... we have incontrovertible evidence of the extent to which one part
> of the common people – notably the literate 'middling sort' had
> become closely involved with the central issues of the day.[13]

Professor Collinson, on the other hand, has sounded a warning. 'Historians will do well not to jump to hasty conclusions about the "better sort",
or to assume too lightly that the meaning of puritan evangelism was a
class war of a kind.' He draws attention to three more studies of religion
in society in the Kent and Sussex Weald, which 'all failed to discover
any clear-cut difference of class between the reformed and unreformed
elements ... We conclude it is premature simply to equate the godly
elite of early Stuart England with a social elite, or even with the broad
band lying across the middle rungs of the social ladder.'[14] Dr Ingram's
study of Keevil, in Wiltshire, likewise fails to find a correlation between
prosperity and religious belief.[15] In view of the fact that the results of
microscopic studies of nine communities have been summarized here,
it seems extremely likely that further village studies will produce further
varied results: that what we are in fact faced with is a variety of puritans
and sectarian groups, formed of an infinite mix of different social and
economic compositions. It is likely that a true analogy would be with the
very wide variations between parish and parish, even in the same area,
in literacy levels, which Dr Wrightson brings vividly to our attention. In
Cornwall, for instance, the worst

> parish for which we have evidence has an illiteracy rate of 92 percent,
> but the best had a rate of only 54 percent. In Essex, the worst parish
> had a rate of 82 percent, yet the best had one of only 36 percent ...
> doubtless such variations owed their existence to a host of local fac-
> tors – The important point to grasp, however, is that despite the gross
> social bias in the attainment of literacy, there were places whether great
> cities or tiny hamlets, in which a much more widespread literacy had

---

[12] Wrightson and Levine, *Poverty and Piety in an English Village*, pp. 158–62.
[13] Wrightson, *English Society*, pp. 213–14, 217.
[14] Collinson, *The Religion of Protestants*, pp. 239–41.
[15] Martin Ingram, *Church Courts, Sex and Marriage in England, 1570–1640* (Cambridge, 1987).

been achieved. Some husbandmen, artisans, labourers, servants and women could read and write.[16]

It seems therefore that a change of procedure is indicated. If instead of attempting further community case-studies, and coming up with more variants to confuse ourselves, we take the social and economic composition of whole heretical or sectarian groups, there is some hope of finding an adequate sample of the members of these groups to illustrate their social antecedents with conviction. This particular method is capable of providing proof. I touched on the subject in 1985, and then wrote:

> The distribution of reformed beliefs has not yet been adequately studied at the village level. No one, to my knowledge, has looked properly at the social backgrounds of the later Lollards, and this could be done with precision . . . I have also looked at the social distribution of post-Restoration dissent and have found it certainly did not spread downwards. The deaf old fenwoman, a day-labourer who was converted to Quakerism by the written word, was one proof of that. So also were the villages where dissent concentrated at the bottom of the social structure, or spread evenly through it. But there were other communities where dissent did make more appeal to the more prosperous. We simply do not know enough yet, and it would be unwise to generalise on the basis of less than a full examination of all the varieties of dissent across at least the whole of two contrasted counties of England. This has not yet been done.[17]

Now it has. Thanks to the enormously hard and enthusiastic labour of Dr Derek Plumb, Dr Christopher Marsh, and Dr Bill Stevenson, we now know, in a way we did not, of the social and economic spread of the later Lollards in the mid-Thames valley area of Buckinghamshire, Berkshire, and Oxfordshire, of the Family of Love in the 1570s and 80s in Cambridgeshire, the Isle of Ely, and at the royal court, and of the social background of Quakers, Baptists, Open Baptists, Independents and even Mugpletonians in no less than five counties, (Buckinghamshire, Bedfordshire, Cambridgeshire, Huntingdonshire, and Hertfordshire). Dr Eric Carlson has explored the backgrounds and bias of the churchwardens in Cambridgeshire who made the all-important presentments to the church courts on which the historian relies so much. Dr Tessa Watt has investigated the nature of the cheap 'godly' print which increased in volume from a trickle to a flood in this period. Dr Michael Frearson has investigated the roads and routes along which the carriers and pedlars who distributed this cheap print travelled.

---

[16] Wrightson, English Society, p. 194.
[17] Margaret Spufford, 'Puritanism and Social Control?', in Fletcher and Stevenson (eds.), Order and Disorder in Early Modern England, pp. 46–7.

Because the results produced by the first three were so full, we were encouraged onwards to tackle a question first explicitly argued as long ago as 1661,[18] and rather more recently by Dr Christopher Hill.[19] For a very long time, historians of dissent have supposed there might be linear continuity between radical dissenters: that later Lollardy might have been the seedbed from which, more than a century later, the post-Restoration dissenting sects finally put out their fully grown shoots. Our possession of lists of names of the later Lollards in Buckinghamshire and over the border into Hertfordshire, and Dr Plumb's identification of a 'gathered church' around Amersham in the 1520s, as well as the names of the early Friends attending the Upperside Meeting in exactly the same area in the seventeenth century collected by Dr Stevenson, together with the lists of Baptists attending Ford and Cuddington 'gathered church' in south Buckinghamshire immediately after the Restoration, suggested power-fully to us that it might be worth tackling this old historical chestnut yet again, by using surname evidence and genealogical techniques, and attempting to trace family and linear linkages between late Lollards and post-Restoration dissenters.

To our delight and our own astonishment, this painfully laborious and tedious exercise proved possible: thanks to the work of Mrs Nesta Evans (Chapter 7) we now have a continuity through time, and through family, of radical dissenters focussed on exactly the same market towns. We have carried out this work for two of the seven main areas designated as 'likely' by Dr Hill. These were Kent,[20] Essex,[21] the Chilterns, Berkshire, the West Riding of Yorkshire, Gloucestershire, and the midlands around Coventry. These other areas deserve further investigation, using the same surname techniques by other historians, since the ecclesiastical court records are unlikely to prove continuity of dissenting opinion through time, unless it be that of 'popish recusants'.[22]

---

[18] *Semper Fidem: Or, a Parallel betwixt the Ancient and Modern Fanaticks* (1661).

[19] 'From Lollards to Levellers', in Maurice Cornforth (ed.), *Rebels and their Causes: Essays in Honour of A.L. Morton* (London, 1978), now most accessible in *The Collected Essays of Christopher Hill*, vol. II: *Religion and Politics in Seventeenth-Century England* (Brighton, 1986), pp. 89–116.

[20] There is a thesis which suggests that such continuity may be very likely in Kent. Robert J. Acheson, 'The Development of Religious Separatism in the Diocese of Canterbury, 1590–1660' (University of Kent at Canterbury, PhD, 1983). Dr Acheson writes: 'other examples, such as the Knotts of Dover and Eythorne, the Innises of Dover and Prescotts of Guston, tend to lend some credence to the idea that the family played a crucial role in the perpetuating of dissenting attitudes over a number of generations, although there is clearly much research before this can be estab-lished reasonably firmly'. I am much indebted to Dr Jacqueline Bower for abstracting this thesis for me.

[21] See Appendix A.

[22] Margaret Spufford, 'The Quest of the Heretical Laity', in Derek Baker (ed.), *Schism, Heresy and Religious Protest*, Studies in Church History, (Cambridge, 1972), pp. 225–6.

Despite being an interested party, and also believing both that proof of the social and economic spread of radical dissent is possible, and that we have achieved it in this volume, I stand by my cautious view that 'genuine popular devotion of a humble kind leaves very little trace upon the records of any given time. The believer, especially the conforming believer, makes less impact than the dissentient. At no period is it possible to distinguish the conforming believer from the apathetic church-goer who merely wished to stay out of trouble.'[23] The case I cite of the post-Restoration yeoman William Coe of Mildenhall,[24] half of whose diary concerns his tippling in the alehouse, and the other half his meditations on reception of Holy Communion, illustrates my meaning well. We are dealing with a huge spectrum of people, ranging, no doubt, from the non-believer[25] through those induced by social pressure to conform to avoid trouble, via genuine conformists of conviction, and those who were prepared to buy and read the new 'small godly' books, to the people to whom the practice of religion was a conscious and deliberate act of belief, like 'our' Calvinists (Table 1), and to those who were prepared to face court prosecution and fines for it, and, ultimately, to those who could, and did, face martyrdom. This spectrum must be expressed statistically in the very limited way that early modern statistics will allow. The Communicants' Returns of 1603, and the Compton Census of 1676 can be used yet again.[26] In this volume, we produce further tables of statistics, this time of the taxable status of dissenters of particular persuasions. But these people are not reducible merely to statistics, not only because we are here reducing such a wide spectrum of conviction, and the lack of it, into a Procrustean bed of similarity, but also because statistics in themselves suggest the passivity of the subjects.

Charles Booth wrote a magnificent plea for dispassionate thinking in his plea for the empirical social survey, in 1887:

> To judge rightly we need to bear both in mind, never to forget the numbers when thinking of the percentages, nor the percentages when thinking of the numbers. This last is difficult to those whose daily

---

[23] Small Books and Pleasant Histories: Popular Fiction and its Readership in Seventeenth-Century England (London, 1981, p/b Cambridge, 1985), p. 194 and argument to p. 196.

[24] See below, pp. 96–7.

[25] Michael Hunter, 'The Problem of "Atheism" in Early Modern England', Trans. Royal Hist. Soc., 5th Ser., 35 (1985), pp. 135–57.

[26] Discussed briefly in Margaret Spufford, 'Can we Count the "Godly" and the "Conformable" in the Seventeenth Century?', Journal of Ecclesiastical History, 36 (1985), pp. 435–7. Dr Keith Snell, of the Department of English Local History at Leicester, has embarked, with Paul Ell, on computer analysis and mapping of the religious statistics that exist for England. His initial results appear as K.D.M. Snell, Church and Chapel in the North Midlands (Leicester, 1991). He intended to work backwards to end up with the Compton Census. These analyses will provide us with a magnificent new tool. See below, p. 43 n. 134.

experience or whose imagination brings vividly before them the trials
and sorrows of individual lives. They refuse to set off and balance the
happy hours of the same class, or even of the same people, against
these miseries; much less can they consent to bring the lot of other
classes into the account, add up the opposing figures, and contentedly
carry forward a credit balance. In the arithmetic of woe they can only
add or multiply, they cannot subtract or divide. In intensity of feeling
such as this, and not in statistics, lies the power to love the world. But
by statistics must this power be guided if it would move the world
aright.[27]

It has sometimes seemed to me recently that we have fallen into the
equal, and opposite, error: in the 'arithmetic of woe' sometimes current
historians can only subtract or divide; they cannot add, or multiply.
Dependence on statistics, which are entirely necessary, by depersonaliz-
ing the subjects, is also inherently misleading, and suggests a flaw in the
historian's relation to the people who are the subject of his or her study,
and a lack of proper respect for the human beings involved, which was
splendidly objected to by Richard Cobb in 1971.

I do not care to learn that members of the upper bourgeoisie of Elbeuf
possessed from 6–20 servants, that members of the middle bourgeoisie
of Elbeuf possessed from 2–6 servants, and that members of the lower
bourgeoisie of Elbeuf possessed from 0–2 servants. I do not know what
sort of a non-person a 0 servant can be: and I even find it distasteful
thus to equate the number of servants to visible signs of wealth and
status, along with knives and forks and silver teapots, pairs of sheets
and household linen, even if this may in fact be a useful measurement
for the assessment of relative wealth. Perhaps I am being sentimental,
but it disturbs me to see poor country girls sweating it out below stairs,
or freezing in the attic, the object of the lust of the Master and his sons,
being further humiliated, long after their death, thus being forced into
graphs in the galleyships of . . . doctoral candidates.
    These girls after all, however poor, possessed their own identity, and
faces, sometimes pretty ones, though generally pock-marked, often a
generous and open disposition, a great deal of naivety, a proneness to
revere and obey their fathers and to love and slave for their brothers,
even if their intellectual baggage was as limited as their wardrobe.[28]

What Cobb is objecting to, with a force for which 'passion' is not too
strong a word, is not the use of numbers, but the degree of depersonaliza-
tion that may go with them, the loss of the 'wealth and variety of human
motivations . . . the myriad variations of human lives'. We have used

---

[27] Quoted by Brian Jackson in his 'Introduction' to Beatrice Webb, *My Apprenticeship*
(Harmondsworth, 1971), p. 14.
[28] Richard Cobb, 'Historians in White Coats', *Times Literary Supplement* 3 Dec. 1971,
pp. 1527–8.

statistics, or at least samples of different sorts of dissenters frequently in this volume, but have tried strenuously to remember the persons, and the passions, behind the numbers.

Our first object, as a group of scholars coordinating our work on the project, then, has been pinpointing the social and economic position of radical dissenters, and even, if possible, some practising conformists, very precisely, by identifying them in taxation returns, and in assessments for poor rates and those in receipt of relief. We wanted to know how far down society practising nonconformists did spread. We are now in a position to make an answer, which is not even tentative, to half of Dr Duffy's first, huge question: 'Was there such a thing as popular Christianity: can we find a genuinely plebeian religious context into which to fit [Pepys'] bible loving shepherd?'[29] The reader will find below, p. 19, an example of a very real Quaker shepherd, distrained of his breeches in 1674. Dr Stevenson provides a genuine sans-culotte to answer Dr Duffy, as well as a statistical frame to prove this poor man was not unusual in his society. This answer will, from the nature of the evidence, always be confined to that end of the spectrum of believers who were prepared to be persecuted for their beliefs: it therefore applies only to a tiny minority. We can speak definitely of the plebeian origins and backgrounds of bible loving shepherds, but they are always going to be Lollard, or Quaker, or Open Baptist bible loving shepherds, in trouble with the authorities, and therefore visible to us. But that tiny minority, of whom we can speak precisely, was quite definitely extended to the poorest taxable members of society. There were Lollards taxed on only their wages in 1524–5,[30] and Quakers, Baptists, Independents, and even Muggletonians who were exempt from the Hearth Taxes on the grounds of poverty in the 1670s.[31] Specific radical religious beliefs were found among the very poorest. Dr Stevenson even has a General Baptist vagrant. But we can only speak of the 'genuinely plebeian religious context' of 'heretics',[32] not of the orthodox.

---

[29] Duffy, 'The Godly and the Multitude', p. 41.
[30] See below, Table 4, p. 114, and pp. 12–13.
[31] See below, Table 10, p. 338, and pp. 18–19, 334 *et seq.*
[32] I have not engaged at all in this essay with the changing definition of heresy through time. See, for instance, Anne Hudson, 'Lollardy: The English Heresy?', first published in Stuart Mows (ed.), *Religion and National Identity*, Studies in Church History, 18 (Oxford, 1982), reprinted in *idem*, *Lollards and their Books* (London, 1985), p. 162, when she points out that knowledge of the Pater Noster and the Creed in English itself was evidence of heresy. Under fifty years later, a woman of the diocese of Ely was presented to her ecclesiastical court for not knowing the Lord's Prayer and the Creed (see below, p. 75).

The huge *lacuna* in this argument is that we could only look for those whose beliefs were unacceptable to their own societies, and were therefore victims of persecution: we could not search for the 'godly', the moderate Calvinists who made up the acceptable English protestants about whose social diffusion there is so much debate. In 1986, Dr Duffy 'granted that puritanism seems to have been most successful amongst the middling and better sorts'. But need we? Is there any theological or social reason why the forms of protestantism, Calvinist orthodox belief, and 'godliness', accepted, and indeed welcomed, by ecclesiastical authority after the 1570s should not spread socially as widely as either Dr Plumb here shows Lollardy did, or Dr Stevenson shows Quaker, Baptist, and Independent beliefs did? There is simply no reason for us to know of the spread of 'godly' beliefs, since they were not presented in ecclesiastical courts, but were a matter for rejoicing. No one needed to flinch after 1558, if a volume of Perkins or Foxe, or even Calvin, was found open on the table in the hall by the churchwardens, as they did when a copy of the Bible in English was found in 1537.[33] There was no need for such an episode ever to be recorded. We cannot know of the spread of either Calvinist conformity, or conformist devotion, although we have attempted an examination of Calvinist dedicatory clauses in wills, which give us a minimum estimate of the number of the convinced 'godly', and a picture of their social distribution. We may perhaps draw a cautious analogy from Dr Judith Maltby's work, showing that in a handful of Cheshire parishes, parishioners whose social and economic level she has identified, including those on poor relief, signed petitions in favour of the prayer book in the late 1630s.[34] The key and vital point is that the overseers of the poor in her parishes did not necessarily sign, even if the poor did. The overseers may not, therefore, have been standing at the church door with a quill in their hands, to enforce conformity on the poor. Prayer book conformists also then crossed the social and economic spectrum, and included some of the very poor, as dissenters did. But we can never estimate the number of conformists who had their own convictions. Like dissenters, they may have been another small minority, or they may not.

Our examination of the minimum number of the Calvinist 'godly' to be found from their wills demonstrates their wide social diffusion but does little to make their real numerical strength amongst the 'common sort' apparent to us. In part this is because the churchwardens themselves

---

[33] A.G. Dickens, *Lollards and Protestants in the Diocese of York, 1509–1558* (Oxford, 1959), p. 8 n. 1, which points out that the works of Calvin appear on a list of prohibited books dated 1542. See below, p. 71.

[34] Judith Maltby, *Prayer Book and People: Religious Conformity before the Civil War* (Cambridge, forthcoming).

frequently were members of the self-styled 'godly', and, like their earlier Lollard predecessors, they could be heretical.[35] They therefore failed to present behaviour of which they did not disapprove, although the ecclesiastical courts might have taken a different view. The vigorous Lollard, John Tyball, from Steeple Bumpstead, who succeeded in converting his own curate to Lollardy in 1526, had become churchwarden of Steeple Bumpstead along with another Lollard, Thomas Hemsted.[36] Dr Plumb adds other examples of Lollard churchwardens in Buckinghamshire.[37] Dr Marsh shows that the Family of Love had the same habit of providing active wardens for their parish churches.[38] So did puritans seeking further reform in church government: no less than one third (twenty-two) of the wardens or questmen in the nine villages with numerous petitions for reform in church government in south-west Cambridgeshire in 1640 signed a petition for the abolition of episcopacy.[39] The post-Restoration dissenters did not, of course, provide churchwardens, but they did provide every other responsible parish officer in their communities.[40] It is because of the decisive hand of the churchwardens in making presentations on doctrinal grounds, and therefore laying down what the historian may, or may not, know now that I asked Dr Carlson to look specifically at the beliefs and role of wardens in the delicate borderland of south-east Cambridgeshire, from which some Lollards may have come, in which the Family of Love flourished, as did the Quakers and Independents, and yet in which, according to the ecclesiastical records, the state of affairs was so often 'omnia bene'.[41]

We had very much hoped that Dr Carlson's general study of churchwardens in this area, combined with Mrs Evans' study of thirty-six parishes centring on Haverhill would put Dr Marsh's particular study of the Familist stronghold of Balsham village in context, and that we would therefore produce results as full as those for the Chilterns. The impossibility of the Haverhill project (Appendix A and Map 4) has hamstrung this ambition to work in depth on a second area. However, we do know much more about churchwardens: the particular findings of importance are their lack of fear of presenting their social superiors within the village, their own change to a higher social status after the Restoration, and their complete willingness, in this area, to present dissenters then. It is fascinating that almost all the names of the nonconformists for whom we only

---

[35] See below, ch. 9, pp. 369–72.
[36] Anne Hudson, *The Premature Reformation: Wycliffite Texts and Lollard History* (Oxford, 1988), pp. 479–80.
[37] See below, Derek Plumb, p. 106, 124–5, 133.
[38] See below, Christopher Marsh, p. 203.
[39] Margaret Spufford, *Contrasting Communities*, pp. 268–9.
[40] See below, Bill Stevenson, pp. 368–72.
[41] Or, 'all well'.

had numbers previously from the Compton Census can be supplied from the wardens' presentments to the ecclesiastical courts. It is well worth trying this matching exercise elsewhere. Yet the presentments still depended on the wardens' individual convictions, and these, and therefore the thoroughness of the presentments, may have depended on the area.

The churchwardens of Sarratt on the Hertfordshire–Buckinghamshire border were unusually obstinate, undiplomatic, or just plain honest in their replies to the question concerning parishioners. In 1680, they answered 'Who can tell what to say concerning this? Some come to Church and some stay at home.' In the following year they replied 'Wee do humbly suppose that no parish if they will write truth can say omnia bene to this querie for some go to church and some to other meetings, but we have never a papist in the towne so far as we know.' The tone of truculence was maintained, and reflected the parishioners' own attitudes, for in 1687 an unfortunate warden reported 'Widow Green when I asked why she did not come to church told me to my face she went elsewhere, and she would goe whither she list for all of me.' In the face of the attitude of Widow Green and her many fellow conventiclers in this area riddled with nonconformity, there may have been relief as well as a measure of rudeness in the final reply in the series, in 1688, 'If we should tell you the names of such as come seldome to church they are excused by the late liberty granted and may goe whither they please, therefore here we must be silent.'[42] The pity of it is that we have found no late Elizabethan or early Jacobean churchwardens similarly moved to frankness.

Dr Plumb is concerned, in his essay, to attack the old contemporary slur, which has been picked up by modern historians, that later Lollards were 'weavers and threshers'.[43] He demonstrates the influence of dominant men in their own societies who were Lollards, like Robert Sanders, a dyer of Amersham, with a small manor, who dominated his market town with an assessment of £200 in the 1524/5 tax list.[44] Dyers were always prosperous, but this man's taxable capacity was astonishing. He, and many others discussed by Dr Plumb were all very unlike 'weavers and threshers'. But as well as this, Dr Plumb demonstrates conclusively the

[42] Churchwardens' presentments of the Archdeaconry of St Albans, 1679–88, Herts. RO ASA 17/1 and 2.
[43] Derek Plumb, see below, pp. 103, 108–9.
[44] Derek Plumb, 'John Foxe and the Later Lollards of the Mid-Thames Valley' (Cambridge PhD, 1987), pp. 248, 261–4, 409–11.

diffusion of Lollard beliefs throughout all levels of their rural societies, with a slant, but no more than that, towards the top of rural society. Almost a fifth, 18–20 per cent, of his Lollards or suspected Lollards were taxed on substantial sums in goods of £10 or more in the Great Subsidy or the musters, 46–8 per cent in the middle ranks were taxed on 30s to £9, but 32–6 per cent were only taxed on wages of 30s and under. In society at large in our focal area[45] 13 per cent of all the taxpayers of 1524–5 were paying on £10 or more, 48 per cent on 30s to £9, and 39 per cent on wages of 30s and under. In other words, the Lollards, or those suspected of Lollard sympathies, represented an (almost exact) proportionate cross-section of society at large, except that there were rather more better-off Lollards, and slightly fewer Lollard wage earners. However, even so, nearly 40 per cent of suspected Lollards were wage earners, and these poor people were certainly not indifferent to this type of nonconformity. We can never again regard Lollards as merely 'weavers and threshers': there were far too many really prosperous rural taxpayers involved; but nor can we regard them as a 'rural elite'. Lollardy was a heresy which permeated the whole of local society in areas where it took root.[46] This permeation was partly assisted because the heresy was so much a family affair, and it seems increasingly apparent that the siblings and cousinhood within families sprawled across the whole social and economic structure. This widthwise spread of families, which did so much to blur the distinctions and differences in rural society in the early modern period, deserves further investigation.[47] The Funge family, of Great Wycombe, Penn, and Amersham, are a good example, including a wage labourer and a miller amongst their number. Millers, like dyers, but less so, are usually prosperous people.

[45] We have analysed the sums on which all 1,466 taxpayers were assessed in eighteen parishes round Amersham in our study area.

[46] Derek Plumb, see below, pp. 136–63, esp. 162–3.

[47] I drew attention to it in Contrasting Communities in the case-study of Johnson alias Butler, pp. 354–5, 197, and particularly the bottom two illustrations, p. 198. David Cressy, 'Kinship and Kin Interaction in Early Modern England', Past and Present, 113 (1986), pp. 38–69, together with his Coming Over (Cambridge, 1987), has transformed the views of some of us. This widthwise spread is unfortunately not visible in the Family Reconstruction Forms of the Cambridge Group, which has done so much to revolutionize our knowledge of early modern family structure and demography, because of the way that the forms are laid out. Motoyasu Takahashi is producing material on seventeenth-century Willingham which demonstrates that this widthwise spread across social and economic divisions did occur there, and also that more heads of households within different economic groups witnessed each other's wills than heads of households in the same economic groups. Interestingly, the witnesses were not always, although they were usually, witnesses to dying men who were poorer than themselves. Sometimes the poor were called in to witness the more prosperous. See Table 10 in Margaret Spufford and Motoyasu Takahashi, 'The Spread of Families across the Social and Economic Structure in Sixteenth and Seventeenth Century Willingham and Chippenham' (forthcoming).

Perhaps the most unexpected point that Dr Plumb brings to our attention is the apparently total integration of the Lollards within their own local communities, as well as within their own gathered church. Part of this integration depended on the superior economic status of 20 per cent of them, of course; gentlemen who held even minor manors, had influence. So did yeomen who employed wage labour. But several Lollards, over half a dozen in this area, were also churchwardens in their own parishes. In the towns they were burgesses, bailiffs, and guild members.[48] They were not alienated from, but integrated into, their own societies. It is this integration which has proved one of the most surprising and fruitful findings in our joint enterprise.

It is a matter of deep regret to us that Dr Richard Davies' brilliant article[49] was in preparation, and in the press, at the same time as Dr Plumb's thesis, and this Introduction. Almost every word is relevant to us. However, all is not lost. Although Christopher Hill's suggestion of the continuity of nonconformity was not based on family descents, Dr Davies called for just the follow-up of W.H. Summer's assertions made in 1906 on these lines[50] which is exactly what a large part of this volume is about. Moreover, Dr Davies did not perform Dr Plumb's laborious exercise of tying suspected Lollards to their subsidy or muster returns, and therefore could not make the statement summarized by me above. He thought, for instance, the leading Collins family were wealthy.[51] Nor did he know of the spread of families across the whole social and economic spectrum. Therefore, although we would entirely agree with his stress on the wealth and respectability of the more influential Lollards, who were indeed not a 'debased proletarian lump', and his diagnosis that the strength of the local movement lay in 'personally-linked clusters'[52] in which these wealthier citizens and yeomen were very highly influential, we have also tried to look at his 'still-obscure majority'. We hope very much that in this exercise of investigating the social and economic spread of Lollards and their sympathizers, and later dissenters round Amersham, we have avoided, on the one hand, the doom of regarding this social and economic spread as determinants (look at the influence of the not-so-wealthy Collins family)[53] and, on the other, the horrid fate of 'choking on a surfeit of undigested anecdote'. We would disapprove of either extravagance quite as much as Dr Davies.

---

[48] Plumb, 'Foxe and the Later Lollards', pp. 174, 202, 252, 148–51.
[49] 'Lollardy and Locality', *Trans. Royal Hist. Soc.*, 6th Ser., 1 (1991), pp. 191–212.
[50] Ibid., p. 205. W.H. Summers, *The Lollards of the Chiltern Hills* (London, 1906), and *Our Lollard Ancestors* (London, 1904).
[51] Davies, 'Lollardy and Locality', pp. 207 and 210.
[52] Ibid., pp. 197–8 and 199.
[53] Pace Ibid., p. 207.

Christopher Marsh provides a very interesting contrast to both Dr Plumb's and Dr Stevenson's results, with his findings on the small mystical group known as the Family of Love, which flourished at court, in south-east Cambridgeshire and the Isle of Ely, and attracted much vilification in the late 1570s. The members of this group, as he shows from detailed work on the parish of Balsham (Chapter 5) were indeed part of something like a 'rural elite' whose prosperous members provided officers for the parish church. They also dominated the social relationships of the whole community, and the major economic decisions of the manor court. The distinction between their social spread and that of both the Lollards and post-Restoration dissenters is complete. It seems to be accounted for by their predominantly devotional stress on the baptism of the believer realizing in him, or herself, the reality of the Resurrection in this present life, and their unwillingness to evangelize or explain their beliefs unless contact had been already made with a potential member already far advanced in 'godliness'.[54] But despite their social dominance, and lack of spread across the economic spectrum, they were again completely integrated into their own society. They were churchwardens, and manorial officials within it.[55] Of all the contributors to this volume, Dr Marsh makes the largest claims for tolerance in practice at the local level, and makes them not solely on account of the economic dominance of his 'most detestable Sectaries or Hereticks that ever reigned on earth'. Yet he only adds to the similar findings for the, much larger, groups worked on by Dr Plumb and Dr Stevenson.

Our next investigation, of belief in election amongst the generality of people, also started in the 1570s. If it is true that there was a general Calvinist consensus among the educated literate protestants who formed the true elite in the Elizabethan and Jacobean church, we can do a little to investigate the spread of this orthodoxy amongst the Common Sort of Christians,[56] by looking at the clauses bequeathing the soul in wills, which

[54] Christopher W. Marsh, 'The Family of Love in English Society, 1550–1630' (Cambridge, PhD, 1991), pp. 24, 137, 392–3, 400–5. This was published under the same title by Cambridge University Press in 1994,

[55] See below, pp. 216–18, 231.

[56] Peter Lake, 'Calvinism and the English Church 1570–1635', Past and Present, 114 (1987), pp. 32–76, especially pp. 32–3. Dr Lake deliberately restricts his study to avoid discussion of popular religion, as I am here deliberately avoiding the culture of the truly educated, rather than the literate, or semi-literate. The quotation is from George Gifford, A Brief Discourse on Certain Points of the Religion which is among the Common Sort of Christians which May be Termed Country Divinity (London, 1581).

Table 1. The social and economic spread of the 'elect' in will dedicatory clauses, diocese of Ely, 1575–1630

Date	Status					Total 'elect'	Total wills, consistory and archdeaconry courts	Percentage of 'elect' rounded to nearest %
	Yeomen	Husbandmen	Widows	Craftsmen[a]	Labourers and servants			
1575						0	81	0
1580						0	104	0
1585						0	77	0
1590	1					1	160	<1
1595		1				1	165	<1
1600		1	1			2	107	2
1605	1	2			1	4	133	3
1610	1	1	1			3	178	2
1615	1			1 (Unknown)	1	4	212	2
1620		1		2	1	4	169	2
1625	1			2	1	4	280	1
1630	2	1	1	4	1	9	274	3
Total	7	7	3	9 1 (Unknown)	5	32	1,940	1.6
1590 and after	7	7	3	9 1 (Unknown)	5	32	1,678	1.9

[a] Carpenter, smith, collarmaker, shoemaker, bricklayer, tailor, shepherd.

have been so much argued about as evidence amongst historians.[57] The current view is that idiosyncratic and strongly flavoured dedicatory clauses give an absolute minimum of individual testators with strong convictions, once the problems of possible duplication by the same scribe have been dealt with. Calvinist dedicatory clauses were nothing if not idiosyncratic; it was very rare for a testator to mention election in his or her will. It therefore seemed worthwhile to take cross-sections of surviving wills for the diocese of Ely every five years between 1570 and 1630, to see the minimum impact the doctrine of predestination and election to salvation had had upon the 'common sort'. Ely was possibly unusual in the social spread of its testators; the habit of making wills spread amongst ordinary people there at the end of the sixteenth century. From the second half of Elizabeth's reign, at least a quarter, and possibly well over half, the wills passing through the consistory court were made by labourers and husbandmen. In the 1620s and 1630s, 22 per cent of those who were given an occupational status were called labourers.[58]

The survey of dedicatory clauses shows that amongst ordinary literate or semi-literate people, that minimum group which felt impelled to mention election in its wills was small indeed. There were no testators who did so in 1575, 1580, or 1585; 1590 saw the first lone yeoman who left his soul to 'Almighty god my Saviour and redemer hoping through the merittes of Jesus Christe to have remission ... of my sinnes, and after this life ended I hope my soule shall have a place of rest amongest the elect of god'. Over the next forty years, another 31 testators out of over 1,600 amongst the surviving wills in the sample joined him. Their social composition was interesting: these Calvinists of conviction covered the complete social spectrum from yeomen to labourers and servants, through a cross-section of petty craftsmen from smiths to bricklayers.[59]

---

[57] There is by now an extremely long, and argumentative, discussion on the way will preambles can be used, or should not be used. Professor Dickens first used them to show the progress of the Reformation in *Lollards and Protestants*, pp 171–2 and 215–17. I refined this by demonstrating the importance both of the scribe and his normal formulas and idiosyncratic clauses in a paper which appeared in *Local Population Studies*, 7 (1971), pp. 28–43. See below, p. 122, for the importance of a radical will preamble as one of the indicators of Lollardy before 1550. This harmonizes with the latest, very extensive discussion and survey of the opposing opinions in Christopher Marsh, 'In the Name of God? Will-Making and Faith in Early Modern England', in G.H. Martin and Peter Spufford (eds.), *The Records of the Nation* (Woodbridge, 1990), pp. 215–49. Dr Marsh concludes that 'Full and expressive dedicatory clauses were more likely from unusually religious testators, and such clauses are undoubtedly evidence of personal conviction. The reverse is not true; short preambles certainly did not invariably reflect lack of strong faith', p. 248.

[58] Motoyasu Takahashi, 'The Number of Wills Proved in the Sixteenth and Seventeenth Centuries. Graphs, with Tables and Commentary', in Martin and Peter Spufford (eds.), *The Records of the Nation*. p. 209.

[59] I was mistaken in my opinion (*Contrasting Communities*, pp. 340, 343–4) that yeomen were more likely to consider themselves 'elect', but correct in my impression that

There was no bias towards the most prosperous end of rural society amongst these convinced Calvinists. Belief in election, like prayer book conformity, and dissent, also crossed the social spectrum. But if 'godliness' was in any sense connected with the reception of Calvinist beliefs in the mind of convinced puritan divines, it is no wonder that they felt a sense of despair at times. Only 1.9 per cent of the testators in our sample, admittedly an absolute minimum, confessed to belief in election overtly (Table 1). The picture is exactly as it is in cheap godly print. The 'godly' ballads stressed the saving power of faith, just as the dedicatory clauses of wills professed a general acceptance of salvation by faith alone, but in the ballads, too, mention of election is almost absent.[60]

Dr Stevenson's work started after the Commonwealth. He had more post-Restoration dissenters to identify, after the population explosion up to 1650, and therefore comes up with a massive group of more than 750 non-conformists of all denominations identified in the relevant Hearth Taxes of 1671–4 for Bedfordshire, Cambridgeshire, and Huntingdonshire. He collected enough members of the Quakers, Congregationalists, Baptists, and Open Baptists to form satisfyingly large samples for each sect.[61] The number of hearths on which a man paid tax indicates his economic

---

those who proclaimed Calvinist beliefs, as opposed to the very common generally reformed protestant emphasis on salvation through Christ's death and passion alone, were very rare.

[60] See below, p. 247–8. I am exceedingly grateful to Dr William Sharman who hunted down the wills of the 'elect' for me. The question that then arises is whether these small numbers are in proportion to the sizes of the occupational groups amongst the testators of Ely at large. Between 1600 and 1639, a total of 5,924 testators left wills in the consistory court. Of those of known status 1 per cent of them were gentry, 17 per cent yeoman, 22 per cent husbandmen, 20 per cent labourers, 19 per cent craftsmen, 21 per cent women. It would be ridiculous to percentage the tiny group of those who declared themselves elect to show whether or not the numbers were truly evenly distributed amongst the will-makers, but if we do so, women are grossly under-represented. Amongst the male godly, the number of yeomen is about the same as the testamentary population at large; husbandmen and labourers are very slightly under-represented, but the difference is too small to be certain. Craftsmen are over-represented (31 per cent of the total elect, 19 per cent of the will-making population with occupations). The difference just could be significant, but again, the numbers are too small to be certain. Takahashi, 'The Number of Wills', Table VI, p. 211. These figures may be marginally refined in the 'Introduction' by Dr Carlson to the three-volume index to the Ely Consistory Court Records to be published by the British Record Society.

[61] W. Stevenson, 'The Economic and Social Status of Protestant Sectaries in Huntingdonshire, Cambridgeshire and Bedfordshire (1650–1725)' (Cambridge, PhD, 1990), p. 251. His careful initial examination of the inventory value and rateable values of those paying on particular numbers of hearths shows that this use of the Hearth Taxes is indeed a meaningful exercise, pp. 5–22.

status. His thumbnail economic and social profiles of the 'better sort', the 'middling sort', and the 'meaner sort', who adhered to the various sects, reinforce the picture given by the taxable capacity of dissenters in the Hearth Taxes and their complete social spread, from those exempted from the Hearth Tax on the grounds of poverty and inability to pay, to those very comfortably off.

'It is the very "ordinariness" of sectaries which is so striking' he writes. 'They were not confined to any particular social rank or sub-group . . . they range from lowly servants and labourers, to humble craftsmen and husbandmen, small retailers, prosperous wholesalers, yeomen, professionals and gentlemen.'[62] The contemporary slur so often used by the bishops in 1669 against them, that the congregations consisted simply of 'mean mechanicks' and the 'vulgar sort' was wrong.[63] All the major sects did contain substantial proportions of the 'meaner sort'. Well over a third, 38 per cent of all the dissenters identified by Dr Stevenson were exempt from the Hearth Tax on the grounds of poverty, or paid on only one hearth. It may well be that this proportion, high though it was, was not, unlike Dr Plumb's Lollards, in proportion to that section of society at large (Table 9, p. 335 below). It is still extremely significant, and cannot be brushed aside. The total comparative analysis of the Hearth Tax to establish this was beyond our resources, but is now under way (p. 43 below, n. 134). Alongside them, in chapel, conventicle, and meeting-house, sat the other two-thirds, significant numbers, indeed, of the 'middling' and 'better' sorts.[64] Both the post-Restoration episcopate's denigratory remarks, and the recent trend of interpretation which suggests that the literate 'middling' sort of the common people were much the most receptive audience to which piety and godliness appealed, are mistaken, judging by these figures.

Amongst the Huntingdonshire Quakers, for instance, was the Quaker gentleman Nurse Parnell, of King's Ripton, who left in his will not only his 'Mansion House' belonging to the manor of King's Ripton, and a dove house, but also the family farmhouse and five cottages, as well as 179 acres of land and an undisclosed amount of freehold. The inventory value was £351. The gentleman Nurse Parnell was a trustee of the 'middling' grazier Edward Neale, who lived in a house taxed on two hearths, and left goods valued at £236 in 1684. But 42 per cent of the Huntingdonshire Quakers were either exempt from the Hearth Tax on the ground of poverty, or taxed on one hearth only. Amongst them were two Quaker shepherds. William Bavin of Bluntisham had his breeches, worth 5s, dis-

---

[62] Ibid., pp. 343–4.
[63] Ibid., pp. 287–8.
[64] Ibid., pp. 345

trained for non-attendance at church in 1674; and could probably ill-afford them. He received 4s out of a legacy to be distributed 'amongst poor friends' in 1696. The value of the goods in his inventory was only £18 1s 2d. The second shepherd, Robert Chappel of Hemingford Grey, made his will in 1683, and could only mark it, even though he was 'merry' and 'in good health'. His goods were worth only £9 9s 9d the following year, but his widow gave 5s to the building of the St Ives Meeting House in 1690. 'Clearly, piety and godliness were not confined to the elite', Dr Stevenson writes.[65] It seems clear from this massive sample of dissenters and their distribution that we must abandon the myth that religious opinion after the Restoration was economically and socially determined.[66]

Dr Stevenson, like Dr Plumb and Dr Marsh, has come up with much evidence of the integration of dissenters into their own local communities, as well as their closeness to their co-religionists.[67] His evidence is particularly impressive for its width and scope. He has Quakers, Open Baptists, and Presbyterians serving as parish constables and overseers of the poor, including a remarkable case of a Quaker, who had been persecuted and had filth thrown into his shop, and at his meeting in 1661, being elected alderman of Huntingdon in 1672. His sectarians also left bequests to the non-sectarian poor of their own parishes. Quakers wrote and witnessed wills for non-Quakers. He has nonconformists frequenting alehouses, football matches, and fairs. He chronicles the beginnings of public sympathy for Quakers from non-Quakers, including the payment of fines extorted from Quakers being paid for them by well-wishers and neighbours, and non-Quakers attending Quaker funerals as a sign of respect. Conversely, both Quakers and Baptists allowed the interment of non-Quaker and non-Baptist kin and sympathizers in their own burial grounds. His most striking evidence of all comes from the most delicate and solemn moments, births and deathbeds, when the mother giving birth and the dying testator were most vulnerable, and most needed to trust those assisting them. Non-Quaker midwives attended Quaker

[65] Ibid., pp. 83, 91, 47, 95–6.
[66] See above, pp. 1–4.
[67] I am both surprised and delighted to be set right on this: I wrote in 1972 of the alienation dissenters must have felt from their own community. *Contrasting Communities*, pp. 346–7. It is particularly interesting that I was heavily influenced in what I then wrote by the tensions that I perceived in a village like Orwell, where seven warrants for the arrest of the 'phanaticks' were issued by their own co-villagers in a single year. One of the cases that influenced me was that of Mary Cundy, a Muggletonian poor widow of Orwell (Stevenson, 'Economic and Social Status', pp. 212–352) who died excommunicate, and was 'buried with the burial of an Asse' in a close next to the churchyard in 1686. Dr Stevenson noticed, however, as I had not, that Widow Cundy had received continuous poor relief at 1s a week from 1671 to 1686, and had had her rent paid from 1676. Her opinions did not prevent substantial support from her co-villagers.

women in childbirth in Buckinghamshire, and vice versa. And, quite extraordinarily, one of the teachers at the Fenstanton Baptist Church was the most prolific scribe and witness of wills to the whole parish community from 1659 to 1722, sometimes cooperating with the rector. On one truly remarkable occasion, the rector acted as a witness with a practising Quaker, to the will of a testator with a practising Baptist sister.[68] I had been much too simple in believing the sectarian battles after the Civil War necessarily lead to a breakdown of harmony in human relations at a parish level, and in the transaction of essential community business.[69]

Although Dr Plumb and Dr Stevenson present their cumulative findings from a much wider area, which has given them both an adequate sample for decisive examination of the social and economic backgrounds of these dissenters, they both then change focus to concentrate on the Chiltern area of south Buckinghamshire, which we have tried to put under the microscope. Just as the late Lollard meetings in Buckinghamshire had been socially mixed, so also were dissenting meetings of all sects. Dr Stevenson found men living in houses with only one and two hearths which were all licensed as meeting-places, like the poor husbandman who was a Presbyterian teacher in Bury in Huntingdonshire, the Quaker husbandman of Oakington in Cambridgeshire, and the Baptist deacon who was a fisherman at Stretham in the Isle of Ely.[70] In these houses, microcosms of rural society, including the more prosperous, gathered, unified by their common religious enthusiasms. It is a delightful and remarkable coincidence that one of the Quaker meeting-houses which still survives in Amersham in Buckinghamshire, a focal point of both Lollards and Quakers in the Chilterns, is a cottage belonging to Joseph Winch, which had two hearths, and was licensed in 1689. By that time, a bay had been added to form a meeting-house (Plate 7).[71]

The focus of the Upperside Meeting in Buckinghamshire, which covered approximately the same area as the Lollard meetings in south Buckinghamshire five generations before, was again in and around Amersham (Map 7). According to the Compton Census of 1676 (Table 2), no less than 25 per cent of the inhabitants of Amersham itself were noncon-

[68] Stevenson, 'Economics and Social Status', pp. 291, 297–8, 324, 310, 304–6, 328, 331, 320–1, 324.

[69] Dr Wrightson points this out, Wrightson and Levine, Poverty and Piety in an English Village, pp. 167–9. On the other hand, his more prosperous nonconformists did not cooperate with their co-villagers so much in the delicate matter of will-making and witnessing, ibid., pp. 169–71.

[70] Stevenson, 'Economic and Social Status', p. 347.

[71] Buckinghamshire: An Inventory of Non-Conformist Chapels, and Meeting-Houses in Central England, Royal Commission for Historical Monuments, HMSO (1986), p. 5. A bay was added in 1689 to form a meeting-house, and the cottage was also added to in the eighteenth century, when the meeting-house was further extended. It has also been refronted. I am much indebted to Mr Stell for his help with this illustration.

formists. The national average was around 4 per cent. The other old
Lollard centre over the border in Hertfordshire, Rickmansworth, also
stood out in the Compton Census as quite abnormal, with 15 per cent
of dissenters. The proportion and weight of local inhabitants prepared
to be persecuted, or counted, for nonconformity, had shifted around a
little: the Lollard village of Hughenden had only 9 per cent of dissenters,
whereas Chalfont St Giles, which had had no Lollards, now had 36 per
cent of dissenters, and contained not only the Quaker meeting at Jordans,
which belonged to the Russell family, who were on the social border
between yeomen and gentlemen, but also a meeting of Independents,
and even of Fifth Monarchy men. But although there were shifts in the
concentrations of dissenters within the area, the outlines of the area dominated by Lollards in the 1520s, and by post-Restoration dissenters in the
late seventeenth century, remained the same (Maps 2 and 7).

Dr Stevenson's work on the members of the Upperside Quaker Meeting has been severely handicapped by the poor condition, and, for six
parishes, the disappearance, of the Hearth Tax returns. Furthermore, the
exempt poor are recorded for only three of the twenty-one parishes
covered by this meeting. However, he has been able to reconsider the
social origins of ninety of the first generation of Quakers belonging to
the Upperside Meeting, previously examined by both Professor Cole and
Professor Vann.[72] Professor Cole used only marriage registers for the
occupational status of early Friends. Professor Vann used a much wider
group of documents, but unfortunately defined anyone who farmed as
little as twenty acres of land as a yeoman. Professor Cole concluded that
the first generation of Quakers were drawn from the 'urban and rural petit
bourgeoisie'. Professor Vann, not surprisingly in view of his definition of
a 'yeoman', concluded that they were drawn from the 'middle to upper'
bourgeoisie, with a predominance of substantial yeomen and traders.

Dr Stevenson's re-examination demonstrates that 34 per cent of the
ninety Quakers belonging to the Upperside of Buckinghamshire Meeting
between 1655 and 1685 were in fact labourers and husbandmen.
Labourers, husbandmen, and craftsmen made up 54 per cent of the
whole. The first generation of Buckinghamshire Quakers was, according
to Dr Stevenson, 'a rural agrarian movement, made up primarily of the
lowest strata of agriculturalists – the "lower" and "middling" sorts'. But
it did also have its yeomen, its professionals, and, unusually, its gentlemen. Isaac Pennington, Thomas Ellwood, and William Penn must not be
forgotten. Thomas Ellwood, an eager young convert to the sect, would

---

[72] Stevenson, 'Economic and Social Status'. Dr Stevenson discusses the arguments in
W.A. Cole, 'The Social Origins of the Early Friends', *The Journal of the Friends' Historical
Society*, 48, 3 (1957), and Richard T. Vann, 'Quakerism and the Social Structure in
the Interregnum', *Past and Present*, 43 (1969), pp. 263–7.

even travel on foot when his horse was impounded by his father, from meeting to meeting in Buckinghamshire, Berkshire, and Oxfordshire,[73] according to his own autobiography.

This migrant pattern, explicitly set out by Thomas Ellwood in his auto-biography, was one followed before him, not only by the reading and teaching Lollards like Alice and Robert Collins, but also by the itinerant teachers of the whole sect.[74]

'Dissent as a phenomenon transmitted within the family deserves more attention', I wrote in 1972.[75] Recently, Dr Anne Hudson has written:

> amongst the Steeple Bumpstead group forced to abjure in 1528 was William Bocher, plough-wright; attached to the abjuration is a note that Bocher came from bad stock, since his great-grandfather was said to have been burned for heresy. Also mentioned in the 1528 proceedings is Joan Bocher, widow, and apparently the same family; this is the woman later notorious as Joan of Kent, who died at the stake in 1550 as an Anabaptist, after a life of persistent heresy. Allowing twenty-five years for each generation, this indicates that heresy continued in the Bocher family for over a hundred years.[76]

She has thus provided us with the earliest example known so far of dissent continuing in the family.

Another, tantalizing possible early example of family connection is between the Lollard tailor of Witham, the uncommonly named Chris-topher Raven, who knew people in Colchester, and William Raven of St Ives in the 1550s, who travelled to Colchester, and was present at a meet-ing for Christian exercises 'having . . . fled beying in danger for Religion'.[77] There had been a Christopher and Dyonise Raven of Witham who

---

[73] H. Morley (ed.), The History of Thomas Ellwood, Written by Himself (London, 1885).

[74] See below, pp. 37, 54–5, 134, 136, 144, 271–5. Notice, however, Dr Davies' stress on their relative lack of importance.

[75] Contrasting Communities, p. 280. Several of us goggled at a piece in The Times (third leader, 23 August 1991) titled 'All in the Genes', which stated 'Already it is known that genes play a large role in obesity, alcoholism, cancer, heart disease, premature senility and even religious belief – where identical twins in different families have similar attitudes.' This suggestion was further elaborated in a lecture by Dr Richard Dawkins given in Edinburgh on 15 April 1992, and reported in the Independent under the title 'Notions of the Deity nourished by human gene soup' the following day. It has been set out by Dr Dawkins in his Selfish Gene (2nd edn, Oxford, 1989). I regret to say that we have not followed up the literature on this, but it opens an interesting, and different, insight on this study. I am grateful to Andrew Brown of the Independent for his help.

[76] Hudson, Premature Reformation, p. 479.

[77] Margaret Spufford, Contrasting Communities, pp. 246–7. It was an exceptionally lively meeting. See below, p. 79.

abjured in 1511.[78] According to Foxe, Christopher Raven was still alive receiving 'good men and women that were in trouble and distress' in 1563.[79] But the will of Christopher Raven of Witham, tailor, complete with a dedicatory clause referring to the 'elect'[80] was proved in February 1541/2.[81] His widow, Joan, also made a strongly protestant will in 1571/2.[82] Their son, John, was a pillar of the Witham community: he was an almshouse trustee, an aletaster, a churchwarden in 1588, a Quarter Sessions juror, and a parish constable,[83] before dying in 1599, and leaving his soul, in a strongly idiosyncratic clause,

> into the hand[es] of allmighty god my maker & to Jesus Christe my alone Savio[ur] and redemer moste assuredlie and stedfastly beleveinge that all my sinnes are purged and cleane washed awaie by his moste p[re]cious bloode & my body to the earthe from whence it came untill the gen[er]all daye of Judgm[en]t, at w[hi]ch time I doe undoutedly beleve I shall w[i]th theise my eyes behoulde my alone lord and savio[ur] Jesus Christe to my endles ioye and comfort.

In the lives of these four Ravens of Witham, from Lollard to puritan churchwarden, which cover the entire sixteenth century, we have another example of radical belief in a family which spanned a century. Yet another John Raven of Hadleigh in Suffolk, not so far off the road between St Ives and Colchester, established four almshouses for the aged poor under Edward VI.[84]

What we do not know yet is whether Christopher Raven's son, John, the puritan churchwarden of Witham, knew his possible relation, William Raven of St Ives, who had visited Colchester in the 1550s. He was there converted to the Family of Love. His subsequent career has been traced by Dr Marsh.[85] He died in 1598 and had a very grand funeral in St Ives, indicating his achievement of a remarkable degree of civic status. In 1676,

[78] T.W. Davids, *Annals of Evangelical Nonconformity in the County of Essex* (London, 1863), and J.E. Oxley, *The Reformation in Essex* (Manchester, 1965).
[79] Hudson, *The Premature Reformation*, p. 477.
[80] See above, pp. 16–18, for the rarity of such clauses, and below, p. 122, for their significance at this date.
[81] Will of Christopher Raven, Essex RO D/ACR 4/185.
[82] Joan Raven, Essex RO D/ABW 31/190.
[83] John Raven, Essex RO D/P 30/25/64; D/DB w M26; D/ACA 16/113v, 16/119, 16/153; D/ACV 1/63; Q/SR 107/15; D/DBW M26 and will; D/ACW 4/123. I owe all these references on the activities and wills of the Raven family of Witham to the great kindness of Mrs Janet Gyford.
[84] Samuel Lewis, *Topographical Dictionary* (London, 1831). I owe this reference to the kindness of Dr Margaret Aston, who points out to me that Lollard influences interacted with others in a noticeable way in Hadleigh.
[85] Marsh, *The Family of Love*, index entry under Raven, William, p. 303.

Dr Stevenson has recorded a General Baptist family surnamed Raven as well as a Quaker, William Raven, all from villages near St Ives.[86]

A shorter, but very illuminating dissenting genealogy is provided in the diary of Isaac Archer,[87] incumbent of Chippenham in Cambridgeshire, and Great Welnetham and Mildenhall in Suffolk until his death in 1700. Isaac was the son of a puritan lecturer of Halstead in Essex, who refused to use any set form of prayer. His uncle had ministered to the separatist congregation at Arnheim. His grandparents were 'godly' people. Isaac's spiritual genealogy, in short, was very much like that of the Presbyterian dissenter of Yorkshire, Oliver Heywood, who wrote 'spiritual biographies' of all his forebears back to his great-grandparents.[88] Isaac Archer's diary is, however, perhaps unique amongst spiritual writing, at least until Edmund Gosse wrote Father and Son (1907), in the insight it gives into the close and tortured relationship between himself and his father. It makes it possible to understand how a tradition of dissent could accommodate apparently successful external adolescent rebellion, however painful, and yet still mark the young man, or woman, out for life. Although Isaac was able to conform, since he could find 'nothing inconsistent with Holy Scripture' in the prayer book, he was never comfortable within the established church and, in consequence, the nonconformists in the parishes where he was an incumbent were treated very tenderly indeed.[89]

Possibly the most remarkable illustration of dissent, or extreme religious conviction following a family line, which this time, interestingly, was nourished and nurtured and perhaps passed on by its women, is that demonstrated by the Diary of Elizabeth Bury, whose elegy was written by Isaac Watts.[90] The really remarkable thing about Elizabeth, which no

---

[86] E.B. Underhill (ed.), Records of the Churches at Fenstanton, Warboys, and Hexham, 1644–1720, Hanserd Knollys Society (London, 1854), p. 255 (1676). Hunts. Monthly Meeting Sufferings Book, Cambs. RO, R. 59.25.3.1 (1692). The Baptists were of Hemingford Grey and Abbott, the Quaker from Bluntisham.

[87] Mr Mathew Storey of St Edmund's College, Cambridge, is editing this for publication by the Suffolk Records Society.

[88] J. Horsfall Turner (ed.), Autobiography, Diaries, Anecdotes and Eventbook of Oliver Heywood (Brighouse, 1881); and W.J. Sheils, 'Oliver Heywood and his Congregation', in W.J. Sheils and Diana Wood (eds.), Voluntary Religion, Studies in Church History, 23 (Oxford, 1986).

[89] So tenderly, indeed, that they do not appear in the records at all, presumably because of the sympathy of the incumbent. Chippenham, where he was vicar, had from the diary, large numbers of nonconformists, whose meetings he even attended himself, but only one man appears as a nonconformist in the Compton Census of 1676. He had failed to pay his tithes, the one certain means of alienating this impecunious incumbent's tolerance.

[90] Samuel Bury (ed.), An Account of the Life and Death of Mrs Elizabeth Bury, Who Died May 11th 1720, Aged 76, Chiefly Collected out of her own Diary, Together with Her Funeral Sermon ... (2nd edn, London, 1971). For Elizabeth herself, her stepfather Nathanial Bradshaw, her second husband Samuel, his father, Edward, who wrote 'small godly'

one has hitherto noticed, is that her father, Captain Adam Lawrence of
Linton, was the grandson of a probable member of the Family of Love
of Balsham, whose father had cousins who were certainly members of
the Family. Adam Lawrence, born in 1581, had married a Suffolk gentlewoman, Elizabeth Cutts, in 1641, when he was sixty and she was only
twenty-two. It is almost certain that this marriage was made for her; but
in that case, Elizabeth's father, Henry Cutts of Clare, Esq., 'a Person learn'd
in the Law . . . and a zealous Promoter of the Interest of the Gospel' was
satisfied that Adam Lawrence was a suitable, and godly, match for his
daughter. This was not at all surprising. In 1645, Richard Baxter found
Captain Lawrence, this descendant and relation of Familists, the only
'orthodox' officer in Colonel Cromwell's regiment. He became his
friend.[91] Elizabeth's own pious papers and writings came into the hands
of her own daughter Elizabeth's second husband, who wrote of his
mother-in-law in his Introduction to a selection from his wife's *Diary*:

> She was an eminently serious, heavenly and experienced Christian; an
> Ornament to her Family, a Blessing to her Children and the Delight of
> all her Friends: She lived long to adorn her Profession, to exemplify
> Religion and to testify her Constancy and Resolution for the Interest of
> Christ . . . The solemn Transactions between God and her Soul, her
> sweet and near Communion with God . . . and the weekly solemn
> Remembrance she had of her Family in her Closet . . . fully appear by
> her own Papers.

This lady, married to a man of Familist descent, bred a veritable horde
of 'godly' children, who in turn, chose 'godly' husbands. She had four
children by her first marriage, and herself chose as her second husband
a Fellow of Trinity, Nathaniel Bradshaw, who became extremely well-
known as the ejected minister who nourished a Congregational flock
round and about Willingham in Cambridgeshire. They had six more children. Nathaniel Bradshaw was 'a laborious Catechist in his Family, to
whom he constantly expounded the Scripture Morning and Evening'.
Between their mother's exercises in her closet and their father's more
public ministrations, it is no wonder so many of the ten led such remarkably devout lives.

books, her half-brother-in-law the Rev. Thomas Salmon of 'Mepal' or Meppershall
in Bedfordshire, see *DNB*, pp. 476–7, and *VCH Beds.*, II, pp. 292, 479–80, 475–6. For
Bradshaw, see also Margaret Spufford, *Contrasting Communities*, p. 293. For Elizabeth
Bury's first husband, Griffith Lloyd, see J. and J.A. Venn, *Alumni Cantabrigiensis*, 4 vols.
(Cambridge, 1922–7), p. 94, and *VCH Hunts.*, II, p. 314 (Hemingford Grey). We are
very deeply indebted to Mrs Jill Leech, who sent us this *Diary* as an interesting
general example, without the least knowledge that it would link Christopher
Marsh's Family of Love and William Stevenson's post-Restoration dissenters. Serendipity is a remarkable ally, although not a methodology.
[91] C.H. Firth and Godfrey Davies, *The Regimental History of Cromwell's Army* (Oxford, 1940),
I, pp. 10, 16 n. 1, 58, 62, 67. Lawrence was killed in 1648, outside Colchester.

Elizabeth, the second daughter, selections from whose *Diary* we have, was a very remarkable woman indeed, not only because she took 'especial delight in Hebrew and frequently quoted the Original in common Conversation, when the true Meaning of some particular Texts of Scripture depended on it', and also practised medicine with some competence. After her conversion at the age of ten, she regularly rose at 4 a.m. to have time for prayer before family worship, after which she withdrew to her closet again for study of divinity, Hebrew, and prayer. In her old age, she modified this regime to rise as late as 5 a.m. We know little of her first husband, a graduate, barrister and JP, except that according to his successor, 'they lived together . . . with such a mutual Love and Pleasure as to be taken Notice of by all their Neighbours; envied by some, and glorified by others'. After his death, she turned down three very eligible offers from two knights and a bishop, since she was not 'easy in the Communion of the Established Church'. She chose instead Samuel Bury, Presbyterian minister of the congregation at Bury St Edmunds, and no less a person than a collaborator with Calamy in compiling lists of nonconforming ministers, since 'The People of God were always the People of her Choice.' She favoured the company of ejected ministers, but, like Isaac Archer, 'had a true Affection . . . for all serious Christians . . . whether under a Cloak or a Cassock'. But she delighted in 'the Company of the Godly . . . and would diligently frequent their Prayer-Meetings'. The Sacraments were immensely important to her, and she never missed Communion for twenty-three years, unless illness prevented her.[92] Her interior life was indeed godly, and so was that of her household: there is a very interesting account of her prayers, readings, and instruction of her servants.[93]

Here, then, we have the descendant of a Familist on the paternal side, whose father was approved of by Richard Baxter as 'orthodox', whose mother chose a man who became an Independent ejected minister as her second husband, and who herself chose a nonconforming minister as her own second husband. Three more of her sisters, or half-sisters, married men who were marked out by their religious practices or ministry, 'hoping for some Blessedness with the Perfect', and one of these women also wrote a set of spiritual papers. Truly, Dr Marsh's Family of Love seem to have left a potent spiritual legacy to its descendants, as did the Cutts family into which they married.

There are other, much humbler examples. Dissenting opinions seemed to have descended in the family amongst adherents of all sects, in south-

---

[92] See below, p. 95.
[93] For all the quotations above, see Elizabeth Bury's *Diary*, Ch. 1, pp. 2, 3, Ch. 2, pp. 5, 6, Ch. 13, pp. 28–9, Ch. 6, pp. 16–17, Ch. 10, pp. 21–2, Ch. 7, p. 18, Ch. 15, p. 31, Ch. 5, p. 14, Ch. 16, p. 34, Ch. 10, pp. 24–5.

ern Cambridgeshire in the seventeenth century. The Conders and the Crabbs were both Congregationalist. The Conders at least were descended from puritans. Old Richard Conder was a yeoman, an 'ancient professor' who regularly met with a group of like-minded farmers in the mid-seventeenth century who marketed at Royston, and whose custom it was 'when they had done their marketing, to meet together, and spend their penny together in a private room, when, without interruption, they might talk freely of the things of God; how they had heard on the Sabbath-day, and how they had gone on the week past etc.'. On one of these occasions, the conversation turned to their conversions. Old Richard Conder gave an account of his horror at hearing the _Book of Sports_ read in his parish church in 1633, and how he dated his conversion from that time.

> When our minister was reading it, I was seized with a chill and horror not to be described. Now, thought I, iniquity is established by a law, and sinners are hardened in their sinful ways! What sore judgments are to be expected upon so wicked and guilty a nation! What must I do? Whither shall I fly? How shall I escape the wrath to come? And God set in so with it, that I thought it was high time to be in earnest about salvation ... So that I date my conversion from that time; and adore the grace of God in making that to be an ordinance to my salvation, which the devil and wicked governors laid as a trap for my destruction.

Richard Conder signed the petition against episcopal government in 1640, even though it was his wife who first joined the Congregational Church in the 1650s. Their son wrote an account of the formation of the church, and the Conders remained pastors until 1781. It was old Richard's great-grandson who, in 1740, was given an account of the scene in the inn at Royston by an old man then aged ninety or more, who, as a boy, had been allowed to sit in the corner while his elders discussed 'by what means God first visited their souls'.[94]

The Crabbs of Little Wilbraham were slightly less spectacular. Moses Crabb, water-miller, had a small conventicle in his house in 1669. Ten years later, four Crabbs and a Crabb son-in-law were presented by the churchwardens for joining conventicles, and the validity of Sarah Crabb's marriage was questioned. In 1716, Sarah Crabb, aged twenty, daughter of Widow Crabb of Little Wilbraham was baptized as a Congregationalist in Cambridge, along with her eighteen-year-old sister, 'after her experience of the work of God laid upon her soul in the law of the church'. She was presumably the grandchild of the Sarah whose marriage was doubted[95]

[94] Margaret Spufford, _Contrasting Communities_, pp. 225–6, 231–2, and Trans. Cong. Hist. Soc., 21 (1972), pp. 77–9.
[95] Margaret Spufford, _Contrasting Communities_, p. 296.

and the fourth generation to experience spiritual conviction of this sort within the Congregational Church.

The Metcalfes of Melbourne were, however, quite as colourful as the Conders. Benjamin Metcalfe was one of the puritanically inclined parish officials of 1637–8, and later signed the petition against episcopacy. His son, another Benjamin, was born about 1626, and became a corporal serving with Cromwell's Ironsides. We do not know, and would like to, whether he served under Captain Adam Lawrence. In 1640, Benjamin senior was responsible for leading a riot, when he turned away the collectors of ship-money at the end of a pitchfork. His son, on his return to Melbourne about 1651, founded the Baptist Church there, which was noted with disgust by the bishop in 1669. It survived, and a Richard Metcalfe was deacon of it between 1705 and 1707. He was probably the great-grandson of old Benjamin who led the riot in 1640, and again the fourth successive generation of his family to lead the Baptists.[96] Dr Jacqueline Bower has been able to trace similar descents among the General Baptists of Kent.[97]

It was high time to draw these anecdotal, but suggestive, fragments together, and produce a scientific study. We chose the Chilterns.[98] The coincidence of the Lollard area of south Buckinghamshire, which had a dense population of Lollards in 1524 and 1525, and the Quaker area of Upperside Meeting in south Buckinghamshire 130 years later persuaded us to take the area around the market town of Amersham for our microscopic study.[99] We were encouraged in this because detailed examination by Dr Plumb has shown that Lollards were 'self-contained ... within three or four parishes adjacent to each other' and within walking distance of each other (see Map 1). The dominant groups were at Amersham, Chesham, Hughenden, and the Missendens. There was a scatter of Lollards in the Wycombes and Penn and other parishes further afield. There had been a conventicle which 'used to resort and confer together of matters of religion' in Thomas Man's house in Amersham[100] before 1511; after that Thomas and Alice Harding, who later moved to Chesham, had a house which was the resort of 'known men'.[101] Thomas Harding was himself burnt in 1532. He may have been a mercer. He was taxed on £10 in the Great Subsidy, and also had goods at Great Missenden and Penn.[102]

[96] Ibid., pp. 269, 279–80. See above, p. 26.
[97] Jacqueline Bower, 'The Congregation of the Dover General Baptist Church 1660–1700' (Leicester, MA, 1983), chapter 4.
[98] See above, p. 21–3, and below, pp. 40–2 Derek Plumb, pp. 135 et seq.
[99] See above, Ch. 7.
[100] Foxe, IV, p. 228; Plumb, 'Foxe and the Later Lollards', p. 395.
[101] Foxe, IV, p. 227; Plumb, 'Foxe and the Later Lollards', pp. 379–80.
[102] For a consideration of his views, see Hudson, Premature Reformation, pp. 505–7; Plumb, 'Foxe and the Later Lollards', p. 379.

Robert Bartlet of Amersham, who was very wealthy, taxed on £40 in the
Subsidy, identified a large group of Lollards, including men and women
from West Wycombe and Little Missenden for 'resorting many times
together, reading and conferring'. Isabel Bartlet of Amersham identified
Lollards from Hughenden.[103] Richard Ashford, a smith, had a group reading the Acts of the Apostles 'for two hours together' in his house at
Chesham.[104] There is a very full description of a meeting in Hughenden
in 1530.[105] Dr Plumb's identification of the varied places of origin of those
present at these conventicles helps us to articulate the bones and muscles
of this gathered church.

It appears from these interwoven detections of each other by the Lollards under persecution, and from the reconstructions of such meetings,
that people resident in Amersham, Chesham, and Hughenden resorted
to each other's meetings, as did adherents from the settlements round
about. There is a strong case for regarding them as integrated members
of a single group.[106] Members resident around the extreme periphery of
the area would also attend other meetings within their reach, like those
at Staines, and even at Burford. Special occasions, like weddings, called
for much more general long-distance travel.

We considered the whole question of the definition of 'normal' catchment areas for a market town, and whether these coincided with the
areas within which most marriages were made, and also with the areas
within which short-term population movement took place. We needed
to examine these questions, to be quite sure of the appropriate area
throughout which we should examine surnames to try and find 'our'
dissenters. We assumed, as a working axiom, that the area from which a
'gathered church' was drawn may well have largely coincided with marketing, marriage, and mobility areas.[107] We ended up with twenty-one
parishes around Amersham in south Buckinghamshire and three in west
Hertfordshire.

We began by comparing the surnames of those taxed in the chosen
area in 1524–5 and the 1660s. We found 29 per cent of these surnames
in the population at large, reoccurring in the 1660s. We then took the
fifty-nine surnames of the known Lollards of the 1520s, and compared
them with the surnames of known Quakers and Baptists in the 1660s.
Forty-eight, or 81 per cent, reoccurred as dissenters five generations later.
Five more Lollard names reoccurred in the 1660s not as dissenters, giving
us the extraordinary total of 90 per cent of Lollard names persisting over

---

[103] Foxe, IV, p. 222; Plumb, 'Foxe and the Later Lollards', p. 344.
[104] Foxe, IV, p. 230; Plumb, 'Foxe and the Later Lollards', p. 344.
[105] Foxe, IV, p. 584; Derek Plumb, see below, pp. 160–2.
[106] Despite Dr Richard Davies, views. See below, pp. 133–5.
[107] See below, Ch. 7, pp. 275–7, 291–2, 326–8.

time. The Lollards of 1524–5 were by no means all prosperous;[108] but we checked this remarkable stability by taking a 'control' group of the wealthiest individuals taxed on £5 or more in the 1524–5 Subsidy.[109] There were 215 of these. The wealthiest may be supposed to be the least mobile in rural society: 45 per cent of these surnames reappeared in the 1660s. Those bearing Lollard surnames, despite the poverty of some of them, were therefore far more static even than the most prosperous in south Buckinghamshire in 1524–5. I believe, indeed, we have stumbled across the most static group so far known amongst the population of early modern England.[110] We have done much, I believe, to strengthen Dr Davies' assertion that Lollardy had been 'built soundly, along the grain of English society: its strength lay in personally-linked clusters ... the hallmark of Lollards was their substantial local self-sufficiency'.[111] This self-sufficiency seems to have been so important that it kept them in their localities.

Mrs Evans has carried this study on by taking nineteen of the most idiosyncratic surnames common to both late Lollards and post-Restoration Quakers and Baptists[112] and trying to trace the families through to see if there was an actual genealogical connection. She has analysed the parish registers of the fifteen parishes in our area for which the registers open early, plus the surviving relevant wills for all of them, both locally and in the Prerogative Court of Canterbury.

It proved possible to connect six of these families in the limited time at our disposal (see Appendix B for these genealogies). We fully expected only to be able to connect prosperous families, for whom the evidence from wills would be the most substantial, amongst the Lollard and Quaker congregations, despite the proven wide social and economic spread of both. We were therefore particularly pleased that one of the six families, the Dells of Chesham and Chartridge, was a labouring family. There is also a delightful irony in the doubts of the 'gentle' Quaker Russell family over the marriage of their daughter, Mary, with a smith from the next parish, who, if they had but known it, was descended from one of the most prominent and wealthiest Lollard families of the 1520s, the Bartlets.[113] Lastly, Mrs Evans showed that it is possible to trace dissenting

---

[108] See above, p. 13, and below, Derek Plumb, p. 114, Table 3.
[109] We would like to record here our gratitude to Mr Richard Wall for his invaluable advice and help in this area.
[110] See below, pp. 315–16, 330. We consider the importance, or lack of it, of being of a freeholder in this 'stable' group, below, pp. 302–3.
[111] Davies, 'Lollardy and Locality', pp. 199, 211.
[112] Again, we would like to record our gratitude to the Marc Fitch Fellow at Leicester, Dr David Postles, for his help in this area, as well as our gratitude to his predecessor, Mr Richard McKinley.
[113] See below, p. 138.

Table 2. The centres of Lollardy and later nonconformity in Buckinghamshire, Hertfordshire, and Middlesex

Parish name	Lollards 1524 No.	Lollards 1524 % of taxpayers	Nonconformists in 1676 No.	Nonconformists in 1676 % of total	Opening date of register if searched for nineteen families	Quakers No. 1669	Quakers In Upperside Meeting	Baptists No. in Ford/Cuddington	Others	LOLLARDS 1636	Licensed meeting-place in 1672. Licensed preachers Q	B	O
Buckinghamshire													
Amersham	115	93.4	215	24.9	1561	79	Yes	56 (132)[a]	P., 'Jews'	M	M	M	P, Pre.
Beaconsfield	6	7.0	12	1.8	1631	10	No					P	M
Bledlow	0				1592	3	Yes	5	Sect not given				?
Chalfont St Giles	0		78	35.7	1584	39	Yes				M[c]		M
Chalfont St Peter	0				1539	18	No		Ind. Fifth Monarchy[b]				P/M
Chenies	2	9.5	11	8.3	1592		No						M
Chesham with members (including Chesham Bois)	34	19.4	(3)[d]	5.7	1538	45	Yes	1		M	M		M, Ind.
Denham	2	3.3	4	1.3	1653	1	No						
Dorney	2						No						
Fingest	0				1607		No						
Hambledon	1	1.2			1566		No						

High Wycombe	3	1.7			1674	73	No	4	Pre. Ind.				M	M Pre. M Ind.
Horton/ Colnbrook	1	2.7					No							M Ind.
Hughenden	26	?	17	8.8	1559	2	No			M				
Iver (near Staines)	5	5.2	9	1.9	1605		No							
Marlow, Great	12	12.9	50	4.1	1592	5	No							
Marlow, Little	2	5.0			1559		No							
Missenden, Great	9	8.3	25	6.1	1678	24	Yes	1						
Missenden, Little	24	[e]	2	1.3	1559	2	Yes	2	Ind.				M	Ind. M
Penn	2	3.1	20	6.0	1563	10	No	2						
Risborough, Monks	0				1587	17	Yes							
Risborough, Princes	7	9.8[f]	38	5.5	1561		No	2		1530 M				
Upton	1						No							
Wendover	1	2.7[g]					No							
West Wycombe	4	5.3			1581	3	No							M Ind.
Wooburn	2	4.2	12	5.6	1653	11	No				M			
Wraysbury	2	6.0					No							
Hertfordshire														
Kings Langley	1		5	1.6	1538	3	No							
Rickmansworth	8	6.3	50	15.3[h]	1653	35	No			M		M	M	
Sarratt	1				1560	1	No							
Ware	5						No							
Watford					1539	50	No						M	P M

Table 2 (cont.)

Parish name	Lollards No. 1524 taxpayers	Lollards % of 1524 taxpayers	Nonconformists in 1676 No.	Nonconformists in 1676 % of total	Opening date of register if searched for nineteen families	Quakers No. 1669	Quakers In Upper-side Meeting	Baptists No. in Ford/ Cuddington	Others	Licensed meeting-place in 1672	Licensed preachers 1636 Q	B	O
Middlesex													
Harrow	2						No						
Ruislip	2	4.2					No						
Staines	11	16					No			M			
Uxbridge	12						No			M			

Note: the meeting-houses in Table 2 are not the same as those on Map 7, as they come from different sources.

B=Baptist
Ind.=Independent
M=Meeting
O=Other
P=Preacher
Pre.=Presbyterian
Q=Quaker

[a] 132 names mentioned but only 56 were baptized members. Amersham Baptist Church was separate from Ford.
[b] Independent meeting-place and preacher; Fifth Monarchy meeting and preacher.
[c] Jordons.
[d] Chesham Bois only.
[e] Subsidy survives only for hamlet at Walton in Little Missenden.
[f] Defective percentage because part of 1524 Subsidy illegible.
[g] Defective subsidy return.
[h] 1677 not 1676.

Sources: Plumb, John Foxe and the Later Lollards'; Whiteman (ed.), The Compton Census of 1676; W.T. Whitley (ed.), The Church Books of Ford or Cuddington and Amersham in the County of Bucks, Baptist Historical Society (London, 1912); Bucks. RO D/A/V/4 Visitations of the Archdeaconry of Buckingham 1636–7; George Lyon Turner (ed.), Original Records of Early Nonconformity under Persecution and Indulgence (London, 1911).

genealogies through a female line, although the exercise is so time consuming that only two were completed.[114]

These results are very dramatic. The most convincing is the continuity of over 80 per cent of dissenting names compared with the 29 per cent of the population at large. Further genealogies could be added, but will only serve to gild the gingerbread. The main point is proven.

There is, of course, a major disadvantage. It is unsatisfactory only to establish pedigrees through four or five generations from late Lollards to early Baptists or Quakers, without finding the middle generations involved either in clandestine, subversive 'radical' dissent, or in popular and much more acceptable Elizabethan 'puritanism'. There are a few extremely important pointers to both the former, and the latter. In the Visitation Book for 1636–7 are the most interesting entries of all, demonstrating the existence of conventicles at Great Chesham and Wooburn.[115] These suggest the continuance of clandestine group dissent just where we would most expect it, in the old Lollard centre north of Amersham, and down on the river next to Marlow. Both places later produced Quakers for the Upperside Meeting. It is also extremely interesting that, despite the reasons for absence from church or Communion being very seldom given, we know from the churchwardens' presentments of 1584–6 that a parishioner of Chesham Bois refused to receive Communion because the minister was not a preacher, which sounds like orthodox 'puritanism', while Henry Dell, one of 'our' families for which we have a dissenting genealogy, was presented for 'disquieting our minister in the time of the communion' which sounds more radical.[116] The Lollard Butterfields, who had Quaker descendants, had a daughter they called 'Grace' round the turn of the sixteenth and seventeenth centuries: the Lollard Hardings, who had Baptist descendants, had a daughter named 'Christian' around 1620. We also found a 'Nathan' and a 'Lazarus' in the 1630s. But this, though highly suggestive, is not enough. We can only plead the truth, problems with the records. There was a complete gap in the records for the archdeaconry between 1584–6 and 1633–4 (below, pp. 36 n. 117, 304–5). It seems highly suspicious that ten of 'our' nineteen families were in trouble in the ecclesiastical court the year the records reopened. The quality of the evidence concerning early sixteenth-century Lollards and post-Restoration Quakers and Baptists in Buckinghamshire is unfortunately therefore not matched during the intervening years. The paucity of evidence for 'hot' protestantism in this period is probably due to several other factors as well: acceptance by the community of dissen-

---

[114] See Appendix B, Gate of Chesham and the Nash and Child families of Amersham.
[115] Bucks. RO D/A/V/4.
[116] Both cases from Bucks. RO D/A/V/1(b).

ters, and failure on the part of churchwardens to make presentments.[117] If the honest churchwardens of Sarratt,[118] who were quite out of control of a parish well placed for attendance at conventicles, were anything to go by, radicals and the 'hotter sort of protestants' would not necessarily have been presented in this area at all. In view of the patchy survival of records, the frequent election of churchwardens who were themselves 'radicals' or the 'hotter sort of protestant', and the proven local tolerant attitude to dissenters, we cannot think that the absence of other evidence of active dissent or 'hot' protestantism between 1530 and 1660 in the area covered by the Quaker Upperside Meeting can be taken as proof that it did not exist.

But we still, lamentably, lack the kind of hard evidence produced so liberally by the quirky records of the Archdeaconry of Essex for the 1570s and 1580s, used with such effect to suggest the possible origins of congregational independency by Professor Collinson in 1966. Professor Collinson himself wrote 'The process can be closely observed in Essex, where the local records, and especially the act books of the archdeaconry courts of Essex and Colchester, are exceptionally informative.'[119] He was

---

[117] All the relevant records at Aylesbury have been searched for the nineteen family names on which we focussed. These records are: D/A/C/1b office and instance cases 1553, 1554–5; D/A/C/2 acts of court 1561–77; D/A/C/23 register of depositions 1578–9, 1581–4; D/A/V/1(b) churchwardens' presentments 1584–6; D/A/C/8 proceedings in instance cases 1620–1, 1632–3; D/A/C/8 Act Book for 1620–1 and 1632–3; D/A/V/2 Visitation Book 1633–4; D/A/V/3 Visitation Book 1635; D/A/V/4 Visitation Book 1636–7; D/A/V/5 church inspections 1637, 1674, 1754 (last year omitted); D/A/V/6 Visitation Book 1662; D/A/V/7 Visitation Book 1664; D/A/V/8 Episcopal Visitation 1664; D/A/V/9 Visitation Book 1666–72; D/A/V/10 Visitation Book 1673–84; D/A/C/24 original depositions 1680–4, 1687; D/A/V/11 Visitation Book 1686–1714. The Lincolnshire Record Office also holds some churchwardens' presentments for this archdeaconry; the only complete set, for 1597, has also been searched as have lists of excommunicants for c. 1600–3; these too are at Lincoln. Irritatingly, no reason is given for the excommunications, but none of our nineteen families were amongst them.

Our major failure, and the one possible future hope for filling this gap in the centre of our time-span, lies in the consistory court records of the diocese of Lincoln. These records have never been properly listed, and papers of the consistory and archdeaconry courts are mixed up in a large number of boxes. There are no deposition books for these courts at Lincoln. We were going to try a 'lucky dip' exercise for a limited time on these boxes: the member of our group who had used ecclesiastical records most came over from the States in the summer of 1991 specifically to undertake this. His visit coincided, appallingly, with the closure of the Lincoln Record Office for removal to new premises. We have never since had the opportunity to fill this, very important, hole in our evidence. A proper search is likely to be very lengthy and may be completely unrewarding, in view of the normal limitations of ecclesiastical records discussed above. However, it would be well worth a doctoral student embarking on it to see if 'hard' evidence of continuity can be found.

[118] See above, p. 12.

[119] Reprinted as 'The Godly: Aspects of Popular Protestantism', in *Godly People: Essays on English Protestantism and Puritanism* (London, 1983), especially pp. 9–11. There is a gentle

entirely, and, from our point of view, lamentably, right. The Essex evidence is exactly the kind of evidence required to prove our case conclusively, but the archdeaconry officials of Buckinghamshire appear to have defined their task very differently from their opposite numbers in Essex.

The very stability of these Lollard dissenting families and their sympathizers at one end of our chronology, and their Quaker and Baptist heirs at the other, will have made them more influential in their communities. Dr Hey has just considered the massive, disproportionately large, social importance in their own areas of those, possibly minority, core groups of families who did remain in the same region over time.[120] Meanwhile, our findings do much to underline Dr Davies' suggestion that historians have overplayed 'the key role of the social marginal in the transmission of information – all those loveable tramps, pedlars, vagabonds, migrants and friars', like our itinerant teachers and preachers of both Lollards and Quakers, who did much to connect Dr Hill's seven radical areas. Dr Davies emphasizes that such preaching strangers could only be successful if they were accepted by a stable social network, including figures of substance. This network should be bound by long-term and active personal ties.[121] Surely we have demonstrated that Lollardy took firm root in the Chilterns, in due course to be replaced by Quaker and Baptist adherents, in just such a stable network. All Dr Davies did not know was that the kin network extended across the social spectrum, and therefore bound adherents of different economic status firmly together. But stability is indeed the outstanding mark of this group, and its descendants.

This stability, together with the nature of early sixteenth-century, and post-Restoration dissent, running completely across the social spectrum, is our most important finding. It leads to the conclusion, which is of enormous importance to the history of religious dissent, that the dissenters themselves were integrated into their local communities in a way which we had not previously dreamt. In turn, Dr Plumb, Dr Marsh, and Dr Stevenson find this. Dr Marsh asks us, as a result, to rethink all our assumptions about the presence, or absence, of toleration in early

---

later modification on p. 18. I discussed the idiosyncratic nature of the Archdeaconry of Essex records as long ago as 1974, *Contrasting Communities*, pp. 250–9, especially pp. 257–9.

[120] David Hey, 'Stable Families in Tudor and Stuart England' (forthcoming). I am most grateful to Dr Hey for letting me see this piece.

[121] Davies, 'Lollardy and Locality', pp. 194–5, 199–200, 202–4. It is extremely revealing that exactly the same point had been made earlier about the stable devout households, whether rural or in prominent towns, which formed the core of the Old Dissenting denominations of the eighteenth century, amongst which Philip Doddridge's perpetual travels formed a link. Alan Everitt, 'Springs of Sensibility: Philip Doddridge of Northampton and the Evangelical Tradition', in Alan Everitt, *Landscape and Community in England* (London, 1985), pp. 215, 240.

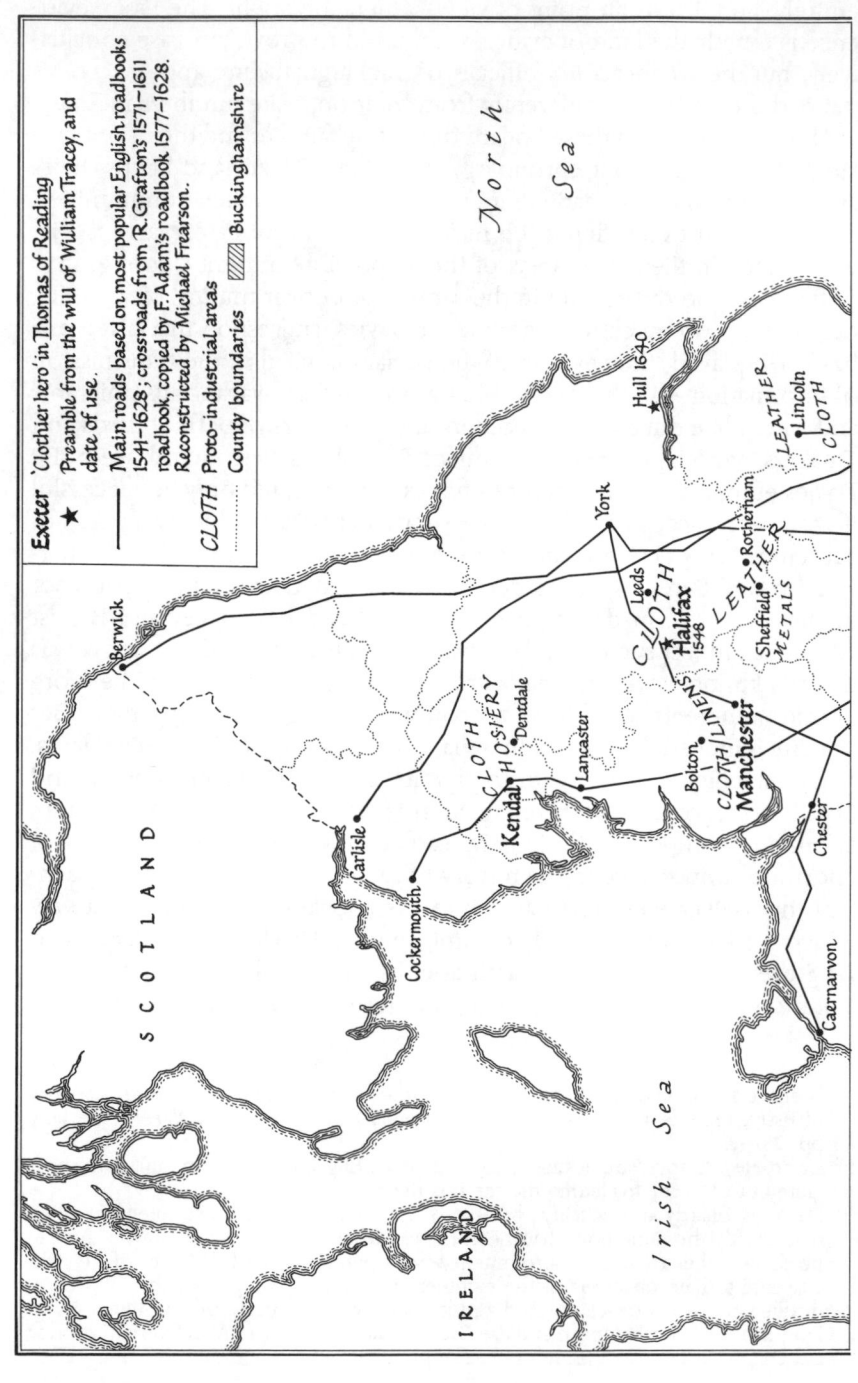

Exeter ★ 'Clothier hero' in Thomas of Reading
Preamble from the will of William Tracey, and
date of use.

Main roads based on most popular English roadbooks
1541–1628; crossroads from R. Grafton's 1571–1611
roadbook, copied by F. Adam's roadbook 1577–1628.
Reconstructed by Michael Frearson.

CLOTH Proto-industrial areas

.... County boundaries ▨▨ Buckinghamshire

SCOTLAND

IRELAND

Irish Sea

North Sea

Berwick

Carlisle

Cockermouth

Kendal
CLOTH HOSIERY

Pentdale

Lancaster

York

Leeds
C L O T H

Halifax
1548

Bolton
CLOTH/LINENS

Manchester

Chester

Caernarvon

Sheffield
METALS

Rotherham
L E A T H E R

Hull 1640

LEATHER

Lincoln
CLOTH

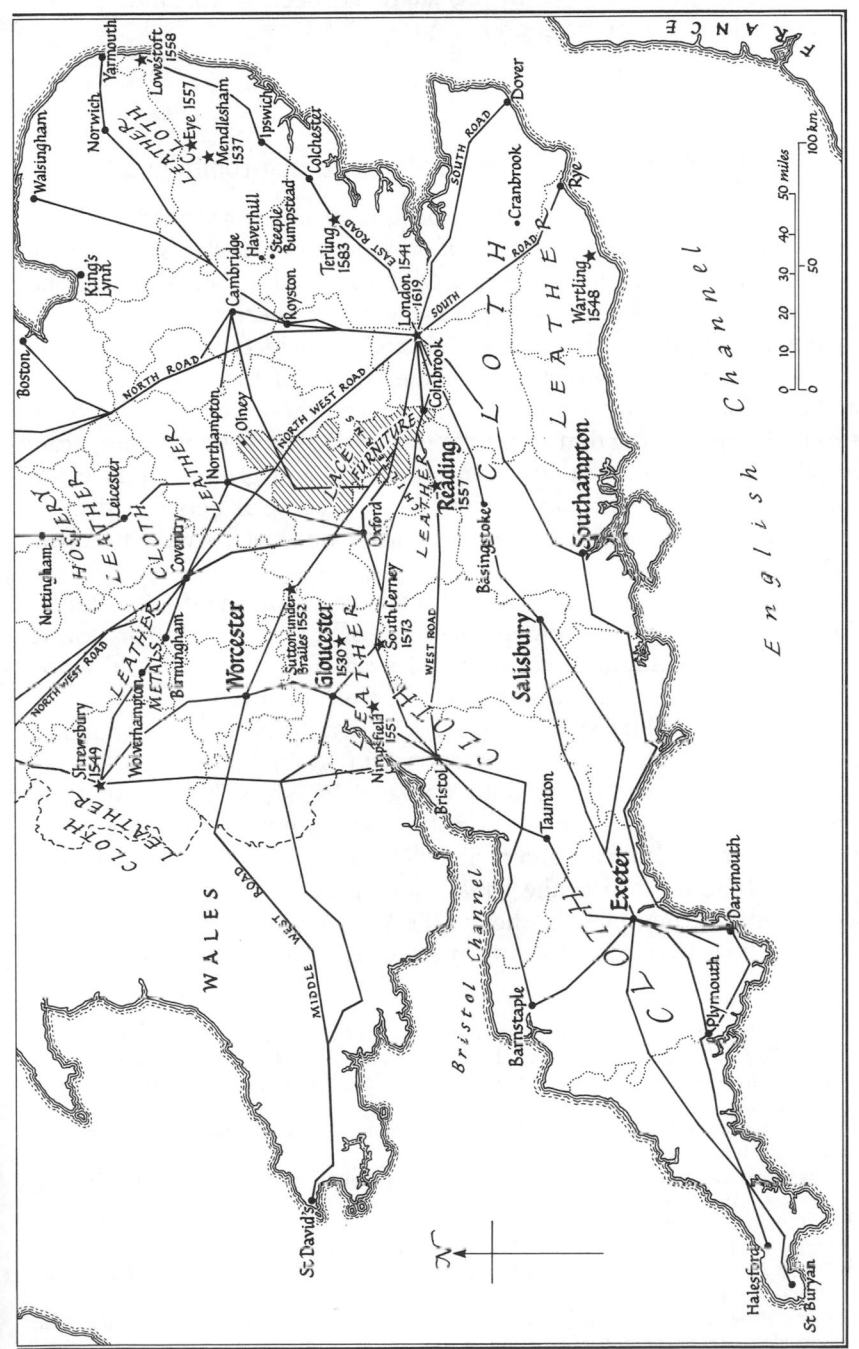

Map 1. Roads, industry, and dissenting connections c. 1600

modern English society. Truly, this study has been worth undertaking, for its implications are profound.

The distribution of dissent, by-employment, and communications

The concentration of dissenters through time in the wooded Chiltern area of south Buckinghamshire, infested first with Lollards, and then with Quakers and Baptists, has caused me to think more widely about the possible connections between areas where there were 'Industries in the Countryside', in the sixteenth and seventeenth centuries, that is, areas of by-employment, or, in the jargon of the 1970s and 80s, areas of 'proto-industrialization', and areas where there was also a strong dissenting tradition. We have established dissenting stability: can we also establish dissenting communications, and give a rationale for these apparent, superficially inexplicable, associations between dissent and handicraft regions? Many of these handicraft regions were in forest areas.[122]

Joan Thirsk first wrote on 'Industries in the Countryside' in 1961.[123] She considered the Wealden parishes of Kent, with their forest resources, large populations, scattered small farms, and the development of the cloth trade, where clothiers were involved in dairying on the side. She considered the wood-pasture and dairying area of Suffolk, with its weak manors, high population, and, again, its cloth trade. She considered the 'cheese and butter' area of Wiltshire. The great cloth area lay only in the dairying part of the county, not on the wide open chalklands of Salisbury Plain.[124] She did not consider our woodlands of the Chilterns,[125] nor the great cloth area with its metal trades alongside[126] in the huge parishes of the West Riding of Yorkshire, nor, indeed, the early industrializing metal area in the west midlands,[127]

---

[122] John Bossy, 'The Map of Christianity in Early-Modern England', in Edward Royle (ed.), *Regional Studies in the History of Religion since the Later Middle Ages* (Conference of Regional and Local Historians, 1984), and J.D. Gay, *The Geography of Religion in England* (London, 1971).

[123] F.J. Fisher (ed.), *Essays in the Economic and Social History of Tudor and Stuart England in Honour of R.H. Tawney* (Cambridge, 1961), pp. 70–88.

[124] For the social distinctions between these areas, see Ingram, *Church Courts, Sex and Marriage*, pp. 74–80.

[125] Although she later made some very suggestive comments on them, in her Preface to *The Rural Economy of England: Collected Essays* (London, 1984), pp. vii–viii.

[126] David Hey, *The Fiery Blades of Hallamshire: Sheffield and its Neighbourhood, 1660–1740* (Leicester, 1991).

[127] Marie Rowlands, *Masters and Men in the West Midlands Metalware Trades before the Industrial Revolution* (Manchester, 1975).

which spread into the Forest of Arden. She did consider the stocking knitting area on the western side of the Pennines, centred on Kendal and Dentdale. This was a different type of area with vast parishes with very large populations which could support themselves, despite tiny farms, on their stocking knitting and their extensive moorland common rights. She concluded that 'the location of handicraft industries is not altogether haphazard, but is associated with certain types of farming community and certain types of social organisation'. She defined the common factors as a populous community of small farmers on relatively secure tenures pursuing a pastoral economy, either dairying, or breeding or rearing livestock, on generous pasture commons. She suggested that further studies of other rural industries which she did not then consider, like lace making, which we find in the Chilterns or, I suggest, furniture making and fuel export, which we also find in the Chilterns, should pay attention to these factors.

These English areas in which handicraft industries flourished, and did, or did not, take off as the bases for later fully industrialized areas, were enumerated very conveniently, and amplified into a complete list (see Map 1) by Professor Donald Coleman in his withering summary of a debate on 'proto-industrialization', which, mercifully, does not concern us here. He concluded that, geographically, all that these various regions with early industry had in common was that they lay in valleys and wooded uplands with mixed pastoral farming and easy access to grazing on the waste.[128]

---

[128] D.C. Coleman, 'Proto-Industrialization: A Concept too Many', *Economic History Review*, 2nd Ser., 36, 3 (1983), pp. 435–8, esp. pp. 441–2. He listed the four main woollen textile areas of East Anglia, the West Country, the south-west, and the West Riding of Yorkshire; some lesser woollen areas on the borders of Shropshire and Wales, the Westmorland industry around Kendal, the southern area from the Kentish Weald into Surrey, Berkshire, and Hampshire, and scattered manufacturing areas around Coventry, Northampton, and Lincoln. He also distinguished two different textile zones, Lancashire, which turned to linens and fustians, and the hosiery knitting area in the Vale of Trent. Lastly, there was the west midlands region of small metalwares. It is extremely interesting that Dr Clarkson's enumeration of areas where the leather crafts were extremely important shows a high degree of coincidence between these and the areas listed by Professor Coleman. Dr Clarkson specifically mentions High Suffolk and Norwich, 'western England', including Gloucestershire, the Forest of Dean, Oxfordshire, the West Riding of Yorkshire especially Sheffield, the borders of Shropshire and Wales, Kendal, the Weald of Kent and Sussex, and Reading, Northampton, and areas of Lincolnshire, Northampton, and Leicester, and Birmingham, Walsall, and Wolverhampton. L.A. Clarkson, 'The Leather Crafts in Tudor and Stuart England', *Agricultural History Review*, 14 (1966), pp. 25–39 *passim*. The most recent major addition to the literature is the series of studies in Pat Hudson (ed.), *Regions and Industries: A Perspective on the Industrial Revolution in Britain* (Cambridge, 1989), which is helpful on early industry round Kendal, the Weald, Lancashire, and the west midlands. The 'Introduction' assumes the connection between wood-pasture and dissenting regions (pp. 18–19). The Scottish chapter, on the other hand, points out that lack of employment for women in large-scale

There is a very high correlation indeed between the lists of areas where early industry flourished, made by these agrarian and economic historians, and that made by Dr Hill of areas in which there might have been linear continuity between radical dissenters.[129] 'Both Lollardy and later heresy are found especially in clothing counties, and in pastoral, forest, and fen areas', he wrote. Again, he stressed large parishes, weaker ecclesiastical and manorial control and resources for the poor and vagrants, as the best conditions for radicals.[130]

If there is indeed a strong correlation between areas of handicraft industries and areas where there is a tradition of questioning, radical religious belief, the question we have to ask is 'Why?'. Why should regions with early industry, or by-employment, also produce more dissenters? What sort of crude determinism have we here?

Before I even embark on this discussion, I would like to enter a strong *caveat* to it. I do not myself believe in any economic determinism for religious conviction or dissent, although there may be conditions that foster it. The scattered information now at our disposal, together with my own examination of seventeenth-century nonconformity in south Cambridgeshire, that great corn and malt area so despised by Defoe because it had no by-employment at all,[131] and Dr Stevenson's new examination of dissenters in areas of his counties which were mainly arable,[132] show very plainly that dissenters were to be found everywhere. This must never be forgotten. Not all John Bunyan's poverty-stricken Open Baptists in open-field Bedfordshire were lace makers.[133] We desperately need the Compton Census returns of 1676 properly mapped to show us the distribution and concentration of

cereal-growing areas could generate proto-industrialization. We also have new local studies of the Sheffield metal region, in which dissent was prominent (Hey, *The Fiery Blades*), and, as an anti-deterministic warning, a parish in the coal-producing area of the north-east. In the large, pastoral manor of the latter, there was only a very minute dissenting presence (David Levine and Keith Wrightson, *The Making of an Industrial Society: Whickham, 1560–1765* (Oxford, 1991), pp. 84–9, 369–75). This demonstrates the considerable caution that must be exercised. R.C. Richardson, *Puritanism in North-West England: A Regional Study of the Diocese of Chester to 1642* (Manchester, 1972), pp. 3–10, finds a strong correlation between puritanism and pastoral areas in eastern Lancashire south of the Ribble, especially around Manchester and in eastern Cheshire. But in the northern part of the diocese, including pastoral Richmondshire in the Dales, where there had been Lollards, and the Kendal area, puritanism 'never developed sufficiently to become a problem'. Pastoral determinism is not enough: it seems much more likely that the commercial links of Liverpool and Manchester with London were responsible. See below, p. 48, and Dr Bossy's corrective, n. 122, above.

[129] See above, p. 6.
[130] Hill, 'Lollards to Levellers', in *Collected Essays*, II, *passim*, esp. p. 91.
[131] *Contrasting Communities*, pp. 225–38, 279–80 esp. Map 12, p. 224.
[132] See above, p. 18, and below pp. 333 *et seq*.
[133] See below, p. 336.

nonconformists then.[134] The maps so far made of these returns, together with those of the licences for protestant nonconformists issued in 1672[135] are suggestive, but not conclusive, since they are organized only by diocese, and diocesan boundaries do not correlate with those of farming regions. After they are mapped with more subtle determinants in mind, we will begin to see whether there really were greater concentrations in those areas I now go on to discuss. But even after these patterns have become plainer, we must still avoid complete determinism. The man I know who was most sublimely ignorant of historians' models, and even of the seventeenth-century opinions of John Aubrey, was Stephen Duck, a day-labourer working on Salisbury Plain early in the eighteenth century, who wrote the elegant verses of *The Thresher's Labour* after borrowing copies of Shakespeare, Dryden, Virgil, Seneca, Ovid, *The Spectator*, *Paradise Lost* (which he had to read twice with the aid of a dictionary), and Pope's *Essay on Criticism* from a friend who had been in service in London. He knew all about sweat, muscle-fatigue, and arable routine. Indeed, he vividly portrayed the social polarization of the great chalk uplands. None of this stopped his passion for both reading and writing. *The Thresher's Labour* is well worth reading. Such men, and the Conders and the Metcalfes of south Cambridgeshire, were too important, in the corn-growing regions they represent, ever to subsume into the handy generalizations that make our lives more convenient. As Professor Bossy writes, 'The closer we get to the creativity of real life, the larger such individuals will loom, putting their clumsy feet into the shapely machinery of the model.'[136] It is well worth remembering that part of this Cambridgeshire group of 'ancient professors', who became Independents, met at Royston, when they had done their marketing. Royston was the great market

---

[134] The unmapped text is available in Anne Whiteman (ed.), *The Compton Census of 1676: A Critical Edition*, Records of Social and Economic History, NS, 10 (Oxford, 1986). The Department of History at the Roehampton Institute has in hand a pilot project mapping and analysing the Hearth Tax returns from Surrey. We hope to extend it to the rest of England, and also to map the distribution of dissenters in the Compton Census on the same base. It would be particularly good to superimpose maps of density of taxable and exempt population in the Hearth Taxes, and the distribution of dissenters in 1676, on top of Joan Thirsk's farming regions, and the map produced now from the sixteenth- and seventeenth-century road books of communications by Michael Frearson. Then we can see how these things really interlock.

[135] Andrew Browning (ed.), *English Historical Documents*, vol. VIII: 1660–1714 (London, 1966), pp. 415 and 425. These should be compared with the simplified map of farming regions in Joan Thirsk (ed.), *Agrarian History of England and Wales*, V, part I, (Cambridge, 1985), p. xx. The patterns produced by the ecclesiastical returns have been examined by Professor Bossy in his splendid piece (n. 122 above).

[136] Bossy, 'The Map of Christianity', p. 17. Stephen Duck can be found in my 'First Steps in Literacy', *Social History*, 4, no. 3 (1979), pp. 424–5.

for local barley travelling overland. The rest went downriver to King's Lynn. The dangers of oversimplification are self-evident. East Anglia's overseas trade was concentrated on the Netherlands, and by far the most important export was corn, until the coming of the New Draperies. The Low Countries were the chief foreign market for Norfolk grain. So it may well be that the substantial middlemen in the corn trade played exactly the same function as brokers of ideas from Reformed Europe as the clothiers did. It does not sound, from the corn export and import figures, as if the kind of contact made between those merchants and sailors from Hull who met, and imported, such an exciting group of new ideas along with their grain in 1528, to the distress of the York diocesan court,[137] can have been unusual.[138]

The first person to notice the correlation between forest or pastoral areas and time for reading, leading to dissent, or 'fanatic', opinions was John Aubrey, writing in the 1680s about the contrast between the 'cheese and butter' county of north Wiltshire, and the great chalklands of the south. He wrote:

> In North Wiltshire, and like the vale of Gloucester (a dirty clayey country) ... hereabout is but little tillage or hard labour, they only milk the cowes and make cheese ... These circumstances make them melancholy, contemplative and malicious ... And by the same reason they are generally more apt to be fanatiques ...
>
> On the downes, ... the south part, where 'tis all upon tillage, and where the shepherds labour hard, their flesh is hard, their bodies strong: being weary after hard labour, they have not leisure to read and contemplate of religion, but goe to bed to their rest, to rise betime the next morning to their labour.[139]

---

[137] See below, p. 56.

[138] See above, p. 42. Neville Williams, 'The Maritime Trade of East Anglian Ports, 1550–1590' (Oxford, DPhil, 1952), pp. 82, 84. Professor Everitt concluded that East Anglia was the most important area for exports in the corn trade. Between 1500 and 1570 the proportion of corn exports from east-coast ports rose to 50 per cent, and by 1640, it was 75 per cent. King's Lynn or Yarmouth exported nearly 60 per cent of all England's grain exports, and 'the principal destination of English grain, at least from eastern counties, was the Netherlands: Antwerp and the other great cities of the Scheldt, Amsterdam and those of Holland'. Alan Everitt, 'The Marketing of Agricultural Produce', in Joan Thirsk (ed.), *Agrarian History of England and Wales*, vol. IV: 1500–1640 (Cambridge, 1967) pp. 524–6. See also John Chartres, 'The Marketing of Agricultural Produce', in Thirsk (ed.), *Agrarian History of England and Wales*, V, part II, pp. 448–50. R.B. Westerfield, *Middlemen in English Business, particularly between 1660–1760* (New Haven, 1915), has very little on the export trade, or, to our purpose, on the middlemen in the trade. He does emphasize the role of Dutch merchants importing corn from the Baltic to supply London between 1550 and 1660 (pp. 160–1).

[139] John Aubrey, *The Natural History of Wiltshire*, ed. John Britton (London, 1847), p. 11. I am particularly indebted to Adam Fox for this reference.

Among contemporary historians, the first to notice the correlation between forest, pastoral, fen areas and dissent later amplified by Dr Hill was Professor Everitt. He wrote on seventeenth-century dissent in Kent:

> Dissenters were everywhere most numerous in the forest parishes, and in the Wealden area of Mid-Kent they comprised as much as 17% of the population . . . What is the explanation of this remarkable prevalence of Dissent in the forest parishes, and its equally curious absence from the chalk downlands? It is significant that in chalk and limestone regions in other counties at this time, such as the Lincolnshire and Leicestershire Wolds, the Old Dissent often seems to have been conspicuous by its absence. It is equally remarkable how prevalent it was in woodland regions in other shires, such as Rockingham Forest in Northamptonshire, and Macclesfield Forest in Cheshire.

Professor Everitt then went on to say: 'In the past, the predominance of Dissent in rural areas like the Weald has usually been attributed to the cloth industry. Quite why there should be this apparent association between sectarian Christianity and cloth has always seemed, to one student of history at least, something of a mystery.' But he qualified this:

> When one looks more closely into the distribution of rural Dissent, however, it becomes clear that it also flourished in many districts where there was no cloth manufacture to speak of. The truth rather seems to be that the link was only an indirect one, and that clothmaking and Nonconformity were probably fostered independently by certain local characteristics peculiar to the society and settlement pattern of these areas. What were these characteristics so far as Dissent is concerned?[140]

Professor Everitt was the first, but not the last, student of history to be perplexed by this apparent peculiar association between dissent and cloth.[141] When I first realized it, Hogarth's print of the *Idle and the Industrious Apprentices* came to mind. The tipsy idle one has a sheet headed *Moll Flanders* pinned above his loom, the other is diligently applying himself to his work and has four broadsheets pinned above

---

[140] Alan Everitt, 'Non-Conformity in Country Parishes', in Joan Thirsk (ed.), *Land, Church and People: Essays Presented to Professor H.P.R. Finberg* (Reading, 1970), pp. 188–9.

[141] The biggest single group of 'clothiers' to come up in an index of probate accounts for Kent which are mainly seventeenth century, now being produced under the auspices of the ESRC under the direction of my husband, Dr Peter Spufford, was based at Cranbrook in the Weald, which is also the base for Professor Collinson's notable case-study of puritanism. Patrick Collinson, 'Cranbrook and the Fletchers: Popular and Unpopular Religion in the Kentish Weald', in P.N. Brooks (ed.), *Reformation Principle and Practice: Essays in Honour of A.G. Dickens* (London, 1980).

his. The fourth of these records the possible rewards of diligence, since it is the story of that very successful apprentice, 'R. *Whittington*, Ld. Mayor'. I wondered if weavers could actually read while working at their looms.[142] No less a person than Richard Baxter provides independent confirmation of the most forcible kind: 'it was a great advantage to me that my neighbours were of such a trade as allowed them time enough to read or talk of holy things; for the town liveth upon the weaving of Kidderminster stuffs, and as they stand in their loom they can set a book before them or edify one another'. He returned to the subject in his 'Last Treatise' and wrote about the opportunity and ability to read amongst the three notoriously dis- senting trades, shoemakers, tailors, and weavers, culminating in the re-iterated evidence of weavers reading as they worked. 'I have known many that weare in the Long loome that can set their sermon notes or a good book before them and read and discourse together for mutual edification while they worke.'[143] Some of these weavers obvi- ously read as they worked. It sounds as if others were read to.[144] There is a print of 1636 showing a weaver reading to a fellow-worker.[145] I do not think it is out of the way also to suggest that there might well have been more time to develop the skill of reading in wood- pasture, fen, and mountain grazing regions? Dairying and grazing are precisely the activities which allowed time for the development of by-employment. They would also allow time for reading, in the way that the full-scale arable routine does not. Baxter wrote about oppor- tunities for reading for arable farmers, 'But so the poore husbandman can seldom do.' It was a theme of his, and a worry to him. 'Abundance, [of people] bred up in toil and poverty, cannot read, nor cannot have their children taught to reade.' This was not mere hyperbole, nor did he mean all the poor could not read, for he went on to lament: 'I find those that can read are so poore that they cannot spare money to buy a Bible nor a smaller book.' Some were obviously too poor to read, but equally some of the very poor could read, and non-readers were relatively rare. At the Episcopal Visitation of Braddenham in the

---

[142] Mrs Ursula Priestley and Mrs Nesta Evans have assured me that only the simplest pattern would permit this dual activity. Mrs Priestley is an expert on the Norwich stuffs and Mrs Evans on the production of coarse linens in wood-pasture Suffolk. However, Richard Baxter is an independent contemporary authority, whose obser- vation must over-ride them.

[143] F.J.M. Lloyd Thomas (ed.), *The Autobiography of Richard Baxter, being the Reliquae Baxterianae* (London, 1931), and Frederick J. Powicke (ed.), 'The Reverend Richard Baxter's Last Treatise', *Bulletin of the John Rylands Library*, 10 (1926), p. 184.

[144] Cuban cigar rollers apparently contribute to a common fund to pay a reader to read to them as they work. Personal communication from Francis Spufford.

[145] Tamsyn Williams, 'Polemical Prints of the English Revolution 1640–1660' (London, PhD, 1987), Plate 195.

Archdeaconry of Buckingham in 1664, there was a genuine lament. 'There are only 2 or 3 poore families who by reason of their poverty have not bred up their children to reading, and therefore our Minister knowes not what to do with them.'[146]

On the other hand, the tradition of the literate shepherd was a very real one, and it had some foundation in fact, as Thomas Tryon's fellow-shepherds, who taught him to read,[147] and our 'sans-culotte' shepherds show.[148] There may well have been a contrast between arable and pastoral regions in this. The skill of reading does not leave quantifiable signatures behind it, so it is no good looking for more signatures in such regions. But it might well be worth looking for small sums for book ownership in a group of wood-pasture and moorland parishes, versus a group of open-field parishes. The example of the labourer in the Forest of Arden, who was lodging in someone else's house in 1614, but still had in his room 'Sertayne small bookes' valued at 10s, and 'one penne and inke horne',[149] is a tantalizing one. So also is the, very early, example of the poor weaver-barber of a market town in the clothing area of Suffolk, who, as early as 1576, left four chests containing sixty-seven books, which were only worth 13s 4d in all.[150]

The most profitable idea on the reasons for the pattern of the distribution of dissent arising out of this joint project stems from the importance of seventeenth-century communications and the road network. What all these areas with early industry, which were mostly, but not all, cloth areas, had in common was transport networks and trade communications of one kind and another. The dissemination of ideas, both religious and political, go along with trade communications and marketing. More than improved seeds and agricultural techniques were exchanged at inns and alehouses and nodal points for marketing.[151] So also was print, cheap and not so cheap, and verbal information and news.

---

[146] Bucks. RO D/A/V/8, Episcopal Visitation of Archdeaconry of Buckingham, 1664.

[147] See below, p. 69.

[148] See above, p. 19. G.H. Jenkins, Literature, Religion and Society in Wales, 1660–1730 (Cardiff, 1978), pp. 303–4, discusses reading shepherds.

[149] Victor Skipp, 'Economic and Social Change in the Forest of Arden, 1530–1649', in Thirsk (ed.), Land, Church and People, p. 111.

[150] David Dymond, 'Three Entertainers from Tudor Suffolk', Records of Early English Drama, 16, no. 1 (1991), p. 3. For the possible nature of these books, see below, Ch. 6. Strength is added to this suggestion by the very high degree of literacy in the wood-pasture parish of Eccleshall, Staffordshire, which is the poorest rural parish we yet know: Poverty Portrayed: Gregory King and Eccleshall in the 1690s, Staffordshire Studies (forthcoming, 1995?).

[151] Probably best summarized in Alan Everitt, 'The English Urban Inn, 1560–1760', in Everitt, Landscape and Community in England, pp. 168–73. Also Tessa Watt, Cheap Print and Popular Piety, 1550–1640 (Cambridge, 1991), pp. 178–9, for the printing and distribution and appearance in alehouses of 'popish reliques'.

I first mapped the roads given in the *City and Country Chapman's Almanack* for 1688[152] in my work on pedlars and chapmen. Pedlars were always mobile, suspect people, in trouble for disseminating seditious literature and books, both papist and protestant.[153] Now there is a thesis which presents in detail the sixteenth- and seventeenth-century road networks, as a background to the study of the distribution and content of the early political newsbooks.[154] A very much clearer picture emerges.

First, there is no doubt of the extent of purely commercial contact between the early industrial areas inside England. The focal point of all roads was London. Dr Richardson drew forcible attention to the way in which economic ties with London and provincial cities like Manchester and Newcastle upon Tyne were inseparable from the spread of puritanism and, he could have added, dissent.[155] An anonymous writer of the mid-seventeenth century declared that puritanism spread 'by means of the City of London, the nest and seminary of the seditious faction, and by reason of its universal trade throughout the kingdom with its commodities conveying and deriving this civil contagion to all our cities, and corporations, and thereby poisoning whole counties'.

Manchester was described in the 1640s as 'the very London of those parts, the liver that sends blood into all the countries thereabouts'. And the blood circulating in both veins and arteries was the merchants. The habits of Richard Heywood of Bolton, merchant, were described:[156]

> when he was abroad his design and practice was to hear the best preachers; he travelled to London once or twice every year and he constantly heard old Mr Edmund Calamy at Aldemanbury . . . and such like. His practice at London was to furnish himself with the best books, the most plain, practical, experimental treatises in divinity, such as Calvin, Luther in English, Mr Perkins, Dr Preston, Dr Sibbs, wherein he took much pleasure in reading.

But we can add less well-known examples. A Lancashire chapman, Robert Marler, regularly rode down to Norwich, where he had a favourite inn, in the 1580s to sell Lancashire coarse linen at fairs and markets in

---

[152] Margaret Spufford, *The Great Reclothing of Rural England: Petty Chapmen and their Wares in the Seventeenth Century* (London, 1984), Map 3 p. 19. I deal more fully with the development of the map and its diffusion at a humble social level in 'The Pedlar and the Historian', *Folklore* (forthcoming). There is a very valuable article which has a bearing on the subject by Victor Morgan, 'The Cartographical Image of the Country', *Trans. Royal Hist. Soc.*, 5th Ser., 29 (1979), pp. 129–54.

[153] Margaret Spufford, *Small Books and Pleasant Histories*, pp. 11, 113, 116–18; idem, *The Great Reclothing*, pp. 25, 43, 85–6.

[154] Michael Frearson, 'The English Corantos of the 1620s' (Cambridge, PhD, 1994). I would especially like to record my gratitude to Michael, whose ideas in supervisions have helped me formulate the concepts and questions in this section.

[155] This passage is all drawn from Richardson, *Puritanism in North-West England*, pp. 11–13.

[156] Horsfall Turner (ed.), *Autobiography*, p. 84.

Norfolk. But he also dealt in packhorses: he had a close friend in Rother-ham in the great wool-textile packhorse-owning belt of the West Riding. So there was a regular interchange between Lancashire, the West Riding, and East Anglia, demonstrated in this one man's trading.

An admittedly anachronistic chapman of Manchester, whose inventory was dated as late as 1742, had highly unusual appraisers who bothered to list his books. He was a very earnest character indeed. As well as a prayer book and a psalm book, he had *A Week's Preparation* valued at 7d, *Sherlock on Death* at 1s 2d, *Sherlock on Judgement* at 1s 6d, *Sherlock on Providence* at 2s 0d, *The Whole Duty of Man* at 1s 2d, *A Pattern of Catheistical Doctrine* [sic] at 1s 8d, and *The Saints Interest in God* at 10d. Only the elevenpenny *Merchant's Manual* bore on his work directly.[157] We know such men had sixteenth- and seventeenth-century predecessors,[158] not only because of Dr Watt's work, and the chapman who supplied Richard Baxter's father with *The Bruised Reed*, but also because of the dissenting bookseller who took out a licence to peddle books round Sheffield in the 1690s.[159]

The horses sold at Chester Fair both in the sixteenth and seventeenth centuries supplied, and connected, the northern 'industrial' areas, Lanca-shire, Yorkshire, and Westmorland. In 1673–9, packhorses were sold at the fair to a stuff-weaver from Kendal, a clothier from Halifax, and a cloth worker from Leeds.[160] Michael Frearson has found a Gloucestershire clo-thier who himself employed more than twenty carriers.[161] These carriers would have been working from the great Gloucestershire western broad-cloth region towards London, along the 'Middle West Road' that passed through Colnbrook in south Buckinghamshire. It was not accidental that Thomas Deloney, who had been a weaver himself, wrote two 'realistic' novels glorifying clothiers between 1597 and 1600, *Jack of Newbury* and *Thomas of Reading*. *Thomas of Reading* had clothier 'heroes': six from the west, from Reading, Gloucester, Worcester, Exeter, Salisbury, and South-ampton, who regularly travelled together on the 'Middle West Road' and the 'West Road'. They met the three northern 'heroes', who were clothiers from Kendal, Manchester, and Halifax, somewhat bizarrely (see Map 1) at Basingstoke, all on their way to London. The major part of the

---

[157] Borthwick Institute, York, Trans. CP 1744 (inv. of David Jackson, deceased). I am indebted to Dr W. Sheils for noticing this case for me. I excluded the whole group of textile chapmen from my study of chapmen and pedlars, because there were so many of these specialists that they overbalanced the work (unpublished paper on wool and textile chapmen). Some of these chapmen did have very pious character-istics.

[158] See below, Ch. 6.

[159] Margaret Spufford, *The Great Reclothing*, pp. 85–6.

[160] Ibid., pp. 20, 74, 86. Peter Edwards, 'The Horse Trade of Chester in the Sixteenth and Seventeenth Centuries', *Journal of the Chester Archaeological Society*, 62 (1979).

[161] Frearson, 'The English Corantos', pp. 57–8.

cloth export trade was of course focussed on London, where the cloth was marketed through Blackwell Hall.[162] Thomas Deloney's clothier heroes, like the real Robert Marler, had favourite inns which formed regular stops, on which they stayed on all their journeys. The 'plot' of *Thomas of Reading* in fact hinges around Thomas' murder on his return home from London by the innkeeper at Colnbrook, who decided to divest him of the profits.

The growth in carrying services out of London in the seventeenth century has been chronicled. It is notable that there was a remarkable expansion in these services to, for instance, the difficult country of the north, which included the textile area and stocking knitting area around Kendal and Dentdale, between 1637 and 1681, and again between 1681 and 1715. It is possible that the increasing number of carriers' services to areas like Kendal, and to the west midlands metal region, directly reflect the increasing volume of their trade.[163]

In stressing the regularity and increasing frequency of trading connections and their flow along the arterial highways, I do not mean to imply either ease or speed. Dogged endurance was necessary. Professor Everitt has reminded me that 'travail' and 'travel' are the same word. The fears of the young lad, Thomas Gent, who immigrated from Ireland in the late seventeenth century and walked down from Chester to London to find work were both real and well founded. He was nearly pressed for the army on the way, and only had 2d left by the time he reached St Albans. He intended to pay this for his bed, and fast until he got to London, but a kindly landlord fed him. When he was much older, in 1714, he was offered a job with a printer in York. The carrier wanted 25s for his fare, which he could not afford. So he walked the distance, but did the whole journey between Tuesday and the following Sunday, partly because 'a gentleman's servant, with a horse ready saddled, and himself riding on another, overtook me, and for a shilling, with a glass or so on the road, allowed me to ride with him in my road as far as Caxton'. On yet another journey, when he was older still, he was accosted by a fellow who stepped out of a hedge:

> I neither liked him nor his style, when luckily, an honest countryman, on horseback, passing by, I went to him, told him I did not like the company I had met with, and desired him to bear me away behind him and I would satisfy him for his trouble; accordingly, I lost my

---

[162] D.C. Coleman, *Industry in Tudor and Stuart England* (London, 1975), p. 26.

[163] John Chartres, 'Road Carrying in England in the Seventeenth Century: Myth and Reality', *Economic History Revue*, 2nd Ser., 30 (1977), pp. 76–81; idem, 'The Capital's Provincial Eyes: London's Inns in the Early Eighteenth Century', *The London Journal*, 1 (1977), pp. 29–33; David Hey, *Packmen, Carriers and Packhorse Roads: Trade and Communications in North Derbyshire and South Yorkshire* (Leicester, 1980).

ill-looked chap, met the opportunity of a coach the last day's journey, and got safe to London.[164]

If travel was alarming for an able-bodied young man, well able to win a fight with fellow-apprentices, how was it for the frailer, the younger, and the women?

Travellers on foot were also lucky, and thankful, to get rides on carts as well as on spare horses, and riding pillion, as was the family of pedlars who hitched a lift on a load of hops to a Dorset fair. Less well-educated travellers than Thomas Gent, like the pedlar who walked down from Lincolnshire to Stourbridge Fair in 1615, and took at least four days over it, cannot have been atypical either in the time it took, or his mental and geographical confusion. The night before he reached Cambridge, he spent at St Neots. The night before, 'he knoweth not'. The night before that, he was on the Great North Road, at Wansford, but where he spent the previous night, again, 'he knoweth not'. The case of women and travellers with children, like the chapwoman who travelled all the Yorkshire fairs, had a baby of unknown fatherhood in an outhouse at Ripon, and after that had her 'Child along with her', must have been even worse. The roads must have been full of such human flotsam, juveniles, orphans, and vagrants, those who preyed upon them and the poor walking from job to job, or in search of work.

Yet despite this, we can easily demonstrate the comparative regularity and frequency of trade and marketing connections. We can then proceed to demonstrate the literacy, and the interest in print, which clothiers had as a group. David Rollinson, working in Gloucestershire which is, incidentally, one of Christopher Hill's regions where there may have been a continuity of radical ideas from the Lollards onwards, finds that 'in Gloucestershire, clothiers and cloth workers were much more likely to own books than any other sector'[165] from his examination of inventories between 1660 and 1680. Clothiers were thought to be a significant group by contemporaries, and were 'identified with traffic in illicit ideas' in the seventeenth century. When George Fox was imprisoned in Cornwall, many clothiers entering the county were arrested as 'suspicious persons'.[166] I should dearly like to see a similar investigation of book owner-

---

[164] *The Life of Mr Thomas Gent, Printer of York: Written by Himself* (London, 1832, written in 1746), pp. 5–7, 18–19, 54–5.

[165] Personal communication to Michael Frearson. I am deeply indebted to both Dr Rollinson and Michael Frearson for giving me permission to use this information, and drawing my attention to it, respectively. Dr Rollinson 'sees no reason why this pattern wouldn't carry back to the 1620s and 30s'. In further correspondence, he takes it back to the early sixteenth century, and qualifies his earlier conviction that clothiers were the group most likely to own books by the important addition of the yeomen, who were also likely to have reading time.

[166] R.T. Vann, *The Social Development of English Quakerism, 1655–1755* (Cambridge, Mass., 1969), p. 13.

ship by clothiers, compared to the rest of the population, carried out amongst the clothiers of Kent and the West Riding. I have little doubt it would produce similar results.

Why are the literate habits, the book ownership, and the trading patterns of clothiers and perhaps of leather workers, and even middlemen in the corn trade, important? The vicissitudes of the English export trade in cloth, or the growth of the re-export trade, or even the grain trade, do not concern us here, but the important point about the cloth trade is that in the late sixteenth century, 85 per cent of the exported cloth of England went to markets in northern Europe. Until the coming of the New Draperies, East Anglia's most important export to the Netherlands was corn. Even in 1700 'the total sale of English cloth in northern and central Europe was much the same as it had been before the Civil War, but more than half of it was now of the New Draperies'.[167] The predominance of north and central Europe as England's main market meant constant contact with areas alive with the ideas of the Reformation. This was so even before the migrations all over Europe of textile workers from the southern Netherlands, from the arrival of the first wave of Calvinist refugees in the 1560s, to the next influx caused by the Eighty Years War there, from the Revolt of the Netherlands in the 1570s, to the Peace of Westphalia in the 1650s. The war 'was one of the main causes of the massive emigrations of tens of thousands of specially skilled workers who, for religious, psychological, or economic reasons, left the region to spread their industrial know-how over the whole of Europe'.[168] This migration was substantial enough to be called 'a diaspora'. These workers brought reformed ideas with them. They had different contacts, and established themselves in different areas, like the French glassmakers who, for example, established the first glassworks of their new technology in England, in the Weald, and then moved to a forest in Staffordshire,[169] the Huguenot and Dutch immigrants who helped drain the

---

[167] Ralph Davis, *English Overseas Trade, 1500–1700* (London, 1973), p. 39. Only 15 per cent were the 'New Draperies' destined for France and the Mediterranean. Dr Rollinson stresses to me the strong trade links between Gloucestershire and the Netherlands. His *The Local Origins of Modern Society* (London, 1992) has much material on the links between cloth making and religious radicalism.

[168] Herman van der Wee, 'Structural Changes and Specialization in the Industry of the Southern Netherlands, 1100–1600', *Economic History Review*, 2nd Ser., 28 (1975), pp. 217–18. For an overview of both French and Dutch settlement, see Robin D. Gwynn, *Huguenot Heritage: The History and Contribution of the Huguenots in Britain* (London, 1985), pp. 29–41. For the importance of these workers in England, see Coleman, *Industry in Tudor and Stuart England*, pp. 30–1; Andrew Pettigree, '"Thirty Years On": Progress towards Integration amongst the Immigrant Population of Elizabethan London', in John Chartres and David Hey (eds.), *English Rural Society, 1500–1800: Essays in Honour of Joan Thirsk* (Cambridge, 1990), pp. 297–313.

[169] G.H. Kenyon, *The Glass Industry of the Weald* (Leicester, 1967), pp. 13–16, 86, 185, 200, 211, 214, 217 and Map, 213.

Fens,[170] and on a different scale, the very important Huguenot immigrant who moved from Paris in the late 1540s and published religious pictures with suitably protestant content, which spread all over England, through the medium of pedlars.[171]

Professor Vann suggests that the clothiers should not be confused with the weavers who worked for them in their own homes, and, I would add, the tailors who made up the cloth, although, as he says 'there was a long tradition of Lollardy and Separatism amongst weavers of this sort'.[172] He does not regard this as especially pertinent. I do: and would add to these the leather workers, the Lollard butchers, tanners, and shoemakers, right through to George Fox himself, who also seem to be conspicuous throughout the history of separatism. Michael Frearson has found a very remarkable account book of a shoemaker and glover of Gloucestershire, who listed his books in 1627. They included two Bibles, a Testament, three psalters and two catechisms, several practical aids to living, like a statute book, 'the bookes of the assize of Bread', and one on 'the duties of constables tything men, and such, low and lay ministers of the peace' as well as 'divers Almanackes bound together'. But they also included two books on travel to Turkey and Persia, and then a revelatory list indicating that the Bibles, psalters, and catechisms were not merely for display. He had cheap copies of *The Rich Cabinet, The Garden of Spiritual Flowers, A Godly Garden of Comfortable Hearbes, Smug the Smith, A Supena [sic] from Heaven,* and *The Treasure of Gladness.*[173] Such men need not have been separatists at all: but they were men of conviction, who were, because their shops were places where people met, waited, and talked, profoundly influential. The leather workers were also linked by wholesale suppliers, both of skins and bark.[174] Behind all leather workers lay the links of the cattle trade, which, like the clothiers, moved all along the roads of England.[175] This stress on migrant workers, as well as trade connections, may be perverse, especially in view of work[176] which dem-

---

[170] Their memorials may be found in Thorney Abbey church and they may have been partly responsible for building the chapel which survives, from the very late Commonwealth, possibly, at Guyhirn in the Isle of Ely. It is dated 1660. Dr Christopher Stell has kindly advised me on this.

[171] Watt, *Cheap Print*, pp. 182–191. Giles Godet's blocks were re-used by his trade heirs, some of whom were also French.

[172] Vann, *Social Development of Quakerism*, p. 13 n. 16.

[173] I am deeply grateful to Michael Frearson for allowing me to use this very striking example. See below, pp. 266–8, 285.

[174] L.A. Clarkson, 'The Organization of the English Leather Industry in the Late Sixteenth and Seventeenth Centuries', *Economic History Review*, 2nd Ser., 13 (1960–1), *passim*. See also below, p. 62.

[175] See ibid., and below, pp. 62, 128–9 for Buckinghamshire bark on the Thames for tanning.

[176] Jan Lucassen, *Migrant Labour in Europe 1600–1900* (Beckenham, 1987), pp. 30–4. One has to distinguish, though, between unskilled labourers and travelling craftsmen.

onstrates that seasonal migrant labour is less likely to be drawn from areas where people possess their own looms, whereas spinners, who spun in the winter and often worked away in the summer, were a frequent source of it. If this model applies to England, our own areas of early industrial by-employment may not have supplied mobile workers. We lack a full study of these people.

Yet there is much highly suggestive material in a study of the origins of trade unionism, which demonstrates that 'tramping' in search of work, carrying the required certificate of former service, guaranteed a welcome and hospitality for a 'brother' from another town who could not get work. Many of the surviving Masons', Carpenters', and Bricklayers' Arms stand as surviving monuments to the ubiquity of the custom. Masons' payments, if work could not be found, to 'travelling brothers' or 'strange felaus' are recorded as early as 1583. The system was copied by the weavers and combers of the wool trade. Wool and silk weavers in Coventry were making such payments under the Commonwealth. The new wave of French Huguenot immigrants after the 1670s took to the road in the hope they might find work in Canterbury, Coventry, Reading, or even Manchester. These were all towns where their predecessors had settled by the 1630s.[177] Various individual examples I have cited demonstrate this considerable mobility amongst young workers in the cloth trade. Meanwhile it is likely that the key people were 'craftsmen on the move', the travelling middlemen with supplies, the wool and textile chapmen, who regularly moved from 'industrial' region to region, and worked with both clothiers and smaller fry. Robert Marler is only one of many possible examples. An elegantly demonstrated local example of the way radical religious ideas flowed along the road network, in this case undoubtedly coming from the Low Countries, has just been provided for the Family of Love.[178]

Men and women who travelled to work in the harvest as seasonal labour were required to have a certificate from their local vicar or a leading citizen, testifying they would not linger after harvest. R.A. Leeson, *Travelling Brothers: The Six Centuries' Road from Craft Fellowship to Trade Unionism* (London, 1979), p. 72.

[177] David Levine, *Family Formation in an Age of Nascent Capitalism* (London, 1977): chapters 3 and 6 mainly deal with eighteenth-century migrants or migrant workers. The chapter on 'Vagrants and Vagrancy' by Paul Slack in Peter Clark and David Souden (eds.), *Migration and Society in Early Modern England* (London, 1987) does not really concentrate on migrant labour. Leeson, *Travelling Brothers*, pp. 15, 39, 54, 56–8, 62, 64–5, has a great deal of early material, after making his introductory claim that almost every trade in the early nineteenth century had a 'tramping system' which was nearly universal, and had very early roots. He demonstrates journeymen's movements, and reciprocal guild agreements from at least the late fourteenth and early fifteenth centuries.

[178] *The Great Reclothing*, p. 86; Marsh, *The Family of Love*, Map 2, p. 61, and pp. 60–3. This example illustrates such corrections in our second study area, see Map 4 and Appendix A.

We have sketched a general picture of good internal communications linking the areas of England with early handicraft industry, where there may have been more time for reading, as well as for by-employments. These 'industrial' areas were, in turn, linked with reformed areas of the Continent, both by very strong trade connections and inflows of immigrant labour avoiding religious persecution. The elusive connection between dissent and cloth becomes more comprehensible set in a general context of trade relationships. The great interest shown by clothiers, who traded mainly with Reformed Europe, in books becomes highly significant.

However, it is possible to be more precise. The general point can be demonstrated in a series of particular examples. The Lollard communities of the 1420s in Kent and East Anglia, and in London, as well as our focal point of Amersham and the upper Thames valley seem to have been 'in repeated contact with each other'. A Kentish priest from Tenterden and Gillingham had a regular missionary circuit in East Anglia and Suffolk, which probably included Colchester. A woman who had learnt her heresy in Coventry in the 1490s travelled to Northampton, to London, where she married a man who became a heretic, on to Kent, and back to Coventry. A priest who had learnt his heresy in Bristol preached in Windsor and Wallingford, and also had connections with the East Anglian group. A Lollard missionary from London who knew a large group of Lollards in London including seven tailors[179] moved to Essex in the 1520s: there again, he was in touch with tailors and weavers. The London circle in turn connected with the Collins family, who were readers and teachers in the upper Thames valley in the 1520s. The conclusion from all this is that 'the reoccurrence of certain towns and areas within heretics' itineraries suggests there was widespread awareness of places friendly to their views'.[180] The later evangelists behaved in exactly the same way, with the same information at their disposal. In 1655 a woman from Westmorland who had travelled to Norwich to preach there and in Norfolk, was arrested with 'diverse papers ... conteyning directions for travails into several counties and places in this Commonwealth'. She, like her Lollard predecessor, knew exactly where to go. So did other Quaker missionaries likewise furnished with lists of names, places, and information about the roads.[181]

---

[179] Out of a total of twenty-four.
[180] See above, p. 23, for itinerant evangelists. All this information comes from Hudson, Premature Reformation, pp. 138, 140 1, 474–7, and Margaret Aston, Lollards and Reformers: Images and Literacy in Late Medieval Religion (London, 1984), pp. 78, 81–3, 86–7. See also Davies, 'Lollardy and Locality', p. 208. but note also his warnings against paying too much attention to the importance of itinerant evangelists, pp. 194, 200.
[181] Vann, Social Development of Quakerism, pp. 10–11.

In his detailed examination of heresy cases in the diocese of York under Henry VIII, Professor Dickens drew attention to a group of immigrant heretics, who were called 'Dutchmen', who, he suggested, were Netherlanders rather than Germans. One of these immigrants in the late fifteenth century was a bookbinder, whose sons were both imprisoned and one burnt for heresy. One of them, a painter, moved from Yorkshire to Colchester, where he betrayed himself by writing scriptural sentences on the borders of newly painted cloths for an inn in the marketplace. Again the centrality of the inn for diffusion of belief, or for religious argument, is relevant. A cloth worker, born in Dewsbury, illustrates both mobility and heresy in the cloth trade within England very nicely for us: he was apprenticed in west Suffolk, and worked as a journeyman in Waldingfield and the later puritan centres of Ipswich and Hadleigh. A group of merchants and sailors who took a cargo from Hull to Amsterdam in 1528, continued to Bremen and loaded with a return cargo of wheat. They illustrate the possible effects of overseas trade for us. In their five weeks in Bremen and Friesland they observed Lutheran practices, and talked too freely of them when they were back home. They, too, ended up in the diocesan courts. In 1546, there were Dutch merchants present at Anne Askew's burning, who later gave an eye-witness account of it. As Professor Dickens says, 'books, Dutchmen and heresy' all figure prominently in the records.[182]

A very intriguing little fragment of information which gives us much information about contacts, drawn from the diffusion of the highly complex and idiosyncratic will preamble of William Tracey, gentleman, of Gloucester, has just come to light. Tracey had been Sheriff of Gloucestershire, and knew William Tyndale, who described him as 'a learned man, and better sene [sic] in the works of St Augustine ... than ever I knew doctoure in England'. Tracey died in 1531, his will was refused probate because of the preamble, was condemned in convocation, and he himself dug up and posthumously burnt.

The will was published in Antwerp in 1535, with a commentary by Tyndale.[183] It found its way, either in manuscript or print, as a formulary into the wills of a handful of testators in Gloucester, Bristol, Shrewsbury, Reading, London, Sussex, Suffolk, Halifax, and Hull (Map 1). The trade connections are obvious.[184]

In the 1570s, trade connections were again apparent in the small, deliberately low-key, but important mystical fellowship of the Family of Love.

---

[182] Dickens, *Lollards and Protestants*, pp. 17–23, 24–32, 34, 48–9, 246–7.

[183] *The Testament of Master William Tracie* (Antwerp, 1535, republished 1546, 1548).

[184] I am very grateful indeed to John S. Craig and Caroline J. Litzenberger for allowing me to use their paper, 'Wills as Religious Propaganda: The Testament of William Tracy', *Journal of Ecclesiastical History* (forthcoming, 1994), and supplying me with a list of places where the preamble has been found.

They followed the teachings of Hendrick Niclaeus, which were translated from 1574: their leading evangelist seems to have been Christopher Vitells, whom we first hear of embroiled in an argument at an inn at, almost inevitably, Colchester. Vitells imported 'Naples fustian' and 'narrow say' from Antwerp. He belonged to a group of dyers, weavers, and merchants.[185] By 1586, there were said to be 1,293 Dutch settlers in Colchester, of whom over a third were children born in England,[186] which argues for some length of settlement. It may be significant that one of Vitells' leading adherents was yet another man connected to the leather trades, a glover at the port of Wisbech, who had a large number of 'heretical' books concealed behind his chimneystack.

Not only those considered by their own society to be heretics were brought together by trade connections. It can be no accident that the ripples from a puritan synod held in St John's College, Cambridge, reached Stourbridge Fair in 1587. It may have been a regular preaching, and possibly meeting, place. Stourbridge Fair was the only fair in England which had international importance. It specialized in wool and hops, but also sold barley, malt, sheep, and cattle. Puritans regularly discoursed there to locals, travellers, and above all merchants from all over the country, and possibly abroad.[187] William Perkins himself preached there in Elizabeth's reign, and urged his merchant hearers to 'carry home this lesson to your great towns and cities where you dwell'.[188]

The fair continued to draw the attentions of preachers, both orthodox and unorthodox. Thomas Symonds of Norwich, a master worsted weaver, who became the first important Quaker in Norwich,[189] first heard of the Quaker missionary Anne Blaykling, who was imprisoned in Cambridge itself in 1654, on a business visit to Stourbridge Fair. He visited her in prison and was converted. Professor Vann suggested, in his turn, that 'commercial ties, especially in the cloth trade, were often converted into channels of evangelism. One of the reasons for the predominance of wholesale traders amongst early Friends is that such men, as they made the trips required by their business, were exposed to new ideas.'

Stourbridge Fair continued to act as a magnet to evangelists, presumably because of the numbers present, its unholy character crying for con-

---

[185] Marsh, 'The Family of Love', chapter 6; idem, *The Family of Love*, pp. 78–9.
[186] Gwynn, *Huguenot Heritage*, p. 30.
[187] The information initially comes from Patrick Collinson, 'The Puritan Classical Movement in the Reign of Elizabeth I' (London, Ph D, 1957), p. 772 n. I have not found it in print, and only owe the detailed reference to Professor Alan Everitt, who draws on it. See *Contrasting Communities*, p. 261.
[188] Patrick Collinson, *The Elizabethan Puritan Movement* (London, 1967), pp. 320–3. The sermon on Zephaniah is printed in Ian Breward (ed.), *The Work of William Perkins* (Appleford, 1970). I owe this reference, as much else, to the kindness of Professor Collinson.
[189] Vann, *Social Development of English Quakerism*, pp. 13, 67–70.

version, and also the ease of moving there relatively unobserved. In 1678, Ludovic Muggleton, who considered himself one of the candlesticks from the Book of Revelation, wrote to his kinsmen: 'I had great hopes to have seen you at Cambridge. I went about the fair at Sturbridge to find you out, and so did several others of our friends, persons of quality, from London, and out of the country, *knowing that I would be there.*' The fair was a recognized meeting-place for the very curious Muggletonian sect, who seem to have intermarried between Cambridgeshire and Kent. It may not be impious to suggest that their common trading interests in hops, malt, and barley may have been one of the causes for the spread of the sect in these two counties. 'The most that have received it, is here in London, and in Cambridgeshire and in Kent' wrote Muggleton.[190]

I therefore suggest that areas both of early 'industrial' activity and of noticeable export, or even import, of trade in cloth, cattle, leather or of grain, may also have been areas where nonconformity was more common because in the first place, as John Aubrey had noticed, by-employments and handicrafts gave more time for reading; secondly, there were normal, and frequent, trade connections between them; and thirdly, these internal trade connections were reinforced by strong external trade connections with protestant Europe.

What does this thesis have to say to our study of the wooded Chilterns of Buckinghamshire, and the dissenters within them? We have been heavily handicapped, in view of the conditions Dr Thirsk and Professor Coleman spelt out for the development of by-employments and early industry,[191] in our work on south Buckinghamshire by three things. Because no probate inventories for the county survive 'Unfortunately, no detailed study of farming in the Buckinghamshire Chilterns has been made.'[192] We therefore do not know about inheritance customs, and whether we have an area of small farms created by partible inheritance either. The region was somewhat improbably, in view of its topography, officially labelled as 'sheep–corn' rather than pasture, with a cereal export trade down the Thames to London, in the *Agrarian History of England and Wales*, but an emphasis on timber growing was heavily stressed. The lack of a farming study was to some extent rectified by a volume of probate inventories from the Prerogative Court of Canterbury for Buckinghamshire which

---

[190] Margaret Spufford, *Contrasting Communities*, p. 229.
[191] See above, pp. 40–1.
[192] Thirsk (ed.), *Agrarian History of England and Wales*, V, part I, J.R. Wordie, chapter 10, particularly pp. 327–8. This absence is probably accounted for by the absence of probate inventories.

appeared in 1988.[193] The author emphasizes the very great difference between the north and south of the county, and the greater emphasis on cheese and butter making and pig-fattening in the latter. Open fields did exist there, but they were very small, and the landscape was dominated by small closes, and considerable patches of woodland, heath, and common. Arable farming was not communally organized. The parishes of the three hundreds with which we are concerned[194] were certainly much larger than those in north Buckinghamshire, but by no means on the scale of those of the Weald of Kent and Surrey, or the vast parishes of Westmorland and Lancashire. But outside the nucleated settlement pattern were numerous isolated farms and hamlets with tell-tale woodland names, of which the dissenters took full advantage. The site for the monthly meeting at the home of Thomas Ellwood, Hunger Hill near Beaconsfield, was, for instance, chosen because 'it was actually in an outlying portion of Hertfordshire, and therefore could not be disturbed by the Buckinghamshire authorities'.[195] We do not in south Buckinghamshire have a pattern of large manors and weak manorial control; on the contrary, we have parishes heavily manorially sub-divided, and therefore perhaps weakly controlled, with some absentee lords.[196] This absenteeism was combined with an immensely strong puritan tradition amongst some lords who were resident in the county.[197] John Hampden's power base as a JP was at High Wycombe. Some of these puritans became dissatisfied and became themselves Quaker converts, like Isaac Penington of Chalfont St Peter, son of the regicide, and his wife, Lady Mary Springett,

---

[193] Michael Reed (ed.), *Buckinghamshire Probate Inventories, 1661–1714*, Buckinghamshire Record Society, 24 (Aylesbury, 1988), pp. xiv–xvi and no. 51, pp. 103–4. These inventories are all from the PCC. It is only fair to add that the Chiltern Hundreds were overwhelmingly arable in the agricultural returns of the late eighteenth century.

[194] Burnham, Desborough, and Stoke. See below, pp. 282, 89–90, 92–3.

[195] Robert Huxter, *Jordans Meeting* (Jordans Preparative Meeting, Buckinghamshire, 1989). There were other notable examples of the attempted use of county or ecclesiastical boundaries in this way: Brigflatts Meeting-House, near Sedbergh, which is the oldest Quaker meeting-house in the north, lies near the border of three counties, and two dioceses. Coleshill, a hamlet of South Amersham, and a separate manor, was also a detached part of Hertfordshire (*VCH Bucks.*, III, p. 150, inside Burnham Hundred) and was held by Henry Child, who became a Quaker. But the inadequacy of these devices is shown, because we know of Henry Child, and indeed many other Quakers, from the Volumes of Sufferings. The authorities did not fail to pick them up.

[196] We also have some late Lollards who were so economically dominant in their communities that they were able to protect lesser brethren. The widows of Robert Sanders of Amersham (see above, p. 12) taxed at £200 in 1524–5, and of Robert Bartlet of Amersham, taxed on the still very considerable sum of £40, were able to threaten lack of employment to those who did not comply with their wishes. Plumb, 'Foxe and the Later Lollards', pp. 248–9, 254, 263–4, 265–6.

[197] J.T. Cliffe, *The Puritan Gentry: The Great Puritan Families of Early Stuart England* (London, 1984), pp. 141, 161, 200.

who was herself daughter and widow of puritans. Thomas Ellwood, son of a puritan gentleman, was also a Quaker; so, of course, were the Penns of Penn, and the Archdales of the manor of Temple Wycombe. It cannot be an accident that the manor of Chalfont St Giles was held by the regicide, Sir George Fleetwood, from 1628. He had been an MP for the county in the Long Parliament. The rector of Chalfont from 1623 preached before the Commons in 1643, was a member of the Westminster Assembly in 1644, and was deprived for nonconformity in 1661. The parish, which had had no Lollards, was alive with Quakers, along with its neighbour of Chalfont St Peter; the Penington house at Chalfont Grange was there, as well as Jordans itself, and the other Quaker meeting at Seer Green. This was the village in which Thomas Ellwood chose a house which he described as a 'pretty little box' in which the blind Milton could take refuge during the plague of 1665.[198] So it may be that some of the considerable, but much divided manorial control there was in the Chilterns was in favour of, or at least not violently against, sectarian nonconformity, and gave it a certain amount of early protection. It would not do to over-estimate the degree of this protection after the Restoration, however, from the amount of time that all these gentlemen spent either in prison or in exile themselves.

We do not know whether there was a high density of population in the late seventeenth century either: the Hearth Taxes are defective and especially lack lists of the exempt, who would be heavily involved in by-employment. To add to this, Buckinghamshire is a 'heavily under-represented county' in the massive *Population History of England*.[199] However, one of the things we are better informed about in Buckinghamshire than most counties, is that it had a mass of small freeholders, like much other manorially divided, and heavily wooded country. We know John Hampden's 3,000 mounted friends and neighbours set a precedent when they rode into London with the Buckinghamshire Protestation to Parliament on 11 January 1642, in a cavalcade three by three, which stretched, with their freeholding supporters, from the Royal Exchange to Newgate. Very unfortunately, no signatures survive for their petition, to match with our dissenters. We simply know the freeholders were very active in the well-organized demonstration.[200] In the early eighteenth century, it was said to be impossible to win a Buckinghamshire election without the

---

[198] Monica Harcourt-Smith, *The Vache and its Owners: A Short History of the Vache, Chalfont St Giles* (Chalfont, n.d.) and *Guide to Milton's Cottage* (n.p., n.d.).

[199] E.A. Wrigley and R.S. Schofield, *The Population History of England, 1541–1871: A Reconstruction* (London, 1981), pp. 43, 485. Only one of the three parishes where detailed work has been done on the registers, Princes Risborough, even abuts on our area.

[200] Anthony Fletcher, *The Outbreak of the English Civil War* (London, 1981), pp. 191, 196–8, and personal communication.

support of the voters of the Chilterns. The county has a remarkable survival, in the shape of half a Poll Book of 1685, with names, parishes, and some occupations given. The immediate question arising therefore, was were 'our' dissenters free to be dissenters because they owned their cottages?[201] The surviving half Poll Book is drawn from all parts of the county, and forms a representative sample.[202] There were 388 freeholders voting in the parishes of the area of the Quaker Upperside Meeting and the Cuddington and Ford Baptist Meeting.

Amongst these 388 voters' surnames, 215, or 30 per cent, of those who had paid tax on £5 or more in the Great Subsidy of 1524/5, well over a century before, reoccurred.[203] But this survival rate was not significantly different at all from the 29 per cent of the population at large which remained static between 1524/5 and the 1660s. There was therefore no correlation between being a freeholder with a 'static' surname in the Poll Book. But no less than 59 per cent of the 'Lollard' surnames did reoccur amongst the freeholders in the Poll Book. Unfortunately, the Returning Officer was entitled to tender them an oath which the Quakers could not take. This may well be why, of all the 388 freeholders voting in the parishes of the Quaker Upperside Meeting, only six were certain, and another seven possible, dissenters. It does not look as if there was any causal connection between the liberty of being a freeholder and the liberty to be a dissenter; it seems in view of these tiny figures as if this determinism, too, does not work. But in view of the theoretical existence of the oath, we cannot be absolutely certain. Therefore, despite the existence of this remarkable source, it is still impossible to tell whether there was any causal relationship between being a freeholder and the liberty to be a dissenter. However, there were a large number of people of Lollard descent amongst freeholders, who were not themselves dissenters, but bore the surnames of dissenters, and were therefore likely to be related to dissenters (see pp. 302–3).

When it comes to by-employment in this woodland area, we are better off. The new paper industry took root in England in the sixteenth and seventeenth centuries. There were paper mills at High Wycombe. The greatest concentration of mills in the seventeenth century was in the home counties, particularly in Buckinghamshire, because of the 'powerful magnet of London, the greatest market for paper, and the centre of rag supplies'. In the outbreaks of plague of 1636–7, the Privy Council ordered the closure of the paper mills in Buckinghamshire and

---

[201] Personal information from Dr John Broad. The question was asked by Dr Ted Collins.

[202] Advice from Dr Kevin Schurer, of the Cambridge Group. Bucks. RO Poll Book, D/C/3/61.

[203] See above, p. 31.

Middlesex, because of the danger of infection spread by rags. Most rags came from London. So here was a very strong connection, making for frequent trade communications with the capital, by road, or by river.[204]

One of the centres for lace making was also at High Wycombe where materials were distributed early in the seventeenth century, and where the mayor complained in 1623 that 'Wee find that by reason of the trades of clothing and bone lace makeing are much decayed and do daylie fayle, the poore are greatlie hindered and impoverished and growne into such multitudes that wee knowe not measures to set them on work.'[205] Indeed, one of the dissenting freeholders of 1685 was a lace maker of Amersham.

No one as far as I know has yet worked on furniture making in the sixteenth and seventeenth centuries and its export to London; this, with the concomitant supply of fuel to London by river from the coppice beechwoods, and tanning bark for the leather industries, looks as if it was the real 'industry' of our area. We do know of the tremendous increase in joined furniture in houses below the gentry level in rural Suffolk between the late sixteenth and the late seventeenth centuries,[206] and the increase of comfort in London,[207] and perhaps we can deduce enough from the inventories of very prosperous men in Buckinghamshire who were living on the Thames, owning inns or barges there, who had in stock on the wharves as much in one case as 1,200 loads of beech billet wood worth £160, and over 1,000 more loads cut in the woods. As well as wood for furniture, wood for fuel went down river to London: so did oak bark for tanning for the leather trades. Marlow, which had been a Lollard centre, was also a centre for shipping wood and bark (William Grinder, the prosperous Lollard of Little Marlow who often attended the Amersham conventicle, was a woodseller);[208] tanning, leather, and dissent, I have suggested, also have a connection through the trade communications involved. Here they are perhaps demonstrated.

Brushes, brooms, and wooden spoons were made in Chesham; furni-

---

[204] D.C. Coleman, *The British Paper Industry, 1495–1800* (Oxford, 1958), pp. 37, 49, 65.

[205] G.F.R. Spenceley, 'The Origins of the English Pillow Lace Industry', *Agricultural History Review*, 21, 2 (1973), esp. pp. 84 n. 1 and 85. But note the warning about the spread of the new industry to arable districts, which does not fit Dr Thirsk's pattern, by the mid-seventeenth century, pp. 86–93.

[206] Rachel Garrard, 'The Social Significance of the Domestic Interior, with Reference to Sixteenth and Seventeenth Century Britain' (Cambridge, PhD, in progress, 1991).

[207] Peter Earle, *The Making of the English Middle Class: Business, Society and Family Life in London, 1660–1730* (London, 1989), pp. 292–4. Unfortunately, he concentrates on upholstery. Christopher Gilbert, *English Vernacular Furniture, 1750–1900* (Yale, 1991), has a compendious bibliography of work on individual items of furniture, which probably includes some seventeenth-century information. I am grateful to Dr Snell for the reference.

[208] See below, Ch. 3, section III, and Reed (ed.), *Buckinghamshire Probate Inventories, 1661–1714*, pp. xv–xvi, 316. It is likely, from this example, that bark was so cheap it was not often listed in an inventory.

ture was made in High Wycombe. Another of our dissenting freeholders was a carpenter in Amersham, as well as a deacon, overseer of the poor, and prison visitor for the Baptist Church. We also have the inventory of a joiner of Wendover, on the northern edge of the hills, south of Aylesbury. He worked in oak, ash, and beech; his inventory included the value of framed bedsteads 'already sent upp to London' and 'Eleaven bedsteeds ready made upp for London'.[209] They will have travelled by carriers' cart. For we also know that of all the counties in England, Buckinghamshire was best supplied with most frequent, regular road communications in 1637. There were more carriers' services during the week from London to it than anywhere else, quite apart from heavy river traffic on the Thames. It is no accident that one of Egbert van Heemskerck's famous satirical paintings of Quaker meetings has always been reputed to be set at the 'Bull and Mouth' Inn at Aldersgate, where one of these services arrived.[210] If heresy flourished in Buckinghamshire, it was not because the county was remote, but the contrary. Dissent, dissenters, and dissenting print all reached it easily.

We therefore end up with a paradox. From our investigations, the five generations of radical dissenters in south Buckinghamshire, from Lollards to Quakers and Baptists, are one of the most static groups of early modern people we know about, deeply rooted in their own local marketing and gathered church areas. But their dissenting ideas were conveyed to them by one of the best serviced road networks in England, as well as the River Thames: on these roads and on this river travelled not only the itinerant teachers and preachers, from the early Lollards to the Quakers, who must have been one of the most mobile groups in the whole population, but also a multiplicity of clothiers, wholesale leather and wood traders, and cloth and leather workers, who not only brought with them their craft expertise and goods, but also radical ideas to exchange.

In view of the evidence of the social integration of our heretics, from Lollards to Quakers, into their own village communities, as well as the mutual support they obviously gave each other in their 'gathered churches' and conventicles, we suggest this relative immobility over time

---

[209] Ibid., pp. xv–xvi and 103–4. Judging from the values of the eleven, nearly twice that number had already been sent to London. Dr Reed wondered how the bedsteads were to have been sent up to London. We now know. See below, Michael Frearson, p. 277.

[210] Reproduced in Joan Kendall, 'The Development of a Distinctive Form of Quaker Dress', Costume, 19 (1985), p. 60. It may only be a happy accident that the author commented on the dress of the three gentry at this meeting, that the clothes were suitable for gentlemen like Ellwood and Penn. Dr Harry Mount of Christchurch, Oxford, is working on a book on early genre painting in England, and we intend to cooperate. He has an article in press on Heemskerck's Quaker Meeting pictures, Journal of the Warburg and the Courtauld Institutes (forthcoming). See below, pp. 286–7.

was the result of social acceptance in their own localities. They did not want to move because their neighbours, on the whole, tolerated them, and these 'known men' also upheld each other.

'I bought me a primer', or, 'how godly were the multitude?' The basic religious concepts of those who could read in the seventeenth century

The diffusion, or lack of it, of religious belief through the various strata of rural society in the sixteenth and seventeenth centuries has been for some years a major research interest of mine. My focus has also been not on the 'rabble that cannot read'[211] but rather on the spread of reading skills amongst the 'poorer sort', the way this was accomplished, and its significance in terms of the availability of all sorts of elementary informa- tion to the 'poorer sort', from their religious concepts to the very pressing economic matter of how to draw up a bond for debt, which, as we discover, affected large numbers of very humble people in society indeed.[212] The subject has an immediate bearing, almost too obvious to underline, on the diffusion of radical, and, indeed, conforming, religious belief. The historical figure of Sister Sneesby, a day-labourer in her widowhood, a deaf old fen woman who was a General Baptist and was reduced in 1654 to a state of great spiritual distress by reading Quaker writings, has haunted me ever since I first made her acquaintance.[213] The Baptist messengers who 'found [her] in a very sad and deplorable condition' advised her to 'continue reading the' Scriptures. She literally could not hear the words of the Quaker evangelist: here was one poor woman who could not be influenced by the oral word. But she was still converted from her General Baptist beliefs to Quakerism by the printed word, and held the new beliefs sufficiently strongly to be imprisoned for them. Print was a potent weapon.

How rare was this woman? Or how typical? The evolution and content of cheap print for the new mass market represented by Sister Sneesby has been my concern. It has been heightened by my realization that one

---

[211] Quoted Duffy 'The Godly and the Multitude', p. 31.
[212] For general indebtedness amongst the poorest groups in society also, see my 'Unre- liability of the Probate Inventory' in Chartres and Hey (eds.), *English Rural Society*, pp. 139–74. A nice example is provided by John Aves of Chippenham, who wrote wills for parishioners. He also signed a bond for a local baker, presumably for bread, worth £4 10s. When he died, his goods were only worth £9 6s 2d, and because of this bond, his household possessions were put up for auction by the parish to pay his arrears of rent, and bury him. His widow bought the cradle at the sale. Margaret Spufford, *Contrasting Communities*, pp. 210, 339.
[213] Margaret Spufford, *Contrasting Communities*, pp. 216–17.

of the first defences of those in danger of being taken up as vagrants was to invest in printed paper to sell. Vagrants and print, usually considered opposite points of the compass from each other, were not necessarily unfamiliar with each other, and cheap print and religion were, as we shall see, inseparable.[214] In this murkiest of all areas, it is worth recording that the first recourse of the destitute, those who were in very real danger of being whipped as vagrants,[215] was sometimes to acquire 'some pictures and ballads and other paper wares' on credit, as did a shipwrecked sailor with no possessions, in the far-from metropolitan north, or 'books and ballads' as did an ex-servant whose husband beat her, who 'went about the country from place to place' bartering her paperware for food or a night's lodging in a barn.[216] Four such vagrants, an almanac seller, two ballad singers, and a woman selling the London Gazette were 'drawne after the Life' by Marcellus Laroon in 1687.[217] Vagrants are usually excluded from discussion of the theological beliefs of the common people, and their opinions thought to be too opaque for study by the ecclesiastical historian. It is quite extraordinary that we have a record of a vagrant who was an active member of the Fenstanton Baptist Church in 1653, when the church agreed to take the financial responsibility for her, if she was allowed to settle in the village of Melbourn.[218] She seems likely to have been a chapwoman, or pedlar, since the members of the church 'upon diligent search found that the best way for the satisfying of her necessities was to provide her a stock to trade withal, as formerly she was accustomed' and to that end supplied her with £1 to buy goods.[219] Here we have a vagrant General Baptist. We cannot any longer agree that 'Christopher Hill must be right to locate puritanism in the ranks of the economically independent', if, indeed, he would have included radical believers like General Baptists under that multiform umbrella.[220]

When she wrote her doctoral thesis on the widows of Abingdon in 1983, Dr Barbara Todd devoted the beginning of it to a consideration of contemporary marriage manuals.[221] She was well aware that these manuals, or their contents, were highly unlikely ever to have reached the hands of the widows of Abingdon at all, but wrote a brief and revealing

[214] See below, Tessa Watt, Ch. 6, passim.
[215] Paul Slack (ed.), Poverty in Early Stuart Salisbury, Wiltshire Record Society, 31 (Devizes, 1975).
[216] Margaret Spufford, The Great Reclothing, pp. 25, 43.
[217] Sean Shesgreen, The Criers and Hawkers of London: Engravings and Drawings by Marcellus Laroon (London, 1990), pp. 100, 150, 186.
[218] Stevenson, 'Economic and Social Status', p. 355 n. 17.
[219] Underhill (ed.), Fenstanton Records, pp. 82–3, 86.
[220] Collinson, 'The Godly: Aspects of Popular Protestantism', p. 4 See below, pp. 334–6.
[221] Barbara Todd, 'Widowhood in a Market Town: Abingdon, 1540–1720' (Oxford, DPhil, 1983).

little footnote, which caught my eye, pointing out that we were then
wholly ignorant of the contents of the ballads which would have formed
the reading matter, and therefore formulated any concepts of marriage
drawn from the printed word, of these women themselves. Now the
picture is different, in both the secular and the religious sphere which is
here my concern.

Thanks to Dr Tessa Watt, we now know what the favourite 'godly'
ballads of the early seventeenth century were, and when the trade in
'small godly' books began.[222] Dr Carlson has examined the ideas on marriage contained in ballads. Thanks to Helen Weinstein, we know the
religious instruction any small seventeenth-century child who learnt to
read would have, and what the religious content of the mass of late
seventeenth-century ballads was.[223]

The concepts familiar to the seventeenth-century humbler sort, unedu-
cated at grammar school, but familiar with hornbooks, primers, or even
with the sung word at alehouse and market, can now be familiar to us
too. In his paper on the 'Godly and the Multitude' Dr Duffy raised two
main questions. The second, more answerable, one was 'did orthodox
Christian belief have a place in the literary culture of the multitude?'[224]
This thanks to Dr Watt and to Helen Weinstein, as well as to Dr Plumb
and Dr Stevenson, we are now able to answer. It did indeed, although,
as always, we can speak much more clearly for unorthodox belief. The
cross-fertilization between the work of these post-doctoral scholars is
nowhere more apparent that in Dr Watt's reconstruction[225] of the possible contents of the bag of 'lytle bookes' which a pedlar was hawking in
1578[226] in the churchyard of the village of Balsham, dominated by Familists, where Dr Marsh analyses society for us.[227] That pedlar, we now know,
is quite likely to have had at least one of the three Familist ballads in
circulation in his bag, translated from the Dutch of Hendrick Niclaes.

The study I made of the brief accounts of their schooling given by the
'spiritual autobiographers' of the seventeenth century, some of whom

---

[222] Watt, *Cheap Print*, chs. 2, 3, 7, and 8.
[223] Eric Josef Carlson, 'Marriage and the English Reformation' (Harvard, PhD, 1987),
chapter 5. Forthcoming under the same title from Blackwell, Oxford. We will come
to know also from Helen Weinstein's work a great deal on the attitudes to sexuality
and to marriage which would have been highly relevant to Dr Todd, 'Rudimentary
Religion and National Identity in Late Seventeenth Century England' (Cambridge,
PhD, in progress, 1994).
[224] Duffy, 'The Godly and the Multitude', p. 41. We have absolutely no doubt about
seventeenth-century culture in general: no less than 42 per cent of the whole output
recorded in the STC for 1640 can be classified as religious. Tessa Watt, below, p.
258.
[225] See below, Ch. 6.
[226] Margaret Spufford, *Contrasting Communities*, p. 208.
[227] See below, Ch. 5.

came from very humble backgrounds,[228] showed they learnt to read between four and six. The autobiographers began to learn to write at seven. This system applied even in the case of child prodigies from very much more privileged backgrounds, like Gregory King. Gregory was born in 1648, and began school at two. 'At 3 years old he read the Psalter, and at 4 the Bible very distinctly.' At five and a half, he was sent to the Free School of Lichfield to learn his Accidence, and by the time he was six, he was removed to the upper school by the headmaster, 'because he found him very forward in respect to his age, and very inclinable to his booke'. His forwardness was all the more noticeable because he was abnormally small. In his sixth year, 'the Grammar and Sententiae Pueriles were his entertainment'. Yet despite all this, 'being arrived at his *seventh year his father taught him to write*' while he was kept at home by a threat of smallpox. He started Hebrew at nine, despite some difficulties, since the Bible was almost as big as himself, and Greek at ten. Neither his parents nor his master was ever inhibited by any fear of making an exhibition of the child, which they seem to have done on all possible occasions. Yet it never crossed their minds to teach him to write early.[229] Seven was the established age.

They were not atypical of society at large in this. Records of the ages of entry and books on which boys started to learn to read at the school at Aldenham in Hertfordshire, run by the Brewers Company, survive, remarkably, for 1689, 1695, and 1708. Cumulatively, they covered 127 boys, whose ages at entry varied from three to twelve, but 68 per cent of whom came in at five, six, and seven. Of these, 60 per cent overall could read: but only 10 per cent could read if they entered aged three or four, as opposed to nearly a third of the five year olds, just over half of the six year olds, and three-quarters of the seven year olds. This tells us that reading skills were frequently acquired either at home or at a dame-school.[230]

---

[228] 'First Steps in Literacy', pp. 417, 434–5.
[229] 'Life of Gregory King', in J. Dallaway, *Inquiries into the Origin and Progress of the Science of Heraldry* (Gloucester, 1793), pp. xxvi–xxvii.
[230] Unpublished paper by Mr Newman Brown on Richard Platt's school founded at Aldenham, Hertfordshire in 1601. I am much indebted to Mr Newman Brown for access to this paper, and to Dr Roger Schofield for drawing it to my attention, with interpretations. The paper is in the records of the Cambridge Group.

We know far too little about dame-schools. I drew attention to the prevalence of women teaching reading only, in 'First Steps in Literacy'. The impression I gained then is heavily reinforced by the eighteenth-century autobiography of James Raine, 'Memoir of his Childhood', in Angela Marsden (ed.), *A Raine Miscellany*, Surtees Society 200 (Newcastle upon Tyne, 1991), pp. 37–48, 14–17, who was taught by no less than three schooldames, two of whom were the wives of day-labourers, but could read, before going on to a series of three masters in tumbledown hovels who could teach writing, when he was five. He was also heavily influenced by both grandmothers who told him stories and rhymes drawn from print. One of them

Six and seven were also the ages at which a child could begin to cope with a full working day, and earn wages which would be significant in a meagre family economy. The importance of the social hierarchy in determining writing skills, and the much wider diffusion of reading skills, is immediately explained, since in general only a parent of the rank of yeoman or above could afford to dispense with a child's earnings from the family budget. Labourers and husbandmen needed the pence they could earn, and if there was great economic pressure, the children's earnings were needed before they were six, and therefore before they could read. Hence Richard Baxter's plea in 1674 to the rich to have pity on the poor 'so full of cares how to pay their rent and debts, that they have no heart to think of the greater business of their soules', unable even to '*spare their children from work while they learn to read*'.[231] This was the case of the often quoted Thomas Tryon, the most expansive of the spiritual autobiographers I found, born in 1634, son of a building craftsman, whose father was only able to spare him for school for a short time after he was five.

The value of his account of eventually mastering reading and writing lies in the detail he gives of the way his thirst for literacy was satisfied, and more particularly in the group which taught him to read, but could not teach him to write.

had an early seventeenth-century *Life of Christ* with 'rude woodcuts', a copy of Aesop's *Fables* with woodcuts, and an 'immense bundle of penny histories and ballads' from which he learnt the *Seven Champions* and *Robin Hood*; the other knew Watts' *Hymns* by heart. However, he is too late for our purposes.

The problem with schooldames appears to be not that they did not normally exist, but they were not normally licensed. If they had been, the diocese of Norwich ought to have recorded them. There is an unpublished thesis by D.M. Meads, 'An Account of the Education of Women and Girls in England at the Time of the Tudors' (London, PhD, 1929), p. 237, in which it is stated that select women in each ward of the city of Norwich were 'to work or learne letters at their house or houses' and were to 'teach the most poorest children whose parents are not liable to pay for theyr learninge'. Meads also points out that the Norwich Visitation Articles enquired 'whether the schoolmasters or schoolmistresses that teach in your parishes either openly or privately'. Despite this, the unpublished Appendix to David Cressy, 'Education and Literacy in London and East Anglia, 1580–1700' (Cambridge, PhD, 1972), demonstrates conclusively the paucity of licences issued to women. There were none in Norfolk, despite the Visitation Articles. I am much indebted to Karen Smith-Adams, who in her hunt for licensed midwives (Cambridge, PhD, in progress, 1992) has kept her eyes open for licensed schooldames for me, and has only found one. She would undoubtedly have found them, had they been licensed. Mrs Caroline Bowden, 'The sixteenth-century ideal of women and the relationship between this and education' (London, MPhil, in progress, 1992) gave me the reference to Meads. In view of the frequency with which schooldames are mentioned, we must conclude that there were many women teachers of reading, but that they are unfortunately normally an untraceable group in the records.

[231] My italics. Richard Baxter, *Poor Man's Family Book* (1674), pp. 101–2, quoted Duffy, 'The Godly and the Multitude', p. 35.

> All this while, tho' now about Thirteen Years Old, I could not Read; then thinking of the vast usefulness of Reading, *I bought me a Primer*, [my italics] and got now one, then another, to teach me to Spell and so learn'd to Read imperfectly, my Teachers themselves not being ready Readers: But in a little time having learn't to Read competently well, I was desirous to learn to Write, but was at a great loss for a Master, none of my Fellow-Shepherds being able to teach me. At last, I bethought myself of a lame young Man, who taught some poor People's Children to Read, and Write; and having by this time got two Sheep of my own, I applied myself to him, and agreed to give him one of my Sheep to teach me to make the Letters, and Joyn them together.[232]

The difficulty Thomas found in learning to write, as opposed to learning to read, seems very important. Although his fellow-shepherds as a group were not 'ready' readers, they did, again as a group, possess the capacity to help him to learn to spell out words. He was not dependent on only one of them to help him. But although these Gloucestershire shepherds could read, they could not write at all. The point about the much greater diffusion of reading skills in seventeenth-century society is strongly reinforced. When Bishop Lloyd of Lichfield had a survey made of his own manor of Eccleshall in Staffordshire, which was so inquisitively detailed that it must have made him one of the most unpopular of landlords on record in the 1690s, he wrote, of just a single one of the many labourers who lived in the little market town, 'Neither he nor his wife can read.' This man, with his wife, stood out as unusual. Abnormality caused remark.[233]

If reading was indeed a widely diffused skill, the absence of which was unusual and worthy of remark, we need to know what basic concepts, basic mental furniture and imagery, had been conveyed to these people who could sound out their letters after a fashion. Thomas Tryon assists us: 'I bought me a primer.' This was not, it seems from the way he wrote it, a difficult thing to do; he had no trouble obtaining a copy. More extensive examination of the distribution network of cheap books and pedlars' goods shows how right this impression is.[234] John Floyd of

---

[232] *Some Memoirs of the Life of Mr Tho: Tryon, Late of London, Merchant: Written by Himself* . . . (London, 1705).

[233] Transcript of the Survey of the Township of Eccleshall, 1697, compiled by N.W. Tildesley (1969) in the William Salt Library, Stafford. This is even more significant because Eccleshall turns out to be, according to the Hearth Taxes, the poorest community we yet know of in Stuart England (Margaret Spufford, 'Eccleshall', *Staffordshire Studies* (forthcoming, 1994)). It may well be extremely relevant that the enormous parish was primarily pastoral, with a great deal of by-employment. See above, pp. 44-7. Aldenham, above, p. 67, was also in a wood-pasture area.

[234] In 1583, Roger Ward was in trouble with the Stationers' Company for printing 'the little primer and the usual psalter'. The year before, he had sent 1,500 copies of *The ABC with the Little Catechism* to Shrewsbury, where he had a shop. Tessa Watt, below, p. 263.

Radnor was a pedlar with a horse in 1675;[235] and amongst the hooks and
eyes, and the buttons and pins he jogged round the Welsh borders selling
were half a dozen primers valued at only 8d the lot. Robert Carr was a
chapman at Newcastle upon Tyne in a very much larger way of business.
In 1677, he had amongst the goods in his shop and warehouse six dozen
primers at 12s, or 2d each, and no less than nineteen dozen hornbooks,
at either 6d a dozen or 5d a dozen.[236] These were presumably wholesale
prices. But even marked-up, the hornbooks would not have cost more
than a penny or a halfpenny each. Children less highly motivated than
Thomas Tryon could certainly acquire them, even more easily than
primers. There is some evidence that first classes of 'petties' began to
learn to read automatically with hornbooks. Small James Fretwell, who
went to grammar school at four and a half was, understandably, put into
the 'hornbook-class, which my master at first sight thought most suitable
for me'.[237]

Even in the first part of the sixteenth century, a print-struck dedicated
youth could obtain a primer. An example exists of a twenty-year-old
apprentice in Chelmsford in 1538 who was so excited by hearing poor
men read the New Testament aloud, after the royal orders to place the
English Bible in all churches, that he decided 'I will learn to read English,
and then will I have the New Testament and read thereon myself.' He,
too, 'bought him a Primer' and clubbed together with another apprentice
to buy an English New Testament, which they hid in their bed-straw.[238]

Lollard conventicles, which in places like Amersham and Hughenden
involved a very considerable part of the whole settlement, included as
we have seen, all ranks of taxpaying society.[239] Thomas Man, who was
martyred in 1518, sought refuge with Andrew Randall of Rickmansworth,
who was worth only £2 in the Subsidy, but was a reader of *The Wicket*.
Prestige and esteem in Lollard communities were not based on prosperity. The regard in which Richard and Alice Collins,[240] who were sought
as readers and preachers all over Berkshire and Oxfordshire, were held
is ample proof. Richard paid tax on goods to the value of £6 13s 4d in
1524. The Lollard conventicles, just like the Quaker meetings later, which,

---

[235] John Floyd of Norton, Radnor, prob. 1676, Herefordshire and Worcestershire
Record Office.
[236] University of Durham, Department of Paleography and Diplomatic, Probate 1686,
Robert Carr.
[237] Margaret Spufford, 'First Steps in Literacy', p. 128.
[238] Margaret Aston, 'Lollardy and Literacy', *History*, 62 (Oct. 1977), p. 368. A revised
version may conveniently be found in her *Lollards and Reformers*. But William Maldon
may have been able to construe Latin before he taught himself to read English, and
he may have had much more trouble buying his primer, and paid more for it as
well.
[239] Derek Plumb, see below, p. 114.
[240] For Alice Collins, see Margaret Aston, 'Lollardy and Literacy', p. 355.

as we now know, often included descendants of the same families,[241] were socially mixed.[242] Economic standing, and standing within this heretical group, were not equivalent. Nor, interestingly, did reading ability, which was immensely important to this group of Lollards, go with economic status in it. The conventicle was riddled with books, readers, and rote-learners;[243] the written word was immensely important, and those who could read it, or possessed texts, were not necessarily the most dominant economically. Benedict Ward of Beaconsfield, one of the Chiltern Lollards who had been persecuted in Bishop Longland's investigation in 1518–21, taught Thomas Pope his 'christe crosse rowe'. He had then given Thomas Pope a book of the Ten Commandments, the Gospels of Matthew and Mark, and five parts of the eight Beatitudes. This enterprising man, eaten up with zeal, had begun by teaching the alphabet. It is even more interesting that he was a fuller, taxed only £1 on goods, the lowest taxable figure in the Great Subsidy of 1524–5.[244] Andrew Fuller of Uxbridge, labourer, taxed on £1 in wages in 1524–5, still dealt in books worth 4s 6d.[245] Francis and Alice Funge, from Little Missenden, were only a little better off. He was taxed on £2. But despite comparative poverty, the pair possessed the Gospels in English: they very unwisely left their Bible on a table in the hall, where the churchwarden saw it.[246] This particular group of Chiltern Lollards owned a wide selection of books[247] and 'resorted many times together reading and conferring'.[248] The Christ cross row, the alphabet, could and did then lead straight into the other contents of the hornbook, the Creed, the Lord's Prayer and what were, early in the sixteenth century, the exceedingly dangerous mysteries of the Gospels themselves.

Apart from surnames and ancestry in common, the other remarkable feature the Lollards of the sixteenth century and the Quakers of the seventeenth century had in common was their books. The existence of a Buckinghamshire Quaker lending library, begun in 1692, with the prices of purchase added to the titles,[249] is tantalizing evidence that the Quakers shared the Lollard passion for reading. We do not know, of course, which Quakers borrowed and read the books. We do know that the library

---

[241] See below, pp. 296, 298–9.
[242] Derek Plumb, see below, Chs. 2 and 3.
[243] Hudson, 'Lollardy: The English Heresy?', in idem, Lollards and their Books, pp. 162–3; idem, Premature Reformation, pp. 471–2, 475–6.
[244] Plumb, 'Foxe and the Later Lollards,' pp. 423, 406, and Foxe, IV, 226, 234.
[245] Plumb, 'Foxe and the Later Lollards', p. 50.
[246] Ibid., pp. 329–30.
[247] Hudson, 'Lollardy: The English Heresy?', in idem, Lollards and their Books, p. 162.
[248] Foxe, IV, p. 222. See also below, pp. 137, 156–60.
[249] I owe this reference and the subsequent comment to W. Stevenson. Bucks. RO, NQ2/22/1. The library seemed to include an up-to-date cross-section of attacks on Quakers, and their printed responses.

included many titles bought for 2d, like *Corrupted Coyn Made Good by Caesar: Corrupted Man Made Good by Christ, A Few Lines in True Love,* and *A Faithful Testimony against Extravagant and Unecessary Wiggs,* as well as much more expensive and weighty works, like *Essays about the Poor,* price 4s, *The Poor Mechanick's Plea,* at 3s, and *The Fig-Leaf Covering Discovered,* at 9s. But we cannot be sure that any one of the Quaker labourers whom Dr Stevenson has found read 'small godly' books, as did their predecessors, like Andrew Fuller of Uxbridge, the Lollard labourer. It remains from the example of Sister Sneesby, a very likely, but unproven, possibility. We do not know, either, whether a tradition of reading skills was fostered in, and descended in, these dissenting families of the Chilterns along with their openness to new religious and radical ideas. It, too, is a likely, but unproven, possibility.

So what did the possessor of a sixteenth- or seventeenth-century hornbook or primer absorb, as he or she sounded out the letters of the alphabet? The general rule about ephemera, the more common or cheaper the object, the less likely is it to survive, applies to hornbooks. There are not even two dozen survivors in England.[250] Amongst the survivors in the Bodleian are seven seventeenth-century examples. The first carries the verses of Psalm 100:

1. Make a joyful noise unto the Lord, all ye lands.
2. Serve the Lord with gladness; come before his presence with singing.
3. Know ye that the Lord he is God: it is he that hath made us, and not we ourselves; we are his people and the sheep of his pasture.

The second carries the black letter alphabet, both lower and upper case, followed by crosses in each case. This introduction, or conclusion, to the alphabet was normal. Alphabetism was so closely associated with basic Christian tenets that the alphabet itself, with its attendant crosses, was known as the 'Christ cross row'. Immediately after the alphabet and its crosses on the hornbook in John Johnson's collection in the Bodleian came the first words the child learning to read was to learn, 'In the name of the Father, and of the Son, and of the Holy Ghost, Amen', followed by the Lord's Prayer. The association of basic Christian instruction and

---

[250] For what follows I am much indebted to Helen Weinstein's unpublished paper on English seventeenth-century primers and hornbooks, and her notes, which she kindly lent me, on the hornbooks surviving in the John Johnson collection in the Bodleian Library. She also used extensively A.W. Tuer, *A History of the Hornbook,* 2 vols. (London, 1896). Her thesis, nearing completion, on 'Rudimentary Religion and National Identity in Late Seventeenth Century England', which there has been no opportunity to incorporate here, will add much more to our understanding of this subject. John Harthan, *Books of Hours and their Owners* (London, 1977), considers both manuscripts and printed books of hours. See particularly pp. 14–19, 169–74.

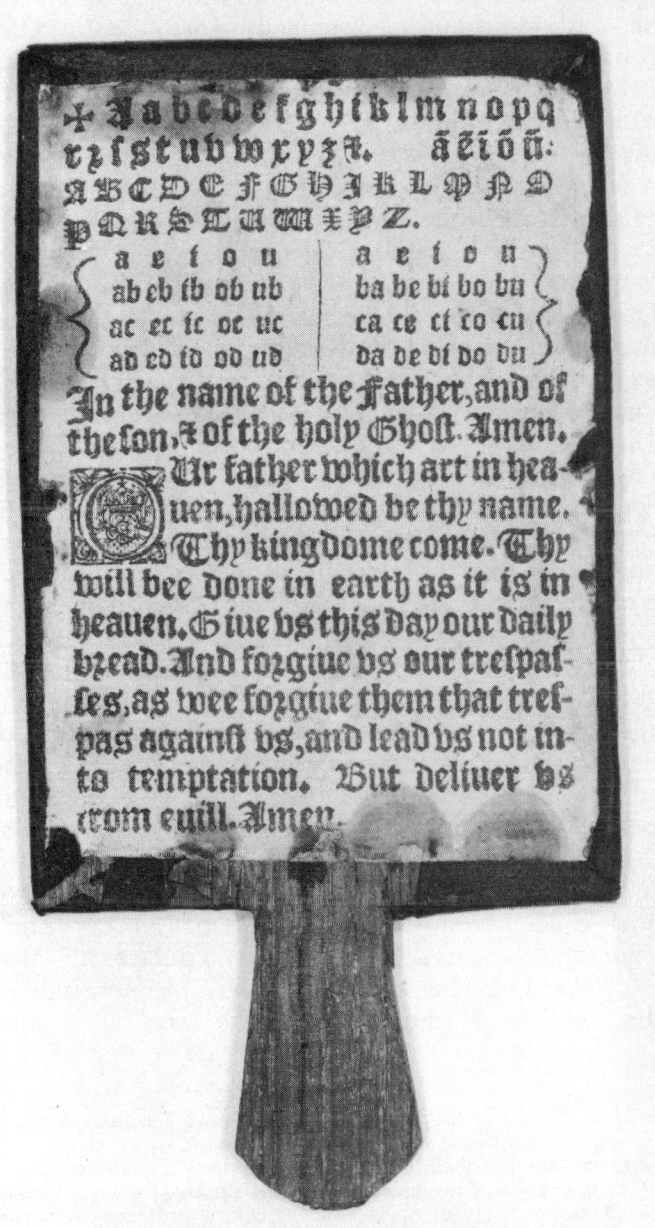

Plate 1. Seventeenth-century hornbook

learning to read was so profoundly intertwined that it is inseparable: the child who had learnt to read learnt to sound out the letters of the alphabet and the words of the Lord's Prayer, and perhaps the Creed, from his or her hornbook. He or she would proceed to the primer, which is defined by the Oxford English Dictionary both as 'a prayerbook or devotional manual for the use of the laity' and as an 'elementary schoolbook for teaching children to read'. The two functions in the sixteenth and seventeenth centuries were not different, or distinguished, from each other, but the same. One of the earliest vernacular translations of the primer, of 1539, contains an almanac, a calendar, the alphabet, and the seven petitions of the paternoster, on the same page. This is followed by the Creed, the Ten Commandments, various graces, anthems and psalms, and ends with the Litany. The pattern was followed by the other surviving primers from the mid- to the late sixteenth century. At the school at Aldenham, admittedly in the late seventeenth century,[251] all entrants under five, and most five year olds who could not read, were taught to do so from a primer. From six onwards, a New Testament, Old Testament, or 'Testament' became the more frequent first book. At Elizabeth's accession, the *ABC and Catechism*[252] which differed from the primer essentially only by being cast in question and answer form, joined the primer on the market.[253] It covered the Creed, the Commandments, the Lord's Prayer, and, from 1604, the Sacraments. Dr Ian Green estimates that by the early seventeenth century, there were something like one and a quarter million copies of either the official Catechism, or its many alternatives, in circulation in a population of about four million.[254] No one has yet estimated the number of primers in circulation. Nor has anyone, I think, stressed the very basic and simple point that those who had learnt to read had also learnt basic Christian tenets, and had at least a basic familiarity with them. If you could read, you were also religiously indoctrinated.

No wonder Richard Baxter was distressed about the poor 'unable to spare their children from work while they learn to read'. And that high proportion of 60 per cent of the entrants who came to Aldenham school in the 1690s and could already read[255] were therefore already familiar with the Lord's Prayer, the Creed, and the Ten Commandments. The

---

[251] See above, p. 67.
[252] H. Anders, 'The Elizabethan ABC with the Catechism', *The Library*, 4th Ser., 16 (1936), pp. 32–48.
[253] The contents are described by Ian Green, 'Children in Understanding: The Emergence of the English Catechism under Elizabeth and the Early Stuarts', *Journal of Ecclesiastical History*, 37 (1986), pp. 309 and 405. Our knowledge of this whole subject will be transformed when Dr Green's *Religious Instruction in Early Modern England circa 1540 to 1740* appears.
[254] Green, 'Children in Understanding', p. 425.
[255] See above, p. 67.

converse does not hold true: those who were instructed in the articles of the Catechism could not necessarily read them. More than a century earlier, in 1569, a woman called Lucy Neales of Swaffham Bulbeck in the diocese of Ely was presented by her churchwardens because she had received Communion 'and colld not say the lords prayre nor the articles of hir beleffe'.[256] She was to learn them within the next three weeks. The case probably reflected both the reforming Bishop Cox's drive for catechizing to be properly performed and the contemporary desire that those who had not learnt the articles of the Catechism should not 'be admitted to the supper of the lorde'.[257] Lucy Neales probably learnt the Lord's Prayer and the Apostle's Creed exactly 'like a parrat', in a way of which George Herbert would have thoroughly disapproved.[258] But cases like hers illustrate very clearly the need for children to get as far in reading, at least, as the hornbook. Then they would know these essentials. This inextricable association between learning to read and the basic reading materials which form the fundamental 'articles of belief' explains the entries in the churchwardens' accounts at Ashwell in Hertfordshire, between 1636 and 1641, for 'teaching the children'.[259] This was churchwardens' business. It is a logical extension of this that Herbert Palmer, minister at Ashwell, was the author of 'the most daring departure from the norm' amongst alternative catechisms,[260] and was also known for his habit of giving a Bible to any child who had learnt to read.

The ABC, the 'Christ cross row' could, and did, lead straight on to the 'articles of belief' and the Lord's Prayer. It could also, as we have seen, lead straight on to trouble, in the form of heresy, although the definition of trouble changed, of course, over time. It was no accident that one of the broadsides of the evangelist of the Family of Love, Hendrick Niclaes, published in 1575, was called 'All the letters of the A.B.C.'.[261]

ABC ballads, in which each stanza began with a letter of the alphabet in order, were part of a group of aphoristic ballads which appeared right from the beginning of registration in 1557. Indeed, there is an earlier survival, 'An ABC to the christen congregacion' of 1549.[262] Nothing could

[256] EDR B/2/4 fol. 55v.
[257] Green, 'Children in Understanding', p. 410.
[258] George Herbert, 'The Parson Catechising', in A Priest to the Temple, or, the Country Parson his Character, and Rule of Holy Life, in F.E. Hutchinson (ed.), The Works of George Herbert (Oxford, 1941), p. 256. Herbert exhorted the country parson to take pains to apply 'himself with Catechizings, and lively exhortations, not on the Sunday of the Communion only (for then it is too late) but the Sunday or Sundayes before the Communion, or on the Eves of all those dayes. If there be any, who not having received yet, are to enter into this great work, he takes the more pains with them' (p. 258).
[259] Herts. RO Cat. D/P7 5/1. I am very grateful indeed to Mrs Karen Smith-Adams for collecting this reference for me.
[260] Green, 'Children in Understanding', pp. 423–4.
[261] Quoted below, Tessa Watt, p. 242.
[262] Watt, Cheap Print, pp. 101–2.

be more familiar, safer, or therefore tempting than to couch an introduction to a new heresy in ballad form in the known terms of the hornbook, the primer, and the ABC with catechism. But despite the possible misuses of reading skills for spreading heresy, sixteenth- and seventeenth-century puritans and divines were still concerned to use them for spreading orthodoxy.

The late Tudor and early Stuart extensions of basic literacy[263] and the existence of a new reading public in the early seventeenth century led to the development of a specialist trade in deliberately 'small' books for purchasers who would previously only have been interested in buying broadside ballads.[264] Dr Watt has very convincingly traced the origins of the 'small godly' book trade back to the 1620s and 30s, and to the works of John Andrewes, a Wiltshire preacher who had, significantly, been a schoolmaster, and whose works were indignantly repudiated by another John Andrewes, minister of St James, Clerkenwell, who wrote that although he did reckon himself 'the meanest amongst the many thousands who are called to the Sacred Priesthood' yet he himself had never played 'the Marketplace Theologian' and, he implied, the pedlar. He also, equally significantly, wrote that his namesake had written various other books, and amongst them 'Christ-crosses etc.'.[265] So John Andrewes, who pioneered the 'small godly' book, began by teaching the Christ cross row, just like the Lollard Benedict Ward before him, but he went on to introduce a whole new genre, the cheap 'small godly' book, which was to dominate the ballad publisher's trade after the Restoration,[266] no doubt to the satisfaction of the Sister Sneesbys. For we now know from Dr Stevenson's work that Sister Sneesby was not at all unusual: indeed the group of 'three or four poor women sitting at a door in the sun, and talking about the things of God' in Bedford, who set John Bunyan, he wrote, on the road to salvation,[267] tell us that. The Bedford Open Baptists

---

[263] David Cressy shows a sharp rise in the number of schoolmasters found at visitations in rural Essex and Hertfordshire from 1580 to 1592, followed by a decline in the 1620s. There was a similar picture in Norfolk and Suffolk, with a boom in the number of masters teaching in the 1590s. Cressy, 'Education and Literacy'. The Cambridgeshire and Kent chronologies were not dissimilar. But the teachers may have become more available at a very different time in north-eastern England: in the dioceses of Coventry and Lichfield, and Chester, the great increase in the number of masters teaching came after the Restoration. Margaret Spufford, *Small Books*, pp. 19–21.

[264] Watt, *Cheap Print*, pp. 278, 288 *et seq.*, 306–17.

[265] Ibid., p. 307 and n. 51. The title of Andrewes' first work is in fact misleading: *Christ his Crosse* (1614) is a long treatise of ten sheets quarto. But he began as a self-confessed schoolmaster, and must have taught those learning to read their 'Christ-crosses etc.'. See below, pp. 266–7.

[266] Margaret Spufford, *Small Books*, Table 2, pp. 134–5.

[267] John Bunyan, *Grace Abounding to the Chief of Sinners*, ed. R. Sharrock (Oxford, 1962), p. 14.

turn out to be the poorest of all the sectarian groups looked at by Dr Stevenson, with more members exempt from the Hearth Tax.[268]

Dr Duffy stresses the motivation of the authors of the godly chapbooks collected by Samuel Pepys, which dominated the cheap book trade in the 1680s, as a desire to save the poor. 'Some of these books were avowedly written by preachers seeking every means to reach the hearts of the poor. If others were simply parrotted by hard-headed businessmen with an eye to the market, that in itself is eloquent testimony to the acceptability of the message they contained.'[269] Dr Watt, looking at an earlier period concurs in the verdict that cheap religious print was profitable, and therefore popular. 'Publishers . . . do not seem to have had any special interest in their readers' souls, but only in their purses: they printed what they thought would sell . . . If these publishers were businessmen, not evangelists, then the godly ballads must have been saleable.'[270]

In his Ford Lectures of 1979, which appeared in 1981,[271] Professor Collinson expressed doubts about the attraction of religious material, when he was considering the contemporary view of catechizing expressed by Eusebius Paget, as the only way to overcome the 'slow mental processes of the "ruder sort" ', and the only way in which children, and especially servants, could be taught. As Professor Collinson wrote,

> Even a captive audience had first to be captured. Many shepherds, carters and milkmaids were beyond the catechiser's reach. And those who willy-nilly were subject to the disciplines of a religious household, or parish, were initiated through the catechism into the lower reaches of a literate, print-based culture to which their occupations and natural inclinations made them strangers . . . The intention was . . . to implant a religion consisting of patterns of printed words in heads which had little use for words of this kind and which must have found it very difficult to convert the words into authentic and meaningful experience.

The advances made in the study of cheap print and its distribution and marketing in the decade since 1981 have been immense. It is no longer possible to think of the mass of the 'ruder sort' being strangers to a print-based culture which never came their way, and which would have made no sense if it had. My Small Books, drawing attention to the bestselling post-Restoration 'small godly' chapbooks and the prosperity of their specialist producers was in the press at the same time as The Religion of Protestants and was followed by the Great Reclothing of Rural England (1984),

[268] Stevenson, 'Economic and Social Status', Table 40, p. 251, pp. 227–39.
[269] Duffy, 'The Godly and the Multitude', p. 49.
[270] Watt, Cheap Print, pp. 50–2, 74.
[271] Collinson, The Religion of Protestants, pp. 233–4.

drawing attention to the strength of the distribution network. Dr Duffy refined, corrected, and strengthened my work on the chapbooks in 1986. In 1986 also, Professor Collinson gave the Anstey Memorial Lectures at the University of Kent, in which he had considerably modified his opinions.

> What should be grasped by the social and cultural historian who may have been too much swayed by recent talk of the growing division of elite and popular cultures in early modern Europe is that all this fertile imagery was as accessible to the obscure and ordinary bible scholar and sermon-goer as it was to the erudite ... the imaginative world of the Bible became the mentality of the literate or scarcely literate lay person, whose mental powers are consistently underestimated by those historians who assume that Protestantism was a message which must have passed clean over his head. The proof is in the many tedious but still deeply impressive letters printed in Foxe's book, written by or to the artisan martyrs of the Marian persecution, which suggest minds so steeped in the cross-references and resonant concordances of Scripture as to be incapable of exercising themselves in any other way.[272]

In 1991, Dr Watt's *Cheap Print and Popular Piety, 1550–1640* which examines godly ballads and pictures and their content and diffusion, as well as pinpointing the appearance of the 'small godly' chapbooks as a genre, revolutionized our knowledge of the pre-Civil War cheap print available to the multitude. Moreover, the stress on the availability of 'godly' print in this essay omits the many attractions of its 'merry' counterpart, also a booming, and probably even more booming part of the cheap book trade.

Quite apart from all this new work, some common-sense suggestions indicate the way in which 'the imaginative world of the Bible became the mentality of the literate or scarcely literate lay person' and the reasons why the 'ruder sort' were never as far removed from the written word, and its inseparable religious message, as Professor Collinson initially thought.

The major part of this difficulty is removed once the essential link between learning to read and religious information is made plain, and it is realized that although the humblest in society might well be beyond the private catechizer's reach in the 1570s, they were not necessarily, when too young to earn, beyond the reach of the hornbook, and may thus have become familiar with the Lord's Prayer and the Creed, just as Thomas Tryon and Sister Sneesby were. 'Patterns of printed words' were not necessarily unfamiliar. Nor was their content necessarily devoid of

---

[272] Published as *The Birthpangs of Protestant England: Religions and Cultural Change in the Sixteenth and Seventeenth Centuries* (New York, 1988), p. 124.

meaning. For another part of the difficulty is removed when we remember that, in a way now unfamiliar to us, in the sixteenth and seventeenth
century religion was 'news', a matter for rowdy argument, emotional
involvement, and anxiety, just as in extreme cases, it was dangerous. The
dockers in the Port of Alexandria in the fourth century sang pro- and
anti-Arian songs;[273] we know that English alehouse society could relish a
rude song about the Mass.[274] An Italian visitor, according to Isaac Walton,
wrote scoffingly to a friend in his own country

> That the common people of England were wiser than the wisest of his
> nation; that here the very women and shopkeepers were able to judge
> of predestination, and determine what laws were fit to be made con-
> cerning church-government; then, what were fit to be obeyed or abol-
> ished. That they were more able (or at least thought so) to raise and
> determine perplexed cases of conscience, than the most learned col-
> leges in Italy. That men of the slightest learning, and the most ignorant
> of the common people were mad for a new, or super, or re-reformation
> of religion; and that in this they appeared like that man who would
> never cease to whet and whet his knife til there was no steel left to
> make it useful.[275]

No doubt he was indulging in hyperbole. Yet we do know that religion
was material for common argument: the best story is still the account of
the husbandman, the servant, and the two 'women Gospellers' sitting up
all night in an inn in Colchester in 1555, unable to stop arguing about
the divinity of Christ.[276] Even the 'godly' or sectarians in agreement with
each other made their presence loudly felt. In 1584, Thomas Settle, curate
and preacher at Mildenhall, who had Brownist leanings, held meetings
at an inn there at which the innkeeper testified in the ecclesiastical court;
the practice of those at the meeting was to shut themselves 'privately in
one chamber, and ther use certayne prayers whereof the noise might be
hard to the furtherside of the streate, so as the other gestes of the house
complayned of the disquiet they recyved therebye'.[277]

One of the outstandingly interesting subjects awaiting a suitably qualified research student is an examination of the so-called 'conscience' and

---

[273] Personal communication from Professor Rowan Williams, for which I am very grateful. Professor Henry Chadwick tells me that Arius himself wrote 'Songs for sailors
and millers and travellers, fitted to various tunes', Philostorgius, History, ed. Bidez,
II, 2, p. 13.

[274] Margaret Spufford, Contrasting Communities, p. 208.

[275] Isaac Walton, Lives (1796 edn), p. 238. I am grateful to Dr Judith Maltby for this
reference.

[276] See above, pp. 23, 57, Margaret Spufford, Contrasting Communities, pp. 246–7.

[277] John S. Craig, 'The Use of Churchwardens and Parish Accounts: A Suffolk Study,
1560–1600' (typescript 1991), p. 39. Dr Craig won the John Nichols Prize for this
piece, and I am much indebted to him for allowing me to use the example.

commonplace books kept by divines in the late sixteenth and the early seventeenth centuries, recording the religious doubts and anxieties brought to them both by members of their flocks, and by travellers from long distances seeking spiritual counsel.[278] There is a considerable group of these books: until they are examined we do not know whether any of them record the social status or background of the troubled seeker. But if any of them do, there is some hope that we may have a source which might reveal much of the theological and spiritual questioning and distress of the post-Reformation period, and even tell us how extensive it was. We may have examples of the post-Reformation alternative to auricular confession.[279] We might even have a source showing us whether religious debate was endemic, in the way that Sir Keith Thomas demonstrates the popular ubiquity and social spread of astrological belief from the surviving astrological case-books.[280] Certainly one of the protagonists in the Colchester inn, the husbandman, set off for Oxford to get his confusion over the divinity of Christ, which troubled him deeply, sorted out by Bishop Ridley and Mr Latimer. This is the kind of consultation that just might have been recorded.

The third and last part of the difficulty of imagining how 'patterns of printed words' can have had any authentic meaning for labourers and servants is overcome when we consider the nature of the religious ballads that survived for a long period of time in the late sixteenth and seventeenth centuries, for it is possible to establish those which were truly popular, which sold, and reprinted, and sold, again and again. We can do this by emphasizing those which were re-registered again and again in the seventeenth century.[281] Even if we suggest that 'small godly books' were only for those who already considered themselves 'godly' amongst the multitude, we are left with the ballads, which must have reached the widest market amongst those who could read at all. They will have followed hornbook, and primer, in natural sequence. The concepts or themes in them would have formed a sort of lowest common denominator of beliefs familiar to the multitude. The familiarity and felicity with

---

[278] The first of these commonplace books recording various sayings of Richard Greenham, pastor of Dry Drayton in Cambridgeshire, rather in the manner of Luther's *Table Talk*, is currently being edited by Dr Kenneth Parker, with an Introduction by Dr Eric Carlson and Dr Parker, from Rylands Library MS 542. It, unfortunately, does not name, or identify, the social status of the troubled inquirers. Richard Napier of Northamptonshire refused to attempt to treat puritans besieged by self-loathing. M. Macdonald, *Mystical Bedlam* (Cambridge, 1981), cited Collinson, *Birthpangs of Protestant England*, p. 76.

[279] Professor Collinson drew attention to the enormous importance of this post-Reformation *lacuna* in his presidential lecture to the Ecclesiastical History Society in the summer of 1988.

[280] Thomas, *Religion and the Decline of Magic*, pp. 362–82.

[281] See below, pp. 83, 244–51.

which the 'ruder sort' used the ballad format themselves is the most powerful argument of all for their easy and complete absorption of the genre. There are very numerous survivors of ballad-type 'libels' preserved in Star Chamber as the basis for suits. These are now being worked on by Adam Fox.[282] He finds that a displeased lower social group, annoyed or outraged by a social superior breaking the accepted conventions of social, economic, or moral behaviour, very frequently took its revenge by versifying on the event in the local alehouse. People from the lowest ranks of provincial society could, and did, frequently make up scurrilous rhymes. The form was familiar and useable by them, and, indeed, seems to have been enjoyed by all ranks of society. The perpetrators from the 'common sort', who, of course, could frequently read, but not write, then paid someone acquainted with the other literate skill a quart or two of wine to write the libel down. Copies then appeared pinned to the church door, the stocks, the market cross, even the haystacks. The victims would scarcely have taken their injured reputations to the Star Chamber, as they did, had they not been exposed by this action to the laughter of a reading public. But the real nub of the matter is that the 'common sort' were not only readers of verses, godly or ungodly, but happy enough with the form actually to create verses themselves.

There was a deliberate puritan move to reach this reading public by writing 'godly' ballads[283] from the 1550s to the 1570s, and over one third of the ballads then printed were 'godly'. The effort languished in the 1580s, when renaissance taste no longer encouraged such exercises by the educated, and when in the 1570s and 80s the *Whole Book of Psalms* was established as a much better, scripturally based godly source for godly songs for the populace, as Calvinism dictated.[284] Dr Watt has examined all the surviving titles registered with the Stationers' Company, and the actual surviving ballads of the sixteenth century, and compared them with the bulk entries made for copyright purposes by the newly organized 'ballad partners' who came to monopolize an increasingly profitable trade from James I's reign on.[285] These entries were made in 1624, 1656, and 1675 with a further two in catalogues of the eighteenth century. Comparison of the originally registered titles and survivors, and those

---

[282] A.P. Fox, 'Aspects of Oral Culture in Early Modern England' (Cambridge, PhD, 1993). I am particularly grateful to Adam Fox for reading, and checking, this passage for me.

[283] Noted by Collinson, *Birthpangs of Protestant England*, pp. 108–12, and discussed in full, by Watt, *Cheap Print*, pp. 40–2, 47–50. However, despite the decline in new titles, the requesting of old favourites has to be borne in mind. Tessa Watt, below, p. 244.

[284] It was first printed by John Day in 1562 and ran to nearly 500 editions over 125 years. Watt, *Cheap Print*, pp. 54–7.

[285] Ibid., chapters 2 and 3, *passim*.

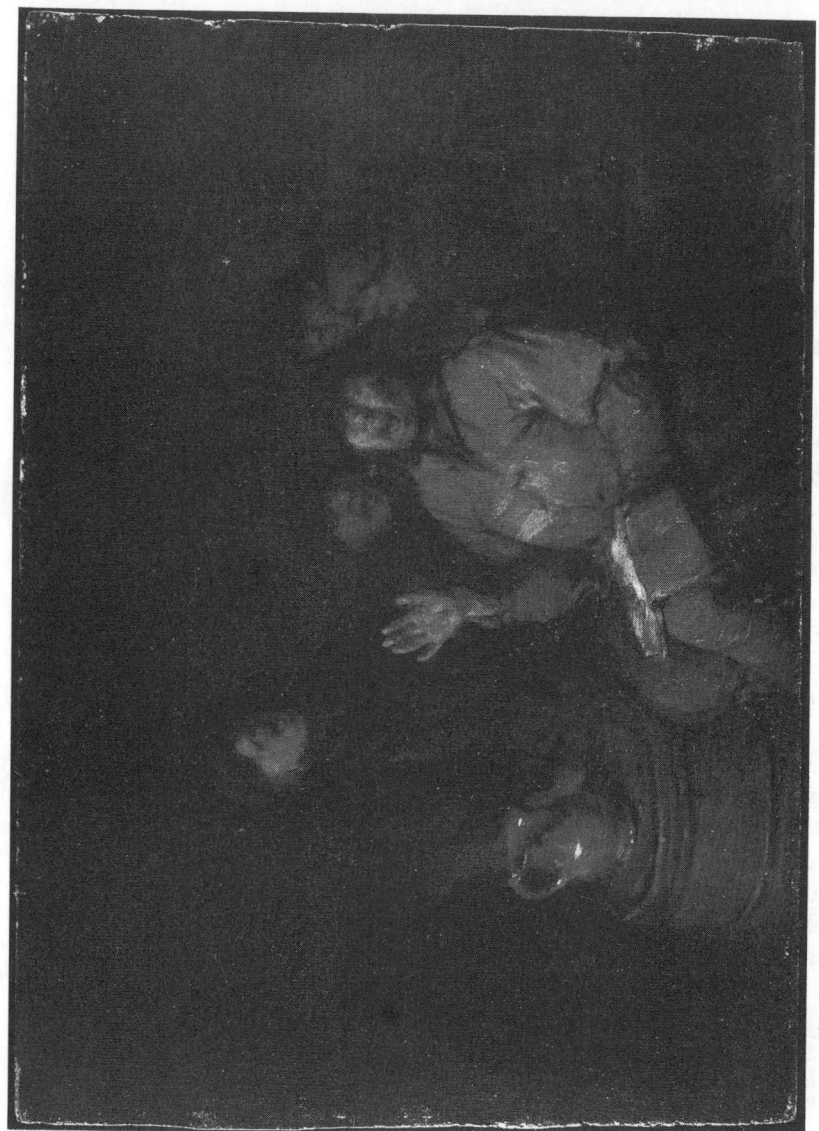

Plate 2. The Singing Peasants, attributed to *Egbert van Heemskerck*, n.d.

re-registered in the bulk entries, showed which caught the public imagination and which remained popular. Unpopular titles which did not sell were dropped by the ballad syndicate. The results are very striking. Thirty-four ballads have a claim to be long-lasting; they survived over a quarter of a century. A notable eight of these survived a full century or more. The titles or texts of 119 more, which did not survive, are known. All of these ballads, both 'short' and long-lived, were primarily written in the sixteenth century, and are mainly the outpourings of the Elizabethan reformers, written before 1586.[286]

The thrust of these ballads was directed in four ways.[287] Amongst the religious-political group, only a group of four songs on protestant martyrs lived on to the seventeenth century. Martyrs and sufferers for religion were attention-catching, thumbnail-sketches from Foxe, and it is no accident that three of the four sufferers who caught the public imagination were women.[288] The ballad of 'The Duchess of Suffolk' was still for sale in 1754. There was certainly matter here for milkmaids. Anne Askewe, stripped, as Dr Watt says, of her own intelligent defence of protestant doctrine and turned into a 'cardboard cut-out' of a weak and victimized woman, a figure attracting immediate sympathy, whose ballad began 'I am a woman poor and blind', stayed in print until 1675. It is noteworthy that her own 'Balade ... made and sunge when she was in Newgate'[289] did not open with this tear-jerking appeal for sympathy, but with the fighting lines

> Lyke as the armed knyght
> Appoynted to the fielde
> With thys world wyll I fyght,
> And fayth shall be my shielde.

It was a good deal more trenchant, and possibly less immediately attractive, than the popular version.

Secondly, a substantial group of the ballads were calls to social reform, to collective responsibility for plague, to repentance, apocalyptic warnings of general judgement to come. The dramatic qualities and human interest of 'Christ's teares over Jerusalem' kept it in print for over eighty years, although moral warnings did not, in general, prove popular. Calls to contemplate protestant martyrs, to collective repentance, and moral

---

[286] Ibid., pp. 82 et seq.
[287] Tessa Watt, below, pp. 240–2.
[288] See below for 'The Duchess of Suffolk', Tessa Watt, pp. 245–6.
[289] That is, if the twentieth-century editor has got the text right. The seventeenth-century examples in the Pepys collection do indeed open 'I am a woman poor and blind'. Anne Askewe in J.C. Squire (ed.), A Book of Women's Verse (Oxford, 1921), pp. 1–3. I am much indebted to Dr Germaine Greer for finding this for me, and to Helen Weinstein for checking the seventeenth-century versions.

behaviour were balanced by a group of 'thoroughly protestant' ballads stressing the saving power of faith. 'Justification by faith alone is made an encouraging proposition in these ballads', death-bed scenes were immediately catching; they were also topical, immensely familiar, and personally relevant to a seventeenth-century audience. Dr Watt's 'archetypal' ballad of personal faith was attributed to the irreproachably post-Reformation parish clerk of Bodnam and contains the lines

> . . . my sinnes, oh Lord, I do confesse,
> Like sands in Sea are numberlesse.

> [Yet] If thou thy mercy doth extend,
> That I my sinfull life may mend.

> *Which mercy thy blessed Word doth say,*
> *At any time obtaine I may.*[290]

There is, as Dr Watt says, little or no sense of a predestined elect. Grace is offered to all and available to the last minute.[291] But alongside a sixteenth- and seventeenth-century reformed tradition ran an unchanged fear of the Last Judgement. Vivid pictorial representation of the torments of a man in hell might well be found by the side of the clerk of Bodnam on the cottage wall. The fear of death dominated seventeenth-century religion.[292]

Attempts to tell scripture stories, and make them attractive, did not, in general, prove best-sellers. The ballads that succeeded were the ballads that featured adulterous love or beautiful young women: the archetypal ballad here was 'David and Bathsheba', probably first registered in 1569–70 and still for sale in 1754. And no wonder, for when David

> . . . went forth to take the ayre
> All in the pleasant moneth of May,
> from whence he spide a Lady faire . . .

> She stood within a pleasant Bower,
> all naked, for to wash her there;
> Her body, like a Lilly Flowere,
> was covered with her golden haire.

Despite the additions to the text of Holy Writ, this ballad got past the censorship.[293]

Amongst the didactic ballads of the New Testament, only the story of the prodigal son succeeded, where the grain of mustard seed and its like disappeared without trace. The basic story of Christ's life and death, with

---

[290] My italics.
[291] Tessa Watt, below, pp. 242 and 247–8.
[292] Margaret Spufford, *Small Books*, pp. 138, 140–3, 201–5, and Tessa Watt, below, p. 249.
[293] Tessa Watt, below, pp. 249–50.

a stress on the Nativity stories, and above all the miracles of Christ, did attract, however, when the parables did not. 'When Jesus Christ was 12 years old', was reprinted for a century and was still on the stock list in 1675, and was in a position to compete successfully, as Dr Watt has written, 'with any of the contemporary miracles described in the sensational news ballads', from teaching in the temple onwards to the resurrection. It had a rousing chorus

> Then praise the Lord both high and low
> Which all these wondrous works doth show,
> That we to heaven at length may goe
> Where he in glory raigneth.[294]

So where does this consideration of basic reading matter and popular balladry get us? Taken together, the materials of hornbooks and primers, and of the most popular of all the godly ballads which those of the less godly might certainly be expected to hear roared in the alehouse in the seventeenth century, form a sort of common denominator of the most basic religious concepts we can presume to be familiar in popular seventeenth-century religion. We may, perhaps, at least make an analogy with 'passive smoking'.

If you learnt to read at all, the first words you puzzled out were religious; after that, there were plenty of ballads to keep you going and if the martyrdom of Anne Askewe, 'I am a woman poor and blind', did not attract you, there were always the attractions of Bathsheba whose

> ... body, like a Lilly Flowere
> was covered with her golden haire.

A print-based culture had, then, much to offer shepherds, carters, and milkmaids, even if we consider the 'godly' cheap print alone. I am not suggesting here 'the fundamental religiosity of the ordinary people of seventeenth-century England',[295] although I believe we have proved in this volume, as in a scientific study, that numbers of the ordinary people of seventeenth-century England, from rich to very poor, were profoundly involved in religious practices from the beginning to the end of the century and its predecessor. But I am suggesting that there was in the seventeenth century a kind of general familiarity, in the alehouse, the cobbler's shop, the miller's, the baker's, and many cottages, even of those exempt from taxation on grounds of poverty, with religious discussion and argument, which no longer exists in contemporary society.

---

[294] Tessa Watt, below, p. 250–1 and 'Cheap Print and Religion, c. 1550–1640' (Cambridge, PhD, 1988), pp. 161–5.

[295] Keith Thomas, 'From Edification to Entertainment', review of Tessa Watt, *Cheap Print and Popular Piety, 1550–1640*, *Times Literary Supplement*, 23 Aug. 1991, p. 5.

The importance of the Lord's Supper to dissenters

In stressing the huge spectrum of religious belief in the sixteenth and seventeenth centuries[296] we have first examined the social antecedents of various radical dissenters through time, and added limited discussion on 'elect' and involved conformist groups. I have attempted to examine the distribution of dissent at large, and its connection with by-employments, trade, and communications. We have then looked at the religious information and songs, that would be familiar to any members of the 'common sort', however unconvinced, who had learnt to read, or who joined in alehouse groups singing ballads. In looking at the religious opinions of those only familiar with the ballads, however 'godly', we are looking at one end of the spectrum.[297] I want to close by looking at the other end, the convinced, and considering the importance repeated ritual actions had for the participants, and how these ritual experiences might have been interpreted.[298] For this purpose I have taken a group whose attendance must certainly have been voluntary, and not a matter of social compulsion or pressure, and attempted to look at the practice of celebration of the Lord's Supper amongst post-Restoration dissenters, a group of whose convictions we can have no doubt, and see whether we can at all gauge what their attendance meant to them.

The Elizabethan theory of reception of Communion was set out by Bishop Cooper of Lincoln in 1580. He composed a homily on the 'right use of the Lord's Supper' in 1580, to be read 'before everie celebration of the Lord's Supper, in all such Churches and Parishes as have not a sufficiently hable preacher' so his words were probably heard by a considerable number of people in the diocese. He wanted his people, even the 'unlearned and ignorant', to understand the benefit of the Sacrament, and particularly how the reception of the outward elements 'quickeneth, stirreth, strengtheneth and increaseth

---

[296] See above, p. 7.

[297] We must not suppose, however, that the convinced, and those who frequented alehouse society, were necessarily different. The case of the widow of Gamlingay, who caused offence to the Gamlingay branch of the Open Baptist Meeting, is witness of that. She became high-flown with ale at a village feast, and sang various unsuitable songs and danced on the table. 'First Minute Book of Gamlingay Old Meeting', (in the keeping of the chapel) entry for 1721. It was not drinking at, or even keeping, an alehouse, but doing so immoderately, like Widow Robinson, or opening the alehouse on the Lord's Day, that was frowned upon. See H.G. Tibbutt (ed.), *The Minutes of the First Independent Church (now Bunyan Meeting) at Bedford 1656–1766*, Bedfordshire Historical Record Society, 55 (Luton, 1976), subject index, p. 232, 'drunkenness' *passim*, and Brother William Wilshire, alehouse keeper, p. 138.

[298] I owe the original remark which stimulated me to think about this last section and the exegesis of 'fat things' to Dr Duffy. He is in no way responsible, however, for any errors into which I have fallen.

our faith, that we may eat the body and blood of Christ more effectually and fruitfully'.[299] These are strong words, even possibly shocking in their purport to someone outside the Eucharistic tradition. There was a drop-off in attendance in Brussels amongst nominal Catholics when they were first exposed to the Mass in the starkness of the vernacular after Vatican II. These words cannot have been less startling, surely, to the Elizabethan peasant? Bishop Cooper would have his worshippers in the diocese of Lincoln in the 1580s say to themselves, 'Even as certainly as my taste feeleth the sweetness of bread and wine … even so the taste of my faith and sense of my heart doth feel the sweetness of Christ his body and blood broken and shed for me and all mankind upon the cross.'[300]

Ian Green has traced over 280 different catechisms published before 1549 and 1646, excluding the longest forms.[301] The most popular of these went through as many as fifty-six editions. One of the four elements expounded in the majority of these catechisms was the doctrine of the Sacraments, which only appeared in the official prayer book catechism from 1604 onwards. Until then, the importance of the omitted subject had been the motive behind the appearance of many of the alternative catechisms, which had preparation for Communion as one of their major objectives. They emphasized the 'understanding of the precise nature and purpose of the sacrament, and the need for a rigorous self-examination before each Communion'.[302]

We cannot know, however, whether, or how many, of the 75 per cent of those who were eligible to receive Communion in the diocese of Lincoln in Easter Week 1603 and actually did so[303] had taken any of Bishop Cooper's words to heart, or whether their reception meant to them anything of which their bishop and reformed pastors would have approved.

---

[299] John E. Booty, 'Preparation for the Lord's Supper in Elizabethan England', *Anglican Theological Review*, 49 (April 1962), no. 2, pp. 1, 131–48.

[300] Ibid., p. 146.

[301] Green, 'Children in Understanding', pp. 309–400, 402, 405, 410–11. Nowell's catechism did have a full treatment of the Sacraments, but it was a quarto of 176 pages. Even the abbreviated octavo version was 94 pages long. Ibid., p. 406.

[302] George Herbert laid down 'the time of every one's first receiving is not so much by yeers, as by understanding: particularly, the rule may be this: When anyone can distinguish the Sacramentall from common bread, knowing the Institution and the difference hee ought to receive, of what age soever. Children and youths are usually deferred too long, under pretence of devotion to the Sacrament, but it is for want of instruction: … Parents and Masters should make hast in this … which while they deferr, both sides suffer.' *A Priest to the Temple, or, The Country Parson his Character, and Rule of Holy Life* (printed 1662), in Hutchinson (ed.), *Works of George Herbert*, pp. 258–9.

[303] Margaret Spufford, 'Can we Count the "Godly" and the "Conformable" in the Seventeenth Century?', pp. 435–6.

We do know that in the rapidly growing parish of St Saviour's, Southwark, in late Elizabethan and Jacobean London, between 80 and 98 per cent of potential communicants made an annual Communion.[304] In this 'open' parish, where the aim was not to exclude the ungodly from Communion, some of the people who received were the kind of people who, in their behaviour or beliefs, were the despair of the Elizabethan reformers. In 1618, at St Saviour's in Southwark, Communion tokens were delivered to Jane Toby, a single woman living in the churchyard, who had two bastard children living in her household. A third bastard child of hers was baptized in 1621.[305] So members of what Peter Laslett has described as the 'bastardy prone sub-society' were, or could be, receiving Communion. It is not irrelevant that the stricter dissenters were willing to accept such women into fellowship, after due repentance. In 1713, the Bedford Open Baptists received Ann Muns, 'who desired communion two yeares since but having formerly been guilty of uncleanness, and having two bastards, was desired to waite longer, and having from that time behaved herself well . . . and giving in a very satisfactory experience was with the rest received'.[306] This is not at all unimportant, considering the points from which we started, Dr Duffy's statement of the current belief amongst social historians 'that the poor were hostile, or resistant, or at best indifferent to Protestant Christianity',[307] or Sir Keith Thomas' belief that sections of the population 'below a certain social level' managed without religion altogether.[308] We know from Dr Plumb's and Dr Stevenson's work that many of the dissenters were very poor and certainly did not manage without religion, and we know from Dr Maltby's work that some conformists in favour of the prayer book were on poor relief. We also know, from these examples, that some few at least of these poor had not led entirely reputable lives, at least before repentance.

However, we seek securer ground. If we consider the importance that practice of the celebration of the Lord's Supper had to dissenters in the late seventeenth century, we shall be considering only the tiny group of 4 per cent of the population who were counted as dissenters in 1676.[309] But we shall be quite sure that we are moving away from a consideration of that part of the population which had at least a general acquaintance

---

[304] J.P. Boulton, 'The Limits of Formal Religion: The Administration of Holy Communion in Late Elizabethan and Early Stuart London', *The London Journal*, 10 (1984), pp. 135–53.

[305] Ibid., p. 143 and p. 153 n. 65.

[306] Tibbutt (ed.), *The Minutes of the First Independent Church . . . at Bedford* (1713), p. 137.

[307] Quoted above, pp. 1–2.

[308] Quoted by Professor Collinson, above, p. 3. The reference is to Thomas, *Religion and the Rise of Magic*, pp. 189–90.

[309] Whiteman (ed.), *The Compton Census of 1676*; George Clark, *The Later Stuarts 1660–1714* (Oxford, 1956).

with popular religion and religious practice but might not be convinced, to a group of whose convictions we can be certain. For the dissenters of 1676 were a hunted and persecuted people. For them, it was very costly to practise, whereas, in 1603, it had been costly, in a minor way, not to conform. I want to try both to establish the pattern of the routine sacramental actions in which these dissenters engaged, and end by using their own literature, the words of Isaacs Watts at the very end of the seventeenth century, and of Philip Doddridge's account of him in the early eighteenth century, to try and see what these repeated ritual experiences might have meant to them.[310]

Cranmer and Calvin had both wanted a weekly Communion or Lord's Supper: Calvin wrote that the custom of communicating once a year was 'a veritable invention of the devil'.[311] The Anglican Church did not manage to avoid this condemnation, although there are some hints that a monthly celebration was held by at least some Elizabethan and Stuart reformers. A vicar who grumbled at Redbourn in Hertfordshire in 1585 of his flock's unseemly eagerness to receive, celebrated once a month, after divine service and his sermon.[312] George Herbert in the early 1630s wished for a monthly celebration, but if this was not possible, 'at least five or six times in a year: as at Easter, Christmas, Whitsuntide, afore and after Harvest, and at the beginning of Lent'.[313] If we move away from parochial Communions to the conventicles of the godly, in which the separatist churches may often have been rooted, we find that some of the puritan exercises, like the 'eager and vast crowds ... flocking to perform their practices' under the jaundiced eye of an imprisoned Jesuit in Wisbech Castle in 1588, ended with a Communion. He estimated the number involved, no doubt wrongly, as high as 1,000.[314] In the same way the very different minister at Denton Chapel in the 1630s, John Angier, held monthly Communions, which attracted 'hundreds' of 'godly folk', some of whom travelled thirty miles to attend. Professor Collinson writes that 'monthly sacraments' seem to have been a special feature of life in the north-west.[315] Only local research would show whether this practice was rooted in earlier popular belief. When Richard Baxter established his monthly Communions which 'gather the faithful from a wide catchment

---

[310] This section of text forms part of the Annual Theme Lecture given to the United Reformed Church in 1988. I am extremely grateful to the editor, Dr Clyde Binfield, for his kindness to me then, and for allowing me to reprint this text now, and to the members of my audience for their very helpful suggestions.

[311] Stephen Mayor, The Lord's Supper in Early English Dissent (London, 1972), pp. xiv–xv, and 10.

[312] Collinson, The Religion of Protestants, pp. 211–12.

[313] Herbert, in Hutchinson (ed.), Works of George Herbert, p. 259.

[314] Quoted, in extenso, in my Contrasting Communities pp. 262–3.

[315] Collinson, The Religion of Protestants, pp. 263–4.

area' in Kidderminster in the 1650s[316] he seems to have been building on long-established puritan practice.

Post-Restoration dissenters, excluding the Quakers, of course, seem, in general, to have lived a much richer sacramental life than their Anglican counterparts, although they still did not achieve the weekly Communion desired by both Calvin and Cranmer. This is a change that has been missed. Stephen Mayor in the *Lord's Supper in Early English Dissent* (London, 1972) writes, indeed, 'it is of course true that the early Dissenters gave a smaller place to the Eucharist than many Christians have done ... For those who believe it to be absolutely central to the Christian faith, the place they gave it was inadequate.'[317] The magnitude of the change, to a Lord's Supper not three times a year, but monthly, or at least six-weekly, on Baxter's model, may have been missed because of the format of the surviving seventeenth-century Church Books. They place very little emphasis on the substance of the routine meetings of which they record the dates: they hardly ever describe the 'normal' events, which are assumed. The bulk of the business recorded is dealing with the errant and the aberrant, not the normal. Yet careful reading seems to show that groups of dissenters, separated in doctrine from Arminian to Calvinist, and in geography from Cambridgeshire and Bedfordshire to Yorkshire, celebrated monthly, and sometimes even more frequently. This was true of the Open Baptists of Fenstanton and of Huntingdonshire in the 1650s[318] and of Bunyan's Open Baptist Church on the Bedfordshire border where the members agreed in 1659 'to entreat our brother Wheeler, brother Donne, brother Gibbs and brother Breedon to give their assistance in the worke of God in preaching and breaking of breade

---

[316] Patrick Collinson, 'Towards a Broader Understanding of the Early Dissenting Tradition' (1975), reprinted in *Godly People*, p. 537.

[317] *The Lord's Supper*, pp. 158–9.

[318] Underhill (ed.), *Fenstanton Records*. Up to the beginning of 1654, the Church Book only gives details of disciplinary disputes. In 1655, it becomes evident that every general meeting opens with prayer, supplication and an exhortation, before the discipline, and business. (See, for instance, pp. 127, 135.) During that year, the minutes also record that the meeting closes with praise, and a dismissal (p. 147). Soon afterwards, the 'observation of some ordinances of God' or 'the Most High' were recorded after the business, before the praise and the dismissal (p. 179). Once the standard description varied helpfully, 'After which praise was rendered to God: then we broke bread together', before the dismissal (p. 200). One explanatory clause was sometimes added 'And so (the day being spent) the assembly were dismissed' (e.g. p. 201). This is interesting in view of the stress in the church that the 'breaking of bread' should, scripturally, follow supper (pp. 36–7, 61, 67–70, 188). The general meetings were held monthly. It is impossible to say whether the change in recording in 1655, and the regular monthly 'observation of some ordinances of God', represents simply a change in the detail of the minutes, or a genuine change in church practice. Anyway, by 1655, the breaking of bread, one of the 'ordinances of the Lord', took place monthly.

once every moneth or 3 weeks, one after another on the Lordes dayes'.[319]
It also seems to be true of the strict Calvinist Church of Guyhirn and
Isleham in north-east Cambridgeshire, which covenanted in 1687,[320] and
the church of the non-conforming Presbyterian, Oliver Heywood, in the
West Riding of Yorkshire in the 1680s and 90s.[321] The magnitude of the
change involved in the lives of the dissenters of 1676 by the routine of
the constantly repeated practice of breaking bread together in the sacrament of the body and blood of the Lord seems very important indeed.
It is a change that does not seem to have been stressed in the literature.
It was, of course, theologically possible because the gathered churches
were a people set apart, or in Isaac Watts' words:

> A Garden wall'd around,
> Chosen and made peculiar Ground[322]

and so no longer faced the problems of discipline and the barring of
unworthy recipients of Communion, whilst still collecting the tithes
essential to economic survival, which had caused the incumbent Ralph
Josselin not to celebrate for nearly nine years in Earls Colne,[323] or Richard
Baxter during his whole time in Bridgnorth.[324] On the contrary, for the
members of these gathered churches, 'preaching the Gospell and
breaking of bread', were inextricably interlinked[325] or as the same Church
Book put it 'the nature of fellowship [is] the Word, prayer, and breaking
of bread'.[326] Withdrawal from this sacrament ordained by Christ was
therefore an offence, as a long letter of rebuke written by Bunyan's church
to one of its members in 1669 shows. One of the chief accusations was:

> In your so long neglecting to be consciably found in the godly prac-
> tise of the Lord's Supper, concerning which, had you bene tender, had
> not the table of the Lord bene too meane in your thoughtes, how could
> you for years have absented your self. And if by that bread and that
> cup, we show to our selves and each other the Lord's death, we had
> seen it by that but seldom had we therein taken you for example. And
> considering that appointment is such as is oft to be put into practise, [my

[319] Tibbutt (ed.), The Minutes of the First Independent Church . . . at Bedford, p. 35.
[320] Kenneth A.C. Parsons (ed.), The Church Book of the Independent Church (now Pound Lane
    Baptist) Isleham, 1693–1805, Cambridge Antiquarian Records Society, 6 (Cambridge,
    1984), pp. 29–30 1693/4 Covenant, nos. 5, 6, and 12, and p. 62, 1756 Covenant nos.
    4, 16, and 63.
[321] Horsfall Turner (ed.), Autobiography, pp. 1, 32–3, and 35–6.
[322] Considered in Donald Davie, A Gathered Church: The Literature of the English Dissenting
    Interest, 1700–1930 (London, 1978), pp. 28–30.
[323] A. Macfarlane (ed.), The Diary of Ralph Josselin, 1616–1683 (London, 1976), pp. 77, 96,
    234–7.
[324] N.H. Keeble (ed.), The Autobiography of Richard Baxter (London, 1974), p. 18.
[325] Minutes of the First Independent Church at Bedford, p. 35 (entry for 1660).
[326] Ibid., p. 20.

italics] and that for the help of our faith, both as to our remembering the Lord, and discerning of his body and blood, we cannot but judge you guilty.[327]

The rules promulgated by the Soham church in the 1690s laid down that 'abstaining from any instituted ordinance which the Lord may call us too . . . is also a breach of covenant'.[328] At a later renewal of the Covenant in the same church, the point was emphasized. There was no acceptable excuse for 'forsaking the assembling of ourselves together . . . to worship God . . . when we break bread in the Lord's Supper, for there all ought to assemble with the church let what gospel man soever preach'.[329]

What, then, did this increased frequency of celebration of the Lord's Supper, which I suggest is a very significant change, mean to these post-Restoration dissenters? The Savoy Declaration of 1658, drawn up by delegates from Independent Churches,[330] was orthodoxly Calvinist in its doctrine:

> Sacraments are holy Signs and Seals of the Covenant of Grace, immediately instituted by Christ to represent him and his benefits, and confirm our interest in him . . . Our Lord Jesus Christ in the night wherein he was betrayed, instituted the Sacrament of his Body and Blood, called the Lord's Supper . . . for the perpetual remembrance and shewing forth of the Sacrifice of Himself in his death, the sealing of all benefits thereof unto true believers . . . and to be bond and pledge of their communion with him, and with each other.[331]

Richard Baxter wrote a programme of meditation for the communicant in his *Christian Directory* and emphasized the presence of Christ

> When you behold the consecrated bread and wine, discern the Lord's body, and reverence it as the representative body and blood of Jesus Christ; and take heed of profaning it, by looking on it as common bread and wine; though it be not transubstantiate, but still is very bread and wine in its natural being, yet it is Christ's body and blood in representation and effect. Look on it as the consecrated bread of life, which with the quickening Spirit must nourish you to life eternal . . .
>
> Even as in delivering the possession of house or lands, the deliverer giveth you a key, and a twig, and a turf, and saith 'I deliver you this house, and I deliver you this land': so doth the minister by Christ's authority deliver you Christ, and pardon, and title to eternal life.[332]

---

[327] Tibbutt (ed.), *The Minutes of the First Independent Church . . . at Bedford*, p. 43.
[328] Parsons (ed.), *The Church Book of the Independent Church (now Pound Lane Baptist)*, p. 29 1693/4 Covenant, nos. 5, 6, and 12, and p. 62, 1756 Covenant nos. 4, 16 and 63.
[329] Ibid., pp. 62–3.
[330] Fully laid out and discussed in Mayor, *The Lord's Supper*, pp. 79–85.
[331] Stephen Mayor, *The Lord's Supper*, CXXVIII, p. 79, and XXX, p. 81.
[332] Richard Baxter, *Christian Directory*, in idem, *Works*, 4 vols. (London, 1673), IV, pp. 337–8, quoted Mayor, *The Lord's Supper*, p. 137.

This metaphor of the twig, strange to us, must have been extremely familiar to all copyholders who were given entry to their lands 'by the rod, at the will of the Lord'. He is using a homely and important analogy to humble readers.

But the theology of the Savoy Declaration, and the devotional directives of Baxter still do not tell us of the relative importance of the Lord's Supper in the lives of ordinary seventeenth-century dissenters, and what they made of this increasing sacramental activity. Was Sir Keith Thomas right after all in postulating that seventeenth-century religion was really increasingly rational and socially cohesive; was the religion of dissenters, at least, as it emerged into the industrial eighteenth century, one 'from which the primitive "magical" elements had been very largely shorn'?[333]

To examine what seventeenth-century dissenters made of the sacramental activity of the Lord's Supper, I would like to turn to the literature.[334] John Bunyan was writing for the same rural audience whose doings are recorded in The Minutes of the First Independent Church of Bedford, and whom we know from Dr Stevenson's work to be poorer than the rural average. His verse disappoints us: his poem written in A Book for Boys and Girls or Country Rhimes for Children, printed in 1686, on the Sacrament is more concerned to warn against the dangers, than to stress the benefits, of reception.

> Two sacraments I do believe there be,
> Ev'n baptism and the Supper of the Lord:
> Both mysteries divine, which do to me,
> By God's appointment, benefit afford:
>
> But shall they be my God, or shall I have
> Of them so foul and impious a thought,
> To think that from the curse they can me save?
> Bread, wine, nor water me no ransom bought.[335]

Bunyan's prose is more revealing. Christian in the Palace Beautiful sat down, when supper was ready, to 'a Table ... furnished with fat things, and with Wine that was well refined; and all their talk at the Table, was about the Lord of the Hill'.[336] In turn, Mr Greatheart brings a token from the Lord to Christiana which is a 'Bottle of Wine'. And at supper in the inn where Christiana stays, which is a forerunner of the 'Supper of the great King in his Kingdom' is a 'Bottle of Wine, red as Blood', which is

[333] Thomas, Religion and the Decline of Magic, pp. 766 and 760–5.
[334] I should stress again both the importance of Professor Davie's A Gathered Church, and my debt to Dr Duffy's original remark on the meaning of 'fat things', which led me to consider this whole topic.
[335] A Book for Boys and Girls or Country Rhimes for Children (1686).
[336] John Bunyan, Pilgrims Progress (Oxford, 1904, reprinted 1945), p. 65.

the 'juice of the true Vine, that makes glad the Heart of God and Man'.[337]

But for more extensive, and real, insight into the importance of the Lord's Supper to the late seventeenth- and early eighteenth-century dissenters, we have to turn to the great hymn writer of the Old Dissent, Isaac Watts. The evidence of popular addiction to his work, and the hold it had on the common people comes, not only from the print runs, but also from the particular evidence of his successor, and friend, Philip Doddridge. Doddridge was born as late as 1702, and ministered to the very important dissenting congregation in Northampton.[338] We owe to him a hymn still regularly sung at the Eucharist in Anglican Churches.[339]

He gives us an irreplaceable and unique glimpse into the importance in the lives of rural people who formed the sort of congregations in Bedfordshire and Cambridgeshire which we have been talking about, of the hymns of his senior, Isaac Watts. In 1731, he wrote to Dr Watts, who was then aged fifty-seven,

> [When] preaching in a barn, to a pretty large assembly of plain country people, at a village a few miles off . . . we sung one of your Hymns . . . these were most of them poor people who work for their living. On the mention of your name, I found they had read several of your books with great delight, and that your Hymns and Psalms were almost their daily entertainments. And when one of the company said, 'What if Dr Watts should come down to Northampton?', another replied with a remarkable warmth 'The very sight of him would be like an ordinance [i.e. the Lord's Supper] to me.'[340]

[337] Ibid., pp. 279 and 311.

[338] But, much more importantly for these purposes, we owe to him his letters. Geoffrey F. Nuttall (ed.), *Calendar of the Correspondence of Philip Doddridge, D.D. 1705–1751*, HMSO Joint Publication 26 and Northamptonshire Record Society 29 (1979). I am particularly grateful to the Rev. Ronald Bocking of the United Reformed Church, who spent some time after my lecture searching for, and sending me, references to the observance of the Communion Service in the Castle Hill church of Northampton while Doddridge was minister there. The tradition was a monthly evening celebration. The date varied according to the phase of the moon, so that the worshippers could get safely home by moonlight. Malcolm Deacon, *Philip Doddridge of Northampton* (Northampton, 1980), p. 72; C. Stanford, *Philip Doddridge* (London, 1880), p. 127; John Stoughton, *History of Religion in England*, 6 vols. (London 1881), VI, p. 94.

[339] *Hymns Ancient and Modern, New Standard* (1983), no. 259. I was tempted to quote this hymn itself as evidence of Eucharistic attitudes amongst dissenters, but Professor Everitt has convinced me (personal communication) of the great shift in religious sensibilities between the Old and New Dissent, and therefore of the changed world of feeling inhabited by Doddridge himself. His own writing cannot therefore properly be used as evidence for the tone of seventeenth-century dissent. See Everitt, 'Springs of Sensibility', pp. 201–45.

[340] Nuttall (ed.), *Calendar of the Correspondence of Philip Doddridge*, p. 62. Professor Davie in *A Gathered Church* drew attention to Lesley Steven writing on Isaac Watts' hymns. Steven wrote that for many years 50,000 copies of Watts' psalms and hymns were printed annually. And Davie comments: 'We a century after Lesley Steven have no way of dealing with such phenomena, no method by which to translate the quantit-

At the very end of the eighteenth century, we get another glimpse. Small James Raine, son of a blacksmith, had a blind grandmother, who had lived in an almshouse, who took 'particular pleasure in teaching me Watts' Hymns' which the little boy 'was not slow in committing to memory'. She had no need of a book to teach him, either.[341]

Isaac Watts had himself been born in 1674, and may properly be regarded as a late seventeenth-century author; his hymns were already being sung from manuscript in the dissenting chapel in Southampton in 1694 and 1695,[342] and were published in 1707.[343] He himself wrote that he had 'just permitted [his] verse to rise above a flat and indolent style' and was 'sensible that [he had] often subdued it below' the esteem of the critics, 'and because I would neither indulge any bold metaphors, nor admit of hard words, nor tempt the ignorant worshipper to sing without his understanding'.[344] So Isaac Watts had deliberately pitched his words and their meaning at the type of congregation worshipping in a barn, 'plain country people ... poor people who work for their living' whom Philip Doddridge later observed singing them with such enthusiasm. Isaac Watts wanted them to understand the words. And what words, and what meaning, they were. If the Holy Communion, or the Lord's Supper was 'instituted by Christ to represent Him and His benefits' in the words of the Savoy Declaration of 1658, then the dissenters singing in Southampton in the 1690s, and in barns in Northamptonshire in the 1730s, were certainly not practising a religion 'from which the primitive "magical" elements had been shorn'. For the Lord's Supper symbolized more to seventeenth-century dissenters and believing conformists than the unity and bonding between believers: it also represented bonding and union with 'God'.[345] Mrs Elizabeth Bury's Diary, meditating on reception, is very clear on this.[346]

> Gracious Assistance this Morning, better than Health: Awake, O North Wind, come thou South, blow upon my Garden still, and fill me with

ative facts of so many copies printed and sold year after year, into the quality of consideration of how they condition the sensibility of the English-speaking peoples. But what we can, and should do ... is to confess and insist ... just what a vast lacuna this reveals in our pretentions to cultural history.' The correspondence between Doddridge and Watts suggests that Watts' influence was indeed enormously widespread and should not be underestimated amongst the common people. Margaret Spufford, Small Books, p. 8. See also above, James Raine, n. 230, pp. 67–8.

341 Raine, 'Memoir of his Childhood', p. 17.
342 Davie, A Gathered Church, p. 30.
343 Bernard Manning, The Hymns of Wesley and Watts: Five Informal Papers (Epworth, 1942), p. 81.
344 Quoted Davie, A Gathered Church, p. 24. My italics.
345 Thomas, Religion and the Decline of Magic, p. 766.
346 Bury (ed.), An Account of the Life and Death of Mrs Elizabeth Bury, pp. 34–5, and quotation for 12 March 1693, p. 82.

thy Gales throughout this Day – Oh! how lovely, Lord! were thy Taber-
nacles all this Day! how much more glorious thy House, the City, the
Kingdom, the Paradice, to which I have been invited! If under thy
Shadow such Delight, what will the unvail'd Glory be? Until the Day
break, and the Shadows fly away, make haste my Beloved.

Mathew Storey has written, considering Isaac Archer's private
reflections in his *Diary* on receiving the Sacrament of Holy Communion,

The great question which is raised in the context of the Eucharist in
dissenting communities is whether it was regarded mainly as a ritual
identification of the limits of a 'gathered' community, or whether it was
seen as an essentially personal event, expressing 'bonding and union
with God'. Functionalist sociology would persuasively suggest that the
more clearly and narrowly defined a religious group is, the more suggestive of that community's self-definition and significance any ritual
(like Communion) will be: 'Such a group may itself become the focus
of intense emotional concern for its members, and religious exercises
necessarily include occasions for the celebration of the existence of the
group, and the dedication of men to its continuance and its goals.'[347]
    The sorts of controls exercised by ministers of 'elect' puritan commu-
nities may, at first sight, appear to bear this out; controlled access to
the Communion table ensured that the very specific identity of the
'godly' community remained inviolate. Only men and women with zeal
for 'exercises' and in possession of an impeccable and unspotted moral
life were to be admitted to the celebration of the Lord's Supper. However, in spite of the obvious awareness of the Pauline injunction to
recognize the true body of Christ on earth in the attempt to avoid
the scandal which might attach to the presence of an evil-liver at the
Communion, the examination and regulation of communicants may
equally have derived from a concern that the believer's 'vertical' relationship with God was in its proper order. It is true that before the
reception of the Communion elements, it was absolutely vital that all
was well between fellow-believers, especially in self-consciously
'gathered' communities. However, the act of receiving the elements,
given the believer ought to have been reconciled in any dispute, placed
him in direct communion with God, and it is this aspect of the
Eucharist's meaning which is so powerfully emphasized in Archer's
numerous but brief accounts of the sacrament. As has been noticed
earlier, each occasion of Communion was an opportunity to focus
intensely upon the believer's personal relationship with God, precisely
because the elements of bread and wine, however their substance was
understood, signified both the means and goal of personal salvation.[348]

[347] Bryan Wilson, *Religion in Sociological Perspective* (Oxford, 1982), p. 35.
[348] I am very grateful to Mathew Storey for permission to quote him, and for his help
with this section. *The Diaries of Isaac Archer and William Coe*, ed. Mathew Storey, Suffolk
Record Society 36 (1994).

We must not forget the significance of that parishioner, unmentioned in his Diary, of whom Isaac Archer certainly cannot have been proud, William Coe. He, also, living in Mildenhall at the same time that Isaac was incumbent there, wrote a Diary. He mentioned in it that he sat 'through many good sermons' and also, specifically, that he once begged forgiveness at the Lord's Supper for having 'thought evilly of his Vicar'. He was a cheerful and bibulous yeoman, an amazing mixture of piety and excess, addicted to good company. He regularly got drunk in the alehouse, and regularly played cards there. What is of interest is that he equally regularly repented of these sins, which he confessed in the privacy of his own Diary, especially before receiving Holy Communion, which he also regularly did. It is apparent from the diary entries that, however monotonous his falls from grace must have appeared to his incumbent, and, indeed, to himself, this reception was personally very meaningful to him. We must remember the 'ordinary' conformists like Coe, whose faith meant a great deal to them, although it might appear negligible to the historian and even to their own contemporaries, as well as Dr Maltby's less wayward conformists,[349] and the dissenters we have singled out for study here, because the importance of the beliefs of the latter are so much more readily detectable.

The difficulty arising out of Religion and the Decline of Magic seems to stem from this issue in sacramental theology, which is outside both the scope of this essay and the competence of its author. However, in his very full and excellent study of the 'horde of popular superstitions', perversions of belief and 'corpus of parasitic beliefs' which certainly clustered round the Christian Sacraments, and especially the Mass,[350] Sir Keith deliberately excluded consideration of both the central doctrine of the Mass,[351] or the Holy Communion, and its end.[352] In his brisk review of the substitution of the Mass by Holy Communion by the reformers[353] he therefore concentrated on the abolition of 'any of the old notions concerning the temporal

---

[349] See above, p. 10.
[350] Thomas, Religion and the Decline of Magic, pp. 35–40.
[351] Unless this is taken to be the 'magic' of transubstantiation.
[352] Indeed, I can find only one reference in the book to the vision of God which is the ultimate end for the believer, unless this is comprehended within the functions of religion as 'a route to immortality' in the important definitional paragraph at the beginning of chapter 2. I may, of course, have missed others in a work of such length. In the opening words of the shorter Westminster Catechism of 1647, 'man's chief end is to glorify God and enjoy Him for ever'. The Catechism was the product of the Westminster Assembly, and was aimed at revising the Thirty-Nine Articles in a puritan direction. The single reference I have found to the vision of God in Religion and the Decline of Magic, is at p. 40, although Sir Keith does have many references to all those highly dubious 'appearances' and 'apparitions' which were recorded, mainly by the unlettered in pursuit of political programmes. Ibid., pp. 175–8, etc.
[353] Ibid., pp. 60–2, 65.

benefits which might spring from communicating or from contemplating the sacred elements'. He seems to be quite unaware that those same reformers, led by Calvin himself, took a very different view of the function and importance of Holy Communion to that propounded by Durkheim of a religious ritual affirming the collective unity of a society.[354] Naturally, the reformers emphasized that too,[355] as St Paul had, before them, and as had medieval preachers also. It is profoundly significant that the pronouns, in the hymns I cite, are in the first person plural, not singular. But this was all secondary. The emphasis on primitive or medieval religion as primarily offering 'the prospect of a supernatural means of control over man's earthly environment', and therefore essentially magical, in functional terms, naturally leads to a stress on the increased 'rationality' of religion, once it was perceived to have lost that capacity. But the religious meaning of the Lord's Supper, which survived not only in theological teaching but in the minds, and more importantly, the feelings, of believers (as we have seen from the diarists) was not comprehended within this 'magical' definition, and was not therefore lost with it, either.

Fenner, who died in 1587, propounded in his *Whole Doctrine of Sacraments* that the faithful Christian receives spiritually not only the whole benefits of Christ, but also Christ himself, as both God and man: Richard Baxter seems to have used the same emphases later. It was true that to Fenner conceptual understanding was essential to sacramental worship, so the Christian communicant had to be knowledgeable. Most puritan preachers between 1600 and 1630 concentrated on the Sacraments as a practical benefit: the Lord's Supper was 'comforting' to fearful Christians. Despite the difficulties propounded by election, it demonstrated God's covenant relationship with man.[356] If the right reception was vital to the efficacy of the Sacrament, then we are entitled to ask whether the general body of the communicants had any 'right' idea of what they were doing. We are then immediately taken not only to the great list of contemporary titles of works on preparation, but also back to the avalanche of alternative catechisms.[357] These alternative catechisms would not have been printed unless they were saleable.[358] Their *raison d'être* was apparently the

---

[354] Ibid., p. 205. For Calvin, see Heiko A. Oberman, *The Dawn of the Reformation* (Edinburgh, 1986), pp. 245–55.

[355] Thomas, *Religion and the Decline of Magic*, p. 631. E. Brooks Holifield, *The Covenant Sealed: The Development of Puritan Sacramental Theology in Old and New England, 1570–1720* (New Haven and London, 1974), p. 37.

[356] Brooks Holifield, *The Covenant Sealed*, pp. 23–4, 35–7, 39–41, 51–7.

[357] Discussed pp. 74, 87, 261. Three-quarters of a million copies of the independent catechetical works were on sale by the early seventeenth century.

[358] See below, Tessa Watt, p. 263. Roger Ward stocked large numbers of these catechisms in his shop in Shrewsbury in 1585, and would surely not have been in trouble with the Star Chamber for infringing the monopoly of printing *The ABC with the Little*

provision of the missing section on the Sacraments in the official catechism. It was no longer missing after 1604. So there is a good chance that some of the recipients of Communion, as well as Bishop Cooper's flock in the diocese of Lincoln,[359] had at least some idea what the Sacrament, in reformed doctrine, was supposed to mean. The real point of the matter was not the subsidiary 'horizontal' bonding established between communicants, the 'social function' of religion, but the 'vertical' relationship established between the communicant and the external being he or she called 'God'. This relationship was not merely intended as a remedy, or a solution of temporal ills, and, indeed, as Sir Keith writes, it became less and less relevant for these purposes. Perhaps religion survived, but with elements that to Dr Isaac Watts and the congregations that sang his hymns, and even to conformists like Coe, seemed decidedly supernatural, simply because its content was far greater than the solution of these practical problems, and pressures, which were increasingly capable of rational solution.

The last section of Isaac Watts' *Hymns* were those 'prepared for the holy ordinance of the Lord's Supper'.[360] And to Isaac Watts, in accordance with the doctrine of the Savoy Declaration, the Lord's Supper was more than a memorial.[361] In his own 'flat and indolent style', suitable for 'poor people who work for their living',

> This holy bread and wine
> Maintains our fainting breath
> By union with our living Lord
> And interest in His death.
>
> Here have we seen Thy face, O Lord
> And view'd salvation with our eyes;
> Tasted and felt the Living Word,
> The bread descending from the skies.

In the face of this set of beliefs, which were not about 'the prospect of material relief by divine means' at all, these late seventeenth- and early eighteenth-century dissenters do not seem to have been condemned to the mere 'stoicism [which] had become the basic religious message for

---

Catechism by printing 10,000 copies of it, and sending 1,500 of these to Shrewsbury, had it not been financially worthwhile for him to do so.

[359] See above, p. 86. Bishop Moreton of Durham, bishop from 1632 to 1659, arranged to have common prayer books and catechisms given to children and servants who could read. 'Many thousands of Catechisms' were distributed, paid for by him, in the 1630s. J. Freeman, 'The Parish Ministry in the Diocese of Durham, c1570–1640' (Durham, PhD, 1979), p. 294. I owe this reference to Judith Maltby.

[360] Manning, *The Hymns of Wesley and Watts*, p. 80.

[361] Ibid., p. 104.

those in misfortune'.[362] Their beliefs were both more complex, and less easy to trace, than that. However, it behoves the historian to attempt to give them the due weight and emphasis that they gave these beliefs themselves.

Modern anthropologists seem to accept Professor Geertz's discussion, which implies that historians are right to take cognizance of what the subjects of their studies themselves thought they were doing.

> The tracing of the social and psychological role of religion is thus not so much a matter of finding correlations between specific ritual acts and specific secular social ties ... More, it is a matter of understanding how it is that men's notions, however implicit, of the 'really real' and the dispositions these notions induce in them, color their sense of the reasonable, the practical, the humane, and the moral. How far they do so ... and how effectively they do so ... all these are crucial issues in the comparative sociology and psychology of religion ... The anthropological study of religion is therefore a two-stage operation: first, an analysis of the system of meanings embodied in the symbols which make up the religion proper, and, second, the relating of these systems to social-structural and psychological processes. My dissatisfaction with so much of contemporary social anthropological work in religion is not that it concerns itself with the second stage, but that it neglects the first, and in so doing takes for granted what most needs to be elucidated.

He has earlier demonstrated his meaning by elucidating what a Bororo 'really' means when he says 'I am a parakeet'.

> A man who says he is a parakeet is, if he says it in normal conversation, saying that, as myth and ritual demonstrate, he is shot through with parakeetness and that this religious fact has some social implications ... we parakeets must stick together, not marry one another, not eat mundane parakeets, and so on, for to do otherwise is to act against the grain of the whole universe ... Having ritually ... slipped ... into the framework of meaning which religious conceptions define, and the ritual ended, returned again to the common-sense world, a man is ... changed. And as he is changed, so also is the common-sense world, for it is now seen as but the partial form of a wider reality which corrects and completes it.[363]

Durkheim himself first wrote in 1915,

> The theoretical importance which has sometimes been attributed to primitive religions has come to pass as a sign of a systematic hostility to all religion, which ... vitiates them in advance.

[362] Thomas, *Religion and the Decline of Magic*, p. 766.
[363] Clifford Geertz, *The Interpretation of Cultures: Selected Essays* (New York, 1973), pp. 124–5. I am much indebted to Professor Daryl Feil for bringing this to my attention, and answering my questions.

There is no occasion for asking here whether or not there are scholars who have merited this reproach, and who have made religious history and ethnology a weapon against religion. In any case, a sociologist cannot hold such a point of view. In fact, it is an essential postulate of sociology that a human institution cannot rest upon an error and a lie, without which it could not exist. If it were not founded in the nature of things, it would have encountered in the facts a resistance over which it could never have triumphed. So when we commence the study of primitive religions, it is with the assurance that they hold to reality and express it . . . one must know how to go underneath the symbol to the reality which it represents and which gives it its meaning . . . The reasons with which the faithful justify them may be, and generally are, erroneous; but the true reasons do not cease to exist, and it is the duty of science to discover them . . .

In reality, then, there are no religions which are false. All are true in their own fashion.[364]

In his 'Introduction' to the second edition in 1976, Robert Nisbet wrote:

an aspect of the book that has been too often neglected by its critics [is that] . . . from the beginning . . . Durkheim leaves us in no doubt that his dominant objective is that of portraying religion in the terms which, he tells us, have been crucial in the minds of the religiously committed themselves. Durkheim is severe on those rationalists who have thought their analysis of religion complete when they have delineated religion in assertedly scientific fashion without regard to the elements which are dominant in the minds of the religiously devout.[365]

I therefore feel entirely justified in emphasizing the importance of the relationship with 'God' into which the seventeenth-century worshipper felt himself brought by his or her attendance at the Holy Communion, or the Lord's Supper, his becoming 'shot through with parakeetness', as it were. The secondary social bonding involved has been so much emphasized that this is a balance that needs redressing.

Professor Geertz addressed a warning to writers on this subject.

One of the main methodological problems in writing about religion scientifically . . . [is] to put aside at once the tone of the village atheist and that of the village preacher, as well as their more sophisticated equivalents, so that the social and psychological implications of particular religious beliefs can emerge in a clear and neutral light.[366]

It may well be that, as is the fate of all those who try to redress balances, I have fallen into the opposite error from the sophisticated equivalent of

[364] Emile Durkheim, The Elementary Forms of the Religious Life, trs. Joseph Ward Swain, introd. Robert Nisbet (London, 1915, 2nd edn, 1976), pp. 2–3.
[365] Ibid, p. ix.
[366] Geertz, Interpretation, p. 123.

the 'village atheist', and become a 'village preacher'. It is technically difficult to write about beliefs, which were passionately held, dispassionately,
yet still convey their original force.

Yet it is probable that religion survived magic, not because of its social
function, but precisely because it retained that contact with the supernatural which enough people continued to find necessary to them, while
magic, with its pretensions to reorganize, or control, a universe which
was increasingly rationally perceived, withered away.

CHAPTER 2

The social and economic status of the later Lollards

DEREK PLUMB

I

It has long been argued that the later Lollards were of little economic and social significance among their peers, and of no significance at all in the theological developments of the Reformation. They were, the argument goes, an isolated group, alienated from their communities and discarded by most when the ideas of Luther and Calvin swept across much of Europe.[1] The latter point is difficult to argue against, although it is now being questioned. The former argument is less securely founded.[2]

I am here seeking to establish the place within their communities of those accused of heresy during the purges of the early sixteenth century. Many of those accused of Lollardy during that period were no doubt heretics; and those accused were surely only a few among a greater

I should like to thank those who have read drafts of this chapter and for their comments and advice. I would especially like to thank Dr Margaret Aston, Prof. Claire Cross, Dr Christopher Haigh, Dr Diarmaid MacCulloch, Dr Anne Hudson, and Dr Richard Davies, who then kindly lent me his typescript before publication. Of course, any errors are my own. Much of the discussion is based on the work I did for my thesis: 'John Foxe and the Later Lollards of the Mid-Thames Valley' (Cambridge, PhD, 1987).

[1] See, for instance, Margaret Bowker, The Henrician Reformation: The Diocese of Lincoln under John Longland, 1521–1547 (Cambridge, 1981); Christopher Haigh (ed.), The English Reformation Revised (Cambridge, 1987); idem, review article: 'The English Reformation: A Premature Birth, a Difficult Labour and a Sickly Child', Historical Journal, 33,2 (1990); Diarmaid MacCulloch, Suffolk and the Tudors: Politics and Religion in an English County, 1500–1600 (Oxford, 1986); J.J. Scarisbrick, The Reformation and the English People (Oxford, 1984); Joyce Youings, Sixteenth-Century England (Harmondsworth, 1984).

[2] Not all historians dismiss the Lollards thus. Imogen Luxton, 'The Lichfield Court Book; a Postscript', Bulletin of the Institute of Historical Research, 44, 109 (1971), pp. 120–5, and, more recently, Anne Hudson, The Premature Reformation: Wycliffite Texts and Lollard History (Oxford, 1988), have shown Lollards in a rather better light socially, and Diarmaid MacCulloch, in The Later Reformation in England, 1547–1603 (Basingstoke, 1990), whilst discussing the various strands of belief important to the development of the English Reformation, makes the point that Lollard and Zwinglian traditions were the two theological factors of most importance, relegating Lutheranism to a minor role. I discuss the description of Lollards put forward by several historians, below.

group: many no doubt managed to escape the questioning of the bishop's officers.[3] I have attempted to show here that those named by John Foxe, both suspects and those subsequently made to abjure, were not unimportant members of their communities, but significant individuals by right of their financial and social standing.[4] Using a wide variety of evidence, I believe it is possible to show that the Lollards of the mid-Thames valley, although 'different' in the beliefs they held, in their concentrated geographical distribution, in their widespread connections, and in their close, secretive associations, were also assimilated into their societies, economically and socially, and that their heterodoxy did not result in their ostracism from their communities. Indeed, it could be argued that the social status of Lollards of the early sixteenth century was little changed from that of the groups we know of immediately after the formation of the sect in the 1380s: Lollardy was very much a sect containing a high proportion of numbers of the 'better' or 'chiefer' sort.[5]

II

The threat of heresy was all too apparent when the death of William Atwater, Bishop of Lincoln, on 4 February 1521, resulted in the elevation of John Longland to the see. Longland, a native of Henley-upon-Thames (itself a centre of Lollard activity), obtained papal provision to the diocese on 20 March 1521, and was consecrated on 5 May following. He was personally installed as bishop on 13 September 1522.[6]

Within the new bishop's huge diocese we are here concerned with only that area, an enclave, at the southern tip of the diocese. It was

[3] I make no attempt in this essay to discuss the developing, or stagnant, theology of the Lollards. Dr M. Aston and Professor A. Hudson have successfully sought out and demonstrated the importance of Lollard literature; and if Dr MacCulloch's latest argument is correct, the Lollards are surely ripe for a theological renaissance of their own. Evidence of connections with individuals who were to the fore in developments during the English Reformation given here must strengthen the arguments of those who seek to prove the importance of Lollardy in the theological changes of the 1520s and 1530s.

[4] The names are taken from Foxe. Most of the evidence referred to here is to be found within volume IV, pp. 123–4, 219–43, although other pages will occasionally be referred to, Foxe is our only source for these proceedings. As he makes clear himself, he was examining preliminary proceedings (interrogatories), and not the formal charges which would have subsequently been brought before the ecclesiastical court. The list he produces contains suspects (on whom we may wish to form our own judgements). Only a proportion of those listed are said by Foxe to have abjured (Foxe, IV, p. 242).

[5] See below, Tables 3 and 4, p. 114.

[6] See John F. Davis, *Heresy and Reformation in the South East of England, 1520–1559* (London, 1983); Norman P. Tanner, *Heresy Trials in the Diocese of Norwich, 1428–31* (London, 1977); and John A.F. Thomson, *The Later Lollards, 1414–1520* (Oxford, 1965), for three examples of work done on the early heresy hunts and subsequent trials. Bowker, *Lincoln*, pp. 4 and 12.

unusual in being the point at which four dioceses met: Salisbury, Winchester, London, and Lincoln. The Lollards were particularly strong in the mid-Thames valley, within the Chiltern parishes of southern Buckinghamshire, in parts of Oxfordshire, and (over the episcopal border) in parts of Middlesex, Berkshire, and Hampshire. This study seeks to discuss individuals from all four dioceses, many of whom had connections throughout the area, and farther afield.

Besides the ecclesiastical formalities referred to above, a royal proclamation had been issued, on 20 October 1521, which required 'all mayors, sheriffs, bailiffs, and constables' to be determined in 'aiding, helping, and assisting the said right reverend father in God [Longland], and his said officers' to search out, to apprehend and to punish those suspected of heresy.[7]

The October 1521 proclamation had clearly signalled Henry VIII's determination to overcome the threat both of Lollard and Lutheran heresies. Longland was probably instrumental in persuading Henry to issue the proclamation. The high profile that heresy had already shown within the parishes was of particular concern to the bishop. He became, in John Foxe's phrase, 'a fierce and cruel vexer of the faithful poor servants of Christ'.[8] In 1521, the Lutheran threat to the church in England was no bigger than a man's hand. Lutheranism was certainly of some concern to the ordinaries, but that threat was nothing, apparently, which the church could not handle. The incipient unbelief of much of the bishops' indigenous flock itself was of more concern in 1521. Had they been given the chance, could they have become, as Professor Dickens has suggested, 'a springboard of critical dissent from which the Protestant Reformation could overleap the wall of orthodoxy'?[9]

Whatever the possibilities, as a consequence of Longland's determined searching out of these domestic heretics, and of similar purges in the dioceses of London and Salisbury, we know a great deal about the Lollards living in and around the Thames valley during the decades leading up to the Reformation, and beyond. The evidence, found by John Foxe (or more likely by one of his lieutenants, possibly the future incumbent of London and Canterbury, Edmund Grindal) was in now long-lost special episcopal registers. It tells us much about the Lollards of the mid-Thames valley.

Whilst Longland and his brother-bishops were searching out heretics, and seeking to defend the English church against the threat from abroad,

---

[7] Foxe, IV, pp. 241–2.
[8] Ibid., p. 219.
[9] A.G. Dickens, *The English Reformation* (London, 1967), p. 60. Dickens first put forward his views in *Lollards and Protestants in the Diocese of York* (2nd edn, London, 1982), especially chapters 2 and 7. Professor Dickens continually stresses the way Lutheran heresy built on Lollard foundations.

Wolsey was desperately trying to satisfy Henry VIII's desire for war, which meant that he had to ensure the supply of men-at-arms, and of sufficient money. The war was likely to be more expensive and lengthy than any hitherto known, and Wolsey's work seemed unending and incapable of success. He turned to new devices to achieve his master's requirements. The Musters of 1522 and the Subsidies of 1524–5, the result of that need, play an important part in our investigation.[10]

It is difficult to tell how successful the ecclesiastical authorities, led by the Bishop of Lincoln, were in actually changing people's minds or changing their beliefs, rather than simply making them conform outwardly. We know from isolated events during the 1520s and 1530s that in some cases the church was not at all successful in its aims. The Lollards' continuing commitment to heterodoxy, and their desire to learn of developments happening elsewhere, is amply shown in the actions of John Tyball, a Lollard and one-time churchwarden of Steeple Bumpstead in Essex, who admitted to having travelled from Essex to London, with others, in order to search out Robert Barnes, former prior of the Augustines in Cambridge (then under 'house arrest' at his Order's house in Bishopsgate), to obtain a copy of Tyndale's Bible from him.[11]

Another individual continually in trouble with the church authorities was Thomas Harding, a member of an Amersham family which had been accused of heterodoxy regularly since the early years of the sixteenth century. Meetings were held at his house.[12] During May 1532 he was charged with being a relapsed heretic. When he was arrested, he had in his possession a small library of books, including Tyndale's Obedience of a Christian Man and a New Testament in English. This is further evidence that Lollards were being fed anew by the ideas of reformers affected by Luther's ideas.[13] He admitted the charge, and was thereafter burnt by the secular arm.[14] His former trials, and the presumed questioning of his family and friends, had not deterred him (nor them perhaps). His descendants and relations continued to be dissenters until the eighteenth

[10] See Plumb, 'Foxe and the Later Lollards', for a full discussion of the economic background to this period.

[11] John Strype, Ecclesiastical Memorials . . ., 2 vols. (London, 1721), I, part II, pp. 54–5. This incident also shows how heretics or nonconformists continued to be members of the church, and totally involved in their society. Robert Barnes was burnt during the conservative reaction which followed Thomas Cromwell's execution.

[12] There are several monuments to the Harding family, dating from the eighteenth century, in the churchyard of the Baptist Chapel in Amersham; see Buckinghamshire: An Inventory of Non-Conformist Chapels, and Meeting-Houses in Central England, Royal Commission for Historical Monuments, HMSO (1986), entry for Amersham.

[13] Foxe, IV, p. 580.

[14] Lincs. RO, Reg Longland (Linc), I, fols. 228r-v. See Hudson, Premature Reformation, pp. 144, 183, 470, 505–7.

century (Appendix B, pp. 412–14). There are other instances showing evidence of a continuation of dissent, as we shall see.

It has been said that the evidence from Harding's trial shows that, by the 1530s, 'Lollardy had ceased to be the Creed of weavers and threshers, and was now to be fed and changed by the graduates who supported Luther, and who, like Tyndale, went abroad in order to publish books for their fellow-countrymen.'[15] Whether Lollards had ever been merely 'weavers and threshers' is a matter we shall continually consider below.

III

According to John Foxe, 'Four principal points they [the Lollards] stood in against the Church of Rome: in pilgrimage, in adoration of the saints, in reading Scripture-books in English, and in the carnal presence of Christ's body in the sacrament.' Auricular confession was attacked, and they argued strongly that the Bible was the sole source of salvation. Consequently they attacked the teaching of the church regarding the efficacy of good works which they considered to include the worship of saints, the undertaking of pilgrimages, and the saying of masses for the departed.[16]

Many of those who were examined in 1521–2 had been challenged a decade earlier, in 1511, by Bishop Smith. Smith had been generous in his dealings with the Lollards, often charging those who abjured simply to return home, and 'live as good Christian men should do'.[17] Longland did not exhibit quite the same feelings towards the heretics in his diocese. His questioning of those arrested and challenged in 1521 was searching. He required detailed information about the earlier seeking-out of heretics. Had they been questioned by Bishop Smith? Did their belief about the Sacraments err in any way from the orthodox? Were they members of an heretical sect? Did they know of other 'known men'? To these and other questions were added demands for information about the more recent activities of the heretics. Residents of the market town of Amersham and of the village of Chesham specifically, and of the Chiltern parishes generally, were affected. The pressure was similarly put on

---

[15] Bowker, *Lincoln*, p. 146; see MacCulloch, *Later Reformation*, pp. 68–9, for a discussion on the importance of Lollard ideas during this period.

[16] Foxe, IV, p. 218. Diarmaid MacCulloch has suggested to me that we might be better employed in emphasizing the Lollards' stress on moral legalism. He suggests that it 'might be better to locate their disagreement with the official Church in the definition of what a good work was'. Ritualism was insignificant as far as the Lollards were concerned, and did not fall within the definition of good works, although charity did.

[17] Foxe, IV, p. 219. Andrew Hope has suggested that this description fits better with our knowledge of Atwater rather than Smith.

suspected heretics in adjacent dioceses. In Berkshire, groups were found in several parishes east of Wantage, as well as elsewhere. In Oxfordshire, the area around Burford and Witney was infiltrated by heretics. In the mid-Thames valley overall, including Oxfordshire, Berkshire, and Middlesex, the number of those arrested and interrogated was over 400. Around fifty individuals were subsequently made to do penance; several were burnt.

In the diocese of London, heretics were to be found in considerable numbers. Bishop Cuthbert Tunstall sought out Lollards and Lutherans in the city itself and in Essex. The latter county, with its neighbour, Suffolk, was the entry-port for a considerable number of English Bibles and other printed heretical literature.[18] In Berkshire and elsewhere, information passed on as a result of Longland's inquiries was used to seek out heretics who themselves had contact with those in Oxfordshire and Buckingham-shire.[19] Foxe's evidence of the purges is corroborated by the information given in four certificates of excommunication dated 22 January 1522, when Thomas Barnard, James Morden, Robert Rane (or Rave), and John Scrivener are named as having been handed over to the secular arm for burning in *causa heretica*.[20]

It is sometimes argued that the later Lollards lacked a sophisticated theology. They were, it is said, by the turn of the century, reliant on manuscripts, or copies of them, which were about a hundred years old, and members of a group which had, it appeared, little or no new thinking inculcated into their beliefs during that time. They were, apparently, intel-lectually moribund.[21] Yet Lollards came together to read, discuss, and encourage each other in their beliefs. These meetings may have been less stimulating than the discussions of Wyclif's *De civili dominio*, but they were not without intellectual content. As will be seen, it is unlikely that Lollards were ever merely the 'weavers and threshers' of Dr Bowker's imagination. It is difficult to know with certainty where they fitted into the develop-ments of the 1530s and 1540s. They did, however, because of Foxe's championship of their cause, mainly for propaganda purposes, become the subject of considerable venom from those seeking to denigrate the

---

[18] Strype, *Memorials*, discusses a considerable underground movement of book importers and booksellers.

[19] Hudson, *Premature Reformation*, pp. 446–507, discusses the communication between the various ecclesiastical authorities.

[20] Foxe, IV, p. 245; PRO C85/115/13.

[21] See Andrew Hope, 'Lollardy: The Stone the Builders Rejected?', in Peter Lake and Maria Dowling (eds.), *Protestantism and the National Church in Sixteenth Century England* (London, 1987), pp. 1–36. I am grateful to Mr Hope for generously allowing me to read his article in manuscript form early on in my period of research. See Dickens, *Lollards and Protestants*, especially chapters 2 and 7, for evidence of Lollards' continuing discussion and debate of theological issues. See also MacCulloch, *Later Reformation*, for a reappraisal of the development of Lollard beliefs and teaching.

English Reformation, for whatever reason, theological or political. This denigrating of heretics was not unusual. It led to a dismissal of them socially and economically, as well as theologically and intellectually, an attitude which has not unduly altered during the consequent centuries, and which seems to have continued into the present era.[22]

IV

Professor Joyce Youings, during her examination of the social and economic history of the sixteenth century, whilst accepting that Lollards, together with later 'reformist groups', 'gave rise to the formation of separate fellowships, of secret or "underground" groups', nevertheless claimed in 1984 that 'the early Tudor Lollards were mostly humble craftsmen, able to maintain a certain detachment from society at large'.[23]

Writing in the same year as Professor Youings, Professor Jack Scarisbrick, reflecting on the existence of Lollardy within that county, commented on the 'extraordinary phenomenon of Buckinghamshire'.[24] The Lollards, Scarisbrick went on to say, exhibited all the signs of 'deeprooted upland semi-paganism'.[25] Two years later, Dr Diarmaid MacCulloch, looking particularly at the Lollards of Suffolk and Norfolk, felt able to describe Lollardy as a 'proletarian ghetto'.[26]

The following year, 1987, Dr Christopher Haigh developed the attack further. He pointed out that 'usually Lollards were drawn from weavers and other artisans', and that they 'do show that there were dissidents from the late-medieval Church', and indeed that some of them were organized into an underground sect. But they seem also to show that heresy was rare. He goes on to make the claim that the Lollards 'were much disliked by their orthodox neighbours'.[27]

[22] A full discussion of the polemical battle carried out during the Elizabethan and Jacobean period can be found in Plumb, 'Foxe and the Later Lollards', pp. 15–59. Dickens, *Lollards and Protestants*, has argued against such presumptions, see especially chapters 2 and 7.

[23] Youings, *Sixteenth-Century England*, p. 180.

[24] Scarisbrick, *Reformation*, p. 6.

[25] Professor Scarisbrick fails to produce evidence to substantiate his statement. See Hudson, *Premature Reformation*, p. 469. Professor Hudson, in the course of discussing the Lollards of the early sixteenth century, and commenting on Scarisbrick's discussion of the sect, says, 'The description of early sixteenth-century Buckinghamshire Lollardy as "semi-paganism" (p. 6) . . . and the more general comment along similar lines (p. 46), must be supposed to derive from ignorance of the sources.'

[26] MacCulloch, *Suffolk*, p. 150. Dr MacCulloch seems to have revised his ideas on this aspect of the English Reformation recently; see above, n. 2. Dr MacCulloch has recently written to me to say that he 'gladly jettison[s] the "proletarian" part in view of your own researches', but argues that Lollards are in a ghetto because of their failure to break out of their early fifteenth-century intellectual world. Additionally, he says, the later Lollards seem to have left the gentry unaffected.

[27] Haigh (ed.), *Reformation Revised*, p. 5.

Dr Haigh has recently continued his critical appraisal of later Lollardy in a review article, in which Professor Anne Hudson's most recent publication was the first item considered.[28] Dr Haigh again argues that the available evidence can only emphasize the total lack of enthusiasm for the Reformation in England, and the equally minimal influence the Lollards had in society, even in their strongholds, such as Amersham in Buckinghamshire. He cites two recent articles, by Mr Andrew Hope and myself, which, he says, suggest that 'no more than ten percent of the population in 1521' were heretics and sympathizers.[29] The Lollards, he says, were 'a weak foundation for a future Reformation'.[30]

The existence of comparatively large Lollard groups in such areas of high and concentrated population as Essex, London, the Thames valley, and Kent would seem to preclude such a sweeping dismissal of their status and relevance to events in England during the years leading up to the Reformation. Lollards existed in areas of high population, and it is surely dangerous to dismiss them, as so many historians still do, simply because we have little evidence of their involvement in the mainstream Reformation as we comprehend it. That they existed in areas later to the forefront in the radical developments of the 1550s should also be noted. That they also existed in areas subsequently in the forefront of radical puritanism cannot be dismissed in a sentence.[31]

The Lollards of the early sixteenth century, far from being aliens within their societies, far, indeed, from being 'semi-pagans', were very much part-and-parcel of the parishes and hamlets they inhabited, and were fully involved in secular and ecclesiastical matters within their societies and ·communities. Not only that, they could be found throughout all levels of society, from the wealthiest in the parish, to the farm labourers taxed on wages of £1 a year, who had little but the clothes on their backs to call their own. That was certainly true of those accused of being involved

---

[28] Haigh, 'Premature Birth', pp. 449–59.

[29] Hope, 'Lollardy'; Derek Plumb, 'The Social and Economic Spread of Rural Lollardy: A Reappraisal', in W. J. Sheils and Diana Wood (eds.), *Studies in Church History*, 23 (Oxford, 1986), pp. 111–30.

[30] Haigh, 'Premature Birth', p. 451. To my mind, a committed phalanx of 10 per cent of the population is a pretty sure foundation upon which to secure any change.

[31] See Dickens, *Lollards and Protestants*, chapters 2 and 7; see also Christopher Hill, 'From Lollards to Levellers', in Maurice Cornforth (eds.), *Rebels and their Causes: Essays in Honour of A. L. Morton* (London, 1978), pp. 49–67. Areas such as Penn and Amersham in Buckinghamshire, Cranbrook and Tenterden in Kent, and Colchester, Steeple Bumpstead, and Braintree in East Anglia were all Lollard strongholds and later radical protestant parishes. See below, pp. 127–30 for the tangled, but very real connection between Maurice Smart, the Lollard, and Jack of Newbury's reforming son, who assisted Coverdale, and Thomas Cromwell. In London several parishes north of Cheapside were continually the home of radicalism from the 1520s to the 1640s. The parish church of St Stephen in Coleman Street was a 'Lollard church', and later sheltered the five members of parliament sought by Charles I.

in the Lollard heresy within the mid-Thames valley, the area covered by the southern parishes of Buckinghamshire, Oxfordshire, and Middlesex, as well as several parishes of Berkshire.

Perhaps the most important point to emerge from my recent studies is that of the wide social spread of Lollardy, and the relative affluence of so many of those suspected of heresy. There were variations from village to village, from town to town, of course. In some places it seems likely that Lollardy was spread throughout all social and economic levels of the settlement, as at Hughenden in Buckinghamshire, and Rickmansworth in Hertfordshire. In the former the sect was very strong, a significant and important part of the community; in the latter it was seemingly a smaller group, yet economically disparate.[32] In other parishes, whilst Lollards were still found at all economic levels, it seems likely that the majority were from the higher economic strands from society, as at Newbury and Henley. Where they were liberally spread throughout all economic and social levels in the parish, within such strongholds as Amersham, they ran them to a large extent.

The economic spread of Lollardy is seen in Tables 3 and 4. We have to remember that we are sometimes talking here about men who were usually at the top of the financial table, and who were considered by the government to be worthy of extraordinary treatment, as in the 'Anticipation'. The 'Anticipation', engineered by Wolsey to gain an early payment of the Subsidy of 1524, considered all those worth £10 or over to be rich enough to participate. Some so dealt with were suspect Lollards – and they were in the upper strands of county society.

In two remarkably consistent tables we see, clearly demonstrated, the wide spread of those suspected of heresy throughout the economic levels of the most all-encompassing fiscal return of the early modern period.[33] We cannot know how many of the poorest and the vagrants escaped from the tax altogether: all we can say is that a proportion of Lollards not very different from that in society in general were found amongst the poorest of those taxed. The taxable poor were involved in unpopular religious activities, even if these brought them into trouble. But we also see how many of those actually named during the purges were from the

---

[32] Plumb, 'Foxe and the Later Lollards', chapter 5, pp. 169–87, chapter 8, pp. 320–3. However, Dr Aston has recently shown the depth of iconoclasm in the parish of Rickmansworth during this period: 'Iconoclasm at Rickmansworth, 1522: Troubles of Churchwardens', *Journal of Ecclesiastical History*, 40, 4 (Oct. 1989), pp. 524–52. It is impossible to say for sure, but it seems likely that the information we have of heresy in the parish is incomplete. I am grateful to Dr Aston for allowing me to read her article in manuscript form.

[33] The figures, taken from my thesis, relate both to those named by Foxe, and to those found in other contemporary sources. For details, see the appendix of names in Plumb, 'Foxe and the Later Lollards'.

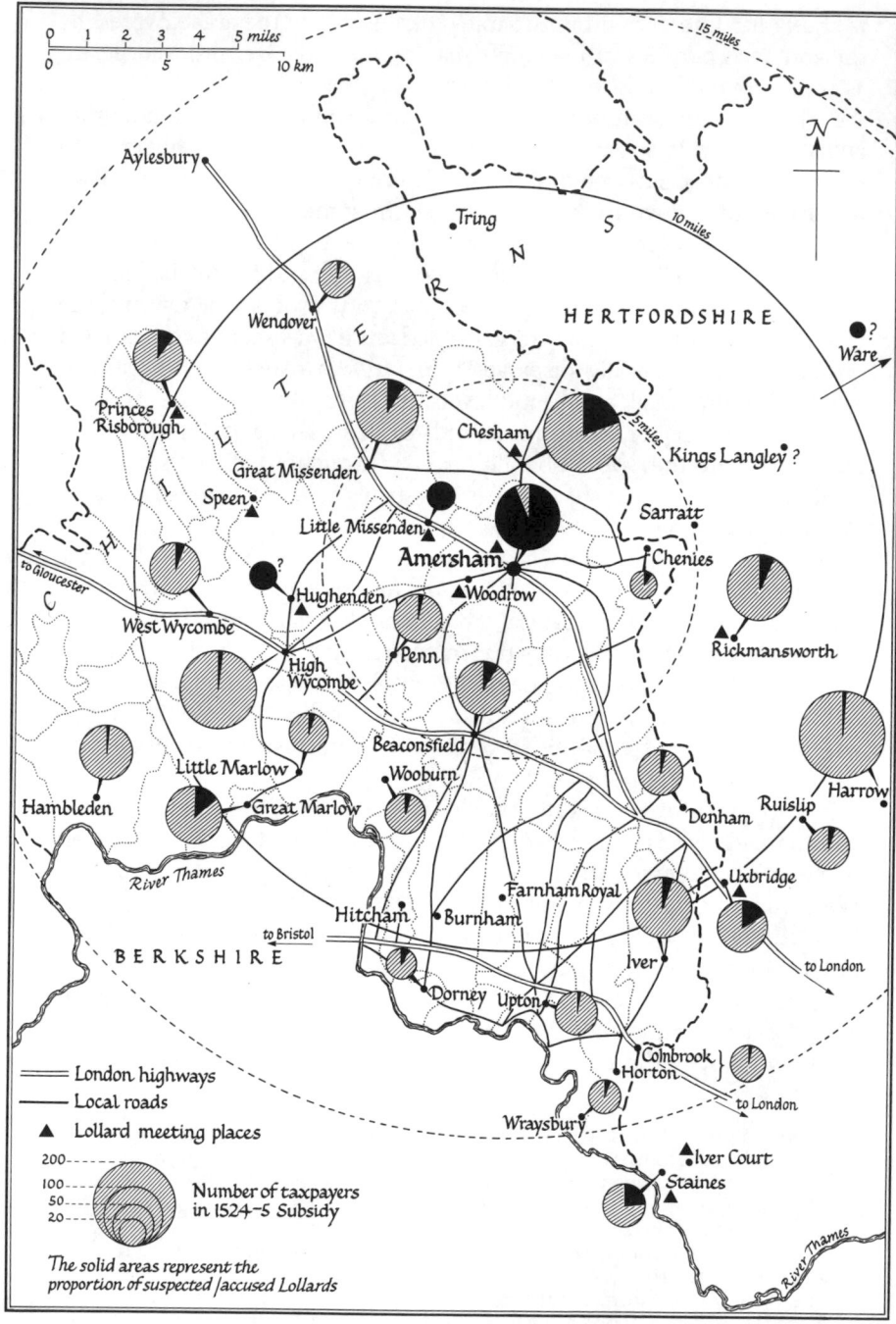

Map 2. The distribution of the later Lollards in the Chilterns

better-off members of their communities. The figures show that nearly 20 per cent of suspected Lollards and their closest family were found at the economic peak of their societies. It must be assumed that political and social status followed. Nearly a half of their number were in the middle ranks of their parishes. Of the others, at the lower economic levels, many were widowers, widows, or younger sons who had enjoyed, or would later enjoy, greater wealth, and had kinship links with their families.[34]

The pattern varies from parish to parish. In some parishes we find apparently isolated individuals named as Lollards: the Lollard is the only person suspected in that particular parish. In other parishes we find families similarly on their own, or with only tenuous contacts with others listed in Foxe, but who later can be seen to have contacts with others of similar beliefs. Some families show evidence of continuity of dissent through the decades of the Reformation. There are parishes where Lollardy must have affected all aspects of religious, social, and economic life.

In those parishes where Lollards were few in number they possibly had little influence on the everyday life of their peers; yet they were often among the richest men living in the parish, and that fact alone indicates authority or standing.

It is when we look at the figures in these tables that the true impact of my examination of Lollardy in its social and economic framework becomes clear. There were, indeed, poor Lollard sympathizers: almost as many as those taxed in society at large. But the important Lollards, of course, were those influential individuals in the middling and upper social levels who were just a little better represented among Lollards than their economic peers in society in general. It was because of these 'well-shod sympathizers' of Lollardy, 'figures of substance and stability in the eyes of those around them' that the group took such firm root in the Chilterns.[35] And there was a slight proportional bias towards the wealthier members of society.

In the rest of this chapter, I shall examine what can be known of Lollard individuals taxed in 1524 or 1525 on various sums from £45 and £40 down through £25 and £23 to £12, and £7, to the poorest and one of the most influential, Richard Collins, husband of Alice, of West Ginge who had goods valued at £6 13s 4d. This is still above average by rural standards.

We turn first to one or two affluent individuals amongst suspected Lollards living apparently isolated from fellow-nonconformists. Andrew

---

[34] PRO E179. See above, pp. 110–11 and Margaret Spufford and Motoyasu Takahashi, 'The Spread of Families across the Social and Economic Structure in Sixteenth and Seventeenth Century Willingham and Chippenham' (forthcoming).

[35] Richard G. Davies, 'Lollardy and Locality', *Trans. Royal Hist. Soc.*, 6th Ser., 1 (1991).

Table 3. *The economic status of suspected Lollards from the Muster Certificates of 1522*

	Lollards			All suspect Lollards	Percentage of total residents
	Certain	Probable	Possible		
£10 and over	34	4	6	44	20
+£4 to £9	12	8	6	26	12
+30s to £4	35	22	23	80	36
30s and under	21	23	27	71	32
Totals	102	57	62	221	100

Table 4. *The economic status of suspected Lollards from the Subsidy Returns of 1524–5*

	Lollards			All suspect Lollards	Percentage of suspect Lollards	Total taxpayers in eighteen parishes	Percentage of total taxpayers
	Certain	Probable	Possible				
£10 and over	23	7	11	41	18	194	13
+£4 to £9	13	4	9	26	12	154	11
+30s to £4	28	16	31	75	34	545	37
30s and under	16	18	45	79	36	573	39
Totals	80	45	96	221	100	1,466	100

Maysey, at 'Burton' as Foxe calls it, was such a man. He was the only person named in Foxe resident in the parish, which was actually called Black Burton. He had been named by the peripatetic Lollard preacher, Robert Pope. He was the richest man in the parish, listed in the Subsidy of 1524–5, with goods worth £40. We know nothing else about him, but his financial status must surely have enabled him to be of some influence locally; and his status allowed him to worship as he saw fit, with a modicum of freedom. Another 'lone' and less affluent but still prosperous heretic, of whom we know more, was Robert Livord, who was named as living at Steventon in Berkshire. Steventon was on the edge of a group of Lollard parishes east of Wantage. Apart from Robert Livord, and his brother William, we are told by Foxe of only three other Lollards in the parish: Father Amershaw, Mr Smart, miller, and John Sympson.[36] Robert Livord had travelled the several miles to Burford in Oxfordshire for a reading group, and had travelled again to attend the marriage of Joan Burges, at Upton, a settlement next to Burford. He knew two leading teachers in the sect, Robert Pope and Robert Collins, amongst others.

[36] The name of Smart will be found often in subsequent pages, with interesting and exciting consequences.

Robert Livord and his brother William came from a wealthy family, as a dispute in the latter years of the fifteenth century shows. Sometime between 1485 and 1500 Agnes Livord, 'late the wife of William Lyford' was the plaintiff against Thomas Bradley of Hanney in a case brought before the Court of Chancery.[37] She was possibly the widowed mother of the brothers later accused, but her husband William may have been the Lollard named by Pope, and Robert his young brother, or perhaps actually their son. Bradley was feoffee to uses of messuages and lands at Livord, West Hanneygrove, Locking and Tilwick. Agnes Livord had, she claimed, been joint holder of six messuages and some 200 acres of land. Bradley had taken hold of these lands by force.

The family's landholding was considerable, and Robert himself was a substantial man. In the Subsidy for the parish of Steventon, he was one of the richest men in the parish, with £10 in goods, whilst Joanna, possibly his brother's widow, or his mother, had a respectable £3.[38] Robert Livord's will does not exist; but the inventory of his goods, taken after his death in 1545, does.[39] Livord's inventory confirms his status: his life-style was one of considerable domestic comfort for the mid-1540s. He and his wife slept on featherbeds, and there were as many as six pairs of sheets. Even after the Restoration, the ability to change the sheets was one of the key indices of money to spend on 'luxury' goods. There were, astonishingly, three curtains, almost unknown at this date in rural society,[40] as well as a painted cloth hanging in the hall. There were also two tables, again unusual for the date because they were folding, thirteen pewter plates, four pewter porringers with saucers, and a pewter basin. Pewter was one of the other indices of prosperity thirty years later to William Harrison. Mistress Livord had two gowns decorated with lambs' fur, and her kirtle was violet. Robert himself had a gown lined with cloth, as well as his working clothes. The farm entries in the inventory show an emphasis on livestock, since he had twelve cows and three bullocks, as well as six horses, a number which itself indicates some considerable wealth. They were valued together at £12 5s. The cattle and horses explain the three loads of hay. He also had eight pigs fattening, as well as six 'bakyn' hoggs at the 'Rose'. But despite this emphasis on milk and bacon production, Robert Livord also had his own plough with harness and cart, valued at 7s. His five acres of wheat was not so striking, but his 420

---

[37] PRO C1/100/51.
[38] PRO E179/73/134.
[39] Berks. RO D/A1/201/116a. It is actually of Robert and his wife Joanne. See Plate 3.
[40] For sheets and curtains and pewter, see Margaret Spufford, *The Great Reclothing of Rural England: Petty Chapmen and their Wares in the Seventeenth Century* (London, 1984), pp. 113–14, 115–116.

pounds of hemp in store was: it looks as if he combined dairying with hemp growing for coarse 'linen', in a typical way. There were thirteen skips, or 'staulls', of bees valued at 10s 10d.[41] The total value of the goods in the house was £23 16s 8d. Livord was very comfortably off: he was a Lollard yeoman.

Another parish with isolated Lollard individuals living within it was Hungerford, lying to the west of Newbury, on the border with Wiltshire. It was a large settlement, having something over 100 souls eligible to pay taxes at the 1524–5 Subsidy.[42] According to the first list (10 January 1524) 106 persons were eligible to pay a total of £17 11s 10d; on 8 January the following year some 114 persons were due to pay £14 9s 6d. Only three suspects from this parish are found in Foxe.

John Eden (variously called Eding, Edon, or Ledisdale) was named by Robert Pope, John Edmunds, Robert Collins and Roger Dods. Dods said that Ledisdale had read from the Bible at Robert Burges' house at Burford. It is likely that the various detectors were also present. John Ludlow was also named by Pope. Thomas Hall was named by Pope, Collins, and Dods. Hall was also at Burges' house (with Eden) where he, too, read; they probably met Livord from Steventon there. Ledisdale and Hall probably travelled together to Burford expressly to read; they were obviously able to draw the attention of some leading figures in the sect.

In the Subsidy Return for Hungerford is an entry for 'John Lodelale', who was taxed on the large sum of £25 in goods. Ledisdale was the fourth richest man among 104 taxpaying residents listed for the parish. Once again we find a suspected Lollard at the very top of the taxpaying table of a parish. Other members of the family emerged; Thomas Edon had goods valued at 20 marks, George Lovsdale had goods at 10 marks. John Hull, with goods at £4 was also named, with Thomas Gray, who had goods of 40s, Edward Kember, John Taylor, and William Burges with wages of 20s. All of them may have been related to the members of those families named as suspected Lollards elsewhere, living at Hendred, West Hanney, and Burford.

John Edon or Ledisdale was involved in a dispute before the Court of Requests.[43] In 1548 Katharine Hull, late wife of Richard Hull, of the town of Oxford, was in dispute with John Edon, 'otherwise called Lydisdayle, . . . of Huddon by Hungerford'. 'Wydowe' Hull was in dispute with Edon over a 'messuage, tenement, or Inne called the Crown' and twenty acres

---

[41] The year may not have gone well. An entry for 'twenty staulls' has been crossed out, as has another entry, for five acres of 'whete in the feylde prased at 25s'. For the common combination of dairying and hemp or flax growing, see Nesta Evans, *The East Anglian Linen Industry, 1550–1850* (Aldershot, 1985).

[42] PRO E179/73/121.

[43] PRO Reg 2/18/14/1–2.

of meadow, 'in the town and in suburbes and in four other small lots and houses in Oxford'. As was often the case, a group of feoffees to uses was installed in the holdings. In other words a trust was set up to escape death duties. Hull claimed that Ledisdale or Edon had illegally entered the properties.

'Edon or Lydisdale, a yeoman of Huddon or Hiddon', by Hungerford, rejected the charge. He claimed he had handed over money to the couple 'seized' of the property, referring to a deed dated 3 March 1523, which had granted the said properties to John and his wife Helen. The couple said to have been in possession were Edmund Smart of Shawe, yeoman, and his wife, Katharine. And Edmund Smart, as we shall see, was at least in contact with, and was probably one of, a group of Lollards living around Newbury. He may even have been the 'one Smart', named by Pope, or the Mr Smart, miller, of Steventon, referred to above.[44]

Edon or Ledisdale owned the Crown Inn at Oxford. Members of the sect considered him an important enough member of their group to travel to Burford to hear him. Oxford may well have been the site of another Lollard meeting-place of which we know nothing. We do, however, know much of the general importance of inns as points from which ideas, as well as other goods, were diffused.

The cases of Maysey, Livord, and Ledisdale are graphic examples of individual Lollard suspects living in a parish who show signs of economic dominance within their communities. With Edon, additionally, we are presented with evidence of a geographically and socially extensive series of connections. Surely Ledisdale and Livord were not outcasts; and surely their views were known to those they dealt with.

V

It was not only individuals who seem, at first, to have been isolated, yet financially dominant, within their community. A close examination of two of the families mentioned by John Foxe demonstrates how they were able to maintain connections with others listed in Foxe, and how they continued in their heretical beliefs well into the turbulent years of the 1530s. One such family is obviously wealthy; the other apparently not so, but it too may show signs of the rising affluence of a family who may have been moving into the ranks of the yeomanry.[45]

The first of these two, the Durdant family, was said by Foxe to live at 'Iver by Staines'. Staines lay on the eastern bank of the River Colne, and on the north bank of the Thames. Two of the manors of the town, Staines

---

[44] See above, p. 114 and below, p. 128.
[45] See below, pp. 158–60, for a similar family background, that of the Funge family.

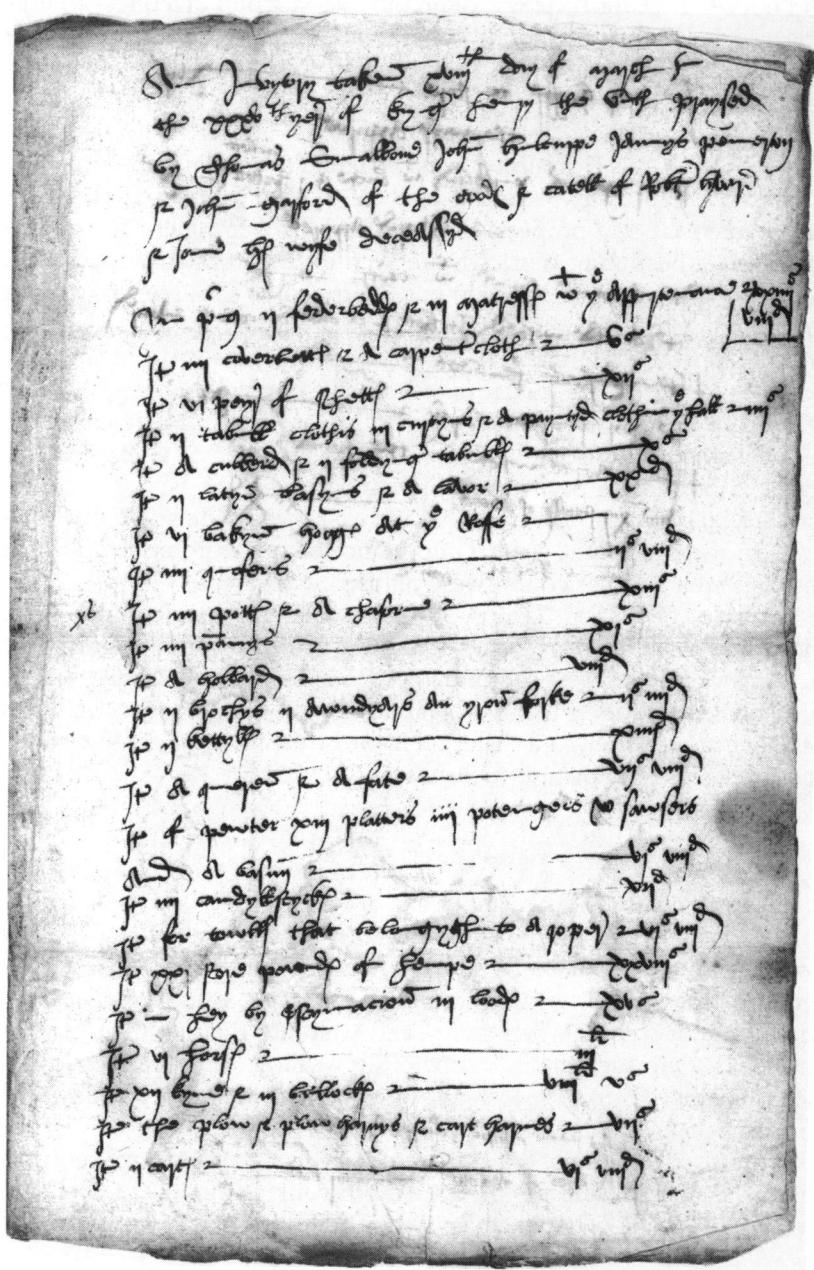

Plate 3. Inventory of Robert Livord, Lollard of Steventon in Berkshire

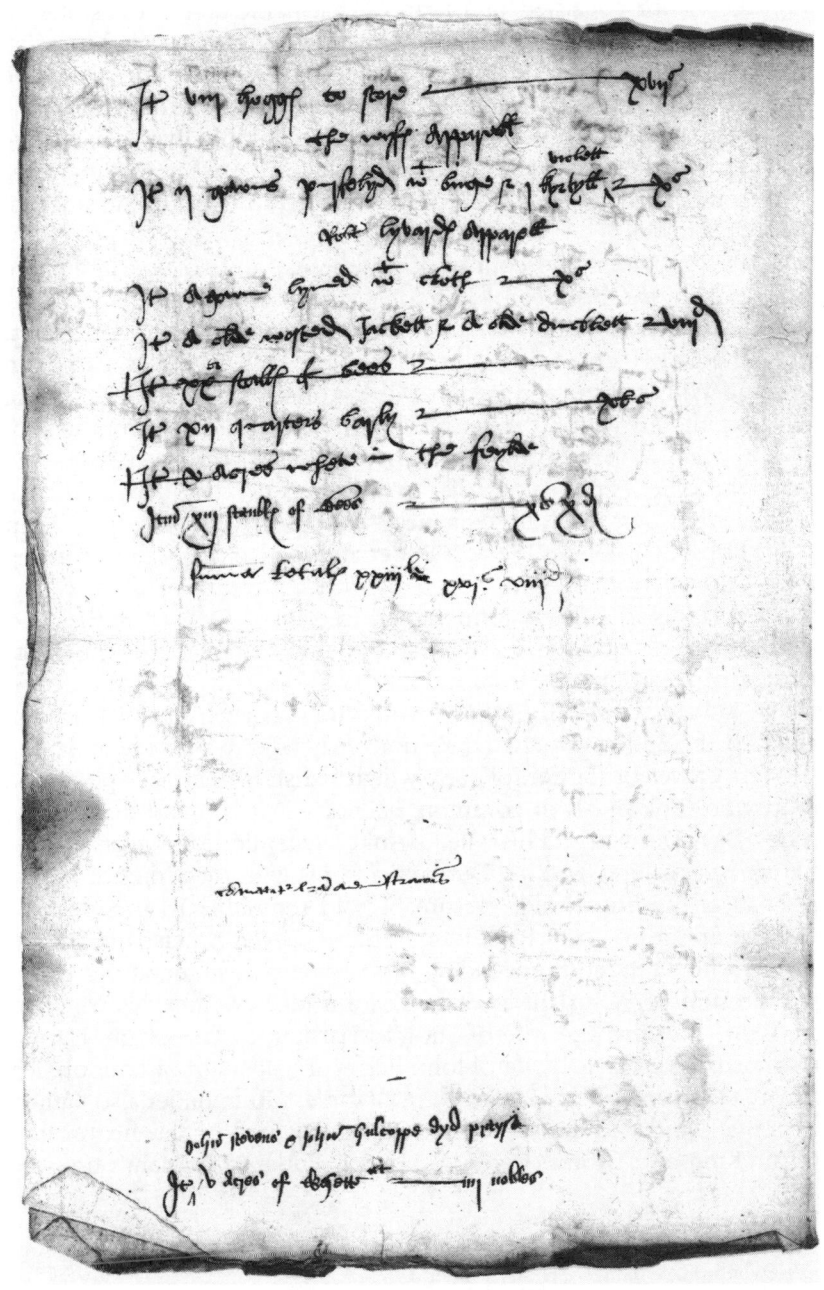

and Yeoveney, belonged to the Abbey of Westminster. By our period the latter manor consisted of a farm of that name and a few scattered homesteads. The village, if it had ever existed, was no longer in existence.[46] The name 'Yeoveney' was distorted over the centuries. At some time, especially during the fifteenth and sixteenth centuries, the name was usually expressed as 'Iveney', 'Iveneia', or simply 'Iver'. According to one source, the manor was situated on flat land between two branches of the Colne, to the north of the town of Staines and near to the adjacent parish of Stanwell.[47]

Staines was within the county of Middlesex, and so was under the jurisdiction of the Bishops of London. A large group of heretics, their places of residence usually unnamed, faced the Bishop of London's court during the early years of the sixteenth century. Richard Butler, named in 1518, and William King and Robert Durdant, both named in 1521, are of particular interest within this group. They were accused, with others, of speaking against the real presence. Richard Butler, forced to give evidence before the court, gave details of a group meeting at Robert Durdant's house at Iver Court, 'near unto Staines', when Butler, William King, John Butler, Robert Carder, and Jenkin Butler attended all night for a reading group. Thomas Holmes, who detected groups all over the Thames valley, included in his detections John Butler, carpenter, Richard Butler, and William King of Uxbridge, stating that they read all night at the house of Durdant of Iver Court by Staines. Holmes also mentioned Joan Cocks, wife of Robert Wywood, husbandman, who was a servant of Durdant, and knew the Butlers. The two detections may refer to the same meeting.

Robert Carver or Carder, of Iver (which parish is unclear), spoke of a group who took meals in common. Nicholas Durdant and his wife, of Staines, Davy Durdant and his wife, of Ankerwyke, along the river Thames in Buckinghamshire, 'and old Durdant' and his wife, sat at dinner, whilst the head of the household, presumably old (or Robert) Durdant, read from the Epistles of Saint Paul. John Scrivener, from Amersham, named a group who attended the wedding of Durdant's daughter, at old Durdant's, presumably 'Durdant by Staines': John Merrywether, his wife and son, Isabel Harding, the wife of Thomas Harding of Amersham, Hartop of Windsor, Joan Barret, wife of John Barret, a goldsmith of London, Mr Stilman, tailor, and Henry Miller, were all there.[48] John Butler also named a group at Durdant's house: Robert Carder, Richard Butler, his brother William King, and Thomas Carder, who took Butler to Durdant's house.[49]

---

[46] *VCH Mdx.*, III, p. 19.
[47] J.E.B. Glover, *The Place-Names of Middlesex* (Cambridge, 1942), pp. 19–20.
[48] Elsewhere Foxe names a Henry Milner.
[49] See below, Ch. 3, sections VIII and IX and Map 3 for this group. The Carders and the Butlers were related.

If Foxe is accurate, we see here an apparently isolated house of one family actually being the centre of a house group, perhaps even a gathered church of the type later to be seen among puritans, at the other end of the century.[50] Foxe said that Robert Durdant lived at Iver Court. In 1494–6, and 1522, Robert Durdant is named as the holder of the manor of 'Yeoveney', holding of Westminster Abbey.[51] Nicholas Durdant was in possession by 1525.[52]

The Subsidy Roll for the Hundred of Spelthorne exists.[53] The entry for Staines shows that Robert Durdant was taxed on £13 6s 8d. Out of forty-seven taxpayers, Durdant was the second richest. He is the only identifiable Lollard in the parish: once again we find an example of a single, wealthy, Lollard apparently living in isolation.

At the same time, Robert Durdant's son Nicholas was living in the adjacent parish of Stanwell. Among a total of fifty-one taxpayers listed in the Subsidy Return for that parish, we find the only known Lollard listed is Nicholas himself. He paid 3s 6d on goods assessed at £7 and was the seventh most prosperous man there. He had, once again, the only name we can identify with certainty as a Lollard. But Thomas Cowper, with goods at £4, John Saunders, a labourer with wages of 26s, and Nicholas Tredway, also a labourer, who had 20s in wages, were also listed, and were possibly connected with Lollard families elsewhere.[54] They may have been related to such families living across the River Colne, who had connections with Middlesex.

The wills made by members of the Durdant family add to our knowledge of these heretics' social and economic position. Robert Durdant, leader of the groups at Iver Court, and lessee of the manor of Yeoveney, died at the end of November 1524, at Staines. Within six days of the will being written, probate had been granted. The preamble to the will is non-committal. Religious bequests are similarly lacking in any sense of commitment. He gave 8d to St Paul's, the mother church; 12d to the high altar at Staines; and 4d to every altar in his parish church. There are no other bequests to the church, and those he gave may have been given merely to smooth the passage of his will through probate. His wife was the residuary legatee, and she and his son Nicholas were executors. An interesting bequest was that to Simon Clerk 'for his labour in the nyght

[50] Dr Aston has reminded me that gathered churches were no new thing among Lollards. They were found during the trials in Norfolk during the early years of the fifteenth century. See Tanner, *Norwich*.

[51] *VCH Mdx.*, III, p. 19; WAM 16905–6, 30501.

[52] WAM West Reg Bks, II, fol. 161b, IV, fol. 85; WAM 16810. (The family were finally made to surrender the lease in the 1660s.)

[53] PRO E179/141/115.

[54] See the Collins family, below pp. 123–6, for an example of social and economic spread.

to me a gentse crestenines' (*sic*): Clerk received two bushels of malt and two bushels of wheat for his efforts.[55]

Robert Durdant's son Nicholas, who was also named as attending the groups at Iver Court, made his will on 12 September 1538.[56] He left his soul to Almighty God 'trusting emdombredly [*sic*] that by the merits of his onlie sonne Jhus Christe to be one of his *elect*' (my italics).[57] The importance of this preamble can not be stressed too much.

There has been much discussion about the importance, or lack of it, of the religious preambles to wills, which space does not permit here. However, my exhaustive examination of 373 wills made between 1480 and 1550, which included fifty made by known Lollards named in Foxe, showed that a conservative, or non-committal will preamble could not be trusted as an indication to the practice of the testator during his or her lifetime, but a radical will preamble could.[58] Forty-three Lollard wills had conservative or non-committal preambles, but seven had radical openings to their wills. Only ten radical preambles were written amongst the whole group of 373, and two of the three not known as Lollard had enough contact with Lollard families to make their position suspect. A radical preamble made before 1550 must always be taken very seriously.

Nicholas Durdant is a shining example of a Lollard maintaining his nonconformity throughout the years of the Reformation and, we must assume, becoming part of any reforming group living locally, no longer simply a Lollard but now a mainstream reformer. He seems to have taken advantage of the relaxing of control in the 1530s. He left his wife Eleanor her dowry 'and she to make no farther title to no parte of my goods nor landes nother corne nor cattell'. His son Andrew received the farm and moveable goods. William Grinder, a Lollard living along the river at Hedsor, was one supervisor.[59] The other supervisor was 'Master Doctor Haynes'. Haynes is probably Simon Haynes, a Cambridge graduate, who became Dean of Windsor in 1535, and later assisted in the compilation of the first English Liturgy.[60]

The witnesses to Nicholas Durdant's will included Henry Hobbes, who was probably the Lollard from Hughenden, and Thomas Holmes.

---

[55] GLRO 9171, 56.

[56] PRO Prob 11/27/22.

[57] See below, p. 125.

[58] Plumb, 'Foxe and the Later Lollards', pp. 54–62, especially p. 59 and Table 2, p. 60.

[59] In Foxe, William Grinder is simply listed with others from Amersham; we now know he lived at Hedsor. In the Muster he is said to have goods valued at £25; in the Subsidy (for *Marlow Parva cum Hedsor*) he is listed with £20.

[60] See J. and J.A. Venn, *Alumni Cantabrigienses*, 4 vols. (Cambridge, 1922–7), p. 341. Perhaps the 'Simon Clerk' mentioned in Robert Durdant's will, above, is the same person. Iver Court was well within range of Windsor. See DNB, 'Heynes'. As Dean of Exeter he showed, says Dr Aston, 'iconoclastic zeal'.

Holmes was said by Foxe probably to have been burnt before this date. The witness may have been a relative, possibly a son, but, as there is no extant evidence of Thomas Holmes being handed over to the secular authorities for burning, it is possible that Foxe was wrong; nor should it be forgotten that Holmes was an intimate witness to several of the meetings at Staines. This may well be the same man.

Nicholas' wife, Eleanor, made her will on 8 April 1539.[61] Probate was given on 23 April. She too had attended the meetings at the elder Durdant's house. Her husband's continuing nonconformity, expressed in his will, did not show itself in her will, if the preamble is anything to go by. She left her soul to 'almighty god and to our blessed lady and to all the holy company of heaven'. However, this apparent conservatism did not extend to her feeling for the church. There are no religious bequests, although the curate at Staines, Sir Robert Russell, received the large sum of 3s 4d. Her brother William Mylls was the residuary legatee and executor. Her son, Andrew, had presumably already settled and established himself on the family holding. Her servant Margery was given Eleanor's chamber.

This individual Lollard family was central to a thriving group of heretics which met at their house. They were of considerable importance socially and economically. They also demonstrate that such a group could, and did, maintain their beliefs throughout the period, and that they could declare those beliefs when the climate changed in their favour.[62] The evidence from the Durdant family wills implies continuity of dissent. They did not, however, abandon their local clergyman, and it would seem probable that the curate, Sir Robert Russell, actually knew of their leanings, and may well have supported or been sympathetic to them. This example shows very well how Foxe's information may be amplified by the use of subsidy, testamentary, and central court information.

Another family which was of enormous importance amongst the later Lollards were the complex Collins family. We find economic and social diversity amongst the family itself, if we take only two examples, John Collins of Betterton, who was almost as prosperous as Robert Durdant, who had been taxed £13 6s 8d, and Thomas Collins of nearby Ginge.

Betterton 'vill' was part of the parish of East Locking. The Muster Certificate for the parish is extant.[63] The settlement at Betterton was small, no

[61] GLRO 9171, 10,328.
[62] For the continuing discussion on the continuity of dissent see Hill, 'Lollards to Levellers'. At its most controversial, the argument suggests a descent from Lollards to Baptists. A less demanding hypothesis seeks to show a continuity of Lollard thought into the maelstrom of the English Reformation, the 1530s, and 1540s. Dr MacCulloch's latest work would seem to suggest this factor to have been of considerably more importance than hitherto suspected: see above, n. 2.
[63] PRO E315/464/53v–6.

more than a hamlet. Only seven individuals were listed as eligible for muster. John Collins was one of them, and was rather more prosperous than Robert Livord. He was listed as a householder, with £12 in goods, and his son, also John, had goods of £7. The latter was required to supply a bill. The other five residents are listed as servants, presumably, of John Collins senior. Collins senior was comfortably off. He was probably a yeoman, possibly a minor member of the local gentry. Some of his apparent wealth had been achieved two decades earlier, when he enclosed land in the parish, apparently illegally. As a consequence, he was the subject of inquiry by one of Wolsey's commissions on enclosure, which toured the country during 1517–18.[64]

'John Colyins the elder, of Beaterton, . . . a hamlet to the south of East Lockinge' had enclosed thirty-five acres of land in 1498, for pasture. Three people had been displaced, and a messuage destroyed. The land enclosed was valued at 15s yearly. Collins was a copyholder of the monastery at Poughley, which monastery, according to the Muster Certificate, was 'chief lorde there', holding lands valued at 20 marks per annum.

The same John Collins of Betterton, 'in the parish of Lockyng', made his will in 1528.[65] The will gives no indication of Lollard sympathies. He bequeathed his soul to 'almighty god and our lady saint Mary and all the holy company of heaven'. Several bequests to lights in the church follow. Sir John Greneway, the curate, was left 3s 4d 'to pray for my soul'. The will shows that John Collins had a daughter named Alice. None of the witnesses are connectable with the Lollard families, nor do they seem to have been resident nearby. His son John was a legatee.

That Collins put his newly gained land to good use is suggested by two of the legacies in his will. His son Richard was given ten sheep and a cow, and his daughter Joan got twenty sheep. Presumably this was only a part of his flock. His thirty-five additional acres would have supported much more livestock. Here we have a Lollard of estate and standing, who maintained that estate throughout the period of persecution and fear. He was an enterprising farmer, who built up his holding and prospered as a result. His son John was, as we shall see, a churchwarden and pillar of the society he lived in. His family's heterodoxy in no way hindered his rise in society.

In 1539, on 19 February, Dom John Grenwey of East Hendred confessed to immorality with Alice Collins, 'late of the parish of Lockinge'. He was ordered to offer a 21 lb wax candle before the third Sunday in Lent to the principal image in the church at Locking.[66] William Whyte and

---

[64] I.S. Leadam (ed.), *The Domesday of Inclosures, 1517–18*, 2 vols. (London, 1897), I, p. 116.
[65] Berks. RO D/A/191.
[66] Berks. RO, MSS Berks. Archdeaconry, c3, fol. 40b. It is difficult to establish who Alice was. She may have been the daughter of John.

John Collins, presumably churchwardens, were to enforce the penance.[67]

John Collins' relative, 'Thomas Collins of Ginge', was not so financially secure. He lived at West Ginge, which was also part of the parish of Locking. It was a settlement which seems to have been even smaller than Betterton, with only six individuals listed eligible for muster. Half of those listed were of the Collins family: Richard Collins, householder, who had goods to the value of £6 13s 4d, Thomas Collins, householder, with goods of 40s, and William Collins, named as Thomas' son, who had goods of 40s. These are an important group. The hamlet was dominated by the family.[68] We see before us an interesting and important group of Lollards. Foxe listed Thomas as the father of Richard, William, and John. The last lived at Burford. The entries in the Muster Return suggest that Richard, the eldest son, had already taken over the family holding in West Ginge, leaving his father Thomas retaining a smaller holding. William, the younger son, still lived with his father.

Richard Collins and his wife Alice were very important teachers in the sect. He was a reader of texts as well as a reciter of passages; she was a roving preacher to groups in Berkshire and Oxfordshire. Yet he was neither a member of the dominating wealthy elite, nor a wage labourer. He was among the seven per cent of middling taxpayers resident in the parish of Locking.

'William Colyns', the Lollard, of West Ginge in the parish of Lockinge, and brother of Richard Collins, made his will in February 1543.[69] The preamble left his soul to 'almighty God my only maker and redeemer, desiring my soule to be associated & in company with the blessed virgin Mary and all the *elect* company of heaven' (my italics). This Lollard declared his belief at a dangerous time of conservative reaction. We can be sure we are viewing the statement of a confirmed nonconformist.[70] 'Alis' his wife was his executrix. The only religious bequests were of half a bushel of barley to the parish church at Locking for prayers for his soul and 2d to the mother church at Salisbury. Eight children received small bequests, including his sons Richard and John. His overseers and witnesses were John Coxshall and Robert Carpenter. Essentially, the group which gathered round William's bedside, for he was 'sike in body' when he made his will, were the taxpaying residents of this hamlet. Whether their relationship went as far as mutual beliefs it is impossible to say.

---

[67] Ibid., fol. 42. John Collins was possibly the son of Richard, or the man of that name living at the hamlet of Betterton.

[68] This virtual domination of the place by members of the Collins family deserves emphasis. As Dr Aston has remarked, 'In such a pattern of settlement it becomes easier to understand the strength of nonconformist behaviour and beliefs, and [subsequently] the conservation of texts.'

[69] Berks. RO D/A1/223.

[70] See above, Nicholas Durdant, p. 122.

Lollardy was a way of life to the Collins family. Their economic standing was diverse, but it did not, however, indicate their standing within the heretics' society. Richard and Alice Collins were quite as prominent as the more prosperous Durdants.

VI

The few men and women named as Lollard suspects from Newbury and the surrounding parishes in Berkshire, were also, previously, mere shadows to us. Within the large, urban community they lived in, or were associated with, it is possible they were of little political consequence, but what we learn of them from sources other than Foxe should make us at least pause and consider their position within their local society. Yet another parish initially suggests isolated individuals secretly maintaining their heretical beliefs. A further examination shows a very different picture.

Newbury was the most important settlement in southern Berkshire and northern Hampshire. It was not surprising that a Lollard group not only existed but had far-reaching connections in a market town with considerable trading contacts both to the north and south. It was a large town, with an important grain market.[71] It was a centre for broadcloth production as well as an important marketing centre. In the two Subsidy Returns it is listed as having 358 and 414 eligible inhabitants, paying £121 and £120 3s 11d.[72]

Bishop Langton's register supports the discussion of the town by Foxe, who asserts that there was a large group of Lollards living there at the turn of the century. During the 1490s a series of trials of suspected heretics had indeed taken place. The group was large, although perhaps not as large as Foxe claimed. William Brigger, then resident just over the county boundary in Hampshire, had been taught by Richard Sawyer of Newbury. William Carpenter or Herford or Daniell, John Edward, Robert Elton, Alice Hignell, Richard Hilling, William Lye of Woodhay, who was an associate of Richard Sawyer or Pitfin, William Smart, and Thomas Taylor were all named during trials in 1491.[73] Although they took place out of

---

[71] J.G.A. Clay, *Economic Expansion and Social Change: England 1500–1700*, 2 vols. (Cambridge, 1984), II, p. 13; Joan Thirsk (ed.), *Agrarian History of England and Wales*, vol. IV: 1500–1640 (Cambridge, 1967), pp. 473, 478, 495.

[72] PRO E179/73/121, E179/73/124. Examination under ultra-violet light failed to reveal more than several groups of names from the roll. It is impossible to make any judgements as to numbers, names, or amounts taxed. All one can say is that the number of taxpayers was large; Newbury was urban in all senses. I failed to find any relevant entries.

[73] Reg Langton (Sarum) ii, fols. 35–42. Places of residence are rarely given; however, it is likely that, like trials in Buckinghamshire some years later, those tried were

our period proper, the trials should be noted for one reason at least: the name of William Smart.[74]

An early will made at Newbury was that of Thomas Collins, written in 1494.[75] Collins gave money to the church at Speen, as well as to the parish church of St Nicholas at Newbury, where Maurice Smart and John Winchcombe later worshipped. He gave a considerable number of sheep away as bequests, and left his holding in Chepestreet, Newbury, to his wife Constance. There is, sadly, no obvious connection with the ubiquitous Collins family elsewhere. However, Thomas was presumably a relative of Walter Collins and possibly connected to the Lollard family of that name, living east of Wantage. One of the supervisors of the will was John Zemand, whom I take to be the man who later emerged as a suspect Lollard, John Semand.

The Lollard evangelists Robert Pope, John Hacker, and Thomas Man later all visited the town, and Hacker's daughter and son-in-law, Elizabeth and John Fitton, were among those resident there, according to Foxe. Robert Pope named Humphrey Shoemaker, John Semand, a fishmonger, whom we now meet as an heretic, and Robert Geydon and his wife from the town; John Edmunds named Thomas Quicke, a weaver; and John Gardiner named William Ramsey of 'Newbery'. It is a very great pity that the Subsidy Returns of 1524 and 1525 are in such poor condition that these people are untraceable.

Only the fishmonger, John Semand, of the group listed by Foxe as living at Newbury, has left an extant will. It leads on to a treasure hunt of tantalizing excitement. He made it in 1532, leaving his soul to 'Almighty God, to our blessed lady saint Mary and to all the holy company of heaven', and asking for his body to be buried in 'our lady's chancell' in the parish church at Newbury. This place of burial suggests he was another prosperous Lollard.[76] He left 2d to the 'mother church of Sarum' and an unknown sum to the high altar, for 'tithes forgotten'. Additionally he gave 12d to the parish church for rebuilding. His servant John Myllyt, possibly an illegitimate son, was his residuary legatee and his executor. Semand instructed Myllyt to 'find Elisabeth my wyff mete and drink as long as she dus lyve and for to give unto her everywyle 4d of lawful money of England'. The supervisors of the will are named as William

---

brought to a central point from all over the archdeaconry, which was equivalent to the county. Since D.M. Smith, *Guide to Bishops' Registers of England and Wales* (London, 1981), gives full details of the whereabouts of the bishops' registers of the period, the information is not given here.

[74] See above pp. 114, 117, see below p. 128.
[75] PRO Prob 11/10/11.
[76] Berks. RO D/A1/1184.

Helier and Walter Collins. These two, and 'syr Roger Harbatyll', were witnesses to the will. Members of the Helier family are mentioned in Foxe, living in the parishes east of Wantage: however, connection is at present impossible.

Walter Collins of Newbury, supervisor and witness to Semand's will, was also son-in-law to Maurice Smart, and we shall next consider him. Both Semand's own will and that of Smart suggest several Lollard connections.

The parish of Shaw cum Donnington, adjacent to Newbury, was small and rural in character. The two subsidies for the parish give totals of twenty-six and twenty-eight taxable individuals; the total taxes payable were given as £9 4s 0d and £7 12s 2d.[77] Foxe mentions only two people from the parish: William Squire and his unnamed brother were both named by Robert Pope. One entry in the Subsidy is of interest. It will be remembered that the surname Smart has come to our attention several times before.[78] In the Subsidy of 1524 for Shaw a 'Morice Smert' is listed as paying taxes on the very substantial sum of £45 in goods.[79] He was the wealthiest inhabitant, and his is the only relevant entry. He is the wealthiest man we have so far considered in detail.

The will of 'Morrys Smart', tanner, of Newbury, made in 1550, is extant.[80] The preamble to the will is non-committal. He left his soul to 'almighty God' and 'my body to the churchyard or church to be buried': the preamble was not abbreviated. There were no religious bequests. He gave '40s or cloth for shyrts & smokes' to the poor of Shaw and Spene, the parish between Shaw and Newbury, without any conditions being set down. He also left lands, at Witney, Oxfordshire, to his wife 'during her widow estate', then to John Shipton, one of his sons-in-law. In fact he left a large family; several daughters married into local families. Among the other legatees was Margaret Smart, the daughter of Edmund Smart.[81] She was left 40s in 'lawful English money so that she might marry'. We shall come across Edmund Smart later, when the connection between Maurice Smart and named Lollards becomes assured. Another daughter, Isabel, married Richard Hyne.[82]

---

[77] PRO E179/73/121, E179/93/124. The second document is unclear.
[78] William Smart was accused in 1491 for reading illicit literature to Sawyer, together with William Carpenter. Richard Smart was burnt at Salisbury in 1503–4. Richard's residence is not given. William Smart was part of the group connected with Newbury, although his place of residence is not specifically given. Robert Pope had named 'one smart', a miller of Steventon, among a group of Berkshire Lollards. Maurice Smart was father-in-law of Walter Collins, supervisor to Semand's will.
[79] PRO E179/73/121.
[80] PRO Prob 11/33/22.
[81] See above, p. 117.
[82] Nearly 150 years later, in 1683, a Robert Hyne of Shaw, also a tanner, was named as a Quaker, VCH Berks., I, p. 398. I shall resist temptations to suggest connections;

This intriguing treasure hunt stops at the additional evidence to be gleaned from the Subsidy Roll for 'Woddespene', or Speen.[83] This settlement was adjacent to Newbury. One resident taxpayer was Edmund Smart, rated at £47 in goods, and no doubt the father of Margaret Smart, the legatee of Maurice Smart, and also the man who had been in possession of Ledisdale's Crown Inn at Oxford.[84] Maurice Smart also had lands in Speen.

Maurice Smart's occupation as a tanner, like several others listed by Foxe in Witney and South Oxfordshire, together with his possession of lands at Witney to leave to his wife, is reasonably suggestive of connections with Lollard groups there. Evidence produced below will substantiate the connections. A sentence in the will adds another clue to Lollard connections:

> I give unto John Smart 26s 8d of lawful English money to be paid yearly during his natural life at the feast of Saint Michael the Archangel, the nativity of our lord god, the annunciation of our lady and the nativity of St John Baptist by even portions and the said 26s 8d to be paid and borne by Walter Collins of Newbury in the county of Berks, mercer, and John Shipton of Shawe in the said county, tanner.

John Skipton and Walter Collins were his sons-in-law, since the latter had married Smart's daughter Joanne. Walter Collins had been supervisor of the Lollard John Semand's will.[85]

Smart had several servants. He was wealthy, despite the paucity of religious bequests. They point more to a refusal to give to the church than to an inability to do so. He had land at Speen, apart from that at Witney. His daughter Isabel Hynde received £20, and every grandchild (of which there were several), received £6 13s 4d at their marriage. Alice Smart, a servant, and presumably a relative, received £10. The only clerk to appear in the will was a legatee: George Barton, the parson of Bradfield.

If Maurice Smart was related to the William Smart accused in 1491 and the 'Mr Smart' named by Pope, or as is quite likely from his taxable capacity, was that individual, and if, as seems likely also, he had contacts at Witney who most probably included Lollard craftsmen, then we have before us a previously unknown example of the intercommunication which Foxe alludes to in his discussion of the Chiltern groups, and also a suggestion of continuity, no matter how tenuous. Here is a mutually supportive group, continuing in one way or another from the 1490s to

---

this particular case is perhaps another where a concentrated, parish study might yield important evidence of continuity of dissent among families in the era from the trials of the early sixteenth century to the 'sufferings of the Quakers'.

[83] PRO E179/73/121.
[84] See above, p. 117.
[85] See above, pp. 127–8.

1550. Whilst the little evidence we find in the wills could not be used to prove Lollardy, we have shown the beginnings of the contacts the sect needed to continue and thrive, though 'underground'. The lack of religious bequests in the second will may be due to a lack of interest towards the local church, but may also be due to the prevailing religious climate: 1550 was right in the middle of Edward VI's reign, and radical changes were taking place in theological and liturgical thinking. The first will shows no more than ambivalence towards the church. The giving is perhaps the minimum required, rather than offerings voluntarily made.

A final point emerges from the will of Maurice Smart. One of the overseers of the will was Master John Wynchecombe of 'Bughelbure', who was a son of the famous clothier entrepreneur, 'Jack of Newbury'. A second overseer was Master Thomas Winchcombe of Newbury. John Winchcombe the elder, alias Smalwoode, had died in 1520, having made his will the previous year.[86] There was much legend built around Jack, some of it probably apocryphal.[87] His will gives us no assistance. However, his son was definitely an enthusiastic reformer. He gave financial assistance to the government at the time of the northern rebellions, in 1536–7. In 1538–9 he assisted Miles Coverdale during the latter's visit, undertaken at Thomas Cromwell's instigation, to detect popish books and 'the hindrance of religion'.[88] Cromwell later gave Winchcombe an order for 1,000 kerseys, presumably for services rendered. This is the kind of link, like that between Nicholas Durdant and 'Master Doctor Haynes',[89] that illustrates a very real connection between Lollardy and mainstream reformers.

The families and individuals discussed above were accused of heresy, or had close personal and social contacts with such persons. Yet they all, apparently, seem to have kept their place in society generally, especially with regard to religion. They were outward conformists in every respect. Other families seem, at first sight, to have had an unorthodox individual within them, and yet remained untainted with heresy. It is extremely important that such Lollards were of the 'better', or 'chiefer' sort.[90] They were for the most part, dominant members of their society, with contacts

---

[86] PCC Prob 11 Ayloffe fo. 27.
[87] Winchcombe employed hundreds of weavers who worked from their homes. He was said to have supplied 100 of his men, fully equipped, for the battle of Flodden, in 1513, and to have entertained Henry VIII and Katharine of Aragon at his house; see DNB, XXI (London, 1976), pp. 154, 156. He lived at Bucklebury, two miles north-east of Thatcham, the residence of several of those accused in the 1490s.
[88] VCH Berks., I, pp. 22–3; LP, XIV, pp. 245, 253, 396, 444; DNB, XXI, p. 626, Coverdale had consorted with Lollards at Steeple Bumpstead in Essex, see Foxe, V, p. 40.
[89] See above, p. 122.
[90] Henry French, 'The "Middle Sort" of People in Essex and Suffolk, 1630–1720: A Social and Economic Study' (Cambridge, PhD, in progress, 1993), considers the terminology of the 'better', 'chiefer', and 'middling sort'.

throughout the region, and with substantial estates. Lollards used that wealth and position to sustain their beliefs. Did they also use their standing to develop a system of 'gathered churches'? That is a question we consider in the next chapter.

CHAPTER 3

A gathered church? Lollards and their society

DEREK PLUMB

I

Lollards were not insignificant members of isolated communities.[1] They were found at all levels of rural and county society and they were totally integrated into that society. Their beliefs, which must have been known to their orthodox neighbours, did not cause them to be ostracized. It might even be argued, given the importance of the city of London in economic and demographical terms in early modern England, that Lollardy was also important within England's premier urban society.

Given that Lollards continued to lead a normal economic and social life throughout the early sixteenth century, how did they maintain their faith? How did they organize their 'church'? To what extent did they turn their backs on the established church? I am not looking here at their beliefs as such, although these will often come into our discussions, but to their ecclesiastical organization. That Lollardy was 'a faith produced in houses, not in churches'[2] might seem a statement that does not need making, for the family and the home were most important factors in continuing the maintenance of the faith, as the church could never be. Where we find evidence of continuity, it is through families,[3] and many of those families were sufficiently well-off to have servants who themselves were agents of the sect. Indeed, servants played an often under-

---

[1] For a full discussion of the social status of Lollards, see Derek Plumb, 'John Foxe and the Later Lollards of the Mid-Thames Valley' (Cambridge, PhD, 1987), chapter 2, pp. 15–29. Since I completed my thesis, most historians have accepted the overwhelming evidence, much of it produced by myself, showing that Lollards were no mere 'threshers and weavers', but important and fully integrated members of their societies.

[2] Richard G. Davies, 'Lollardy and Locality', *Trans. Royal Hist. Soc.*, 6th Ser., 1 (1991), p. 195. I am grateful to Dr Davies for allowing me to read his paper in manuscript.

[3] The Phipps of Hughenden, the Popes of Amersham and West Hendred, the Scriveners of Amersham and Chesham, and of course the Hardings of the same two villages give us ample examples of continuity of belief going back to the 1460s. How many more families continued to teach heresy within the confines of their homes during this period?

rated part in the dissemination of Lollard texts and in the intercommunication of the various groups in south-east England. According to Dr
Davies, 'kinship ... turns up as the major conduit for the spread and
maintenance of Lollardy ... [if] ... Wyclifitism was what you knew, Lollardy was whom you knew'.[4]

But how far did that 'kinship' spread? Were there really isolated groups
in hidden communities who scarcely spoke one to the other? How did
heterodox groups ensure the continuity of their beliefs? How did they
practise those beliefs, and how did they overcome the threat to their
existence that the established church, by its very nature, posed? Did they
carry on their own sacramental regime or did they rely on the established
church for the 'essentials' of Christianity? Were the Lollards of the mid-
Thames valley, especially those in the Chiltern hills, members of a
'gathered' church? These questions are difficult to answer. A secret sect,
even one that fraternizes with its orthodox neighbours, is, by definition,
difficult to search out.[5]

Dr Davies, in his necessarily broad examination of Lollard society,
attempts to answer some of these questions. He makes some assumptions which the evidence I have gathered together would seem to contra-
dict. The evidence discussed below, together with that examined in
Chapter 2 above, shows clearly that Lollards had a very high profile in
their communities. In will making, land and commodity dealing, and in
their participation in everyday activities in the parish, Lollards were there,
dealing with their fellow-heretics and with many others of their neighbours, who were, apparently, orthodox in their beliefs. I find it hard to
believe that the orthodox neighbours of Lollards were unaware of the
latter's heresy.

Dr Davies thinks differently. 'Lollards were always wary of letting their
orthodox neighbours know too much.'[6] Many of those discussed below
were among the richest in their parishes. Others were much involved in
local parish activities, holding office in the church or in the parish, holding land of other residents, or carrying out their businesses in the locality.
Either many apparently orthodox members of their communities, themselves often among the richest in the parish, participated in the processes
mentioned above, with Lollards, known or otherwise, or many more
were Lollards than we have evidence of.

There was continuity as well. Dr Davies is cautious,[7] yet many of the
families we discuss could trace their heterodoxy back to ancestors alive

---

[4] Davies, 'Lollardy and Locality', p. 212. There is enough evidence from the investigations undertaken by the church to suggest that locality, as much as relationships,
was important for the propagation of heresy.
[5] S. Brigden, *London and the Reformation* (Oxford, 1989), p. 87.
[6] Davies, 'Lollardy and Locality', p. 203.
[7] Ibid., p. 205.

in the mid- to late fifteenth-century, and as Mrs Nesta Evans shows below
(Chapter 7 and Appendix B) nonconformity was amazingly continuous
in the genealogical lines of several families, and in several areas, in the
Chiltern Hundreds, extending into parishes in Hertfordshire and
Middlesex.[8]

The importance of peripatetic missionaries was almost certainly greater
than Dr Davies suggests.[9] They were not only preachers and teachers, of
course. Several brought books and texts into the centres of heresy, and
others, less well known to us, came from London to preach to gathered
groups behind closed doors. The meeting at Speen, in Hughenden in
1530, when Nicholas Field of London spoke to a group at John Taylor's
house, is but one example. Field could have been a local man made good
within reformist circles. There are others of whom we know something:
William Littlepage, Thurstan Harding, Thomas Man, the ubiquitous
Hacker, and others, were well known and spoken of in revered tones,
but there were others who travelled from parish to parish, from county
to county, from diocese to diocese, in order to preach, read, and no
doubt give aid in whatever ways they could. One remembers Alice and
Robert Collins (not always working together), Isabel Harding, James
Morden, John Ledisdale, and so on. Their contacts were widespread.
Some of them attained enormous spiritual status among members of the
sect.

What concerns me particularly is Dr Davies' argument that 'the Lollards
in 1511 and 1521 reflected the geography (of the Chiltern Hundreds)'.[10]
According to Dr Davies: 'Physical geography played its part in the sect's
life.'[11] True, the county is divided by the Chilterns and heresy was a
manifestation of the area south of the Icknield Way which ran along the
foot of the hills on the north, but it really will not do for Dr Davies to
say that: 'The Chesham Lollards had some reasonable [sic] contact with
those in Amersham, much less with those in the Missendens and next
to nothing with those in Hughenden ... Their lives, though only six
miles apart, were in a different world.'[12]

The evidence below, selected from a cornucopia of evidence found by
myself when I examined in detail the lives of the Lollards of the mid-
Thames valley named by Foxe, shows how widespread and fluid were
the connections between Lollards and their neighbours, whatever their

---

[8] See below, Chs. 7 and 8, and Map 7, p. 295, for the similarity between the areas
   within which later Lollards and Quakers in the Upperside Meeting practised their
   faith and met together.
[9] Davies, 'Lollardy and Locality', p. 202.
[10] Ibid., p. 207.
[11] Ibid., p. 206.
[12] Ibid., p. 207.

religious proclivities. From London to Hambledon, from Amersham to Chelmsford, from Uxbridge to Wycombe, Lollards communicated with each other (Map 3). To paraphrase Dr Davies, Lollards were only too pleased to jog over the hill, to wade through rivers, to suffer the appalling roads of the area ... to share an epistle with each other.[13]

I hope that by looking at some of the evidence we have of groups meeting together in the area, we can answer some of the questions I posed above, and which Dr Davies mentioned in his paper. I therefore intend to examine in turn the members of groups meeting in particular places named by each other, and all their local connections which I can find.

II

The Chiltern Hundreds lay conveniently close to London for local sectaries to have used the valuable connections and support to be found in that city.[14] South Buckinghamshire not only had several market towns within the area,[15] but also acted like a funnel, not just for local produce but for all traffic moving from the north-west of England, Wales, and the West Country to London.[16] The ebb and flow of such economic activity meant that the Lollards of the area were given considerable opportunity to maintain contacts with others elsewhere, as it doubtless did to traders in wool, clothing, and associated trades. The possible connections between Lollardy and those particular trades has been discussed in Chapter 1. Traffic along these trade routes would consist not just of traders of food and domestic produce. The carriers of books would lose themselves among the carts of those on the road. Indeed the carts themselves might

[13] Ibid., p. 207.
[14] There is little doubting the importance of south Buckinghamshire in the annals of Lollard history. From the earliest days of the sect the area to the south of the Icknield Way is mentioned. K.B. McFarlane, *John Wycliffe and the Beginnings of English Nonconformity* (London, 1952), passim; idem, *Lancastrian Kings and Lollard Knights* (Oxford, 1972), pp. 139–232; Thomson, *The Later Lollards*. It was most certainly the hiding place and the breeding ground of heresy throughout the fifteenth century. The trials which took place from the 1460s until the years of the Reformation time and again show the central place the parishes and settlements of the area had in the workings of the sect.
[15] Amersham, Beaconsfield, Chesham, Colnbrook, High Wycombe, and Marlow were all market towns (Map 5, p. 282). See Julian Cornwall, 'English Country Towns in the Fifteen-Twenties', *Economic History Review*, 2nd Ser., 15, 1, (Utrecht, 1962–3), pp. 54–9. For a full discussion on the geography of the area see Thirsk (ed.), *Agrarian History of England and Wales*, IV; Michael Reed, *The Buckinghamshire Landscape* (London, 1979); and my thesis, passim. Lucy Toulmin Smith (ed.), *The Itinerary of John Leland in or about the Years 1535–1543*, 4 vols. (London, 1908), IV, gives a delightful description of the area. All the market towns mentioned had resident Lollard groups.
[16] See below, Michael Frearson, Ch. 7, pp. 275–87, for roads, carriers, and books, and p. 284 Map 6, for inns and alehouses in the Chiltern Hundreds.

be used to transport books from town to town, surreptitiously. At the end of a tiring day an inn might be the scene of similar undercover transactions.[17]

Visits from peripatetic preachers gave support to the groups and supplied much-needed texts, but beliefs needed constant nurturing by others living nearby. It was within local communities that the individuals of the sect, if they were to survive at all, would gain much of their comfort and strength. There was no conflict between the evangelism of outsiders and this essential local nurturing in a stable environment.

Not surprisingly, those living in the parishes between the slopes of the Chilterns and the River Thames were well aware of what was going on elsewhere. Indeed, it has been suggested recently that 'the continuity of religious dissent [in the Chiltern Hundreds] is in part attributable to good communications'.[18] Just as Mrs Evans has shown the continuity of Lollard families in the area under discussion, so she shows (Chapter 7) that Quakers and Baptists of the area were often descendants of Lollards, or lived alongside members of families whose ancestors had been Lollards. Dr Peter Spufford demonstrates the quite extraordinary, and abnormal, stability of the dissenting local population. Lollards met together frequently. There are many gatherings mentioned in Foxe, or at least suggested by the wording he uses. I happen to believe that the typographical layout used in the original edition of *The Acts and Monuments* is particularly important in understanding relationships among the heretics. Below, we look at a few of the groups he listed. This type of study may well result in us entering a cul-de-sac, but it equally often opens up a vista which we may at least glance down.

III

Robert Bartlet, a member of a large and affluent Lollard family living at Amersham, named a group meeting before 1511 who 'had resorted together many times, reading and conferring among themselves . . . if any came in amongst them that were not of their side . . . (they would) keep all silence'.[19] Presumably Bartlet was intimate with this group, even if he did not attend all their gatherings. He named Elizabeth Dean, wife of Richard Dean of West Wycombe, Emma Tilesworth, wife of William

---

[17] Dr Frearson mentions an inn in Broad Street, London, and another around the corner in Friday Street where books were bought and sold. The area had long been so used. During the 'persecution in London for the Six Articles' many were accused, including 'The good man of the Saracen's Head in Friday-Street', Foxe, V, p. 446. I have not footnoted references to Foxe, except occasionally. The majority of the evidence regarding the Buckinghamshire Lollards is found in volume IV, pp. 221–46.

[18] Frearson, Ch. 7, pp. 275–87.

[19] Foxe, IV, p. 222.

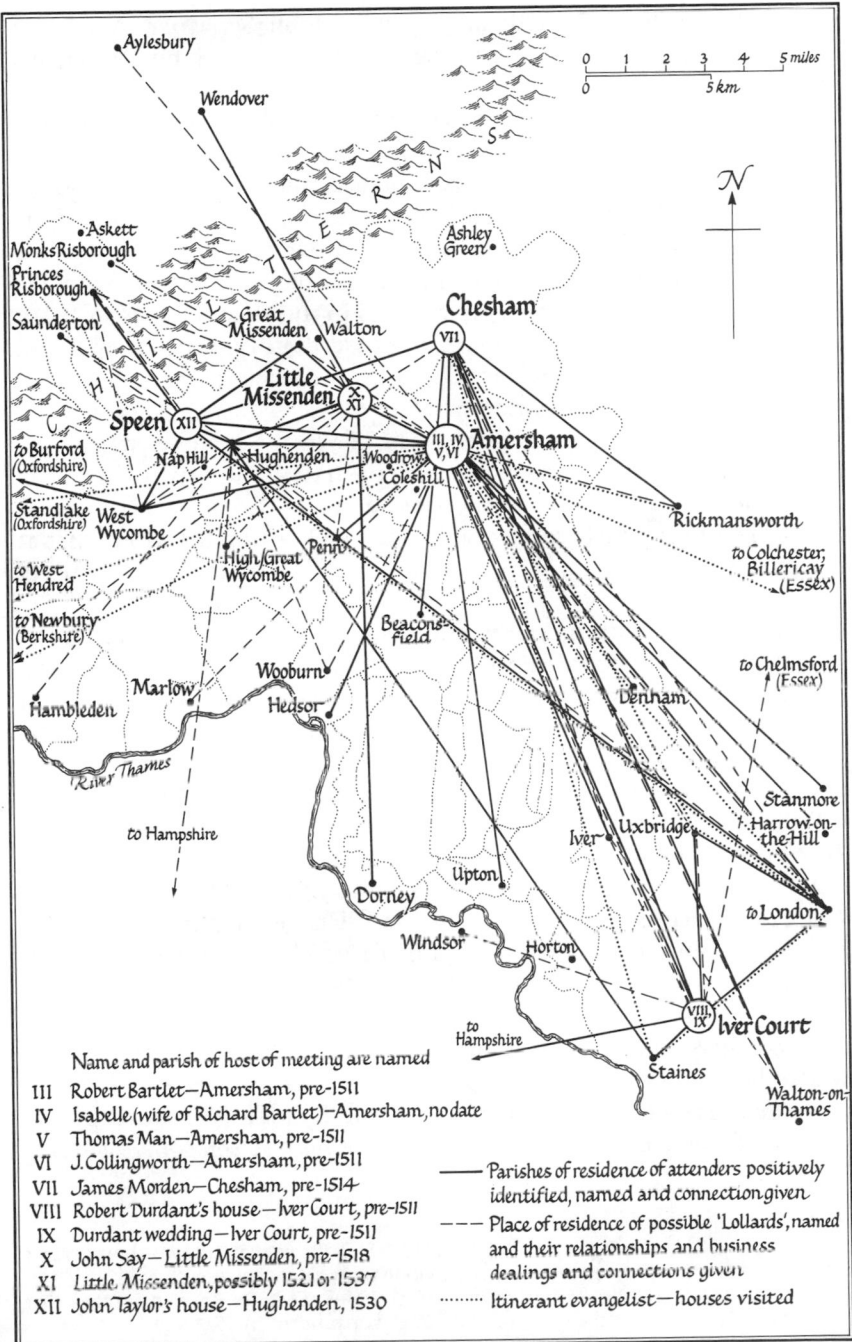

Map 3. Lollard meetings and their connections in the Chilterns

Name and parish of host of meeting are named

III   Robert Bartlet—Amersham, pre-1511
IV   Isabelle (wife of Richard Bartlet)—Amersham, no date
V   Thomas Man—Amersham, pre-1511
VI   J. Collingworth—Amersham, pre-1511
VII   James Morden—Chesham, pre-1514
VIII   Robert Durdant's house—Iver Court, pre-1511
IX   Durdant wedding—Iver Court, pre-1511
X   John Say—Little Missenden, pre-1518
XI   Little Missenden, possibly 1521 or 1537
XII   John Taylor's house—Hughenden, 1530

——— Parishes of residence of attenders positively identified, named and connection given

——— Place of residence of possible 'Lollards', named and their relationships and business dealings and connections given

········ Itinerant evangelist—houses visited

Tilesworth, William Grinder and his wife, John Scrivener, Alexander Mastel, William Tilesworth, Thurstan Littlepage, and John Bartlet, his brother.

Robert Bartlet was a rich man. He had borne a faggot at the burning of William Tilesworth, in 1511, having been 'put out of his farm and goods'.[20] In the Muster for Amersham he had lands worth 15s and goods worth £40: a rich man indeed. He is not named in the Subsidy for Amersham. Presumably he was in exile from the town under the terms of his penance. Katharine Bartlet, widow, his mother, was listed, with £8. Robert had been mentioned several times in the examinations in 1521–2: he knew many in Amersham, had visited the house of Thomas and Alice Harding to discuss matters with William Tilesworth, and was forced to name others during the inquiries.

Elizabeth Dean, wife of Richard Dean of West Wycombe, was apparently not rich. Neither was her husband. In 1522 he was listed in the Muster at West Wycombe, with goods valued at £2, and land valued at 1s. In the Subsidy Richard was said to have £2. When the group met at Taylor's house at Speen, Richard was there. He was then said to be of Chesham.

Later in Foxe, William Tilesworth was said to be a goldsmith, 'sometime apprentice of John Barret'.[21] Connections with London are found continually when searching for Lollards in the mid-Thames valley. Often those with such connections were craftsmen, and comfortably off. Emma, wife of William Tilesworth, was presumably so. The family are found in London in dispute with the ecclesiastical authorities into the 1550s.[22]

William Grinder and his wife are well known to us (see above, Chapter 2). William did penance at Tilesworth's burning. He was said by Thomas Coupland not to be able to say the Creed in Latin. John Hacker said he was of Cookham, on the River Thames.[23] His geography was not that bad. In the Muster, Grinder was found at Hedsor (part of Little Marlow) with goods worth £25. In the Subsidy for *Marlow Parva cum Hedsor* he was listed with £20. He was a wealthy man. His wife no doubt travelled in style to Amersham. At the same time, possibly, William was preoccupied with a dispute in the Court of Chancery.[24] Grinder was a woodseller, and his trade is likely to have connected him with London (see above, pp. 58, 62–3). Following the cancellation of an agreement to sell some 'standing

---

[20] Foxe, IV, pp. 123–4.
[21] Foxe, IV, p. 228. The Significat, PRO C85/115/10, confirms that Tilesworth was burnt in 1511. The meeting discussed here obviously predates that event.
[22] Brigden, *London and the Reformation*, pp. 97–8, 104–5, 568. Dr Brigden implies that William Tilesworth is the son of the Dr Tilesworth burnt in 1511.
[23] Foxe, IV, pp. 123, 227, 240.
[24] PRO C1/511/69.

timber at Wooburn' he was suing John and Margaret Colverhouse. The latter was 'executrix' and late the wife of John Puttenham. Grinder claimed that they had failed to pay for the cancellation of the sale. The result of the case is unknown, but the parties in it are found in the Muster Returns and Subsidy Rolls for Wooburn, Penn, and Wycombe: they were all comfortably off.

Some years later, no doubt now an 'elder' among the Lollards, William Grinder was a supervisor for the will of Nicholas Durdant, son of Robert Durdant, at Stanmore.[25] Durdant was not poor himself, of course, being the holder of the manor of Stanmore. William Grinder and his wife moved around the Thames valley during the early decades of the six-teenth century: on business no doubt, but also maintaining contact with fellow-heretics.

Given that the meeting described by Robert Bartlet took place before 1511, John Scrivener is no doubt the elder of that name, found in Foxe. He too did penance at the burning of William Tilesworth, who was his one-time apprentice.[26] He came from heterodox stock. William Scrivener was burnt in 1511, along with Tilesworth: perhaps the name was a mis-take on the signification.[27] He seems to have been much involved in arguments with his neighbours, often culminating in an appearance before the archdeacon's court. In 1489 he was in dispute over the estate of Christine Guloffer, with Isabel Lovechilde or Screvener (sic). In 1490 he was involved in a case at Amersham, with John Fisher, and Thomas Russell and John Salter of Chalfont St Giles. John Bartlet, the Lollard, was his compurgator. Later, when he was named as the son of Robert Scriv-ener, the case appeared before the Court of Chancery, with Robert Derby and Thomas Scrivener named.[28] It was a dispute over land, as were so many of the cases we read of.

John Scrivener was certainly dead by 1522. Sybell Scrivener, presumably the Isabel mentioned above, was listed in the Muster as a widow living at Amersham. She had land worth 10s and goods worth £2. She made her will on 12 August 1526, whilst living at Amersham.[29] She left her soul to 'my savyor Jesu &c', perhaps an indication of less than total commit-ment to the established thinking of the day. Her tenement at 'Whyllaynd', worth 10s in 1522, she gave to her daughter Elizabeth. The residue legatee

[25] PRO Prob 11/27/22.
[26] Tilesworth was previously named as the apprentice of John Barret, goldsmith of London; presumably Tilesworth, and Scrivener, were also goldsmiths. The thought occurs that the trade was associated with heretical practices. Other evidence from London certainly suggests this to be the case. See Brigden, *London and the Reformation*, passim.
[27] PRO C85/115/10.
[28] Bucks. RO DA/We/141/144; PRO C1/108/88.
[29] Bucks. RO DA/We/154/14.

in an otherwise uninteresting document was Thomas Saunders the younger, who is listed in the Muster with £40 in goods, and was the son of Richard Saunders' brother, also Thomas. The 'godly elite', if we apply such a label to the Saunders family, obviously deigned to mix with their social inferiors, not that Scrivener was at the bottom of the social scale, of course. The Saunders and Scrivener families were probably related.

Alexander Mastel is an enigma. Only in 'far-away' Denham do we find anyone of that surname in the documents to hand: in the Muster, John Mastel (who had named the daughter of John Phip of Hughenden) had land worth £1, and at adjacent Horton he was listed with goods worth £20. The figures in the Subsidy showed he was taxed on land worth £1 and goods worth £12. John was another litigious Lollard. In 1491 he had faced the archdeacon's court, having been accused by the rector of Denham of a misdemeanour. Later, in the Court of Requests, he was in dispute with John Salcoke of Amersham, who later detected several Lollards, and others over a piece of land. He then appeared in Star Chamber in dispute with Thomas Durdant, of Denham, over an issue of which we know nothing.[30] Mastel is another example of an argumentative individual being involved in the seeking out of heretics, and we may well wonder whether such matters coloured the views of those involved, on both sides, but especially those who became leading witnesses against heretics. 'Alexander' may well have been a mistaken Christian name for 'John', since the surname is uncommon.

Thurstan Littlepage is another enigma, if only because of the problem we have in deciding on his real surname: We are sorely tempted to say 'Will the real Mr Littlepage, Harding, Africke, or Page step forward, please?' Such are the very different names which many of the same individuals we are aware of answer to, in the pages of Foxe. This chapter is not the place to attempt to untangle that web, but I would suggest that Thurstan Harding, listed in the Muster for Little Missenden with £7 in goods, may well be the same man.

The last member of the group mentioned by Robert Bartlet, who 'had resorted together many times, reading and conferring among themselves' was his brother, John Bartlet. John, as we noted above, had been involved in a case involving John Scrivener in 1490. In the Muster and Subsidy for Upton, a parish near the Thames, a John Bartlet is found: in the Muster he has land worth 1s 8d and goods worth £6 13s 8d; in the Subsidy there are two entries, each giving £2. If this is the same man, then we have another example of the variation of economic, and so social, standing of a group of individuals who, coming from a variety of backgrounds in the area, gathered together to follow their faith.

---

[30] Bucks. RO DA/We/1/137v–8; PRO Req 2/4/145; PRO Stac 2/17/151.

IV

Isabel Bartlet, wife of Richard Bartlet and sister-in-law of Robert Bartlet, in her turn named Richard Hobbes and Henry Hobbes of Hughenden; Herne's wife; Herne, widow of Amersham; and Thomas Cooper of Amersham, husbandman.[31] Why did she name this particular group as she did?

Isabel had married into the large and heretical Bartlet family of Amersham, but she was a Lollard in her own right. She had been a member of the sect before their marriage, and had to be put under some pressure before she detected her husband. As we have already established, the Bartlet family were comfortably off, and leaders in the heterodox community in Amersham. What was the connection between Isabel and the groups she named?

Isabel, then a widow, made her will on 23 February 1547, whilst living at Amersham.[32] The will is badly damaged. Important details, names, etc., are illegible. But we can rescue something from the document. Katharine Bartlet, her daughter, who was possibly named after her grandmother, or the shrine of that name in the parish church, was given all her household. Her brother, one Partridge, was supervisor of the will. Several of that name are found in the Muster at Ashley Green, Chesham. William Pope was overseer. Others mentioned as legatees, include Joanne Good, members of whose family can be found in Hughenden and Missenden but not in Amersham or Chesham. Agnes White and Thomas Wor. . .y also received small legacies.

According to Foxe, Richard Hobbes and Henry Hobbes were of Hughenden. 'Mr' Hobbes and his unnamed sons were named by Thomas Holmes. They are not named by anyone else, although Roger Dods of Burford named two brothers Radulph and William Hobbes living at West Wycombe. Henry, of course, was present at the making of Nicholas Durdant's will at Staines in 1538. The Hobbes family are not found at Hughenden, and this appears to be a mistake of Foxe's.

William Hobbes, of West Wycombe, made his will in 1525.[33] He appeared before Bishop Smith, probably during the 1511 trials, being handed over by the curate of West Wycombe. William Hobbes is found in the Muster for West Wycombe with land valued at £2 and goods at the considerable figure of £12. His son, John, was also listed, with £1 in goods.

In his will Hobbes made no provision for his soul; there is no religious preamble at all. He left 8d to the high altar at Wycombe, and a bushel of

---

[31] Foxe, IV, p. 224.
[32] Bucks. RO DA/We/7/117.
[33] Bucks. RO DA/We/2/64.

barley for the repair of the bell. His widow, Elizabeth, was given a tenement at 'Parke yate', with three closes attached, together with 'kyne, 2
weynars, a black amllyng horse and the sorele fore horse'. The bequests
to his children show he had considerable numbers of livestock and several acres of crops. The flock of sheep alone comes to over fifty head.
Hobbes the Lollard was affluent. His witnesses were led by the vicar, Sir
Robert King, and include members of the Ravening family, who are found
in Hughenden and West Wycombe. Unfortunately, connections with the
family in 'Hughenden' known to Isabel Bartlet are difficult to make.

Isabel Bartlet also named 'Herne's wife' and 'Herne, widow of Amersham'. Thomas Halfeaker of Amersham, who was well aware of the Bartlets' participation in heretical goings-on, named 'Herne's wife, now the
wife of Waiver'. Elsewhere in Foxe mention is made of Heron or Horne.
These appear to be variants on the same family name.[34] The family is
mentioned by William Littlepage, Thomas Holmes, Robert Pope and
John Hacker, as well as by Isabel Bartlet and Halfeaker.

In the Muster Certificates, Roger Herne or Heron is found at Little
Missenden, with goods worth £1 6s 8d; Laurence Herne is found at Hughenden with goods at £1, Thomas Heron is found at Saunderton, adjacent
to Hughenden, but down the Chiltern scarp, with goods worth £1, John
Heron or Horne, who was a carpenter, is found at Hambledon, also
adjacent to Hughenden, with goods worth £1. John is also found in the
Subsidy for Hambledon with £1. Overall, the family seem to have been
labourers and craftsmen, barely liable to taxation. What connection did
they have with Isabel Bartlet, other than their faith? Isabel Bartlet's connection with the west of the county, the area around Hughenden, and
possibly West Wycombe, was obviously strong. Can we show any other
connections between the Bartlet family and the parish of Hughenden?
The answer is a resounding yes!

John Wellysbourne made his will at Hughenden in 1521.[35] We are not
here interested in the detail of the will. His daughter was 'Mastres Anne
Bartlet'. One of his executors (the other being his wife) was Thomas
Widmore, whose wife was named and who was related to John Phip.[36]

John Widmore, of Nap Hill, Hughenden, made his will on 31 July 1547,
'being sike in body but hole and perfect remembrance lawde be unto
almighty god'.[37] His soul is bequeathed to 'Almighty God my maker,
saviour and redeemer, and to the glorious virgin Mary his most blessed

---

[34] Foxe, IV, pp. 224, 226, 228, 235, 584 (Herne); 226, 240 (Heron); 229 (Horne).
[35] Bucks. RO WA/Wf/1/40v. Wellysbourne is found in the Muster for Hughenden with
     £2 in land.
[36] Foxe, IV, pp. 226, 235, 237, 240.
[37] Bucks. RO DA/Wf/2/100 (original), DA/We/6/398. Nap Hill is halfway between
     Hughenden and Bradenham.

mother and all the company of heaven'. The mother church of Lincoln received 2d and the lights at Hughenden 4d. Christian Herne, his servant, and presumably related to the Herne family above, received half a quarter of barley. Joanne his wife, and Katharine his daughter were to share the house, and were to be joint executors. One of the witnesses, Thomas Barnard, may be related to the Barnards at Amersham and Chesham.

Laurence Herne of Hughenden, named by Robert Pope, made his will on 15 May 1556, probate being given on 18 June.[38] He was dying. The religious preamble was conservative, yet there were no bequests to the church at all. The Muster Certificate suggested that Herne was poor, yet legacies and bequests suggest he had improved his financial position since the 1520s: perhaps he had come into his inheritance. His wife Alice received six sheep, and each of his two sons, Edward and Thomas, received two sheep and two lambs. Two other bequests included lambs. He had a reasonable flock; presumably a good number of sheep went to his son John (or had already been handed over). His wife and John, his son (possibly the Lollard of Hambledon), were residue legatees. The witnesses were all Lollards, or of Lollard families: Thomas Clerk the elder, Thomas Wydmer, and Frances Howse. It is perhaps indicative of more than any official relationship that the wealthy Thomas Wydmer was present at the poorer man's will making.

William Fastendich made his will at Hughenden in 1557, on 8 March.[39] A man of that name had been accused of criticizing the sacrament around 1530.[40] Probate was awarded on 30 March. He was living at Wooburn.[41] 'Ffist and cheflye I beqth my soule to the mercye of all mightye god the father and sonne & the holye ghoste'; there was no mention of Mary in this late Marian will. There were no religious bequests. Agnes Bartlet, daughter of John Bartlet of Wooburn, received William's great coffer. Thomas Bartlet received a pewter platter. William asked Robert Stowe to settle an agreement previously made between himself and Richard Harding. It seems probable that John Bartlet was his son-in-law, for John's children are among those receiving legacies. Those legacies would be paid after the sale of several items of pewter, including 'my great pan'. The witnesses are not known to us. Fastendich of Hughenden gives further evidence of connections across the rivers and hills, with Chesham.

Thomas Cowper of Amersham, husbandman, is the odd man out in this group. Perhaps he was an anchorman; perhaps the contact for the group. Cowper lived at Woodrow in Amersham. He may be listed in the

---

[38] Bucks. RO DA/Wf/2/299 (original), DA/We/8/201.
[39] Bucks. RO DA/Wf/3/87 (original), DA/We/8/276.
[40] Foxe, V, p. 454.
[41] Possibly the manor of Woburn in Chesham, rather than the parish of Wooburn. The documents are unclear.

Subsidy for Stanwell with goods at £4. His son Roger is found in the Muster for Amersham with land worth 16s 8d and goods worth £20. In the Subsidy Robert is found listed with £18. Thomas no doubt knew Isabel Bartlet. No wonder Isabel Bartlet mentioned the group from Hughenden. She was related to them, and knew only too well of their connections and involvement in the sect.

V

John Scrivener named a group that met at the house of Thomas Man at Amersham, before 1511: Thomas Grove, of London, butcher; William Glasbroke, of Harrow-on-the-Hill; Christopher Glasbroke, of London; William Tilesworth, of London, goldsmith (sometime apprentice of John Barret). The group often met together and conferred 'of matters of religion'.[42]

Scrivener is already known to us, of course. As we saw above, he was much involved in everyday activities in Amersham and elsewhere. He was also, obviously, deeply involved in the activities of the sect. He was burnt in 1521.

Thomas Man was one of the peripatetic preachers so important to the sect. He had contacts in areas from Amersham to London, from Uxbridge to Billericay, from Colchester to Newbury. With his wife, he taught and preached throughout the Lollard communities. He was said to be one of four 'principal readers or instructors in the sect', and to have spent some time on the run from the authorities. He fled from Colchester to Newbury, then to Amersham. He hid in the home of Andrew Randall at Rickmansworth, and at the home of William King at Uxbridge. He was finally caught, and, still being 'obstinate', was burnt at Smithfield in 1518.[43] Evidence would suggest a Lollard pedigree of which we know little. In 1528 Thomas Vincent faced the Bishop of London. He was said to be the father-in-law of one burnt for heresy about fourteen years earlier. Vincent's daughter was married to Thomas Austy, who knew Hacker. Man was no doubt on friendly terms with them all.[44] Man and his wife do not appear in the records for Buckinghamshire, although they were both members of the sect. Nor does Thomas Grove, who, although said to be a butcher of London, may well have been another local with London connections. He was wealthy, being able to offer the bishop's officers the large sum of £20 to escape doing open penance. He had refused to go

[42] Foxe, IV, p. 228.
[43] Foxe, IV, pp. 208–14, 226, 229, 230. Man was said to be 'obstinate' in 1511, when Tilesworth was burnt. PRO C85/115/10.
[44] John Strype, Ecclesiastical Memorials . . ., 2 vols. (London, 1721), I, part I, p. 115; LP, IV (ii), 4029.

to church, hiding instead at the house of William Tracher at Amersham.

Grove may have lived at Penn for a time. A man of that name was involved in a court case with John Gardiner of Great Missenden who was possibly another Lollard. They were plaintiffs in the case,[45] which may have originated in the conditions of the will of Richard Gardener of Chesham, made in 1493, when a Thomas Grove was a witness. But that is mere supposition.

William Glasbroke, of Harrow-on-the-Hill, is not so difficult to pin down. He and Christopher Glasbroke of London (their relationship is not given) appear elsewhere in Foxe. Thomas Halfeaker said Christopher was a miller. William's sister, Joan, was named by Thomas Holmes. Glasbroke may have had local connections, which drew him to Amersham, and from which he gained his faith. In 1491 a John Glasbroke had been named in a case involving residents of Chesham.[46]

In the large parish of Harrow-on-the-Hill over 200 were eligible for taxation in 1524. William 'Glasbrocre' is listed, with 20s in wages. Here we have social status changing through the life-cycle, for when Glasbroke made his will, written at Harrow in 1548, he was said to be a yeoman.[47] Just like Nicholas Durdant (above, Chapter 2) he saw the new religious climate of Edward VI's reign as a sign for him to declare his opinions. He 'yealds [his] soul into the hands of God, trusting that through his marcy I have and shall have full remission of all my synnes by the merites of christes passion', then moves straight into the 'temporall riches' he wishes to dispose of.

His reasonable estate was balanced by his debts. He left instructions that all 'my horses, my cartles and my ploughes be solde to pay my debts withall'. His three cows, and all his hay and wheat, except 'sixe quarters of wheat to sowe the grounds' were also to be sold. He seems to have been heavily in debt; his moveables were also to be sold for similar purposes. The residue, if there was any, went to his wife Joyanne (possibly his 'sister' Joan). His elder son James got his house in Harrow, on the condition that his younger son John was allowed to live there, paying James 16s yearly. The lease of a house in Sudbury, a village in the south of the parish, he gave to James. His executors were Sir Richard Rade, knight, Mr Sithcott, gent, and his sons John Glasbroke and James Glasbroke. The witnesses are unknown. They are not in the Subsidy. There are no religious bequests, despite his apparent 'wealth'; perhaps he could not afford it.

Glasbroke is another example of the lone Lollard, a common enough feature of this study, who gives no indication of Lollard connections,

---

[45] PRO Req 2/3/339.
[46] Bucks. RO DA/We/1/138v.
[47] PRO Prob 11/32/16.

yet is 'named' as such, and supports that contention by declaring his nonconformist beliefs early on. He may have had to visit Amersham to meet fellow-practitioners while he kept his views very private in his home town.

William Tilesworth, of London, goldsmith (sometime apprentice of John Barret), was the last member of this strange group covertly meeting in Amersham. We found him above (in group III), meeting with a group at Amersham involving 'known men' from Hughenden and Amersham. It was at Tilesworth's burning, in 1511, in Stanley Close, Amersham, that Thomas Man had been referred to as 'obstinate'.[48] His wife moved to Hawkwell in Essex after her husband's death. His sons (if such they were) Robert and Thomas lived in Abchurch Lane and Budge Rowe in London, practising their trade as tailors (see Chapter 1, pp. 53, 55). They were to the fore in Lollard circles.[49] Of the family in Amersham, there is no other information.

The group is frustrating to the seeker of information on Lollards. It is indicative, however, of the lengths individuals would go to hear their faith propounded. There can be no doubt that such meetings were going on all the time, behind closed doors.

VI

The importance of women in Lollardy; their role as teachers, preachers, and readers, as well as simply that of encouraging matriarchs supporting their offspring has been much discussed.[50] There is plenty of information in Foxe which suggests they had an importance far and away above that which their legal place in society, or in the established church, would suggest.

Roger Bennet named a group of women who met together at holidays in Amersham 'when they go and come from the church' at the house of J. Collingworth, 'and there to keep their conventicle': they were the wife of John Milsent; the wife of William Rogers; Mrs Robert Stamp; and the

[48] PRO C85/115/10.
[49] BL Harleian MS 42, fol. 13r; Brigden, *London and the Reformation*, pp. 104–5.
[50] See Margaret Aston, 'Lollard Women Priests?', in *Lollards and Reformers: Images and Literacy in Late Medieval Religion* (London, 1984), pp. 49–70 (originally published in the *Journal of Ecclesiastical History*, 31 (1980), pp. 441–61); Claire Cross, 'Great Reasoners in Scripture: The Activities of Women Lollards, 1380–1530', in Derek Baker (ed.), *Medieval Women*, Studies in Church History, Subsdia 1 (Oxford, 1979), pp. 359–80; John Davis, 'Joan of Kent, Lollardy and the English Reformation', *Journal of Ecclesiastical History*, 33 (1982), pp. 225–33. See also R.A. Houlbrooke, 'Women's Social Life and Common Action in England from the Fifteenth Century to the Eve of the Civil War', *Continuity and Change: A Journal of Social Structures, Law and Demography*, 1 (2) (1986), pp. 171–89.

wife of Robert Bartlet.[51] Why Bennet should know of this meeting in particular we cannot say. Perhaps it is an example of Foxe being selective as he rushed his way through the register he was examining. Perhaps Bennet taught the group (he was said to be 'especially to be noted').

The women's group meeting was from families steeped in heresy. Roger Bennet, Mrs Milsent, and Robert Bartlet had all abjured in 1511. The others had contacts with several Lollards in the county.

Bennet was comfortably off. In the Muster for Amersham he is listed with land worth 15s and goods worth 6s. In the Subsidy he is taxed on £8. Despite his heretical history he was overseer to the curate of Amersham, Robert Fleming, when he made his will in 1525. Fleming left his 'bybill with the lyer and the comen glosse conteyning in 6 wolyms and the concordance' to the abbey at Missenden.

Bennet made his will on 10 March 1544, at Amersham,[52] leaving his soul to 'Almighty God my maker and redeemer trusting by the faith that I have in the passion of my saviour to be saved'. Bennet left 2d to Lincoln and 4d to the high altar at Amersham. Additionally he gave the church an altar cloth, 'the pryce 3s 4d'. The poor were to get 3s 4d, with no strings attached, and the highways were to have 3d spent on them.

His daughter Alice,[53] who was not yet twenty years old, received £10 upon reaching that age, which Thomas, his son, was to pay out of the estate. Thomas, and Joan, Roger's wife, were to share the estate, although Thomas was to have possession of the 'farme house and the stock there [also] all my landys wythe all my tenement'. Should there be no heirs of his children, Roger required the 'parson of Agmondesham [Amersham] with the churche wardens for ye tyme beynge shall sell the sayde landis and tenement' distributing the money raised from the sale 'one parte to poure peple and an other to maydes mariage' another part towards the maintenance of the highways, and 'the iiiith to the churche of Agmondesham'. 'Em' Benet of Amersham, widow of William, lately dead, was given 2s yearly at quarterly payments, and Emma Bowther received 4s 4d.

Thomas, Roger's son, was sole executor. Thomas Bland was supervisor, as he was to Alice Saunders, and the witnesses were Mr Pollyns, clerk, Nicholas Herne, found in the Muster at Askett in Monks Risborough, adjacent to Hughenden, with 6s 8d in land and £2 in goods, and Richard

---

[51] Foxe, IV, p. 224.
[52] Bucks. RO DA/We/4/186.
[53] Alice was a servant of Alice Saunders, the wife of Lollardy's most prominent resident in Amersham. Saunders gave Alice 20s and her maser, or drinking cup, when she made her will in 1543. PRO Prob 11/29/29. It is an example of the Saunders' connections with less affluent members of the sect. Were the Saunders family integrated into the sect, despite their status? Dr Davis thinks not, 'Joan of Kent', p. 204.

Batten. None of these is found at Amersham. John Clypson and William Dowghte, Roger's apprentices, received 3s 4d each, 'if their seve my sone Thomas'.

Roger's trade or craft is not known to us, but his comfortable existence does come across. This Lollard, whose daughter was well thought of by another leader of the sect in the parish, and who taught others, was willing to endow the parish church upon his death. It gives yet another indication of the fact that Lollards were not separatists; seeking change and reform perhaps, but not desiring a break from the church. Of course, there was the added point that the actual building of the parish church was a social centre, but in Roger's case the bequests show a religious attachment as well. This was the man who named the group of women meeting at Collingworth's house.

Mrs Isabel Bartlet was discussed above, when we considered a group from Hughenden. Isabel Bartlet knew others at Woodrow, of course, and members of the Herne family of Hughenden, as well as the Bennets.

Joan Collingborne, presumably the same person as the host of the group Bennet named, was named by a group in 1521. She was said to have spoken to, and presumably taught, Joan Timberlake and Alice Tredway some ten years earlier regarding the faith. In the Muster for Amersham, John Collingborne is listed as a non-resident, with £2 in land. There were other connections with Lollardy in the Collingborne family. John Collingborne was the executor of Isabel Saunders, mother of Richard, when she made her will in 1497.[54] John Collingborne himself made his will at Aylesbury in 1524. There are no obvious connections with Lollards.

As we already know, Mrs Milsent was the wife of another affluent Lollard, and a pillar of the local community. John Milsent was listed in the Muster for Amersham with £3 in land and £30 in goods. In the Subsidy for Chesham he was present with £13 6s 8d. In 1505 he had been listed as *iconomi* at Chesham, with William West and John Bukett. Of course, as we saw above, Milsent was still practising his heterodoxy in 1532, when he faced the manor court.[55] His holding in Amersham, 'Thomas Milsent's Land', a perch in area, was held by Simon Harding in 1541, and by Roger Harding thereafter.[56]

Lest we begin to suspect that the group meeting at Mrs Collingworth's house were all of a particular social position in Amersham, Mrs Rogers brings us back to earth with a bump. Her husband, a tiler according to Roger Bennet, was listed in the Subsidy for Chesham with £1. Bennet said he was a 'known man'. Was he an employee of Bennet?

---

[54] PRO Prob 11/11.
[55] Bucks. RO D/BASM 18/202.
[56] Frederick G. Lee, 'Amersham Churchwardens' Accounts', in *Records of Buckinghamshire*, Buckinghamshire Archaeological Society, 7 (Aylesbury, 1897), p. 46.

Robert Stamp, whose wife was also at the meeting, was of Woodrow. Bennet said that his wife, like several others, had not finished her penance. Stamp had goods worth £4 in the Muster Certificate at Woodrow, and in the Subsidy he was listed with £2 at Penn.[57]

It was a diverse group, as we have found before. Their beliefs, and perhaps the employment of their husbands, brought them together. Their divergent financial and social position did not seem to matter. It seems too much to ask that they did not discuss heretical doctrine, and other practising Lollards, at some time during their meetings. We should stress the obvious: all these women will have known about the contacts both of Robert Bartlet (mapped in group III) and his sister-in-law, Isabel Bartlet (mapped in group IV). They therefore knew, or knew of, numerous other people suspected of Lollardy across the Chiltern divide, in Hughenden, the Missendens, and West Wycombe, as well as those connecting to the Staines group.

VII

A small group met at Chesham to hear James Morden recite the Ten Commandments in English: Thomas Tredway of Chesham, Robert Pope, and John Morden and his wife (James' uncle and aunt).[58]

This meeting is another which predates the inquisitions of 1521–2. John Morden died in 1514, having apparently divulged the secrets of the sect to his son-in-law, Richard Ashford (or Nash or Tredway). The scene Ashford described when facing the Bishop of Winchester's court is emotional, but requires a considerable stretching of the imagination.[59] Richard Ashford lived at Walton-upon-Thames, and knew the Butlers at Iver, as well as his in-laws and their associates at Chesham and Amersham.

James Morden of Chesham was one of those sad characters burnt merely because of his long-standing commitment to the sect, rather than because of any status he held within it. He was handed over to the secular authority on 23 January 1522 and was burnt with Barnard, Rave, and Scrivener.[60] He held lands at Chesham and an inquisition post mortem regarding lands held by him and Barnard was held at Chesham later the same year.[61] On 1 May lands belonging to 'James Morden and Thomas

---

[57] As we have seen, individuals could move around during their life, depending on their employment, or their marriage. Historians tend to imagine a static society. This was not the case. See below, pp. 309–10, 315–16.

[58] Foxe, IV, p. 225.

[59] Reg Fox (Winton) iv, fols. 18–19v. Considerable credulity is indeed required if we are to believe that Ashford did not know of his wife's family's heterodoxy until his father-in-law's declaration to him – but it's a nice story!

[60] PRO C85/115/13.

[61] PRO E150/17.

Barnarde, recently burned, [were] given to Thomas Warde the king's har-
binge, Geo Ducworth, yeoman of the Mouth, in the cellar of Queen
Katharine, and Rob Coly, yeoman usher of the king's hall: Grant in fee
all messuages and lands in Amersham Bucks late of Thomas Barnarde
and Jas Morden, burnt as heretics'.[62]

Chesham shows signs of considerable Lollard presence. In the Muster
Certificate some 15 per cent of those listed were named Lollards, or of
Lollard families. In the Subsidy the figure is also 15 per cent.

James Morden was not poor. His servant, John Jennings, was a book
or text-carrier. James Morden is called a labourer by Foxe, but obviously
he was not simply that. In 1511 he had faced Bishop Smith and been
made to do penance. He failed to carry out the instructions given him.
He was taught by Agnes Ashford of Chesham, whom he named. He
taught others, including his sister Marion Morden, and he named his
brothers Richard and Radulph, as well as Marion. Not surprisingly, we
do not find James Morden in other sources.

Marion Morden, widow of Ashley Green, Chesham Leicester, made
her will on 13 May 1521, and she was dead before 16 September, when
the will was proved.[63] She therefore escaped the trials which began
shortly afterwards, which presents us with a problem. Whose widow was
she?

She left her soul to 'God Father Allmyghty and to Our Blissid Lady seynt
Mary and to all the seynts in hevyn' and asked to be buried alongside her
husband, in the churchyard. It was a very conservative will: she left 4d to
Lincoln, 12d to the repair of 'Our Lady chapel within the parish church', a
good sheep to the lights, and 6d for the torches.

The bequests suggest various family connections, the most important
of which is a young ewe sheep to Marion Morden, the daughter of 'Herry'
Morden. It is often the case that a bequest to the children of one's spouse
is couched in such terms: it could be that Marion the testator is the
mother, or step-mother, to the heretics James and Marion Morden. However, that is supposition. It seems that Marion was related to the Butterfields: she left Marion Butterfield, possibly a niece, 'a pugge ewe
sheep'. Robert Butterfield, of an unknown parish, was named by Thomas
White and Thomas Clerk, also of unnamed parishes.[64]

To Isabel Ashford, a member of a Lollard family, she gave 'an handyll
panne and on lambe when she ys cum to her full age'. Several members

---

[62] LP, III (ii), 3062 (pat 15 Henry VIII pl m8).
[63] Bucks. RO DA/We/1/8.
[64] Butterfield is found in both the Muster and Subsidy for Chenies, the parish adjacent
to Chesham. In the manor court roll for Isnamsted Latimer (Buckinghamshire
Archaeological Society 64/48), in Chesham parish, alongside Chenies, Robert Butterfield is noted as absent in a sitting of the court during 1527.

of the Weedon family, many of whom are found at Chesham, were legatees.[65] Marion's daughter Joan was residuary legatee, which argues against Harry being her son. Her overseers were Robert Weedon and Thomas Harding of Chesham, who was later burnt. Robert Hutton, yet another Lollard, was supervisor.

Richard Morden and his wife Emma, of Chesham, were detected by his brother James, and by John Hill. Richard is found in the Muster and Subsidy for Chesham, with lands valued at 10s. There is no extant will for him, but his wife left a will, made on 6 February 1541, probate being awarded on 19 March.[66]

We have a record of Richard's and Emma's burials, from the extant church register.[67] He was buried on 3 February, and Emma followed him to the grave three days later, the very day she made her will.

Emma Morden left her soul to 'almighty God and to our lady and all the company of heavene'. Lincoln received 2d, as did the high altar. She left a cloth to make a corporal. Her daughter Alice Schorte received 'my red cow and a kettell, my beste kyrtell and my best peticote and the white coveryng on my bed'. Richard Morden, her son, received a brass pot, and 'all my schepe not bequeathed' and 'Emps' Chamber, her daughter, received her black cow, a kirtle, a coverlet from her bed, a gown, and a violet kirtle.

John Hill and John Weedon, both mentioned in Foxe, were the executors, and James Dell was a witness. The others involved are not known to us. No priest is named, but that may have been due to the haste involved.

Members of the Hill, Dell, and Weedon families were named by Foxe. John Hill especially turns out to be important to us. John Hill knew the Bartlets and named them when he was questioned in 1511 and 1522. In fact we are talking of two Lollards of that name, father and son.

John Hill and his wife Florence died in 1523, within days of each other. Their wills are extant, and so is the inventory of their household goods.[68] Space precludes a discussion of those documents, except to say that Hill was very well off and held a large holding, well stocked with sheep and cattle. His son, also John, was the main beneficiary. Several Lollards, Roger Bennet, Robert Andrew (a former churchwarden), and William Tracher were mentioned.

John junior came before the manor court of the manor of Chesham Higham and Chesham Bury held on 15 April 1532. Several men, including

[65] One reference to the family is found in Foxe. John a Weedon, with William Dorset, of King's Langley of Hertfordshire, was named by John a Lee.
[66] Bucks. RO DA/We/4/5.
[67] Bucks. RO Chesham Parish Register, burials.
[68] Bucks. RO DA/We/2/5, DA/We/2/6, DA/We/2/8.

John Hill, Thomas Tredway alias Bose, Roger Harding and John Milsent were accused of 'hirise' (heresy). (Thomas Harding, a patriarch of the sect, was burnt the same year.) It was ordered 'to each of them that they henceforth not come together secretly under penalty for each of them of 20d'.[69] Apart from the evidence of continuity into the 1530s we see here, it is of particular importance to us that we find others, of which we find no other information, in Foxe or elsewhere, accused of heresy. Apart from Tredway, Harding, Milsent and Hill, Thomas Bedimaker, Henry Goodlade, and William Hales were also accused. This additional evidence supports my contention that many others were involved in such parishes as Hughenden and Amersham.

John Hill junior was found again in a document drawn up on 2 November 1541 by the churchwarden at the time, Thomas Bland, who was a witness to many Lollard wills, when he produced a detailed table of landholding in Amersham.[70] John Hill held half a perch of land in 'Batchelor's Land'. Robert Hill, possibly his brother, held the land thereafter.

The same document lists 'Cumsutlatt's Land', a perch of which was held by Walter Tredway. In a footnote, Lee states that the Tredway family later moved to Beaconsfield, when one member of the family, Thomas, 'a warm adherent of the Tudor Revolution', was knighted and granted arms.[71] It is possible that this was the same Thomas Tredway who had met with James Morden.

Robert Pope, as we found above, is difficult to locate, but Thomas Tredway, the final member of this small group, we have already come across, accused of heresy in 1532. Tredway was the son of Agnes Ashford, and so related to John and James Morden. He named several Lollards in 1521–2.[72] He lived at Chesham. In the Muster he had goods worth £1. His father, Walter, was a non-resident and had land worth 9s (presumably Cumsutlatt's Land, mentioned above) at Amersham, and land worth £1 6s 8d at Little Missenden, where he lived. In 1519–20 Walter was churchwarden at Chesham, with Henry Salcott and Richard Cutler.[73]

When Walter made his will in 1546 he described himself as a yeoman of Amersham. His will confirms that status.[74] He left lands to his several children, including Thomas. A tenement at Coleshill, Amersham, 'now in the hands of John Hill', went to his son Richard. The farm he was dwelling in went to Thomas. Other lands, in Rickmansworth in Hertfordshire, went to his several children for the rest of the term of the rent,

[69] Bucks. RO D/BASM 18/202.
[70] Lee, 'Amersham Churchwardens' Accounts', pp. 43–51.
[71] Ibid., p. 47.
[72] Foxe, IV, pp. 225, 230–1.
[73] Bucks. RO DA/We/1/106v.
[74] Bucks. RO DA/We/8/80.

eleven years. When we remember that the Ashford/Nash/Tredway family had connections with the Butlers at Iver, who in turn had connections with Uxbridge, we see yet again, a group meeting, this time one which seems to have strong family connections, with connections with areas geographically distant. In this instance we see an affluent section of Lollard society at Chesham meeting together. Their beliefs were continued into the 1530s, apparently unchanged and unaffected by the continuing threats of the church, including the burning of one of their number.

VIII

Thomas Holmes, a prolific detector, named John Butler, carpenter; Richard Butler; and William King, of Uxbridge. They all met together at the home of Durdant by Iver Court by Staines, and read 'all the night in a book of Scripture'.[75]

Durdant we have already met. He was comfortably off; his home was the venue for meetings and readings throughout the early years of the sixteenth century, and probably before. His family were on intimate terms with intellectual reformers, and his son declared his radicalism on his deathbed. We may also have come across Thomas Holmes at Nicholas Durdant's bedside, so the connection suggested in Foxe would seem obvious.

The Butlers had connections throughout the area. They knew Lollards in Uxbridge and in Chesham. John and his brother Richard visited the house of Richard Ashford.[76] John was married to Alice, the sister of Richard Woolman, of Uxbridge. The Woolman family were much involved in Lollard practices.[77] John had listened to John Colet preach in London, and had gone to London with Mrs Henry Vulman (Woolman) to a 'corner house in Friday-street, where the good man of the house, having a stump foot, had divers ... books, to the intent that they should hear them read'.[78] The Butlers are not found in Muster Certificates nor in Subsidy Rolls. At Iver, Robert Carde is found in the Muster with £2 in goods. Roger Carde is listed with £1 in goods. John Carter is listed in the Subsidy for Iver with wages at £1 6s 8d. Carter is probably Carder or Butler.[79]

William King of Uxbridge had also been at Durdant's house at the all-night reading party. His mother had been named by Richard Vulford.

[75] Fox, IV, p. 226.
[76] Reg Fox (Winton) iv, fols. 18–19v.
[77] PRO Req 2/1/69, 2/36.
[78] Foxe, IV, p. 230.
[79] Robert Carder went to the house of Richard Ashford or Nash with his sons John and Richard. Trinity College, Dublin, MS D.3.4 fol. 128v; Reg Fox (Winton) iv, fols. 18–19v.

A group had come to his house to listen to Thomas Man, the peripatetic preacher.

The Subsidy at Uxbridge lists several Lollards. Henry Woolman had goods valued at £10, John Baker, a miller, had money worth 40s, William King had goods at 40s, and Andrew Fuller, a wage earner, taxed at the lowest level of 4d, was on 20s per annum. Richard Taylor who was also named, had wages of 20s. He may be the Richard Taylor involved in the argument which took place across the river at Iver, involving the vicar of Iver. Richard Fuller, taxed on wages of 40s, was presumably a relative of Andrew Fuller.

In the Court of Requests, a case brought by Richard Woolman was heard.[80] The case involved a messuage with a 'curtilage and a pece of lande thereto being with the apperternances lying and being at Wox-brige'. The holding was seised of Richard Jararede and Thomas Bartilot. Richard's father, Robert Woolman, the Lollard, together with John Botler (Butler, another Lollard) and his wife Alice, had been given possession, by deed, with the holding descending to any heirs of the three. Only Robert had had an heir, the 'orator' Richard Woolman. But William Woolman, younger son of Henry Woolman, brother of Robert, had 'wrongfully entered' into the holding, and was still there.

It seems Richard had difficulties regaining the holding, for he addressed his plea to the court again, shortly afterwards, this time calling himself 'of London, draper'.[81] Whilst repeating the charge against his cousin, for taking the holding 'by violence and power', he disclosed that Alice Butler was his sister, being the daughter of Robert Woolman. John Butler was the son of Robert Carder.

Many of the gatherings mentioned in Foxe in this area were of close friends and relatives. They travelled considerable distances to read and pray. Once again family and social ties are seen in a group detected to the authorities. Connections with London were frequent and important.

IX

In a rare insight into Lollard sacramental activity, John Scrivener named a group who met to celebrate a wedding of one of their number. John Merrywether and his wife and son were there; so were Durdant by Staines; Old Durdant; Isabel, wife of Thomas Harding; Hartop of Windsor; Joan Barret, wife of John Barret, of London; Henry Miller; and

---

[80] PRO Req 2/1/69, 2/36.
[81] The Drapers' Company could list many who were 'known men'. See Brigden, *London and the Reformation*, chapter 2.

one Stilman, tailor. They gathered in a barn and heard an Epistle of St Paul read, 'at the marriage of Durdant's daughter'.[82]

John Scrivener of Amersham we already know about. Presumably he was at the Durdant wedding. If so, we have yet another example of Lollards overcoming the geography of the area, which Dr Davies thought was inhibiting to them.

John Merrywether and his family are not found elsewhere.

'Durdant by Staines', and 'Old Durdant' were Nicholas and his father Robert. They too have been the subject of our scrutiny.

Isabel Harding travelled from Chesham to be at the Durdant wedding. The Harding family proliferated. They often surfaced using the name Africke, or Littlepage, or Page. Isabel's husband Thomas would later be burnt when the authorities, rather belatedly really, caught up with him.[83] His wife was probably as important as her husband within the sect. She had her penance remitted in 1515, presumably after having abjured in 1511.[84] The Hardings lived for much of their married lives at Chesham, and Thomas is duly found in the Muster and Subsidy for the parish. In the former he has lands worth £1 6s 8d and goods worth the very substantial £32. In the Subsidy he was listed with £20. So he was another Lollard who was wealthy in rural terms. With Robert Weedon he was the executor for the will of Marion Morden, a member of another important Lollard family, whom we considered above.[85] Isabel Harding spent her time teaching. She spoke to the Bartlet brothers about William Tilesworth, whom she must have known and at whose burning she was present. She taught Richard Bennet and the daughter of Isabel Tracher. She taught Joan Norman, who, said Foxe, was later burnt. No doubt she spoke at the wedding. She was a busy lady.[86]

'Hartop of Windsor' is not known to us.

Joan Barret's husband John was mentioned above. He had recited from the Gospels in front of his wife and servant, John Scrivener said, when Barret was said to be a goldsmith of London. John Scrivener was his apprentice, as was William Tilesworth, who was burnt in 1511. Thomas Walker named Barret when he appeared before Bishop Fitzjames of London. He lived, said Walker, in Cheapside.[87] Not surprisingly, Barret and his wife are not found in documents relating to Buckinghamshire and Middlesex. But the wedding again shows how Lollards travelled considerable distances to be in the right place at the right time.

[82] Foxe, IV, p. 228.
[83] Reg Longland (Linc) i, fol. 288r–v.
[84] Linc Ep Recs C.j.2, fols. 23v–4.
[85] Bucks. RO DA/We/1/8.
[86] Foxe, IV, pp. 123, 221, 224, 227, 228.
[87] Trinity College, Dublin, MS 775 fol. 124; Herbert, London Chronicle (1836), ii, 273.

Henry Miller was also at the wedding. He is another Lollard of whom we know little. He was 'counted a great heretic' said Thomas Holmes, who knew the Durdants, of course. Perhaps it is not surprising that we do not know more about him: according to John Scrivener he had fled to Chelmsford, and then to Kent.[88]

'One Stilman, tailor' also attended the Durdant wedding. He is either John or Thomas Stilman, probably the same person. John Stilman was burnt in London in 1518. He had been taught by Stephen Moone and Richard Smart around 1498 and 1504, respectively, within the diocese of Winchester. William Phips of Hughenden knew him. He had abjured at Reading in 1508, and in 1514 was named by Thomas Watts of Dogmersfield, Hampshire.[89] Thomas Stilman was named by Thomas Holmes. He was also named by John Phip, who told how Stilman had escaped from the Lollard's Tower, by St Paul's Cathedral in London.[90] Stilman was obviously an extraordinary man. To add to his other attributes, he travelled a considerable distance to be at the wedding at Staines.

Stilman mixed with a varied group of heretics. One can only be impressed that the Durdant marriage should draw so many from so far. Durdant was obviously well thought of and the house was obviously of more importance than we might at first think. What did the neighbours think of it all?

X

If we move to the north-west, Foxe tells us that Christopher Shoemaker, said to be of Great Missenden, came to the house of John Say, of the same parish, several times, to read to Say and teach him in 'the true Gospel'. John Okenden and Robert Pope later confirmed this, having been involved in the teaching of Say. Shoemaker, says Foxe, was later burnt at Newbury, in 1518. John Say was later named by Thomas Holmes, with his son William Say, when he was said to be of Little Missenden. Holmes named him again, and this time said Say was of 'Missenden'. John Say subsequently named Christopher Shoemaker, John Okenden, and Robert Pope.[91]

Christopher Shoemaker is not found in any source I have examined. Robert Pope mentioned a Humphrey Shoemaker of Newbury, a strange coincidence. Henry Shoemaker, with wages of £1 per annum, was listed

---

[88] Foxe, IV, p. 228. John Scrivener said Miller was a wiredrawer.
[89] Foxe, IV, pp. 207–8, 229. Trinity College, Dublin, MS D 3.4 fol. 125. Reg Audley (Sarum), fols. 147v–8v. Reg Fox (Winton) iii, fols. 73v–4.
[90] Foxe, IV, pp. 226, 228, 230.
[91] Foxe, IV, pp. 217, 226, 229.

in the Subsidy for Walton, a hamlet in the parish of Great Missenden.[92] Henry was probably Christopher's son, and might have been 'Humphrey'.

John Say survived the episcopal searching out of heretics in 1521–2. He was resident in Little Missenden when the Muster Certificate for the parish was produced, in 1522.[93] He had goods worth £3 6s 9d and no lands. His son, William, was also in Little Missenden when the Muster Commissioners produced their Certificates. He had goods worth 10s. Two years later, when the Subsidy Rolls were prepared, a John Say was said to be of Princes Risborough and to have wages at £1 per annum. He may, of course, not have been the same man.

No amount of threatening could keep John Say away from the truth as he saw it. He was found again at a meeting at Speen, a hamlet on the Princes Risborough side of the parish border with Hughenden, in 1530, when a group met at the house of John Taylor to hear Nicholas Field speak (see section XII, p. 160). Say was then said to be of Princes Risborough.[94]

John Say made his will on 27 August 1561, whilst living back at Great Missenden. Probate was granted on 1 October.[95] He left his soul to 'my maker and redeemer, Jesus Christ', and his body to be buried in the churchyard at Great Missenden. The poor were to receive 20d. Among the bequests his son William, the Lollard, received 26s 8d and two ewes. Several other children received similar bequests. Joan, his wife, was his executrix. Sir Edward Dene and Christopher Medcalfe were the witnesses. Say was comfortably off.

John Okenden was apparently from Wendover, a parish on the road to Aylesbury. In 1519–20, when living at Wendover, he faced the archdeacon's court.[96] Two years later, in 1522, he was listed in the Muster for Wendover, with land worth 5s and goods worth £1 13s 4d.

[92] A.C. Chibnall and A. Vere Woodman (eds.), Subsidy Roll for the County of Buckingham Anno 1524, Buckinghamshire Records Society, 8 (1950); PRO E179/78/161 (Aylesbury). I have not normally footnoted references to the Subsidy below.

[93] A.C. Chibnall (ed.), The Certificate of Musters for Buckinghamshire for 1522, Buckinghamshire Records Society, 17/18 (London 1973); Bodleian Library MS Eng hist. e 187. I have not footnoted references to the Muster Certificates individually.

[94] Foxe, IV, p. 584. The meeting is discussed fully below. John Say is not mentioned by Foxe, but the details of the meeting are found in Reg Longland (Linc) 26, fol. 180b, where he is listed. See John Fines, 'Studies in the Lollard Heresy: Being an Examination of the Evidence from the Dioceses of Norwich, Lincoln, Coventry and Lichfield, and Ely, during the Period 1430–1530' (Sheffield, PhD, 1964), pp. 200–1, and in idem, A Biographical Register of Early English Protestants and Others Opposed to the Roman Catholic Church, 1525–1558 (Abingdon, 1981; Chichester, 1985). According to Dr Fines, Thomas Lound of London and John Symondes of London were also in attendance.

[95] Bucks. RO DA/We/14/40, DA/Wf/6 (original).

[96] Bucks. RO DA/We/1/60.

Of Robert Pope there is no trace. He knew several throughout the region and named many. He visited houses in Amersham, West Hendred, Standlake, and probably elsewhere. He escaped the examination of the Muster Commissioners and the Subsidy Collectors, and his will, if he made one, has not survived.

The indications are that the small group associated with John Say were not rich. They were smallholders and labourers, or both. Say himself was better-off but still not affluent. Apart from Pope's extended connections, communications extended only to adjacent parishes, but they did extend beyond natural geographical boundaries, west to east.

XI

John Funge named his brother Francis Funge, at a meeting we deduce from the evidence to have been in Little Missenden, with Thomas Clerk. Francis Funge and Alice his wife named Thomas Clerk and Robert Rave of Dorney. Thomas Clerk spoke against the real presence to them. Fourteen years previously Rave had criticized the Sacrament and pilgrimages.[97] It was an apparently intimate gathering.

Thomas Clerk was of Hughenden, of course. The Funge family thought nothing of moving around and changing their name. At High Wycombe, John Coke or Funge was listed in the Muster with £1 in goods. Roger, possibly his brother, had goods at £3. At Penn, Cecily Coke, their mother, was listed with goods at £3. John Funge was listed at Penn with goods worth £2. He was a servant. Robert Sunge (sic) was listed at Amersham with £5 in goods. Robert Funge was listed at Penn with goods worth £7. At Amersham Richard Sunge (sic) was listed with goods worth £3. At Penn Francis Funge was listed with goods worth £2, and James Funge was listed at Great Wycombe as eligible for muster. In the Subsidy, John Funge the elder was listed with £2. At High Wycombe James Funge was named with wages of £1. At Amersham John Funge was named with £5 and Richard Funge with £3. At West Wycombe, Francis Funge had £2, at Great Wycombe Roger Funge had £2 and Cecily Coke had £3.

Richard Funge or Coke was accused of an unknown offence by Thomas Payvour of Penn in 1496.[98] Funge was probably the father of the brothers named in Foxe.

Cecily Coke or Funge made her will in 1535, on 24 January. The date of probate is not given.[99] She was the mother of John and Francis Funge. Mrs Funge left a conservative will. The curate, Sir Christopher Lyng, was

---

[97] Foxe, IV, p. 233.
[98] Bucks. RO DA/We/1/194.
[99] Bucks. RO DA/We/3/112.

asked to say a trental of masses for her husband's soul. Her son, the Lollard John, received a quarter of barley, but nothing else apparently. The few other bequests are similarly meagre. There is no reference to Francis Funge, the other brother. He was a witness to the will of Henry Honer, in 1535, when Honer was living at Beamond End, Little Missenden.[100] Honer may well have been a relative of the Abbot of Missenden Abbey we noted above. Roger and John Coke or Funge were witnesses, and John Fryer, the Lollard book-runner and servant of Master Penn, and Roger Funge were overseers to the will of Henry Littlepage, 'yeoman of Chepping Wycombe', on 5 September 1551. Probate was awarded on 28 September 1557.[101]

In 1559, on 3 January, John Funge, 'otherwise called Francis', a miller, made his will at West Wycombe.[102] Again the preamble was conservative. The only bequests were 2d to Lincoln and 2d to Wycombe high altar for tithes unpaid. The bequests are as few and minimal as those of his mother, Cecily. The family were apparently not particularly well off. Witnesses gave us no further information.

John Funge had 'named' his brother Francis. Francis, and his wife Alice had named several others. In the various tax and muster returns they were found at Great and West Wycombe. Much of the probate evidence also showed them connected to those parishes. Yet they were mentioned in wills made at Missenden, and John died in Little Missenden.

Their residence at Little Missenden is confirmed by the evidence found of their heresy in that parish.[103] In 1537, Francis Fonge (sic), of Little Missenden, had been visited by churchwardens of Lye (Lee), who 'asked his charity for their church'. They unfortunately saw a book of the Gospels in English, and asked Alice about it. She was questioned and denied transubstantiation and the efficacy of the blessed water. She was consequently charged and questioned. We do not know the result.

Robert Rave, the final member of this small group, is found in the Subsidy for West Wycombe, with £2.

The Funge family seem insignificant in the pages of Foxe, yet we can surely believe that the family were steadfast in maintaining their faith into the Reformation proper, and that their contacts, from West Wycombe to Amersham, from Penn to Little Missenden, meant that their house (or houses) were points of contact for other Lollards, despite the relatively low social standing they had. Indeed, we might also note that, despite that low social standing, Alice Funge spent some of her time reading from the Gospels. It should also be noted that those at Amersham were

---

[100] Bucks. RO DA/We/3/150.
[101] Bucks. RO DA/We/8/162.
[102] Bucks. RO DA/We/11/133.
[103] LP, XII (ii), 221.

not the only ones to maintain their faith throughout the period of the Reformation. To what extent Lutheranism affected Lollards it is difficult to say, but it is possible that the text Mrs Funge had open in her hall was a copy of Tyndale's text.

XII

The Funge family and the groups at Amersham were not the only Lollards continuing to meet during the 1530s. In 1530, as the Reformation parliament was agonizing over what to do about the 'King's Great Matter', members of several families met at the home of John Taylor at Hughenden, to hear Nicholas Field of London read from the Scripture and speak to them.[104] The group, according to Foxe, consisted of William Wingrave, Thomas Hawkes of Hughenden, Robert Hawes of West Wycombe, John Taylor, John Hawkes, Thomas Herne of 'Cobshil', Nicholas Field, Richard Dean, Thomas Clerk the younger, and William Hawkes of Chesham, who had not found it too difficult to join a group meeting in Hughenden, despite Dr Davies' doubts over the terrain. The group were sought by the authorities, and we are fortunate that details are extant.[105]

According to the register, the group had met at the house of John Taylor, of Speen, a hamlet between Hughenden and Princes Risborough, to hear Nicholas Field of London speak. Apart from the group listed by Foxe, the register shows that John Say of Princes Risborough, John Simons of London, and Thomas Lound of London, were present.

John Say we have already met. He had been of the sect for decades. He was by 1530 a middle-aged man, perhaps an elder of the sect.

Thomas Lound had spent two years in Germany, with Martin Luther. He had been arrested by the English authorities and cast into prison. He had taught John Ryburn, of Speen.

John Taylor, the host, had previously been host to another small group, when John Simons, presumably of London, had read to Taylor and John Ryburn. Taylor was comfortably off. In the Muster for Great Missenden he had land worth 10s and goods at £9. In the Subsidy he had land at 18s and goods at £6. He was a witness at the making of the wills of two Lollards: Thomas Potter, at Hughenden, in 1558, and Robert Wingrave, also at Hughenden, in 1558.[106]

Nicholas Field may be the man of that name from Hughenden who, with his wife, was accused by John Bishop in 1505.[107]

[104] Foxe, IV, p. 584.
[105] Lincoln Episcopal Register, 26, fol. 180b.
[106] Bucks. RO DA/Wf/4/356, DA/Wf/4/248.
[107] Bucks. RO DA/We/1/168.

Thomas Clerk the younger was the member of an important and prosperous family in Hughenden, much involved in parish affairs and business. His father, also Thomas, had been churchwarden in 1495, with Nicholas Widmore.[108] In the Muster he was listed with land worth £3 and goods worth £12. In the Subsidy he had £8. He was also listed at High Wycombe with land worth £3 and goods worth the very large sum of £40. Thomas himself had £30 in land and £2 in goods in the Muster for Hughenden. Thomas Clerk the younger was a witness to the wills of Laurence Herne at Hughenden in 1556 and to William Fastendich at Hughenden, in 1546.[109]

The Clerk family were steeped in heresy. Their family was related to the Widmore, Africk, and Phips families, and Thomas Holmes, who seems to have known everyone, named them.

Thomas Hawkes of Hughenden, John Hawkes, and William Hawkes of Chesham, were presumably of the same family. It is probable that Robert Hawes of West Wycombe was also related. This is the only evidence we have of their heresy. They appear nowhere else.

The Muster at Hughenden lists a Thomas Hawkes with no lands or goods, simply eligible for muster. At Great Missenden a Thomas Hawkes had goods worth £2. At Princes Risborough, Robert Hawes had goods worth £5 and William Hawkes had lands worth 10s and goods worth £1. At Little Missenden, John Hawkes is listed with land worth 2s and goods worth £2. They were not well off, it would seem. During the 1490s Thomas was often before the archdeacon's court for minor offences. He would seem, therefore, to have been of a similar age to Thomas Clerk.[110]

Thomas Hawes of Princes Risborough made his will on 27 May 1554.[111] His son Richard obtained his horses, carts, gear, and plough-gear. Richard's wife got all the brass pots in the house. Their sons Thomas and Henry Hawes were beneficiaries. Robert, another son, probably the Lollard, gained the best cot. Alice Coke, conceivably Alice Funge, was a witness. Probate was given at Missenden on 3 October.

Richard Dean we noted above. He had travelled from West Wycombe. Thomas Herne, of 'Cobshil', was probably the son of Lawrence Herne, whom we discussed above. Thomas is found in the Muster at Saunderton, adjacent to Princes Risborough, at the foot of the scarp, with only £1 in goods.

William Wingrave is probably Robert Wingrave. No one called William is found in any source, but evidence of Robert abounds. In the Muster for Hughenden he had goods worth £5. In the Subsidy he is listed at £3.

---

[108] Bucks. RO DA/We/1/183v.
[109] Bucks. RO DA/Wf/2/229, DA/Wf/1/228.
[110] Bucks. RO DA/We/1/132, DA/V/1/1, 1v, 14, 193v.
[111] Bucks. RO DA/We/8/45.

There are several references to the family in the Muster and Subsidy for High Wycombe. Robert is listed with £5 in goods in the former, and with £5 in the latter. Robert Wingrave is also much in evidence in the will making in Hughenden. He knew the heretic John Phip, whom Foxe called a physician, John Wellysborne, and Thomas Widmore. He was a witness at the making of all their wills. Robert Wingrave himself made his will on 31 July 1558.[112] His daughter was married into the Rydinge family, and his fellow Lollard, John Taylor, was a witness. His son Thomas, who is listed in the Muster and Subsidy for High Wycombe, is the main beneficiary.

John Simons of London may well have been a local man. He is found in the Muster for West Wycombe with goods worth £1 and in the Subsidy with wages at £1 per annum. It is not inconceivable that a local man returned to join in a group meeting for a Bible reading or preaching having previously known of the heresy in his home parish, and possibly having met with men like the Tilesworth brothers whilst working in London.

XIII

We have seen how diverse and important was Lollard society. Lollards were mixing with each other, of course, but the evidence from their wills, from the archdeaconry records, and from the records of the central courts all show that Lollards lived a conventional life among neighbours who were well aware of their proclivities. I suspect there may often have been other adherents we know nothing of. Lollards were not at all insignificant, socially and financially. A large proportion of those listed by Foxe were of the middle ranks of rural society, but others were of greater importance; they were members of the gentry and yeomanry. Yet others were poor, and we have caught only a glimpse of those Lollards at the very bottom of society. They remain shadows, although we are aware of their presence.

Of equal importance is that there is ample evidence of continuity throughout the difficult years from 1500 to 1540. We have discussed three cases of groups meeting during the 1530s, in Hughenden, the Missendens, and Chesham. They were three from many such groups.

Similarly important has been the overwhelming evidence that Lollards were not insular, either socially or with regard to contacts with groups and individuals elsewhere. Contact with London was continuous. Contact with others in parishes some distance away was also continuous, and of course that contact was made easier with so many of the Lollards having

---

[112] Bucks. RO DA/Wf/4/356.

land in various parishes or dealing in businesses which took them far away from home. Landholding and business dealings often led to disputes and to appearances in courts, locally and in London.

This has been a brief examination of only a few of those named during Longland's searching out of heresy. It has nevertheless shown clearly that Lollard communications were much more widespread than Dr Davies argued in his article.[113] Lollards were not only able to sustain a high profile within their own communities; they retained strong contacts with relatives and friends elsewhere, across the geographical divide so restricting in Dr Davies' eyes. Indeed, geography failed totally to hinder those determined to remain in contact with their spiritual brothers and sisters, wherever they may have been; nor did it stop the peripatetic wanderings of those individuals crucial to the dissemination of the Gospel to Lollards 'gathered together' in the house groups, such as those we have discussed above. This intercommunication puts paid to Dr Davies' idea of isolation: it is graphically shown on Map 3, based on the material I have discussed above. Lollards were both very securely stable within their own environment, and also a people on the move. The 'known men' (and women) were known to each other, and to others, from the mouth of the Thames to its source, from the uplands of Oxfordshire to the riverside towns of Staines and Windsor, from the pastures of Hampshire to the reed lands of Essex. One can only guess at what other connections existed among the heretics.

Lollards remained a force in society during the years of the Reformation. They held on to their beliefs and they secured for themselves and for their descendants a nonconformist base from which later sects were to spring. But the thought arises time and again that Lollards were normal sixteenth-century gentry, yeomen, artisans, farmers, craftsmen, labourers, and full-time members of their communities, their guilds, and their parish church. Their own society accepted them as such, and there are grounds for supposing that their physical stability made them the dominant 'core' group within that society.[114]

[113] See above, pp. 14, 132–7, and n. 2.
[114] See below, Ch. 7, pp. 311–12, 324–5.

CHAPTER 4

The origins, function, and status of the office of
churchwarden, with particular reference to the diocese
of Ely

ERIC CARLSON

I

A volume on rural English heterodoxy and nonconformity seems an odd
place for an essay on those ecclesiastical Dogberrys and pillars of local
Anglicanism, the churchwardens.[1] Perhaps if it could be shown that rural
dissenters flooded – or even trickled – into the ranks of the churchwardens and their assistants, such an essay would appear well placed. While
that cannot be shown to have been the case in Cambridgeshire,[2] these
men are nonetheless an integral part of the world of rural dissent. Since
their duties included reporting any deviations from official religion to the
authorities, they had it in their power to bring about the end of that world
and they, through inaction or connivance, kept that world spinning on
its axis. Professor Collinson's recent observation that 'ecclesiastical and
social historians should have a particular desire to interview the consciences, minds and pockets of extinct churchwardens'[3] seems particularly apposite and it is in that spirit that this essay is written. Moreover,
it investigates the behaviour of wardens in part of the area round the
market town of Haverhill, which contained Lollards, Familists, and post-

[1] The author wishes to thank Dr Margaret Spufford, who suggested that I write this
essay and aided me in countless ways during its writing; Dr John Craig, who shared
his unpublished work on Suffolk churchwardens and assisted my own research in
Cambridge; and Mr Neal Enssle, who helped me sort my data and without whom
I could not have completed this essay. This project was made possible by financial
support, which I gratefully acknowledge, from the National Endowment for the
Humanities (grant FE-25921–91); the Gustavus Adolphus College Research, Scholarship and Creativity Fund; and the Pilgrim Trust, channelled through the Marc Fitch
Fund.
[2] Lollard churchwardens were identified in Essex and Buckinghamshire: Andrew
Hope, 'Lollardy: The Stone the Builders Rejected?', in Peter Lake and Maria Dowling
(eds.), *Protestantism and the National Church in Sixteenth Century England* (London, 1987),
pp. 23–4; Derek Plumb, 'John Foxe and the Later Lollards of the Mid-Thames Valley'
(Cambridge, PhD, 1987). Dissenting churchwardens have been identified in Terling
(Essex): Keith Wrightson and David Levine, *Poverty and Piety in an English Village: Terling,
1525–1700* (New York and London, 1979), pp. 168–9.
[3] Patrick Collinson, *De Republica Anglorum: Or, History with the Politics Put Back* (Cambridge,
1990), p. 34.

Restoration dissenters, which we hoped to investigate (see Map 4 and Appendix A).

Historians have had good cause to be aware of the churchwardens' importance in the post-Reformation church. In the 1630s, for example, George Herbert described the office as 'the greatest honor of this world'.[4] The late seventeenth-century Archdeacon of Suffolk, Humphrey Prideaux, explicitly compared churchwardens to village constables: 'Churchwardens are officers of the parish in ecclesiastical affairs, as the constables are in civil.'[5] Yet churchwardens have not received modern scholarly attention comparable to that given their civil counterparts; they have as yet no Joan Kent.[6] Instead, printed works both scholarly and popular have been primarily bland catalogues of their duties, peppered lightly with highly impressionistic comments about their elections and qualifications for office.[7] For this essay, a systematic study of 'the consciences, minds and pockets' of a large sample of churchwardens has been undertaken: over 1,200 wardens from the twenty parishes of the two most south-easterly of Cambridgeshire's hundreds, Radfield and Chilford.[8]

These parishes were chosen for two reasons. Although none was a 'dissenting centre' (as defined by Dr Spufford) after 1660, they had a tradition of nearly continuous exposure to and interest in religious

---

[4] F.E. Hutchinson (ed.), *The Works of George Herbert* (Oxford, 1941), p. 270.

[5] Humphrey Prideaux, *Directions to Church-Wardens for the Faithful Discharge of their Office* (2nd edn, Norwich, 1704), p. 1. I am grateful to the Rev. Dr Judith Maltby for this reference.

[6] Joan R. Kent, *The English Village Constable 1580–1642: A Social and Administrative Study* (Oxford, 1986).

[7] An exception, limited in geographical scope, is Marjorie Keniston McIntosh, *A Community Transformed: The Manor and Liberty of Havering, 1500–1620* (Cambridge, 1991). Important earlier works are: J. Charles Cox, *Churchwardens' Accounts from the Fourteenth Century to the Close of the Seventeenth Century* (London, 1913); Abbot Gasquet, *Parish Life in Medieval England* (London, 1906), chapter 5; W.E. Tate, *The Parish Chest. A Study of the Records of Parochial Administration in England* (3rd edn, Cambridge, 1969), chapter 2; Sedley Lynch Ware, *The Elizabethan Parish in its Ecclesiastical and Financial Aspects*, Johns Hopkins University Studies in Historical and Political Science, ser. 26, vols. 7–8 (Baltimore, 1908), chapter 1; A. Tindal Hart, *The Man in the Pew, 1558–1660* (New York, 1966), chapter 3.

[8] Parishes: Great Abington, Little Abington, Babraham, Balsham, Bartlow, Brinkley, Burrough Green, Carlton cum Willingham, Castle Camps, Dullingham, Hildersham, Horseheath, Linton, Pampisford, Shudy Camps, Stetchworth, Westley Waterless, Weston Colville, West Wickham, and West Wratting. Chilford and Radfield Hundreds are treated in the *VCH Cambs.*, VI. Names of wardens were compiled from parish register transcripts (EDR, H/3 class); diocesan court act books (EDR, B/2 and D/2 class); miscellaneous court papers (EDR, B/9 class; K/4–7, 11, 15, 21; CUL, Add. MS 6605); and original parish registers housed in the Cambs. RO. Sidesmen have not been included because the sources did not permit making a complete list of these officers during this period. In addition, a sizable percentage of those identified served as churchwardens during the survey period.

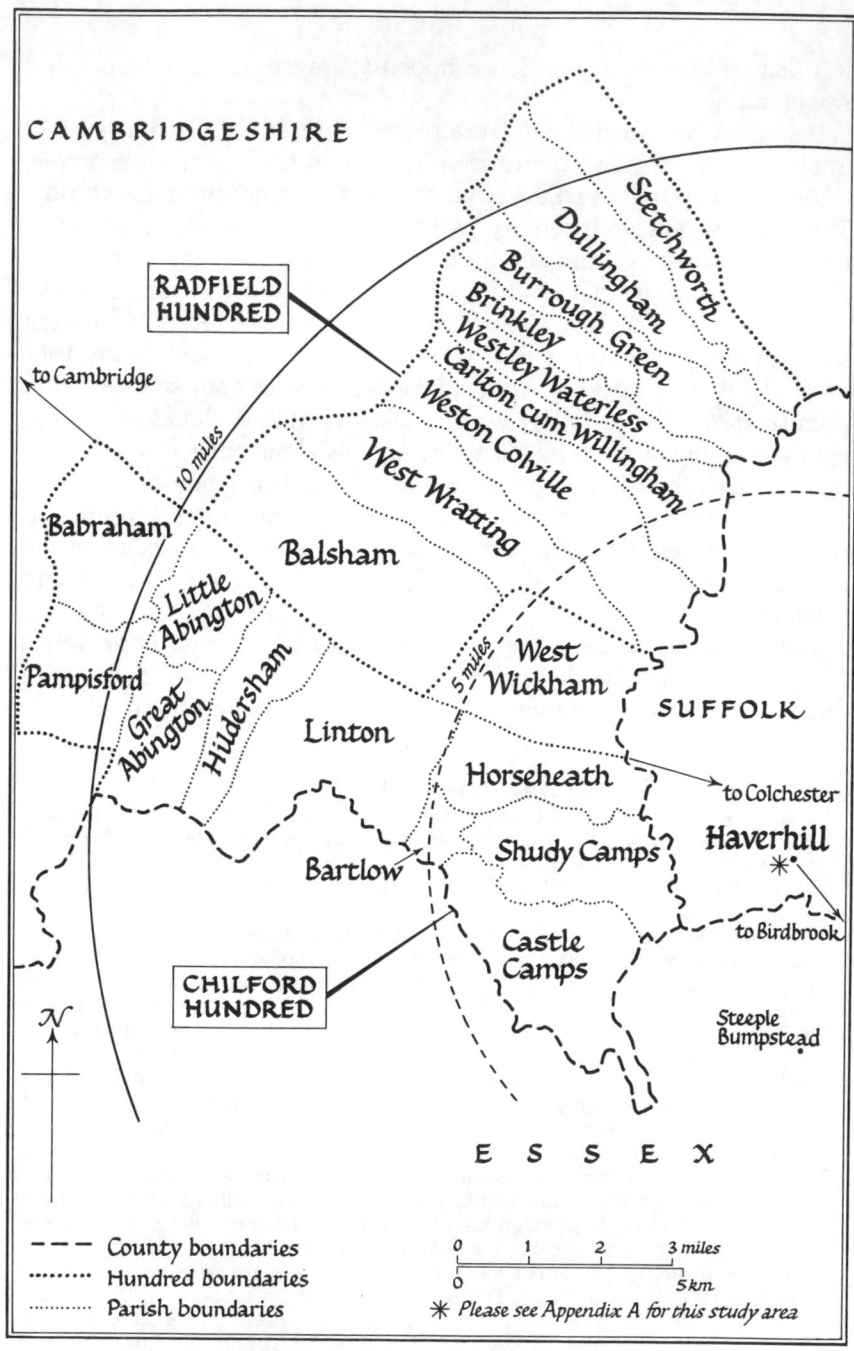

CAMBRIDGESHIRE

RADFIELD HUNDRED

Stetchworth

Dullingham

Burrough Green

Brinkley

Westley Waterless

Carlton cum Willingham

Weston Colville

to Cambridge

10 miles

West Wratting

Babraham

Balsham

Little Abington

West Wickham

Pampisford

Great Abington

Hildersham

SUFFOLK

5 miles

Linton

Horseheath

to Colchester

Haverhill
✳

Bartlow

Shudy Camps

to Birdbrook

CHILFORD HUNDRED

Castle Camps

Steeple Bumpstead

N

E S S E X

- - - County boundaries
······· Hundred boundaries
·········· Parish boundaries

0   1   2   3 miles
0   5km

✳ *Please see Appendix A for this study area*

Map 4. Chilford and Radfield Hundreds, Cambridgeshire

eccentricity that predated the Reformation.[9] While I am not aware of any Lollards identified in these villages, they can be found in the neighbouring Essex parishes of Birdbrook, Finchingfield, Helions Bumstead, and Steeple Bumstead,[10] and those in Steeple Bumstead were aggressive proselytizers.[11] Given the scale of commerce, population exchange, and overlapping landholding between the villages of northern Essex and south-eastern Cambridgeshire,[12] it is impossible to accept that villagers in this sample were not exposed to Lollard influences, directly or indirectly. Starting in the 1560s, Balsham and Shudy Camps were identified as centres of the heretical Family of Love. Familist influence may have spread well beyond these two parishes, as well. As late as 1609, Balsham residents were associated with the sect.[13] Puritanism of a sometimes quite confrontational variety can be detected in parishes such as Weston Colville[14] and might well have been present in less virulent strains elsewhere, and Bishop Wren's efforts met widespread resistance in the late 1630s.[15] Babraham's churchwardens, for example, reported: 'We have diligently inquired into the Articles given us charge by the Reverend Father in God Matthew Lord Bishop of Ely: find nothing worthy of presentment, but have all things performed decently in our church. We have none refuse to receive the Communion.'[16]

Thirteen adult male members of a Baptist church in Dullingham can be identified in 1657,[17] many active resisters of the restored church in the 1660s.[18] Although the numbers involved were not unusually high, post-Restoration nonconformity was a feature of many parishes in this

---

[9] Margaret Spufford, *Contrasting Communities: English Villagers in the Sixteenth and Seventeenth Centuries* (Cambridge, 1974), part 3.
[10] Communication from Dr Derek Plumb. See Appendix A for our abortive attempt to trace dissent through time in these parishes.
[11] Hope, 'Lollardy', pp. 23–4
[12] For example, William Brown of Helions Bumpstead, a Lollard centre, also held land in Linton, a centre of nonconformity after 1660: EPR, WR C35: 169.
[13] EDR, B/2/38, fol. 18; Gonville and Caius College, Cambridge, MS 53/30, fols. 72v–3r. See Felicity Heal, 'The Family of Love and the Diocese of Ely', in Derek Baker (ed.), *Schism, Heresy and Religious Protest*, Studies in Church History, 9 (Cambridge, 1972), pp. 213–22; Christopher Marsh, '"A Graceless, and Audacious Companie"? The Family of Love in the Parish of Balsham, 1550–1630', in W.J. Sheils and Diana Wood (eds.), *Voluntary Religion*, Studies in Church History, 23 (Oxford, 1986), pp. 191–208. I am grateful to Dr Marsh for aid in identifying Familists in my sample parishes.
[14] Discussed in Eric Josef Carlson, *Marriage and the English Reformation* (Oxford, 1994), chapter 7.
[15] The manuscript record of the 1639 visitation is EDR, B/2/52. See Margaret Spufford, *Contrasting Communities*, pp. 265–71.
[16] EDR, B/9/37.
[17] E.B. Underhill (ed.), *Records of the Churches of Christ Gathered at Fenstanton, Warboys, and Hexham, 1644–1720*, Hanserd Knollys Society (London, 1854), pp. 238–9.
[18] EDR, B/2/54, fols. 8r, 22v–3r.

sample.[19] In the 1660s, Baptist and Quaker meetings were held in Shudy Camps, Balsham, Linton, Castle Camps, and Horseheath.[20] The 1676 Compton Census identified nonconformists in ten parishes.[21] Church court records make it possible to identify by name Quakers, Baptists, and other obstinate absentees from church from those, as well as two more, parishes.[22] In addition to men from Linton, one of the trustees of the Linton Congregational meeting-house in 1698 was from Bartlow.[23]

A further reason for sampling these parishes is the quality of the records and supporting material. Ecclesiastical court records and parish registers, both originals and annual episcopal transcripts, made it possible to compile a list of churchwardens which is remarkably complete, and the same court records made it possible to observe those wardens at work. Records of a number of lay subsidies and Hearth Taxes made it possible to study the relative wealth of the wardens at a number of different points in time. Wills, which are preserved quite completely for Cambridgeshire from the mid-sixteenth century, provided information about their religious views and occupations.

With their tradition of dissent and good records, these twenty parishes are both an appropriate and a manageable basis for a study of rural churchwardens and their connection to nonconformity. While no such study can pretend to be definitive or representative, the results reported here may place in sharper relief the landscape of the world of rural dissent. Moreover, it is hoped that they will provoke others to investigate rural churchwardens in other parts of England, so that our picture of their place in the rural world will resemble more a mural than a snapshot.

II

When the eleventh-century canonist Bourchard was Bishop of Worms, he established a system in which seven men were chosen in each parish to assist the bishop in his visitations by informing him of their neighbours' misdeeds, and he helpfully provided them with a set of questions

---

[19] William Stevenson, 'The Economic and Social Status of Protestant Sectarians in Huntingdonshire, Cambridgeshire and Bedfordshire, 1650–1725' (Cambridge, PhD, 1990).

[20] From Bishop Laney's survey (1669), in G. Lyon Turner (ed.), *Original Records of Early Nonconformity under Persecution and Indulgence*, 3 vols. (London, 1911), I, pp. 39–41; Margaret Spufford, *Contrasting Communities*, pp. 223–5.

[21] Great Abington, Balsham, Castle Camps, Dullingham, Horseheath, Linton, Shudy Camps, Stetchworth, West Wickham, and West Wratting: Anne Whiteman (ed.), *The Compton Census of 1676: A Critical Edition*, Records of Social and Economic History, NS, 10 (London, 1986), pp. 162–7. (Bartlow, Burrough Green omitted from original.)

[22] Bartlow and Brinkley.

[23] CUL, Palmer MS B.30.

to aid them in this undertaking.[24] This scheme anticipated in notable ways what became the functions of churchwardens, but it was not from this unpopular practice that the office was to evolve.

When the first beings who resembled churchwardens emerged from the ecclesiastical primordial slime can never be known with precision. The office originated in the need of English parishioners to maintain property given to their parish churches.[25] In that role, under the title of 'parish procurators', modern scholars first detect them in Bristol in 1261 where they are assigned responsibility for a house left by Alice Hayle to provide maintenance for a light in the church of All Saints. Many other obligations – such as maintaining, repairing, and enlarging parish churches – also began to fall to the laity, and the funds to meet these responsibilities had to be raised and administered. All of this was delegated to members of the parish community who, although known by a variety of names, 'were soon to be indistinguishable from the churchwardens of the sixteenth and seventeenth centuries'.[26] Less than a century after their first known appearance, churchwardens had become 'a generally established feature of parochial life'.[27]

Official cognizance of churchwardens was first taken in 1287, in a statute of the synod of Exeter, but at no time before the Tudors did the central government (lay or ecclesiastical) attempt to standardize the office or its duties. Bishops transferred many responsibilities to congregations, including the upkeep of the nave and the provision of liturgical vessels and vestments,[28] but they did not dictate how the congregation was to meet its obligations. The office of churchwarden – and this is essential to understanding its response to local religious nonconformity – was from the first a local construction designed to address the needs of each emerging parish community to take collective action.[29] As such, it fits neatly among the other offices and institutions of collective activity in the robust village self-government which

---

[24] Georges Duby, *The Knight, the Lady and the Priest: The Making of Modern Marriage in Medieval France* (New York, 1985), p. 61.
[25] What follows depends on Charles Drew, *Early Parochial Organisation in England: The Origins of the Office of Churchwarden* (London, 1954). See also Emma Mason, 'The Role of the English Parishioner, 1100–1500', *Journal of Ecclesiastical History*, 27 (1976), pp. 17–29.
[26] Dorothy M. Owen, *Church and Society in Medieval Lincolnshire* (Lincoln, 1981), pp. 115–16.
[27] Drew, *Early Parochial Organisation*, p. 7.
[28] F.M. Powicke and C.R. Cheney (eds.), *Councils and Synods with Other Documents relating to the English Church*, vol. II: *AD 1205–1313* (Oxford, 1964), pp. 128, 367, 1006, 1122–3, 1385–8. References taken from Clive Burgess, '"A Fond Thing Vainly Invented": An Essay on Purgatory and Pious Gesture in Later Medieval England', in Susan J. Wright (ed.), *Parish, Church and People: Local Studies in Lay Religion 1350–1750* (London, 1988).
[29] Susan Reynolds, *Kingdoms and Communities in Western Europe, 900–1300* (Oxford, 1984), pp. 79–100.

flourished at that same time.[30] Most of all, it reflected the absolute determination of medieval English villagers to be in control of their own milieux to whatever extent was possible.[31]

This local initiative has meant that there is a certain degree of messiness in the historical record. As Charles Drew observed, the evolution of churchwardens 'had none of the smooth inevitability which historical developments are so apt to assume when observed from the privileged viewpoint of posterity'. Instead of producing a uniform model of parochial organization, the process resulted in 'a norm to which there were throughout the Middle Ages, and later, plenty of exceptions [since] nowhere did "approved local custom" play a greater part than in the parish'.[32] Nevertheless, when we first encounter Tudor churchwardens, the very real local variations in practice fade next to the sort of uniformity provided by the agreed categories of their duties and their universal recognition as a stable and standard part of local government.

Under Henry VIII, the churchwardens received their first mandated civil duties. These included providing arms for soldiers and relief for maimed veterans.[33] Delegating responsibility to villagers in this way paralleled what had been happening for some time with peasant juries, which had, by 1450, become the bodies through which 'the crown routinely met the country' for a variety of administrative, military, and judicial matters.[34] Just as the crown was to turn to parliament to provide a semblance of consensus for the religious changes of the 1530s and after, it would also require the churchwardens to serve as its agents enforcing local conformity with the new settlement. The consequences could surely not have been anticipated at the time, but this step was to transform the office and place the churchwardens in a novel and perhaps awkward position in relation to their neighbours, whose agents and trustees they now were to have been.

---

[30] A complete list of works is beyond the scope of this note. See: Warren O. Ault, 'Village Assemblies in Medieval England', in *Album Helen Maud Cam*, Studies Presented to the International Commission for the History of Representative and Parliamentary Institutions 23 (Louvain and Paris, 1960), pp. 11–35; idem, 'Manor Court and Parish Church in Fifteenth-Century England: A Study of Village By-Laws', *Speculum*, 42 (1967), pp. 53–67; idem, 'The Village Church and the Village Community in Mediaeval England', *Speculum*, 45 (1970), pp. 197–215; Anne Reiber DeWindt, 'Peasant Power Structures in Fourteenth-Century King's Ripton', *Mediaeval Studies*, 38 (1976), pp. 236–67; idem, 'Local Government in a Small Town: A Medieval Leet Jury and its Constituents', *Albion*, 23 (1991), pp. 627–54; Marjorie Keniston McIntosh, *Autonomy and Community: The Royal Manor of Havering, 1200–1500* (Cambridge, 1986).

[31] Reynolds, *Kingdoms and Communities*, p. 58.

[32] Drew, *Early Parochial Organisation*, p. 25.

[33] Cox, *Churchwardens' Accounts*, p. 2.

[34] R.B. Goheen, 'Peasant Politics? Village Community and the Crown in Fifteenth-Century England', *American Historical Review*, 96 (1991), pp. 42–62.

In 1552, the English laity were for the first time required by statute law to attend their parish churches 'upon the Sundays and other days ordained to be holy days'. The second Edwardian Uniformity Act ordered that

> all ... persons inhabiting within this realm ... shall diligently and faithfully, having no lawful or reasonable excuse to be absent, endeavour themselves to resort to their parish church or chapel accustomed, or upon reasonable let thereof to some usual place where common prayer and such service of God shall be used in such time of let ... and there to abide orderly and soberly during the time of the common prayer, preachings or other service of God there to be used and ministered; upon pain of punishment by the censures of the church.

Archbishops, bishops, and ordinaries were charged with the statute's execution and they were authorized to make full use of ecclesiastical censures to 'reform, correct and punish' all violators.[35] Any explicit plan for getting the necessary information into the hands of the bishops was noticeably missing.

The religious settlement of 1559 restored these provisions with very little change. In addition to ecclesiastical church censures, the new law provided that 'every person so offending shall forfeit for every such offence twelve pence, to be by the churchwardens of the parish where such offence shall be done, to the use of the poor of the same parish, of the goods, lands and tenements of such offender by way of distress'.[36] The churchwardens were not officially charged with any responsibility beyond levying and collecting the fine.

The duty of identifying absentees was originally to be vested in 'three or four discreet men' in every parish, appointed by the local ordinary. These men were to call upon those found 'slack or negligent in resorting to church, having no great or urgent cause of absence' and admonish them to mend their behaviour; if that failed, they were to 'denounce them to the ordinary'.[37] Although some parishes had officers 'to view the comers to the church',[38] normally this burden was passed to the churchwardens as well.

Growing anxiety about threats from English Catholics meant that, almost immediately, concerns began to surface about the results. To

---

[35] 5/6 Edw. VI c. 1 §§ 1–2.
[36] 1 Eliz. I c. 2 § 3.
[37] W.H. Frere (ed.), *Visitation Articles and Injunctions of the Period of the Reformation*, vol. III: 1559–1575, Alcuin Club Collections, 16 (London, 1910), p. 22.
[38] Frederic Ouvry (ed.), 'Extracts from the Churchwardens' Accounts of the Parish of Wing in the County of Buckingham', *Archaeologia*, 36 (1855), p. 237. The example is from 1568.

improve the thoroughness of their reports, wardens were sent out of
the church to search the parish during the service and find those who
were absent 'negligently or wilfully' from church.[39] This procedure
exposed more card players and alehouse haunters than Roman Catholics, and it had the added disadvantage of keeping the wardens from
being present for the service, where they were also responsible for
keeping order and assuring that no one left early. Another solution
was to arrange formally to record attenders. In Prescot (Lancs.), the
vicar and wardens prepared a parish census and the wardens crossed
off the names of those present each week.[40] Parish pew charts were
drafted for that purpose. Ickleton (Cambs.) wardens used a primitive
pew chart to make a rather oblique presentment in 1597:

> Absent from church All the men in the long stool except 2.
> All the men in Ed: Swan stool except 2.
> 3 absent out of Symon Swan his stool.
> Many of the bachelors. Some man's whole household
> Thirloe his stool was empty & twenty more in the whole church.[41]

While expected to report both on absences and their collection of
the 12d fine in their quarter bills,[42] wardens rarely did so.[43] When the
subject was acknowledged at all, it was met more likely than not with
something similar to this from 1582 by the wardens of Barton (Cambs.):
'There have not been any forfeiture of xii[d] levied or gathered neither
hath there been any cause to gather or to levy any such forfeiture so
far as we know.'[44] Wardens also described disturbances caused because
pews were filled to overflowing and parishioners could not comfortably be accommodated.[45]

Most scholars have, however, chosen to believe that wardens were
deliberately concealing violators, preferring to perjure themselves since
wardens were under oath to present anyone so much as 'vehemently
suspected' to have committed any of the offences named in the

---

[39] Visitation article from York, 1571, quoted in Kenneth L. Parker, *The English Sabbath:
A Study of Doctrine and Discipline from the Reformation to the Civil War* (Cambridge, 1988),
p. 63.

[40] Christopher Haigh, *Reformation and Resistance in Tudor Lancashire* (Cambridge, 1975),
p. 273.

[41] EDR, B/2/16, fol. 59r.

[42] See, for example, Bishop Cox's visitation articles and injunctions for 1571, in Frere
(ed.), *Visitation Articles*, p. 299.

[43] In their 1579 quarter bill, the wardens from Sawston reported: 'We doubt not but
that many have deserved by reason of willfullness or otherwise to have paid the
forfeiture . . . but if it had been truly taken according to the statute, either the poor
men's box should have been better stored with money, or else the church many
times better filled with people.' EDR, D/2/10, fol. 154r.

[44] EDR, B/9/1, no. 44.

[45] For example, EDR, B/2/11, fol. 175v, B/2/18, fol. 18v.

bishop's articles, than incommode themselves or their neighbours.[46] This view – that they could or would blithely ignore both the state of their souls and the rule of law – over some transitory inconveniences deserves some consideration. Wardens certainly might face abuse and be threatened with violence when they attempted to collect the fine[47] but this in itself did not deter them. After all, we know of the abuse only because of wardens who did carry out their duties. Some other motive must have been in play.

When the churchwardens of Westley Waterless reported 'that they could not levy the 12d of any, for that they knew not of any to be absent from church'[48] they were using the word 'absent' in something other than a literal sense. This is made abundantly clear by a London minister, who noted in 1580 that he and the parish officers had been ordered to investigate and report those in the parish who did not attend church or receive the Communion but that the 'investigation [was] not to extend to any others than such as do *obstinately for religion* refuse' to attend.[49] When Lucas Barefoot was presented for his absence by the wardens of Eltisley (Cambs.), he dutifully appeared in court, describing how he and his wife alternated Sundays attending church so that one of them could tend their two small children. The case was dismissed, and it is easy to imagine that the wardens also received a few tart words from the judge on the subject of wasting everyone's time.[50] Barefoot was as far from absent 'obstinately for religion' as one could be. A few cases like this were bound to make the point to wardens that the courts did not consider such absences worth presenting. Failing to present could, as Martin Ingram has observed, demonstrate 'a robust regard for distinctions between the serious and the trivial' on the part of the wardens.[51] Moreover, the 1559 royal injunctions had explicitly provided that an admonition should precede presentment. In 1584, Robert Heddley of Pampisford was named as 'a slack comer to church', but it was noted that he had been 'sundry times admonished' without success, and only after that failure was he presented.[52] Apparently, then, to say that no one was absent was to say that no one had been absent 'obstinately for religion', or that any who had,

---

[46] For example, this line of argument is used in Haigh, *Reformation and Resistance*; and Roger B. Manning, *Religion and Society in Elizabethan Sussex: A Study of the Enforcement of the Religious Settlement 1558–1603* (Leicester, 1969).

[47] See below, pp. 188–9.

[48] EDR, D/2/10, fols. 9r, 16v. They were ordered to investigate and send names of non-attenders to the court, but were later dismissed without giving the name of a single parishioner.

[49] CUL, MS Mm.1.29, fols. 36v, 40r (emphasis mine).

[50] EDR, D/2/8, fol. 124v.

[51] Martin Ingram, *Church Courts, Sex and Marriage in England, 1570–1640* (Cambridge, 1987), p. 328.

[52] EDR, D/2/16, fol. 59r.

had been brought to conformity through the efforts of the wardens or minister.

The more punctilious, particularly those in parliament alarmed about the imagined Catholic menace, were unsatisfied by this approach and remained convinced that too many were absenting themselves without penalty. In 1571, a bill was offered to require 'every subject not sick or in plight' to attend the parish church once every quarter and receive Communion annually. The fine for non-attendance was to be £12, and for non-Communion it was to be 100 marks. Sir Owen Hopton moved 'that the presentation of such defaults should not depend upon the relation of the churchwardens, who being simple men and fearing to offend, would rather incur the danger of perjury than displease some of their neighbours'.[53] To prove his assertion, Hopton offered what is unhelpfully described in the report as 'experience'. The bill tried to circumvent the churchwardens by using 'promoters', or, more vulgarly, informers, who would receive the statutory fine in return for their information. This made some who might support the principle behind the bill uneasy, and William Fleetwood was long-winded on the subject of the 'evils and inconveniences' caused by past use of informers.[54] The queen's objections to requiring Communion stopped the bill.

In the 1580s, new recusancy legislation provided for enormous fines to be paid, not into the local poor relief coffers, but directly to the Exchequer, and the secular courts began enforcing the laws.[55] Churchwardens continued to be required, via episcopal visitation articles, to report on those who did not attend their parish churches. In 1604, Canon XC required that churchwardens and sidesmen

> shall diligently see that all the parishioners duly resort to their church upon all Sundays and holy-days, and there continue the whole time of divine service; and none to walk or to stand idle or talking in the church, or in the church-yard, or church-porch during that time. And all such as shall be found slack or negligent in resorting to the church (having no great or urgent cause of absence) they shall earnestly call upon them; and after due monition (if they amend not) they shall present them to the ordinary.[56]

Claiming that the churchwardens 'often . . . do forbear to discharge their duties', however, the canons also provided that the minister could present offenders if the wardens and sidesmen did not.[57]

---

[53] T.E. Hartley (ed.), *Proceedings in the Parliaments of Elizabeth I*, vol. I: 1559–1581 (Leicester, 1981), pp. 201–2.

[54] Ibid., p. 210.

[55] 23 Eliz. I c. 1.

[56] E. Cardwell (ed.), *Synodalia* (Oxford, 1842), p. 297.

[57] Canon CXIII, in Cardwell (ed.), *Synodalia*, pp. 309–10. This was a significant departure from past practice. In Elizabethan Ely diocese, there had been a number of ugly

Early Stuart bishops based their visitations on the 1604 canons, but Roman Catholics were no longer the only concern when seeking out non-attenders. Archbishop Abbot's 1616 articles sought information from the churchwardens on 'conventicles or private congregations' and required that they name any people suspected of being 'Anabaptists, Libertines, Brownists, of the Family of Love, or of any other heresy or schism'.[58] By 1638, Bishop Wren of Ely had made conventicles more important than papists, and moved the subject of religious conformity to the first chapter of his articles.[59]

Visitations ceased on 1 August 1641 after parliament struck down episcopal disciplinary authority and made it illegal for them to 'minister unto any churchwarden . . . any corporal oath whereby [they] may be charged or obliged to make any presentment of any crime or offence or to confess or to accuse [themselves] of any crime, offence, delinquency or misdemeanour'.[60]

Although in the 1570s and 1580s there had been some discussion among puritans and Presbyterians of whether wardens should be replaced by elders, and the Dedham classis discussed the issue without finding a solution,[61] they were not abolished along with bishops. During the 1630s, they had gained credibility with those who previously might have seen them as episcopal toadies. In 1632, the Bishop of Rochester stated his fear that they were the base from which 'to hatch a lay presbytery',[62] and William Prynne sanguinely offered a programme of civil disobedience to be carried out by wardens, encouraging them to throw up a series of procedural obstacles when bishops attempted to carry out their visitations. Churchwardens were urged to demand to see a lawful patent and ask whether the articles had been approved by convocation, parliament, and the king: 'If not (as none of them are) then bid them keep them for waste paper, or to stop mustard pots.'[63] Although they stopped a good deal short of that, the litany of *omnia bene* heard by Wren in 1638–9 is ample testimony to the turning of this particular worm.[64]

---

conflicts when ministers had tried to interpose their own presentments in the wardens' bills: see Carlson, *Marriage and the English Reformation*, chapter 7.

[58] E. Cardwell (ed.), *Documentary Annals of the Reformed Church of England*, 2 vols. (Oxford, 1844), II, pp. 179–80.

[59] *Articles to be Inquired of within the Diocess of Ely in the First Visitation of the R. Reverend Father in God Matthew Lord Bishop of Ely* (London, 1638).

[60] 17 Car. I c. 11 § 2.

[61] Donald McGinn, *The Admonition Controversy* (New Brunswick, NJ, 1949), pp. 470–7; R.G. Usher (ed.), *The Presbyterian Movement in the Reign of Queen Elizabeth as Illustrated by the Minute Book of the Dedham Classis*, Camden Society, 3rd Ser., 8 (1905), pp. 73, 79.

[62] Quoted in Paul S. Seaver, *The Puritan Lectureships: The Politics of Religious Dissent, 1560–1662* (Stanford, 1970), pp. 138–9.

[63] W. Prynne, *Briefe Instructions for Churchwardens and Others to Observe in all Episcopall or Archdiaconall Visitations and Spirituall Courts* (n.p., 1637), p. 1v.

[64] See, for example, EDR, B/9/3–6. See n. 16, above.

This litany may be explained by noting that in the nine villages in west Cambridgeshire which produced numerous petitioners in favour of the abolition of episcopacy well over a third of the fifty-eight wardens and questmen who held office in 1637 or 1638 signed the petition.[65]

The order originally intended for the post-episcopal English church would have replaced churchwardens with elders, elected by those who had taken the Covenant and were not servants without families.[66] There was little national enthusiasm for the Scottish-style church order and it was implemented fitfully. When the 'Act for the relief of religious and peaceable people' repealed uniformity and required only that everyone go somewhere on the Sabbath for 'prayer, preaching, reading or expounding the Scriptures, or conferring upon the same' in 1650,[67] parliament effectively removed the rationale for the elders. A number of ministers, like Richard Baxter, rejected the use of elders in favour of maintaining moral discipline as a ministerial prerogative, and many of their old disciplinary activities passed to the JPs, but the wardens themselves continued to be elected and assigned duties.[68] For example, in 1657 they were designated as among the officers responsible for enforcing new Sabbath laws and given authority to demand entry into any place where they suspected the Lord's Day was being violated. They were also to report to the mayor or JPs anyone who deliberately disrupted or disturbed a minister or preacher in pursuit of his duty.[69]

In July 1661, the Ecclesiastical Causes Act restored the powers of the church courts as they had been in 1640.[70] Visitations were one of the last parts of the machinery reinstated; no full-scale episcopal visitations were undertaken until 1662 after the passage of a new Act of Uniformity.[71] Parliament then added a number of additional burdens to those who did not conform, and the churchwardens were in the centre of the struggle to enforce these punitive acts.[72]

[65] Margaret Spufford, Contrasting Communities, pp. 268–9.
[66] John Morrill, 'The Church in England, 1642–9', in John Morrill (ed.), Reactions to the English Civil War 1642–1649 (London, 1982), pp. 89–114, esp. pp. 96–7.
[67] C.H. Firth and R.S. Rait (eds.), Acts and Ordinances of the Interregnum, 1642–1660, 3 vols. (London, 1911), II, pp. 423–5.
[68] Claire Cross, 'The Church in England 1646–1660', in G.E. Aylmer (ed.), The Quest for Settlement 1646–1660 (London, 1972), pp. 99–120, esp. pp. 103–7. The process of shifting many disciplinary functions to the JPs was well under way before the Interregnum: see Anthony Fletcher, Reform in the Provinces: The Government of Stuart England (New Haven, 1986), esp. pp. 262–81; McIntosh, A Community Transformed, pp. 256–7.
[69] Firth and Rait (eds.), Acts and Ordinances of the Interregnum, II, pp. 1167–8.
[70] The exceptions were High Commission and the ex officio oath, which were explicitly not to return: 13 Car. II st. 1 c. 12.
[71] 14 Car. II c. 4.
[72] The discussion following is based primarily on: I. M. Green, The Re-Establishment of the Church of England, 1660–1663 (Oxford, 1978), pp. 128–40; Ronald Hutton, The Restoration: A Political and Religious History of England and Wales, 1658–1667 (Oxford, 1985); Paul Seaward, The Cavalier Parliament and the Reconstruction of the Old Regime, 1661–1667

The Quakers were most offensive to the Cavalier parliament. Their disruptive behaviour in the 1650s and refusal to take the Oath of Allegiance made them the greatest source of social and political anxiety. In 1662, they were singled out for particularly heavy fines. Parliament planned to expand the Quaker Act in 1663 and to institute fines for churchwardens who failed to make reports to JPs, and for JPs who failed to prosecute on reports. In the aftermath of the aborted rebellion in August 1664, nonconformist meetings were seen by many to be seedbeds of sedition and parliament pressed ahead, passing the first Conventicle Act. This Act subjected anyone over sixteen who attended a religious gathering of more than five persons to a fine of £5 for a first offence, £10 for a second, and £100 or transportation for a third. Churchwardens who failed to report offenders would be fined £5. The Act expired in 1668, but it was replaced by one with essentially the same provisions in 1670, which was in force until toleration was granted in 1689.

Churchwardens initially may have resisted their assigned roles and some resisted the return of visitations. Having been restored during the Interregnum to something closer to the original form of the office, wardens found that the Restoration meant the return of irksome episcopal demands.[73] There is some evidence that they resisted these demands even more aggressively than they were accused of doing in the 1630s. Gilbert Sheldon found wardenly intransigence so effective in frustrating his assault on nonconformity that he launched a campaign to reconstruct London vestries in order to secure more cooperative officers,[74] though Tim Harris has observed that in the London visitations of 1664–80 there was a continued 'general unwillingness of churchwardens to present religious delinquents'.[75] Peterborough's Bishop William Lloyd complained of the 'falseness and perjury of the churchwardens'[76] and wrote to the Archbishop of Canterbury in 1680 that 'defects can never be known by the presentments of the churchwardens [who] will forswear themselves over and over rather than bring expense on themselves or their neighbours'.[77] Parish priests imitated their ordinaries. The rector of Saddington

(Cambridge, 1988), chapter 7; and Anne Whiteman, 'The Re-Establishment of the Church of England, 1660–1663', Trans. Royal Hist. Soc., 5th Ser., 5 (1955), pp. 11–31.

[73] Andrew M. Coleby argues that they also found distasteful losing the independence gained in the previous decade: Central Government and the Localities: Hampshire 1649–1689 (Cambridge, 1987), p. 131.

[74] Paul Seaward, 'Gilbert Sheldon, the London Vestries, and the Defense of the Church', in Tim Harris et al. (eds.), The Politics of Religion in Restoration England (Oxford, 1990), pp. 49–73.

[75] Tim Harris, London Crowds in the Reign of Charles II: Propaganda and Politics from the Restoration until the Exclusion Crisis (Cambridge, 1987), p. 71.

[76] John Spurr, The Restoration Church of England, 1649–1689 (New Haven, 1991), p. 193.

[77] Susan Doran and Christopher Durston, Princes, Pastors and People: The Church and Religion in England 1529–1689 (London, 1991), p. 187.

accused wardens of 'dancing after the pipes of some grandees in the parish and according to their dictates presenting a perjured *omnia bene* at the Visitation'[78] – lines which could have come from the mouth of Sir Owen Hopton in 1571. These by-now ritual laments have too often been taken at face value. Examining them in the light of practice shows that they were not entirely justified.

Cambridgeshire wardens produced lists of Quakers, Baptists, and other 'slack comers to church', even for the restored Matthew Wren, the last active Laudian bishop, who had had so little success with them in 1639.[79] These were absent 'obstinately for religion', would not be reconciled to the church through any amount of admonition from their neighbours, and thus deserved to be presented according to the standards which had long been applied – and they were, regularly and without concealment.

The accuracy and completeness of these presentments can be tested against the Compton Census of 1676, and the results are startling in light of the negative reviews typically received by post-Restoration wardens. In every parish from Chilford and Radfield Hundreds reported to have nonconformists in 1676, it is possible from church court records to identify by name virtually every person counted by the Compton Census. For example, the six nonconformists noted in 1676 from Great Abington can confidently be identified as three members of the Amye family (Thomas, his wife Mary, and their daughter Margaret), the Quaker widow Mary Smith and her son Robert, and Joan Barker. These continued to be presented regularly until 1689, although by then death had reduced them to Robert Smith and Joan Barker.[80] In Castle Camps, four of the five nonconformists of 1676 can be named: the Quakers John and Anne Washtail, Barbara Bunyard (who had at one point been host to a meeting at her house), and Milo Boddenham.[81] The Washtails had been fixtures in Castle Camps' presentments since 1663.[82] Barbara Bunyard (or Bunyon) soon moved to Shudy Camps, where she was also presented, joining the three Quakers, all in one family, described in Bishop Lacey's survey. These were the Salmons, who were regularly presented in the 1670s and 1680s.[83] In Dullingham, most of the seven Compton nonconformists were

---

[78] John H. Pruett, *The Parish Clergy under the Later Stuarts: The Leicestershire Experience* (Urbana, Ill., 1978), p. 118.

[79] Castle Camps, Dullingham, Linton, and Stetchworth presented non-attenders at Wren's visitation: EDR, B/2/54, fols. 8r–9v, 22v–3r.

[80] EDR, D/2/54, fol. 41r, B/2/62, fol. 18r, B/2/65, fol. 42r, B/2/66, fol. 43v, D/2/56, fol. 9v, B/2/70, fol. 8v.

[81] EDR, D/2/54, fol. 52v.

[82] EDR, B/2/54, fols. 23r, 25r.

[83] EDR, D/2/54, fols. 14r, 41r, and unpaginated section, B/2/63a, fol. 9v, B/2/66, fol. 14v, D/2/56, fol. 14r, B/2/70, fols. 7v, 38v. Joan Salmon, a widow, and her sons Robert and John were the original family members identified. John soon disappeared, Joan died, and Robert continued to appear, but with his wife Sarah.

remnants of the Baptist Church noted above: the Fyson family, Edward Prick, and the widow of either John or Thomas Pratt. They were joined by Thomas Ranew and his wife and, in the 1680s, William Bridge.[84] Around 1679, Henry Fyson moved to Stetchworth, where he joined an established nonconformist group, married, raised a family, and continued to be presented for refusing to attend church.[85] This pattern of close correspondence between the Compton Census and church court records can be repeated in all of the sample parishes. If the repeated presentments of the same people has something of a round-up-the-usual-suspects feel to it, it is the case nonetheless that committed nonconformists – those absent obstinately for religion – were presented in rural Cambridgeshire. This is not evidence to support the notion of widespread, perjured *omnia benes*.

Rural south-eastern Cambridgeshire might not be typical in this regard.[86] In 1683, in the Hertfordshire parish of Sarratt, the wardens did not name anyone, saying that they did not think it right to turn people over to the church courts who were already being punished by the civil courts. This excuse rings hollow given evidence from other places of wardens' reluctance to perform their statutory duties in that respect. In August 1673, for example, Andover's wardens knew of a conventicle, but refused to act and were fined £5.[87] Enforcing the Conventicle Acts was hopeless, frustrated, according to a Wiltshire justice who tried, by 'these country officers'.[88] Indeed, earlier returns from Sarratt show that, even more fundamentally, people could not see Baptists and Quakers as a problem: 'No parish if they will write truth can say omnia bene to this query, for some go to church and some to other meetings', the wardens wrote, and named none of the Baptists and Quakers who they freely acknowledge lived among them, but concluded that 'we bless God that we have no papists'.[89]

Official toleration, granted in 1689, was supposed to provide that everyone would continue to attend some church (as had been the case in the

---

84 EDR, B/2/54, fols. 8r, 22v–3r, D/2/54, fol. 52v, B/2/63a, fol. 7r, B/2/66, fols. 44v–5r D/2/56, fol. 25r.

85 EDR, B/2/66, fol. 15v, B/2/70, fol. 40r.

86 Indeed, other areas of the county might also have behaved differently. There is evidence of widespread nonconformity, and at least one conventicle meeting in the parish of Chippenham and its neighbours, but only one parishioner was presented here, and numbered in the Compton Census as a nonconformist, and he had refused to pay tithes. The semi-conforming incumbent may have been responsible. Mathew Storey, 'The Diary of Isaac Archer, 1641–1700' (Cambridge, PhD, in progress, 1993).

87 Coleby, *Central Government and the Localities*, pp. 140–1.

88 Anthony Fletcher, 'The Enforcement of the Conventicle Act 1664–1679', in W.J. Sheils (ed.), *Persecution and Toleration*, Studies in Church History, 21 (Oxford, 1984), pp. 235–46.

89 Churchwardens' returns for Sarratt provided by Nesta Evans.

1650s), but many went to none. Churchwardens were again among those responsible for enforcing church attendance but now they proved unwilling to do so. A Norfolk parson whined in 1692 that the local officers would do nothing about irreligion in his parish: 'No churchwarden or constable will present any for not going to church, though they go nowhere else but to the alehouse.'[90] Humphrey Prideaux lamented in a 1692 circular letter sent to his clergy that he had tried assiduously to move the wardens on this issue,

> yet have always found them so obstinately bent against putting [absentees] into their presentments, that ... whatever I have said unto them either from the obligation of their oaths or any other argument to press them to their duty in this particular, I have not yet been able to prevail, that any more than six or seven only from one parish ... have ever been presented to me on this account.[91]

By 1692, churchwardens had essentially given up this task. It had perhaps never been to the liking of any but a few and had grown increasingly distasteful as they could see no conceivable reason for persecuting peaceful residents of their villages, including members of their own families, who chose to worship God in a different way. They probably would not have denied the danger of irreligion. Indeed, it was likely to be seen as a genuine threat to the social order of which they were a part. But the churchwardens of the 1690s could easily see irreligion and atheism living in the same space as drunkenness, theft and all manner of other secular offences and could as easily be dealt with by the justices. Their work in that respect was done.

III

No formal rules governed churchwardens' elections until 1571, when Archbishop Parker's canons stated that wardens were to be elected by the parishioners and minister according to parochial custom, and no churchwarden was to continue in office for more than one year unless re-elected.[92] These terms were revised in the Canons of 1604. Canon

---

[90] Pruett, *Parish Clergy under the Later Stuarts*, p. 118.
[91] Prideaux, *Directions to Church-Wardens*, p. 35.
[92] 'Aeditui pro consuetudine suae quique parochiae, parochianorum suorum, et ecclesiastici sui ministri suffragiis eligentur; alioqui aeditui non erunt; nec amplius quam unum annum durabunt in illo munere, nisi forte iterum eligantur.' Cardwell (ed.), *Synodalia*, p. 122. In the course of providing for administering the Poor Law Statute of 1536 (27 Hen. VIII c. 25), a provision was added that 'no churchwarden, collector, or collectors of any the foresaid charitable alms shall continue in his or their said offices and rooms above the space of one whole year'. The wording is ambiguous, but probably nothing more was meant than what was provided in the 1571 canon. In any event, the statute was thrown over by the notorious Vagrancy Act of 1547 (1 Edw. VI c. 3) which made no provisions along those lines.

LXXXIX provided that the churchwardens were to serve one-year terms but could be re-elected. They were to be chosen by the joint consent of the minister and parishioners, but if they could not agree, then the minister was to choose one warden and the parishioners the other. In Canon XC, it was specified that election was to take place during Easter week.[93]

Canon LXXXIX was a staggering reversal of centuries of lay self-government. Until 1604, churchwardens had been exclusively the agents of their parishioners, and though it was in everyone's best interests if those chosen could work with the parish's clergy, it would have seemed impertinent to suggest that he ought to have any rights in choosing the wardens. Canon LXXXIX, of course, reflected the changes that had taken place in the office over the previous century. At some point, burgeoning responsibilities had nudged wardens across some invisible Rubicon and they could be seen no longer as purely local officials ministering to local *desiderata*. Instead, they found themselves under the Tudors turned irreversibly into agents of the central governments of church and state as well. Given these duties, it might seem appropriate to grant some role to the minister in electing the churchwardens, even to the point of personally choosing one. In Fen Drayton (Cambs.), a dispute arose in 1594 over the procedure for electing wardens from which one cause paper survives. In it, the wardens responded to articles presented by the curate and said that his predecessors

> every year successively were present at the election of the churchwardens ... and amongst the parishioners [they] did yield their consent ... to the election by the said parishioners made, and did sometime name a churchwarden, but if such a man ... was disliked by the parishioners they (the said parishioners) would and did name another man.[94]

The will of the parish was still the most important. Ten years later, the power balance was shifted canonically, and this most basic office of lay self-government formally became something very different.

What precise impact the canons had is unclear. No records, for example, make it possible to know if Fen Drayton's election process changed. Before 1604, the few surviving records suggest little uniformity in election schedules. In the London parish of St Bartholomew Exchange, elections normally took place in December in the late 1560s, while in neighbouring St Margaret Lothbury, the parish ordinances adopted in 1571 specified election day as the Sunday before All Hallows.[95] By 1606

---

[93] Cardwell (ed.), *Synodalia*, pp. 296–7. Sidesmen, according to Canon CX, were to be chosen much like churchwardens, except that if the parishioners and minister did not agree, the ordinary would choose. The canon provided for choosing more than two sidesmen, apparently as the parish determined the need.

[94] EDR, D/2/19, fol. 50v.

[95] Edwin Freshfield (ed.), *The Vestry Minute Books of the Parish of St Bartholomew Exchange in the City of London 1567–1676* (London, 1890), pp. 1–2; Edwin Freshfield (ed.), *The Vestry Minute Book of the Parish of St Margaret Lothbury in the City of London 1571–1677*

they had abandoned these practices and began holding elections during Easter week. In Cambridge, the parish of St Mary the Great had been holding its elections on Easter Monday already during Henry VIII's reign; beginning in 1606, they shifted to Tuesday 'by general consent'.[96]

It is difficult to be certain to what extent rural Cambridgeshire parishes conformed. In 1634, a resident of March was presented for alleging that one of the churchwardens had bribed the curate in order to obtain his office 'this Easter last'.[97] Casual references of this sort are rare. Some parishes apparently did not even bother to hold annual elections: not until 1624 did Horseheath fill a vacancy caused by the death of one warden two years earlier.[98] The number of parishes in which the same two men held office in tandem for years at a time also cast doubts on the frequency of elections. However, since there was little patterning to that practice, no formal policy of biennial or triennial elections seems to have existed. Rather, it is possible that elections were called only as needed – when an incumbent became incapacitated (though not even death apparently provoked an election) or decided that he had had enough, or when someone else in the community expressed a desire to serve.

Wren's 1638 visitation articles asked if churchwardens were 'chosen by the minister and parishioners yearly in Easter week'[99] as did his next visitation, held in 1662 after his restoration.[100] None of the surviving responses from either year indicates any deviation from the canon.[101] Whether these were formulaic responses or reflect actual practice is impossible to tell, and Bishop Wren, who had more serious concerns, was unlikely to wrestle with parishes over the timing of elections. Wren's successors, Benjamin Laney, Peter Gunning, and Simon Patrick, dropped Easter week elections from their visitation articles.[102]

(London, 1887), p. 1. I am grateful to Dr Ian Archer for calling my attention to London vestry books.

[96] J.E. Foster (ed.), *Churchwardens' Accounts of St Mary the Great Cambridge from 1504 to 1635* (Cambridge, 1905), pp. 89–90, 292.

[97] EDR, B/2/46, fol. 65r.

[98] EDR, B/2/40, fol. 137r, H/3/23–4.

[99] *Articles . . . of . . . the First Visitation of . . . Mathew [Wren]*, chapter 6.

[100] *Articles of Enquiry, (with Some Directions Intermingled) for the Diocese of Ely: In the Second Visitation of R. Reverend Father in God, Matthew Lord Bishop of that Diocese; Anno Dom. 1662* (London, 1662), chapter 6, no. 1.

[101] The surviving returns are EDR, B/9/5, B/9/8–9, B/9/11–16, B/9/18a.

[102] For example, *Articles for Visitation concerning certain Matters Ecclesiastical: Exhibited to the Ministers, Church-Wardens and Side-Men of every Parish within the Diocess of Ely. In the Second Episcopal Visitation of the Right Reverend Father in God Benjamin by Divine Permission Lord Bishop of Ely* (Cambridge, 1691), p. 8; *Articles of Visitation and Enquiry within the Diocess of Ely: In the Second Episcopal Visitation of the Right Reverend Father in God Peter by Divine Permission Lord Bishop of Ely in the Fifth Year of his Translation* (London, 1679), p. 15; and *Articles to be Enquired of, and Answered unto, by the Churchwardens and Sworn Men, in the Primary Visitation of the Right Reverend Father in God, Symon Lord Bishop of Ely, in the First Year of his Translation, M DC XCII* (London, 1692), p. 6.

A number of English parishes, especially in London, established bodies known as select vestries, typically ranging in size from twelve to forty members, and empowered them to conduct virtually all parish business from levying taxes to electing parish officers.[103] Many of these were in place before 1604 and their electoral duties continued thereafter. The prescriptions of Canon LXXXIX for election of wardens by the parishioners were clearly not followed literally, but the canonical spirit was observed, since select vestries were not usurpers but were delegated by parishioners to speak for them.

Even in parishes with formally open vestries, participation in elections might be quite limited and real choices non-existent. St Margaret Lothbury, divided by two city wards, elected one churchwarden to represent each ward. A ward usually presented three candidates at election time, and the winner was chosen 'by erecting of most hands'. However, very few actually voted and the vote was more of a formality than might appear. In 1654, Thomas Biggs had already served one year as the warden for the west ward. Junior wardens were routinely assured of re-election and a turn as senior wardens, and Biggs was no exception. In spite of a foreknown result, there were two other candidates: Richard Bromer and Arthur Vigors. Bromer finished second, and in 1655 he was elected junior warden representing the west ward. In that election, Vigors was placed second, followed by Thomas Smith. Predictably, Bromer was re-elected in 1656 and served as senior warden. Vigors, meanwhile, vanished from parish assessment records and may be presumed either to have moved or died. The voters dutifully raised their hands to place Thomas Smith second to Bromer in 1656, from which position he could expect to move into the junior warden's post in 1657.[104] The result of this scheme was that, barring death or removal, the parish knew who churchwardens would be several years in advance. This is typical of elections throughout this vestry minute book before and after 1604.

In rural Cambridgeshire, there is no formal evidence of select vestries. This does not mean that they did not exist. The 1584 example of Pittington parish in Durham diocese shows that rural parishes were not beyond creating a select vestry 'to order and define all common causes pertaining to the church' and to choose the churchwardens, in order to avoid the 'molestation or troubling' of the whole parish.[105] Since people considered select vestries acted for the entire parish, it is impossible to

---

[103] Ian W. Archer, *The Pursuit of Stability: Social Relations in Elizabethan England* (Cambridge, 1991), pp. 69–74; Jonathan Barry, 'The Parish in Civic Life: Bristol and its Churches, 1640–1750', in Wright (ed.), *Parish, Church and People*, p. 155.
[104] Freshfield (ed.), *Vestry Minute Book of . . . St Margaret Lothbury*, pp. 102–5.
[105] *Churchwardens' Accounts of Pittington and Other Parishes in the Diocese of Durham from A.D. 1580 to 1700*, Surtees Society, 84 (Durham, 1888), pp. 12–13, 26.

preclude their existence from statements at visitations that the wardens had been chosen 'by the parish'.

On the other hand, there is evidence of many uncanonical election procedures. Wren and his successors asked at every visitation if 'the churchwardens of the parish [are] yearly and duly chosen, by the joint consent of your minister and parishioners, or one of them by your minister and the other by your parishioners'.[106] While possible to answer this with a simple 'yes', some wardens read the 'or' as meaning that they were to indicate which method was used. Rather than being used only in case of disagreement, having the minister automatically choose one of the wardens had become a standard option in some parishes. In 1685, Burrough Green's wardens matter-of-factly informed Bishop Gunning, 'We the churchwardens were chosen one by the minister and the other by the parish.'[107] No division or disagreement had arisen to be resolved in this way. Other parishes adopted a form of cooptation. In the large parish of St Mary the Great in Cambridge town, the incumbent churchwardens chose two men, each of whom chose three more men, and those eight then chose the new wardens.[108] The rural parish of Madingley, according to its 1662 return, had wardens 'chosen by the minister and [outgoing] churchwardens yearly in Easter week according to the Canon'.[109] Only the timing was 'according to the Canon'!

The wording of Canon LXXXIX unambiguously implies that more than one churchwarden was to be chosen in each parish, and this was the case in Cambridgeshire parishes until the Restoration. In the decades following, probably because of the decline in business and (as will be seen below) an increased reluctance to serve, some parishes shifted to electing a single churchwarden. Moreover, this was not concealed from the authorities. In 1666, Impington reported with an unmistakable, and repeated, singular noun, 'The churchwarden is chosen by the minister and parishioners and the last warden hath continued by the space of two years.'[110] The annual catalogues of parish officers show that of our sample parishes five stopped electing a second warden at some point after 1680: Little Abington from 1683, Babraham from 1692, Bartlow from 1685, Hildersham from 1681, and Pampisford from 1693. Since the source of this information is an official record kept by the bishop, and no action was taken to reverse this, episcopal consent to this practice may be assumed.

The term served by churchwardens is a complex puzzle. A two-year term such as the sole Impington warden had was not uncommon. As

---

[106] *Articles ... in the Primary Visitation of ... Symon [Patrick]*, p. 8. Identical wording was used by Bishops Gunning and Laney in their Visitation Articles.

[107] EDR, B/9/52, p. 17. See also B/2/46, fol. 65r (March parish).

[108] Foster (ed.), *Churchwardens' Accounts of St Mary the Great*, pp. 89–90, 138.

[109] EDR, B/9/18a, fol. 1v.

[110] EDR, B/9/52, p. 17.

we have seen, in some London parishes junior wardens were routinely elected to a term as senior warden in the following year. The certainty of this can be seen in the vestry minutes of St Christopher le Stocks in 1639, when Gilbert Morewood paid a £20 fine when elected 'underchurchwarden' to be excused from that and from 'the place of upperchurchwarden which would fall upon him the next year'.[111] Havering parishes followed a practice similar to that in London, as did Southover in Sussex.[112]

In none of the twenty sample parishes can such a pattern be found. In fact, the evidence unambiguously demonstrates that rural Cambridge-shire parishes had no set pattern of service. A few examples will make this abundantly clear. From 1599, when churchwarden lists can be estab-lished in almost unbroken succession, to 1642, when many parish records ceased to be kept systematically, parishes exhibit a wide range of experiences with the terms of their wardens. In Great Abington, from 1599 to 1614, eighteen men served. While some were chosen more than once during that period, in only three cases did the same person serve in two consecutive years. Eighteen men also served from 1615 to 1630. Consecutive terms begin to be somewhat more common towards the end of that period, but the longest was three years. During the turbulent 1630s, six new men joined the list of wardens. No individuals emerged as dominant figures. Its smaller neighbour, Little Abington, likewise had no long consecutive runs of service but, unlike Great Abington, some men virtually dominated the lists. Between 1599 and 1621, William Cowell served at least twelve terms and John Loftes served seven, but neither served more than three years in succession. In 1625, Edward Gilson and John Evered joined together and served in tandem for three years. In 1629, Evered joined with Thomas Gilson for another four years, a pattern matched by William Amye and Samuel Bevis, who served from 1639 to 1642. What is striking about Little Abington's evolution is the tendency not towards a staggered-term system but the adoption, by acci-dent or design, of yoked pairs.

Balsham shows signs of this pattern much earlier. Between 1599 and 1614, fourteen men were churchwardens. Eight of those served in yoked pairs with multiple, consecutive terms. Unlike Little Abington, however, Balsham experienced a dramatic opening-up of the wardenship from 1615 to 1642. At least thirty-three men served and, although the number of veterans increased noticeably in the 1630s, consecutive terms were almost unknown. Only three men served more than two terms during

---

[111] Edwin Freshfield (ed.), Minutes of the Vestry Meetings and Other Records of the Parish of St Christopher le Stocks in the City of London (London, 1886), p. 40.
[112] McIntosh, A Community Transformed, p. 224; William Hudson, 'Extracts from the First Book of the Parish of Southover', Sussex Archaeological Collections, 48 (1905), 16–37.

that period. Burrough Green, although working from a smaller pool, appeared much like Balsham. From 1602 to 1614, eleven individuals were wardens; from 1602 to 1607, the office was filled by three pairs serving for two consecutive years. Twenty-one new men and only three veterans were chosen from 1615 to 1630. Only Thomas Ellis, Thomas Gilbert and John Woolard served consecutive terms, and Thomas Ellis was the only man to serve a total of more than two terms during those years. Then from 1631 to 1642 the parish returned to a very few men serving as many as four consecutive terms.

Hildersham had the closest to an overlapping rotation, but it was clearly very informal. Richard Smith, who began serving in 1606, was joined in 1610 by John Runham. Runham continued in office until 1613, but Smith withdrew in 1611. Other examples of this type can be found in the parish: a flexible and *ad hoc* practice of having a novice serve with a veteran for a year or two before the more experienced man 'retired'. Hildersham wardens tended, once experienced, to serve many terms, though rarely for more than two or three years running. Only twenty-four men were wardens in Hildersham from 1599 to 1641, and only three of them served for the first time in the last decade.

Shudy Camps began, like Burrough Green, with a series of pairs serving consecutive two-year stints until 1609, and then followed with typically one-term wardens. From 1614 to 1640, although over twenty men served, two dominated the list. William Woolwood served a total of seventeen times beginning in 1614, including unbroken service to 1625, and Edward Rolph, who joined him in 1620, served for eight years.

Linton, the most 'urban' of these parishes, could be expected to have a different experience. A market town, with a larger population and greater social and economic diversity due to its numbers of merchants and craftsmen, might be expected to have a much more formal structure. However, this was not the case. Only twelve men were wardens from 1599 to 1615. Most served for several consecutive years; only three served fewer than three terms. From 1616 to 1642, thirty-seven new names and that of only one veteran appear on the list. The veteran John Fulwell served three consecutive terms, as did Edward Cornell, but with those exceptions, no one served more than two terms and even that was a rarity.

Describing more parishes would exhaust the patience of the reader and add nothing. From 1599 to 1642, the variety of experiences found is bewildering. The only things that they have in common are these. First, there is no trace of any formal system of staggered terms or regular formal terms in office. The only common practice which emerges is the yoked pair of men serving (usually) for two or more years as a team, entering and leaving service together. (One can almost hear the 'I'll-do-it-if-you'll-do-it' conversations in the alehouse on Easter Monday evening!) While a sizable proportion of the qualified men who wished to serve probably did so, almost every parish experienced wild fluctuations from decade to decade in the number of men serving for the first time or serving more than one term.

Frustratingly little information exists on the wardens serving during the Civil War and Interregnum. The names of four men who were wardens in Great Abington from 1648 to 1653 have been unearthed. At least two can be identified as veterans of office in the 1630s, while a third may be either the veteran or his namesake son. The fourth is very probably the son of a previous warden. In Little Abington, two new men – Daniel Ward and Richard Loftes – are known to have served from 1649 to 1653. Seven of Horseheath's wardens from 1642 to 1652 can be identified. Thomas Glasscock and Thomas Lord each served one term before the Civil War as well. They, together with Henry Hatley, were the wardens from 1642 to 1649. Suddenly, in 1650, an entirely new cast stepped on stage: Robert Whiskin, Edward Flower, William Petyt and William Flanders. In Shudy Camps, veteran wardens served from 1648 to 1650, but then seven new men divided the remaining terms in the 1650s. Lawrence Mynot, whose first term was in 1659, served in 1660 as well but none of the other wardens of the 1650s reappear in later decades. In Linton, there is a similar pattern: two veterans of the late-1640s served until 1652, and then a series of new men appeared. None was to serve after the Restoration.[113] With the exception of Great Abington, then, the Interregnum saw a complete change in the personnel of the office. Records are too patchy to say much about these wardens' terms of service, but it is clear that they were not men who served as part of a normal pattern of office holding since they disappeared rather dramatically from office after the Restoration.

The churchwardens of the Restoration and beyond served under markedly different terms. In parish after parish, it is possible to notice a dramatic reduction in the number of men holding the office and an equally dramatic increase in the length of time individuals served. Little Abington is an extreme example (and it had only one warden beginning in 1683): only six men held office from 1662 to 1694. More typically, Burrough Green and Shudy Camps had fourteen wardens from 1661 to 1691. From 1662 to 1699, fifteen men served in Hildersham, which chose only one warden from 1681, and eighteen in Great Abington, which continued to have a pair every year. In all of these parishes the trend was towards long consecutive terms served by men without prior experience.[114] For

[113] CUL, Palmer MS A.20A.
[114] Possible exceptions are Henry Hammond of Hildersham and William Hammond of Shudy Camps, but the names are so common that they may be new men as well.

example, William Drury and Richard Whiskin of Burrough Green served six consecutive terms each, while William Hardy of Shudy Camps served continuously from 1673 to 1684 and John Smee of Great Abington served fifteen terms. Balsham and Linton, the two centres of nonconformity, were somewhat anomalous. In Linton, twenty-seven men served from 1662 to 1698. Although this meant that the office was far less exclusive than in other parishes, individuals still tended to have multi-year terms and, after 1671, usually with the same partner. With thirty different men serving from 1661 to 1699, the Balsham wardenships were by far the most open. No individual served more than five terms. A return to having pairs of men serving two-year stints was typical, especially after 1689.

The dramatic change observed after 1660 in most parishes raises the question of whether it was difficult to find men willing to serve, a piece of a larger question on which scholars have not been entirely consistent. Before the Reformation, according to Clive Burgess, the office was attractive precisely because of its burdens: 'The effort and sacrifice involved in discharging the task was itself a good work, the profit accruing to all further benefiting their own souls. Service as a warden would redeem worldly success in much the same way as almsgiving.'[115] However they might outwardly conform, people could hardly be expected to abandon the piety of a lifetime overnight. But by the 1570s, perhaps, this motive would have disappeared and all that would be left would be a heap of unredeemed, unredeemable busyness.[116] Ralph Houlbrooke has written that the office 'was not one eagerly sought after'[117] and Christopher Haigh has described it in Tudor Lancashire as so 'onerous and unpopular', that in some places 'no-one could be found who was willing to serve'. He attributed this to 'the abuse the conscientious officers received from parishioners'.[118]

Cambridgeshire wardens did receive abuse. When Thomas Wells of Foxton presented Allin Hall for being absent from church, Hall questioned his honesty and fitness for office 'and did use diverse other quarrelling and brawling words'.[119] Landbeach wardens were called 'fools and asses' by a victim of their presentment, who also offered his theory that there had been a shortage of qualified candidates when they had been elected.[120] Most abuse never went beyond 'evil and naughty language', as it was described when William Foster of Ely was presented for using it.[121]

[115] Burgess, ' "A Fond Thing Vainly Invented" ', p. 78.
[116] Cox, Churchwardens' Accounts, pp. 5–6.
[117] Ralph Houlbrooke, Church Courts and the People during the English Reformation, 1520–1570 (Oxford, 1979), p. 152.
[118] Haigh, Reformation and Resistance, pp. 18, 230.
[119] EDR, D/2/10, fols. 229r, 239r.
[120] EDR, B/2/11, fol. 151v.
[121] EDR, D/2/9, fol. 29v.

There were occasional threats of physical violence, as when a churchwarden of St Peter's parish in Cambridge went to collect the non-attendance fine from Stephen Kercher and Kercher 'said he would break his pate that came to fetch any distress out of his house'.[122]

The material burdens of the office are equally undeniable. In addition to the time that might be spent in drawing up quarter bills and appearing in court, churchwardens might be fined if the court considered their presentments to be deficient and they might also be temporarily out of pocket for sizable sums of money carrying out curial orders to repair broken windows and gaps in churchyard fences.

Unsurprisingly, there is evidence of people trying to avoid the office. Ronald Marchant claims that 'churchwardens, once elected, were compelled to serve and could not resign'.[123] In a sense that was true. While the *electus* might refuse to take the oath of office, he could be excommunicated for doing so.[124] A simpler strategy might be to plead old age or disability, such as John Stockwell of Salisbury who sought relief from election in 1676 'by reason of the failure of his eyes and other infirmities',[125] or 'great business and employments' which would keep one away from the parish, such as did Richard Bowdler of London in 1612.[126] An even simpler strategy was adopted by Edward Riche of Langford (Essex) in 1599, who was reported 'drinking himself drunk to the end that it might be a reasonable excuse for him not to be churchwarden'.[127]

Parishioners might see in a reluctant warden someone who would be uninterested in misdeeds that a more eager officer might take as an excuse to have them before the archdeacon. However, they also relied upon the wardens to administer charitable bequests and maintain communal property. Both their purses and their local pride dictated the choice of someone who would be responsible, if unenthusiastic. Thus, rather than compelling the reluctant to serve, many parishes adopted by-laws which allowed them to pay a fine to be excused from serving.[128] In 1568, St Mary the Great in Cambridge approved a 10s fine for refusing the office. This was raised to 40s in 1621 when it was noted 'that we find

---

[122] EDR, D/2/10, fol. 201v, see also 124v. Cases of actual violence (as opposed to threats) do not appear in the church court records, since assault was a criminal offence. However, it is noteworthy that there are not even any passing references to actual violence in the ecclesiastical records.

[123] Ronald A. Marchant, *The Church under the Law: Justice, Administration and Discipline in the Diocese of York 1560–1640* (Cambridge, 1969), p. 183.

[124] F.G. Emmison, *Elizabethan Life: Morals and the Church Courts* (Chelmsford, 1973), p. 233.

[125] Stockwell was fined, but at a lower rate than 'one who hath ability to serve': Cox, *Churchwardens' Accounts*, p. 6. See also Emmison, *Morals and the Church Courts*, p. 233.

[126] Freshfield (ed.), *Vestry Minute Books . . . of St Bartholomew Exchange*, pp. 68–9.

[127] Emmison, *Morals and the Church Courts*, p. 233.

[128] See, for example, Cox, *Churchwardens' Accounts*, pp. 5–6.

much trouble from year to year in choosing of churchwardens' because too many found the fine less bothersome than the job.[129]

Against this has to be weighed some rather contrary evidence. In 1634, John Neale of March (Isle of Ely), was presented 'for saying in an abusive and scandalous manner' that one of the churchwardens, William Walham, had bribed the curate to choose him for office at the previous Easter.[130] That such an accusation was considered slander, and not simply risible, means that the possibility was imaginable. If the office were so odious, and one could pay money to be excused from it, why would anyone pay to be chosen for it? Indeed, if reluctance to serve was a problem, why would volunteering not be more than enough to secure it?

Was the office onerous and unpopular, or an honour worth a hefty bribe? A case from Richard Gough's famous description of Myddle provides the answer. Gough reported that William Parker bribed the rector's brother with a side of bacon in order to be made churchwarden because he 'affected to be accounted somebody' in the parish.[131] For all its inconveniences, the office marked its holder as a man trusted by his neighbours. In London, a term as churchwarden was part of an accepted *cursus honorum* of local office and could be a prerequisite for serving in higher offices.[132] In a village, it could be the highest office to which one could aspire. The Jacobean vicar of Stapleford Abbots in Essex described the offices through which a person could proceed: 'one that is able to do the King and country good service, we make him a constable, a sidesman, a head-borough, and at length a churchwarden; thus we raise him by degrees, we prolong his ambitious hopes, and at last we heap all our honours upon him'.[133]

Not all who filled the office could have done so for the honour, which must have dimmed after several years of quarter bills, annual accountings, and leaky roofs. And indeed the average village did not have the population necessary to sustain a more formal hierarchy of office holding like that of London which would guarantee an individual a year or two as warden and then either a move on to something better or an untroubled retirement from public office. As shown above, many Cambridgeshire wardens served several non-consecutive terms and others actually found themselves stepping backwards into service as sidesmen. John Glasscock of Hildersham, for example, served as churchwarden in 1595 and 1600, and as sidesman in 1599, 1604, and 1606–8. Robert London of Little Abington was sidesman from 1604 to 1606, churchwarden in 1608, and

[129] Foster (ed.), *Churchwardens' Accounts of St Mary the Great*, pp. 163, 371.
[130] EDR, B/2/46, fol. 65r.
[131] Richard Gough, *The History of Myddle*, ed. D. Hey (Harmondsworth, 1981), p. 239.
[132] Archer, *Pursuit of Stability*, pp. 51, 65–9.
[133] Quoted in J.A. Sharpe, *Crime in Seventeenth-Century England* (Cambridge, 1983), p. 173.

sidesman again from 1610 to 1615. Even Linton, with its larger population and more 'urban' environment, demonstrably had no formal *cursus hono-rum*. For the period 1600–35, it is possible to identify thirty sidesmen, only seven of whom later served as churchwardens.[134] Even more striking is the lack of previous service as sidesmen by those serving as wardens. From 1620 to 1635, an unusually high number of 'new' men became wardens. Of the twenty-three who held that office for the first time, only three had been sidesmen.[135]

Since the office was not part of a formal pyramid of village honours, and its burdens and irritations were undeniable, why is there no evidence of evasion and, until the 1660s at least, no shortage of parishioners to fill the office? No one who has served on the faculty of a school or university should have difficulty cutting through this particular Gordian knot. While we typically cringe at the thought of service on a major faculty committee, we serve conscientiously – and sometimes for several years running – either out of a desire to serve (altruistically, or for rewards such as tenure) or a silent pride (often smothered in half-felt complaints about overwork) in being trusted by one's colleagues. Villagers knew that self-government was a great deal of work, but it was also a fundamental value. The office of churchwarden, created by their ancestors, was thus faced by candidates with an understandable mixture of attraction and repulsion. Ultimately, they served because they were needed. As John Craig has said of Suffolk wardens, 'Holding the office of churchwarden was a mark of status and honour within local communities that was rarely spurned.'[136] Only after 1662, with the onerous but respectable task of maintaining order in the community finally lost to the justices, and when much of the remaining responsibilities consisted in harassing dissenting neighbours, when the office's genuine community service involved had been suffocated under the weight of distasteful repressive legislation, was it difficult to find men willing to take their turn.

IV

Nothing has yet been said about the qualifications which would or might be considered before someone might be considered for election as churchwarden. Nowhere in the canons or parish by-laws are those quali-fications stated, and yet they are important to ascertain if we are to create a profile of the 'typical' warden.

---

[134] Moses Browne, William Willows, George Maye, William Wright, Henry Lawrence, Thomas Barker, and John Jurden.
[135] George Maye, John Jurden, and Thomas Barker.
[136] J.S. Craig, 'Co-operation and Initiatives: Elizabethan Churchwardens and the Parish Accounts of Mildenhall', *Social History*, 18 (1993), p. 364.

In Cambridgeshire, women were never elected as churchwardens.[137] While being male was a necessary condition for election in the shire, it might not be sufficient. Nick Alldridge's study of churchwardens in Chester shows a relationship between age and office holding consistent with a clear, formal hierarchy. For example, in St Mary's parish between 1560 and 1630, the mean age of sidesmen was 26.5, of wardens 33.2, and of auditors and sessors 45.5.[138] Even barring a formal 'pyramid' like that described by Archer for London or Alldridge for Chester, an age profile like this reflects the natural inclination that parishioners would have to demand a level of experience and maturity before entrusting someone with the material wealth of the parish as well as the right and duty to discipline them.

Determining the ages at which Cambridgeshire churchwardens were first elected has proved to be extremely difficult. A careful study of the parish baptismal registers of Castle Camps has resulted in a secure identification of only ten churchwardens of all those elected before 1640. These men ranged in age from 23 to 54, with a mean of 40.5.[139] In addition, there is a suggestive correlation between the dates of marriage and election among the Castle Camps churchwardens. Thomas Whitney married in 1622 and was elected in 1627; William Jaggard married in 1606 and first served as warden in 1608. For those married outside the parish, a rough substitute for their marriage date may be the baptismal date of their first child, since that would normally be between a few months and two years after marriage. Robert Mascall's son Thomas was baptized in 1603 and Robert became a churchwarden in 1607; Edward Brady's son William was christened in 1605 and Edward was elected four years later. The pool involved here is admittedly small, and much more study needs to be undertaken before drawing any solid conclusions. However, these correspondences are consistent with the fact that in the sixteenth and seventeenth centuries marrying and establishing a family was the bridge by which one crossed over into adulthood; in other words, marriage at whatever age, not age alone, determined full adult membership in the

---

[137] This was not universally true: women were elected elsewhere, such as in Devon and Somerset: Cox, *Churchwardens' Accounts*, p. 7; Pearl Hogrefe, *Tudor Women: Commoners and Queens* (Ames, Iowa, 1975), pp. 27–8.

[138] Nick Alldridge, 'Loyalty and Identity in Chester Parishes 1540–1640', in Wright (ed.), *Parish, Church and People*, p. 107.

[139] The difficulties are caused in part because so many of the wardens were not native to the village. Common names pose additional problems. Two Richard Flacks – one baptized in 1583, the other in 1596 – fit the age profile, since Flack was first elected in 1634. These general figures correspond with Marjorie McIntosh's results for Romford (1580–99). In her sample of ten wardens, seven were aged forty to fifty-nine when elected; in mine, six fall within that range: McIntosh, *A Community Transformed*, pp. 235–6.

local community.[140] No one who had not demonstrated the responsibility necessary to establish and manage a household could be trusted with the management of the parish 'household goods' and property, nor with the quasi-parental task of correcting and disciplining members of the parish family.

Were a certain social rank and wealth additional qualifications? Here we find confusion and contradiction among historians. Village church-wardens have been described as men of little (if any) wealth and status in their communities. They have been called 'the meanest and lewdest sort of people', men 'of humble origin' who 'seldom had any social standing or influence'.[141] Such comments seem to be based primarily on dismissive remarks made by contemporaries. When Sir Thomas Smith considered the role of 'day labourers, poor husbandmen, yea merchants and retailers which have no free land, copyholders, all artificers' in the Commonwealth, he noted that these 'low and base persons', fit only to be ruled and not to rule others, 'in villages . . . be commonly made churchwardens',[142] and puritan critics of episcopal church government libelled its agents as 'the meanest and lewdest sort of people' in order to undermine support for it. These classifications, entirely unsubstantiated, have helped some historians explain what they see as the failure of eccle-siastical courts to enforce conformity to the religious settlement: humble villagers knew that presenting 'their betters' to the church courts required a 'luxurious independence' which they could ill afford and were easily badgered into silence if they dared to consider it.[143]

A thoroughly different picture emerges from the work of several other historians: churchwardens were the 'principal parishioners', 'substantial member[s] of the community', and a 'virtually random cross-section of the upper half of parish society'. Summarizing recent research, Dr Sharpe writes that wardens were 'recruited almost exclusively from the upper stratum of village society'.[144] Indeed, in the 1630s, George Herbert wrote that the parson 'suffers not the place [of wardens] to be vilified or debased by being cast on the lower rank of people, but invites and urges the best unto it'.[145] Higher social status was no guarantee of ardour in pre-

---

[140] Eric Josef Carlson, 'Courtship in Tudor England', *History Today*, 43 (1993), pp. 23–9.
[141] Respectively, Haigh, *Reformation and Resistance*, pp. 18–19, 231; Manning, *Religion and Society*, pp. 24–5; Penry Williams, *The Tudor Regime* (Oxford, 1979), p. 271. Williams later described the wardens as 'lesser gentlemen, merchants, and yeomen' (p. 451).
[142] Sir Thomas Smith, *De Republica Anglorum*, ed. Mary Dewar (Cambridge, 1982), pp. 76–7.
[143] Haigh, *Reformation and Resistance*, pp. 18–19, 230–1; Manning, *Religion and Society*, pp. 24–5; Williams, *Tudor Regime*, p. 261.
[144] Respectively, Marchant, *The Church under the Law*, p. 183; Margaret Steig, *Laud's Laboratory* (Lewisburg, Pa., 1983), pp. 176–7; Ingram, *Church Courts, Sex and Marriage*, p. 324; J.A. Sharpe, 'The People and the Law', in Barry Reay (ed.), *Popular Culture in Seventeenth-Century England* (London, 1985), pp. 255–6.
[145] Hutchinson (ed.), *Works of George Herbert*, p. 270.

sentment, however, since good-neighbourliness might hinder where fear and social deference did not.

This contradiction may in part be explained by change over time. Clive Burgess has argued that 'busy and successful' men were eager to serve before the Reformation because of the spiritual profit earned by performing such a good work.[146] Low status is assigned to wardens by three historians writing about the sixteenth century, largely after the Reformation, while those whose focus is a later period describe wardens of higher status. Dr McIntosh's study of the parishes in Havering, which bridges these two centuries by extending to 1620, shows that the status of churchwardens rose, beginning in the 1580s as more gentry, moved by a 'desire to enforce their own social attitudes', held the office.[147]

By examining the wealth of the churchwardens of our twenty sample parishes, it is possible to test these suggestions in a systematic way and with a larger sample over a longer period of time than has been attempted in any previously published study of rural parishes.[148] The 1599 and 1640 Subsidies and the 1674 Hearth Tax have been selected and transcribed, and the assessments for each parish set out in tables. Only churchwardens from the year of each assessment and from one year on either side have been used. This was done to provide the largest sample possible which did not risk distorting the results, since the chance of significant change in an individual's wealth during that brief time was minimal.[149] Having done this, it is possible to take an economic snapshot of the wardens of these rural parishes at three very different points in time: the days of glory of the Elizabethan settlement after Whitgift and his supporters had successfully turned back parliamentary efforts for further reformation; the high-water mark of Laudian aggressiveness in the diocese of Ely; and the period in which the 1670 Conventicle Act would have been in effect. Results from nine representative parishes are given in Table 5.[150]

The first column in Table 5a reproduces the results of the diocesan census of households prepared in 1563 at the request of the Privy Council.[151] While there is no secure basis on which to calculate the numbers

---

[146] Burgess, ' "A Fond Thing Vainly Invented" ', p. 78.

[147] McIntosh, A Community Transformed, pp. 231–5, 238.

[148] Ian Archer studied the wardens of two London parishes in this way, but for a short period only: Pursuit of Stability, pp. 65–6. My study will soon be complemented by the results of Dr John Craig's study of Suffolk churchwardens.

[149] Since many wardens served multiple consecutive terms, this rarely yielded the maximum possible of six names per parish.

[150] All twenty parishes were studied; nine are chosen for illustrative purposes which represent the range of experiences in the hundreds, including a market town (Linton), parishes with a range of sizes and populations, and both with nonconformity and without.

[151] D.M. Palliser and L.J. Jones, 'The Diocesan Population Returns for 1563 and 1603', Local Population Studies, 30 (1983), pp. 55–8.

of households in Cambridgeshire between the diocesan survey of 1563 and the 1662 Hearth Tax, there were no mortality crises in these parishes which would cause the numbers of households to be lower in 1599 or 1640 than in 1563. Indeed, since this was a period of population growth, the number of households in 1563 can safely be assumed to be a marked understatement of the case in 1599 and 1640.[152] Bearing that in mind, the 1563 data accent what a small percentage of parishioners were assessed for these taxes. Fewer than half, and perhaps as few as a third, of households had a member assessed in 1599. The proportion plunges in 1640 to something closer to 20 per cent. What were called the subsidymen (and include a few subsidywidows) were the economic elite of their parishes.

With that in mind, it is striking how few churchwardens were part of that group in either of the first two sample periods. Taking both samples together, thirty seven (56 per cent) churchwardens were not assessed at all. In Linton and Hildersham, none of the churchwardens were assessed in 1599, and the same is true for Westley Waterless and Weston Colville in 1640. Assessments from 1599 and 1640 are not, of course, strictly comparable, nor are the assessments from the same years in different parishes, so even this survey, despite its statistics, must be taken as no more than impressionistic.

The hypothesis that wardens' social-economic profile rose from 1599 to 1640, supported by some historians, must be considered from the evidence as not proven. These results do not suggest any pattern which can be applied in even a majority of the twenty parishes. Neither, of course, is it contradicted from these data. What is clearer, however, is that the numbers of those not assessed at all, together with those assessed at the lowest levels, make up an overwhelming majority of wardens. Most pre-Civil War wardens were, at the time of their service,[153] in or below the economic middle group in their parishes.

The question which then presses upon us is: how far below? It is possible to be quite clear about the relative wealth of churchwardens who were not subsidymen by examining a document recently discovered in the Ely diocesan records: the detailed record of a Brinkley parish rate assessed in 1636 to cover expenses incurred by the wardens.[154] Of forty men and one woman assessed, fourteen men were rated at the minimum of 12d, and seven were rated at or above 14s. (The range of this upper group was from 14s to 30s 6d.) The remaining nineteen men and one woman were assessed

---

[152] Margaret Spufford, *Contrasting Communities*, chapter 1.
[153] I do not use the occupational or social labels in wills for this survey because the wills identified for the sample wardens are almost invariably made too many years after their service to reliably reflect their status or occupation at the earlier date.
[154] EDR, K/15/2.

Table 5. Tax assessments on churchwardens and other inhabitants of nine Cambridgeshire parishes

(a) 1599 Subsidy

Parishes	1563 households	Numbers assessed (entire parish)								
		4s	5s 4d	6s	8s	10s 8d	12s	13s 4d	16s	>16s
Little Abington	15				2	2	1c	2		1
Balsham	80	8			10		3	1c	1	3
Brinkley	29	1		1c	5		2			3
Burrough Green	34	5		1	6c	3cc				
Hildersham	17	3			4	1		1	2	1
Linton	92	9	1		10	5	2			3
Shudy Camps	30	5			5c	6	3		5	3
Westley Waterless	15	2c			2c	3		1c		1
Weston Colville	26	4		1	1	3cc			3	2c

c = churchwarden (1598–1600) assessed.

Churchwardens not assessed: Little Abington 1, Balsham 2, Brinkley 0, Burrough Green 1, Hildersham 2, Linton 4, Shudy Camps 3, Westley Waterless 1, Weston Colville 1.

Sources: 1563 Household Census: BL, Harley MS 594, fols. 198–201; 1599 Subsidy: PRO, E179/83/307.

(b) 1640 Subsidy

Parishes	Numbers assessed (entire parish)								
	8s	10s 8d	12s	16s	21s 4d	24s	26s 8d	32s	>32s
Little Abington				4c					1
Balsham	10		7c	4c				1	1
Brinkley	4cc		1	1	1				4c
Burrough Green	7c			2cc					
Hildersham	3c		1	2	1				
Linton	14c			3c					1
Shudy Camps	6c		2c	3cc		1			
Westley Waterless	1		1	1					
Weston Colville	4		3	3		1	1		

c = churchwarden (1639–41) assessed.
Churchwardens not assessed: Little Abington 1, Balsham 3, Brinkley 1, Burrough Green 0, Hildersham 3, Linton 4, Shudy Camps 2, Westley Waterless 4, Weston Colville 4.
Sources: PRO, E179/83/404. (Rates twice those of 1599.)

Table 5 (cont.)

(c) Lady Day 1674 Hearth Tax

	Total 1674	Exempt[a]	Charged @ numbers of hearths					
			1	2	3	4	5	6 or more
Little Abington	16	–	2	7	2c	4		1c
Balsham	99	22	27c	26c	12c	6	3	3
Brinkley	34	7	7	6c	3c	4	2c	5
Burrough Green	54	25	19	6cc	2			2c
Hildersham	20	–	4	6	4	1		5cc
Linton	181	31	47	42c	23	16c	10c	12c
Shudy Camps	45	8	13	7	7c	6c	2c	2
Westley Waterless	16		9c	4			1c	2
Weston Colville	44	8	14c	11c	7	1	1c	2c
Radfield/Chilford Hundreds (all)	1,077[b]	244[b]	322	227	122	67	36	59
Radfield/Chilford Hundreds (churchwardens only)	65[c]	0	13	12	11	8	7	9

c = churchwarden (1675–7) assessed.
[a] All exempt listed with one hearth, except two @ two hearths in Linton.
[b] In parishes for which exempt listed, average 24 per cent of total households. Figure of actual exempt listed in original adjusted to assume 24 per cent in parishes for which exempt are omitted: 207 exempt listed + 37 assumed = 244 exempt.
[c] In the entire sample (twenty parishes), five churchwardens do not appear in the 1674 Hearth Tax.
Source: PRO, E179/244/23.

between 2s and 12s, with all but five at or below 5s. When the Brinkley wardens from 1633 to 1639 are identified on this list, a striking pattern emerges: all five of the men who were wardens during that period and rated in 1636 fall in the middle group rated between 12s and 2s.[155] No one in the lowest rated group (12d) served as churchwarden. The 1640 subsidymen, in contrast, are drawn almost exclusively from the group assessed at the higher levels, 14s and above. Of the seven men assessed in both 1636 and 1640, only two men, the erstwhile wardens Thomas Clarke and Thomas Marsh, were from the middle group. This demonstrates two things. Churchwardens before 1640 were 'men of substance [but] not the most substantial men of the parish',[156] if, of course, Brinkley was typical. At the same time, a third of those who were considered worth taxing to pay the parish's expenses were not of substance enough either to administer those shillings and pence once collected or, by serving as wardens, to incur the expenses which necessitated them.

Identifying churchwardens from 1673 to 1675 against the Lady Day 1674 Hearth Tax shows that the Restoration did not restore churchwardens precisely as they were before the Civil War. Indeed, the office in the last four decades of the century was filled by men of markedly higher wealth and status. In Chilford and Radfield Hundreds, 793 households (73.6 per cent) had two hearths or less, while only 284 (26.4 per cent) had three or more. Of all churchwardens from the twenty parishes, thirty five (58.3 per cent) were assessed on three or more hearths. As Dr Spufford has shown, and Dr Stevenson has further demonstrated, the Hearth Tax can be used as a general guide to social and economic position, especially at the level of three hearths and above since 'persons with three or more hearths were almost certain to be yeomen or extremely prosperous craftsmen of a similar status'.[157] One hearth households account for over half of all hundredal households, but just thirteen (21.6 per cent) of those of churchwardens. Since, as Dr Spufford's research shows, some substantial yeomen had houses with only one or two hearths, the Hearth Tax figures are likely to understate the extent to which the social-economic position of churchwardens had shifted upwards since the 1640s. For example, the probate inventory of William Folkes, yeoman of Westley Waterless, indicates a valuation of £324 7s 4d, and a house of ten rooms

---

[155] James Howton (1633): 12s; Thomas Clarke (1634–5): 12s; Thomas Martin (1634–5): 5s; John Carter (1633, 1636–8): 4s; Ambrose Mortlock (1636–8): 2s. William Day (1633) was not rated in 1636.

[156] See Craig, 'Co-operation and Initiatives', pp. 362–4.

[157] H.M. Spufford, 'The Significance of the Cambridgeshire Hearth Tax', *Proceedings of the Cambridge Antiquarian Society*, 55 (1962), pp. 53–64; Stevenson, 'Economic and Social Status', pp. 5–22.

but only two hearths.[158] John Rule, a Balsham churchwarden in 1670, was considered a yeoman when he made his will in 1674, but was charged on only two hearths in the same year, and the sometime Linton church-warden John Skinner was also called a yeoman in his 1677 will but taxed on only one hearth in 1674.[159] While the middle group which tended to dominate the office earlier, probably represented by some one and most two hearth householders, certainly did not disappear by the 1670s, the wealthiest and most socially influential people of the parish began serving as wardens in numbers and proportions which would have defied ima-gining thirty years before.

This survey's implications for theories about presentments are unmis-takable: social inferiority or intimidation simply cannot account for the failure of wardens to present those who did not attend church. For the earlier decades, the numbers of those economically below the wardens is so great that, if any were 'slack comers to church' or absenting themselves 'obstinately for religion', there should have been no obstacle to pre-senting them, yet that rarely occurs. For the 1660s–80s, the social status of wardens is so high that virtually no one should have been spared on that account, except perhaps members of the wardens' own social class. The parish of Dullingham illustrates how little account should be taken of arguments that deference or fear barred presentment: Thomas Ranew and William Fyson, presented for nonconformity regularly in the 1670s, were four hearth householders in 1674, while the churchwardens who presented them were all assessed on either two or three hearths. The social and economic profile of wardens certainly changed from the late 1590s to the 1670s–80s but, interesting though that may be, it fails to explain who would or would not be presented for religious practices. Indeed, throughout this period the social and economic status of war-dens has, on its own, little merit as an explanation of their activities.

A final possibility remains to be explored: that the wardens of rural Cam-bridgeshire concealed the ecclesiastical eccentricities and deviations of their neighbours, from sermon-gadding away from their parish churches to conventicle-holding and everything in between, because they were in something more than casual sympathy with their practices. In other words, were a number of churchwardens themselves people of religious convic-tions which put them on or beyond the margins of the national church?

The possibility is not an idle one. Steeple Bumpstead Lollards mono-polized the office for a time and used it to good effect, and in their

---

[158] Spufford, 'Significance', p. 58. Probate inventories must not, of course, be taken by themselves as an indication of real net wealth: Margaret Spufford, 'The Limitations of the Probate Inventory', in John Chartres and David Hey (eds.), *English Rural Society, 1500–1800: Essays in Honour of Joan Thirsk* (Cambridge, 1990), pp. 139–74.
[159] EPR, CW1674, CW1677.

study of Terling, Keith Wrightson and David Levine argue for a close connection between a budding 'Protestantism of conviction' in the 1580s, which flowered into a 'whole generation of parish notables of striking personal piety' dominating village office holding in the early 1600s, and increasing prosecutions over church attendance and receiving Communion and, finally, in resistance to Laud.[160] The office of churchwarden was sought by, and of use to, those of strong religious convictions.

How can the convictions of rural churchwardens be studied? For many years, historians have turned increasingly to wills for evidence of religious beliefs.[161] This is because most wills from the period begin with a preamble in which the testator commends his or her soul to God, sometimes accompanied by extended expressions of piety and faith. Religious preambles must be used with great caution as indicators of personal piety since they were routinely supplied by the will's scribe rather than directly a statement of the testator's beliefs.[162] By studying a large enough sample of wills from one area, however, it is possible to filter out scribal formulas and look for evidence of profound and distinctive piety.

The wills of churchwardens from Chilford and Radfield Hundreds were examined in this way to see if 'a Protestantism of conviction' could be detected, but the opposite is the case: the sample is almost completely free of identifiably personal statements of piety. Most wills repeat mechanically some scribal conventions. Some of these are quite elaborate, but are repeated practically verbatim in so many parish wills as to render unlikely the possibility that they reflect the especial views of the testator. Those wills in which the precise arrangement of words is unique employ phrases and formulas which were a part of typical testamentary vocabulary, making it impossible to conclude anything from them about the personal views of their user.[163]

---

[160] Wrightson and Levine, *Poverty and Piety in an English Village*, pp. 155–69.

[161] Some recent examples from this now long list are: Claire Cross, 'The Development of Protestantism in Leeds and Hull, 1520–1640: The Evidence from Wills', *Northern History*, 18 (1982), pp. 230–8; idem, 'Wills as Evidence of Popular Piety in the Reformation Period: Leeds and Hull, 1540–1640', in D.M. Loades (ed.), *The End of Strife* (Edinburgh, 1984), pp. 44–51; and Peter Heath, 'Urban Piety in the Later Middle Ages: The Evidence of Hull Wills', in R.B. Dobson (ed.), *The Church, Politics, and Patronage in England and France in the Fifteenth Century* (Gloucester, 1984), pp. 209–34.

[162] Margaret Spufford, *Contrasting Communities*, pp. 320–44; Christopher Marsh, 'In the Name of God? Will-Making and Faith in Early Modern England', in G.H. Martin and Peter Spufford (eds.), *The Records of the Nation* (Woodbridge, 1990), pp. 215–49. See also J.D. Alsop, 'Religious Preambles in Early Modern English Wills as Formulae', *Journal of Ecclesiastical History*, 40 (1989), pp. 19–27; and Michael L. Zell, 'The Use of Religious Preambles as a Measure of Religious Belief in the Sixteenth Century', *Bulletin of the Institute of Historical Research*, 50 (1977), pp. 246–9.

[163] For a more sanguine view of what can be learned from such minor variations, see McIntosh, *A Community Transformed*, pp. 188–95.

In every parish, a few wills use the neutral commendatory clause in which the testators offer their souls 'to Almighty God my maker', but most wardens' wills begin with a more elaborate statement. Thomas Webb of Linton, for example, offered his soul 'into the hands of Almighty God my maker and to Jesus Christ my saviour and redeemer hoping steadfastly through his merits, death and passion that after this transitory life is ended my soul shall rest with the elect in his everlasting life'. On the surface, this seems to be quite an intense declaration of personal faith. Five more Linton wardens, however, have identical phrasing in their wills.[164]

Even when there is some deviation from a precise formula, the wardens' preambles stick so close to familiar themes and conventions that it is difficult to read much between the lines. For example, William Cockerton of Balsham offered his soul to God 'my only Saviour and Redeemer by whose merits and passions I hope and confidently believe to be saved', and John Smith of the same parish commended his soul to God 'hoping assuredly through the merits of Christ Jesus that I shall inherit eternal life in the kingdom of heaven'. Even John Taylor, erstwhile member of the Family of Love, used phrases repeated by other testators in many parishes when he offered his soul 'into the blessed protection of Almighty God hoping by the death, merits and passion of Jesus Christ his only son and my redeemer to be made partakers [sic] of his most blessed and glorious kingdom'.[165] These preambles appear to be unique within the sample, but even if designed by the testators, they use such familiar themes and word choices as to render them nugatory to historians in search of exceptional piety. All they can show is a general shared vocabulary of orthodox protestantism which would be quite unexceptional in their day.

After 1660, the typical preamble is worded differently, but again within narrow parameters. The most popular form in Balsham returned the testator's soul 'to God that gave it me hoping assuredly through the only merits, death and passion of my alone and blessed Saviour and redeemer Jesus Christ to have free pardon and remission of all my sins and to enjoy eternal happiness with him in the highest heaven'.[166] If rarely this elaborate, most wills touched on these themes, especially that of hoping through the merits, death, and passion of Jesus to have pardon and remis-

---

[164] EPR, WR C27: 99v (Thomas Webb); CW1637 (Robert Tofts); CW1639 (Philip Newman); CW1642 (Matthew Sherman); WR C28: 128, 187 (Thomas Barker, William Willow). See above, Table 1, for the rarity of Calvinist clauses. There was either a Calvinist group, or a Calvinist scribe, in Linton.

[165] EPR, WR C24: 170r; C26: 86v, 114. Taylor was presented for his continued Familist association in 1609: EDR, B/2/28, fol. 18.

[166] EPR, WR C31: 228v (John Rule), 386 (Henry Chapman); C34: 5v (Edmund Marsh), 88 (Henry Leader), 98v (John Taylor).

sion of one's sins.[167] Some add a hope 'to be partaker in everlasting life' or 'eternal happiness'.[168]

At best, wills reveal Cambridgeshire wardens as conventionally pious according to the tenor of their times; at worst, they throw up a smoke screen obscuring their piety from our gaze. There is little additional evidence to suggest that wardens held distinctive religious views and might, therefore, be insinuating themselves into the office in order to use it to pursue a pious agenda. In Balsham, a gaggle of Familists held church office between 1561 and 1599.[169] Richard Marsh was a churchwarden in 1567; his son Richard served in 1599.[170] William Taylor served as churchwarden with Marsh in 1599, and seven Familists served as sidesmen, all in the 1570s.[171] Finally, Thomas Bridge was a warden in Shudy Camps in 1561.[172] (Unfortunately, no records survive which identify the wardens from the 1580s, when the Family was under attack from the authorities.) This is not an unimpressive list, but at no point did Familists hold a monopoly over parish office. Even in 1599 when both wardens were Familists, the sidesmen elected, Matthew Starr and Thomas Chapman, cannot be connected with the sect. This is not the sort of pattern that could support using the office to push a Familist agenda. It is likely that these men held office because their social and economic position in Balsham, as Dr Marsh has shown, entitled them to it.

In 1609, Edmund Rule, John Taylor, and William Taylor were presented as Familists, and the churchwarden William Rule was cited for failing to present them himself. While it was unclear why suddenly they came to the attention of the court, until Dr Marsh engaged in a little gravedigging in 1992 (Chapter 5 below), since their sympathies must have been unchanged since the 1580s, here is possible evidence that wardens deliberately concealed nonconformity out of sympathy for the nonconformists. Indeed sympathy was at work here, but not sympathy for their views: Edmund Rule and the Taylors were elderly men, and one was blind and

---

[167] For example, see the Balsham wills, covering the period from 1664 to 1698, of Giles Taylor (EPR, WR C29: 245v), Richard Norden (C31: 353v), Edward Martin (C34: 113v), William Carter (C35: 284), and John Flacke (C35: 344). The cheap, popular almanac *Fly* included a section on will-making which provided a preamble in which the soul was bequeathed 'into the hands of Almighty God my Maker, hoping that through the meritorious death and passion of Jesus Christ my only Saviour and Redeemer to receive free pardon and forgiveness of all of my sins': Bernard Capp, 'Will Formularies', *Local Population Studies*, 14 (1975), p. 49.

[168] For example, Robert Appleyard (EPR, WR C29: 140v), and Giles Taylor and Richard Norden (previous note).

[169] I have used the names of those imprisoned in 1580 and probable Familists identified by Dr Marsh: see above, n. 13.

[170] EDR, B/2/6, p. 42, B/2/17, fol. 38v.

[171] EDR, B/2/3, pp. 87, 98 (William Tassell), B/2/6, p. 42 (Thomas Baker), p. 151 (William Cornell, and two John Smiths), B/2/8, p. 20 (John Taylor, Henry Marsh).

[172] EDR, B/2/3, pp. 87, 100.

another deaf.[173] Such men as these were threats neither to the monarch nor the church. They were pious eccentrics who were being allowed to carry their idiosyncracies quietly to their graves.

From the 1590s onward, a number of once or future wardens were presented for violations of the Sabbath, usually either for carting or for allowing illicit activities such as card playing or drinking in their houses.[174] Many of these presentments were made by the minister against incumbent wardens, who were naturally unlikely to present themselves. Moreover, ministers clearly expected wardens to meet a higher standard of behaviour as an example to the parish.[175] These cases were invariably dismissed, for even when the violations were admitted, those accused demonstrated that they acted out of necessity or that neither work nor play interfered with attending services. In either case, they affirmed both the importance of the Sabbath and of conformity. These few cases, and their results, only emphasize that wardens were not the 'godly', but can comfortably be counted in the unquantifiable mass of the 'conformable'.[176] Presentments of Sabbath-breaking wardens are few, and other cases are virtually non-existent, but if these men were rarely at the wrong end of presentments before, during, or after their time in office, this is not surprising. They were those who most appreciated that if the peace of the community was broken it had to be repaired; they did not need to be dragged into court to do so.

V

In 1609–10, the parish of Dullingham was torn apart by suits and countersuits over the behaviour of Thomas Harrington, a former warden and one of the wealthiest men of the parish. First, Harrington was presented for refusing to sit in his appointed seat. He responded that he was not placed with 'men of his calling, ability and wealth but with them who receive alms of him'. The court was convinced of this and ordered the wardens to provide him with a more appropriate seat, which they did. Satisfied with the new provisions, the judge dismissed the case. Harrington was soon back, accused of wearing his hat during the service and of missing services on several occasions. Each time, he was dismissed with a pious admonition.[177]

---

[173] EDR, B/2/28, fol. 18.
[174] EDR, B/2/11, fol. 196v, B/2/13, fols. 72r, 121v, 130r, 165v, B/2/16, fols. 145r, 161v, 212v.
[175] EDR, B/2/40, fol. 13r, D/2/23, fol. 118Av.
[176] See Margaret Spufford, 'Can we Count the "Godly" and the "Conformable" in the Seventeenth Century?', *Journal of Ecclesiastical History*, 36 (1985), pp. 428–38.
[177] EDR, B/2/28, fols. 53v–4v.

These presentments were only the momentary surfacings of a much deeper problem, as soon became clear. Relations between Harrington and the vicar were so strained that the vicar turned to High Commission for relief, alleging Harrington to be 'a railer and reviler of the ministers of the word of God'. In March 1610, the ministers of Brinkley, Stetchworth, and Westley Waterless were delegated to hear witnesses in the case. The picture of Harrington which emerges is both unedifying and amusing. There was universal agreement that he was one of the best customers of alehouses as far afield as Newmarket and Bury. His friends reported having to tie him on to his horse in order to get him home, as well as leaving him leaning against an alehouse wall for the night when he was beyond moving. From the testimony of his drinking companions the story of his problems with his vicar, John Dunch, emerged.

A few years earlier (the witnesses disagree as to when), Dunch had caused the pew built by Harrington's father to be removed and put a new reading desk and seat for himself in its place. The Harrington pew, at the head of the north side of the nave, had been a source of pride and prestige, and Thomas was enraged by its removal. He began routinely to refer to Dunch as 'Mr Fucker' or 'our Fucker' despite the admonitions of his friends. Moreover, he began threatening to take direct action, including removing the reading desk and dumping it into the village pond. Many witnesses also recounted that Harrington, refusing any seat offered to him in place of his father's, promised to bring a stool and sit in the middle aisle during the service, saying that if Dunch pointed at him during the sermon, he would 'point at him with two fingers (holding his two fingers out forked-wise)'. This seems to have been nothing more than bold talk, and his actions never went beyond urinating in several parts of the church, including at least once while he was churchwarden, to the understandable offence of many in the parish. Harrington also seems to have been responsible for starting or encouraging rumours that Dunch's wife Margaret was having an affair with their servant, Lambert Lorkin.[178] How the case ended we do not know, but the bad blood continued, for when Thomas Harrington died in 1627, he was not buried by Dunch. His name was left out of Dullingham's burial register for the year, and had later to be added in another hand.

The case tells us much both about churchwardens and their world. Harrington appears to be as unfit to carry out the responsibilities of the office as it is possible to be. Perhaps a majority in the parish shared that view. He was, after all, elected only once. His election took place early in his controversy with Dunch, and he had many supporters. Even those who might have been repulsed by his quotidian behaviour might be

---

[178] EDR, K/6/105, K/11/25, K/11/68–9.

forced to agree that his complaint was justified, since they believed without question that church seating ought to reflect the village's social hierarchy. Electing him warden gave him responsibility for the church's interior, the *locus* of his grievance, but when he made ill use of his year, he was not given a second chance. His social position entitled him to seek and hold the office, but that still depended on the consent of his neighbours.

It is easy to see Harrington's drunkenness and vulgarity and read into that godlessness or irreligion. His occasional presentments for not attending services or leaving his hat on during morning prayer seem to confirm that. Such a view is, however, inaccurate, for at the heart of his case was his own insistence that he be allowed to attend the church of his father, and attend it as his father had done. In refusing to remove his hat (as apparently did others in the parish), he showed disrespect for the vicar, who had denied him the respect he himself deserved by removing his pew. Harrington absented himself from his own parish, but he attended the church in neighbouring Stetchworth, showing that his absences were not 'for religion' (or lack thereof) but because he was not at peace with the vicar and churchwardens. If he expressed himself crudely, even obscenely, to our ears, that should not be allowed to deafen us to the message: Harrington wanted to be in his parish church on Sunday because it was part of who he was as a member of his community and his family.

Is Thomas Harrington typical of rural churchwardens? In many ways obviously not, since the disturbances at which he was the centre are without parallel in seventeenth-century Cambridgeshire. But in other respects he is. The parish church to him was more than a house of prayer; it was a reflection of the parish's history and hierarchy. Attending church was as much (if not more) a statement of his role in society as it was of religious convictions. Wardens and those who chose them took attendance at church seriously and acted upon this. If they blinked at nonconformity, the reasons must be sought not in religious sympathies, but in their understanding of their village society and the role of each person in it. For, finally, the wardens were the trustees of that society in many ways, not only of its church ornaments but also of its values and aspirations.

If there is a connection between churchwardens and nonconformity, perhaps it may be found in this: although Harrington's behaviour might tempt us to see this as a conflict of the 'godly' against the unregenerate, the surviving materials from this case make clear that this was not so. Dunch was no puritan, nor were his churchwardens a godly vanguard. Harrington's struggle with Dunch and his supporters, including the wardens who presented him, critically undermined the church's authority in Dullingham. The parish services became the stage on which conflicts of class and honour were played out, rather than God worshipped. As a result, Dullingham became by the 1650s, and remained into the 1680s, a centre of dissent in Cambridgeshire. Could it be that the proper question is not whether churchwardens failed to present nonconformists, but whether their failure to maintain peace and social harmony in their parishes might itself engender dissent?

CHAPTER 5

The gravestone of Thomas Lawrence revisited (or the
Family of Love and the local community in Balsham,
1560–1630)

CHRISTOPHER MARSH

Between February and November 1609, an episode of extraordinary passion and drama took place in the south Cambridgeshire parish of Balsham. The bare facts – and bare they certainly are – were as follows.
Thomas Lawrence, an elderly member of the mystical religious fellowship known as the Family of Love, died and was buried in the churchyard.
A gravestone was laid over him. Some time shortly afterwards, three other
villagers – a churchwarden, a questman, and the parish clerk – went into
the churchyard and deliberately violated the grave. They pulled the stone
from the ground, perhaps exposing Lawrence's shrouded corpse to the
air, and prevented the dead man's friends from replacing it. In June, the
violent and symbolic action of the three church officers became the subject of a characteristically abbreviated church court presentment – our
only *written* source in this matter.

A few months later, a counter-presentment was made, and three of the
dead man's closest friends – Edmund Rule, John and William Taylor –
were accused of belonging to the Family of Love.[1]

This essay is unapologetically intensive in its focus. The aim is to set the
events of 1609 as deeply into their context as the evidence – some written
on paper, some set in stone – will allow. There is far more to the tale of
Thomas Lawrence's gravestone than the consistory court records reveal,

---

[1] EDR, B/2/28, fols. 17r–19r. These folios form the basis for this essay, and the reference will not subsequently be repeated. For a comprehensive account of the Family
of Love's history in England, see Christopher Marsh, *The Family of Love in English Society,
1550–1630* (Cambridge, 1994). The facts about Thomas Lawrence's death known
are that he made a will on 17 January 1608/9, which was granted probate on 10
May 1609 (PRO, PCC 40 Dorset). His burial took place on 26 Feb. 1608/9 (Balsham
parish registers, Cambs. RO).

and the historian is presented with a rare and irresistible opportunity to explore the *mentalité* of the principal actors on both sides, and almost to feel the atmosphere in a Jacobean village. The essay is also intended as a comment upon historical method, and a reminder of the fragility and partiality of many of the paper sources which historians use with varying degrees of trust and confidence. For between the lines of the ecclesiastical court record (or, more literally, beneath the soil of southern Cambridgeshire) there lie concealed several elements crucial to an understanding of the situation. As new layers of meaning are revealed, the significance of this conspicuous village drama changes markedly.

How should the action of the three church officers be explained? What drove them to commit so violent an act, and to break a deeply rooted taboo against the disturbance of newly buried bodies? Did that act reflect the contempt in which a deviant religious minority was held by other contemporaries, as initially it certainly seems to? How indulgent, and how imaginative is the microhistorian allowed to be, before he or she turns into something more like a novelist?

Just as the microbiologist may hope to move from examination of a few minute cells towards a new treatment for cancer, so the historian can aspire to develop a deeper understanding of a society by occasionally staring obsessively at tiny groups of its smallest constituent units. It may not be wise to do this all the time, but the microscopic approach remains a valuable feature of the methodological repertoire. Paradoxically, it is sometimes possible to tell far more about a society by scrutinizing one household, one individual, or three church officers and a dead 'heretic' than by standing back and attempting to observe the totality. As Giovanni Levi has recently put it, 'Phenomena previously considered to be sufficiently described and understood assume completely new meanings by altering the scale of investigation. It is then possible to use these results to draw far wider generalisations.'[2]

The trick, of course, is to bear the wider questions and possible implications continually in mind. This essay aims to contribute to the growing debate over the effects of committed religious belief on social relations in early modern England. Most modern commentators would probably share Lawrence Sasek's opinion that 'there was little religious tolerance in England until after the civil wars', and the violation of Thomas Lawrence's grave certainly seems to support this view. When, in 1974, Margaret Spufford argued that seventeenth-century dissenters had

---

[2] Giovanni Levi, 'On Microhistory', in Peter Burke (ed.), *New Perspectives on Historical Writing* (Cambridge, 1991), p. 98. See also Edward Muir and Guido Ruggiero (eds.), *Microhistory and the Lost Peoples of Europe* (Baltimore and London, 1991).

to choose between membership of their 'natural communities' and membership of an 'alienated' religious group, she expressed a widely held assumption about the nature of early modern English society.[3]

It is gradually becoming clear, however, that early modern attitudes were rather less straightforward than we might at first imagine. Several factors may conspire to mislead the unwary analyst. For example, the rhetorical polarities that seem to have been built into early modern patterns of thought may give an impression of conflicting opposites – godly/ungodly, conformist/nonconformist, even church/alehouse – where an impression of broad spectrums may be equally valuable. Of course, the polarities are not to be written off completely – rhetorical and intellectual conventions are one vital layer of 'reality' – but they must be assessed critically.

A second contemporary rhetorical tactic is equally relevant. Literate commentators (and doubtless others too) were apparently in the habit of describing a situation as they wished it to be, rather than as it actually was, without drawing the distinction. Queen Elizabeth I was hailed as a glorious, reforming, protestant prince by individuals who knew, or feared most strongly, that she was nothing of the sort. The idea, clearly, was to persuade her to *become* such a godly paragon. In the present context, the significance is that when early modern writers gave the impression, as they often did, that dissenting groups were unpopular and profoundly alienated, they may not have been reflecting things as they were, but as they ought to have been. Again, we cannot step lightly from rhetoric to reality.

A third problem is more obvious and better known. All societies are characterized by conflict and concord in varying measures, but the documentary sources upon which historians have little option but to rely are frequently biased in favour of friction and dispute. A hypothetical village community existing in total, unbroken peace would generate no court records, no polemical literary tracts, no fiery sermons. Early modern people are most historically visible when locked in combat with their neighbours. Moreover, moments of conflict – fierce quarrels over gravestones, for example – appear extremely compelling in comparison to periods of relative tranquillity.

It is, therefore, one of the challenges facing social historians to compensate for the unbalancing effect of these factors. One of the ways in which this can be attempted is by asking of the more mundane available sources – wills, records of land transactions and parish registers, for

---

[3] Lawrence A. Sasek, *Images of English Puritanism* (Baton Rouge, 1989), p. 14; Margaret Spufford, *Contrasting Communities: English Villagers in the Sixteenth and Seventeenth Centuries* (Cambridge, 1974), pp. 346–7.

example – the sort of questions more usually explored through court records and the literature of controversy. Another might be by considering not what court records include, but what they exclude. The known nonconformist whose name makes no appearance in the documents of dispute may have as much to tell us of early modern society as the one whose name is recorded. The difficulty is in persuading the first individual to say his or her piece. This essay will endeavour to put some of these ideas into practice, by reconstructing the background – broadly conceived – to the spellbinding local controversy of 1609.

We are dealing here with one of the most obscure of early modern dissenting groups, and a few words of introduction may therefore be appropriate.[4] The Family of Love was a small, closely-knit fellowship of mystical believers, founded by a Messianic Dutchman named Hendrick Niclaes in the middle of the sixteenth century. Niclaes, who identified himself only as 'H.N.', wrote numerous inspirational works, frequently impenetrable to the uninitiated, many of which were translated into English during the 1570s. The books, with titles like *Terra Pacis* and *The Prophetie of the Spirit of Love*, were imported secretly along well-worn trade routes linking eastern England with the Low Countries, before being distributed amongst H.N.'s deeply committed disciples. The Family had members, both male and female, in a variety of social and geographical settings, including the court of Elizabeth I, but they were apparently most numerous in Cambridgeshire and the surrounding counties. It seems that the Familists, whose religious backgrounds were diverse, had generally been recruited to the fellowship during the late 1550s or early 1560s by one of H.N.'s foremost followers, an itinerant, bilingual craftsman or merchant named Christopher Vittels.

The Familists' faith was mystical and profoundly inward, characterized fundamentally by a quest for spiritual transformation and the attainment of a mysterious state of union with God. When an individual had achieved this state, he or she was in some sense perfect and without sin. Followers of H.N. also emphasized allegorical interpretations of Scripture, and were accused of denying the literal reality of Jesus Christ, the Resurrection and the creation of the world. The fellowship was extremely secretive, and though its members undoubtedly nourished hopes of global success, they generally chose not to evangelize. In some circumstances, this fact combined with a certain spiritual arrogance to produce a belief that it was permissible for Familists to dissemble unashamedly

---

[4] For a much fuller account, see Marsh, *The Family of Love*.

when challenged by hostile outsiders. Partly for this reason, the Family of Love supplied no martyrs. The same belief, in another guise, appeared as a willingness to conform to the requirements of the established church.

The high degree of collective introversion also helps to account for the fact that the Family's members were generally drawn from the middling and wealthy sections of local society. It was probably through trading networks that H.N. first found his English following, and Familists rarely strove actively to carry their belief beyond these networks.

The Family of Love had members in over twenty parishes in Cambridgeshire and adjacent counties, but nowhere were they more numerous than in the nucleated village of Balsham, ten miles south-east of Cambridge (Map 4: Balsham was intended also to fall within our second study area, see Appendix A). Within this parish, which was lucky enough to combine arable open-fields with extensive heath and some pasture, the nine Familist families prospered disproportionately. The heads of Balsham's Familist households were generally yeomen, farming substantial acreages of land and contributing to parliamentary taxation.[5] Thomas Lawrence, the man whose grave lay at the centre of such controversy in 1609, was wealthy enough to have held a sub-manor of several hundred acres.[6] John Killingworth and Richard Hasell were wealthier still, and the former died as an 'esquire' in nearby Pampisford.[7] Others were less privileged, but none was in any danger whatsoever of falling on the poor rates.

It is estimated that, during the 1590s, over half of the parish's 4,550 acres of land was held or farmed by members of the Family of Love, or their immediate relations. The wills of Balsham's Familists – and most of them died testate – also convey a remarkably consistent impression of material well being. The household goods they listed – featherbeds, blankets, posted bedsteads, chairs, pewter or silver cups and plates, cupboards, and chests – reflect the unpretentious prosperity of the region's yeomen, though we should also note the occasional cushion or 'hutch of walnut tree'.[8] One of the Familist families – the Tassells – was probably responsible for the construction of Balsham's most beautiful surviving

---

[5] PRO, E179, 82/244 (5 Eliz), 82/248 (10 Eliz), 82/257 (14 Eliz), 82/294 (35 Eliz), 83/307 (41 Eliz), 83/351 (7 James), 83/358 (19 James).

[6] PRO, PCC 16 Mellershe; Ely CC, C12.397 (will of William Lawrence, Thomas' father).

[7] PRO, E179, 82/294 (35 Eliz), 83/307 (41 Eliz); GLRO, Charterhouse MS, Acc. 1876, MR2/549. In 1617, the Killingworth estate in Balsham, held by John's son, amounted to 538 acres of freehold. For John's will (probate 1617), see PRO, PCC 55 Weldon.

[8] PRO, PCC 22 Pyckering (William Tassell), 40 Dorset (Thomas Lawrence), 48 Clarke (William Taylor), 16 Soame (Richard Hasell, died in Bottisham), 19 Rudd (Thomas Diss, died in Kirtling), 35 Wallopp (William Lawrence, died in Great Massingham, Norfolk); Ely CC C22.306 (Henry Marsh), C26.86 (John Taylor).

house, certainly one of the largest that stood in the Elizabethan village. The interior walls, intriguingly, were covered with paintings, some of which remain partially visible today.[9]

⌒⌒

The dispute of 1609 appears at first as indisputable evidence of the radical dissociation between members of the Family of Love and their neighbours. The action against Thomas Lawrence's grave was taken, after all, by three parish officers, elected representatives of their community. They presumably spoke for a considerable body of the villagers.

It is certainly not difficult to construct a wider context that supports this view. Any number of literary comments were recorded which suggest the Family of Love's status as an ostracized, persecuted, isolated 'sect'. To the preacher, John Dyos, this was no family of love, but 'a familie of Sathan ... a familie of all vice and vilanie'.[10] To others, the Familists were wolves in the sheepfold, vile spiders creeping through society, or 'shamelesse dogges thrusting themselves (for a fatter soppe) into houses of great wealth'.[11]

Literary enemies of the fellowship sometimes sought to create an impression of the Family as a group whose members stood apart from local society, partly by choice and partly by compulsion. William Wilkinson alleged that Familists could meet one another only in houses that were 'far from company', standing 'out of the common walke of the people' with whom they dwelt.[12] Another writer scorned H.N., claiming 'that all men, especially the true Church and servantes of God, are against him, and his Familie'.[13] John Rogers, in *The Displaying of an Horrible Secte of Grosse and Wicked Heretiques*, alleged that members of the Family reserved their charitable gifts for fellow-heretics. This charge became something of a commonplace, and earned a line in Thomas Middleton's satirical play, *The Family of Love*.[14]

[9] One of the manorial maps drawn in 1617 (GLRO, Charterhouse MS, Acc. 1876, MP2/3) identifies Robert Tassell, son of the Familist, Bartholomew, as the occupant of this house. The house was probably built in the second half of the sixteenth century by Bartholomew, or his father, William. I am very grateful to Mr and Mrs Sanders, the current owners of the house, for their help, and to Pamela Tudor-Craig, Lady Wedgewood, for commenting on the paintings.

[10] John Dyos, *A Sermon Preached at Pauls Crosse the 19 of Juli 1579* (London, 1579), fol. 62r–v.

[11] William Wilkinson, *A Confutation of Certaine Articles Delivered unto the Family of Love* (London, 1579), II(v); John Rogers, *An Answere unto a Wicked & Infamous Libel Made by Christopher Vitel* (London, 1579), A8r–v; John Knewstub, *A Confutation of Monstrous and Horrible Heresies* (London, 1579), fol. 4v.

[12] Wilkinson, *A Confutation*, fols. 30v–1r.

[13] *A Supplication of the Family of Love* (Cambridge, 1606), p. 32.

[14] John Rogers, *The Displaying of an Horrible Secte of Grosse and Wicked Heretiques* (London, 1578; 2nd edn, 1579), H3r–12r (no. 31); Thomas Middleton, *The Family of Love*, in Alexander Dyce (ed.), *The Works of Thomas Middleton*, II (London, 1840), pp. 202–3.

In Balsham, comments suggesting social polarity were also recorded. In a document written in 1574, there was talk of 'sinister reports' that had reached those in authority.[15] In 1580, Bishop Cox of Ely headed a commission of inquiry into the Family's existence, and six Balsham men, including Thomas Lawrence, Edmund Rule, and John Taylor, were imprisoned in Cambridge Castle. In a letter to the Privy Council, Cox referred to their 'dampnable heresies' and 'wilfull blyndenes'. He also warned that, if the Familists were left alone, they would 'litely esteme anye authoritie'.[16]

The bishop must have had his local informants, and we are led further still towards the conclusion that the Family's members stood apart from the rest of local society. Some years later, William Lawrence, one of the Familists, recalled his decision 'at that tyme upon some harde and extreeme dealing offred unto him to absente him selfe for A tyme'. He stayed away for longer than he intended, dying as a wealthy yeoman in Great Massingham, Norfolk, early in the seventeenth century.[17]

The Family's attitude to wider society can also be portrayed as deeply hostile. H.N. declared repeatedly that none outside the Family could hope to be saved.[18] He warned his followers to 'keepe not companye with the Craftie and Wicked' and to 'Rest not yourselves among the straunge People'.[19]

In Balsham, there was a very marked tendency for Familists to call will-witnesses from within the fellowship. The will of Thomas Lawrence, for example, was witnessed in 1608/9 by Edmund Rule, John and William Taylor, all three of whom were to be accused of Familism in the court case following Lawrence's burial. Lawrence's executor was John Hasell of nearby Bottisham, another prominent member of the Family of Love.[20]

The Cambridgeshire Familists also maintained an impressive system of endogamy, rarely if ever selecting spouses who were not themselves members of the fellowship. The marital career of Henry Marsh (no relation) amply illustrates the importance attached to the choice of partner. Marsh lost his first wife, of whom little is known, in May 1587. Just over a year later, he married Edmund Rule's niece, a woman who was well over thirty years his junior. In this instance, the need for spiritual compatibility between partners clearly trumped the need for parity of age. Against all the odds, Marsh easily outlived his young bride, for she died within six months. The sixty-year-old Familist again remarried

[15] Inner Temple Library, Petyt MS No. 538/vol. 47, fol. 492. Printed by John Strype, *The Life and Acts of M. Parker* (London, 1711), pp. 471–3.
[16] Gonville and Caius College Library, MS 53/30 (Letter Book of Bishop Cox), fols. 72v–3r.
[17] PRO, SP12, 133; PCC 35 Wallopp.
[18] See, for example, H.N., *Exhortatio I* (Cologne, *c.* 1575), fols. 12r, 43v.
[19] Ibid. fol. 20r; H.N., *Terra Pacis* (Cologne, 1574), p. 5.
[20] PRO, PCC 40 Dorset.

swiftly, the daughter of his co-religionist John Taylor. On this occasion, the age difference was a mere twenty-five years.[21]

The most conspicuous evidence that the Balsham Familists held more orthodox people in low regard is to be found in an intricate dispute, which found its way into the central courts. In 1576, Michael Heneage, brother of Sir Thomas Heneage, formerly Treasurer of Her Majesty's Chamber, purchased the manor of Oxcroft near Balsham from the Familist, Thomas Lawrence.[22] Some years later, Heneage was outraged to find that the grazing rights of his tenants were being denied by two other local landholders, John Killingworth and John Taylor. Both were committed Familists, though Heneage, a duped outsider, failed to gather this information.

The well-connected London esquire took the case to Chancery, but was unable to provide the court with documentary evidence of his claims concerning Balsham manorial custom. A bemused Michael Heneage told the court that he had no idea of the exact contents of the 'deeds and writings' appertaining to his manor, 'nor how they came to . . . the handes or custodie of the said John Kyllingworth and John Taylor'. If Heneage had known that both his adversaries, and the man from whom he should have obtained the documents at the time of purchase, were members of the Family of Love, his confusion – if not his anger – might have been assuaged.[23] Although no official verdict has been discovered, a manorial map of 1617 demonstrates that the Familists' version of local custom had, by then, become the accepted one.[24]

Within this context, the violent action of one of the churchwardens and his associates in disturbing Lawrence's grave in 1609 seems perfectly explicable. The question becomes not 'why did they act the way they did?', but 'why did they not do something similar sooner?' The answer, at this stage, would appear to be that the economic power of the Familists was such that justifiable hostility towards them had of necessity been bottled up for decades.

This picture of aggressive, self-protecting separateness from wider society is, however, no more than a half-truth. Against the background so far

[21] Cambs. RO, Balsham parish registers; Ely CC C22.306 (Henry Marsh), C26.86 (John Taylor). Marsh's third marriage was not, for some reason, registered in Balsham, but it can be deduced from references in these wills. The ages of Marsh and Elizabeth Rule have been calculated from various wills written between 1520 and 1560. When they married, he was close to sixty; she was aged between twenty-one and twenty-six.
[22] Cambs. RO, 'Cambridgeshire Fines, 1199–1603', p. 64.
[23] PRO, C3/241/22, C2/ELIZ/H13/6, C24 (Town depositions), Box 237.
[24] GLRO, Charterhouse MS, Acc. 1876, MP2/3.

presented, the suggestion that the Balsham Familists were in fact amongst the most respected, generous and integrated people in their village may seem ludicrous. Nevertheless, it is perfectly possible to construct an alternative scenario, using various indices of integration, to demonstrate the validity of this claim.

Between 1560 and 1602, broadly the period during which Balsham's Familists were most active, over half of the thirty-six wills written in the village were witnessed by one or more of the fellowship's members. Every one of the nine individual Familists resident in Balsham appeared at some point alongside a testator who was apparently unconnected to the fellowship. If the names of obvious scribes are excluded, Thomas Lawrence, Edmund Rule, and John Taylor – central players in the events of 1609 – were all amongst the six most popular will-witnesses in the parish, including all those who performed the service at any time between the reign of Edward VI and the personal rule of Charles I.[25] Between 1584 and 1602, most strikingly, ten of the thirteen wills written in Balsham carried the names of one or more Familists as witnesses or executors. In one of the exceptions, furthermore, the testator referred his son to the arbitration of William Lawrence in a dispute that seemed likely to arise with another local man.[26] This was the same William Lawrence who, very shortly afterwards, felt moved to depart the parish on account of the 'hard dealings' being offered him. Clearly, there were two sides to his existence.

Depositions in court cases surrounding disputed wills demonstrate conclusively that testators chose their witnesses and executors deliberately and with care. Those individuals who were called to village sickbeds on more than one occasion were trusted and respected local figures, holders of high 'credit'. Will making was a practical action with widely perceived spiritual overtones, and the presence of Familists like Thomas Lawrence on so many occasions indicates that their moral and religious worth was not considered to be in serious question.[27]

Balsham's Familists also served regularly on the manorial homage, the lists of which were headed by the names of Thomas Lawrence or Edmund Rule at every court held between 1592 and 1602. Yet this was no socio-economic stranglehold, for when tenants, out of court, desired the presence of credible villagers to witness, or act as intermediaries in, land transactions, they frequently called not upon their immediate

[25] Ely CC; PRO, PCC, wills written in Balsham (there is insufficient space here to list the specific references for more than 100 wills).

[26] PRO, PCC 5 Windsor (John Cole, 1585/6).

[27] See Christopher Marsh, 'In the Name of God? Will-Making and Faith in Early Modern England', in G.H. Martin and Peter Spufford (eds.), The Records of the Nation (Woodbridge, 1990), pp. 215–51.

neighbours, but upon members of the Family of Love. Edmund Rule fulfilled the duty on a total of twenty-three occasions, for tenants who spanned the economic spectrum.[28]

When the manorial homage – which, numerically, was not dominated by Familists – decided to appoint particular individuals to supervise the enforcement of the arable fields in the run-up to harvest, it turned, as often as not, to the Familists. Four such committees, each of five or six men, were appointed between 1574 and 1602; every one included at least two members of the Family of Love. The most remarkable example was recorded on 16 April 1580:

> It is ordained that if any tenaunt of the manor do reare up any dwelling place for any person to dwell in, that hath nott bene usually dwelt in heretofore, with owt the consent of John Smith, Edmund Rule, Richard Tassell, Thomas Lawrence, Thomas Lawrence Jun and William Lawrence, or foure of them, he shall forfeyt to the Lord – 40s.[29]

The preservation of Balsham's demographic balance – no small matter, as the hefty fine demonstrates – was here entrusted to a group very strongly associated with the Family of Love. Later in the same year, Edmund Rule, Thomas Lawrence, and William Lawrence were arrested by the bishop's agents and 'committed to prison for the heresies of HN'.[30] It is worth remarking that Balsham's social stability was probably more severely disturbed by the enforced absence of the Familists than it ever was by their presence.

Other indices convey the same impression of the Familists' trusted and integrated status. Despite belonging to 'a sect most vile', all but one of the Balsham Familists held local office at some stage. In the period between 1560 and 1602, there were five Familist constables, one manorial foreman, twelve supervisors of by-laws, three churchwardens, and five questmen.[31] There are substantial gaps in the record, so this is a minimum estimate. In the Ely diocese as a whole, thirty-two Familists, from nine communities, held a total of fifty-eight offices, both temporal and ecclesiastical, during the reigns of Elizabeth and James.[32] When Bishop Cox informed the Privy Council in 1580 that he had identified the heretics in the fenland town of Wisbech following conference with the churchwar-

---

[28] GLRO, Charterhouse MS, Acc. 1876, MR2/34–8.
[29] GLRO, Charterhouse, MS, MR2/64a and b. The ordinance survives on a separate, undated sheet, but it can be dated very precisely by comparison with one of the other court rolls.
[30] Gonville and Caius College Library, MS 53/30, fol. 73r.
[31] GLRO, Charterhouse MS, Acc. 1876, MR2/34–8; EDR, B/2/3, fols. 87–115, B/2/6, fols. 11–77, 113–198, B/2/8, fols. 1–70, 87–123, 143–87, B/2/11, fols. 7–42, B/2/17, fols. 33–74, B/2/31, fols. 112–38, F/5/34, fols. 5–18.
[32] Marsh, *The Family of Love*, Table 1.

dens there, he was concealing more than he revealed; for the wardens there in 1579–80 were John May and Thomas Peirson, two of the suspected Familists![33]

Local office holding was, of course, a duty as well as an honour, but there can be little doubt that the extent of Familist involvement suggests a thorough degree of trusted integration. Although in Balsham it could be argued that the Familists' economic power accounted for their presence in such offices, the same can certainly not be said of the situation in most of the other parishes, where Familists, though quite wealthy, were spread more thinly on the ground. In Cottenham, for example, John Essex was a smaller fish in a bigger pond, yet he served at least twice as churchwarden and witnessed numerous wills for his orthodox neighbours.[34]

The allegation, made on several occasions, that the Family's voluntary charity was only directed internally appears to have been wholly inaccurate. The name of John Killingworth, the Familist gentleman who conspired against Michael Heneage in the 1590s, is recorded on a charity board in Balsham church, for a gift of £5 he made to the parish's poor in the same decade. The Balsham Familists who made wills all registered generous bequests to the local poor, and the £20 left by William Tassell in 1574 was a local testamentary record.[35]

Within this second, alternative scenario, the Family of Love appears as a tolerated and thoroughly integrated group, despite known religious unorthodoxy. An examination of ecclesiastical court records reinforces this impression. In the years between 1580 and 1608, when the fellowship was firmly established in several parishes, no church court presentment for the Ely diocese so much as mentioned the Family of Love.

The Family's members did not avoid presentment altogether, but the offences of which they found themselves accused were no different from those which occasionally touched the lives of other prosperous and generally respectable parishioners. Edmund Rule was presented, in 1591, 'for suffering his servants to work upon Bartholomewe daye last, and to bind corne upon Sondaye the xxii of August last . . . in divine servis time'. In 1598, Rule's friend William Taylor was reported 'for goeinge to carte upon Sunday morninge in harvest time'. He successfully defended himself by explaining that he had been busy performing a good deed: 'he did onely fetch a loade of corne which lay in danger of spoilinge by cattell oute of

[33] Gonville and Caius College Library, MS 53/30, fol. 126v.
[34] EDR, B/2/8, fols. 143–87, B/2/16, first section (unpaginated); Ely CC C19.220, 265, 272, C20.83, 84, 166, 168, 340, C21.153, C22.155.
[35] PRO, PCC, 22 Pyckering (1574).

his neighbours yarde into his owne yarde and that notwithstanding himself & his servants were at morning prayer'.[36]

So far, an artificial separation has been imposed on the material in order
to demonstrate the radically different interpretations which surviving
evidence will support. There must now be an attempt to weave the two
alternative contexts together, and to assess each in the light of the other.
The drama of 1609 provides a challenging opportunity to attempt this
exercise. Initially, there can be little doubt that the episode sits more
comfortably within the first, more polarized and embittered, context.
Church officers do not, in general, tear up the gravestones of men whom
they love and admire. Nevertheless, the second, softer interpretation has
undeniable weight. How, then, should the events surrounding Thomas
Lawrence's death be understood?

The political situation in Balsham, and in other parishes where the
Family of Love's members lived, possessed an inherent tension; men
who frequently enjoyed considerable authority in local affairs, and were
generally accorded much respect, held deviant and officially outlawed
religious beliefs through the greater portion of their adult lives. Inevitably,
there must have been individuals amongst their neighbours who experienced feelings of jealousy and suspicion. These feelings were not frequently allowed free expression, for various reasons, but any shift in the
underlying social and political structure might have had the effect of
liberating an undercurrent of hostility from the constraints placed upon
it by the distribution of local power and the more tolerant attitudes of
other parishioners.

In Balsham, such a shift had been taking place in the years leading up
to 1609. When the aged Thomas Lawrence composed the preamble to
his will on 17 January 1608/9, he deviated from colourless common form
for a passing moment, 'considering the state of man to be but transitory
and vanishing as the flower which this day groweth and to morrow
withereth'.[37] To the villagers of Balsham, however, the influence of Lawrence and his friends must have seemed anything but transitory. For over
half a century, they had operated as the most powerful self-defining group
in the parish, more like the oak trees on Balsham's boulder clay than the
vanishing flowers on its chalk. Now, finally, their influence was fading as
they grew old and withdrew from village life. Thomas Lawrence and

[36] EDR, B/2/11, fol. 204, B/2/16, fol. 145.
[37] PRO, PCC, 40 Dorset.

Edmund Rule had both handed their land on to their offspring, and with it had passed part of the foundation for the authority they had grown accustomed to exercising.[38] Thomas Lawrence had been a very substantial local farmer, one of Balsham's wealthiest residents; but he was no longer. His burial in the churchyard on 26 February 1608/9 marked the end of an era.[39]

As the elderly Familists declined in prominence, others had risen. Some of the new men, naturally, were the sons of the Familists (William Taylor and William Rule, for example), but others had no connection with the fellowship. The balance seems to have been shifting, and Familist surnames became slightly, but noticeably, less conspicuous in the types of document already discussed. In a sense, the village may have felt released from the influence of the Familists after they had been prominent for so long. This is, of course, no more than imaginative speculation. It can be said with greater certainty that, following the death of Thomas Lawrence, a level of hostility was seen between the Familists and a small number of their neighbours that had no apparent precedent.

One of the men who rose in wealth and influence as the aged Familists declined was named Thomas Teversham. Throughout the 1590s his name had appeared beneath those of Lawrence and Rule on the manorial homages. During the same decade, he was taxed for the first time in a lay subsidy, and his rent in 1597 was one of Balsham's highest, though Edmund Rule paid over twice as much.[40] Teversham acted as an intermediary in several land transfers and was appointed constable in 1596, being succeeded the following year by Rule.[41] In 1602, both men were among the six elected to control the pasturing of sheep. A year later, Rule and Thomas Lawrence passed their land to the next generation, and withdrew from their manorial activities. Symbolically, Teversham was one of the witnesses to Rule's transfer of land, a fact which indicates that relations between the two were cordial enough. At this point, Teversham's name moved closer to the top of the homage, perhaps reflecting his increasing influence, though he now found himself serving alongside William Taylor and Edmund Rule's four sons.[42] Teversham was elected churchwarden in 1608–9, one of the few men not descended from Familists to hold this office in the early seventeenth century. His fellow-warden was Edmund Rule's son William.[43]

Against this background, the happenings of that year can be brought into sharp focus.[44] In February, Thomas Lawrence Senior was buried

[38] GLRO, Charterhouse MS, Acc. 1876, MR2/38.
[39] Cambs. RO, Balsham parish registers.
[40] PRO, E179, 83/307; GLRO, Charterhouse MS, Acc. 1876, MR6/163.
[41] GLRO, Charterhouse MS, Acc. 1876, MR2/37.
[42] GLRO, Charterhouse MS, Acc. 1876, MR2/38.
[43] EDR, B/2/25, fol. 31v.
[44] See above, n. 1.

in the churchyard, and the event was registered by the churchwardens, Thomas Teversham and William Rule. There seems to have been nothing unusual in this, nor in the fact that in March the two wardens were ordered by the consistory court to ensure that a damaged church bell was 'newe cast, & hunge up againe in the steeple there'.

On 26 June, Teversham and Rule certified that this routine task had been performed. On the same day, however, the court clerks recorded a sudden rise in temperature. Thomas Teversham, along with Richard Norden, a questman, and Richard Swinborne, the parish clerk, found themselves presented on an extraordinary charge: 'that they tooke uppe a graveston after yt was laid uppon Thomas Lawrence, it being layd soe by the consente of Wm Rule thother churchwarden there & the best or better sorte of the Townes men there'. The judge ordered that the offenders replace the stone and exhibit a certificate to this effect on 10 July. Teversham duly appeared, and found himself subjected to a further severe reprimand from the judge, who reluctantly agreed not to punish the three men any further, 'althoughe they had wel deservd to have ben suspended'. Their only saving grace was that 'they obeyed the commandement of the judge & layed the ston againe on the grave of Tho Lawrence'. Teversham, licking his wounds, returned to Balsham.

To a limited degree, it is possible to examine the motivations of Teversham and the other church officers. One important trigger appears to have been the fact that they were not consulted over the laying of the gravestone. Most outdoor village graves at this time, even those enclosing the bodies of wealthy yeomen, were marked by nothing more than a wooden cross. Many were completely bare.[45] The laying of this stone was therefore an unusual event, and a statement of considerable social significance. To some observers, it may have seemed no more than Thomas Lawrence deserved; to others, it perhaps looked arrogant and pretentious.

Teversham, as a churchwarden, was justified in feeling that he should have been asked about the laying of a gravestone, and his implicit exclusion from the ranks of 'the best or better sorte' heaped insult upon injury. He was certainly considerably more wealthy than William Rule, the second churchwarden, who was presumably instrumental in presenting Teversham to the church authorities. Rule was also the godson of the dead Familist, and had received 'one hive of bees' in Thomas Lawrence's will (there was no mention of a hornet's nest). It also seems certain that 'the best or better sorte' was a label which applied to a group dominated by the ageing Familists and accustomed to a certain freedom of action in

[45] Clare Gittings, Death, Burial and the Individual in Early Modern England (London, 1984), pp. 143–4.

the village. It is impossible to avoid the conclusion that, in 1609, this evident feeling of local supremacy was increasingly outdated.

In all probability, Teversham was attacking not only the perceived arrogance of the people involved, but their religious affiliation. Little is known of Teversham's own spiritual convictions, though it is conceivable that the recent choice of 'Jeremiah' as a name for his son suggests committed protestant godliness.[46] 'Puritan' commentators, particularly during the reign of Elizabeth I, were unparalleled in the intensity with which they despised the Family of Love. It is possible that Teversham took his lead from preachers like John Knewstub who, in the years around 1580, had channelled all his energy into a drive against the fellowship.[47]

It remains difficult, however, to account for the full passionate force of the action taken against the late Thomas Lawrence and, by direct implication, against his friends and relatives. Tampering with the graves of the recently deceased is a sensitive matter in all cultures and all periods. In this particular case, it is extremely fortunate that additional sources make it possible to recover a vital element of this dramatic episode.[48]

Surviving gravestones within Balsham churchyard almost all date from the nineteenth and twentieth centuries. Four monuments, however, are clearly of much greater age (see Plate 4). They are set in a prestigious position, within feet of the chancel's eastern wall. The gravestones are so similar in design that it seems overwhelmingly probable that they were erected during the same period, and that they are linked in some way. The horizontal constructions visible above ground, though shaped like coffins, did not contain the bodies, which were buried beneath them.

The origin of these weather-worn monuments, fashioned out of limestone, can be established, with some certainty, from a variety of written sources. In 1744, when William Cole made notes on the church, the stones were already attracting considerable curiosity, and were described as 'very old'. At this date, the decorations upon them were clearly visible. Each of the four ridged stone lids bore three identical floriated crosses, but no names or dates.[49]

It seems almost certain that the graves belonged to four medieval rectors. In 1333, for example, a priest named William de Ousthorpe wrote

---

[46] Cambs. RO, Balsham parish registers.
[47] Marsh, *The Family of Love*, chapter 5.
[48] I have been assisted in this work of recovery by many people, and am grateful to them all for their advice and, in some cases, their spadework: Beth Davis, Mr Derrick, David Dymond, the Rev. William Girard, William Godfrey, Ralph Houlbrooke, Caroline Hull, Andrew Jotischky, Julian Litten, Jonathan Marsh, Katie Marsh, Edward Martin, Janet Miller, Warwick Rodwell, William and Joanna Sanders, Josh Schwieso, Margaret Spufford, Bishop Stephen of Ely, Alison Taylor, Robert Taylor, the Venerable David Walser, and Ken Wildsmith. Any errors or extravagances of interpretation are, of course, my own.
[49] BL, Add. MS 5807, fol. 62.

a will which requested burial in the churchyard, near to his predecessors.[50] Furthermore, when the second tomb from the north was opened
in the mid-nineteenth century, it was found to contain not only an
ancient skeleton but the remains of a small pewter chalice, now in Saffron
Walden Museum. This sepulchral chalice can probably be attributed to
the second half of the thirteenth century, and supports the suggestion
that the occupants of these graves were local rectors.[51] Between 1250
and 1350, a large number of similar limestone tombs were erected in
Cambridgeshire.[52]

Thus far, a connection with the Family of Love seems improbable. The
southernmost grave, however, is not what it seems. Shortly before Cole
made his notes in 1744, this grave had been opened, as was the one at
the other end of the group. The two sets of contents, described by Cole
following his conversations with local people, allow an intriguing comparison. The skeleton in the northernmost grave lay in a coffin of stone,
but the occupant of the other grave – to the surprise of the excavators –
lay in a hole 'with . . . brick on the sides & bottom'. The dead person
'had never been put into a Coffin', and it was conjectured that he 'might
formerly have bricked it up as a Vault for himself, & remov'd the old &
first inhabitant away'. The skeleton lay on a bed of gravel which, in comparison to the contents of the other tomb, looked 'quite fresh'.[53]

It is indeed rather unlikely that a brick-lined grave would have been
constructed in a rural Cambridgeshire churchyard during the fourteenth
century, even if the intended occupant was a wealthy cleric. Other excava-
tions, conducted at various dates, reveal that none of the other three
graves in the group make use of bricks. In each, the body was found to
be buried within a makeshift 'coffin' formed of stone slabs. Brick-lined
graves were not in fact common until the eighteenth century. Although
there are examples of early sixteenth-century brickwork in Balsham,
bricks were probably not readily available until the reign of Elizabeth.[54]

---

[50] H.J.E. Burrell, *The Church of the Holy Trinity, Balsham*, p. 8. This booklet is available at
the church.
[51] Saffron Walden Museum, Register No. 1, p. 295. I am grateful to the curator for
showing me the chalice and the documents acquired with it. I would also like to
thank Dr Caroline Hull, who kindly accompanied me to the museum and applied
herself to the problem of dating the chalice.
[52] L.A.S. Butler, 'Medieval Gravestones of Cambridgeshire, Huntingdonshire and the
Soke of Peterborough', *Proceedings of the Cambridgeshire Antiquarian Society*, 50 (1957),
pp. 89–100.
[53] BL, Add. MS 5807. fol. 62r.
[54] Examples of early brickwork in Balsham can be seen in the cellar of Oxcroft Farm,
the external rood staircase at the church, and the chimneys of Nine Chimney House.
It is intriguing, and perhaps not incidental, that two of these examples, Oxcroft and
Nine Chimney House, were associated with members of the Family of Love in the
sixteenth century. I am grateful to the residents of Balsham for permitting me to
inspect their homes.

Their use in the lining of this grave suggests the likelihood of a date after 1570.

The absence of a coffin, either of wood or stone, from the southern-most grave encourages a complementary suggestion. Coffins, according to Clare Gittings, became increasingly common during the seventeenth century.[55] If the body in question, which must have been that of a wealthy individual, had been buried in the later seventeenth century, a wooden coffin would very probably have been present, within the brick vault. It is also likely that the eighteenth-century excavators would have been able to recover the grave's history by consulting the people of Balsham. Instead, they were forced, like us, to speculate. Furthermore, the very notion of reusing an existing monument may imply the absence of an established trade network for gravestones suitable to be placed outside. There had been such a network during the thirteenth and fourteenth centuries, but by the sixteenth century it had largely disintegrated. By that time, brass memorials set into the floor of the church interior were much more fashionable.[56] Overall, then, it can be argued that the second occupant of the Balsham grave is more likely to have been installed between 1580 and 1650 than at earlier or later dates.

The only villager known to have been buried in the churchyard under a stone of any sort in this period was Thomas Lawrence, and it has already been established that his grave lay at the centre of a furious dispute. We can also deduce, from the language used in the court presentment, that his gravestone was horizontal, like the medieval slabs.[57] Early modern churchyard memorials generally stood upright, except for the grander table-tombs sometimes built by the gentry. The rarity of gravestones in Balsham during the seventeenth century is demonstrated by William Cole's slightly later sketch of the churchyard. The only monuments he depicted were the four close to the chancel, and he had no idea whose graves they marked.[58] If the stone being disputed in 1609 was a separate construction, it seems no longer to have been noticeable in 1744.

Is it possible that no such separate stone existed, and that the second occupant of the southernmost medieval grave was none other than Thomas Lawrence, one of Balsham's most prominent Familists? This would certainly help to explain the passions aroused amongst the non-Familist church officers following his death.

Seventeenth-century people lived in a society that was only partially literate, and they were more likely to register statements of identity or

[55] Gittings, *Death, Burial and the Individual*, p. 114.
[56] Butler, 'Medieval Gravestones of Cambridgeshire'.
[57] 'The stone had been laid upon the grave of the sayd Tho. Lawrence' (EDR, B/2/28, fol. 18r).
[58] BL, Add. MS 5807, fol. 61v.

Plate 4. Excavated grave at Balsham, Cambridgeshire

opinion by taking symbolic action than by putting pen to paper. In order to pursue this gripping tale further, it is therefore valuable to modify the perspective of a social historian by adopting that of an (amateur) archaeologist.

In the summer of 1992, the Archdeacon of Ely issued a certificate permitting an archaeological investigation to be conducted in Balsham churchyard. The current rector was reluctant to allow the actual opening of the grave, so we proceeded by digging a trench alongside it, hoping to establish the date of the underground brickwork. The results substantially reinforce the argument that the southernmost of the four graves is indeed that of Thomas Lawrence. It also becomes possible to form a much fuller impression of events in Balsham during 1609 (see Plate 4).

The bricks are impressively regular in colour, texture, and size. They are therefore extremely unlikely to have been manufactured during the period between 1250 and 1350, when the four gravestones were originally set in place. The Balsham bricks are generally of a warm, orange-red colour, though a few are darker, having been overfired. Their texture is smooth, with occasional straw-marks on the surface, and the clay is remarkably free of pebbles and shells. The bricks are unusually large (10.2 × 5 × 2.3 inches, on average), but their dimensions are highly consistent by pre-industrial standards.[59]

There is little doubt, in the opinion of a trio of experts, that the bricks date from the early seventeenth century. According to Mr Robert Taylor of the Royal Commission on Historical Monuments, who kindly came to visit the site, the bricks are too regular to predate the reign of James I. Dr Warwick Rodwell expressed a similar opinion after studying photographs of the grave. On the evidence of the technique used to construct the underground wall, and of the bricks' size, colour, and texture, he concludes that the burial cannot have occurred much earlier than 1609, nor much later. The bricks, he believes, were probably new when used, and belong to the tail-end of the 'Tudor' tradition. Mr Julian Litten of the Victoria and Albert Museum adds that these are properly called 'paviours' rather than bricks, but he confirms that they were laid either in the very late sixteenth century or the very early seventeenth.[60]

It is highly probable, therefore, that the dramatic events of 1609 were played out over this grave, and that Thomas Lawrence is its current occupant. Of the four graves, this one is certainly the most damaged, a fact that is consistent with a history of violent removal and replacement. The

[59] Nathanial Lloyd, *A History of English Brickwork* (London, 1925; repr. 1983); Jane A. Wight, *Brick Building in England* (London, 1972); Nicholas J. Moore, 'Brick', in John Blair and Nigel Ramsay (eds.), *English Medieval Industries* (London, 1991), pp. 211–37.
[60] I am extremely grateful to Mr Taylor, Dr Rodwell, and Mr Litten for their generous comments.

horizontal stone slabs that lie upon the bricks are cracked, and they have slipped out of position. The mock-coffin at the top of the structure has crumbled badly at one end, and two of its corners have been broken off. This grave conveys a powerful impression of disturbance. The other three in the set, though severely eroded, are all in better condition.

If the friends of Thomas Lawrence did indeed reuse an ancient grave for his burial, it is obvious that they cannot have done so surreptitiously. They would first have had to remove the two slabs of the mock-coffin, followed by the huge stone plinth that lay across the original burial. It would then have been necessary to dismantle the real coffin, probably made of additional stone slabs, and perhaps to remove the skeleton of the original occupant. If the grave was that of a priest, as seems likely, it is possible that a sepulchral chalice would also have been discovered. The hole in the ground would then have been enlarged, and lined on the sides and bottom with 600 bricks, extending to a depth of eleven courses. During the Church of England burial service, Thomas Lawrence's body would have been laid in the grave, and the medieval plinth and limestone slabs replaced over the top. Finally, loose earth would have been used to fill any remaining gaps and to restore the original ground level. All this would have taken several strong men several long days. It was not the sort of project that a handful of elderly Familists could have completed overnight. Their activity must, then, have been a matter of public knowledge, a subject for gossip in the village alehouses.

What did the Familists mean by their purposeful and symbolic action? Most obviously, they were paying tribute to Thomas Lawrence as a man of exceptional worth, not only in the eyes of his friends but in the eyes of God. The appropriation of such a well-known local grave would also have been a reaffirmation of the dead man's social prominence, and of his wealth. It might also have been a confident assertion that Lawrence's known religious unorthodoxy was not something that had left him anxious and unsure of his status within the earthly community. The act of reusing this ancient grave connected Lawrence with the past, asserting his significance as a local historical figure. It also made the point that, though the man was dead, his influence and social presence were to continue.

It is impossible to know whether the Familists would have known or assumed that the grave was originally that of a priest. Its location so close to the altar and its clear relationship with the three other graves in the set may have made this the obvious conclusion. If so, Lawrence's friends and relatives may also have been praising him as a religious leader of some renown.

This burial would also have been a statement, surely, about the Family of Love's relationship with the established church. For decades, the Familists had conformed to that church's services and, in a sense, they had deliberately lost themselves within it. Nevertheless, they believed that only H.N.'s invisible church could mark out the true pathway towards salvation. Without it, there was little hope. Anthony Randall, a Devon vicar suspected of Familism under Elizabeth, had asserted clearly that total obedience to the requirements of the established church was an essential element in his doctrine. Yet he had also explained that he belonged neither to the Church of England, nor to the Romanist Church, 'but hoped yet there was a third Church, which should stand where both these shal fall'.[61]

Thomas Lawrence, whose first wife may have been related to the suspected Devon vicar, perhaps held some similar belief.[62] Arguably, the burial of a Familist just outside the chancel of an Anglican church, but within the grave of a Romanist priest, represented the same statement: 'there was a third Church, which should stand where both these shal fall'. The southernmost of the four ancient graves in Balsham churchyard may thus be comprehensible as a sort of coded prophecy, set in limestone. The imaginative and conjectural nature of this interpretation need hardly be emphasized.

It is worth pausing for a moment to wonder just how provocative the Familists' action would actually have been. The bare bones of the long dead were a common sight in early modern English churchyards. Old graves were frequently disturbed as new ones were dug, partly because churchyards were overcrowded, but also because burial places were not generally marked in any permanent way. Bones were frequently removed from the ground, and reinterred in ossuaries or charnel pits.[63] Tombstones were sometimes reused, and they turn up as paving stones and wall slabs. If the Familists did remove an ancient skeleton from the medieval grave, their action may not therefore have been quite as challenging as we might at first be led to believe. The medieval priest, unlike Yorrick, was not remembered personally. There is clearly a distinction to be drawn between the idea of disturbing very fresh graves, which would be a deeply threatening act, and that of disturbing graves that were hundreds of years old. The Balsham Familists were certainly stretching a point, but they may not have been breaking any profoundly important taboo.

Teversham and his accomplices must have felt deeply aggrieved to find themselves charged before the bishop's official for removing the stone.

---

[61] John Strype, *The Life and Acts of John Whitgift*, 3 vols. (new edn, Oxford, 1822), III, pp. 158–9.

[62] Lawrence had married one Margaret Randall in Balsham in 1564/5. 'Randal' was not a common local name, and it may be relevant that Anthony Randall, the Familist vicar, had been a student at Christ's College, Cambridge, at the same date. J. and J.A. Venn, *Alumni Cantabrigienses*, 4 vols. (Cambridge, 1922–7).

[63] Warwick Rodwell, *English Heritage Book of Church Archaeology* (London, 1989), p. 169.

Nevertheless, it was several months before they decided upon official retaliation, a fact which may imply that, despite everything, local opinion remained broadly sympathetic to the Familists. The same impression may be deduced from the harsh manner in which Judge Gager of the consistory court reprimanded Teversham, Swinborne, and Norden. Gager's activities in the church courts at this time were characterized by an attempt to take local attitudes and sensibilities into consideration as he formed his judgements. In a case from Sutton, for example, he was anxious to establish that one group of parishioners had not 'followed theire owne discretions' in drawing up a church-seating plan, but had consulted other villagers, particularly members of the 'better sort'.[64]

Gager was probably as sensitive as he could be to the wider atmosphere in Balsham in 1609. The funeral of Thomas Lawrence had, after all, been marked by the distribution of 40s to the parish's poor, the largest documented dole seen in Balsham for twelve years.[65] In a village still suffering the after-effects of the agrarian crisis of the 1590s, such gestures were not to be lightly dismissed.

The removal of the stone from Lawrence's grave by Teversham and the others was, in contrast, an act of savage aggression in a society which took the matter of Christian burial so seriously. If they disturbed not only the false coffin but the underlying plinth – both are badly damaged – their action would actually have exposed Lawrence's corpse to the air, and to the gaze of all who passed.

Teversham's retaliation was delayed, but it finally came in November 1609 when Edmund Rule, John Taylor, and William Taylor were all presented to the consistory court, 'named uppon a common fame to be of the familye of Love'. All three had witnessed Thomas Lawrence's will making, and all three are likely to have had some involvement in the arrangements for his burial. Was Teversham's accusation aimed specifically at those Familists whom he felt had snubbed him? There were certainly other Familists in the parish whom he did not present. The decision to name Edmund Rule and the two Taylors was a weighty one, for never before had the Balsham Familists been accused before the church courts.

None of the three men appeared in person to answer the charges, but they did send a proxy in the form of John Hasell of Bottisham. Hasell was almost certainly a Familist himself, and was married to the daughter of Thomas Lawrence, deceased, whose lands he had inherited. As Lawrence's executor, Hasell had been entrusted with the old man's wish for a 'decent burial', which had proved something of an understatement in

[64] EDR, B/2/35, fols. 207, 210.
[65] PRO, PCC 40 Dorset.

the circumstances. Hasell is therefore certain to have played an active part in the unfolding drama surrounding the gravestone. He was also related by marriage to Edmund Rule. Hasell presented excuses on behalf of the three accused men, explaining

> that the sayd Edmund Rule & John Tayler thelder ar ould men, of the age of lxx yeres apeece, and that Edmund Rule is stone blynde, and that [John] Tayloure thelder is deaffe and cannot here And that thother Wm Tayloure is sonne of the sayd John Taylor thelder. And they were all three of them in question for thease matters before the Lord Chief Justice of England [Judge Popham] in his latter tyme, in the open Assises at Cambridge Castle & were there delivered or discharged.

The response of the consistory court judge, William Gager, is again intriguing. We might have expected him, as a representative of ecclesiastical authority, to respond swiftly and decisively to this suggestion that heretics lived long and untroubled lives under his jurisdiction. Instead, he made appropriate official sounds about postponing judgement while the new bishop was consulted; and then, it seems, he quietly laid all three cases to rest. No further proceedings were taken. Thirty-five years earlier, Dr Andrew Perne, then vicar of Balsham, had investigated the same Familists with similar restraint.[66]

William Gager, having heard the charges concerning Thomas Lawrence's gravestone, may have felt that Teversham's motivation for making the presentments was not altogether admirable, particularly since two of the three men had already enjoyed their three score years and ten, and were unlikely to enjoy many more. He may also have known that, at higher levels in English society, the apparent concern over the Family which had marked the opening of James' reign had now receded again. It was presumably this earlier anxiety that had stimulated the trial before Lord Chief Justice Popham, for which, lamentably, there are no surviving records.

The final presentment in the Balsham set accused William Rule, Teversham's fellow-churchwarden, of 'refuseinge to sett his hand to the presentment aforesayd'. Asked to turn against his blind father and his dead godfather, he chose, not surprisingly, to place himself at the judge's mercy. The judge responded, once again, by delaying a decision, and the case was never pursued.

The impression, faintly discernible between the lines, that the action of Teversham and his associates in disturbing Lawrence's grave was substan-

---

[66] Inner Temple Library, Petyt MS No. 538/vol. 47, fol. 492. Printed by Strype, *The Life and Acts of M. Parker*, pp. 471–3. Perne had required the Balsham Familists to sign statements of religious orthodoxy, but he had refrained from forcing them to deny their membership of H.N.'s fellowship.

tially unrepresentative of opinion in Balsham is strengthened by a glance at the aftermath to this ugly dispute. The bitterness of 1608–9 seems to have had little long-term impact upon social relations. When one of the accused Familists, John Taylor, made his will in 1616, close to eighty years of age, his only witnesses were William Rule and Thomas Teversham, the warring churchwardens of 1609.[67] William Taylor, another of the Familist suspects, was a churchwarden in 1613, probably chosen by a select group of townsmen which no longer included Thomas Lawrence, Edmund Rule, and Henry Marsh.[68] The fact that these men had all died in Balsham, where they had been born during the 1530s and 1540s, is further evidence of the essential stability of their role within the village. Thomas Teversham, incidentally, does not appear to have held parochial office again.

Even in the year of the dispute, there had been indications that Teversham's action was misleading in its hostility. Two of Balsham's church bells were recast into four, not quite as ordered by the consistory court, and one of the new bells was inscribed with the names of three men, including that of William Taylor.[69] He indulged in the early modern villagers' 'mania for immortalising themselves' just as he participated in other spheres of parish life, and the bell bearing his name rings to this day.[70]

It was also around this time that Thomas Sutton, founder of Charterhouse school and lord of Balsham manor, made his will. It contained a breathtaking series of charitable bequests, and left gifts to an impressive array of Jacobean notables and their offspring, including two who had personally presided over prosecutions of Balsham's Familists. It would seem that Sutton stood firmly on the side of ecclesiastical and civil authority in its duty to exterminate heresy. Yet, even here, the paradox of the Family left its mark, for almost with the next breath Sutton chose to remember one of his Balsham acquaintances, a less illustrious individual but evidently a trusted tenant: 'Item I give to ... Thomas Lawrence thelder of the same town five poundes of like lawfull money.' Lawrence was already dead and buried, unbeknownst to Sutton, but there is no doubting the intended legatee's identity.[71]

The dispute in 1609, though compelling and clearly significant, was something of an aberration, and to dwell on it is to distort the fuller picture

---

[67] Ely CC C26.86.

[68] EDR, B/2/31, fol. 119v.

[69] My information here is taken from a leaflet on Balsham church, by the Rt Rev. W.H. Frere. I am also grateful to the current vicar, the Rev. William Girard, for taking me up into the belfry to see the bell.

[70] W.E. Tate, *The Parish Chest. A Study of the Records of Parochial Administration in England* (Cambridge, 1943; 3rd edn, 1983), p. 100.

[71] PRO, PCC, 101 Wood (1611). Lawrence had regularly been called 'Thomas Lawrence thelder' by his neighbours, until his nephew and namesake departed Balsham.

presented in this essay. If the history of early modern English society is written on the basis of court records and partisan literature – as to some extent it has to be – then, unless considerable guile is employed, a cultural atmosphere marked by stark, conflictual polarities is likely to be discovered. The Family of Love, if such sources had dominated the search, would have emerged as a radical 'sect' whose members spent their lives in stark isolation; ostracized, self-protecting, deceitful, and subversive.

In some sense, they clearly did display several of these characteristics. But the search cannot be allowed to cease there. If the Family of Love is studied both when it was in trouble and when it was out of it, a picture of unimagined depth and subtlety appears before our eyes. The Family's place within English society had many facets, and was characterized by a set of never-ending counterpoints, like the intricate vocal lines of a Tallis motet. Of these, the most fundamental involved a continuous interplay between the urge to despise, shun, and victimize, and the urge to love, tolerate, and embrace. These contradictory impulses affected both the Family's attitude to society and society's attitude to it.

It was this second, warmer impulse that seems to have guided most of the people most of the time, though its more aggressive counterpart found its way into the foreground on several occasions. As in the Tallis motet, it is the return to harmony, the resolution following each discordant suspension, that gives the work its meaning and deserves the final word in any account. An analysis of Tallis' *Spem in Alium* based on the discords alone would be of dubious value.

The wider implications of this extraordinary case are obviously significant. The microscopic approach should draw the attention of historians to the limitations of more mainstream methodologies. Around a compelling Jacobean incident of stark polarity, suggestive of religious bigotry, there hangs a less tangible atmosphere of profound subtlety and complexity, frequently suggestive of considerable resources of tolerance. How commonly do court cases and other sources conceal similar alternative worlds? The written record thrown up by Thomas Lawrence's burial tells us hardly anything of the circumstances, and takes on an almost entirely new meaning when set into context. If the same were to turn out to be true of every reported comment and quotation in *Religion and the Decline of Magic*, imagine the consequences for our understanding of early modern society. Microhistory should not stand alone, but it can fulfil an important role in the process of testing and, if necessary, reshaping initial assumptions, preconceptions, and expectations.

This methodology can, and must, also lead back towards wider generalization – though this, of course, is the difficult part. In the case of the Balsham gravestone, the clearest wider implication concerns, paradoxically, the extent of positive religious toleration in early modern rural society. A substantial group of Familist men (and women) were both accepted and respected within their community, and the flashpoints of tense conflict take on the aspect of occasional lapses from a desirable norm, rather than the norm itself. This level of integration was achieved despite the Family of Love's official reputation as 'the most detestable Sectaries or Hereticks, that ever reigned on earth; yea, and as people not worthy to live in a Common-wealth'.[72] If we are to write realistic history, we need to incorporate both aspects of the 'sect–society' relationship within the way we think.

The Balsham Familists were not able to live as they did simply because they were powerful, nor because people were either ignorant or apathetic concerning their unusual religion. The situation was more positive. We should also think in terms of a widespread though unarticulated belief that they had a justifiable claim to hold deviant religious views, as long as they did not hold them to the detriment of consensual moral and social expectations. This was a negotiated settlement, and one which suggests an impressive flexibility in the thought-world of ordinary villagers (and of ecclesiastical court judges). It also suggests something approaching a concept of privacy, at least where matters of inward belief were concerned. In a sense, it can be argued that a majority of Balsham's inhabitants did not consider the beliefs of Thomas Lawrence and his co-religionists to be any of their business.

The situation in Jacobean Balsham also encourages a more positive perspective on popular religion. If the spiritual ideas and expectations of ordinary rural people continue to be measured according to the standards set by protestant preachers, popular religion will always be found wanting. 'Good fellowship' will continue to be treated negatively, as the polar opposite of 'godliness'. Alehouses will remain centres of irreligion and subversion; churches will remain centres of protestant sobriety and commitment, attended without enthusiasm by most of the people.

In fact, there was a great deal that was positive about majority religion, and that filled the fertile ground between these extremes. People may not generally have been theologically knowledgeable, but they certainly held the traditional goals of social Christianity in high esteem. Their commitment to these goals, on its own terms, was coherent, robust, and impressive.

Good fellowship was an ideal with powerful, though rarely articulated, spiritual overtones, and it is here that we can locate the roots of the tolerance extended to the Balsham Familists. Perhaps the real outsiders in early seventeenth-century English villages were not people like Thomas

---

[72] An Apology for the Service of Love, and the People that Own it, Commonly Called the Family of Love (written c. 1580; printed in London, 1656), p. 54.

Lawrence, who belonged to dissenting religious minorities, but people like Thomas Teversham, who forgot themselves, admittedly under provocation, and, for a time, fell into violent intolerance.

CHAPTER 6

Piety in the pedlar's pack: continuity and change, 1578–1630

TESSA WATT

The common pedlar or petty chapman, trudging along the highways and back-roads of early modern England, is not an obvious bedfellow for the godly dissenters of the present volume.[1] Pedlars and ballad sellers had a reputation as 'masterless' men and women at the nether regions of society; often prosecuted as vagrants, and forced by economic hardship into petty crime.[2] Writers like Shakespeare and Robert Greene described pedlars who doubled as pick-pockets, while the record books show that real chapmen were indeed often accused of theft at fairs and markets.[3] Ballad sellers were not approved of by protestant reformers like Nicholas Bownde, who considered the possibility of printing the psalms as broadsides, but rejected it on these grounds: 'Indeed, many of the common singing men are so ungodly, that it were better for them to leave their mouths stopped, then once to open them to pollute such holy and sacred songs.'[4]

However, despite this disapproval, and whether willingly or unwittingly, the pedlar of print could be a messenger bearing God's word into towns and villages across the country. Richard Baxter, who grew up in the village of Eaton Constantine in Shropshire, recorded how, around 1630, 'a poor pedlar came to the door that had ballads and some good books: and my father bought of him Dr Sibb's *Bruised Reed*'.[5] This book of sermons by the puritan divine helped to strengthen the adolescent Baxter in his convictions, and gave him 'a livelier apprehension of the mystery of redemption'.

[1] The place of publication for printed works referred to in these footnotes is London, unless otherwise stated.
[2] However, the close, and hitherto unemphasized relationship between cheap print and vagrants, who could even be 'godly' dissenters, has been stressed above, p. 65. Ballad sellers and chapmen appear in the 'Register of Passports for Vagrants 1598–1669', in Paul Slack (ed.), *Poverty in Early Stuart Salisbury*, Wiltshire Record Society, 31 (Devizes, 1975).
[3] William Shakespeare, *The Winter's Tale* (written 1610–11), IV, iii–iv. Robert Greene, *The Second Part of Conny-Catching* (1591). BL Harleian MS 6715, fol. 98v.
[4] Nicholas Bownde, *The Doctrine of the Sabbath* (1595), p. 241.
[5] R. Baxter, *Reliquiae Baxterianae* (1696), pp. 3–4.

It is rare to find concrete references in this period to pedlars of print coming directly to the door, and to a small village such as Eaton Constantine. Ballad sellers appear most frequently in the court records of large cities such as Norwich, and they are often to be found at the major fairs.[6] However, we do know that in 1578 a pedlar in Cambridgeshire ventured several miles off the main road to the village of Balsham, where he sold 'lytle bookes' in the churchyard. One of these books was bought by 'a young barber-surgeon who does not appear to have been very prosperous, since he was also a patcher of old clothes, and swore on oath that he would be "worthe nothinge" if his debts were paid off'. His wares cannot have been very expensive; nor did the arrival of this itinerant bookseller, in itself, seem to cause any special remark.[7]

Did this pedlar's visit have anything to do with the presence of the Family of Love in Balsham, and did the 'little books' include the teachings of the Familist leader Hendrick Niclaes? In 1574, just a few years earlier, six Balsham yeomen confessed to holding private conventicles in their houses, and in 1580 four of them were imprisoned as members of the Familist sect.[8] A local leader of the sect in Wisbech owned over half a dozen books of Hendrick Niclaes' teachings, and other followers in the area must have had access to Familist writings.[9] Works which were printed at a Familist press in Cologne in this period included the cheapest and most portable of wares: a broadside of 1575 contains a blessing and grace to be said at table, and another offers an 'abc' for the Family's children.[10]

Our pedlar could have collected these broadsides from one of several booksellers in Cambridge, who were used to acquiring books published on the Continent for their scholarly clientele. The Cambridge stationer and bookbinder John Denys was apparently doing a brisk trade with the Continent, and in particular with the city of Cologne where the Familist works were printed. He died of 'plague' in 1578, the very same year our pedlar visited Balsham. His inventory of 1578 lists a copy of Avenarius' *Precationes* which was printed in Cologne in that same year of 1578.[11] Of

---

[6] David Galloway (ed.), *Records of Early English Drama. Norwich 1540–1642* (Toronto, 1984), pp. 115, 126, 141, 200–1, 237. Walter Plummer of Southwark was stopped at Trowbridge Fair in 1620, 'carrying with him a store of ballads to sing in his travels' (A.L. Beier, *Masterless Men: The Vagrancy Problem in England 1560–1640* (1985), p. 98).

[7] Margaret Spufford, *Contrasting Communities: English Villagers in the Sixteenth and Seventeenth Centuries* (Cambridge, 1974), p. 208.

[8] See Christopher Marsh, above, p. 214.

[9] Spufford, *Contrasting Communities*, p. 208.

[10] STC 18548.5, 'All the letters of the A.B.C. by every sondrye letter whereof, there is a good document set-fourth and taught, in ryme' ([N. Bohmberg, Cologne], 1575). STC 1858, 'A benedictie or blessinge to be saide over the table before meate and a grace or thankesgeevinge to be saide after meate' ([N. Bohmberg, Cologne], 1575).

[11] E. Leedham-Green (ed.), *Books in Cambridge Inventories*, 2 vols. (Cambridge, 1986), I, pp. xviii–xix, 327.

course, the distribution of heretical works was not to be undertaken lightly, and it seems unlikely that an ordinary pedlar would wander the county carrying Familist broadsides to show to all and sundry. If our pedlar did distribute Niclaes' writings it would mean he had special connections with the Familist yeomen and was a regular and trusted supplier. If he did not, the Balsham sect may have got their books directly from a Cambridge bookseller, or perhaps from the London–Cambridge carrier. Certainly the Quakers of the seventeenth century used carriers to send their books, and in 1654 the Atherston–London carrier took the risk of carrying 100 copies of a Quaker pamphlet for distribution.[12] Or the Familists may have been served by a specialist pedlar of their own faith. The London stationer Michael Sparke remembered travelling around the country selling Roman Catholic books, during his apprenticeship between 1603 and 1610, and it may be that the Familists, too, had their own supplier who has escaped the record books.[13]

In the absence of further evidence it seems fair to assume that our Balsham bookseller was an ordinary petty chapman, possibly with a small but risky sideline feeding the Balsham Familists with seditious print. For our purposes, the crucial question is this: how did the wares of this chapman compare with those of Richard Baxter's pedlar in Shropshire some fifty years later? Were these men specialists in print, or did they sell books and ballads among other wares like cambrics and small courtship gifts, as did Shakespeare's Autolycus?[14] For now, we must leave the ribbons and gloves at the bottom of the pack, along with the merry chapbooks and bawdy ballads. In this essay, which must inevitably be speculative, I will describe a cross-section of the religious print which may have been carried by the petty chapman working in Cambridgeshire in the 1570s, and by his fellow-pedlar in Shropshire in the 1630s. Although publishers of the 1570s did produce a number of small and cheap books suitable for pedlars, as we shall see, the 1620s heralded an expansion at the bottom end of the publishing trade, and the rise of a whole new genre of chapbooks.

The pedlar working in Cambridgeshire would have had no shortage of potential suppliers of print, since the presence of the university in Cambridge attracted a number of booksellers. The village of Balsham lay some ten miles south-east of Cambridge, and could have been part of a circuit involving several days walking. The inventory for John Denys

---

[12] See Michael Frearson, below, pp. 283, 285.
[13] [M. Sparke], *A Second Beacon Fired by Scintilla* (1652), pp. 5–6.
[14] Shakespeare, *The Winter's Tale*, IV, iii–iv. In *The Great Reclothing of Rural England: Petty Chapmen and their Wares in the Seventeenth Century* (1984), pp. 88–9, Margaret Spufford examines the items in Autolycus' pack, which included linen, cambrics, and lawns, haberdashery and small courtship gifts, as well as ballads.

shows that many of his books were Latin textbooks and other works for the members of the University, but that his shop also contained psalm books and prayer books suitable for ordinary householders, an assortment of pamphlets valued at as little as twopence each, and a dozen almanacs at a penny per copy.[15]

Assuming that the 'poor pedlar' of Shropshire was travelling by foot, without a horse, it seems likely that he worked a limited local circuit, centring on the town of Shrewsbury. The village of Eaton Constantine was only five miles from Shrewsbury, and well within half a day's walk. The pedlar could have collected his wares from a Shrewsbury bookshop on a sale-or-return basis, or may even have been in the bookseller's employ. By the late sixteenth century we know that the publisher Roger Ward stocked some 2,500 books in his Shrewsbury bookshop; mostly catechisms, prayer books, Latin texts, sermons, psalters, and so on. At the cheap end of the market these included at least 225 copies of sermons, 69 unspecified 'bookes at pence', '22 Almanakes', '20 pictures not colored', and '1 Reame 6 quire ballates' (or about 650 broadsides), all of which might have been sent round to nearby villages with a pedlar.[16] Provincial booksellers like John Denys and Roger Ward may have had their own wares delivered to them by the Cambridge and Shrewsbury carriers, who could be found on Thursdays at specific inns in London, as listed in John Taylor's *Carriers Cosmographie*.[17] Both Cambridge and Shrewsbury were at the end of regular trade routes from the capital. For a carrier travelling by packhorse or waggon, Cambridge was five days' travel on the road north through Hertfordshire, while the journey to Shrewsbury would take two weeks on a route which led through Coventry and Birmingham.[18] The carriers were regularly entrusted with books and letters, and we know of at least one West Country carrier who transported cloth to London and returned to Stroud Water with psalters in the 1550s.[19] Our pedlars may have got their wares directly from the carriers, when London publishers 'sent' ballads and books to the country, specifically for sale by chapmen.

In the testimony of two London stationers brought before the High Commission in 1630, there is evidence of an established distribution system operating between London stationers and country chapmen. Accused of distributing a dangerous book, James Boler and Michael

---

[15] Leedham-Green (ed.), *Books in Cambridge Inventories*, I, pp. 326–40.

[16] Alexander Rodger (ed.), 'Roger Ward's Shrewsbury Stock: An Inventory of 1585', *The Library*, 5th Ser., 13 (1958), pp. 252, 257, 259, 260, 262, 267.

[17] John Taylor, *The Carriers Cosmographie; Or a Briefe Relation of the Innes in and Neere London* (1637). In addition to the Cambridge 'carriers' there were also 'waggons or coaches', found on Thursdays and Fridays at the Black Bull in Bishopsgate Street.

[18] See above, Map 1, and, for speed of travel, see below, pp. 274, 276, 285–6.

[19] See Thomas Seyver of Eastington, described by Michael Frearson, below, p. 285.

Sparke both claimed they were absent when copies of the book arrived at their London shops, and that their servants sent copies to country chapmen.[20] At Boler's house some forty copies were left with a female servant 'the one halfe whereof this examte servauntes before his coming home sent away to some Chapmen in the Country'. Michael Sparke's servants were said to have done the same with about forty copies, which 'they did in his absence send to divers of his chapmen in Oxford & Salisbury and other partes'. The fact that this was thought to be a reasonable line of defence indicates that 'sending away' books directly to country chapmen was a regular and common practice.

Finally, there were apparently large numbers of the London-based chapmen, including some 277 ballad sellers by 1641. Many were in the direct employ of the publishers, according to Henry Chettle's *Kind-Harts Dreame* [1593]:

> no stationer, who after a little bringing them uppe to singing brokerie, takes into his shop some fresh men, and trusts his olde searvantes of a two months standing with a dossen groates worth of ballads. In which, if they proove thrifty, hee makes them prety chapmen, able to spred more pamphlets by the state forbidden then all the booksellers in London.[21]

Even chapmen setting out from London could cover substantial distances. We have evidence of long-distance travel from cases in the Court of Requests from the 1590s, showing that chapmen from the midlands and south-west, as well as the home counties, were following regular trade routes to and from London. In 1595, a Leicester chapman had been bringing the wares of a London haberdasher to a local cordwainer for twenty years. A Nottingham chapman in the haberdashery trade owed £15 to his London supplier in 1608; while a chapman of Taunton in Somerset had, by 1623, run up a bill in silks worth some £120.[22] Long-distance travel was not only a way of life for these established chapmen with their regular suppliers and routes, but for the lesser classes of pedlars who were likely to fall foul of the vagrancy laws. A surviving 'register of passports' for vagrants apprehended in Salisbury includes 'Edward Kerbye, a balladseller, wandering' who had travelled from his 'home' in Holborne, London, in 1630. Four of the vagrants caught between 1598

[20] W.W. Greg, *Companion to Arber. Being a Calendar of Documents in Edward Arber's Transcript of the Registers of the Company of Stationers of London 1554–1640* (Oxford, 1967), pp. 253–5. I am grateful to Michael Frearson for this reference. The book is identified by Greg as *Christ's Confession and Complaint* (ibid., pp. 70, 253).

[21] Henry Chettle, *Kind-Harts Dreame. Conteining Five Apparitions, with their Invectives against Abuses Raigning* [1593], sig. C2v.

[22] PRO Req 2/259/64, Req 2/293/27, Req 2/394/22. For further examples see Tessa Watt, *Cheap Print and Popular Piety, 1550–1640* (Cambridge, 1991), pp. 27–8.

and 1640 who were described in the register as 'chapmen' or 'petty chap-men' were also from the capital. Another London man, Walter Plummer of Southwark was stopped at Trowbridge Fair in 1620, 'carrying with him a store of ballads to sing in his travels'.[23]

Any certain knowledge about the suppliers of our chapmen in Cambridgeshire and Shropshire will probably remain elusive to the historian. However, with a knowledge of publishing in this period we can discuss some of the possible titles carried by these two pedlars, who were separated by a particularly interesting half-century in the development and expansion of the trade in cheap religious print.

Ballads

We are told by Baxter that the Shropshire pedlar carried broadside ballads, and it is likely that the Cambridgeshire pedlar of 1578 also carried this staple of cheap-print pedlars throughout the period.[24] Writing in 1595, Nicholas Bownde places the popularity of ballads in opposition to protestant godliness: it is a disappointment to him that 'in the shops of artificers, and cottages of poore husbandmen ... you shall sooner see one of these newe Ballades ... than any of the Psalmes, and may perceive them to be cunninger in singing the one, than the other'.[25] However, an earlier generation of protestant reformers, writing in the 1560s, 70s, and 80s, was happy to appropriate the ballad form and the ballad tunes for its own purposes, making no sharp break with pre-Reformation attitudes to traditional recreations. A study of ballad titles in the Stationers' Registers reveals an outpouring of 'moralizing' ballads, making up a full 35 per cent of ballads registered in the period 1560–88.[26] If he carried a representative cross-section, one in three of the ballads sold by our Cambridgeshire pedlar of 1578 would have dealt with a religious or moral theme.

The godly ballads which could have been hawked in the churchyard at Balsham in 1578 can be divided into four groups, reflecting the aims of Elizabethan protestant reformers. The first and largest group was religio-political, attempting to galvanize support for the protestant nation, against the papists at home and abroad. Our Balsham pedlar may have carried ballads like 'The cruel assault of Gods fort' (1560–1), a moralization of an earlier song 'Thassault of Cupide upon the fort where the

---

[23] Slack (ed.), *Poverty in Early Stuart Salisbury*, p. 58 and nos. 82, 152, 288, 476. Beier, *Masterless Men*, p. 98.

[24] On the ubiquity of ballads see Watt, *Cheap Print*, pp. 11–13.

[25] Bownde, *The Doctrine of the Sabbath*, p. 242.

[26] See Watt, *Cheap Print*, pp. 42–9.

louers hart lay wounded and how he was taken'.[27] John Awdeley's godly version began with Edward VI building a fort to shield God's truth, continued with a catalogue of the papists who besieged the fort in the Marian period, led by 'generall Gardner' and 'captain Boner'; and of the protestants killed in defending the fort, the martyrs of 1555–6. The ballad ended, of course, with the Lord sending a new 'godly captaine', Elizabeth. Other ballads in the pack were the stories of individual martyrs, like the famous 'John Carelesse' taken from Coverdale, or the story of 'Anne Askew' adapted from Foxe.[28]

The second group of ballads in the pack were directed at the social reform which was meant to go hand in hand with religious reform. Our Elizabethan pedlar would have carried some of the diatribes which poured from the presses in the 1560s and 1570s, expressing the zeal of the new reformers for the transformation of society and its morals. The least imaginative were straightforward catalogues of social ills, from drunkenness to rent-racking, for which the nation could expect to receive collective punishment in the form of the plague and other disasters.[29] A group of apocalyptic ballads warned that the general Judgement Day was imminent, while another version of the alarum theme looked backward to the biblical examples of cities destroyed for their sin, from Sodom and Gomorrah to Jerusalem.[30]

The form of moral lesson which proved to be most palatable to ballad buyers was the aphoristic broadside, presenting a set of handy maxims for behaviour in everyday life, designed primarily to be implanted in the minds of the young. One organizing principle for the aphoristic ballad was the simple 'abc', each stanza beginning with a letter of the alphabet in order; a genre which grew, of course, out of the method by which most readers would have learnt their letters.[31] One of these broadsides would have been of particular interest to some of the householders of Balsham, the members of the Family of Love studied by Christopher

[27] H.L. Collmann (ed.), *Ballads and Broadsides Chiefly of the Elizabethan Period . . . Now in the Library at Britwell Court* (1912), no. 3. *Tottel's Miscellany* (1557), ed. Edward Arber (1870), p. 172.

[28] Miles Coverdale, *Certain Most Godly, Fruitful, and Comfortable Letters* (1564), pp. 634–8. 'John Carelesse' was registered as a broadside on 1 August 1586, amongst a re-registration of old stock. STC 853.5: 'A ballad of Anne Askew, intituled: I am a woman poor and blind' (1624?). Registered on 14 December 1624, but, once again, in a batch of ballads of much earlier provenance.

[29] See Watt, *Cheap Print*, pp. 96–7.

[30] For example, 'Of the horrible and wofull destruction of Sodome and Gomorra' [1570] in Joseph Lilly (ed.), *A Collection of 79 Black-Letter Ballads and Broadsides Printed in the Reign of Queen Elizabeth* (1867), p. 125; 'Of the horyble and woful destruction of Jerusalem' [1569?], in Collmann (ed.), *Ballads and Broadsides*, no. 5. For more information on apocalyptic ballads see Watt, *Cheap Print*, p. 97.

[31] See Helen Weinstein, above, pp. 72 n. 250, 73.

Marsh. This broadside bore the initials of the Familist leader H[endrick] N[iclaes] and was printed in Cologne in 1575.[32] There is no tune, so the abc appears to have been intended for the wall rather than for singing:

A. Attend yee Youngones, and learne Understandinge.
B. Beare-favor to the Love, that she in you may have plantinge.
C. Com to the meekmynded Beeinge of Bounteousnesse.

There is a woodcut of school children in a classroom, and an introduction addressed to the Family's children warns them not to tackle great books 'er-ever yee have well exercised you in the A.B.C., and can perfectly spell all Woordes'. The broadside first appeared just three years before our pedlar was reported to be selling his wares in the Balsham churchyard.

Although most of the moralizing ballads emphasized collective repentance and outward behaviour, our pedlar could also have sold a third group of ballads presenting the more personal side of the protestant message: the saving power of faith. The tone is positive, promising that the offer of grace is infinite and universal, if only the sinner will take the first step.[33] There is no promulgation of predestination in these ballads. One technique often used for this theme was the moral parody of the secular song, most often a love song, of which Christ becomes the object:

> Thou art my saviour sweete,
> foode and delight to mee . . .
> To my tast, honnie sweete,
> to my eare, melodie . . .[34]

This song is based on 'Dainty come thou to me', rendered as 'Jesu come thou to me'. The central protestant doctrine of justification by faith alone is made an encouraging proposition in these ballads.

Finally, the last group of ballads in our pedlar's pack tried to capture the people's imagination with scripture stories, in order to help effect the transition to a book-based religion. Early Elizabethan reformers like William Samuel had high hopes of replacing the old saints' lives and miracles with characters and events from the Bible:

> My mynd is that I wold have my contrey people able in a smale some to syng the hole contents of the byble, & where as in tymes past the musicians or mynstrells, were wont to syng fained myracles, saints

---

[32] STC 18548.5, 'All the letters of the A.B.C. . . .' ([Cologne], 1575). Reprinted in John Holloway (ed.), *The Euing Collection of English Broadside Ballads* (Glasgow, 1971), no. 1.

[33] In 'A christian conference betweene Christ and a sinner' Christ promises he will receive the sinner 'If once I do see thee be sory in heart' (William Chappell and J. Woodfall Ebsworth (eds.), *The Roxburghe Ballads*, 8 vols. (1871–97), III, p. 164).

[34] 'The sinner, dispisinge the world and all earthly vanities . . .' [ent. 1568–9?], in Hyder E. Rollins, *Old English Ballads 1553–1625* (Cambridge, 1920), p. 198.

lives, & Robin hode, in stede thereof to sing, undoutyd truthes, canonycall scryptures, and Gods doynges.[35]

The pedlar of the 1570s could have carried a whole stock of good stories from the Old Testament, some of which are obvious choices for their dramatic quality: Jonah and the whale, Abraham offering Isaac, Daniel in the lion's den, David and Goliath. Lesser-known episodes could be picked because of their relevance to contemporary concerns. The history of 'Manasses kynge of Juda', who brought punishment upon Jerusalem with his graven images and false altars, was an obvious lesson against popish idolatry.[36]

As well as Old Testament stories, the Elizabethan pedlar could have carried quite a variety of titles from the Gospels, especially songs making use of the parables. Ballads were registered on the fig tree and the grain of mustard seed, the ten servants and ten talents, the rich man and the unjust steward, and lessons from the sermon on the mount.[37] By setting them to popular tunes the reformers tried to give unlearned people direct access to the concepts of Christian faith and to provoke further interest in vernacular bible reading: 'as the man that hearyth a parte of a story in the scryptures, & doth not knowe the hole: thys may move the hole to be red'.[38]

The range of ballads which could have been sold in the churchyard at Balsham in 1578 reflects the serious didactic purposes of the early protestant reformers. By the time our Shropshire pedlar visited Richard Baxter's house in the 1630s, the situation had radically changed, and the ballad seller was no longer widely considered to be a potential tool of the Reformation. The writing of moralizing ballads had fallen out of fashion, as can be seen in the Stationers' Register entries. For the period 1560–88, 35 per cent of ballad titles were religious and moralizing; in 1588–1625 the figure drops to 19 per cent; and in 1625–40, to 9 per cent.[39] The decline may partly be attributed to a growing gap between what the reformers perceived to be 'godly' and 'ungodly' spheres of activity. This gap can be seen in Baxter's description of his village of Eaton Constantine, where the neighbours spent each Sunday dancing under a maypole near Baxter's house: 'So that we could not read the Scripture in our family without the great disturbance of the tabor and pipe and noise in the

---

[35] William Samuel, *The Abridgemente of Goddes Statutes in Myter* (1551), A2–A2v. Cited in John King, *English Reformation Literature: The Tudor Origins of the Protestant Tradition* (Princeton, 1982), p. 212.

[36] Arber, I, p. 205 (1562–3), I, p. 378 (1568–9), II, p. 359 (1579–80), III, p. 486 (1611–12), I, p. 401 (1569–70).

[37] Ibid., I, p. 414 (1569–70), II, p. 376 (1580–1), II, p. 376 (1580–1), I, p. 415 (1569–70), I, p. 416 (1569–70).

[38] Samuel, *The Abridgemente of Goddes Statutes in Myter*, A2–A2v.

[39] See Watt, *Cheap Print*, pp. 42–9.

street. Many times I was inclined to be among them . . . But when I heard them call my father Puritan it did much to cure me and alienate me from them.'[40] Ballads, along with the dance tunes to which they were set, were no longer seen by reformers as potential routes to godliness: they had become part of those popular recreations which caused a keen sense of separation of 'the saints' from 'the rest'. The decline of the moralizing ballad can be attributed partly to the ballad's negative associations with bawdy lyrics, lascivious dancing and unsavoury pedlars, and partly to the growing success of the metrical psalms, which were taking over as the definitive godly songs by the seventeenth century.[41]

By the time of our Shropshire pedlar, then, only one in ten of the ballads registered each year were on religious themes. However, the proportion of godly ballads he carried in his pack was undoubtedly higher than this figure, which reflects only the new ballads being written, but not the republishing of old favourites. By 1624, six of the leading ballad publishers had collected together the copyrights to a stock of ballads, formed themselves into a syndicate called the 'ballad partners', and organized themselves for more efficient storage and distribution of the printed sheets. In 1624 they registered a large batch of 128 ballads, most of them old titles, of which a striking one third were still religious in subject matter.[42] These stock ballads tell us little about the situation at the cutting edge of protestant reform, but perhaps much more about the impact of protestantism on a wide public and about their religious tastes.

Many of the old titles registered by the 'ballad partners' in 1624 were reprinted again and again in turn by their trade descendants. These titles can be traced in the later bulk entries made for copyright purposes in 1656, 1675, and 1712, and still later in a catalogue of 1754.[43] From these sources, I have compiled a list of forty-six godly ballads of long duration on the market, of which forty-one can be shown to have lasted more than a quarter century, twenty-eight were sold over a half-century, and eleven of these survived a full century or more.[44] Of these 'stock' ballads, the majority (60 per cent) can be shown to be of sixteenth-century origin. In other words, our Shropshire pedlar of the 1630s would have carried

---

[40] N.H. Keeble (ed.), *The Autobiography of Richard Baxter* (1974), p. 6.
[41] See Watt, *Cheap Print*, pp. 55–73.
[42] Arber, IV, pp. 131–2.
[43] Ballad partners' entries for 1656 and 1675, in Eyre, II, pp. 36–7, 496–501. Entry to Thomas Norris and Charles Brown, 20 September 1712, reprinted in R.S. Thomson, 'The Development of the Broadside Trade and its Influence upon the Transmission of English Folksongs' (Cambridge, PhD, 1974), App. B. William and Cluer Dicey, *A Catalogue of Maps, Histories, Prints, Old Ballads, Copy-Books, Broadsheets and Other Patters, Drawing-Books, Garlands &c* (1754), reprinted in Thomson, 'Development of the Broadside Trade', App. C.
[44] For a full list see Watt, *Cheap Print*, App. A.

a number of the same titles sold by his colleague half a century earlier: ballads which had poured from the pens of the Elizabethan reformers, primarily before 1586.[45] The chapman who reached Richard Baxter's door would have carried a smaller selection of those ballads than our Elizabethan pedlar, selling only those which had proved their commercial success by the early decades of the seventeenth century.

The ballads in that Shropshire pack of the 1630s can give us some measure of how far protestant goals were achieved in each of the four areas discussed above: politicized anti-catholicism, social reform, personal salvation, and scripture stories. From the 'stock' of long-enduring titles we will examine in detail seven ballads which may be considered archetypical, each demonstrating a particular aspect of seventeenth-century piety. The pedlar's pack reflected a religious culture which was far from monolithic, showing a fragmentary reception of protestant doctrine.

The first group of ballads, expressing sixteenth-century anti-catholicism, did not in general survive into the seventeenth century. There is one notable type of exception: a group of four ballads on protestant martyrs, of which three were female.[46] The human image of the martyr seems to have been worth a thousand arguments in the task of embedding anti-catholic feeling in popular consciousness. These songs could have been bought and sung by the maypole dancers of Eaton Constantine for their gripping and tragic stories, regardless of religious content. As they entered into the ballad repertoire, however, they achieved the writers' aim of replacing catholic saints with protestant ones, amongst those readers and singers unlikely to have direct access to Foxe's great volumes.

The most successful ballad in this category, very likely to have found a place in the Shropshire pedlar's pack, was the story of the Duchess of Suffolk's exile during Mary's reign. It was adapted from Foxe by Thomas Deloney, set to the tune 'Queen Dido', and was still for sale in 1754.[47] In addition to the theme of a woman suffering for religion, there was the attraction of royalty travelling incognito, a popular ballad motif.[48] The

[45] For a list of 119 less successful religious ballads published before 1640, see ibid., App. B.

[46] 'A godly and vertuous songe or ballade, made by the constant member of Christe, John Carelesse', in Coverdale, Certain Most Godly, Fruitful, and Comfortable Letters, pp. 634–8. 'A rare example of a vertuous maid in Paris . . .', in Pepys Collection, Magdalene College, Cambridge, II, pp. 24–5. 'A ballad of Anne Askew, intituled: I am a woman poor and blind', Manchester Central Library, collection of ballads, I, p. 54. 'The most rare and excellent history of the Dutchesse of Suffolkes calamity', in Chappell and Ebsworth (eds.), The Roxburghe Ballads, I, p. 287.

[47] Pepys Collection, I, pp. 544–5. First printed in Thomas Deloney, Strange Histories, of Kings, Princes, Dukes . . . With the Great Troubles of the Dutches of Suffolke (1602). Taken from John Foxe, Actes and Monuments (1583 edn), II, pp. 2078–81.

[48] See, for example, 'King Edward the fourth and a tanner of Tamworth', in F.J. Child (ed.), The English and Scottish Popular Ballads, 8 vols. (1882–98), no. 273.

duchess and her husband Bertie flee with their baby to Flanders, accompanied by just one nurse (who later runs away), and dressed as 'people poor'. Being refused shelter, and unable to speak the local language, they are forced to take refuge from the rain in a church porch. The interest of the story is in the temporary inversion of hierarchy:

> loe! here a princess of great blood
> doth pray a peasant for reliefe,
> With teares bedewed, as she stood,
> Yet few or none regards her griefe!

The heroine is thus incorporated into traditional ballad themes and conventions.[49] At the same time as protestant historiography is popularized, much of the specific protestant content and motivation is lost.

Not surprisingly, many of the second group of ballads, the moral diatribes of the Elizabethan reformers, did not survive to be sold by our pedlar of the seventeenth century. Accounts of the destruction of biblical cities did endure quite well, probably because they provided gripping stories, from which the warning to repent emerged secondarily as the moral. The *pièce de résistance* of this genre was 'Christ's teares over Jerusalem', an anonymous ballad based on Thomas Nashe's book of that name, and apparently first printed soon after the book's appearance in 1593.[50] The ballad succinctly combines a metrical paraphrase of Christ's prophecy of the destruction of Jerusalem, a brief but emotive description of the crucifixion and of Jerusalem's fall, and an account of plagues and punishments sent to contemporary England. Sensational details are highlighted:

> Yea, Dogs and Cats they eat, mice, rats and every thing,
> For want of food, 'their Infants young unto the Pot they bring'.

The successful narrative structure, probably the work of a London dramatist, meant the survival of a ballad like 'Christ's teares' for over eighty years, and the still-birth of many attempts by ministers and other amateurs.[51]

Although there may have been room for the emotive piety of 'Christ's teares' in the pedlar's pack of the 1630s, the platitudes of the aphoristic ballads proved to be the most popular form of broadside morality. The archetypical ballad in this vein was 'Solomon's sentences', drawn from Ecclesiasticus but attributed to the wise king Solomon. It was first regis-

---

[49] For similar revelation scenes, see James Kinsley (ed.), *The Oxford Book of Ballads* (Oxford, 1982 edn), nos. 32, 47.
[50] Pepys Collection, II, p. 6. It refers to the Armada which God sent against England 'of late', and to a recent plague, probably that of 1592.
[51] On attribution of the ballad, see Watt, *Cheap Print*, p. 99 n. 98.

tered in 1586, and remained in the ballad stock until at least 1675.[52] The gems of advice chosen by the ballad versifier as most applicable to his Elizabethan audience deal with financial matters, the raising of children, the running of a household. The advice is aimed at young males; the son in the ballad is warned in turn never to smile on his daughters, because they are prone to wantonness. Budding young householders are advised not to go to law with the magistrate and to pay their labourers promptly, implying that at least in 1586 an audience of reasonably wealthy yeomen or tradesmen was expected. There is an emphasis on good works which must have appealed to the pelagian tendency which, according to Richard Baxter, lingered on amongst the parishioners of rural England.[53]

From the practical morality of 'Solomon's sentences' we move to the more personal ballads appealing to the buyer's concern about his or her salvation. Making Christ the object of love songs like 'Dainty come thou to me' was a practice no longer in favour in the 1630s. However, the ballads of faith which did endure took the form of last dying speeches addressed to God: ballads which seem to have functioned as guides to the appropriate mental framework before death. The archetypical ballad of personal faith (surviving at least from 1624 to 1688) was attributed to a parish clerk: 'The earnest petition of the faithful Christian, being clerk of Bodnam, made upon his deathbed, at the instant of his transmutation.'[54]

The melody of 'The clarke of Bodnam' does not survive, but it was described as a 'sweet solemn tune' and may have imitated the toll of the passing-bell, as hinted in the text:

> Now my painful eyes lye rowling, and my passing-bell is towling,
> Towling sweetly, I lye dying, and my life is from me flying.

Ballads like the 'Clarke of Bodnam' took a standard form: confession of complete unworthiness and repentance of sins, followed by prayers for grace, expressions of faith, and hope for reception in heaven. God, whether Father or Son, is a close and kindly figure: 'my loving Father sweet', 'blessed Son', 'sweet Jesus'.[55] They are thoroughly protestant ballads, but there is no sense of a predestined elect. For the clerk, grace is a gift offered by Christ to all and available to the last minute:

[52] 'A most excellent new dittie, wherein is shewed the sage sayings, and wise sentences of Salomon' (1586), in Collmann (ed.), *Ballads and Broadsides*, no. 84. Pepys Collection, II, p. 64.

[53] Baxter commented on this pelagian element amongst his parishioners (*Confirmation and Restauration, the Necessary Means of Reformation and Reconciliation* (1658), pp. 157–65. Discussed in Eamon Duffy, 'The Godly and the Multitude in Stuart England', *Seventeenth Century Journal*, 1, no. 1 (1986), p. 39.

[54] Registered 1624. Chappell and Ebsworth (eds.), *The Roxburghe Ballads*, VII, p. 40. Pepys Collection, I, pp. 48–9.

[55] 'The sorrowful lamentation of a penitent sinner' [ent. 1624], in Chappell and Ebsworth, (eds.), *The Roxburghe Ballads*, VIII, p. 99; 'Clarke of Bodnam'.

Yet though my sins like scarlet show, their whiteness may exceed the snow,
If thou thy mercy do extend, that I my sinful life may mend.
Which mercy, thy blest word doth say, at any time obtain I may.

Here there is little of the insistence on outward and life-long godliness
found in many early seventeenth-century catechisms:

> Q. What if good workes be wanting?
> A. Then is iustifying Faith wanting whatsoever we professe.[56]

Whether or not the clerk of Bodnam would pass the most rigorous catechizing sessions of contemporary reformers, in his general effect he
is undoubtedly the incarnation of a seventeenth-century godliness, the
exemplary protestant on his deathbed. But his was not the only approach
to death available from the pedlar's pack of the 1630s. There was still a
more traditional vision of damnation and salvation, descended from the
art, drama, and song of pre-Reformation catholicism, with little sign of
any break. In more than half the stock ballads dealing with death, a
retributive God is less interested in repentance and faith than in the preparation for salvation with good works, and the promise of Jerusalem is
balanced (if not overshadowed) by the very real threat of hell-fire. If the
ballad buyer found the Bodnam parish clerk too bland for his taste, he
could choose a broadside of 'St Bernard's vision' [c. 1640], with a woodcut
of demons prodding a naked body with pitchforks.[57] Here was a tiny
fragment of the great medieval painting of 'The Doom' which had stood
over the chancel arch in the parish church, now transferred to the cottage
wall.

The ballad of 'St Bernard's vision' is a dramatization of the after-life,
using a narrator who experiences a death-like state, but is then revived
to tell the tale. This device came from a long tradition of clerical vision
literature, made familiar to a wide audience through its influence on the
paintings of 'The Doom'.[58] The first extant copy dates from c. 1640, and
the ballad was one of only half a dozen seventeenth-century religious
titles still available in Dicey's catalogue of 1754.[59] The ballad is subtitled
'A briefe discourse (dialogue-wise) betweene the soule and the body of
a damned man newly deceased, laying open the faults of each other; with
a speech of the divel's in hell'. The lugubrious tune 'Fortune my foe' is
well suited to the wailing and groaning of the body and soul in their

---

[56] James Balmford, *A Short Catechisme, Summarily Comprizing the Principal Points of Christian Faith* (1607), sig. A8v.
[57] Chapell and Ebsworth (eds.), *The Roxburghe Ballads*, II, p. 491. Pepys Collection, II, p. 4.
[58] A. Caiger-Smith, *English Medieval Mural Paintings* (Oxford, 1963), pp. 36, 31. The specific source was the supposititious 'Visio Sancti Bernardi', translated into English metre by William Crashaw in 1613 (STC 1908.5 to 1909.7).
[59] William and Cluer Dicey, *A Catalogue of Maps, Histories, Prints . . .*, p. 65.

pain. The soul berates the body for its sins and pleasures which have brought them both to hell, 'where we in frying flames for aye must dwell'. 'St Bernard's vision' is a powerful argument for the continuity of a medieval religious outlook well into the early modern period.

This group of ballads passes on, almost unchanged, a centuries-old vision of the Last Judgement based on the individual's sins or merits in this life.[60] It is possible that the ballad buyers themselves did not always perceive a contradiction between this traditional scheme of salvation and current protestant doctrine. It is quite possible that if a husbandman was of a mind to purchase a ballad about death, 'The clerk of Bodnam' might do just as well as 'St Bernard's vision', and our Shropshire pedlar probably sold both. The preoccupation with death, and the belief in a tangible heaven and hell, was an area of shared culture spanning the doctrinal rift between conformists and nonconformists, mainstream protestants, and groups like the Familists or Quakers, even between catholics and protestants. The fear of death lay at the core of popular religion long before and long after the Reformation, and on this theme the ballads testify to just how little had changed.

The popularization of Scripture was one of the great aims of reformers at the time of our Balsham pedlar, as we saw, but the Old Testament ballads still on sale in the 1630s did not show the same breadth of themes and lessons. The most popular stories were those involving a beautiful young woman, shown to be either a paragon of virtue, or inconstant and deceitful, or unwittingly the cause of men's destruction. Ballads of 'Constant Susanna', Sampson and Delilah, or David and Bathsheba came closest among the godly ballads to the narratives Child collected, and which we have come to think of as defining balladry.[61] The same ballad clichés were used: the 'maidens' are always 'fresh and gay', 'faire and bright'.[62] The opening of 'The story of David and Berseba' is similar in essence to that of 'Fair Margaret and Sweet William' and other 'traditional' ballads:[63]

> ... It chaunced so, upon a day,
> the king went forth to take the ayre
> All in the pleasant moneth of May,
> from whence he spide a Lady faire ...

---

[60] Only one of these after-life ballads presents the protestant message of the sinner saved by faith alone: 'A comfortable new ballad of a dreame of a sinner, being very sore troubled with the assaults of Sathan' (ent. 1624), Pepys Collection, I, p. 39. See Watt, *Cheap Print*, p. 112.

[61] Child (ed.), *The English and Scottish Popular Ballads*.

[62] Delilah in 'A most excellent and famous ditty of Sampson judge of Israell, how he wedded a Philistine's daughter' (?ent. 1563–4), Pepys Collection, I, p. 32.

[63] Kinsley (ed.), *Oxford Book of Ballads*, nos. 44, 58.

> She stood within a pleasant Bower,
> all naked, for to wash her there;
> Her body, like a Lilly Flowere,
> was covered with her golden haire.[64]

The incorporation of this story into the body of 'folksong' was apparently successful, since the ballad, probably first registered in 1569–70, was still for sale in the Dicey catalogue of 1754.

Like the Old Testament ballads, songs based on the Gospels had narrowed in range between the 1570s and the 1630s. Of the many parable-ballads, only one remained in the pedlar's pack: the story of the prodigal son.[65] The ballad belongs with the stories of ungrateful children and misspent youth which were a continuing strand in popular balladry, like the 'Good fellows resolution' which became the well-known 'Wild rover'.[66] With this exception, the seventeenth-century ballad stock contains nothing of Christ's teachings, but moves back to basic events of his life and death which had been the central themes of pre-Reformation piety: the virgin birth, the passion, and resurrection.

The single most successful ballad from the Gospels was 'A new ditty, shewing the wonderfull miracles of our lord' (known by its first line 'When Jesus Christ was twelve'), which survived on the 'partners' stock-list of 1675, a century after its first registration.[67] In a jogging rhythm it describes how Christ turned the water into wine, fed the multitude with the loaves, raised Lazarus from the dead, healed the lepers, the lame, and the blind. This is a story to compete with any of the contemporary miracles described in the sensational news ballads:

> But yet for all these wonders great, the Jews were in a raging heat,
> Whom no persuasions could intreat, but cruelly did kill him.
> And when he left his life so good, the Moon was turned into blood,
> The earth and Temple shaking stood, the graves full wide did open.

'When Jesus Christ was twelve' is a succinct paraphrase of the plot-line of Christ's life, and may have performed a mnemonic function for its singers, like a musical catechism. However, it is devoid of any of the parables and teachings which the early Elizabethan gospellers had hoped to spread.

---

[64] 'The story of David and Berseba' [?ent. 1569–70?], in Chappell and Ebsworth (eds.), *The Roxburghe Ballads*, I, p. 270.

[65] 'A new ballad; declaring the excellent parable of the prodigal child' [ent. 1570–1?], in *ibid.*, I, p. 393.

[66] 'Good fellows resolution', discussed in Thomson, 'Development of the Broadside Trade', pp. 232–6.

[67] Registered 11 September 1578. Andrew Clark (ed.), *The Shirburn Ballads* (Oxford, 1907), p. 103.

The general picture of popular piety gleaned from the godly ballads in our pedlar's pack of the 1630s is a conservative one. Religion is about the same fear of death and personal judgement which preoccupied medieval Catholics; it is about practical lists of good and bad behaviour; and about stories of miracles, a virgin birth, heroism, and even love and trickery. However, certain protestant lessons, like the centrality of repentance, and the shift from catholic saints to protestant martyrs and Old Testament heroines, had apparently been absorbed by some of their buyers. The incorporation of protestant aims into balladry created new archetypes: the brave Duchess of Suffolk; the wise king Solomon; the faithful clerk of Bodnam. Judging by their longevity, these new saints succeeded in populating the imagination of at least some of the readers and singers in seventeenth-century England.

Pictures

The sales appeal of the ballads was not only a matter of their content, but was also affected by their visual appearance. The broadsides carried by the pedlar in Cambridgeshire in the 1570s would have looked quite different from those sold by the Shropshire pedlar half a century later. The most striking change was the institution of woodcut pictures as a standard feature. Only one fifth of surviving sixteenth-century religious ballads are illustrated, while for the period 1600–10 more than five-sixths are illustrated.[68] There was also more of an attempt than in the sixteenth century to achieve some correlation between text and image.[69]

The increased importance of the woodcut pictures appears to have been closely linked to the development and specialization of the ballad trade in the early seventeenth century. The leading ballad publishers also began to put out large decorative woodcuts as a natural extension of their activities obtaining illustrations for their ballads. These included large poster-portraits of royalty and satirical prints, like 'Fill gut, & pinch belly' (1620), a picture of two monsters, 'one being fat with eating good men, the other leane for want of good women'.[70] One print which could have been carried by both our Cambridgeshire and Shropshire pedlars is a woodcut in the tradition of the 'Four Alls', which survives in a copy of

---

[68] A similar trend can be confirmed for 'secular' as well as 'religous' ballads. Unfortunately, this change of visual appearance cannot be dated precisely because of a gap in the surviving broadsides: the sixteenth-century collections are mostly concentrated in the period from around 1550 to 1572, while the seventeenth-century collections do not begin in full force until 1624–5. For a list of surviving ballads, see Watt, Cheap Print, pp. 333–41.

[69] See ibid., p. 149.

[70] See ibid., Figs. 10 and 11 and pp. 143–6.

c. 1580, and was still available in 1656.[71] This large woodcut (20 in × 14 in) is sloppily coloured in bright hues of blue, purple, orange, and brown, and depicts a bishop, king, harlot, lawyer, and 'country clowne', each with verses proclaiming their importance and power over the others. Of course, Death arrives with his spear to win the contest. The theme of death was common in pictures, as it was in the ballads, but it is a secularized vision, shorn of the spiritual dimension which had been present in medieval wall paintings and in the woodcuts of the *Ars Moriendi*: the angels and demons at the bedside, the weighing of souls, the intercession of the virgin, the divine judge.[72]

Contemporary 'iconophobia' seems to have limited the direct depiction of religious themes on these large woodcut pictures.[73] A Huguenot press in the Blackfriars produced Old Testament scenes and religious allegories, but appears to have avoided potentially idolatrous scenes like the crucifixion or nativity.[74] In the 1578 inventory of the Cambridge bookseller John Denys, a number of pictorial items are listed at the end: 'v other small pictures' (6d), 'a Rolle of the kynges' (6d), 'the storye of David' (6d), 'helias' (6d), 'the storye of Joseph' (7d).[75] A 'story' is a term normally used to describe a picture, and the 'stories' of David and of Joseph were almost certainly series of biblical pictures in the Blackfriars tradition.[76] However, the small number of pictures in stock, and the relatively high price of 6d, does not suggest that Denys was sending out great bundles of these pictures with chapmen like our Balsham pedlar.[77]

The most common form of printed decoration in humble households, according to contemporary accounts, was in fact the broadside ballad. Nicholas Bownde claims to have seen illiterate cottagers pasting up ballads in order to 'learne' them later: 'and though they cannot read themselves, nor any of theirs, yet will have many Ballades set up in their houses, that so might learne them, as they shall have occasion'. In 1624 Abraham Holland mocked the habit in northern villages of sticking up

---

[71] STC 6223. Thomas Warren re-registered the picture in 1656. (Eyre, I, p. 48.) The theme was known in France as 'Les Quatre Verités'. M. Dorothy George, *English Political Caricature to 1792. A Study of Opinion and Propaganda* (Oxford, 1959), p. 9.

[72] On woodcuts' depictions of death in the *Ars moriendi*, see Roger Chartier, *The Cultural Uses of Print in Early Modern France*, trans. Lydia C. Cochrane (Princeton, 1987), pp. 32–70.

[73] On iconophobia see Watt, *Cheap Print*, pp. 131–40.

[74] Giles Godet worked in England from the late 1540s to his death in 1571. Many of his blocks were still being used in 1656 by Thomas Warren. See *ibid.*, pp. 181–91.

[75] Reproduced in Leedham-Green (ed.), *Books in Cambridge Inventories*, I, p. 338.

[76] Susan Foister found that in the inventories of the prosperous classes a 'story' usually referred to a framed painting (Susan Foister, 'Paintings and Other Works of Art in Sixteenth-Century English Inventories', *The Burlington Magazine*, 123 (1981), 275).

[77] Compare Charles Tias' 1664 stock, which contained pictures in 'reams' (Margaret Spufford, *Small Books*, pp. 91–101).

ballads of Chevy Chase or the latest execution over the chimney. Ballads were also used to decorate public places: the standard decor of a country alehouse was 'a painted cloath, with a row of Balletts pasted on it'.[78]

The 'ballad partners' may have avoided religious themes in their large poster-size prints, but the woodcuts they used on their ballads tell quite a different story, testifying to a continued demand for pictures of Christ and other images which one might expect to be considered idolatrous.[79] It may be that the physical size of the pictures was a crucial factor: these small woodcuts of several inches square do not immediately suggest the act of adoration. Not all of the 'hotter sort of Protestants' were happy, however. In William Cartwright's *The Ordinary* (c. 1635), the puritan curate Sir Kit insults his companion, Rimewell the poet:

> Thou art a Lopaz; when
> One of thy legs rots off (which will be shortly)
> Thou'lt beare about a Quire of wicked Paper,
> Defil'd with sanctified Rithmes,
> And Idols in the frontisepiece: that I
> May speak to thy capacity, thou'lt be
> A Balladmonger.[80]

As the reference to 'Idols in the frontisepiece' suggests, even the crude little woodcuts, which ran like a frieze along the top of the ballad sheets, were the subject of criticism and controversy. A Quaker tract of 1655 later singled out ballad makers for special attack on account of the woodcuts: 'the Lord God of glory is arising, who saith, Thou shalt not make any Image of Male or Female, which you do amongst you, and are found upon your ballets, and so out of Gods councell, are amongst the heathen making Images'.[81]

[78] Bownde, *The Doctrine of the Sabbath*, p. 241. Abraham Holland in John Davies, *A Scourge for Paper-Persecutors, or Papers Complaint* (1624), sig. A2v of section by Holland. Wye Saltonstall, *Picturae Loquentes. Or Pictures Drawne forth in Characters. With a Poeme of a Maid* (1631), sig. E10v.

[79] The 1584 inventory of Mrs Hampden of Stoke in Buckinghamshire included 'a picture of Christe' and 'a picture of (as it is termed) the Judgement daye', which were assumed to be incriminating (PRO, SP 12/167/47). Cited in Patrick Collinson, *From Iconoclasm to Iconophobia: The Cultural Impact of the Second English Reformation*, The Stenton Lecture 1985 (Reading, 1986), p. 37 n. 109, where two similar examples are noted.

[80] *The Ordinary*, a Comedy, III, v. In *The Plays and Poems of William Cartwright*, ed. G. Blakemore Evans (Madison, 1951), p. 317.

[81] This tract represents an extreme position against *any* images, not just religious images. However, it does illustrate the point that ballad woodcuts could give offence despite their relatively innocuous proportions, and that they were an ubiquitous form of image, worthy of attack (*A Declaration from the Children of Light*, cited in Hyder E. Rollins, *Cavalier and Puritan. Ballads and Broadsides Illustrating the Period of the Great Rebellion, 1640–1660* (New York, 1923), p. 68).

The continued use of traditional iconography on the ballads may at first have been partly a result of the economic advantages of using old sixteenth-century woodblocks. The discarded blocks acquired by the publishers were sometimes survivals from the pre-Reformation printing houses, like the cut of Christ and his disciples used by Richard Harper in the 1640s, once used by Wynkyn de Worde in 1506.[82] When the old blocks wore out and the publishers had scenes newly cut, they continued to cater to the demand for story-telling images, depicting simple and familiar scenes from the Gospels. 'The sinner's redemption' (1634?) carries a woodcut of Christ between two labourers with hoes; 'The glorious resurrection' (1640?) shows him rising from the grave with the centurions leaping back in alarm.[83] Other broadsides depict the holy family on their flight into Egypt, and the virgin and child.[84] The most frequently used godly woodcut descended from the standard pre-Reformation image of Christ in Glory. On 'The sinner's supplication' (c. 1630) Christ blesses the ballad buyer from the starry vault, with palms raised in benediction and rays emanating from the clouds.[85] When this woodcut wore out the ballad partners had a copy cut, which survives on over a dozen ballads from the 1650s to 80s: it had become a trademark recognizable to the godly-ballad buyer (Plate 5).[86]

The cottager who pasted a ballad like 'The sinner's supplication' on his wall apparently liked to have a figure of Christ to look at, even if only an awkward little woodcut Christ like this. And if some types of religious picture might cause suspicion of popery in a domestic setting, it was apparently a widespread practice to paste up ballads adorned with little woodcuts of the resurrection and the holy family. Recent arguments about the growth of 'iconophobia' have suggested that our pedlar of the 1630s was travelling in a world with a very limited range of religious images, compared with his predecessor of the 1570s.[87] However, the

[82] See Watt, Cheap Print, Fig. 19. Edward Hodnett, English Woodcuts 1480–1535 (2nd edn, Oxford, 1973), no. 477, figure 46.

[83] Chappell and Ebsworth (eds.) The Roxburghe Ballads, II, p. 486, I, p. 388. Reprinted in Watt, Cheap Print, pp. 170–2.

[84] 'Glad tydings from heaven' [c. 1630] in Roxburghe Ballads, BL, I, 134. The virgin and child woodcut is found on post-Restoration broadsides (e.g. Pepys Collection, II, pp. 27, 30), but appears to be of old stock.

[85] 'The sinner's supplication' [c. 1630], in Chappell and Ebsworth (eds.), The Roxburghe Ballads, II, p. 498. This Christ in Glory was a copy of an earlier woodcut used on a pamphlet of 1613, when it already contained several wormholes. See Hodnett, English Woodcuts 1480–1535, pl. 78. For similar images see ibid., figures 66, 117.

[86] This copy from Pepys Collection, II, p. 13. Other copies are in Pepys Collection, II, pp. 28, 29, 47, 63; Wood Ballads, Bodleian Library, Wood. 401. (66), (160); Roxburghe Ballads, BL, II, pp. 141, 248, 422, III, pp. 371, 344.

[87] Collinson, From Iconoclasm to Iconophobia, p. 8; re-stated in Patrick Collinson, The Birthpangs of Protestant England: Religions and Cultural Change in the Sixteenth and Seventeenth Centuries (New York, 1988), p. 117.

Plate 5. *Woodcut of Christ in Glory, from the ballad of 'The sorrowful lamentation of a penitent sinner'*

evidence of woodcut pictures, together with other media like wall painting and painted cloths, suggests that his visual universe had not changed so dramatically.[88] The pedlar of Shropshire could still have carried quite a number of images which helped the villagers who bought them to convert the words of the protestant religion into visualized experience.

Little books

So much for single-sheet wares, but what of more substantial reading matter, the 'little books' sold in the Balsham churchyard? And what were the 'some good books' offered by the pedlar of Eaton Constantine, besides the one named title, Richard Sibbes' *Bruised Reed*? The book bought by Richard Baxter's father was probably the first edition of *The Bruised Reede, and Smoaking Flax,* a collection of sermons by the leading puritan divine, which was not itself very 'little' as books go.[89] Although printed in the very compact duodecimo format, it was a thick book of almost 400 pages, which would have cost 8d or 9d at the halfpenny per sheet

---

[88] For a more detailed exploration of images in this period, see Watt, *Cheap Print,* pp. 131–216.

[89] STC 22479. The first edition, published in 1630 (around the time of which Baxter writes), is available in a facsimile edition by the Scolar Press (1973) with an introduction by P.A. Slack.

prescribed by the Stationers' Company in 1598.[90] This would have been affordable to Baxter's yeoman father, but certainly not to all customers along the pedlar's route.

Book prices must be set against a context of contemporary incomes. Keith Wrightson estimates a basic cost of subsistence of around £11–14 for a family in a normal year, while the wages of a labouring man might total only £9–10. Clearly there was little 'surplus' for luxuries like books and pamphlets. An early seventeenth-century husbandman with an arable holding of thirty acres might have £3–4 'surplus' after food, or an average of 14d to 18d a week.[91] At this level, our chapman would not be able to sell very many books at 9d, although he might do quite a good business in twopenny chapbooks. For this reason I will be concentrating on the very cheapest and 'littlest' books available in this period, examining the type of works which I believe would have been the main stock-in-trade of both our pedlars. However, as the presence of the *Bruised Reed* and one or two rare pedlar's inventories suggest, the pedlars also seem to have carried at least a few books we might describe as 'luxury' wares, for the wealthier households and better-educated readers along the route. The poor young packman, George Pool of Cumberland, was trudging up the hills with a few books worth 9d each, along with his haberdashery, when he died in 1695.[92]

Leaving George Pool's customers, along with Richard Baxter, to their 'good' but costly books, we will look for a cheaper form of chapbook which could have been sold to the same wide audience as the ballads. In the later seventeenth century, it is much easier to identify titles which were published specifically for sale by chapmen. Publishers advertised their trade-lists at the end of their own volumes: 'J. Back, at the sign of the Black Boy on London Bridge, furnisheth country chapmen or others, with all sorts of small books, ballads, and all other stationary-wares at reasonable rates.'[93] Collectors like Pepys and Wood bought these 'small merry books' and 'small godly books' directly from chapmen; and from these collections together with surviving publishers' inventories, Margaret Spufford has been able to reconstruct the chapbook trade of the late seventeenth century.[94]

Unfortunately booksellers before the 1650s did not print trade-lists in their books, nor have we found a chapman's or bookseller's inventory

---

[90] Francis Johnson found that from about 1560 to 1635, prices for normal new unbound books stuck quite closely to this halfpenny per sheet (Francis R. Johnson, 'Notes on English Retail Book-Prices, 1550–1640', *The Library*, 5th Ser., 5 (1950), pp. 84, 93).
[91] Keith Wrightson, *English Society 1580–1680* (1982), pp. 32–4.
[92] Reference from Margaret Spufford.
[93] Notice of 1686 in Margaret Spufford, *Small Books*, pp. 111–13.
[94] Ibid.

to shed light on distribution practices.[95] However, we do know that the chapbook trade after the Restoration was closely connected with the ballad trade, and that ballads were distributed in the countryside from the second half of the sixteenth century.[96] The ballad publishers apparently had direct access to a network of chapmen; at what point did they begin to distribute chapbooks along this network as well?

In order to trace the development of a specialized chapbook trade, I have examined the entire non-ballad output of eight leading ballad publishers, three from the late sixteenth century and five from the early seventeenth century.[97] I looked especially for the format which Pepys later bound together as 'penny merriments' and 'penny godlinesses': this standard 'penny' size format was twenty-four pages or less, in octavo or duodecimo. Pepys used the term 'penny' as a description of an unmistakable size and format, rather than a precise statement about price: in fact, from at least 1637, the standard price seems to have been twopence.[98] In addition to its cheapness (requiring only 1 to 1.5 sheets of paper), the 'penny' format was ideally designed for chapmen, who could have carried large numbers of these small books in their packs. This was to remain the standard format through the eighteenth and nineteenth centuries.[99] I have also looked for precursors of an assortment of longer works which Pepys called 'Vulgaria': these included twenty-four-page quartos called 'double-books' (costing 3d or 4d) and longer quartos called 'histories' (costing 6d or more).[100]

The full results of this investigation are published elsewhere.[101] The search yielded some three dozen extant 'penny books' of the early seventeenth century: not an enormous corpus, but (given the odds against their survival) enough to indicate the beginnings of a new genre. The 1620s was the decade in which the publishers organized themselves into a specialized syndicate for distribution of broadside ballads. The evidence also points to this as the period when ballad publishers began consciously to acquire the copyrights to these small books, which they could sell to the same wide market as their ballads.

[95] John Andrews, bookseller of Pye Corner, appears to be the first to advertise chapbooks as a trade-list in the back of his books, in 1658–9 (see Watt, *Cheap Print*, p. 218).
[96] See ibid., pp. 11–30.
[97] Richard Jones, William Pickering, and John Awdeley; John Wright, Henry Gosson, John Trundle, Francis Coules, and Francis Grove. See ibid., pp. 274–95.
[98] Martin Parker describes his 'twopeny customers' in *Harry White his Humour* (1637). John Andrews, bookseller, lists seven books at 2d in the back of John Hart, *The Plain Mans Plain Path-Way to Heaven* (1659). Johnson, 'Notes on English Retail Book-Prices', pp. 89–90.
[99] See descriptions of chapbook size in Harry B. Weiss, *A Catalogue of the Chapbooks in the New York Public Library* (New York, 1936), p. 3; Victor E. Neuberg, *The Batsford Companion to Popular Literature* (1983), p. 51.
[100] Margaret Spufford, *Small Books*, pp. 130–1, 150–1.
[101] Watt, *Cheap Print*, pp. 274–320 and Apps. H to L.

What, then, of our Balsham pedlar in 1578, plying his wares before the development of this specialist trade? Since there was not yet a trade-list advertised specially for his purposes, he may have sold a whole range of books which could be described as 'little': that is, short, probably unbound, and light to carry. Many of these may have been 'merry' books such as the titles found in the library of Captain Cox the mason of Coventry, recorded in a letter of 1575.[102] Our Balsham pedlar might well have stocked *Adam Bell*, *The King and the Tanner*, and *The Fryar and the Boy*, all printed on just 1.5 to 2.5 sheets in quarto, and costing 1d or at most 2d at the normal rates per sheet.[103]

It is unlikely, however, that our Balsham pedlar sold only little books for entertainment and none for edification. In the late seventeenth century, although the proportion of new religious ballad titles had dropped, the new line of religious tracts made up no less than 32 per cent of the trade-lists of the 'small book' publishers.[104] One third of the ballads being published at the time of our Cambridgeshire pedlar were godly, and the total output of religious print remained very high throughout the period: 42 per cent of the STC works published in 1640 can be classified as religious.[105] If our pedlar's stock was at all representative, at least one in three of his 'little books' would have been godly ones.

Our chapman could have stocked up with these books at the shop of John Denys in Cambridge, who died in 1578, leaving over 759 volumes which are itemized in his inventory.[106] Most of these were specialized works for the University, many in Latin, but the presence of titles like *The Maner of Measurynge of All Maner of Lande* suggests an audience beyond the scholars in their college rooms.[107] There were a number of books in English which were suitable for an ordinary lay audience and valued at prices which would have been affordable to all but the poorest of Cambridgeshire households. Twelve 'almanackes and prognostications' in octavo were listed at only 1d each, while four copies of an account of the voyage of 'captayne Furbisher' were also valued at 1d per copy.[108]

---

[102] Frederick J. Furnivall (ed.), *Captain Cox, his Ballads and Books; Or, Robert Laneham's Letter* (1871). Margaret Spufford, *Small Books*, pp. 51, 66, 77, etc.

[103] See Watt, *Cheap Print*, Table 4. Reprints cost less than new books, an average of ½d per sheet. New pamphlets tended to be sold at a price of 1d per sheet, levelling off to the standard ½d at around four sheets (Johnson, 'Notes on English Retail Book-Prices', pp. 84, 93).

[104] Margaret Spufford, *Small Books*, p. 197.

[105] Calculated from figures given in Edith L. Klotz, 'A Subject Analysis of English Imprints for Every Tenth Year from 1480 to 1640', *Huntington Library Quarterly*, 1 (1938), p. 418.

[106] Leedham-Green (ed.), *Books in Cambridge Inventories*, I, pp. 326–40.

[107] 'Serving of landes', valued at 8d, is identified by Elizabeth Leedham-Green as Richard Benese, *This Boke Sheweth the Maner of Measurynge of All Maner of Lande* (probably the edn of c. 1565). Ibid., I, p. 336.

[108] STC 22265: Dionyse Settle, *A True Reporte of the Laste Voyage into the West and Northwest Regions, & c 1577 Worthily Atchieved by Capteine Frobisher* (1577).

Apart from these, the majority of works at the bottom of John Denys'
price range were religious in content. Nine unbound copies of the
'psalmes in meeter' were valued at 3s 6d, or just under 5d each: a reasonable price for a staple of religious worship for godly Balsham householders at all points on the protestant spectrum. These psalm books were
in the tiny 32° format designed for carrying in the pocket, approximately
3 in × 2 in in size, and could certainly have been described as 'little'
books.[109] Another religious handbook was the 'Right rule of godlie praiers', also in the miniature 32°, valued at 1s for five copies, or just 2½d
each. This was probably *A Right Godly Rule; How All Faithfull Christians Ought
to Occupie and Exercise Themselves in their Dayly Prayers*, based largely on prayers
in the official primer of 1555, which were in turn the inheritance of
generations of Latin primers.[110] *A Right Godly Rule* offered short prayers for
each morning of the week, followed by more elaborate formulae for
specific occasions: 'in adversity', 'at the houre of death', 'before hee goeth
about any wordly busines'.

An alternative to this semi-official prayer book which may have been
carried by our Balsham pedlar was Edward Dering's *Godlye Private Praiers
For Housholders in their Families*: the Cambridge bookshop contained one
copy valued at 2d, and another (presumably old or damaged) at only 1d.
Dering provides for the same daily spiritual needs as other collections,
but his originality comes across in 'passages of honest puzzlement and
even wonder', and his puritan convictions appear in prayers to 'roote
out all remnaunts . . . of idolatry'.[111]

Some of the pedlar's wares may have been educational tools for the
children of Balsham. A sixteenth-century Italian engraving (Plate 6) shows
a pedlar with hornbooks hanging from his pack, and hornbooks would
be reliable wares for an English pedlar too, since every village would
have children of the age to learn their 'Christ cross row'.[112] For godly
households with older children and adults he may have stocked catechisms. Ian Green has shown a barrage of alternative catechisms after 1570,
reaching their first peak in the 1580s, as many of the parish clergy began
to expect more knowledge from their catechumens than was found in
the official Edwardian catechism. He identifies over 250 independent

[109] A surviving copy of the Sternhold and Hopkins psalms in this format is STC 2449.5:
The Whole Booke of Psalmes, Collected into English Metre (1577). A more prosperous yeoman
could have bought a bound copy in various larger formats valued at 6d, 8d, or 10d
in Denys' inventory.

[110] STC 21446.7. The surviving copy dates from 1602, but the work was first registered
to T. Marsh in 1562–3. The 1602 edition is 12.5 sheets in 16°, but the 32° edition
may have been an abridged version. On the official primer, see Helen C. White, *The
Tudor Books of Private Devotion* (Wisconsin, 1951), p. 125.

[111] Ibid., p. 169. STC 6655 or STC 6685.5. Dering, *Godlye private praiers*, sig. C1.

[112] In 1677 Robert Carr, chapman of Newcastle upon Tyne, had nineteen dozen hornbooks in his warehouse, at a halfpenny each or less. See Margaret Spufford, above,
p. 70. I am grateful to Helen Weinstein for finding the engraving.

Plate 6. Engraving of Italian pedlar with book and hornbooks, 1640s

catechetical works: with repeat editions, Green calculates that 'over three-quarters of a million copies of these works were in circulation by the early seventeenth century, in addition to perhaps half a million copies of the official forms'.[113] The Cambridge bookshop in 1578 had seven copies of 'master moores cathechismus', once again by Edward Dering, valued at 8d for the lot, or just over 1d each.[114] This catechism began with an ABC, and proceeded, in only three sheets octavo, with simple questions and answers on the Ten Commandments, the Creed, the two Sacraments, the role of good works and of prayer, the Lord's Prayer and finally a 'prayer contayning the summe and effect of this catechisme'.

As well as these educational tools, our pedlar may have sold a selection of short sermons and pamphlets which, if they came from John Denys' shop, tended to be 'puritan' in bent. Three copies of 'master doctor fulkes sermone', probably *A Comfortable Sermon of Faith* were valued at 4d all together.[115] For 2d you could have *A Conference Containing a Conflict had with Satan, wherein are Plainely Set Downe the True Markes and Tokens, whereby the Afflicted Conscience may Prove It Selfe, whether it be the Childe of God, or the Childe of Satan* (1577) by the puritan divine Andrew Kingsmill. Readers worried about their sins are assured that their torment 'is the very token that you are Gods childe', for the reprobate take pleasure in their sinning, while only the blessed grieve for the wrongs they have done.[116] The neuroses of the godly about their salvation appear to have been good for the sale of cheap godly books in Cambridgeshire. Another work listed at 2d was Pierre de la Place, *A Treatise of the Excellencie of a Christian Man*, which included a discussion of how a man may know himself to be a Christian 'by the effects which the same spirit of God bringeth forth in him'.[117] For 2d you could also have Thomas Lever's *A Treatise of the Right Way from Danger of Synne* (1575), while for 3d or 4d, the Cambridge shop stocked seven copies of Stephen Bateman's *The Golden Booke of the Leaden Goddes* (1577), which described heathen deities leading up to the greatest of 'leaden goddes', the Roman Catholic pope.

Clearly there were quite a number of suitable wares for our Balsham pedlar's pack in the bookshops of Cambridge, the city which served the area. We should not, however, rule out the possiblity that he acquired

---

[113] Ian Green, '"For Children in Yeeres and Children in Understanding": The Emergence of the English Catechism under Elizabeth and the Early Stuarts', *Journal of Ecclesiastical History*, 37, p. 425.

[114] Leedham-Green (ed.), *Books in Cambridge Inventories*, I, p. 335. Edward Dering, *A Bryefe and Necessary Catechisme, very Needefull to be Knowne of All Housholders* (1577).

[115] William Fulke, *A Comfortable Sermon of Faith*, in *Temptations and Afflictions* (1578 edn), a work of 3.5 sheets octavo.

[116] Sig. C3.

[117] Sig. D4v. This book should have been more expensive, at 8.5 sheets octavo. The twopenny copy may have been second hand.

wares directly from London. These could have included ballads, which notably do not appear in the surviving inventories of any Cambridge booksellers in this period, as well as other small pamphlets produced by the ballad publishers. Likely 'chapbooks' from these presses included little pamphlets like *An Epistle of the Ladye Jane to a Learned Man of Late Falne from the Truth of Gods Word* (ent. 1569–70), published by William Pickering.[118] Just as Anne Askew and the Duchess of Suffolk were popular ballad heroines, stories of women suffering for their religion made good chapbook copy. Lady Jane's popularity was confirmed by the reprinting of this pamphlet in 1615, 1629, and 1636 by John Wright.[119] The dramatic narrative of a woman's martyrdom was used as a forum for a defence of protestant doctrine and an anti-papist diatribe. The four discourses 'written with her own hands' included a catechism emphasizing that there were two Sacraments rather than seven, that the Eucharist was not the real body of Christ, and so on. The pamphlets of the sixteenth-century ballad publishers are, like their ballads, artifacts of early-Elizabethan protestantism, with its urgent need to convey reformed doctrine, the sense of the papist enemy not yet vanquished, and the mood of struggle, inspiration, and martyrdom.[120]

Leaving Balsham and our pedlar of the 1570s, it is likely that the Shropshire pedlar of the next century carried many of the same bread-and-butter staples of religious print – the primers, catechisms, and psalm books – acquired from a Shrewsbury bookshop. A book of 1635 was printed 'for William Millard, bookseller in Shrewbury', but unfortunately we know nothing more about Millard or his shop.[121] However, the 1585 inventory of an earlier Shrewsbury bookshop shows the quantity and variety of religious works which were readily available in that county long before the pedlar reached the Baxters' door.[122] Apart from a number of grammar-school texts, Roger Ward's stock was dominated by popular devotional manuals, including '60 prayer books', another '28 bookes of praier gilte', '13 primers', '41 psalters with psalmes', '41 Communion bookes with smale psalmes', and '42 singinge psalmes alone'. Catechisms were also stocked in large batches: forty-three copies of 'pagettes catechismes', twenty-seven of Edward Dering's catechism known as 'mores cat-

---

[118] *An Epistle of the Ladye Jane . . . Wherunto is Added the Communication that she had with Master Feckenham. Also Another Epistle to her Sister, with the Words she Spake upon the Scaffold. MDLIIII* [J. Day? 1554?]. Pickering's edition does not survive.

[119] STC 7281. Wright's version was retitled *The Life, Death and Actions of the Lady Jane Gray. Containing Foure Discourses Written with her Owne Hands* (1615 etc.) and ran to three sheets in quarto.

[120] For a more detailed account of these pamphlets, see Watt, *Cheap Print*, pp. 278–88.

[121] John Terry, *The Defence of Protestancie* (1635 edn). See STC 'Index I. Printers and Publishers' (1991).

[122] Rodger (ed.), 'Roger Ward's Shrewsbury Stock', pp. 247–68.

achismes', thirty-three 'nowells catachisms', nine 'Bezas catac[hisms]', another unspecified '83 catach[i]smes duble', and twenty-five of *The ABC with the Catechism*. Some of the Shropshire pedlar's 'good books' may have been cheap black-letter sermons: Roger Ward's stock included ninety sermons by unnamed authors valued at 2.5d each, and another ninety-three at 3d. (These entries are among the very few which include prices.) The large numbers of copies suggest that by the late sixteenth century this Shrewsbury bookshop was serving a wider catchment area than John Denys' Cambridge shop, and catering primarily to a lay rather than learned clientele.

Roger Ward's shop was the provincial outpost of his business in London, where he was notorious among stationers for his repeated book piracy. In 1582 he was hauled before the Court of Star Chamber for printing 10,000 copies of *The ABC with the Little Catechism*, which was the privilege of John Day. Ward admitted sending his servant John Legge to Shrewsbury with 1,500 of these copies, which were then assembled in that town.[123] Clearly there was a large market for these basic educational tools in Shropshire. Ward was also asked how many he had 'sent out to be sold in the country'. Although he denied selling any copies to chapmen, his testimony contained a number of blatent falsehoods, and presumably there was good reason for the question to have been asked. Roger Ward was in trouble again in 1583 for printing 'the little primer and the usual psalter', and in 1582–3 he put out a pirated edition of 'Dentes Sermons', of which work forty-two copies are listed in his Shrewsbury inventory. This profitable tract was Dent's *Sermon of Repentaunce* (valued at 2d in the inventory of another bookseller in York) which had run to an impressive thirty-seven editions by 1638.[124]

Long-term best-sellers like Dent's suggest a degree of continuity in cheap religious print, but other 'little books' illustrate changes in both content and format by the seventeenth century. Roger Ward's Shrewsbury shop in 1585 contained '20 bookes of Robin consciens & suche', referring to a popular verse pamphlet of sixteen pages quarto, first registered to the ballad publisher John Awdeley.[125] The version of *Robin Conscience* which would have been carried by a sixteenth-century pedlar captures the flavour of Elizabethan protestantism, presenting reformed ideas in a palatable narrative form. The godly Robin chastises his father Covet-

---

[123] Cyril B. Judge, *Elizabethan Book-Pirates* (Cambridge, Mass., 1934), pp. 49–50.
[124] Rodger (ed.), 'Roger Ward's Shrewsbury Stock', pp. 259, 267. STC 6649.5. Robert Davies, *A Memoir of the York Press* (1868), p. 363.
[125] Rodger (ed.), 'Roger Ward's Shrewsbury Stock', p. 252. *The Book in Meeter of Robin Conscience* [c. 1565?]. Another edition printed by Edward Allde [1590?]. Reprinted in W. Carew Hazlitt (ed.), *Remains of the Early Popular Poetry of England*, 4 vols. (1864–6), III, pp. 225–47.

ousnesse for extortion, his mother Newgise for vain apparel, and his
sister Proud Beauty for her wantonness. But more than a morality tale, it
is a protestant manifesto, a conflict between old religion and new religion. The family swears 'By the Masse' while Robin urges them to 'have
a respect unto Christ's Testament'. The vanity of his sister is associated
with the vanity of Rome: her gold chains and embroidered hair are 'the
decking and balming of proud living Idols'.[126] The father warns his son:

> By the masse, yf thou to the Scripture incline,
> Be sure that I wyll never do the pleasor
> Nor yet never helpe the, with none of my treasor.[127]

This paternal diatribe is described in the margin as 'the rebuke and
admonicion of the generacyon of Satan'. As a generational conflict, with
protestant doctrine in the mouth of the son rebuking his parents, *Robin
Conscience* supports the association of the mid-sixteenth-century
Reformation with 'novelty, youth, insubordination and iconoclasm'.[128]

This is the pamphlet as it would have been sold by our pedlar of 1578,
but our Shropshire chapman of 1630 would have carried a rather different
version. In 1630, the ballad writer Martin Parker updated the tale for
seventeenth-century tastes.[129] Gone is the protestant content, gone is the
generational conflict: in this story, morality is linked to social responsibility, as the 'Conscience' figure visits people from various walks of life and
is turned away. The setting in named places around London ('Smithfield',
'Pye corner', 'Southwark') gives the moral a topical, contemporary feel;
yet it is only in the country that 'Conscience' is finally welcomed. Not
with the gentry or yeomanry (who refuse to give up their corn for the
poor), but with the labourers:

> Mongst honest folks that have no lands,
> But get their living with their hands,
> These are his friends that to him stands,
> and's guiding.[130]

Martin Parker was the most popular and prolific of seventeenth-century
ballad writers, and his involvement with these little books suggests they
were aimed at the same public as the ballads. Indeed, the chapbook was
sometimes merely a ballad text printed over a number of octavo pages,
and sprinkled liberally with woodcuts.[131] There was a major change taking

---

[126] Ibid., original printed marginal notes, lines 296–300.
[127] Ibid., lines 71–3.
[128] Collinson, *From Iconoclasm to Iconophobia*, p. 4.
[129] *Robin Conscience, or, Conscionable Robin* (for F. Coules, 1635). Registered to M. Sparke, 20 April 1630.
[130] Ibid., p. 15.
[131] For example, *The Pleasant and Sweet History of Patient Grissell* was first registered as a broadside in 1565–6 (Arber, I, p. 296), but around 1640 the ballad partner John

place in the 1620s and 30s. The ballad publishers were collecting copyrights to small books which they could distribute to the same market as
their ballads, and having these books printed in the 'penny' format (of
twenty-four pages octavo or less) which was to become standard by the
late seventeenth century. In doing so they did not think only of the
dancers on the village green, but also of the sober godly readers like the
Baxter family. The leading 'ballad partner', John Wright, was in fact far
more involved in 'godly' books than 'merry' ones: we have only two
surviving 'penny merriments' with his imprint, compared with five of a
hybrid form I have called 'penny miscellanies', and a full dozen of what
Pepys would call 'penny godlinesses'.

The 'penny miscellanies' were little collections of aphorisms, ranging
from pure humour to pure moralizing and catechizing; most of the
examples including a curious assortment of both, with no sense of incongruity. They would have sat well in the Shropshire pedlar's pack alongside
ballads like 'Solomon's Sentences' and 'An Hundred Godly Lessons'. John
Wright's surviving miscellanies were written by Nicholas Breton, and
included *The Crossing of Proverbs* (1616), *The Soothing of Proverbs* (registered
1617), and *The Figure of Four* (1631), which parented a whole line of 'figures'
of three, five, six, seven, and nine.[132] There were common sense sayings,
practical advice, puns, and anti-female jokes: 'Three things will not prove
well without beating: a Walnut tree, an Asse, and a Woman.'[133] But in all
cases there was a large religious content too: not controversial doctrine,
but simple injunctions for the daily living of a Christian life. Remember
death, fear God, be sorry for your sins, avoid sloth and gluttony, be sober
and chaste (especially if you are female). Most of this might have been
written before the Reformation, although the writers sometimes incorporate the central position of faith in Christ, and, very rarely, a reference
to the elect:

> The sweetnesse of this Name Jesus consists in three things: It is honey
> to the mouth, Melodie to the Eare, and joy to the Hearr [sic].

> The knowledge of God is threefold: Generall, Speciall, and Singular.
> Generall, as the Philosophers: Special, as of the Christians: and singular,
> as of them that are blessed.[134]

Wright took the ballad and spread it out over twenty-four pages octavo, dividing the
text into little chapters, adding a prose introduction and conclusion, and adorning it
with seven woodcuts.

[132] Anon., *The Figure of Three* (1636); Martin Parker, *The Figure of Five* (1645?); D.N., *The
Figure of Six* (1652); Martin Parker, *The Figure of Seven* (1647); and Samuel Smithson,
The Figure of Nine (1662). Later editions of these were included among Pepys' penny
merriments.

[133] Anon., *Figure of Three*, sig. B2.

[134] Ibid., sig. A3.

These writers were poets, not preachers, and their little books may reflect the moderate religion of the majority of the literate public: those who would buy godly advice mixed with merry jests, but might not venture their 2d for a dose of the fire-and-brimstone found in the more puritanical 'penny godlies'.[135]

For those like the young Richard Baxter yearning for more fire in their faith, however, John Wright's trade-list included at least a dozen titles in 'penny book' size. These were largely the work of one author who appears to deserve credit, together with his publisher Wright, for the invention of the 'penny book' formula: John Andrewes, 'Minister and Preacher of the word of God at Barricke Basset in the County of Wiltes'.[136] Another John Andrewes, a minister at St James Clerkenwell in Middlesex, gives us an idea of the reputation of our 'penny godly' author:

> For another there is, who writes both his Names as I do, and hath published divers Books, (as Petitions, Subpoena's, Christ-Crosses &c) ... I doe hereby certifie thee, that I am not the man ... for my part, howsoever I be the meanest among the many thousands that are called to the Sacred Priesthood; yet I may truly protest, that I never played the Circumforanean Theologaster: Istos enim Circulatores, qui Sacram Philosophiam honestius neglixissent, quam vendunt, semper exosus habui.[137]

In other words, by 1621 our Andrewes was known as a 'marketplace theologian' whose books were peddled around the countryside by chapmen of dubious character.

In his own works, our John Andrewes tells how he was called, late in life, from the profession of school teaching to become a minister. He had no regular living in Wiltshire: he was not the incumbent at Berwick Bassett, and must instead have been an occasional preacher or puritan lecturer.[138] He claims to have lost 'to the value of three-score pounds by the yeare in spirituall livings within the Realme of Ireland', and hopes to relieve his family's impoverished situation by success with his books.[139] To this end he acts as his own part-publisher, printing one of his early works at his own cost, and taking over the distribution of two others, no

---

[135] On the moderate religion of 'honest householders' at all levels of society, see Martin Ingram, *Church Courts, Sex and Marriage in England, 1570–1640* (Cambridge, 1987).

[136] John Andrewes, *Christ his Crosse* (1614). For a fuller account of John Andrewes see Watt, *Cheap Print*, pp. 306–11.

[137] 'I never played the marketplace theologian: I have always detested those pedlars who neglect the sacred philosophy which they sell.' Andrewes, *The Brazen Serpent: Or, the Copie of a Sermon* (1621), sig. A3.

[138] Andrewes, *Christ his Crosse* (1614), sig. A4. Alexander B. Grosart (ed.), *Miscellanies of the Fuller Worthies' Library*, 39 vols. (Blackburn, 1868–76), II, 6.

[139] *Andrewes Humble Petition* (for J. Wright, 1623 edn), sig. A4.

doubt increasing his share of the profits.[140] However, Andrewes' little books were destined for life beyond the villages of Wiltshire, and it is quite likely that our Shropshire pedlar carried one or two of them in his pack. By the 1620s John Wright had begun to acquire the copyrights to distribute them along his ballad network, and they were selling so well that their author remarked on the phenomenon in 1630:

> whereas I have formerly published unto the view of the world, many small bookes for the setting forth of Gods glory . . . now seeing that my former bookes are so vendible, and so well likeing unto the children of God, that in short time there have been divers impressions printed, I have therefore now set foorth another booke, intituled *Andrewes Repentance*.[141]

Andrewes' story is not unlike the pattern for later godly chapbook writers shown by Eamon Duffy: that is, ejected nonconformist ministers who turned to evangelical writing as a substitute for the usual pastoral duties.[142]

What were these small books which proved so 'vendible'? As Andrewes said himself, all were variations on the theme of 'repentance'.[143] Sometimes Andrewes focusses on the first step of repentance, the fire-and-brimstone 'alarum' to the unconverted sinner:

> Heare, oh therefore, heare all you that walke after the lusts of your owne hearts, and depart from Bethel the house of God, to starve your soules in Bethaven, the den of iniquity: It is sinne, oh! it is your unrepented sinne that drawes Gods anger towards you, that makes your eyes more dry than the stony rocke, and your hearts more hard than the Adament.[144]

But Andrewes dwells more often on the next step of the repentance process; offering encouragement to the penitent man who is already converted. If, says Andrewes, Satan shows you your sins and tempts you to despair, tell him 'Oh, thou hellish fiend, I say againe, Depart, I doe utterly defie thee, O take thy ugly sinnes againe, which thou hast caused me to commit; and lay them not unto my charge, for I am a member of my Lord and Saviour Jesus Christ.'[145]

Andrewes' style is always immediate and informal, and he includes himself as a companion in the reader's predicament. His books are notable for so often including his name in the title, as if for a loyal following

---

[140] See verses at the back of *Christ his Crosse*, sig. L2v; a variation is repeated on the title page of *Andrewes Humble Petition* (1623 edn). The 1621 *Celestiall Looking-Glasse* was 'imprinted at my own cost and charges'.

[141] *Andrewes Repentance* (1631 edn), sig. A2.

[142] Duffy, 'The Godly and the Multitude', pp. 47–8.

[143] *Andrewes Repentance*, sig. B1v.

[144] *Andrewes Caveat to Win Sinners* (for J. Wright, 1631), sig. A6.

[145] *Andrewes Repentance*, sig. A7.

waiting for his next 'penny godly' to appear. What kind of buyers was he appealing to? Andrewes himself gave some indication that he felt his audience would include those on the fringes of literacy; he addressed himself to hearers as well as readers: 'If thou dost reade or heare this worke . . .'; 'Gentle Readers, or Hearers, whosoever yee are, that are the Children of God'.[146]

The public for these little books did certainly include readers of at least gentry status, such as the Staffordshire lady, Frances Wolfreston. As well as Shakespearean quartos and other literary treasures, marked out with the inscription 'frances wolfreston hor [or her] bouk', Frances collected some fifty 'penny godlinesses'.[147] Those which bear a publication date number five from the 1640s (four of them by John Andrewes), eight from the 1650s, and twenty from the 1660s; a distribution which appears to reflect faithfully the snowballing growth of the trade.[148] However, Frances' copy of *A Golden Trumpet* gives an indication that not all of Andrewes' earlier readers were as well-read and well-off as herself: in 1648, the *Golden Trumpet* had reached its 'nine and twentieth Impression'.[149]

As well as the tracts of John Andrewes, our Shropshire pedlar may have carried other 'penny godlinesses' by the unknown 'George Shawe minister of Gods word', and a few titles by authors better known for more substantial works, like William Perkins.[150] His *Death's Knell or the Sicke Mans Passing-Bell*, which had reached its sixteenth edition by 1637, featured a title-page woodcut of a bed-side scene, with the skeleton figure of Death pulling at the rope of a bell.

At the cheapest end of the publishing trade, the key to survival was less often in finding new authors than in acquiring copyrights to old titles of proven popularity, and moving them into new formats. One piece of verse text illustrates well both the changes and the continuity between the eras in which our two pedlars plied their trade. 'The exhortacion of Robert Smith, unto his children, commonly set out in the name of maister Rogers' appeared in the 1563 edition of Foxe.[151] This was supposed to have been written in prison by the martyr Smith (d. August 1555), and

---

[146] *Humble Petition*, title page; *The Converted Man's New Birth* (1629), sig. A2.

[147] Sale catalogue in BL: Sotheby C.S.413(3), 24 May 1856. For more on Frances Wolfreston see Watt, *Cheap Print*, pp. 315–17; Paul Morgan, 'Frances Wolfreston and "Hor Bouks": A Seventeenth-Century Woman Book-Collector', *The Library*, 6th Ser., 11 (1989), pp. 197–219.

[148] A further dozen were listed in the sales catalogue as 'an one other', or titled but without date: most of these were lumped together with post-1660 books and probably date from that period. It is also very rare for a pre-1640 chapbook to have no date in the imprint.

[149] This work was written before 1630 when its copyright was transferred to John Wright, but there are no surviving copies before 1641.

[150] Watt, *Cheap Print*, pp. 311–15.

[151] Foxe, *Actes and Monuments* (1563 edn), sigs. 3U$_2$–3U$_2$v.

brought to publication by Mathewe Rogers, with whose name the ballad became firmly associated. The popular title was simply 'Rogers Will'. The text was copied into numerous manuscripts of the period, and it became part of the long-enduring stock of godly ballads: both of our pedlars are likely to have carried it in broadside form.[152] It combined two of the most successful godly ballad formulas: the story of protestant martyrdom and the parental advice ballad. It contained the usual predictable maxims to honour God and one's mother, give to the poor, beware lust, and (a small reminder of the situation in which it was composed) to 'abhore that arrant whore of Rome'. The bulk of the text might have been the advice of any parent to his or her children, but presumably the ballad gained weight from its origin in such spiritually significant circumstances:

> where I amonge myne Iron bands
> inclosed in the darke
> afewe dayes before my death
> did diddicate this warke.

In addition to the ballad, our pedlar of 1578 might also have carried 'Rogers Will' in the form of a 'litle booke' which was registered in 1577.[153] The work does not survive, but according to the detailed Stationers' Register entry, it contained four other godly texts, probably also in verse form: 'the complainte of veritye made by John Bradforde', 'the complainte of Raphe Allerton and others beinge prisoners in Lolers [Lollards?] Tower and wrytten with their bloude how God was their comforte', 'a song of Caine and Abell', and 'the saienge of Master Hooper that he wrote the night before he suffered upon a wall with a cole in the newe inne in Gloucester and his saienge at his deathe'. Here was, essentially, a miniature book of martyrs, of a portable size for both chapman and reader, and affordable to many readers for whom Foxe's great tomes would have been out of reach.

This book was not as 'little', however, as the 'penny godlinesses' which developed in the seventeenth century, which were usually the length of only one broadside ballad spread out over sixteen to twenty-four octavo pages. This is exactly what happened to the text of 'Rogers Will' when it got into the hands of the ballad partners Coules, Wright, Vere, and Gilbertson. When they were required to register their stock in 1656, their entry of 'ten little bookes' included the 'Exhortation that a Father Gave

---

[152] 'Mastare Rogers to his childerne', in MS Stowe 958; 'Mathewe Rogers to his childrine', in Cambridge University MS Ff.5.14. First registration probably the entry to William Pickering in 1564: 'An Instruction of a father to his cheldren' (Arber, I, p. 262). Entered as 'Rogers will' in 1624 (Arber, IV, p. 131).

[153] It was entered on 14 October to John Arnold and then on 11 November to James Robotham, neither of whom appear to have been specialists in ballads or other cheap print (Arber, II, p. 319).

his Children' along with other familiar titles like 'Tom Thumb', '100 Godly Lessons', and 'Death's Knell'.[154] *The Exhortation that a Father Gave his Children* survives in a copy printed in 1648 for Francis Coules. Coules was in business from 1624 onwards, and this little book might well have been among the wares of our 1630 pedlar, in an earlier edition which does not survive.[155] The extant copy is just sixteen pages in octavo, with a scene of a martyr at the stake on the title page and back page. A number of generic woodcuts have been spread throughout: a king with his sceptre, a gentlewoman with feathered hat and fan, an old religious woodcut which may represent the coronation of the virgin. The text is exactly the same as that of the ballad.

The changing format of 'Rogers Will' demonstrates the development of the 'penny godliness', and a significant change in the cheap-print trade. At the same time, the longevity of the text itself indicates the conservative nature of much of popular piety. The successful chapbooks like 'Roger's Will', or ballads like 'The Duchess of Suffolk', probably survived because they could appeal to the dancers on the village green as well as to the Baxter family reading their Scripture. From his investigation of church courts in Wiltshire, Martin Ingram argues that respect for the church and protestant values was not limited to the middle and upper strata of parish society, but 'probably applied also to many "honest householders" of the poorer sort, who had a definite, albeit modest stake in the community'.[156]

The pedlar's basic stock of cheap printed wares must have catered to this 'spectrum of unspectacular orthodoxy', within which most villagers fell. There were still variations and contradictions in these godly chapbooks and ballads, from the more traditional piety of 'St Bernard's Vision' to the greater emphasis on faith and the elect found in 'The Clerk of Bodnam' or John Andrewes' little repentance tracts. The resulting patchwork of beliefs may be described as distinctively 'post-Reformation', but not always thoroughly 'protestant'. Piety retained a visual dimension, even if Christ in Glory was now banished to the tiny woodcuts along the top of a ballad. Religious emotion still attached itself to heroic archetypes, even if these were increasingly protestant martyrs rather than catholic saints. Morality still meant good neighbourly behaviour, and hell was still the same fiery place, a final threat as direct punishment for sins committed in this world.

As well as the popular ballads and chapbooks, our pedlars of Cambridgeshire and Shropshire must also have carried a number of books

---

[154] Eyre, II, p. 55.
[155] The existing copy survives only because it was bought by the Staffordshire lady Frances Wolfreston, and preserved for 200 years by her descendants.
[156] Martin Ingram, *Church Courts, Sex and Marriage in England, 1570–1640* (Cambridge, 1987), pp. 123–4, 94.

for the more serious students of religion, as the Baxters' purchase of 'Dr Sibb's *Bruised Reed*' suggests. The presence of large batches of inexpensive devotional manuals in provincial booksellers' inventories indicate that prayer books, psalm books, and catechisms were in demand throughout the country. Many of these could have been staples in the households of dissenters as well as mainstream protestants. Members of the Family of Love, as Christopher Marsh has shown, participated in village life as constables, witnesses to wills, and even as churchwardens; they shared many values with other householders.[157] It seems unlikely that ordinary pedlars would carry the writings of Hendrick Niclaes or other proscribed works, unless they had already established special contacts with local members of the sect. However, the sale of sermons by William Fulke or Arthur Dent might well be the first step of conversion for rural readers, which could then lead to their involvement with local protestants of the 'hotter sort', whether conformists or dissenters. We know how the printed word affected Sister Sneesby, a deaf old fen woman who was converted from her General Baptist beliefs to Quakerism by the reading of Quaker tracts.[158]

The possibility that the poor pedlar at the door could be an instrument of conversion was not lost on early Elizabethan reformers, who wrote broadside ballads urging the reform of society according to protestant ideals. But if the pedlar of the 1570s was considered a potential agent of God's word, his descendant of the 1630s was widely reviled as belonging to a band of masterless men 'who neglect the sacred philosophy which they sell'.[159] The task of stocking the pedlar's pack was increasingly left to publishers like the 'ballad partners', who reprinted godly works with proven commercial appeal; and to ejected nonconformist ministers like John Andrewes of Wiltshire. The evangelical thrust was shifting from the ballads to the developing format of the penny chapbook. 'Marketplace theologians' like Andrewes no longer wrote ballads calling for wide-spread social reform, but instead published little repentance tracts aiming directly at the conversion of individuals.

The chapman, who no doubt weighed up with each step the value of every ounce in his pack, had to carry a basic stock of goods which would appeal to the widest audience: linens and haberdashery, simple luxuries, best-selling ballads and chapbooks, popular devotional manuals. The chapmen of the late seventeenth century were still carrying titles like *The Dying Man's Last Sermon*, *A Book of Prayer and Graces*, and *The Door of Salvation Opened*; in fact, a third of the chapbooks in their packs were apparently

---

[157] See above, pp. 216–18.
[158] See Margaret Spufford, above, p. 64.
[159] Andrewes, *The Brazen Serpent*, sig. A3. The acquisition of paper wares to sell was sometimes the first recourse of the destitute. See Margaret Spufford, above, p. 65.

godly ones.[160] These little books could hardly have been worth their weight in gloves and ribbons if they did not sell. In the dissemination of religious ideas and beliefs, the petty chapman of rural England was undoubtedly an important agent, even if 'good books' were mixed together with bawdy ballads in the jumble of the pedlar's pack.

[160] Margaret Spufford, *Small Books*, pp. 197–201.

CHAPTER 7

The mobility and descent of dissenters in the Chiltern Hundreds

Communications and the continuity of dissent in the Chiltern Hundreds during the sixteenth and seventeenth centuries

MICHAEL FREARSON

To survive means making some contact, no matter how small, with the outside world.[1]

. . . the interest of an inquiry such as this, and one cannot say it too often, lies in the detail of the subject.[2]

There were other people on the roads of England whose motives for travel, unlike those of the chapmen, were solely religious. In the summer of 1658 Richard Hubberthorne, one of the foremost early Quaker protagonists, rode through the Chiltern Hundreds of south Buckinghamshire.[3] He was described by Adam Martindale as 'the famous Richard Hubberthorne, well-known by his pamphlets, and (to speak the truth,) the most rationall calme-spirited man of his judgement that I was ever publickly engaged against'.[4] His journey began in Oxfordshire in the first week of June and ended in Bristol eighteen days later, after he had visited Wycombe, Beaconsfield, Chalfont St Peter, Chesham, London, Reading, Marlborough, and Calne. Like other Quaker missionaries at this time, Richard Hubberthorne 'spread the truth' in the Upperside Meeting area.[5]

[1] Fernand Braudel, The Identity of France, vol. I: History and the Environment (London, 1989), Part II 'The Pattern of Settlement: Villages, Bourgs, Towns', p. 126.

[2] W.G. Hoskins, The Making of the English Landscape (London, 1970 edn), chapter 8 'Roads, Canals and Railways', p. 233.

[3] Letter from Richard Hubberthorne to Margaret Fell, November 1658. FL, Caton MSS, III/127. I am very grateful to Kate Peters, who is completing a Cambridge PhD dissertation on Quaker pamphleteering in 1652–6, for references to Quaker correspondence.

[4] Life of . . . Martindale (Chetham Society, 1845), cited by Ann Hughes, 'The Pulpit Guarded: Confrontations between Orthodox and Radicals in Revolutionary England', in Anne Laurence, W.R. Owens, and Stuart Sim (eds.), John Bunyan and his England, 1628–88 (London, 1990), p. 44.

[5] This strenuous itinerary, sometimes involving more than one meeting a day, was typical of Quaker missionary activity in the mid-seventeenth century. Alaxander

The following year, Thomas Ellwood, a young Quaker convert from Crowell in Oxfordshire, ventured into the Upperside Meeting area 'to be among friends'. On a winter Wednesday he rode 'fifteen long miles ... the ways bad and my nag small' to Isaac Pennington's house in Chalfont St Peters, attended a meeting of Friends in Wycombe on Thursday (returning to Chalfont St Peter the same evening), and went home on Friday. When his disapproving father repossessed his horse on Saturday, Thomas walked back to Wycombe. Later he walked from Chalfont St Peter to Crowell: 'I took my leave of them to depart home, intending to walk to Wycombe in one day, and from thence home in another.' After his father forbade his Upperside visits Thomas walked to meetings in Meadle village, 'four long miles' from Crowell: 'many a sore day's travel I had thither and back again, being commonly in the winter time (how fair so ever the weather was overhead) wit up to the ankles at least'.[6]

Unfortunately, no records survive to show us how Quakerism was introduced into Buckinghamshire, but the example of Anne Blaykling, the Quaker missionary who brought the 'truth' into Norfolk, demonstrates how it may have been done. When she was arrested in June 1655 'with a great concourse of people about her in the highway to the disturbance of the publique peace', Norfolk justices found on her person 'diverse papers . . . conteyning directions for travails into severall counties and places in this commonwealth'. Like later Quaker missionaries, her missionary travels were guided by a planned itinerary of places to visit.[7]

These examples demonstrate the mobility, and determination, among members of one of the later dissenting sects which flourished in the Chiltern Hundreds during the sixteenth and seventeenth centuries. They also raise important questions about the relationship between mobility and the continuity of religious dissent in the area. Was the high level of mobility amongst Quakers typical for the earlier dissenters, as John Earle's 'Shee puritan' of 1627 suggests: 'Her oftest Gossipings are Saboth dayes iournyes, when shee will ride behind her husband fiue mile in Pilgrimage to a coughing Minister when there is a better Sermon at her owne Parish.'[8] John Hampden himself was presented for journeying to a

[6] The History of Thomas Ellwood, Written by Himself (London, 1885), pp. 45–58, 79.
[7] Norman Penny (ed.), 'The First Publishers of Truth' Being Early Records (Now Printed) of the Introduction of Quakerism into the Counties of England and Wales (London, 1907); Norfolk Quarter Sessions Indictments, 12 June 1655, cited by Richard Vann, The Social Development of English Quakerism, 1655–1755 (Cambridge, Mass., 1969), pp. 10, 13. See above, p. 55.
[8] John Earle, The Autograph Manuscript of Microcosmographie (1st published London, 1627; Leeds, 1966), pp. 117–18.

sermon outside his parish.[9] Or was the continuity of religious dissent, and the extraordinary genealogical stability of dissenting families of these parts, the result of geographical isolation? What sort of contact did the dissenting communities of the area have with each other and with dissenters in other parts of the country?

In this essay I would like to suggest that the continuity of religious dissent is in part attributable to good communications. Far from being geographically isolated, the families of the Chiltern Hundreds which participated in the main streams of religious dissent in the period had the opportunity for regular and frequent contact with the other dissenting families in the area, and with dissenters in other parts of the country. Buckinghamshire, and the Chiltern Hundreds in particular, was one of the most mobile and well-connected counties in England. The dissenters of the area used the communications network to spread and consolidate their faith.

The communications network in the Chiltern Hundreds operated on three interconnected levels which linked three overlapping marketing areas. At the most local level, the Chiltern Hundreds contained a large number of stable market towns which lay in close proximity to one another with overlapping market areas. Most inhabitants of the region lived within walking distance of at least two market towns, and so each market town attracted local traders from different parts of the Hundreds. At the second level, the close proximity of the Chiltern Hundreds to London caused these overlapping local market areas to overlap further areas which fed the expanding London market. An increasing proportion of the agricultural and manufactured commodities produced in the Chiltern Hundreds was sent to London in the later sixteenth and seventeenth centuries. At the third level, packhorses, waggons, and barges from the West Country moved along the Chiltern highways and the Thames river to and from London, thereby linking the local market areas with more distant parts of the West Country which also supplied the metropolitan market. The dissenting communities of the Chiltern Hundreds were brought into contact with each other and the outside world by the ebb and flow of local marketing patterns and the strong currents of more distant marketing activities in the West Country and the capital.

The occasions for these contacts were both regular and frequent. Local inhabitants from a wide area were brought together during the weekly market days in the numerous market towns of the Hundreds. They were

[9] PRO SP 16/284/12; *Calendar of State Papers Domestic, 1634–5*, p. 250, cited by J.T Cliffe, *The Puritan Gentry: The Great Puritan Families of Early Stuart England* (London, 1984), p. 161.

also brought into contact with the outside world through the weekly movement of carriers travelling along the highways to and from the capital, the passage of barges up and down the river, and the seasonal markets and fairs during the year. These patterns of communication facilitated contact between local dissenters and dissenters in other parts. Public disputations and lectures were held in market towns on market days when dissenters knew large crowds would gather. The inns where travelling dissenters like Richard Hubberthorne and Thomas Ellwood stayed, and where dissenters sometimes held their meetings, were maintained by the trade of the carrier community. Amongst the goods delivered by carriers in highway towns and villages were also letters and books written by dissenters. Good communications and constant mobility facilitated the formation of dissenting communities near and far.

The agriculture and industry of the Chiltern Hundreds – mostly corn, pasture, market gardening, wood crafts, lace making, and paper making – supported a large population throughout the period.[10] Undoubtedly, much of this production was for local use. The six market towns of the Chiltern Hundreds – Amersham, Beaconsfield, Chesham, Colnebrook, High Wycombe, and Marlow – held weekly markets where these and other goods were traded by local inhabitants from hinterland villages. These market towns were located close together, with most inhabitants living within half a day's walk (seven miles) from at least two (Map 5). Their market days did not clash. The local trade of each market town drew people from many parts of the Chiltern Hundreds.

The regular contact between the inhabitants of different parts of the Chiltern Hundreds is reflected in the seventeenth-century settlement papers of two market towns in different parts of the region, Amersham in the north and High Wycombe in the south.[11] Some of the new incomers in these towns came from nearby villages, but many also came from more distant parts in the Chiltern Hundreds, and also northern Buckinghamshire and the neighbouring counties. Most were crafts and farming families who would have traded in their new town before settling there. The pattern of settlement suggests strong links and mobility between different parts of the Chiltern Hundreds, even amongst the most humble occupations. This is reflected in the widespread places where the Upperside Quakers held their monthly meetings, where Quakers

---

[10] See below, p. 290, above, p. 60.
[11] Amersham settlement papers, 1608–1737, Bucks. RO PR/13/1. L.J. Ashford, 'Newcomers to the Borough during the Seventeenth Century', *The History of the Borough of High Wycombe from its Origins to 1880* (London, 1960), pp. 146–50.

from all parts of the area regularly travelled to be among friends.[12] The internal mobility of the Chiltern Hundreds ensured the dissenting families of the area remained in frequent and regular contact with one another.

The close proximity of the Chiltern Hundreds to London, and the existence of good communications to the capital, ensured that the area was drawn into supplying the London market. In the seventeenth century, Chiltern corn was sold to London buyers in High Wycombe, and transported in large Thames barges down the river from Marlow.[13] Edward Perrat, an Amersham maltster who died in 1665, had malt worth £294 23s 8d (more than half the total value of his goods) destined for London brewers stored in his stable. In 1673, Thomas Price, a turner of Wendover (just on the other side of the Chilterns) had eleven bedsteads worth £8 5s made up for London buyers, and wood cut and framed for several more.[14] Dairy and market garden produce from the Thames valley, paper made in the mills between West Wycombe and High Wycombe, lace from High Wycombe and Great Marlow, and chairs made of Chesham beech were all sent to London.

The London highways on which the Chiltern market towns stood started in the West Country and Wales. Buckinghamshire maintained a unique position in the national network of London highways in the sixteenth and seventeenth centuries. The county acted like a funnel for all the London traffic from the north-west of England, Wales, and the West Country. The London highways of the Chiltern Hundreds carried London-bound traffic from central and southern Wales, Herefordshire, Worcestershire, Gloucestershire, northern Somerset, Wiltshire and Berkshire, Oxfordshire and central Buckinghamshire (Maps 1 and 5). These highways were first mapped by John Ogilby in 1675 as part of his road-atlas Britannia. They were later described by John Sellor in his Buckinghamshire county map of 1680, to which more roads were added by Philip Lea in 1693. Clearly, by this time these highways were already well-established routes to the capital.[15]

---

[12] M.M. Beatrice Saxon Snell (ed.), Minute Book of the Monthly Meeting of the Society of Friends for the Upperside of Buckinghamshire, 1669–1690, Buckinghamshire Record Society 1 (Aylesbury, 1937), Introduction.

[13] T.S. Willan, River Navigation in England, 1600–1750, Oxford Historical Series (Oxford, 1936), pp. 6, 98–9, 100–1, 126–7.

[14] Michael Reed (ed.), Buckinghamshire Probate Inventories, 1661–1714, Buckinghamshire Record Society, 24 (Aylesbury, 1988), pp. 49–51, 103–4.

[15] John Ogilby, Britannia (London, 1675). John Sellor, Buckinghamshire (London, 1680; 1693 edition enlarged by Philip Lea).

The same routes to the capital were described with very little variation
in the popular road-books printed for commercial travellers from the
middle of the sixteenth century.[16] The highways they described were the
roads most known about by the sorts of people who travelled along
them most often; commercial carriers, waggoners, chapmen, higglers,
posts, and market farmers. By following their guides, we shall be able
to find the highways most travelled in the sixteenth and seventeenth
centuries.

A comparison of the Chiltern highways listed in the most popular six-
teenth- and seventeenth-century road-books with John Ogilby's 1675
road-atlas shows that these routes to the capital remained constant
throughout the period (Table 6). The only exception is the Buckingham
to London highway, which was not represented in any road-books before
1675. But other evidence, discussed below, indicates that this highway
was also in use from at least the last quarter of the sixteenth century. The
remaining four London highways from Worcester, Oxford, Gloucester,
and Bristol passed through the Chiltern Hundreds at least a century
before the publication of Ogilby's road-atlas.

While compiling his *Britannia*, John Ogilby often noted the local roads
running off his highways, and because of the high density of highways
for our area, these local roads can be mapped in the Chiltern Hundreds,
with the helpful assistance of Philip Lea's 1693 county map (Map 5).
Since both market towns and highways remained stable here during the
sixteenth and seventeenth centuries, it seems reasonable to assume that
local roads were also much the same throughout the period. The central
and southern parts of the Chilterns appear to have received the most
London traffic. However, the dense network of local roads linked the
London highways and the river into most areas. Most local roads radiated
out from market towns to reach their hinterland villages and other market
towns. These highways and local roads, and also the Thames river, provided the basic infrastructure for communications in the Chiltern Hundreds, and formed vital links with the national communications network.

Some idea of the volume of traffic which passed along the river and
roads of the Chilterns can be gained by a close examination of the location of the inns, alehouses, beds, and stables where travellers and their
horses lodged. In 1577, Chiltern Justices of the Peace recorded thirty-one
inns and 100 alehouses in the six market towns and twenty-three of the
parishes of the area.[17] Twenty-nine of these inns and ninety of the ale-

---

[16] H.G. Fordham, *The Road-Books and Itineraries of Great Britain 1570 to 1850* (Cambridge,
1924); *idem*, 'The Earliest Tables of Highways of England and Wales', *The Library*, 4th
Ser., 8 (1928).

[17] Certificate of the Alehouses, Inns and Taverns in the county of Bucks., 23 September
1577, PRO SP 12/115/73–84.

Table 6. London highways in the Chiltern Hundreds, 1571–1628 and 1675

1571–1628	A	B	1675	C	D	E	F
Bristol highway							
London			London				
Colnbrooke	15	15	Brentford	8	8	10.1	10.1
Maidenhead	7	22	Hounslow	2	10	2.2	12.3
Reading	10	32	Colnbrooke	5	15	6.4	18.7
Newbury	15	47	Maidenhead	7	22	8.7	27.6
Hungerford	7	54	Twiford	6	28	7.4	35.2
Marlborough	8	62	Reading	4	32	5.0	40.2
Chippenham	15	77	Theale	4	36	4.3	44.5
Marshfield	10	87	Woolhampton	6	42	5.6	50.3
Bristol	10	97	Thatcham	3	45	3.2	53.5
			Newbury	2	47	3.1	56.6
			Chiltern	9	56	9.5	66.6
			Ramsbury	2	58	2.7	69.2
			Marlborough	4	62	6.1	75.3
			Calne	10	71	12.5	88.0
			Chippenham	6	77	5.6	93.6
			Marshfield	7	84	9.2	103.0
			Bristol	10	94	12.2	115.0
Gloucester highway							
London			London				
Hounslow	10	10	Brentford	8	8	10.1	10.1
Colnbrooke	5	15	Hounslow	2	10	2.2	12.3
Maidenhead	7	22	Colnbrooke	5	15	6.4	18.7
Henley	7	29	Maidenhead	7	22	8.7	27.6
Dorchester	12	41	Henley	7	29	8.1	35.7
Abingdon	5	46	Dorchester	12	41	13.3	49.3
Farringdon	10	56	Abingdon	5	46	6.0	55.3
Cirencester	12	68	Farringdon	10	56	13.2	68.5
Gloucester	15	83	Lechdale	4	60	6.0	74.5
St Davids	>>	201	Fairford	2	62	3.4	78.1
			Barnesley	4	66	5.6	83.7
			Gloucester	15	81	18.3	102.2
			St Davids	>>	207	>>	269.5
Oxford highway							
London			London				
Uxbridge	15	15	Acton	6	6	8.3	8.3
Beaconsfield	7	22	Uxbridge	9	15	10.1	18.4
High Wycombe	5	27	Beaconsfield	7	22	8.5	27.1
Stokenchurch	5	32	High Wycombe	5	27	5.5	32.6
Tetsworth	5	37	Tetsworth	10	37	12.0	44.6
Wheatley	5	42	Wheatley	5	42	5.4	50.2
Oxford	5	47	Oxford	5	47	5.4	55.6

houses were located on London highways and along the river. As the volume of traffic grew and stable patterns of travel formed during the seventeenth century, traveller accommodation became increasingly concentrated in the highway market towns and a number of highway and river parishes. In 1686, Chiltern justices counted 397 beds and 642 stables

Table 6 (cont).

1571–1628	A	B	1675	C	D	E	F
Worcester highway							
London			London				
Uxbridge	15	15	Acton	6	6	8.3	8.3
Beaconsfield	7	22	Uxbridge	9	15	10.1	18.4
High Wycombe	5	27	Beaconsfield	7	22	8.5	27.1
Islip	20	47	High Wycombe	5	27	5.5	32.6
Ch. Norton	12	59	Tetsworth	10	37	12.0	44.6
Eversham	14	73	Wheatley	4	41	4.5	49.3
Worcester	12	85	Islip	6	47	8.0	57.3
Carmarthen	>>	157	Enston	10	57	12.5	70.0
			Morton	10	67	13.2	83.2
			Broadway	5	72	7.5	90.7
			Pershore	7	79	11.6	102.5
			Worcester	6	85	9.5	112.2
			Aberystwyth	>>	145	>>	199.2
Buckingham highway							
			London				
			Acton	6	6	8.3	8.3
			Uxbridge	9	15	10.1	18.4
			Amersham	9	24	11.0	29.4
			Wendover	6	30	9.5	39.1
			Aylesbury	4	34	5.0	44.1
			E. Claydon	6	40	9.7	54.0
			Buckingham	4	44	6.4	60.4
			Bridgenorth	>>	105	>>	142.0

Key
A C E Distance between listed stage towns
B D F Cumulative distance from London
A B C D Customary miles
E F Statute miles
Sources: the most popular Elizabethan and Jacobean road-book, reprinted thirty-three times between 1571 and 1628, in Richard Grafton's *Litle Treatise* (London, 1571–1611) and Franke Adams' *Wryting Tables* (London, 1577–1628), with distances measured in customary miles (A B), and John Ogilby's road-atlas *Britannia* (London, 1675), with distances measured in customary miles (C D) and statute miles (E F). According to Philip Grierson, one customary mile measured between ten and twelve furlongs, compared with eight furlongs for a statute mile (Philip Grierson, *English Linear Measurements* (Reading, 1972), pp. 15, 30). Slight variations in the measurement of the same London highways in the road-books of 1571–1628 were caused by the arbitrary nature of the customary mile as a unit measurement, and by typographical errors.

in the six market towns and twenty-one of the parishes, of which 360 beds and 545 stables were located on the London highways and the river.[18] Carriage and coaching involved more horses than people, which explains why there were more stables than beds in 1686.[19] The small

[18] Abstract of the particular account of all the inns and alehouses etc. in England with their stable-room and bedding in the year 1686, PRO WO 30/48.
[19] See John Montaine's probate inventory, discussed below.

Table 7. Chiltern traveller accommodation in London highway and Thames river towns and parishes, 1577 and 1686

	1577		1686	
	Inns	Alehouses	Beds	Stables
In Chiltern area	31	100	397	642
On highways and river	29	92	360	545
	94%	92%	91%	85%
Bristol/Gloucester highway (towns/parishes)				
Colnbrooke	8	8	58	59
Langley		2		
Slough		3	10	20
Farnham		2	3	3
Burnham	2	3	3	3
Hitcham				
Taplow				
Oxford/Worcester highway (towns/parishes)				
Iver		2	3	3
Denham	1	2		
Gerrards Cross			4	4
Hedgerly				
Hedgerly Dean				
Beaconsfield parish				
Beaconsfield	3	12	66	64
Wooburn		2		
Rural Wycombe				
High Wycombe parish				
High Wycombe	3	16	82	171
West Wycombe	1	3	20	34
Stokenchurch				
Buckingham highway (towns/parishes)				
Iver		2	3	3
Denham	1	2		
Gerrards Cross			4	4
Chalfont St Peter	2	1	28	48
Chalfont St Giles		3		
Amersham	2	7	26	51
River Thames (towns/parishes)				
Waisbury				
Datchet		2	2	2
Upton		2		
Eton	3	3	18	30
Eton Wick				
Boveney				
Dorney		2		
Taplow				
Hedsor				
Wooburn		2		
Little Marlow		1	2	2
Marlow parish				
Marlow	3	6	27	44
Great Marlow				
Medmenham				
Hambleden		3		
Fawley		1	1	

Sources: Certificate of the Alehouses, Inns and Taverns in the county of Bucks., 23 September 1577, PRO SP 12/115/73–84, Abstract of the particular account of all the inns and alehouses etc. in England with their stable-room and bedding in the year 1686, PRO WO 30/48. Market towns appear in italic.

Map 5. Market towns and days, London highways and local roads, and hundredal boundaries in the Chilterns

proportion of traveller accommodation which was not located on London highways or the river was to be found in parishes located on the cross-roads between the highways, the river, and the market towns. However, the greatest volume of traffic in the Chiltern Hundreds flowed along the London highways and the Thames river, and this pattern remained stable throughout later sixteenth and seventeenth centuries (Table 6, Maps 5 and 6).

The movement of London traffic along the highways and the river was intersected at market towns and cross-road villages by the local traffic of the area, and local traffic also flowed between the market towns along sections of the London highways. The inns where West Country London carriers stayed were also used by London agents who came to trade with local producers, and by local people coming to market or living in the town. The inns of the Chiltern Hundreds were perhaps the most important intersecting points in the communications network where the three overlapping marketing areas met.

Common carriers probably made up the bulk of traffic on Chiltern highways and in travellers' inns and alehouses. They were certainly the most regular and frequent travellers of the sixteenth and seventeenth centuries. Aside from transporting goods and passengers, carriers operated an informal postal service. In 1627 the character writer John Earle described his 'Carrier' thus: 'He is the vault in Gloster church, that converses whispers at a distance: for he takes the sound out of your Mouth at Yorke & makes it be heard as far as London.'[20] Later in the century, the Quakers William Caton and George Taylor both recommended sending letters with the carrier:

> I was moved to write to our friends yt they may send all by ye Carrier, unlese it be some thinge of Consernement for ye Carrier comes Every weeke, & I shall have as much brought me for 2d. as I pay to post 2 or 3s.[21]

> If thou wold anie thinges write back by James Moore if he deliver thee this for he is deare and pretious to mee, and sensiable in the truth of his place.[22]

Even items of 'Consernement' could be sent with the carrier. In 1654 the Atherston carrier delivered the manuscript of Richard Farnworth's

[20] Earle, *Autograph Manuscript* pp. 65–7.
[21] William Caton (Kendal) to Margaret Fell (Lancashire), 26 November 1654, FL, Spencer MSS, 378/7.
[22] George Taylor (Kendal) to Margaret Fell (Lancashire), 25 December 1654, FL, Swarthmoor Hall correspondence, 54/11.

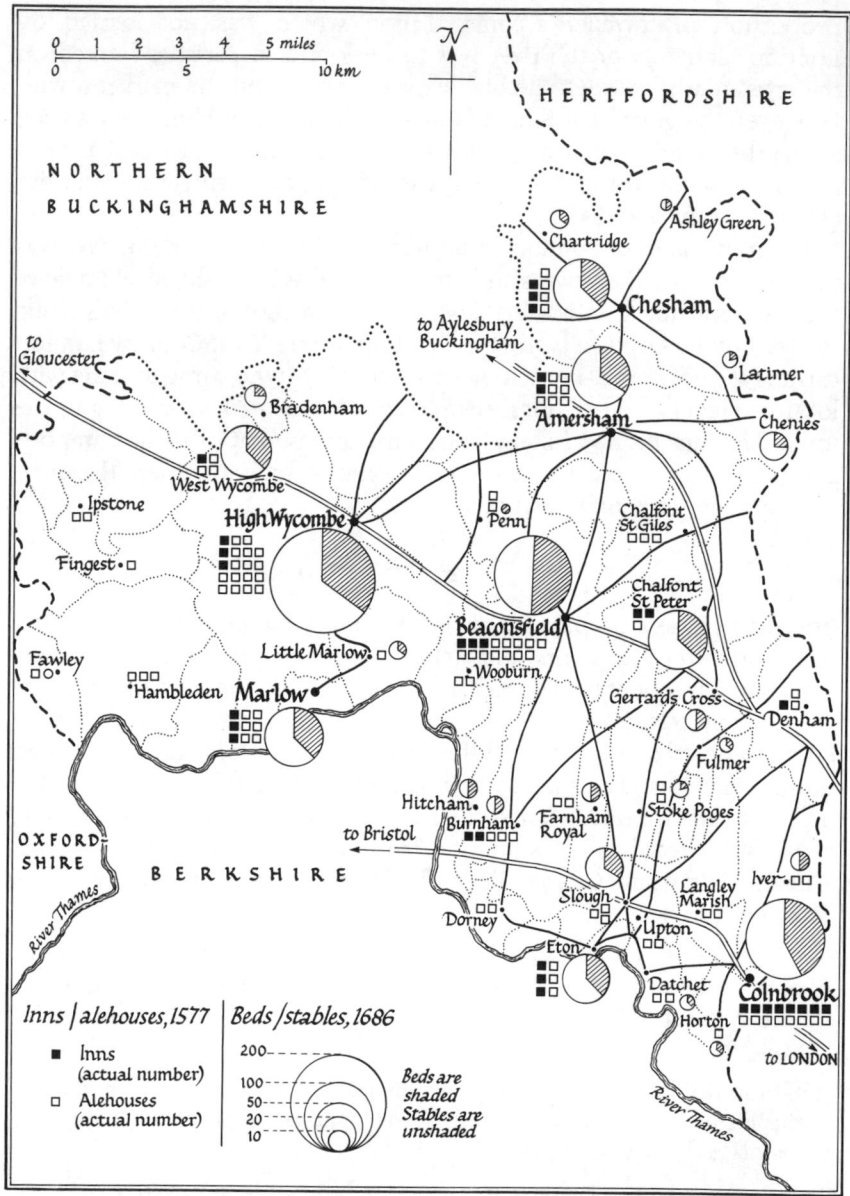

Map 6. Accommodation for travellers in inns and alehouses in the Chilterns in 1577 and 1686

pamphlet *Truth Cleared of Scandals* to Quakers in London for printing, and later transported 100 copies of the same to a Badsley Quaker for distribution.[23] In this case the carrier took a considerable risk. The relationship between Quakers and their carriers was one of trust, and perhaps the same was true of earlier dissenters.

We know that carriers distributed godly books printed in London to country readers. The account and memorandum book kept by John Tayer, a Thornbury shoemaker in the early seventeenth century, contains a list of 'printed Bookes in my howse at Kinton Farme the xth of August 1627'.[24] Aside from Bibles and several books of psalms, and some classical works, John Tayer read godly books: Arthur Dent's *Plain Mans Pathway to Heaven*, *The Garden of Spiritual Flowers*, *A Godly Garden of Comfortable Herbs*, and a sermon by Joseph Hall published in 1624 titled *The Peace Maker*.[25] John Tayer's books were bought for him in Bristol by his brother Edward. Some may have been delivered to Bristol by John Montaine, a London carrier of Bristol who died in 1618. His probate inventory shows us that he was a prosperous carrier worth £134 11s 4d on his death, who owned fourteen horses and their carrying equipment worth £11 9s, slept in a feather bed, cooked on brass, and ate from pewter. He also read chapbooks: six were found next to his bed by his assessors.[26] Another West Country carrier, Thomas Seyver of Eastington in Stroud Water, transported cloth to London and returned with psalters. On his death in 1559 he owed 5s to his London host at the Three Cups in Bread Street, 40s to John Fisher of Bread Street and 8s to Mr Parkington of Friday Street, the last two for psalters.[27] The close proximity of the Chiltern Hundreds to London and the existence of good communications to the capital suggests that this area was also readily supplied with London print.

It is possible to estimate the days of the week when London carriers from Buckinghamshire and the West Country passed through the Chiltern Hundreds on their way to and from the capital. The average distance of one day's travel by packhorse or waggon was about twelve miles in the later sixteenth and seventeenth centuries. By this reckoning, most of the sixty-two London carriers from Buckinghamshire and the West Country recorded in John Taylor's *Carriers Cosmographie* of 1637 travelled through

[23] Richard Farnworth (Leicestershire) to Francis Howgill and Edward Burrough (London), 17 October 1654, FL, Portfolio, 32/56. Richard Farnworth, *Truth Cleared of Scandals* (London, 1654).

[24] Glos. RO D3673.

[25] All of these books were printed in London. *The Garden of Spiritual Flowers* and *A Godly Garden of Comfortable Herbs* were sold in London in the 1620s by Robert Bird at the Sign of the Bible in Cheapside. See STC, III, p. 21.

[26] Bristol Record Office, Inventory, John Montaine 1618/49.

[27] Glos. RO, Will, Thomas Seyver 1559/290. I am very grateful to Caroline Litzenberger for this reference.

the Chilterns towards London in the middle of the week, and passed through early each following week on their way home. It may well have been at these times that locals congregated at the carriers' inns on the London highways, waiting for letters, books, and news from other parts of the country.[28]

Communication between Chiltern dissenters and those in other parts was further strengthened by the meeting of carriers from different parts at their London inns. London's inns were grouped at the end of the highways to the provinces they served, and in them carriers from different parts of the country met and exchanged news, letters, books, and other goods they carried.[29] The carriers from Buckingham, Aylesbury, and the Chiltern Hundreds stayed in the Holborn area, and in the lanes behind St Paul's. Many West Country carriers, who travelled the same London highways as their Buckinghamshire friends, also stayed in the inns at this end of the city. The Saracen's Head in Newgate, for example, catered for Buckinghamshire, Oxfordshire, and Gloucestershire carriers, while the George, the Crown, and the Three Cups in Bread Street catered for Berkshire, Somerset, and Gloucestershire carriers.[30]

The Bull and Mouth inn in Aldersgate, where provincial carriers lodged in the later seventeenth century, is of special interest. It was also the 'Great Meeting place' for London Quakers.[31] The Quakers rented the great hall of Northumberland House adjoining Aldersgate from 1655 to 1696, while the inn occupied the remaining buildings around the inner courtyard. For many years the Bull and Mouth was the scene of the fiercest persecution of Quakers. The Presbyterian Richard Baxter commented that the Quakers 'were so resolute, and gloried in their constancy and suffereings, that they assembled openly, at the Bull and Mouth near Aldersgate, and were dragged away daylie to the Common Goal, and yet desisted not'.[32] Thomas Ellwood was arrested there in October 1662. Quaker tracts were printed at the Bull and Mouth by Thomas Simmonds

---

[28] This estimate of carrier speed of travel is based on the average distances between all the stage towns listed in the road-books printed in Richard Grafton's *Litle Treatise* (London, 1571–1611) and Franke Adams' *Wryting Tables* (London, 1577–1628). John Taylor's *Carriers Cosmographie* (London, 1637) underestimates the number of weekly London carrier services. See Michael Frearson, 'The Distribution and Readership of Corantos in the 1620s', in Robin Myers and Michael Harris (eds.), *Serials and their Readers* (Winchester, 1993).

[29] J.A. Chartres, 'The Capital's Provincial Eyes: London's Inns in the Early Eighteenth Century', *The London Journal*, 3 (1977).

[30] Taylor, *Carriers Cosmographie*, gives details of the carriers' London inns and their days of arrival in the capital.

[31] Francis Howgill (London) to Margaret Fell (Lancashire) March 1655, cited by G. W. Edwards, 'The Bull and Mouth Meeting House, its Site and Environs', *Friends Quarterly*, 9 (1955), p. 78. Above, p. 63.

[32] *Reliquae Baxterianae*, II, pp. 435–7, cited by W. C. Braithwaite, *The Second Period of Quakerism* (2nd edn, Cambridge, 1961), p. 41.

during the Commonwealth period. In 1690, Jeremiah Rolph, the London carrier of High Wycombe, arrived at the Bull and Mouth each Monday.[33] One wonders what stories he was told by his host about the meetings the previous day, and whether he carried any Quaker literature back to Wycombe in his saddle bags.

[33] Thomas Deluane, *Angliae Metropolis* (London, 1690).

The descent of dissenters in the Chiltern Hundreds
NESTA EVANS

Now that the excellent, and frequent, communications both within Buckinghamshire and between the West Country and London through Buckinghamshire have been established, we can consider the possible stability of dissenting families within Buckinghamshire itself. Since the early nineteenth century, writers on Baptist history have been convinced that there were links between Lollards living in and around Amersham in the early sixteenth century, and dissenting congregations of Baptists and Quakers in the same area in the post-Restoration period. They based their belief on the coincidence of surnames between the early sixteenth- and late seventeenth-century dissenters.[1] Until now no one has attempted to prove that these connections really existed, and were anything more than a myth, so to remedy the lack of firm evidence the genealogical links between the two groups have been explored here.

More than a dozen years ago, Mr Michael Watts pointed out that although concrete evidence is lacking, there is a good deal of circumstantial evidence to suggest a link between Lollards and seventeenth-century General Baptists, by way of Tudor Anabaptists. Joan Bocher alias Joan of Kent provides evidence of one such link. In 1528 she was among the Lollards named by Foxe at Steeple Bumpstead in Essex, and in 1550 she was burnt as an Anabaptist. In this year a number of this persuasion were arrested at Steeple Bumpstead and the nearby clothing town of Bocking. Watts wrote that the 'strongest evidence to support the thesis of a continuing radical tradition linking the Lollards and Anabaptists of the early sixteenth century with the General Baptists of the seventeenth is geographic'. It is well known that this sect made rapid headway in the old Lollard strongholds of the Buckinghamshire Chilterns, the Weald of Kent, and the cloth-making towns of north Essex.[2]

---

[1] Adam Taylor, *The History of the English General Baptists*, vol. I: *The English Baptists of the Seventeenth Century* (London, 1818); J.H. Wood, *A Condensed History of the General Baptists of the New Connexion* (Leicester, 1847). W.H. Summers, *The Lollards of the Chiltern Hills* (London, 1906) and *Our Lollard Ancestors* (London, 1904).

[2] Michael R. Watts, *The Dissenters from the Reformation to the French Revolution* (Oxford, 1978), pp. 14–15.

What Watts says of Baptist links with Lollards is probably equally true of Quakers. As far as is known, there were no members of the Family of Love, or Familists, in the Chilterns, but it is interesting that George Fox's library, when he died, included books by the founder of the Familists, Hendrick Niclaes. Some of the Quaker tenets, initially propounded by Fox, were identical with those of the Family of Love. Both men had similar experiences: they were worried by the discrepancy between the church's claim that Christ takes away sin and the obvious imperfections of those claiming to be saved, and they believed that the leading of the Spirit took precedence over the Scriptures. Like the Lollards, the Family of Love was very much centred on families and households.[3]

As a working axiom, the assumption was made that the area from which the adherents of a 'gathered church' was drawn may well have largely coincided with marriage and marketing horizons. The number of market towns in Buckinghamshire remained remarkably stable between 1500 and 1800, with fewer declining into villages than in other counties, such as Lancashire, Staffordshire, and Suffolk.[4] People living in the Chiltern Hundreds were within easy reach of one or more market towns. In the late seventeenth century, Quarter Sessions were held at six Buckinghamshire towns, including Wendover, Chesham, and Amersham, and this was another factor drawing people to these central places.

We have already seen how seventeenth-century Buckinghamshire lay within the orbit of the London market for both foodstuffs and manufactured goods. Did the middle class of Restoration London sit on chairs made in the Chilterns, and wear Buckinghamshire lace? Certainly the rags of the London poor provided the raw material for the High Wycombe paper mills, which in turn supplied the London chapbook printers.[5] In Chesham and elsewhere, wet-nursing London children was another source of income. 'Nurse children' often appear in the burial registers of the Chiltern parishes.

Large scattered parishes are common in the Chilterns, and both Chesham and Amersham, with their numerous outlying hamlets, resemble the extensive parishes found in northern England. The comparative remoteness of these woodland hamlets may have assisted the growth of nonconformity, and provided a relatively safe haven for dissenters. Most of the Chiltern villages consisted of hamlets in woodland clear-

---

[3] See above, Ch. 4, pp. 214–15.
[4] Joan Thirsk (ed.), *Agrarian History of England and Wales*, V, part I (Cambridge, 1985), pp. 410–11; *Index Villaris* (London, 1690); *Great Britain's Vade Mecum* (1720); *Owen's New Book of Fairs* (London, 1792).
[5] Peter Earle, *The Making of the English Middle Class: Business, Society and Family Life in London, 1660–1730* (London, 1989); Margaret Spufford, *Small Books and Pleasant Histories: Popular Fiction and its Readership in Seventeenth-Century England* (London, 1981, p/b Cambridge, 1985).

ings, rather than nucleated settlements. Small open-field communities, such as Chalfont St Peter and Hedgerly, were sparsely populated and typical of townships supported by a poor forest-pasture economy. There was grazing for cattle, and pigs were fed on beech mast, but exploitation of the woodlands was the most important activity here.[6]

Population expansion in the early middle ages led to a reduction in the extent of the Chiltern woods, and the ploughing up of much land that later returned to pasture or woodland. By the seventeenth century the area was again sufficiently well wooded to supply the growing, local furniture trade.[7] Travellers from John Leland to Daniel Defoe all agree on the predominance of pasture and sheep in the Vale of Aylesbury, and of woods and enclosed fields in the Chilterns. In the later seventeenth century the tops of the Chilterns, which are quite extensive and reasonably flat, were ploughed up as a result of the sainfoin revolution on light land. By 1750 these areas were largely arable.[8]

These village communities were not solely dependent on agriculture, and the existence of alternative sources of employment allowed the Chilterns to support a large population. As well as the making of furniture and paper, lace making was a major industry in the county. Pillow or bone lace became very fashionable in the sixteenth and seventeenth centuries, and its manufacture was soundly established on a commercial basis in several counties, including Buckinghamshire, by the 1630s. At the same time, lace making was introduced in these areas as an employment for pauper children. By 1700, lace dealers claimed to employ over 100,000 women and children 'within this kingdom', some of whom earned 7s a week; even a child of six could earn 20d a week. The main centres of lace making in Buckinghamshire were in the north of the county around Olney and Newport Pagnell, but by the 1620s High Wycombe and Great Marlow were also important, and work was put out in the Chiltern villages. By 1700 there were over 200 lace dealers in the county, of whom more than 150 travelled regularly to London to sell lace.[9] Lace making has been described as the most important domestic industry in Buckinghamshire between 1640 and 1750. In the seventeenth century there were lace-making schools at Great Marlow and High Wycombe. When Defoe visited the county, Chesham was the main centre of manufacturing chairs and other items from beech, and this is confirmed by recent research.[10]

---

[6] Thirsk (ed.), *Agrarian History of England and Wales*, V, part I, p. 342.

[7] Pat Preece, 'Wood Products from the Oxfordshire Chilterns before 1830', *Local Historian*, 20, 2 (1990).

[8] Personal communication from Dr John Broad.

[9] G.F.R. Spenceley, 'The Origins of the English Pillow Lace Industry', *Agricultural History Review*, 21, 2 (1973).

[10] Thirsk (ed.), *Agrarian History of England and Wales*, V, part I, p. 348.

As a rule there is a reasonable coincidence between marketing areas, marriage horizons, and the catchment areas of hiring fairs, but unfortunately, there are no records of seventeenth-century hiring fairs in the Chilterns. The parish registers seldom indicate the place of residence of brides and grooms, and there are no sources such as records of horse sales or market courts, or burgess rolls. Dr Frearson has used settlement papers to good effect to demonstrate mobility into these towns, however.[11]

The general conclusion to be drawn from studies of surname distribution, marriage horizons, and marketing areas is that intense local movement takes place mainly within a radius of five to ten miles.[12] There seems no reason why it should not be assumed that the catchment area of a dissenting chapel or 'gathered church' will to a large extent coincide with the local marriage and marketing area.

Analogies with other regions can be drawn on. At Colyton in Devon few marriage partners travelled more than ten miles, but artisans tended to travel further for contacts than did farmers or labourers, because they needed to go to the next little town to find their own kind. Equally, when artisans moved they tended to travel further than rural workers in search of work. In the early nineteenth century, Colyton dissenters travelled further in search of marriage partners, as well as for other purposes, than the population at large.[13]

It would be rash to extrapolate this last finding back to Buckinghamshire in the seventeenth century, when rather than having difficulty in finding partners, dissenters were spoilt for choice in places such as Amersham. In any case there is too little evidence about seventeenth-century dissenting marriages in the county to reach any conclusion about marriage horizons. But we also know that much earlier dissenters travelled sometimes vast distances to find a suitable partner. The extreme example is probably that of the Lollard woman who travelled from Coventry to Kent in the 1490s, finding a marriage partner in London on the way.[14]

Nonconformist congregations, of whatever denomination, were long accustomed to travel to chapels or meeting-houses, for these were not organized on the parish system of the Church of England. In Buckinghamshire, Quaker meeting-houses were mainly found in towns, while some of the Baptist chapels were in rural villages. Margaret Spufford describes market towns as 'the inevitable gathering-centres' for dissenters. She found that in seventeenth-century Cambridgeshire, small market towns such as Gamlingay, Linton, and Soham tended to be centres of

[11] See above, Map 5 and p. 276.
[12] See below, pp. 309–10.
[13] Personal communication from Dr Richard Wall.
[14] See above, p. 55.

dissent, not just because dissent flourished among the artisans who lived in these towns, but because villagers from some miles around were accustomed to travel to them regularly to attend market, and they were also the natural focus of local roads and tracks.[15]

Recent work by Dr Stevenson on late seventeenth-century dissenters in Bedfordshire, Cambridgeshire, and Huntingdonshire shows that both Baptists and Quakers in these counties were predominantly rural dwellers, and yet supports Margaret Spufford's view of market towns as the natural foci for dissent. In the post-Restoration period, nonconformist chapels existed in all the six market towns of Huntingdonshire or in their rural hinterland. For example, Fenstanton, which lies near St Ives, had a General Baptist chapel.[16] The bulk of the members of a gathered church will have lived within travelling distance of their chapel.

The twenty-one parishes covered by the Quaker Upperside Meeting in Buckinghamshire were selected to study the continuity of religious dissent (Map 7) as this area coincided suggestively with the district where Lollards had been most numerous in the early sixteenth century (Map 2). This Quaker meeting covered the Chiltern district of Buckinghamshire, which as we have already seen was particularly suitable for industrial growth and thus able to support a growing population. In the employment opportunities it offered, it resembled districts such as the Forest of Arden, Myddle in Shropshire, and the wood-pasture region of East Anglia.[17]

The scattered nature of many of the parishes may have provided suitable conditions for the development of nonconformity. Several of the market towns, notably Amersham and Chesham, included hamlets within their parish boundaries and these may well have provided suitable meeting-places for small dissenting groups. There were ten hamlets in the parish of Chesham, excluding the separate parish of Chesham Bois. In the seventeenth century the hamlet of Coleshill, although part of the ecclesiastical parish of Amersham, was an outlying portion of Hertfordshire. Its position made it relatively safe from interference by the authorities of both counties, and explains the choice of Thomas Ellwood's house there at Hunger Hill as a Quaker meeting-place.

A recent article about Coleshill in the seventeenth century anatomizes the social structure of this hamlet.[18] Around 1640 there were thirty-eight

---

[15] Margaret Spufford, *Contrasting Communities: English Villagers in the Sixteenth and Seventeenth Centuries* (Cambridge, 1974).

[16] William Stevenson, 'The Economic and Social Status of Protestant Sectaries in Huntingdonshire, Cambridgeshire and Bedfordshire (1650–1725)' (Cambridge, PhD, 1990).

[17] Victor Skipp, *Crisis and Development* (Cambridge, 1978); David G. Hey, *An English Rural Community: Myddle under the Tudors and Stuarts* (Leicester, 1974).

[18] John Chenevix Trench, 'The Houses of Coleshill: The Social Anatomy of a Seventeenth-Century Village', *Records of Buckinghamshire*, 25 (1983), pp. 61–109.

identified houses there, occupied by eighteen freeholders and twenty-three tenants, of whom seven held long leases. A breakdown of the social status of the heads of household shows that three were gentlemen, seventeen yeomen, eight husbandmen and one was a widow. In addition there were six engaged in trade, two labourers and four whose status is unknown. This is a most unusual social structure. Its strong bias towards the middling and better sort, and the preponderance of freeholders and long leaseholders must have made Coleshill an ideal environment for independence of thought and action.

However, the line of argument that the comparative remoteness of the Chiltern woodland hamlets with their abundance of freeholders may have assisted the growth of nonconformity, and provided a relatively safe haven for dissenters, cannot be pushed too far. Much of what we know about these people, from Lollards to seventeenth-century dissenters, comes directly from ecclesiastical records, which show them being burnt, imprisoned, or fined for their beliefs. The long arm of the church and civil courts could and did reach into the fastnesses of the Chiltern woodlands.

Table 2 shows where meeting-houses were registered in 1672. The list of those registered in 1689 differs from the earlier one, but is interesting as it shows that several lay in outlying hamlets. At Princes Risborough eight houses were licensed, only three of which were in the town. Two stood at Loosely Row, and there was one each at Lacyes Green, Darvall's Hill, and Speen. As it happened, there had been a Lollard meeting at Speen in 1530. Three houses were licensed in Chesham town, where there had also been Lollard meetings, another at the hamlet of Whelply Hill and yet another at Ley Green. In the old Lollard centre of Amersham there were two meeting-houses in the town and a third at Woodrow. Even there, Lollards had lived and met. One of the pair in the town itself was a two-hearth house belonging to Joseph Winch, which was licensed as a Quaker meeting-place in 1689, by which time the cottage had been enlarged by one bay to form a meeting-house (Plate 7). Quakers seem often to have felt privacy was desirable for meeting-houses. Jordans, the oldest Quaker meeting-house in the south of England, stands in a remote part of Chalfont St Giles parish; the barn licensed at Burnham was described as being in the 'Wood Liberty', and at Great Missenden the house licensed was at Prestwood.[19]

Dissent in Buckinghamshire flourished not only in the Chiltern region, with its many craftsmen, but also in the north-east of the county on the border with Bedfordshire. The Baptists were far more numerous than the Quakers in this second area, perhaps due to the influence of John

---

[19] Source for 1689 licences for meeting-houses: Buckinghamshire: An Inventory of Non-Conformist Chapels, Meeting-Houses in Central England, Royal Commission for Historic Monuments, HMSO (1986).

Plate 7. *Joseph Winch's cottage, licensed for a Quaker meeting in 1689, Amer-*
sham, Buckinghamshire, with eighteenth-century additions

Bunyan. The Buckinghamshire Lollards were concentrated in the Thames
valley and the Chilterns, so the north of the county would not have made
a suitable comparative study area.

The area of the Quaker Upperside Meeting was chosen to trace the
possible movements of families who were known dissenters in the early
sixteenth century, to see if there was indeed a linear connection with
Quakers or Baptists of the same surname in the later seventeenth century.
In the first place, it was important to demonstrate whether there was
more continuity among surnames of Lollards and Baptists or Quakers
than among the population at large, and secondly whether it is possible
to connect families of radical dissenting opinions from later Lollards to
early post-Restoration dissenters.[20]

In order to discover if this could be done, several different procedures
were undertaken. First, the names of all those assessed for the Lay Subsidy
of 1524 who were living in the twenty-one parishes of the study area
were indexed by name and by parish of residence. For the later seventeenth century there is no listing as comprehensive as the 1524 Subsidy.
The Hearth Tax returns for Buckinghamshire are in poor condition, and
lists of the exempt exist for only a few parishes. The best year for the

---

[20] See Appendix B for details of parish registers investigated, and family names
selected.

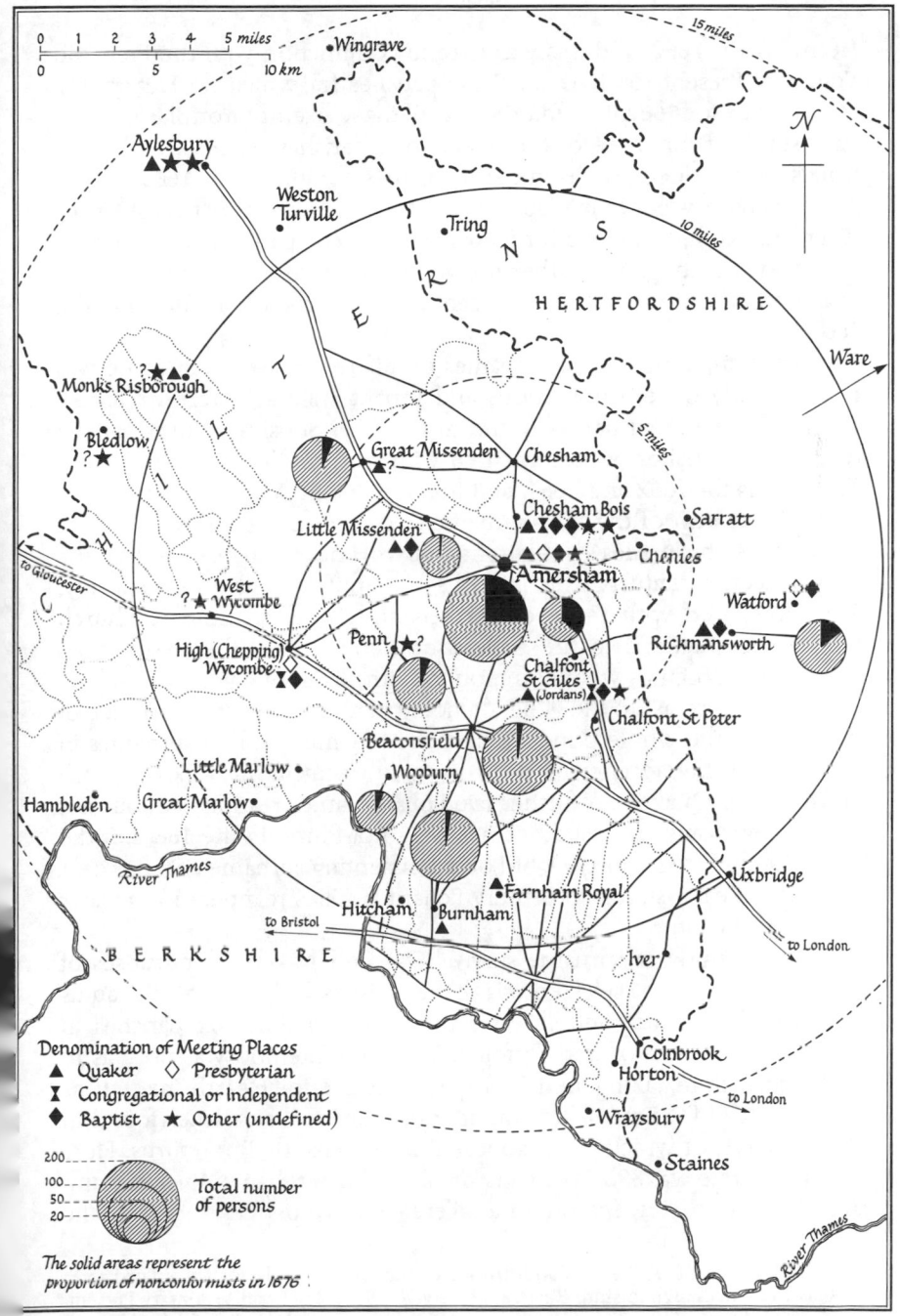

Map 7. The Upperside Quaker Meeting and the strength of nonconformity in the Chilterns in 1676 and 1689

Hearth Tax is 1662, and this was used in conjunction with the Free and Voluntary Present for 1661 for those parishes for which no Hearth Tax returns exist for 1662. In addition, lists of those exempt from Hearth Tax have survived for three of the twenty-one parishes in 1664, and these names were added to the index of names for the early 1660s.[21] The same exercise was carried out for the Hertfordshire parishes of Tring, Rickmansworth, and Watford, which formed part of the Quaker Upperside Meeting. No further use was made of the Hertfordshire material, except to note that 22.5 per cent of 1524 surnames recurred in the 1660s.

When comparing lists of surnames of different dates, each name was counted only once; duplications and variant spellings were excluded. When all the 521 surnames found in the 1524 Subsidy returns for the twenty-one parishes were compared with all those listed in the Hearth Tax returns for 1662 and 1664, and in the Free and Voluntary Present of 1661, 29 per cent of the 1524 surnames recurred in the 1660s.

Secondly, the names of fifty-nine known Lollards persecuted in the early sixteenth century, which had been identified in the 1524 subsidy, were compared with those of Quakers and Baptists found in church lists or presentations to the ecclesiastical courts after the Restoration. Forty-eight surnames were common to both dissenting groups.

In strong contrast to the general finding of a 29 per cent recurrence of surnames in the whole population, of the fifty-nine Lollard surnames in the 1524 Subsidy, forty-eight, or 81 per cent, recur in the 1660s as those of Baptists or Quakers. A further five Lollard names reappeared, but not as dissenters; only six Lollard names were not found in the 1660s. If the five are added to the forty-eight Lollard dissenting surnames, 90 per cent of names of early sixteenth-century Lollard families reappear in the later seventeenth century.

A second study of surname survival was undertaken for purposes of comparison. The area selected was all the parishes within a six-mile radius of Haverhill in south Suffolk. This encompassed thirty-six parishes in Cambridgeshire, Essex, and Suffolk.[22] The same method was used as in Buckinghamshire, taking the 1524 Lay Subsidy and the Hearth Tax returns for 1674 (1673 for Essex). The number of individual surnames found in 1524 was 541, of which 215 reappeared in the Hearth Tax returns. Here the survival rate was 39.74 per cent, markedly higher than in Buckinghamshire. The most likely reason for a difference of 10 per cent between the

---

[21] A.C. Chibnall and A. Vere Woodman (eds.), *Subsidy Roll for the County of Buckingham Anno 1524*, Buckinghamshire Records Society, 8 (1950); Free and Voluntary Present, 1661–2, PRO E179/80/333; Hearth Tax, 1662, PRO E179/80/345, 348, 350; Hearth Tax, 1664, PRO E179/80/358.
[22] See Appendix A.

two areas is that the Hearth Tax returns for the second are in far better condition and include the names of those exempt from the tax.

The parish of Chesham offers unusual opportunities to look more closely at the survival of surnames, and over a longer period than was done for the population of all the parishes in the study area. In 1606 a special church rate was levied for repewing the parish church. The contributors to this rate were listed by Richard Bowle, as were those who paid nothing towards it. In addition Bowle also carefully noted the names of those allotted places after the church had been reseated, and in what part of the building they were placed. Two rate books, dated 1650 and 1671–2, have survived from the middle years of the seventeenth century, and the Buckinghamshire *Posse Comitatus* for 1798 is in print.[23] Finally an up-to-date telephone directory was checked to see how many of the surnames found in the 1520s were still borne by present-day residents in Chesham.

By using the 1522 Musters, as well as the 1524 Lay Subsidy, 122 separate surnames were found in Chesham.[24] Forty-eight of these appeared in Bowle's lists of contributors to the special rate, of persons who paid nothing and of parishioners given seats in the church; that is 39 per cent of the early 1520s names. Most of the names which appear in the two rate books and the 1662 Hearth Tax appear in all three sources, so these three have been treated as one. Of the forty-eight names surviving to 1606, thirty-two, or two-thirds, were still there in the third quarter of the seventeenth century. Over a hundred years later, in 1798, twenty-seven (56 per cent) of the forty-eight names of 1606 were still present in Chesham. The twenty-seven include four names which were not found between 1524 and 1798, so if these are discarded a more accurate survival rate is just under half (48 per cent). The 1990 telephone directory lists twenty-six of the twenty-seven names found in the *Posse Comitatus* of 1798, that is 54 per cent of the forty-eight names found in 1606. Only one name has disappeared from Chesham in nearly two centuries, and that is still to be found in the neighbourhood of the town.

Amongst the forty-eight Chesham names, eleven were those of Lollard families, which were also dissenters in the late seventeenth century; they formed 23 per cent of the whole group. In 1798, nine of the eleven Lollard names were found in Chesham, giving a survival rate of 82 per cent. In 1990 these nine names were still present in the town, so of the

---

[23] 'Richard Bowle's Book', transcribed by J.W. Garrett-Pegge, *Records of Buckinghamshire*, 9 (1909), pp. 329–48, 393–414; Bucks. RO Acc. 38/58 (L) Box 6; Ian F. W. Beckett (ed.), *The Buckinghamshire Posse Comitatus 1798*, Buckinghamshire Record Society, 22 (1985).

[24] A.C. Chibnall (ed.), *The Certificate of Musters for Buckinghamshire for 1522*, Buckinghamshire Records Society, 15 (1973).

twenty-six names which have survived there for nearly 500 years, nine (35 per cent) were those of long-term dissenting families.

The survival rate for the population at large in Chesham was naturally lower than for all twenty-one parishes.[25] An analysis of these census type documents for one parish has also made apparent the unsurprising fact that families disappear from a parish only to reappear there later. Others, which were not present in the 1520s, are there by the early seventeenth century if not sooner, and then persist over two centuries.

In order to test whether the stability of the Buckinghamshire Lollard families was unusual, a control group from the same twenty-one parishes was selected. The group chosen was all those assessed at £5 or more in 1524. This produced 311 individuals, giving a total of 215 names when duplicates and variants had been eliminated. This group made up 41.5 per cent of all the names in the 1524 Subsidy for the study area. Ninety-seven (45 per cent) of these 215 names reappeared in the same 1660s sources as were used for the population at large. A higher survival rate for the richest fifth of the 1524 taxpayers is a result which might be expected, but is still much lower than the 90 per cent for the fifty-nine Lollard surnames found in 1524. Lollards were therefore even more stable than the most prosperous section of rural society, which is usually the most stable.

The next step was to consider whether the Lollards did belong to this most prosperous and settled section of early modern society, or were indeed the most prosperous. There were twenty-seven Lollard surnames amongst those assessed at £5 or more in 1524, that is 13 per cent of this group, and twenty-three (85 per cent) of these names were found in the 1660s. Amongst these twenty-seven Lollard surnames were nineteen known Lollards, or 9 per cent of the 215 names of wealthy 1524 taxpayers. The much higher survival rate for the names of taxpayers who were both assessed at £5 or more in 1524 and were Lollards serves to underline the remarkable continuity of Lollard names.

But the known Lollards assessed in 1524 were by no means all amongst the most prosperous taxpayers. Six were assessed at £1 and ten at £2, and five of these sixteen were taxed on wages. These sixteen poorer individuals are 37 per cent of the known Lollards whose names were found in the 1524 Subsidy return. The five assessed on wages make up 11.5 per cent of all known Lollards. To sum up:

29 per cent of all the 1524 surnames in twenty-one parishes recur in the 1660s.

45 per cent of all surnames in the same twenty-one parishes assessed at £5 or more in 1524 reappear in the 1660s.

[25] See Table 8, below, pp. 315–16, and pp. 324–6.

90 per cent of all Lollard surnames in the same parishes are listed in the 1660s.

81 per cent of 1524 Lollard surnames were borne by Baptists or Quakers in the later seventeenth century.

The sources used for the above analysis are biased towards the better-off, and more stable sections of early modern society; this is especially so of the documents used for the 1660s. Had full Hearth Tax returns, including the exempt, survived for the whole of the study area, a higher percentage of all 1524 surnames might have been found. Even so, nine (56 per cent) of the surnames of Lollards assessed at £2 or less in 1524 recur in the 1660s.

It was shown above that the families of the richest fifth of the taxpayers of 1524 were more stable than the population at large in twenty-one Buckinghamshire parishes. This does not explain the remarkable coincidence between Lollard and dissenting names, for Dr Plumb found many servants and landless labourers amongst the Lollards mentioned by Foxe (Table 4), and 37 per cent (sixteen) of the known Lollards taxed in 1524 were assessed at £2 or less. We have already seen that south Buckinghamshire in the sixteenth and seventeenth centuries was certainly not a remote area, where a slower than usual turnover in population might be expected. There is ample evidence of links between Buckinghamshire Lollards and Quakers and their co-religionists in London, as well as trade between the Chilterns and London.[26]

The astonishingly high degree of stability amongst the surnames of late Lollards and post-Restoration dissenters is therefore not only quite different from that of local society in general in the region, and even from the most prosperous elements of it, but is also completely unexpected in view of the excellent communications of south Buckinghamshire.

In view of this conclusive demonstration of such a high degree of stability in the area of the Quaker Upperside Meeting, the next step was to attempt to make actual, genealogical connections between late Lollards and early Baptists and Quakers in the same area through five or six generations. From the fifty-three surnames which were borne first by known Lollards, and later by Quakers or Baptists, the nineteen most distinctive were selected for further study. All marriages for these nineteen names were traced in the surviving registers of the twenty-one parishes in the study area.[27] Given the constraints of time, it was very encouraging to

[26] See above, Map 5 and pp. 58, 62–3, 277–83.
[27] Dr Richard McKinley kindly advised on which of the fifty-three names were most useful for the study of continuity; six of these are among the selected nineteen. Unfortunately, many of the most distinctive Buckinghamshire surnames are not those of dissenters. The genealogies of the families which have been linked, together with other information about them, are in Appendix B.

find that it was possible to connect six families within this group in the male line.

The methods used to link families were basically those used by genealogists. Work started at both ends, in the early sixteenth and the late seventeenth centuries, thus working both forwards and backwards from the known. The points of departure were Dr Derek Plumb's list of Lollards, and known post-Restoration dissenters. Apart from the fact that some parish registers in the study area begin too late to be of use, and are only partly compensated for by bishops' transcripts, there are serious gaps during the Interregnum and no register starts earlier than 1537. Furthermore, the vital events of the lives of Quakers and Baptists will not be found in Anglican parish registers. Baptist church books record some burials and adult baptisms; Quaker records are superior, but even so, are patchy for the seventeenth century. Wills were therefore as important as registers in tracing families, but inevitably biased the search to those who felt they needed to bequeath something.

Other sources used were parish records, other than registers, the Visitation Books of the Archdeaconry of Buckingham, the original episcopal returns of 1669, and Quaker minute books and books of sufferings. A search was also made of manorial and estate records, but, apart from the discovery of copies of two seventeenth-century rate books for Chesham amongst the papers of the Cavendish estate there, no relevant material was found.

The procedures used to link dissenting families over 150 years have two major limitations: they are less likely to trace the undoubtedly extremely important passing of radical religious opinion through female lines; and the families which are traceable through a century and a half are more likely to be the more prosperous families, which are established with land. But despite this, one of the six linked, reassuringly, is a labouring family, the Dells of Chesham.

The fact that continuity can more easily be established for prosperous families in no way contradicts the findings of Dr Plumb and Dr Stevenson on the complete economic cross-section of the distribution of dissent both among Lollards, and Quakers and Baptists. It only means that it is less easy in general to trace poorer, and therefore more mobile, dissenters, who moved further and more frequently. In any case, this is delightfully undermined by the poor Dells of Chesham.

Women were important in dissenting sects, as has been shown by the work of Sir Keith Thomas on dissenting women and of Professor Claire Cross on Lollard preachers. Dr Plumb's thesis on the Lollards of the Thames valley indicates that women played a considerable part in the early sixteenth-century Lollard community of Buckinghamshire.[28] In

---

[28] Keith Thomas, 'Women and the Civil War Sects', in Trevor Ashton (ed.), *Crisis in Europe 1560–1660* (London, 1965). Claire Cross, 'Great Reasoners in Scripture: The

addition, Margaret Spufford's *Contrasting Communities* demonstrates their importance in seventeenth-century dissent, as does Dr Stevenson's thesis. The lack of information about the descent of dissent through female lines may to some extent be cancelled out by endogamous marriage. A study of marriage in Amersham and Chesham showed a high incidence, particularly in the former, of marriage between dissenting couples.

As the people most likely to teach children reading at home and in dame schools,[29] women are crucial to the transmission of dissenting religious beliefs. The ability to read is difficult to quantify, but it is thought that a considerable number of seventeenth-century women possessed this skill.

Professor Cross and Dr Hudson have shown the important part played by women in Lollardy, and the early records of dissenting churches provide ample evidence of the numerical importance of women amongst their members.[30] Dr Christopher Marsh's research into the Family of Love in Cambridgeshire has established the deep involvement of women in this group.[31] At Fenstanton, Dr Stevenson found that of 184 members baptized into the Baptist Church there between 1645 and 1692, just over 50 per cent were women. At least twenty-three seem to have joined the church together with their husbands, but it was also common here and elsewhere for women to precede their menfolk in joining a dissenting congregation. Between 1652 and 1681, eighty-three individuals were received into the Independent Church at Beccles in East Suffolk; fifty-one (61.5 per cent) of these were women, many of whom were widows.[32]

The seventeenth century, particularly its middle years, saw a great upsurge in published writings by women. An analysis of these publications shows that of 620 works written by women in this century, 285 (46 per cent) are concerned with religion in one way or another. The protestant stress on personal religious experience had encouraged women to keep records of their spiritual lives. One of the earliest of these to be published is the journal started by Lady Hoby in 1599. Quaker women were particularly active in writing; 177 (62 per cent) of the 285 books published by women in the seventeenth century were by female members of this sect, and of 300 women who published spiritual testimonies during the Interregnum, 220 were Quakers.[33] Early Quakerism actively

Activities of Women Lollards, 1380–1530', in Derek Baker (ed.), *Medieval Women*, Studies in Church History, Subsidia 1 (Oxford, 1979); Derek Plumb, 'John Foxe and the Later Lollards of the Mid-Thames Valley' (Cambridge, PhD, 1987).

[29] See Ch. 1, n. 230, p. 67 above.

[30] Cross, 'Great Reasoners'; Anne Hudson, *The Premature Reformation: Wycliffite Texts and Lollard History* (Oxford, 1988), pp. 181–3, 185, 191.

[31] Christopher W. Marsh, 'The Family of Love in English Society, 1550–1630' (Cambridge, PhD, 1991).

[32] Stevenson, 'Economic and Social Status', pp. 34, 354; Suff. RO (Lowestoft) 229/1.

[33] Patricia Crawford, 'Women's Published Writings 1600–1700', in Mary Prior (ed.), *Women in English Society 1500–1800* (London, 1985).

encouraged the participation of women, and separate Women's Meetings were established in a number of places, including the Buckinghamshire Quaker Upperside Meeting. Later Quakerism seems to have restricted the activities of female members.

The obvious importance of women to the transmission and support of dissent encouraged a search for continuity of religious dissent through female lines. For this purpose the marriages of women from the first five families to be traced from Lollards to late seventeenth-century dissenters were selected. Twenty-one women from these Lollard families chose as husbands men from other Lollard families, leaving another thirty-eight who married into families which eventually produced Baptists or Quakers, or both. Three female lines were successfully traced, and others partially so.[34] More than once descendants of Lollard women were found to have married back into families of Lollard origin.

Over twenty years ago Professor Alan Everitt wrote that 'The most satisfactory explanation of General Baptist strength in early eighteenth-century Kent, Sussex and Buckinghamshire is, though, that it represents the legacy of fifteenth- and early sixteenth-century Lollardy.' Professor Everitt also proposed that the survival of radical religious views in these areas was a result of their common characteristics: large parishes with weak manorial structure in forest areas, which provided opportunities for squatters.[35]

Michael Watts also suggested that Lollardy, Elizabethan Separatism, and post-Restoration dissent all appealed chiefly to those who were economically independent. He thought that 'the association between economic and religious independence was chiefly a characteristic of urban areas', but this is surely also true of rural areas, where freeholds and local industries freed men from social and economic pressures just as surely as in towns.[36]

Even if there was a causal connection between being a dissenter and a freeholder in some parts of the country, this cannot be conclusively demonstrated even in Buckinghamshire, where two parts of a Poll Book for the county election in 1685 have survived; they list 63 per cent of the voters. Despite this remarkable survival of an early source offering an opportunity for correlation, the connection cannot be checked, for radical beliefs caused, or could possibly cause, practical disenfranchisement. Until 1696, when they were allowed to affirm, Quakers could not swear an oath. It is therefore probably not significant that although I abstracted

---

[34] See Appendix B for the descendants of Martha Gate of Chesham and Isabel Child of Amersham, and the ancestors of Margaret Tredway (née West).

[35] Quoted in Michael R. Watts, *The Dissenters: From the Reformation to the French Revolution* (Oxford, 1978).

[36] Ibid.

the names of the 388 voters who lived in the parishes of the Quaker Upperside Meeting, only thirteen names of dissenters were found. Six of these can be firmly linked with known Quakers or Baptists, and the other seven were probably dissenters. But we still cannot state, despite this very low correlation between freeholders and dissenting voters, because of the oath possibly involved in voting, that there was no causal connection between the security involved in being a freeholder, and the adoption of radical opinions. We simply do not know. On the other hand, it may be suggestive that the surviving Poll Book nowhere has written 'jurat' or 'affirmavit' by the name of the voter. If they were not asked to swear, there was no causal connection between freeholding, and the liberty to be a dissenter.

The 388 voters did include twenty-eight (59 per cent) of the fifty-three Lollard names which had survived into the later seventeenth century. When the Poll Book was compared with the 1524 Lay Subsidy return, it was found that twenty-three (85 per cent) of the surnames borne by Lollards who were assessed at £5 or more in 1524 re-appeared as voters in 1685. This high survival rate is significant, for only 20 per cent of non-Lollard taxpayers assessed at £5 and over bore the same names as freeholders in 1685. The high level of freeholders among Lollard families may be a reason why they were static.

Dr Anne Hudson, writing on Lollard history, suggests that 'if the community were united in unorthodoxy ... heresy would go unrecorded'. Certainly, our knowledge of Lollards is based almost entirely on the records of persecution and heresy trials, and to a lesser extent we rely on similar records for information about later dissenters. She quotes from Drs Heal and O'Day: 'the depressing possibility that the records indicate only the distribution of small minorities of dissenters and that areas of widespread dissent often pass unrecorded'.[37] This could well be true of parts of Cambridgeshire and East Anglia in the early sixteenth century, even though Dr Carlson shows it was not true of Chilford and Radfield Hundreds in Cambridgeshire after the Restoration (Chapter 4).

Dr Hudson is convinced of the importance of the family in passing on Lollard tenets, and sees it, or rather the household, as the centre of Lollard society. She suggests that in many cases the village was the 'larger circle' of Lollardy, citing as examples the south Norfolk villages of Earsham and Loddon, from which came many of the Lollards tried by the Bishop of Norwich in 1428–31.[38] May this not also have been true of some of the villages and towns of the Buckinghamshire Chilterns in the

---

[37] Hudson, *Premature Reformation*, p. 35, quoting from F. Heal and R. O'Day (eds.), *Church and Society in England Henry VIII to James I* (London, 1977).
[38] Hudson, *Premature Reformation*, p. 134.

early sixteenth century and, indeed, of the Familist village of Balsham in Cambridgeshire later in the century?

Another interesting link between Lollardy and later dissent is the own-ership of Wycliffite texts by men of puritan outlook, such as Francis Russell, Earl of Bedford, in 1566. St John's College, Cambridge, was given a volume containing Wycliffite sermons by John Gent, whose family came from Steeple Bumpstead in Essex.[39]

Dr Hudson makes the point that after about 1440 it was the Lollard community that fostered and maintained heresy, and individual teachers ceased to be important in this respect. The superficial conformity of most late medieval Lollards may have lulled the authorities into thinking that Lollardy had disappeared. This may explain why there were so few pro-secutions for heresy between 1440 and the 1480s, and why the persecu-tion of Lollards was geographically so patchy in the early sixteenth cen-tury.[40] Given the known propensity of Lollards to travel, the considerable number of late seventeenth-century dissenters in the area around Linton and Balsham in Cambridgeshire and Haverhill in Suffolk, and the pres-ence of Familists in these Cambridgeshire villages in the reign of Elizabeth I, it seems improbable that Lollardy did not exist in these places at the same time as it came under attack just over the border in Essex. However much the existence of Lollards may be suspected in Cambridgeshire and Suffolk, there is no way of proving their presence in the face of lack of activity, or at least of surviving records of any anti-Lollard action, by the Bishops of Norwich and Ely.[41]

Dr Hudson says that the Lollard communities persecuted on either side of 1500 'give every indication of being of long standing', and demon-strates the continuity between Lollards of the early and later periods.[42] If Lollards already had a long experience of surviving in difficult circum-stances, this increases the likelihood that they would continue to survive, if not as Lollards, at least as people with minds open to dissenting ideas, after the Reformation.

Unfortunately, there is little evidence of continuing dissenting beliefs or activity in the Buckinghamshire Chilterns between the early Tudor Lollard trials, and the appearance of dissenting sects in the middle of the seventeenth century. It is virtually impossible to trace the transmission of dissenting views and beliefs, or of a dissenting cast of mind, through five or six generations, because of the patchiness, in this area, of the ecclesiastical records. Nothing survives between 1584–6 and 1633–4.

[39] Ibid., p. 207.
[40] Ibid., chapter 10. This view of the importance of the stable core of the community in nurturing dissent has recently been heavily underwritten by Dr Richard Davies.
[41] See below, Appendix A.
[42] Hudson, *Premature Reformation*, p. 456.

However, a surprising, and possibly suspicious, number of 'our' families were named in 1633–4.[43] The best source of information is the visitation records of the Archdeaconry of Buckingham, but these cover only a few years. The earliest surviving document is the churchwardens' presentments for 1584–6. The majority of cases were sexual offences, although a few persons were presented for not attending church. It is unsafe to assume that people absented themselves from church only if they were Roman Catholic recusants or dissenters; there must always have been a few individuals who did not believe that church attendance was necessary, as well as those who did not go because of laziness, drunkenness, or similar reasons. Some non-church goers disliked their parish priest; for instance William Tuchle of Chesham Bois had not been to church for three months and had refused to receive Communion because the minister was not a preacher. In this instance, puritanism seems a likely motive. At Chesham, also in 1584–6, Henry Dell, a member of one of 'our' Lollard families who reappeared as post-Restoration dissenters, was presented for 'disquieting our minister in the time of the communion', but we are not told why he did this. Some clergy were strongly criticized, particularly the curate at Chalfont St Giles, who was described as a swearer, who did not catechize the children, failed to say service on Wednesdays and Fridays, and whose daughters were called harlots.[44]

After 1584–6 no other visitation records survive for the Archdeaconry of Buckingham until 1633–4. This book, and subsequent ones, uses the word 'recusant' to describe some of those who refused to attend church. It is not always clear whether 'recusant' is being used in its modern sense of a Roman Catholic who refused to attend church, particularly as occasionally the phrase 'popish recusant' is found. In 1633 there were presentments for not attending church in nine of the parishes in the study area. Amongst these presentments are ten names from our short list of nineteen. At Chesham a Dell was once more in trouble, this time Richard senior for not going to church for a whole year. At Chalfont St Peter, James Nash was presented three times for absenting himself from afternoon service in his own parish church. On the third occasion he produced an excuse: he had been at Hampden church 'awooing' his wife, who lived there; now that they were married, he would attend his parish church. Thomas Fryer and William Widmore, who were both churchwardens of High Wycombe, absented themselves, along with the other wardens. At Great Missenden, George Weedon and his wife, John Weedon, and John Hoare were presented for not attending church. We

---

[43] See below, pp. 306, 394–6, and above, p. 35.
[44] Bucks. RO D/A/V/1(b) Churchwardens' presentments 1584–5: William Tuchle, fol. 29v; Henry Dell, fol. 47v.

may perhaps omit Lazarus Dell of Little Missenden from consideration, despite his extremely interesting and suggestive Christian name which argues family conviction, because he was presented for incontinency. Possibly he was a disappointment to a 'godly' family, however. Walter Tredway and his wife of Amersham were to appear at a later court. Finally, Nathan Harding, whose name must again be significant, was presented for marrying clandestinely in London, which certainly sounds like a sectarian marriage.[45]

The Visitation Book for 1636–7 contains the most interesting entry of all under Woobum, where Thomas Hornblow was presented for receiving Alice Longe widow and her son John Cardwell 'with divers others, which keepe their meettings or Conventicles'. There is no other information about this conventicle, except that Alice Longe was presented in her home parish of Great Marlow for attending it. It could well have been a Baptist meeting, and in any case it is too early for any of the other sects which first appeared in the seventeenth century. Unfortunately, nothing is known of the three individuals named. In the same Visitation Book Nathaniel and Thomas Dell of Chesham were presented 'for keeping houses of disorderly meetinge of strangers & others in tyme of divine service whose names we know not'. Does this refer to a conventicle or to an alehouse? In this Visitation Book there are presentments for frequenting alehouses or drinking in private houses during service time, but the wording of the Chesham case seems to be unique. On balance it seems more probable that the Dells were conducting a conventicle rather than keeping an alehouse. Richard Dell of Chesham who had been a non-attender in 1633, was still in trouble for not attending church.[46]

The evidence for dissent, in what was to become the Quaker Upperside Meeting area, in the three Visitation Books for the 1630s is suspicious, if not convincing. Also, presentments depended on the churchwardens and, if they were sympathetic to the views of dissident parishioners, they may have been slack in reporting backsliding in such matters as church attendance. The existence of a conventicle at Woobum, and of a probable one at Chesham, is most significant, particularly if this was the tip of an iceberg.

Much later, between 1680 and 1689, the presentments made by the churchwardens of Sarratt just over the border in Hertfordshire make interesting reading. Several members of the Upperside Quaker Meeting lived at Sarratt. In 1680 the churchwardens, in answer to the question concerning parishioners, said 'Who can tell what to say concerning this?

---

[45] Bucks. RO D/A/V/2 Visitations 1633–4.
[46] Bucks. RO D/A/V/4 Visitations 1636–7: Nathaniel and Thomas Dell, fol. 51v; Thomas Hornblow, fol. 62v.

Some come to Church & some stay at home.' The next year their reply was 'Wee doe humbly suppose that no parish if they will write truth can say omnia bene to this querie, for some goe to church & some to other meetings, but we have never a papist in the towne so far as we know.' In 1683 the Sarratt churchwardens asked that two men who had had their goods distrained for being at a conventicle should not be punished by the church court, having already been punished by a civil court. In 1685 the churchwardens reported that 'Most of those that formerly absented themselves doe come to church, and by faire means in time the rest may be persuaded to come who formerly refused, they promise faire.' Then in 1687 the only presentment at Sarratt was the following: 'Widow Green when I asked why she did not come to church told me to my face she went elsewhere and she would goe whither she list for all of me.' Lastly in 1688: 'If we should tell you the names of such as come seldome to church they are excused by the late liberty granted and may goe whither they please, therefore here we must be silent.'[47]

The refreshing candour of the Sarratt churchwardens is most unusual, but how often did the officers of other parishes share their outlook and fail to present offenders? Such behaviour is perhaps less surprising in the 1680s, but, in areas with a long history of dissent, it may have existed earlier, as it undoubtedly must have done in Lollard Steeple Bumpstead.[48]

There is another vast gap in the Visitation Books between 1637 and 1662. The first post-Restoration book is for the Episcopal Visitation of 1662 and it includes a number of presentments for not coming to church. At Burnham, 'Thomas Dell in our parish doth suffer private meetinges in his house contrary to the law in that case provided to our knowledge.' This man was a well-known Quaker. Fourteen individuals, some with their families, were named as Quakers at Burnham, but apart from Thomas Dell none of them appear in the Quaker records. This is evidence of the incompleteness of surviving dissenting records; those whose names we know are clearly only a proportion of the total adherents of dissenting sects. At Penn eight men were presented as 'being reputed anabaptists and quakers'; two are known Quakers. The churchwardens did not always seem able to distinguish Quakers from Baptists.[49]

The 1664 book shows a marked shift in the type of cases presented with absence from church replacing sexual offences as the commonest reason for presentment.[50] In the same year there was also an Episcopal

---

[47] Herts. RO ASA 17/1 and ASA 17/2 Churchwardens' presentments 1609–79 and 1680–9.
[48] See above, pp. 11, 201.
[49] E.R.C. Brinkworth (ed.), *Episcopal Visitation Book for the Archdeaconry of Buckingham, 1662*, Buckinghamshire Records Society, 7 (1947).
[50] See above, Ch. 4, pp. 178–9, for this thoroughness.

Visitation, and both books have long lists of persons presented for not going to church. Amongst these are several names which appear in the genealogies in the Appendix, including the leading Quaker Thomas Dell, and Henry Tredway and his wife Margaret.[51] There are only two more seventeenth-century Visitation Books, for 1673–84 and 1686–1714; the later includes the Archepiscopal Visitation of 1686. Again there are many presentments for failure to attend church or to pay church rates, and also for refusing to baptize children, but after 1686 there are no more as a result of James II's Declarations of Indulgence and the Toleration Act of 1689.[52]

A more general view of the strength of late seventeenth-century dissent in the Quaker Upperside Meeting area can be drawn from the Compton Census, and the places where meeting-houses were registered in 1689.[53]

The long silence from dissent in Buckinghamshire, between the early Tudor Lollard trials and the emergence of new sects in the mid-seventeenth century, must surely be due to the lengthy gaps in the visitation records and to the complicity of many sympathetic churchwardens in the heterodox beliefs of their fellow parishioners.

In conclusion, we can say that the surnames of these families who were both Lollards and post-Restoration dissenters in the Chilterns demonstrated that these families were outstandingly and entirely abnormally stable in the area. This was true even when they were compared with the wealthiest section of rural society there, which is usually the most static. The mobility, or rather lack of it, of radical dissenting families in the Chilterns was 'different' from anyone else. In detail, six of the nineteen families examined with the most unusual surnames were actually connected in the male line through the period. These included one labouring family. Three more dissenting families were traced through the female line. These genealogies were certainly not the maximum number that could be produced, but simply the number that could be produced in the time available for the project. We may certainly say that earlier historical suspicions that heterodoxy descended in the family in the Chilterns are now demonstrably true. Radical dissent was a family affair.

---

[51] Bucks. RO D/A/V/7 and D/A/V/8 Visitations 1664.
[52] Bucks. RO D/A/V/10 and D/A/V/11 Visitations 1673–84, 1686–1714.
[53] See Map 7, p. 295, Table 2, pp. 32–4, and Anne Whiteman (ed.), *The Compton Census of 1676: A Critical Edition*, Records of Social and Economic History, NS, 10 (Oxford, 1986).

The comparative mobility and immobility of Lollard descendants in early modern England

PETER SPUFFORD

It is very clear that, in the sixteenth and seventeenth centuries, families with Lollard ancestry were much less mobile than other families in the Chilterns, even than those families with ancestors taxed on more than £5 in 1524. They stand out as different from their own neighbours.[1] How does the degree of mobility that they exhibited match up with our knowledge of the mobility of other people in rural England at this period? The object of the present essay is to place in comparative perspective the communities from which the members of the Quaker Upperside Meeting were drawn against a general survey of mobility.

Mobility in sixteenth- and seventeenth-century England

The common patterns of movement in much of rural England in the sixteenth and seventeenth centuries were strongly related to the life-cycle. They consisted of very occasional child mobility as a part of a family unit, followed, after leaving home around the age of fifteen to go into 'service',[2] by frequent, annual or biennial, movement for a decade to a decade and a half,[3] often ending with a move at or around the time of

---

[1] See above, pp. 30–1, 296, 298–9.

[2] Gregory King's category of in-servants primarily consisted of servants in husbandry, but also included domestic servants and a certain number of craftsmen who were resident with their masters. Peter Laslett, working from sixty-three surviving listings of inhabitants of the late seventeenth and eighteenth centuries, has reckoned that around one in seven of the population were in-servants at any one time, and that amongst these in-servants, males slightly preponderated, Peter Laslett, 'Size and Structure of the Household in England over Three Centuries', Population Studies, 23 (1969), p. 219, collected in Peter Laslett with R. Wall (eds.), Household and Family in Past Times (Cambridge, 1972), p. 152. Since those who were in-servants were very heavily concentrated in a relatively narrow age band, this seventh part of the whole population appears to have included rather more than a half of the eighteen- to twenty-two-year-old age group at any one time. In other words rather more than half, and perhaps as many as three-quarters of late seventeenth-century Englishmen had the experience of spending some part of their lives as in-servants.

[3] A.S. Kussmaul, 'The Ambiguous Mobility of Farm Servants', Economic History Review, 2nd Ser., 34 (1981), pp. 222–35, and Servants in Husbandry in Early-Modern England (Cambridge, 1982). Donald Woodward (ed.), The Farming and Memorandum Books of

marriage and setting up. Then movement became much less common, apart from seasonal mobility, although there might well be a final move on retirement. All this meant that only a minority, perhaps one fifth, died in the same place as that in which they were born, if they survived to the age of ten. For those who survived early death, it was very much more normal to move away and remain away for the rest of their lives. Even those who did die in their birthplace included many who had moved away and returned later.[4] Most rural mobility, however, took place within a distance of only ten miles (sixteen kilometres), and very little of it exceeded twenty miles (thirty-two kilometres).[5]

Outside this 'normal' pattern there were some exceptional groups. There was the very large group of people who took the road to London, either permanently or for a period of years. As Sir John Reresby put it in the 1680s London 'drained all England of its people'.[6] Provincial cities also exerted a certain magnetism, but it was much less marked. There was the substantial, privileged minority of 'betterment migrants', largely apprentices, who travelled rather longer distances than most, to take up opportunities of advancement, but were then more static than the great majority of the young working population. There were men caught up in the militia, and others in particular occupations, such as masons. Finally there were the small number of desperate young men and women, highly visible though few in number, the 'subsistence migrants', vagabonds who had fallen or taken themselves out of the system, and had often become vagrants rather than true migrants.[7]

Henry Best of Elmsworth, 1642, Records of Social and Economic History, NS, 8 (London, 1984), gives a vivid illustration of hiring practices in Yorkshire in 1642.

[4] This 'normal' pattern for pre-industrial rural mobility was established in the 1970s, before the advent of family reconstitution: R.S. Schofield, 'Age Specific Mobility in an Eighteenth Century English Parish', Annales de Démographie Historique (1970), pp. 261–74; Peter Spufford, 'Population Movement in Seventeenth Century England', Local Population Studies, 4 (1970), pp. 41–50, expanded in 'Population Mobility in Pre-Industrial England', Genealogists' Magazine, 17 (1973–4), pp. 420–9, 475–81, 537–43. A more recently elaborated example, adding the information from family reconstitution, has been provided by Barry Stapleton, 'Migration in Pre-Industrial Southern England: The Example of Odiham', Southern History, 10 (1988), pp. 47–93. The not altogether different patterns of rural–urban mobility were also being established in the 1970s: Peter Clark, 'The Migrant in Kentish Towns', in Peter Clark and Paul Slack (eds.), Crisis and Order in English Towns 1500–1700 (London, 1972), pp. 117–63; John Patten, Rural–Urban Migration in Pre-Industrial England, School of Geography Research Paper, 6 (Oxford, 1973); and Peter Clark and David Souden, 'Rural–Urban Migration and its Impact in Early Modern England', in Migrations, Population and Occupation of Land (before 1800), Eighth International Economic History Congress, Section B8 (Budapest, 1982). Post-Restoration intra-rural and rural–urban mobility were compared in Peter Clark, 'Migration in England during the Late Seventeenth and Early Eighteenth Centuries', Past and Present, 83 (1979), pp. 57–90.

[5] See below, p. 326 and n. 53.

[6] John Reresby, Memoirs (London, 1875 edn), p. 333.

[7] Peter Clark, in 'The Migrant', coined the terms 'betterment' and 'subsistence' for those two groups on which he concentrated his attention. Subsistence migration

The cumulative effect of such individual mobility in terms of patrilineal family mobility can be seen from family reconstitutions. Mrs Nesta Evans' reconstitution of six of the nine very small parishes of South Elmham, from the mid-sixteenth century to the mid-seventeenth produced a total of 1,164 reconstituted families. Of these only fifty-five, under 5 per cent of the total, lasted for two generations, and only six, around a half a per cent of the total, lasted in the same place for three generations.[8] In this part of Suffolk, at any rate, it was extremely rare for families to remain, as used to be supposed, 'from one generation to the next, living in the same houses as their fathers and grandfathers, and tilling the same soil'.[9] Two factors distinguished those few families that remained from the vast majority that did not – family size and status. Those families which had more children reaching adulthood were more likely to include a member who remained in the same place to keep the family going there.[10] There was also a strong positive correlation between the small group who stayed on, and the small group who ran the community. What Mrs Evans found at South Elmham in Suffolk, David Hey had found at Myddle in Shropshire,[11] my wife had found at Willingham in Cambridgeshire,[12] and William Hoskins had found in a group of Leicestershire villages for an earlier period.[13] In all these places, the families that survived for two generations or more were distinctive. They were generally distinguished by larger family size, by belonging to the group which ran the community, and by an appreciable stake in the land. This correlation seems to have held not only in the tiny wood-pasture villages and hamlets of South Elmham and Myddle, but also in the large nucleated village of Willingham

---

was dealt with authoritatively in A.L. Beier, *Masterless Men: The Vagrancy Problem in England 1560–1640* (London, 1985).

[8] Nesta Evans, 'The Community of South Elmham, Suffolk 1550–1640' (East Anglia, MPhil, 1978), pp. 132–4. It must be remembered that migration is not the only reason for the failure of families to survive in the male line, for around 20 per cent of marriages have no children, and a further 20 per cent only produce girls.

[9] Peter Burke, *Popular Culture in Early Modern Europe* (London, 1978), pp. 84 and 302, provided one of the last expressions of this older myth of immobility. It has now become fashionable to overstress mobility.

[10] The average recorded number of children surviving to fourteen in the families which lasted for two or more generations was 4.2, whilst it was only 2.5 in the families which did not last to a second generation. This was not merely a matter of a higher average brought about by a few enormous families. The 'staying' families, as a group, included more families into which five to seven children were born than of any other family size. In terms of numbers surviving to adulthood, slightly larger average numbers at birth were accentuated by both lower infant mortality and lower childhood mortality.

[11] David G. Hey, *An English Rural Community: Myddle under the Tudors and Stuarts* (Leicester, 1974), p. 206.

[12] Margaret Spufford, *Contrasting Communities: English Villagers in the Sixteenth and Seventeenth Centuries* (Cambridge, 1974), pp. 18–22, and see below, pp. 315, 329–30.

[13] W.G. Hoskins, 'The Leicestershire Farmer in the Sixteenth Century', collected in his *Essays in Leicestershire History* (Liverpool, 1950), pp. 131–2.

on the edge of the then pastoral fens, and in the more 'normal' medium-sized villages of midland Leicestershire with their mixed husbandry weighted towards the arable.

Surname survival is a much cruder measure, but it has been looked at for many places and naturally gives a rather lower turnover than the exact genealogical linkage of individual families in detail, for each surname may represent either a single family or a largish group of families. Since it has been undertaken for many places it is possible to postulate what may have been a normal rate of turnover and to underline what may have been abnormal, in terms of either stagnation or instability.

Whether or not a surname-group of families was monophyletic, that is had a common ancestry, may be questioned by historians, even though in the seventeenth century it could be taken for granted. Professor Cressy cites the Lancashire draper who wrote across the Atlantic to Increase Mather in 1686 claiming kinship on the grounds that his wife's first husband shared a surname with Mather and also came from the same parish.[14] Although there may have been a strong likelihood of relationship, there was of course no necessity for people of the same surname in the same place to be monophyletic. This lack of necessary relationship applied to all the four main types of surname – locative (descendants from unrelated migrants scattered outwards from a surname-giving place of origin), occupational (descendants from unrelated people of the same occupation), toponymic (descendants from unrelated people named from common natural features), and patronymic (descendants from unrelated people with the same personal name). Richard McKinley has nevertheless been able to demonstrate how often people with a surname in common, at least in Norfolk and Suffolk, shared in a common ancestry.[15]

As long ago as 1915, S.A. Peyton showed that in Nottinghamshire it was normal for only between 10 and 20 per cent of the surnames in the tax assessment of 1544 to survive in the same place to 1641, just under 100 years later.[16] A generation later E.F. Buckatzsch was only able to gather together three other examples for comparison with Peyton's Nottinghamshire figures.[17] In Bedfordshire, it was normal for half the surnames to survive for the period of forty-four years from 1627 to 1671. This is approximately the same rate of survival as in Nottinghamshire. In Table 8, I have reduced different survival rates for different communities for

[14] David Cressy, *Coming Over* (Cambridge, 1987).
[15] Richard McKinley, *Norfolk and Suffolk Surnames in the Middle Ages*, English Surnames Series, 2 (1975).
[16] S.A.Peyton, 'Village Population in Tudor Lay Subsidy Rolls', *English Historical Review*, 30 (1915), pp. 234–50.
[17] E.F. Buckatzsch, 'The Constancy of Local Population and Migration in England before 1800', *Population Studies*, 5 (1951), pp. 62–9.

different periods, to survival rates per 100 surnames per century. I have assumed a steady compound rate of survival.[18] However, Dr Buckatzsch noted, without emphasizing, that analysis of surnames in the parish registers at Horringer in Suffolk and at Shap in Westmorland produced totally different results.[19] People were moving in and out of seventeenth-century Horringer a great deal more rapidly than was 'normal' in Bedfordshire and Nottinghamshire, but were moving in and out of Shap rather more slowly.

Since Dr Buckatzsch gathered these examples together in 1951 a great deal more has been done. Mr McKinley started his great work on surnames in Norfolk. In none of the 102 places that he examined in Norfolk did as many as 20 per cent of the surnames in the 1523 Subsidy lists or military surveys survive to the 1666 Hearth Tax lists. Over four-fifths of the family name groups had changed in every single place. This is generally a very similar rate to Nottinghamshire and Bedfordshire, although movement was perhaps a little slower in some places.[20]

[18] The survival rate per 100 surnames over a century has been reckoned as

$$100 \left(\frac{S_t}{S_o} \right)^{\frac{100}{t}}$$

where S_o is the number of surnames on an initial taxation list, or in an initial period of the parish registers, and S_t is the number of such surnames surviving on a similar list, or a similar period of parish registers t years later. This is a very rough approximation, for it slightly depresses the rates for survival over a century where the evidence is drawn from periods shorter than a century and exaggerates it where the evidence is drawn from longer periods. This is because the propensity of families of 'stayers' to go on producing 'stayers' means that the proportionate rates of survival will be very slightly greater over longer periods of time than shorter.

In my calculations I have not made any allowance for the differing geographical areas of communities. There is therefore a problem in making comparisons between the smaller parishes of central, southern, and eastern England on the one hand and the extensive parishes of the north and west on the other. Some multi-settlement parishes in the north and west of England were many miles across. This means that in these cases part of the movement within some western and northern parishes was equivalent to that which in other parts of the country would take an individual, a family, or a surname group of families into another parish.

An alternative method is to take the number of surnames at an end point and calculate from the proportion which had already been there at some earlier point in time. This alternative method emphasizes the size of the static core as against the number of in-migrants, whilst my method emphasizes the static core as against the number of out-migrants. It was used for Wigston Magna in Leicestershire by W.G. Hoskins, *The Midland Peasant* (London, 1957), pp. 88 and 195–6, and, with a battery of other demographic tools for Whickham in County Durham by G.W. Lasker and D.F. Roberts, 'Secular Trends in Relationship as Estimated by Surnames: A Study of a Tyneside Parish', *Annals of Human Biology*, 9 (1982).

[19] See below, pp. 317 and 320.

[20] R.A. McKinley, *Norfolk Surnames in the Sixteenth Century*, Department of English Local History, Occasional Papers, 2nd Ser., 2 (Leicester, 1969), p. 44. This was the first fruit of Richard McKinley's work as Marc Fitch Research Fellow in the Department of English Local History at the University of Leicester. He later produced *Norfolk and*

In addition to this sort of wide-ranging survey there has been a large amount of work on individual places. David Hey's analysis of names in the baptism and burial registers of Myddle showed that 42 per cent of the names between 1541 and 1599 were of those he called 'old families'. He found the same percentage between 1600 and 1643, and 40 per cent between 1647 and 1701.[21] At Rowley Regis, a large and fast-growing industrial village in south Staffordshire, I found ninety-six different surnames in the registers between 1540 and 1549. Fifty-five of these were to be found again between 1566 and 1576. Forty were still there between 1603 and 1612 and twenty-five survived the full century to 1640–9. At Earl's Colne in Essex, of 102 different surnames mentioned in the Lay Subsidy of 1524, twelve were still present in the 1673 Hearth Tax.[22] All of these instances fit with the 'normal' surname turnover of Nottinghamshire, Bedfordshire, and Norfolk, as did W.G. Hoskins' examination of Leicestershire taxation returns working backwards from the Lay Subsidy of 1524 to the Poll Taxes of 1377/81. Just under 10 per cent had been present in the same places five generations earlier.[23] It seems that it was normal, from the sixteenth century to the eighteenth, for some 15–25 per cent of surnames to survive for a century, and if Leicestershire was not atypical, for the same rate of survival to reach back through the fifteenth century as well. This meant that it was very ordinary for as many as 75–85 per cent of family name groups to die out or move on over three generations.

This is still much the same picture as Dr Buckatzsch was able to present forty years ago. He used it to emphasize the constancy of migration in pre-industrial England, without highlighting the divergences from this normality. What was generally the case was not necessarily particularly applicable either in all places or at all times.

At Neen Savage in south Shropshire, on one of the principal main roads into Wales, Dr Goodman found that the turnover of surnames was extraordinarily high. Of those found in the parish registers between 1586 and 1595, only 34 per cent were to be found forty years later.[24] An even faster rate of turnover was found by Alan Macfarlane at Boreham in central Essex. By comparing surnames in Subsidy returns he found so much change between 1544 and 1566 that only half of the families assessed at

---

Suffolk Surnames (London, 1975), The Surnames of Oxfordshire (London, 1977), The Surnames of Lancashire (London, 1981), The Surnames of Sussex (London, 1988), and A History of British Surnames (London, 1990). The surnames of a further county were also covered in Mr McKinley's English Surnames series by George Redmonds, Yorkshire, West Riding (London, 1973).

[21] Hey, An English Rural Community, p. 200.
[22] Alan Macfarlane, Reconstructing Historical Communities (Cambridge, 1977), p. 172.
[23] Hoskins, 'The Leicestershire Farmer', pp. 131–2.
[24] Kenneth Goodman, 'Hammerman's Hill' (Keele, PhD, 1979).

Table 8. Comparative mobility in England: surname survival rates
(per 100 surnames per century)

Place	Record	Date	Time-span (years)	Survival	Rate of survival
Region					
Bucks.					
(surnames of Lollard adherents in 21 Chiltern parishes)	Tax	1524–1662	138	53 out of 59	92
Bucks.					
(Surnames of Lollard adherents in 21 Chiltern parishes, borne by Quakers and Baptists)	Tax	1524–1662	138	48 out of 59	86
Bucks.					
(Surnames of those taxed at £5 or over in 1524 in 21 Chiltern parishes)	Tax	1524–1662	138	97 out of 215	56
Cambs., Essex, Suff.					
(35 parishes around Haverhill combined)	Tax	1524–1673/4[c]	150	215 out of 541	54
Bucks.					
(surnames of all those taxed, 21 Chiltern parishes combined)	Tax	1524–1662[b]	138	151 out of 524	40
Parishes					
High survival rates					
Willingham, Cambs.	Tax	1524/5–1662/4	138	21 out of 44	58
	Surveys	1574–1720s	150	22 out of 58	52
Kibworth Harcourt, Leics.	Tenants	1500–1679	179	10 out of 43	44
	Tenants	1593–1686	93	57.5%	55
Burslem, Staffs.	Parish register	1660/84–1735/59	75	62 out of 109	46
Chesham, Bucks.	Tax/list	1524–1606	82	48 out of 122	32
	Tax	1524–1662	138	32 out of 122	38
Shap, Westmld.	Parish registers	1600/24–1700/24	100	28 out of 84	33

Table 8 (cont.)

Place	Record	Date	Time-span (years)	Survival	Rate of survival
Normal survival rates					
Norf. (102 separate places)	Tax	1523–1666	143	<20%	<33
Rowley Regis, Staffs.	Parish registers	1540/9–1640/9	100	25 out of 96	26
Burford, Salop.	Parish registers	1586/95–1626/35	40	57%	25
Coreley, Salop.	Parish registers	1573/82–1613/22	40	56%	23
In Beds.	Tax	1627–71	44	50%	21
In Leics.	Tax	1377/81–1524/5	144	28 out of 289	20
Earls Colne, Essex	Tax	1524–1673	149	12 out of 102	20
In Notts.	Tax	1544–1641	97	10%–20%	10–20
Low survival rates					
Clayworth, Notts.	Lists	1642–88	46	25 out of 78	8
Neen Savage, Salop.	Parish registers	1586/95–1626/35	40	34%	7
Boreham, Essex	Tax	1524–98	74	3 out of 42	4
Horringer, Suff.	Parish registers	1600/24–1700/24	100	2 out of 63	3

[a] Hearth Tax includes exempt.
[b] Hearth Tax does not include exempt.

the latter date had been assessed a mere twenty-two years earlier. By 1598 only three of the forty-two family names of the 1524 Subsidy were represented in the tax list.[25] This is a rate of change nearly as fast as that at Horringer in mid-Suffolk. The families who formed the population of Horringer almost totally changed in the course of the seventeenth century.[26] An apparently even faster rate of change has been deduced for Broomfield, a village very close to Boreham in central Essex, two centuries later.[27] A lower than usual survival rate can also be calculated for Clayworth in Nottinghamshire, one of the first villages to have its listings of inhabitants analysed by historians. It could not then be known that its patterns of mobility were not entirely typical.[28] Possibly the most rapid turnover of surnames yet noticed comes from Whickham in County Durham, where under 7 per cent of the surnames in the baptismal registers recorded from 1629 to 1654 could be found earlier in the period 1577 to 1602.[29] This patently reveals an extraordinarily rapid turnover of population, but, being expressed on a different basis, is not amenable to direct comparison.

What was it that marked out some communities for such particularly low or high rates of mobility? From their work Drs Clark and Souden have been able to pick out some broad regional variations within southern England. Peter Clark suggested lower mobility in Oxfordshire, Gloucestershire, Wiltshire, and Dorset, compared with Kent and Suffolk.[30] David Souden, having analysed nearly 10,000 ecclesiastical court depositions from the ecclesiastical province of Canterbury, concluded 'Time and again, indices of movement show that there was a gradient of rural mobility from west to east, with lower levels of mobility in the western counties, middling values in Oxfordshire and Leicestershire and higher levels of mobility in Norfolk and Suffolk.'[31] Mobility in northern England

[25] Alan Macfarlane, *Witchcraft in Tudor and Stuart England* (London, 1970), p. 148.

[26] Of sixty-three surnames found in the parish registers in the period 1600–24 only two were to be found in the period 1700–24. Quoted by Buckatzsch, 'The Constancy'.

[27] In 1735 the vicar listed sixty-six householders. Fifty years later a list was drawn up of thirty-seven men of an age fit for military service. The two lists had only nine surnames in common. A.F.J. Brown, *Essex at Work 1700–1815*, Essex RO (Chelmsford, 1969), pp. 106–8. It must, however, be objected that the two lists are not strictly comparable.

[28] Peter Laslett and John Harrison, 'Clayworth and Cogenhoe', in H.E. Bell and R.L. Ollard (eds.), *Historical Essays 1600–1750 presented to David Ogg* (London, 1963), pp. 156–84. To make the calculations in Table 8 their listings have been supplemented by W.F. Webster (ed.), *Protestation Returns, 1641/2: Nottinghamshire* (Nottingham, 1984), as abstracted by Dr David Hey, 'Stable Families in Tudor and Stuart England' (forthcoming).

[29] Lasker and Roberts, 'Secular Trends'.

[30] Peter Clark, 'Migration', pp. 75ff.

[31] David Souden, 'Pre-Industrial English Local Migration Fields' (Cambridge, PhD, 1981). He published some of his conclusions in David Souden, 'East, West – Home's Best? Regional Patterns in Migration in Early Modern England', in Peter Clark and

seems to have been generally less than in the south, and here again mobility in the west seems to have been lower than in the east, so that the region with the lowest mobility of all was the north-west of the country.[32] Celia Fiennes commented on how curiously immobile people still were at the end of the seventeenth century in the Lake District.[33] One of the distinctive features of Preston in Lancashire, according to the listing of inhabitants of 1705, was the extraordinarily high proportion of resident children in the population over the age of fourteen, and the correspondingly low proportion of servants.[34] The 'normal' southern English pre-industrial pattern of sending children away in adolescence into service did not apply there, and indeed the general low mobility in the north-west may be accounted for by an alternative tradition of keeping children at home.

However, there do seem to be extremely local differences as well. Dr Goodman compared Neen Savage with two other nearby parishes in the Clee Hills, Coreley and Burford, which had perfectly ordinary rates of turnover of surnames. Neen Savage had a much larger number of resident gentry than either of the other two parishes; indeed, Coreley had no resident gentle family. As a corollary, there were a much larger number of servants at Neen Savage than in either of the other two parishes. However, although Neen Savage offered more opportunities for employment by the gentry, it did not offer so many of the stable opportunities of by-employment, so necessary for more permanent settlement in an agriculturally poor area. Although all these parishes experienced a flow of immigrants from Wales, Neen Savage had the largest numbers of them, and like the beggars in which it also seems to have abounded, rapidly passed them on, first to Cleobury Mortimer, and then further along the road into England. Neen Savage seems to have been a markedly unstable community, without an established core either of substantial yeomen like Burford, or of smallholders with by-employments like Coreley.

In their work on Whickham, David Levine and Keith Wrightson have given us the most revealing picture yet of any community in early modern England. The period of the fastest turnover of surnames coincides with

---

David Souden (eds.), *Migration and Society in Early Modern England* (London, 1987), pp. 314–16.

[32] McKinley, *Surnames of Lancashire*. Mr McKinley emphasized very low mobility of population not only in Lancashire, but also in parts of the West Riding of Yorkshire. Although there may have been less 'normal' movement within the north-west, it was nevertheless a region which produced large numbers of long-distance 'subsistence' migrants, since it was extremely vulnerable to subsistence crises, Andrew B. Appleby, *Famine in Tudor and Stuart England* (Stanford and Liverpool, 1978).

[33] Quoted in the introduction to Clark and Souden (eds.), *Migration and Society*, p. 22. Roger Finlay had to abandon the family reconstitution of Hawkshead, west of Windermere, because immobility had reduced surnames to too small a number.

[34] ESRC Cambridge Group for the History of Population and Social Structure.

its transformation from an agricultural community with some coal mining to one in which the old copyholder community had been swept away by the rapid expansion of the mining. The new mining community was marked by its transience. A quarter of the householders moved out of the parish between Michaelmas 1665 and Lady Day 1666. Of 367 householders at Lady Day 1666, only 43 had been baptized in the parish. An extraordinary proportion were single men. In the 1650s and the 1700s the sex ratio reached 149 men for every 100 women. The multitude of colliers set 'daylie' to work might stay only for a few months, or a single mining season. Indeed miners and mine owners alike regarded the whole coalfield rather than a single parish as the workplace for this free floating body of impoverished labour. Nuptuality was correspondingly low, whilst mortality was disastrously high, as in a man-devouring city. It is no wonder that kinship networks were loose within the parish.[35]

Perhaps all the villages with a high turnover of surnames would look as unstable on close examination. It comes as no surprise that another of these excessively mobile villages, Boreham in Essex, so lacked the bonds of community and personal security that it became a seedbed of accusations of witchcraft. It was not a place so closely linked by ties of kinship and neighbourliness that each individual felt himself safely meshed into a network of communal support. It would be interesting to know how different Boreham was from its neighbours. Did much of Essex share in this abnormally high rate of population turnover? Earl's Colne, a dozen miles (under twenty kilometres) away, had a perfectly 'normal' turnover of population. Historians working on Essex should be aware of this pocket of high mobility. The consequence is that this in itself is likely to have produced idiosyncratic or even bizarre social results. The atypicality of the number of witchcraft cases in this part of Essex is possibly explained. It is probable that communities could only tolerate a certain level of mobility before exhibiting stress signals of this kind.

Conversely, communities with a relatively low level of general movement are likely to have been able to tolerate new or idiosyncratic groups within society, without undue fear and anxiety.

The stability of a community with even a 'normal' turnover, like Myddle in north Shropshire, stands in marked contrast with the instability of Neen Savage and of those Essex villages where there were frequent accusations of witchcraft. Dr Hey has picked out the way in which immigrants were easily absorbed into local society there. Unlike the situation in Neen Savage there were simply not too many of them for the Myddle community to cope with. As an example of the warm acceptance of the

[35] David Levine and Keith Wrightson, *The Making of an Industrial Society: Whickham 1560–1765* (Oxford, 1991), pp. 165–72, 179–80, 185–92.

newcomer, he quotes the story of a Welsh migrant, known as Soundsey Eaven, who could not speak good English. He came to Myddle as a servant, and remained there, having married a local girl. He built himself a 'lytle hut att the higher end of the town'. When this was accidentally burnt, the community readily and handsomely contributed to his rebuilding of a more durable house.[36] Such communal care and neighbourliness could only be so readily extended when there were not too many migrants to absorb easily. Without too many outsiders, there were not so many occasions for uncharitableness towards the poor and unfortunate, and consequently not the guilt and tension which issued according to Dr Macfarlane and Sir Keith Thomas, amongst other things, in accusations of witchcraft.

At the other extreme from the unstable settlements were communities such as Shap, in Westmorland, where a third of the population at the beginning of the eighteenth century was made up of members of families which had the same names as those who had been there a century before.[37] It is not clear if this merely exemplifies the low mobility of the north-west, and was normal for the region, or whether it was brought about by particular circumstances. Shap was exceptionally isolated until the opening of a new west coast route to Carlisle and Scotland. The very high rate of survival of surnames at Shap was matched only by the slowest moving of Richard McKinley's 102 Norfolk communities.

The slowest turnovers that I have yet encountered were those at Willingham, on the edge of the Cambridgeshire fens, and at the large industrial village of Burslem in the nascent Potteries of north Staffordshire, and perhaps Kibworth Harcourt in open-field Leicestershire.[38]

Willingham had a relatively sparse population at the beginning of the sixteenth century, but was much more heavily peopled by the mid-seventeenth century, so that there was a strong inward current of migrants to set against the astonishingly low level of out-migration. It is interesting to observe which families it was that survived so noticeably. They were above all the holders of the customary half-yardlands, which, with their shares of the demesne and the extensive common rights in

---

[36] Richard Gough, *Antiquities & Memoirs of the Parish of Myddle* (Shrewsbury, 1875 edn), p. 162, and Hey, *An English Rural Community*, pp. 187–8.

[37] Quoted in Buckatzsch, 'The Constancy'.

[38] It is not clear whether Kibworth Harcourt provides a fair comparison, since tenants were naturally a smaller and more durable group than taxpayers or those appearing in parish registers. The evidence comes from rentals, surveys, court rolls, and lists of 'inhabitants' prepared in advance of court meetings. The turnover of surnames was noticeably slower here in the seventeenth century than in the sixteenth, and slower in the sixteenth than in the fifteenth. The fifteenth-century surname survival rate, per 100 surnames per 100 years, was a more normal 32, based on rentals 1412 and 1527. Cicely Howell, *Land, Family and Inheritance in Transition: Kibworth Harcourt 1280–1700* (Cambridge, 1983), pp. 67–9, 241, and 248–9.

the still pastoral fen, provided their holders with livings as comfortable as those of yeomen who farmed much larger acreages in midland England.[39] The stable core of families which did not move on was patently more numerous and more substantial here than elsewhere. It was members of these families who provided the motive force to set up an endowed school in the village in the late sixteenth century and to buy out the manorial lord in the mid-seventeenth century.

Kibworth Harcourt was very different. In the seventeenth century it was transformed into a 'closed' village, dominated by a small circle of gentlemen and yeomen farmers, who in both the sixteenth and seventeenth centuries had deliberately been engrossing numerous earlier tenements by marriage and purchase. It was these families who provided a noticeably static core. There were also a few husbandmen or small farmers and a group of landless labourers for whom housing was provided by their employers.[40] With a relatively small and shrinking static core it is surprising that there was not a greater turnover of surnames.

At Burslem well over half the surnames survived in the parish registers for three-quarters of a century from 1660–84 to 1735–59.[41] This is quite different from the volatility of Whickham as it was taken over by coal mining, or even the 'normality' of Rowley Regis, another rapidly growing industrial village in south Staffordshire, or of Eccleshall, a small market town only fourteen miles (twenty-two kilometres) away, with an extensive rural parish. Once again there seems to have been a larger than normal stable core of less mobile families, who combined farming with potting. There may also be a very localized reason why the turnover of surnames in Burslem should be so slow. One of the distinctive features of the even larger neighbouring parish of Stoke-on-Trent, according to the listing of inhabitants of 1701, was that the 'normal' pre-industrial pattern of sending children away in adolescence into service was replaced there by a local tradition of keeping children at home, as at Preston, and perhaps as in much of north-western England.[42] If such a tradition was also current in

---

[39] Margaret Spufford, *Contrasting Communities*, supplemented by the recent, unpublished, work of Mr Motoyasu Takahashi, who is currently completing a doctoral thesis in Japan at Tohoku University at Sendai.

[40] Howell, *Land*.

[41] Lorna Weatherill, *The Pottery Trade and North Staffordshire 1660–1760* (Manchester, 1971), pp. 119–20.

[42] Stoke was second only to Preston in showing both a high percentage of households with resident children over fourteen and a lower percentage with resident servants. Of 223 males over fourteen in the listing who were not married, no fewer than 111 were resident children (50 per cent), only 31 were servants (14 per cent) and 81 were widowers, unmarried, and unspecified. Of 1379 males over fourteen in 29 other listings, as many as 480 (35 per cent) were servants, but only 465 were resident children (34 per cent) and 434 were widowers unmarried and unspecified. ESRC Cambridge Group for the History of Population and Social Structure.

Burslem, a very large measure of the personal mobility that was prevalent elsewhere would have been eliminated, and this would provide an additional explanation for the high rate of survival of family name groups over long periods of time. Even in the mid-nineteenth century the whole area of the pottery towns was marked by a very low level of geographical mobility, and by an extremely strong sense of the very local community.[43] It was patently a great deal more comfortable and secure to live in a very slow-moving community, despite a conservatism almost bordering on stagnation, than it was to live in the dynamic tensions of fast-moving communities where insecurity might even explode into brutal and bloody witch hunts. Insularity and low wage rates were a cheap price to pay for the lack of riot and extremism.

The turnover of surnames must always be a crude measure of mobility, or lack of mobility, compared with the precision to be derived from family reconstitution. Family reconstitution, however, is extremely time consuming, whilst a count of surnames can be undertaken much more rapidly. Comparisons can therefore be made much more widely using the turnover of surnames than in comparing the limited number of places for which family reconstitutions have been undertaken. However, until we have figures for the rates of turnover of surnames for the places for which family reconstitutions have been undertaken, there is no means of seeing what rates of mobility of individuals, as seen in family reconstitutions, correlate with, or are represented by, what rates of turnover of surnames.

Rex Watson attempted, for eight of the parishes of Thriplow Hundred in south Cambridgeshire, to refine upon the simple counting of surnames, in order to compensate for the varying number of families, whether related or not, represented by each surname.[44] His work raised

---

[43] This low level of geographical mobility appears to continue in this area into the later twentieth century, from personal observation.

[44] Rex Watson, 'A Study of Surname Distribution in a Group of Cambridgeshire Parishes 1538–1840', *Local Population Studies*, 15 (1975), pp. 23–32. Instead of considering all surnames, he merely considered the commonest fifty surnames in each place, for each hundred years, and then looked to see how many of them survived into the next hundred years. The elimination of the less common names from consideration should have concentrated attention on the mobility of the larger, core family, name groups, and should have produced a much lower rate of turnover. In his south Cambridgeshire parishes the more common names did persist slightly more frequently, but not as markedly as might have been expected (see above, p. 311 for consideration of family size and persistence). This, Mr Watson suggested, was because his 'common' names were not in fact very common. Prime, the commonest name in Thriplow Hundred only accounted for 1.6 per cent of the total entries in the parish registers between 1538 and 1640. By way of contrast, Hartley, the commonest name in the registers of the chapelry of Colne in Lancashire, accounted for 9.9 per cent of the entries between 1599 and 1653. In other words the range of surnames in Lancashire was much more restricted than that in Cambridgeshire. Mr McKinley's work has confirmed the narrower range of surnames in Lancashire and also in

the question of why some places should have more numerous surnames, whilst others had fewer. Mr McKinley saw the smaller variety of surnames in Lancashire, combined with the lack of dispersal of localized names (in Lancashire the fewer surnames are heavily made up of locative surnames derived from small nearby places rather than from patronymics), as a consequence of a much lower rate of geographical mobility than was normal elsewhere in England.[45] The generalized conclusion may well be that, where there were few surnames and many families per surname, this indicates a relatively closed society, with low mobility in the preceding generations, as well as a high likelihood of a low turnover of surnames in the period under examination. Conversely, a wide range of surnames may well be an indicator of an earlier rapid turnover of families, leading in turn to the expectation of a high turnover of surnames in the period under examination.

It is apparent that just as there was a positive correlation between the number of children and the likelihood of the survival of a family in one place,[46] so there was a similar correlation between the number of branches and the likelihood of the survival of a surname.[47] Surname group survival, like patrilineal family survival, was influenced by the proportion of marriages without children and the proportion with only female children. However, the existence of multiple branches with the same surname presupposes an earlier ability to produce sons, and such an ability is itself inheritable, so that families which are part of a large surname group are *ipso facto* more likely to survive in male lines, although, of course, not necessarily in the same place.

Even if Shap is to stand as the exemplar of this lower mobility pattern of the north-west, we must still remember that, even there, two-thirds, not of families, but of the whole membership of these particularly broad isonymous groups, moved away in the course of three generations. Even relatively low mobility, judged by the standards applicable elsewhere in pre-industrial England, still meant a very great deal of movement. Even in areas of 'low mobility' most family-name groups, let alone families, did not remain rooted in one place for generation after generation. We must not, however, fall into the opposite trap of forgetting the minority of families which did remain for generation after generation and provided

parts of the West Riding of Yorkshire (McKinley, *Surnames of Lancashire*). Mr Watson therefore suggested that the lower rates of turnover of surnames in some places, Shap against Horringer, for example, did not indicate a lower rate of real migration in or out of the parish, but merely that the size of the isonymous groups was so much larger that a similar rate of actual migration had a much slower effect in eroding a few common surnames as opposed to numerous less common surnames.
[45] McKinley, *Surnames of Lancashire*.
[46] See above: p. 311 and n. 10.
[47] Hey, 'Stable Families'.

the static core to each community. The stability of a community seems to have depended on the proportionate size of this static core. It is effectively the size of the static core that we are measuring by calculating the rate of turnover of surnames.

Mobility in the Chiltern Hundreds

How, then, do the villages and small towns of the Chilterns fit into this pattern? Mrs Evans only had time to count the turnover of surnames in one individual parish, Chesham, which was the centre for Chiltern wood working, particularly cart wheels and turned beech furniture. Both Quarter Sessions and hiring fairs were held there. It was also a venue in turn for Lollard, and for Quaker, Baptist, and Independent meetings, and a conventicle in the 1630s between them. For lowland England it was an extensive parish. It contained ten small hamlet communities besides the market town of Chesham itself, and was over five miles (eight kilometres) from east to west and over four miles (seven kilometres) from north to south.[48] Of the 122 separate surnames that she found there in the 1522 Musters and the 1524 Lay Subsidy, no fewer than thirty-two reappeared in the 1662 Hearth Tax and contemporary rate books.[49] Chesham evidently had a relatively large static core which is shown by this very high rate of survival of surnames. It exceeds the rate of survival at Shap and is only exceeded by the rate of survival in Burslem and Willingham, and perhaps that at Kibworth.

Even though it was not on one of the main through roads,[50] Chesham was certainly not isolated like Shap, and the relative immobility of its surname groups over a long period of time presents an astonishing contrast with the evidence produced by Dr Frearson on the importance of the road network through the Chilterns and by Dr Plumb on the frequency of communication amongst the members of his Lollard 'gathered church' in this area. Short-term mobility of individuals need not add up to long-term turnover of families.

Work on other parishes provides interesting comparisons for the existence of a larger than normal group of 'staying' families in Chesham. In Shropshire Dr Goodman pointed to the lack of such a core group in Neen Savage by contrast with the normality of Coreley and Burford. Dr

---

[48] It was not, however, large by the standards of northern and western England. The parish of Eccleshall in Staffordshire, for example, was over three times as extensive as Chesham. It was eight miles (thirteen kilometres) from east to west and nearly nine miles (fourteen kilometres) from north to south.

[49] See above, pp. 297–8. The evidence from the special 1606 church rate suggests that there was less out-migration in the seventeenth century than in the sixteenth.

[50] See above, Map 5, p. 282.

Hey has emphasized the importance of such a core of surviving families at Myddle and in the communities that he has studied in Yorkshire and Derbyshire.[51] At the other extreme, we have also been shown that the stable core was larger than usual at Willingham and Burslem. These examples strikingly illustrate my contention that the key explanation of the varying speeds of movement of families in different places, as it is suggested by the turnover of surnames, lies in the differing sizes of the stable cores of staying families, as opposed to those which lasted only one or two generations.

It does not seem that Chesham was unique in the area. Mrs Evans has counted the turnover of surnames for the whole of the twenty-one parishes in Buckinghamshire from which members of the Quaker Upperside Meeting are known to have been drawn. She found that of 521 surnames found in the 1524 Subsidy returns, 151 reappeared in the defective taxation returns of 1661–4.[52] This gives only a minimum number for the surnames that had survived. Had the Hearth Tax returns been complete, we would know how many more surname groups were still in the area. Nevertheless, this minimum suggests an even higher rate of survival than for Chesham by itself (see Table 8).

However, this does not necessarily mean that the population of the other Chiltern parishes investigated was even less mobile than that of Chesham, since some allowance has to be made for the size of the area involved, from around thirteen miles north of Amersham to eleven miles south, from around twelve miles west of Amersham to five miles east, in all some twenty-six kilometres from east to west and some thirty-nine kilometres from north to south. The problem is to know what sort of allowance must be made for the size of area involved. This is an even more complex problem than that posed by making comparisons between the smaller parishes of central, southern, and eastern England on the one hand and the extensive parishes of the north and west on the other. Some allowance, however, does have to be made. In view of the shortness of the distance moved by so many individuals in pre-industrial England, a great deal of the migration not only of individuals, but of families and of like surnamed groups of families, will have taken

[51] I am much indebted to Dr David Hey for allowing me to see a copy of his forthcoming paper on 'Stable Families in Tudor and Stuart England' in which he contrasts this stable core of families in a number of communities with the large penumbra of mobile short-term residents. I am particularly grateful for being allowed to see his thought-provoking paper at this juncture.

[52] See above, p. 296. Appendix B lists the twenty-one parishes concerned in Buckinghamshire. Members of the meeting were also drawn from three parishes in Hertfordshire, which have been left out of these calculations: Rickmansworth, Tring, and Watford. Had the Hertfordshire parishes been included the rate of survival of surnames would have been correspondingly greater.

place beyond the confines of single parishes, but within the area under investigation.

For the migration of individuals, the evidence of listings and descriptive surveys, the evidence of hiring fairs and marriage and baptism registers, of ecclesiastical court depositions and settlement records, taken together, suggests that most intra-rural migration in pre-industrial England took place within a distance of only ten miles (sixteen kilometres), and that very little of it exceeded twenty miles (thirty-two kilometres). Exceptional proportions of movement over greater distances were to be found amongst those who had applied for marriage by licence, amongst the gentry and richer freeholders, and amongst the deponents in ecclesiastical courts, with their bias against the poor. The distance criterion which applied with hiring fairs, the amount that can be ordinarily walked in a third, or at most half, a day, seems to have applied to all sorts of mobility.[53]. Notions of distance against time were, of course, slightly greater for those sections of society well enough off to travel on horseback; carriers, of course, moved more slowly, with their packhorses or waggons.[54]

The strong bias in ecclesiastical court depositions is towards evidence either from respectable members of the core families who had never moved from their birthplace, or from equally respectable members of society who because of their status were likely to have moved further than most, if they had moved at all. Even so in his analysis of some 7,000 ecclesiastical court depositions from six dioceses Dr Clark showed that of the witnesses who had moved, 59 per cent of rural male deponents and 65 per cent of rural female deponents were living within ten miles (sixteen kilometres) of their birthplaces when they made their depositions, and only 9 per cent of the men and 7 per cent of the women were then over forty miles (sixty-four kilometres) from their birthplaces.[55] Dr Souden brought out some regional variations in the distance of movement among his 10,000 deponents in ecclesiastical court cases: 'In the years before 1660 (when average migration distances were higher) 75 per cent of migrant males in the countryside had moved less than 19 miles (30 kilometres) in Norfolk and Oxfordshire, less than 16 miles (26 kilometres) in Wiltshire, less than 13 miles (21 kilometres) in Somerset.'[56] Hugh Hanley's earlier study of 145 deponents, mainly from north Buckinghamshire rather than the Chilterns, in the archdeaconry court of Buckingham between 1578 and 1584, found much the same migration dis-

---

[53] Peter Spufford, unpublished paper on intra-rural mobility in pre-industrial England read to the Jubilee Meeting of the Economic History Society, Cambridge, 1976 (ts. p. 32).
[54] See above, p. 285.
[55] Clark, 'Migration'.
[56] Souden, 'East, West', pp. 314–16.

tances as Dr Souden was later to find in the neighbouring county of Oxfordshire.[57]

It is therefore evident that a very great deal of the 'normal' migration of individuals in the Chilterns, although taking them outside any particular parish, even a large one like Chesham, still would not, and in fact did not take them outside the Chiltern area under investigation as a whole. The seventeenth-century settlement papers from Amersham and High Wycombe admirably illustrate this movement within the Chiltern 'country'.[58] Although there was a certain amount of linear chain migration in successive generations, much family migration did not go far beyond the limits of individual migration. Just as the frequent personal and family mobility of the pre-industrial past is the bane of genealogists, so the short distance of so much of that movement is their salvation. A number of the families for which Mrs Evans has given details in Appendix B illustrate this relatively short distance movement within the Chiltern area.

Surname studies by Richard McKinley and others have emphasized again and again that although only a minority of surname groups remained in the same parishes for prolonged periods of time, they frequently persisted within the same limited regions. These regions were smaller in scale than counties, and related to the hinterlands of one or more market towns. Some such 'pays' or 'countries' are easier to pick out than others.[59] The Chiltern Hundreds of Buckinghamshire and Hertfordshire seem to have been one such self-conscious 'country'. The core of the Chiltern 'country' was the joint market hinterland of the twin markets held at Amersham (Fridays to 1613, then Tuesdays) and at Chesham (Wednesdays), only three miles (five kilometres) apart. There were six other markets in this Chiltern 'country', all nearer, and some much nearer to Amersham–Chesham than the usual distance between market towns

---

[57] Hugh Hanley, 'Population Mobility in Buckinghamshire 1578–83', *Local Population Studies*, 15 (1975).

[58] See above, p. 276.

[59] Charles Phythian-Adams emphasized the importance of such 'countries' and their boundaries, as well as their neglect by historians, in his inaugural lecture as Hatton Professor of English Local History in the University of Leicester, 'Local History and National History: The Quest for the Peoples of England', *Rural History*, 2 (1991). Dr Malcolm T. Smith of the Department of Anthropology at the University of Durham is currently seeking to determine, from nineteenth-century censuses, whether migration of surname groups, when mapped, then followed an undifferentiated 'isolation by distance' model, or whether migration frequencies were distorted away from a simple distance alone pattern by the cultural boundaries of such 'countries'. I am much indebted to Dr Smith for letting me know what he is doing. He has a team working on different areas of Britain. M.T. Smith *et al.*, 'Isonomyc Analyses of Post-Famine Relationships in the Ards Peninsula, N.E. Ireland: Genetic Effects of Geographical and Politico-Religious Boundaries', *American Journal of Human Biology*, 2 (1990), pp. 245–54, has already appeared. See also the note by Malcolm Smith in *Local Population Studies*, 39 (1987), pp. 70–1.

in southern England.[60] Such a proliferation of markets within so small a region naturally dampened down the distances moved in service and on marriage. Both these sorts of mobility normally related to market areas, and help to explain the abnormal persistence of so many families in the Chilterns.[61]

Professor Everitt, when exploring the farming dynasties of Kent, picked out what he considered the 220 most important farming surnames, which combined well over 4,000 families by the nineteenth century. Some surnames, like that of Denne, were borne by as many as forty families within the county. By picking out such families he was, of course, concentrating on the stable core of 'stayers'. He found that in most cases each surname was predominantly restricted to a small group of nearby parishes within the county, so that, although paramount in that narrow area, they still remained intensely localized in their outlook and connections. This localization was particularly intense in the region around Canterbury.[62] This part of east Kent seems to have formed another self-conscious 'country'. David Souden and Gabriel Lasker established that in this part of Kent there was a close association of surnames between parishes within six miles (ten kilometres) of each other and a weak association between parishes over eleven miles (eighteen kilometres) apart. They have taken this as a measure of the cumulative movement of surname groups of families over the many generations between the adoption of surnames, before 1400 in this part of England, and 1705.[63] This surprisingly suggests

---

[60] These markets were, clockwise, at Wendover, Tring, Berkhamsted, Rickmansworth, Beaconsfield, and Chipping (High) Wycombe. Alan Everitt, 'The Marketing of Agricultural Produce', in Joan Thirsk (ed.), *Agrarian History of England and Wales*, vol. IV: 1500–1640 (Cambridge, 1967), pp. 473–4. All these were within seven miles of Amersham or Chesham. See Everitt, 'The Marketing', particularly pp. 496–502, for market areas and distances between market towns in various parts of England.

[61] See above, pp. 276 and 282 for the network of market towns, each with a tiny hinterland. Market areas here were so small that most people in the Chilterns were within easy reach of at least two market towns.

[62] Alan Everitt, 'Dynasty and Community since the Seventeenth Century', in his collected papers *Landscape and Community in England* (London, 1985), pp. 319–22.

[63] The surnames in the nominative listings from thirty-seven parishes are discussed in David Souden and Gabriel Lasker, 'Biological Inter-Relationships between Parishes in East Kent: An Analysis of Marriage Duty Act Returns for 1705', *Local Population Studies*, 21 (1978), pp. 30–9. However, their intention was not to measure mobility over time, but to establish a 'coefficient of relationship by isonymy' (having the same surname) as a means of helping to describe and explain the geographical 'migration fields' within which so much of the physical mobility of the past took place. The part of Kent covered was dictated by the survival of records, and is an essentially triangular area between, but excluding, the towns of Canterbury, Dover, Deal, and Sandwich. It partially overlaps with the area picked out by Professor Everitt as dominated by a close-knit clanship. However, it must be borne in mind that the area covered is circumscribed both by the sea-coast and by the failure of comparable documents to survive for analysis from the complete market areas of any of the east Kent towns, so that there is no evidence to suggest whether or not

a rather shorter distance of cumulative movement than many studies have suggested for individual mobility elsewhere over a single lifetime.

That the persistence of surnames within such extended areas should have been higher than in individual parishes is therefore not surprising, but the problem remains of knowing how movement within the Chilterns ranked in relation to that in comparable '*pays*'. The only roughly comparable area is a slightly larger group of similar hamlet settlements fifty miles (80 kilometres) to the north-west along the same ridge of heavily wooded hills, around Haverhill on the Cambridgeshire, Suffolk, and Essex borders. Although Mrs Evans began work on this area for the continuity of dissent, she had to abandon it because of the inadequacy of the sources for dissent. She did, however, make a comparison of surnames in a group of thirty-six parishes.[64] This appears to show an even slower turnover of surnames (see Table 8), but migration in this area was probably actually very similar, since the area chosen around Haverhill included fifteen more parishes, and, more importantly, the surviving Buckinghamshire Hearth Tax returns do not include the exempt, whilst those for the Haverhill parishes do. It is unfortunately not yet possible to make comparisons with any other areas, since I am not aware of any other suitable study of the persistence of surnames in groups of communities rather than in single communities.[65] Nevertheless, I have a strong impression that the amount of long-term migration out of either the parishes in the Buckinghamshire Chilterns, or those around Haverhill was particularly low. If so it is the more surprising in view of the extraordinary number of important main roads passing through the region and the ease of communications both towards London and away from it, northwards and westwards.

If such long-term immobility needs explaining, the explanation, as elsewhere, must be in terms of the large size of the core of less mobile families in the region. The preponderance of yeomen amongst the heads of household at Coleshill in 1640 suggests a large static core, as at Willingham.[66] Indeed, the whole Chiltern area had a noticeably large number of such freeholders, on whose votes parliamentary elections depended.[67]

---

slightly longer distance mobility was taking place to other parts of a market hinterland, of Canterbury for example.

[64] See above, p. 296, and Appendix A.

[65] Neither the Souden and Lasker study of 'Biological Inter-Relationships' nor a study of the isolated villages of Otmoor, north-east of Oxford, are comparable. The latter focussed on wider questions of overall interrelationships rather than the narrower field limited by the study of surnames. G.A. Harrison and A.J. Boyce, 'Migration, Exchange and the Genetic Structure of Populations', in *idem* (eds.), *The Structure of Human Populations* (Oxford, 1972).

[66] See above, p. 311, Table 8 p. 315.

[67] See above, pp. 60–1 and 302–3.

We are brought back to the economic resources of a wooded area for providing opportunities for large numbers of families to persist in the male line in numerous hamlet settlements scattered in these wooded hills. Woodland areas in general, like fenland, seem to have offered greater opportunities than open country. In particular, furniture making around Chesham and paper and lace making around High Wycombe would have been the equivalent here of earthenware in the Potteries region of north Staffordshire and of cheese and fish and other resources of the fen in the group of communities on its edge in the north-west of the old county of Cambridgeshire.[68]

The consequence of such a relatively low level of general long-term movement for the communities involved was a durable network of kinship and, presumably neighbourliness. Even within this peculiarly stable communal background the rate of survival of families of Lollard ancestry was extraordinary and exceptional. They were living within a cluster of communities which were amongst the least mobile so far to have been investigated, but, even in such a setting, striking by their own comparative immobility, these families with Lollard ancestors turn out to be themselves by far the least mobile of any group yet looked at by historians anywhere in England (see Table 8).

This extraordinary lack of mobility amongst radical religious families explains why it has been possible for Mrs Evans to trace descent in such a number of these families within the same small geographical area. The very frequent intermarriage between these families can be paralleled afterwards by self-conscious endogamy amongst their dissenting descendants, and earlier amongst their Lollard predecessors. Was there a continous tradition of endogamy? If so it will in part be responsible for the extraordinary lack of mobility, even amongst their noticeably immobile neighbours, since the movement of individuals which frequently took place at the time of marriage will have been eliminated. Did endogamy keep alive the 'nonconformist' flame of the Lollard martyr amongst the later generations of Hardings, whose monuments dominated Amersham Baptist Chapel?[69] Did traces of a religious tradition show up not only in our occasional indications of conventicling and absence from the established church, but also in the fervour of their will dedicat-

---

[68] For the economy and social structure of the Chiltern region see above, pp. 58–63 and pp. 276–7, 289–90, 292. By the early eighteenth century Buckinghamshire as a whole had an imbalance of males and females, that diverged slightly from the national imbalance. Souden, 'East, West', pp. 301, 308, 319. Disproportionately more females might mean excess in-migration of women (making lace?), rather than excess out-migration of men.

[69] Buckinghamshire: An Inventory of Non-Conformist Chapels, Meeting-Houses in Central England, Royal Commission for Historical Monuments, HMSO (1986), sub Amersham.

ory clauses, and their propensity to give their daughters names like Grace and Christian?

If David Hey's conclusions on the importance within communities of their least mobile families can be applied to these Chiltern parishes, there is no need to invoke inherited religious motivation to explain the number of times that members of families of Lollard ancestry were to be found as churchwardens or overseers of the poor. It is clear that their very lack of mobility in itself ensured that, far from being marginal, these people, however heterodox their religious opinions might possibly have been, were at the core of the societies in which they lived.[70] They did not need to be tolerated, for they, like the Balsham Familists,[71] were so integrated into the fabric of society that they themselves could set the tone of what and who was or was not to be tolerated.

[70] See above, pp. 111–14, for the disproportionately large number of suspected Lollards amongst the most highly taxed in these towns and villages in the 1520s.
[71] See Christopher Marsh, above, pp. 216–18.

CHAPTER 8

The social and economic status of post-Restoration dissenters, 1660–1725

BILL STEVENSON

Post-Restoration churchmen and present-day historians have presented very different accounts of the social and economic status of first generation protestant sectarian dissenters. As far as contemporary clergymen and heresiographers were concerned, dissenters were drawn largely from the 'vulgar sort' of people. In the Episcopal Return on the strength and nature of nonconformity of 1669, for example, the Bishop of Ely and his agents described a conventicle of Congregationalists meeting in the Cambridgeshire village of Over as 'Fanatiques' of 'Meane condition'. The Over Quakers were held to be of 'very poore condition, scarce a yeoman amongst them'.[1] The Bishop of Lincoln dismissed the members of a Presbyterian conventicle meeting in Bledlow, in Buckinghamshire, as mostly 'silly women'.[2] Obviously, bishops and their agents had a vested interest in demeaning the status of dissenters. Only 'silly women' and 'meane mechanicks' would forsake the national church; worthy and sensible men would not.

Some historians have presented a totally opposite view. They have stressed the seemingly 'bourgeois' nature of early sectarian dissent. Early Quakers, according to Alan Cole, were drawn predominantly from the 'urban and rural *petite bourgeoisie*'.[3] Cole found little evidence that early Quakerism had a 'proletarian character'. Richard T. Vann preferred to promote early Friends to the ranks of the 'middle to upper bourgeoisie'. The 'stronghold' of early Quakerism, according to Vann, was located among 'substantial yeomen and traders'. Poor husbandmen and artisans were numerically insignificant.[4] Similarly, Barry Reay has suggested that the status of post-Restoration Muggletonians was 'slightly more bourgeois

---

[1] George Lyon Turner (ed.), *Original Records of Early Nonconformity under Persecution and Indulgence*, I (London, 1911), p. 38.

[2] Ibid., p. 78.

[3] W.A. Cole, 'The Social Origins of the Early Friends', *The Journal of the Friends' Historical Society*, 48, 3 (1957), p. 117.

[4] Richard T. Vann, 'Quakerism and the Social Structure in the Interregnum', *Past and Present*, 43 (1969), p. 78.

than the early Friends'; and 'like the Quakers, there were few Muggletonian labourers and servants'.[5]

Moreover, Keith Wrightson and David Levine found that post-
Restoration sectarian nonconformity in the Essex village of Terling was
'essentially an affair of the middling sort of villager'. The radical piety of
Quakers and Congregationalists, like popular piety in general, appeared
to Wrightson and Levine to exist in direct proportion to the economic
and social status of the individual. 'Perhaps', they tell us, 'the matter of
the best road to salvation in the next world exercised only a limited
appeal over the imaginations of those hardest put to keep body and soul
together on earth.'[6]

Furthermore, the growing relationship between godliness and wealth,
on the one hand, and profanity and poverty, on the other, was all part of
an 'undeniable trend' which took place from the protestant Reformation
onwards. Moreover, it was not confined to Terling, nor even to Essex,
but occurred throughout England in general. Indeed, this 'trend', according to Wrightson and Levine, was 'by no means peculiar either to England
or to Protestantism'.[7]

Clearly, there has been a long tradition amongst historians to view
seventeenth-century protestant sectarianism as primarily the prerogative
of the rich and moderately well-to-do, having little or limited appeal for
the poor and 'vulgar' multitude. This chapter will seek to demonstrate
that neither the 'vulgar' label attached to seventeenth-century dissenters
by contemporary churchmen, nor the 'bourgeois' image stressed by
some present-day historians, presents a balanced view of their actual economic status. Rural dissenters of all sectarian persuasions were drawn
from a very wide cross-section of the economic spectrum indeed. They
included significant numbers of the very poor and lowly as well as a
goodly proportion of the 'comfortable', privileged, and wealthy. They
were drawn from all major social and economic categories and sub-
groups, except for the nobilitas major and the vagrant poor.

The four contiguous counties Cambridgeshire, Huntingdonshire,
Bedfordshire, and Buckinghamshire have been chosen as the geographical base for an investigation into dissenter status for a number of reasons.
First, each of them contained comparatively large numbers of a wide
variety of sectarian types during the period 1660–1725. Cambridgeshire,
for example, contained Quakers, General Baptists, Open Baptists, Congregationalists, Presbyterians, Independents, Muggletonians, and French

---

[5] Barry Reay, 'The Muggletonians: An Introductory Survey', in Christopher Hill, Barry
Reay, and William Lamont, The World of the Muggletonians (London, 1983), p. 52.
[6] Keith Wrightson and David Levine, Poverty and Piety in an English Village: Terling, 1525–
1700 (New York and London, 1979), pp. 166–7.
[7] Ibid., p. 14.

Huguenot refugees. Secondly, and somewhat fortuitously, is the fact that reliable Hearth Tax assessments from the early 1670s (showing those exempt from the tax through poverty) are extant for the first three of these aforementioned counties.[8] This provides an economic index with which to compare the relative wealth of individual sectarian groups *inter se* – as well as with the rest of society in general – both in their particular common county settings and on a wider regional basis. Finally, the Upperside of Buckinghamshire provides an area previously studied by both Alan Cole and Richard T. Vann (with greatly conflicting results). This allows a direct comparison and evaluation of their findings with my own.

Table 9 provides cumulative totals of the numbers of hearths contained within the dwelling houses of members of all of the major sectarian groups meeting in Bedfordshire, Cambridgeshire, and Huntingdonshire combined in the four-year period 1671–4. As can be seen, each of the most popular sects attracted a significant proportion of the 'meaner sort'; that is, the exempt combined with one-hearth householders. By far the most significant in this respect was the Bedford Open Baptist Church with a considerable 51.8 per cent of the poor in total. The Quakers and General Baptists appear similarly matched with 40.5 and 37.4 per cent of the 'meaner sort' respectively. Members of unspecified conventicles and Congregationalists, in comparison, each had a similar 28.5 and 27.3 per cent of poorer members respectively. Out of a total of 759 dissenters of all descriptions, 289 of them were either exempt from the Hearth Tax through poverty or occupied humble houses containing just a single hearth. This represents a very significant 38.1 per cent of all dissenters included in the table. Furthermore, as can be calculated from Table 9, 84.2 per cent of all 759 dissenters lived in houses containing less than four hearths, the point at which personal wealth measured in terms of moveable goods begins to escalate.[9]

In terms of collective status overall, the Quakers, General Baptists, and Congregationalists each had an identical mean average of 2.2 hearths per household and a median of two. The Open Baptists were clearly the

---

[8] They are: (a) Hearth Tax, Cambridgeshire, Lady Day 1674, PRO E179/244/23; (b) Huntingdonshire, Lady Day 1674, PRO E179/249/2; (c) Bedfordshire, Lady Day 1671, PRO E179/72/301. The reliability of Hearth Tax assessments as indicators of relative economic status have been tested against other indicators and shown to be very good indeed. They were tested against probate inventory values, poor rate subscriptions, and the Free and Voluntary Present of 1661. William Stevenson, 'The Economic and Social Status of Protestant Sectarians in Huntingdonshire, Cambridge-shire and Bedfordshire (1650–1725)' (Cambridge, PhD, 1990), pp. 5–13.

[9] Stevenson, 'Economic and Social Status' pp. 7, 12, 22. See above, pp. 19 and 43 n. 134. 38% may not have been representative of the size of this group in society at large, but is far too large to consider insignificant.

Table 9. *Cumulative totals of the number of hearths of 759 dissenters in Bedfordshire, Cambridgeshire, and Huntingdonshire, 1671–4*

Sect	Total no. of houses	Number of hearths											
		Exempt		1		2–3		4–7		8+		Mean/med.	
		No.	%	No.	%	No.	%	No.	%	No.	%		
Quakers[a]	405	33	8.1	131	32.4	173	42.7	64	15.8	4	1.0	2.2	2
Congregationalists[b]	128	9	7.0	26	20.3	78	60.9	13	10.2	2	1.6	2.2	2
General Baptists[c]	91	11	12.1	23	25.3	46	50.5	9	9.9	2	2.2	2.2	2
Open Baptists[d]	81	12	14.8	30	37.0	31	38.3	7	8.7	1	1.2	1.9	1
Presbyterians	12	–		2	16.6	5	41.7	5	41.7	–		3.1	3
Unspecified	42	3	7.1	9	21.4	17	40.5	11	26.2	2	4.8	2.7	2
Total	759	68		221		350		109		11			
% of total		9.0		29.1		46.1		14.4		1.4			

[a] Includes two Quaker wives of householders of unknown religious persuasion.
[b] Includes the Congregationalist wife of a householder of unknown religious persuasion.
[c] Six of these are the sectarian wives of male householders of unknown religious persuasion.
[d] Seven of these are the sectarian wives of male householders of unknown religious persuasion.

poorest group by far with a mean of 1.9 hearths per household and a median of only one. The wealthiest group of all was the Presbyterians with a mean of 3.1 hearths per household and a median of three.[10]

Table 10 provides the urban/rural distribution of the same 759 dissenters featured in Table 9. It can be seen, at a glance, that rural dissenters outnumbered their urban brethren in every sectarian division. In total, 573 of the 759 dissenters came from rural parishes. This represents a three-quarters rural predominance overall (75.5 per cent). The calculated rural predominance for each sectarian group (in ranked order) is given as Table 11. As the table shows, rural predominance amongst the differing sectarian groups ranged from two-thirds at its lowest to a hefty 82.8 per cent for Congregationalists at the top of the scale. Even the Open Baptists, who were gathered in and around the county town of Bedford, showed a significant two-to-one preponderance of rural members.

The relative economic standing of individual dissenting groups in comparison to the rest of society at large in the three counties under study is difficult to establish. Christopher Roy Husbands has calculated that composite mean hearth ownership in this period was 2.084 hearths per household in Cambridgeshire, 2.402 in Huntingdonshire, and 2.444 in Bedfordshire.[11] This represents an average of 2.31 hearths for the region as a whole. Although the following conclusions can only be taken tentatively, it can be seen that each of the urban divisions in Table 10 (except the Open Baptists) show a mean number of hearths per household above the 'regional average' of 2.31 hearths and each of the rural divisions (including the Open Baptists) are below it. This tends to corroborate the trend found within the individual counties: urban dissenters, on average, were generally slightly wealthier than the rest of society and their rural brethren were generally slightly poorer; although nonconformist hearth ownership could vary significantly from village to village.[12] Moreover, the relatively high Bedfordshire composite mean of 2.444 hearths highlights the overall relative poverty of the Open Baptists (with a mean of only 1.9

---

[10] This can be explained partly by the smallness of the group, and also by the fact that four of the Presbyterians were former divines ejected by the Anglican Church; and a fifth was a serving Church of England minister, Isaac Archer. The diary of Isaac Archer, the minister of Chippenham, in eastern Cambridgeshire, and the holder of a licence to run a Presbyterian conventicle in 1672, is kept in the University of Cambridge Library (CUL Add. MS 8499). It will be printed as Suffolk Record Society, 36 (1994), ed. Mathew Storey.

[11] Christopher Roy Husbands, 'The Hearth Tax and the Structure of the English Economy' (Cambridge, PhD, 1986), p. 166.

[12] Stevenson, 'Economic and Social Status', pp. 54–8, 141–7. See also Margaret Spufford, 'The Social Status of Some Seventeenth-Century Rural Dissenters', in G.J. Cuming and Derek Baker (eds.), Popular Belief and Practice, Studies in Church History, 8 (Cambridge, 1972), pp. 203–11.

Table 10. The urban and rural hearth distribution of 759 dissenters in Bedfordshire, Cambridgeshire, and Huntingdonshire, 1671–4

Sect	Total no. of houses	Number of hearths										Mean/med.	
		Exempt		1		2–3		4–7		8+			
		No.	%	No.	%	No.	%	No.	%	No.	%		
Quakers													
Urban	106	7	6.6	33	31.1	34	32.1	32	30.2	—		2.6	2
Rural	299	26	8.7	98	32.8	139	46.5	32	10.7	4	1.3	2.1	2
Congregationalists													
Urban	22	3	13.6	4	18.2	9	40.9	5	22.7	1	4.6	2.7	2
Rural	106	6	5.7	22	20.8	69	65.1	8	7.5	1	0.9	2.1	2
General Baptists													
Urban	18	4	22.2	2	11.1	6	33.3	5	27.8	1	5.6	3.0	3
Rural	73	7	9.6	21	28.7	40	54.8	4	5.5	1	1.3	2.0	2
Open Baptists													
Urban	27	5	18.6	9	33.3	11	40.7	2	7.4	—		1.9	1
Rural	54	7	13.0	21	38.9	20	37.0	5	9.2	1	1.9	1.9	1
Presbyterians													
Urban	3	—		—		—		3		—		4.0	4
Rural	9	—		2		5		2		—		2.8	2
Unspecified													
Urban	10	—		2	20.0	4	40.0	3	30.0	1	10.0	3.6	3
Rural	32	3	9.4	7	21.9	13	40.6	8	25.0	1	3.1	2.8	2
Total	759												

Table 11. *The rural predominance of individual sectarian groups in Bedfordshire,*
Cambridgeshire, and Huntingdonshire, 1671–4

Sect	Rural (%)	Urban (%)
Congregationalists	82.8	17.2
General Baptists	80.2	19.8
Unspecified conventiclers	76.2	23.8
Presbyterians	75.0	25.0
Quakers	73.8	26.2
Open Baptists	66.6	33.4

hearths per household), the vast majority of whom came from Bedfordshire parishes.

The occupational distribution of members of the major sectarian
groups show them to have been recruited overwhelmingly from agriculturalists, craftsmen and small retail traders. Tables 12 and 13, for example,
give the occupations of 216 male Quakers in Huntingdonshire and 214
in Cambridgeshire, respectively, over the period 1655–1724. Of the 430
Quakers featured in Tables 12 and 13 combined, 295 of them came from
rural parishes. This represents a weighty rural predominance of 68.6 per
cent.

Table 12 shows that 39.8 per cent of all Huntingdonshire Quakers with
known occupations between 1655–1724 were involved in agriculture as
their major source of employment. Of these, yeoman farmers represent
14.8 per cent of Quaker occupations in total. However, a significant proportion of Quaker agriculturalists came from the lower end of the social
scale. Husbandmen, labourers, and shepherds constitute 19.9 per cent of
all known Huntingdonshire Quaker occupations (and represent 50.0 per
cent of those involved in agriculture alone). Similarly, as Table 13 shows,
45.3 per cent of all Cambridgeshire Quakers in the same period came
from the agrarian sector. Yeoman farmers constitute 26.6 per cent of all
known occupations. Yet, 18.2 per cent of all Quakers in total were either
husbandmen or humble labourers (40.2 per cent of those involved in
agriculture alone). In Bedfordshire, twelve agricultural labourers
recorded during the eleven years 1666–76 constitute a very significant
22.2 per cent of all known Quaker occupations in this period. Labourers
and husbandmen combined account for 33.3 per cent of all known
Bedfordshire first generation Quaker occupations; and 58.0 per cent of
all agriculturalists.[13] In Buckinghamshire, husbandmen and labourers
combined constitute 34.4 per cent of all known occupations within the

[13] Stevenson, 'Economic and Social Status', p. 242.

Table 12. The distribution of known occupations of 216 male Quakers in Huntingdonshire, 1655–1724[a]

Occupation/status	No.	%	Occupation/status	No.	%
Gentlemen	5	2.3	Retail traders (cont.)		
Professional			Hatter	1	
Schoolmaster	2		Butcher	3	
Surgeon	1		Baker	2	
Lawyer	1		Ironmonger	1	
			Shopkeeper	1	
	4	1.9		51	23.6
Agrarian					
Yeoman	32	(14.8)	Craftsmen		
Husbandman	27	(12.5)	Hempdresser	8	
Farmer	4		Woolcomber	6	
Grazier	4		Weaver	8	
Dairy farmer	3		Fuller	1	
Labourer	12	(5.5)	Blacksmith	4	
Shepherd	4		Bodicemaker	3	
			Carpenter	4	
	86	39.8	Thatcher	1	
Wholesale traders and			Bricklayer	1	
large producers			Pattenmaker	2	
Fellmonger	2		Cooper	1	
Tanner	1		Collarmaker	4	
Miller	11	(5.0)	Ropemaker	1	
Maltster	4				
Oil merchant	1			44	20.4
	19	8.8	Servants and others		
			Servant	1	
Retail traders			Carrier	1	
Mercer/draper	3		Drover	1	
Grocer	9		Waterman	2	
Shoemaker	10	(4.6)	Fisherman	1	
Tailor	20	(9.2)	Tin man	1	
Gardener (fruiterer)	1				
				7	3.2
			Total	216	100

[a] In cases where a particular occupation was held by ten or more individuals, the percentage of the whole is given in parentheses.

Upperside of Buckinghamshire Quaker Monthly Meeting between 1655 and 1685.[14] Husbandmen, labourers, shepherds, and other poor agriculturalists also feature regularly in the membership lists of various Baptist, Congregationalist, and Independent gathered churches in Bedfordshire, Cambridgeshire, and Huntingdonshire throughout the period under study.[15]

[14] Ibid., p. 275.
[15] Ibid., pp. 75–6, 162, 165, 235.

Table 13. The known occupations of 214 male Quakers in Cambridgeshire and the Isle of Ely, 1655–1724[a]

Occupation/status	No.	%	Occupation/status	No.	%
Gentlemen	2	0.9	Craftsmen		
Agrarian			Carpenter	15	(7.0)
Yeoman	57	(26.6)	Woolcomber	8	
Husbandman	29	(13.5)	Blacksmith	4	
Labourer	10	(4.7)	Bodicemaker	3	
Farmer	1		Thatcher	3	
	97	45.3	Weaver	3	
Wholesale traders and			Collarmaker	2	
large producers			Glazier	2	
Miller	4		Wheelwright	2	
Fellmonger	3		Basketmaker	1	
Merchant	3		Brazier	1	
Maltster	1		Bricklayer	1	
Tanner	1		Cooper	1	
Retail traders	12	5.6	Flaxdresser	1	
Grocer			Fustianmaker	1	
Tailor	11	(5.1)	Ploughwright	1	
Shoemaker	11	(5.1)	Skipmaker	1	
Baker	9		Servants and others	50	23.4
Butcher	5		Mariner		
Gardener/fruiterer	3		Servant	2	
Shopkeeper	2		Farrier	2	
Draper	2		Stonecutter	1	
Fishmonger	1		Waterman	1	
Hosier	1			1	
	1			7	3.3
	46	21.5	Total	214	100

[a] In cases where a particular occupation was held by ten or more individuals, the percentage of the whole is given in parentheses.

Rural craftsmen were a significant economic component of both Huntingdonshire and Cambridgeshire Quakerism between 1655 and 1725. As Tables 12 and 13 show clearly, 20.4 per cent and 23.4 per cent of Huntingdonshire and Cambridgeshire Quakers, respectively, earned their livings as craftsmen or artisans. In Huntingdonshire, 77.3 per cent of these craftsmen came from the countryside; as did 62.0 per cent in Cambridgeshire and the Isle of Ely.[16] Rural blacksmiths, carpenters, wheelwrights, collarmakers, thatchers, weavers, and suchlike, were a common feature of post-Restoration gathered congregations throughout the period, whether Quaker, Baptist, or Congregationalist.

[16] Ibid., pp. 64, 151.

Quaker retailers were generally present in town and countryside alike. In Cambridgeshire, between 1655 and 1725, for example, 56.5 per cent of retail tradesmen came from rural parishes and 43.5 per cent from the towns.[17] In Huntingdonshire, during the same period, however, there was a 63.1 per cent bias towards urban retailers.[18] Substantial Quaker wholesale traders and large producers came mostly from rural parishes; 63.1 and 58.3 per cent in Huntingdonshire and Cambridgeshire respectively.[19]

Lastly, as Tables 12 and 13 show, gentlemen and professionals did not figure significantly in either Huntingdonshire or Cambridgeshire Quakerism throughout the period under study. In Huntingdonshire, only 2.3 per cent of all Quakers had gentry status and only 1.9 per cent of them were professionals. In Cambridgeshire, no professionals at all were recorded, and only 0.9 per cent of Quakers were gentlemen. In Bedfordshire, between 1666 and 1676, only 3.7 per cent of early Friends were listed as gentlemen.[20]

As we can see, the so-called 'bourgeois' nature of post-Restoration sectarian nonconformity does not stand up to close scrutiny – as least as far as Bedfordshire, Cambridgeshire, and Huntingdonshire are concerned. The three-quarters rural bias reflected in the cumulative Hearth Tax data pertaining to all the major sectarian groups, and the 68.6 per cent rural bias recorded in the occupational distribution of Huntingdonshire and Cambridgeshire Quakers show the 'bourgeois' tag to be a gross contradiction in terms. It is difficult to argue the existence of a dissenting 'bourgeoisie' when around 70 per cent of them lived and worked in the countryside; and even more difficult to do so in respect of the significant proportion of poor husbandmen, lowly shepherds and farm labourers, humble artisans and small retail tradesmen shown to have existed amongst the rural nonconformist rank and file.

Economic profiles

In the early 1940s, when social history as a respectable academic discipline was still in its infancy, G.M. Trevelyan defined it 'negatively' as the 'history of a people with the politics left out'.[21] Today, social and economic history is in danger of becoming the history of a people with the 'people' left out. Although this chapter necessarily contains much statistical data concerning the collective economic status of sectarian groups, I

---

[17] Ibid., p. 151.
[18] Ibid., p. 64.
[19] Ibid., pp. 64, 151.
[20] Ibid., p. 242.
[21] G.M. Trevelyan, *English Social History* (London, 1978 edn), p. 1.

hope to redress the balance by the inclusion of detailed economic profiles of individual dissenters. These profiles have been selected to include
members of a wide variety of sectarian groups, across a broad geographical and temporal scale, and from a wide cross-section of the economic
spectrum.

The 'better sort'

Although the economic hierarchies of all sectarian groups stopped short
of the *nobilitas major*, their upper strata did include gentlemen, professionals, substantial yeomen, some wealthy wholesale traders, and a
smaller proportion of wealthy retailers. As can be calculated from Table
9, only 15.8 per cent of nonconformists of all sectarian persuasions occupied houses containing four or more hearths in 1671–4 (the level of
hearth ownership at which a significant expansion occurred in the value
of moveable wealth). The economic profiles which follow, therefore, are
not typical of sectaries in general, but they do reflect the varying degrees
of wealth enjoyed by the very small minority at the top of the nonconformist economic hierarchy.

Peregrine Doyley of Chatteris, in the Isle of Ely, was a regular delegate
at both Monthly and Quarterly Quaker Meetings from the 1690s well into
the eighteenth century.[22] He was made an executor to the will of the
Quaker butcher Francis Cowper senior, also of Chatteris, in September
1708.[23] He was recorded as being a 'gentleman'. On 8 April 1735, Doyley's
estate passed into the hands of his wife and executrix Elizabeth who,
'being a Quaker', gave the required affirmation to that end. The will upon
which this affirmation was later recorded was made on 7 October 1731.[24]
Doyley left two manors in Suffolk to one son; his freehold tenement in
Chatteris to a second son; another freehold house in Chatteris to a third
son; and a copyhold house to a fourth son. He also left thirty-eight acres
of fenland in Chatteris, plus undisclosed amounts of woodland and
meadowland in the same parish, and undisclosed amounts of arable and
pasture in Suffolk, to be shared amongst his wife and four sons. He made
cash bequests of £100 each to three of his sons; and one of £300 to the
unborn child with which his wife Elizabeth was then pregnant.

The inventory of Doyley's goods, made on 17 September 1734, also
afforded him the title of gentleman; and it shows him to have thoroughly

---

[22] Cambridgeshire Quarterly Meeting minute book, 1673/4–1756, Cambs. RO R59/25/
1/5; Cambridge (later Sutton) Monthly Meeting minute book, 1703–61, Cambs. RO
R59/26/B2/1.
[23] Consistory of Ely, original will, 1710, CUL.
[24] Ibid., 1735, CUL.

deserved that title.[25] The total value of his goods was a substantial £811 5s 6d. His residence appears to have contained at least eight ground-floor rooms; seven first-floor chambers; and a garret. At least five of these rooms contained hearths. Amongst the goods in the hall was a coffee table, a marble table, a clock, some china, two maps, and a screen. Doyley's study contained tapestry hangings; and the closet, a 'parcele of books'. The parlour chamber contained £40 worth of silver plate, various maps, and a tea table. The barn contained 'a Charriott upon Carriage'; and three black mares and three bay geldings. In terms of farm livestock, Doyley kept only five cows and two sheep. He appears not to have been involved in tillage to any great extent, but seems to have lived off debt interest and income from rents. The sizable sum of £500 was either out on loan or due to the deceased in debts. Clearly, Doyley was the archetypal gentleman. He did not work with his hands, and lived an extremely gracious life in the process.

The Quaker gentleman Jeremiah Laundey of Midloe, in Huntingdon-shire, made his will on 21 January 1708/9 (it passed probate on 27 March 1713).[26] The value of his goods, appraised on 6 March 1712/13, was a healthy £385 8s 6d.[27] Amongst the livestock listed were: twenty-five 'Beasts' and a 'filley'; six horses; fifty-one sheep and some pigs. The appraisers of his goods allowed £100 for fifty acres of wheat in the field, and £25 for twenty-five acres of barley. Clearly, Laundey was farming at least seventy-five acres of arable land and kept a fairly substantial number of animals.

Laundey's inventory shows that his house contained at least four upper chambers with a garret above them. There were also at least four ground-floor rooms; plus a buttery, dairy-house, and brew-house. Listed amongst the linen was eleven pairs of 'Window Curtains', which were luxury items in the countryside at that time.[28] Laundey also

---

[25] Ely bonds and inventories, 1735, CUL.

[26] Archdeaconry of Huntingdon wills, probate register 28, pp. 207–8, Hunts. RO.

[27] Archdeaconry of Huntingdon inventories, 1712, Hunts. RO.

[28] Window curtains were extremely rare items in neighbouring Cambridgeshire between 1670 and 1705. Only three sets were found by Richard Kamm in Cambridgeshire inventories for this period. Unfortunately, this Cambridge BA dissertation is unavailable to me. For further details of Kamm's work see Margaret Spufford, *The Great Reclothing of Rural England: Petty Chapmen and their Wares in the Seventeenth Century* (London, 1984), p. 110. Furthermore, Lorna Weatherill has shown that window curtains were still relatively uncommon in the English countryside in 1715. Only 7 per cent of rural inventories listed them, compared to 60 per cent in London. Also, 26 per cent of gentry inventories mention window curtains between 1675 and 1725, compared to only 5 per cent for yeomen and 2 per cent for husbandmen (see Lorna Weatherill, *Consumer Behaviour and Material Culture in Britain 1660–1760* (London, 1988), pp. 88, 168).

possessed several other items which could be considered normal for a person from the higher ranks of society but expensive and rare for persons of a lesser status. He owned a 'Silver Tankerd ... a Clock[29] ... one Gun ... [and] Coffee pott'.[30] Laundey's 'Purse and Apparel' was worth £20; as much, in many cases, as the total value of some Quaker's goods.

Francis Holcroft, an ex-fellow of Clare College, Cambridge, and a former Church of England minister, was the founding father of the Cambridge Congregationalist Church. The extent of his activity as a peripatetic minister in the late 1660s and early 1670s was considerable. In the Episcopal Return of 1669, Holcroft was listed as the teacher to conventicles meeting in Histon, Oakington, Over, Willingham, Stow-cum-Quy, Haddenham, and St Michael's parish, Cambridge.[31] In 1672, he was licensed to be a teacher to a conventicle meeting in Bridge Street, Cambridge.[32] In April 1677, he was bound over for the sum of £10 for 'keeping unlawfull assemblies'; and in January 1680/1 a recognizance for £200 was issued against him.[33] In spite of this, the clerk of the court was courteous enough to afford him the title of 'gentleman'.

Holcroft's goods were appraised on 21 March 1691/2.[34] Although their value was a relatively modest £126 10s 8d, his few possessions reflect his position of former academic, author, and gentleman. His 'library of bookes' was valued at a very substantial £40. He left £38 5s 4d in ready money; a 'parcel of plate' valued at £7; 'two pecis of old gold' and a watch.

[29] Clocks were rare items in the seventeenth century and early years of the eighteenth century. They appear in only four inventories from Lichfield, in Staffordshire, and the surrounding district, between 1568 and 1680 (see D.G. Vaissey (ed.), *Probate Inventories of Lichfield and District 1568–1680*, Staffordshire Record Society (Oxford, 1969), p. 33). In Telford, in Shropshire, and surrounding area, only seven clocks were listed in inventories between 1660 and 1700. From the turn of the century they became increasingly more common. In the first decade of the eighteenth century, however, clocks were still rare. Only six clocks were recorded in the Telford area in the first decade of the eighteenth century whereas seventy-four appear in the forty years which followed (see B. Trinder and J. Cox (eds.), *Yeomen and Colliers in Telford: Probate Inventories for Dawley, Lilleshall, Wellington and Wrockwardine, 1660–1750* (London, 1980), p. 101).

[30] Coffee was rare for all but the wealthiest social groups in the early eighteenth century. Specialized coffee pots do not appear in mid-Essex inventories until 1725 (see F.W. Steer (ed.), *Farm and Cottage Inventories of Mid-Essex 1635–1749*, Essex Record Office Publications, 8 (Chelmsford, 1950), p. 24). Furthermore, as Trinder and Cox found in Shropshire, wealthier social groups only began to drink coffee and tea in the early eighteenth century (Trinder and Cox (eds.), *Yeomen and Colliers in Telford*, p. 113).

[31] Turner (ed.), *Original Records of Early Nonconformity*, I, pp. 38, 40, 41, 42.

[32] Ibid., p. 465.

[33] Book of recognizances, Cambridgeshire Quarter Sessions, 1661–89, Cambs. RO QS/4/1 (unpaginated).

[34] Ely bonds and inventories, 1692, CUL.

The Muggletonian Nathaniel Singleton senior, of Foxton, in southern Cambridgeshire, was an extremely wealthy yeoman farmer indeed. His spacious house contained seven hearths in 1674.[35] He left £80 to be divided equally between four of his grandchildren, and £5 to his Muggletonian servant Elizabeth Dunedge.[36] Singleton's goods, appraised on 6 December 1675, were valued at a hefty £823 19s 0d.[37] He was tilling at least 259 acres of land, and kept five ploughs and three harrows for that purpose. He had £258 10s 0d worth of barley in store; as well as significant quantities of wheat and rye. He kept twenty-seven cows, ten horses, twenty pigs, and 163 ewes and lambs.

The Baptist Clement Cousin of Croxton, in Cambridgeshire, was a yeoman farmer of some standing. He was excommunicated from the Fenstanton General Baptist Church in October 1658 for continual absence from their meetings.[38] By the time of his death he had moved to nearby Eltisley. However, in spite of his excommunication, he maintained some form of bond with the Baptist James Disbrowe of Croxton who witnessed his will in 1685.[39] He made cash bequests of £370 in total to three of his children and stipulated that 'the Child my wife is now big withall', should receive £150, on reaching the age of twenty-four, if a boy, but only £80 should it be born a girl.

Nicholas Apthorp of Gamlingay, in Cambridgeshire, was received into the Bedford Open Baptist Church on 9 May 1692.[40] He was a maltster of considerable means. The total value of his goods, in 1711, was a very substantial £813 17s 1d.[41] Of this, £208 worth of malt lay at Ware market in Hertfordshire. He left his malt house and messuage to his daughter Ann.[42] Besides his malting interests, Apthorp was deeply involved in agriculture. His inventory shows that he was farming at least sixty-three acres of arable land at the time of his death. Nineteen acres of this was enclosed land. He had £120 worth of wheat, rye, barley, oats, and hay in store.

---

[35] Hearth Tax, Cambridgeshire, Lady Day 1674, PRO E179/244/23.

[36] Elizabeth Dunedge of Foxton was presented to the church court of visitation in October 1686 as a reputed Muggletonian. Presented at the same time was one Elizabeth Singleton, wife of Nathaniel Singleton junior, and daughter-in-law, to the seven-hearth yeoman Nathaniel Singleton senior. For further details, see Episcopal visitation, October 1686, Ely diocesan records, B/2/70, fol. 41v, CUL.

[37] Ely bonds and inventories, 1675, CUL. The median wealth of Cambridgeshire yeomen at this time was £180 (see Margaret Spufford, Contrasting Communities: English Villagers in the Sixteenth and Seventeenth Centuries (Cambridge, 1979 edn), pp. 72, 156, 177).

[38] E.B. Underhill (ed.), Records of the Churches of Christ Gathered at Fenstanton, Warboys, and Hexham, 1644–1720, Hanserd Knollys Society, (London, 1854), pp. 245–6.

[39] Archdeaconry of Ely, original will, 1685, CUL.

[40] H.G. Tibbutt (ed.), The Minutes of the First Independent Church (now Bunyan Meeting) at Bedford 1656–1766, Bedfordshire Historical Record Society, 55 (Luton, 1976), p. 96.

[41] Ely bonds and inventories, 1711, CUL.

[42] Archdeaconry of Ely, original will, 1711, CUL.

Amongst his livestock were 110 sheep, three sows and fifteen pigs, four horses and cattle, and fowls and ducks to the value of £22. In spite of Apthorp's significant involvement in agriculture, he was primarily a malt-ster; and a very large producer indeed.

The 'middling sort'

William Proctor and his wife Alice of Willingham, in Cambridgeshire, were both members of Francis Holcroft's Cambridge Congregationalist Church in 1675.[43] William died in 1677, but his widow Alice kept faith with her religion. She was presented to the Vicar General's court in 1683 for her continued absence from the national church.[44] William Proctor [Prockter] was described as a 'knacker and roper' on the inventory of his goods made on 20 May 1677.[45] Amongst his goods, valued £102 7s 2d in total, was a quantity of hides and skins, hemp and working tools valued at £12 6s 0d. Like many small rural craftsmen, Proctor supplemented his income with the profits derived from a small-scale involvement in agriculture. He held five acres and one rood of ground sown with grain. Amongst his livestock were eight cows, two calves, two mares, three colts, seventeen sheep, and two hogs valued at £27 in total. He also had £40 due to him in cash lent out upon bond. Proctor was a classic example of a small rural craftsman and fenland farmer of middling status.

The grocer Thomas Skinner of Over was a typical small retailer of mod-erate status amongst first generation Quakers in Cambridgeshire. He lived in a house containing two hearths in 1662;[46] and paid 1s in the Free and Voluntary Present to the Crown in 1661.[47] In 1674, Skinner paid tax on three hearths.[48] He made his will on 14 March 1680/1.[49] He left his wife Elizabeth one copyhold messuage; one freehold messuage; four acres of arable land; one acre of marshland; and one copyhold close during her lifetime. He left a further two acres of arable land and one half-acre of marshland to three other relatives. Skinner was able to sign his will, even though he died within a few weeks of having done so.

Skinner's goods were appraised on 20 April 1681.[50] Although he had been described as a grocer in his will, he was accorded the status of 'yeoman' on his inventory. Amongst his goods – valued at £92 10s 1d in

---

[43] List of members of the Cambridge Church of Christ, 26 April 1675, Bodleian Library, Oxford, Bodl. MS Rawl. D1480, fols. 123–6.
[44] Vicar General's visitation, 1683, Ely diocesan records B/2/65, fol. 77v, CUL.
[45] Ely bonds and inventories, 1677, CUL.
[46] Hearth Tax, Cambridgeshire and the Isle of Ely, 1662, PRO E179/84/436.
[47] Free and Voluntary Present, Cambridgeshire, 1661, PRO E179/84/433.
[48] Hearth Tax, Cambridgeshire, Lady Day 1674, PRO E179/244/23.
[49] Consistory of Ely, original will, 1681, CUL.
[50] Ely bonds and inventories, 1681, CUL.

total – were £17 3s 9d worth of 'macery' goods, or spices, in his shop. His involvement in agriculture, although evident, was not of a sufficiently high degree to have afforded him yeoman status. He had sixteen acres of grain in the field; eight cows; five sheep; and five mares and a foal. Such a level of involvement would be more in line with husbandman status. However, since Skinner was coherent enough to sign his will (in which he was called a grocer), he would appear to have seen no incongruity in that assessment of his occupational status.[51] Whatever his primary occupation, Skinner's three hearths in 1674, and the value of his moveable goods, suggests that he was a typical member of the 'middling sort'.

The Quaker 'fanatique' George Nash of Over, in Cambridgeshire, was buried 'without a minister' on 3 December 1678.[52] He was no doubt interred in his own orchard, which had been used as a resting-place for at least twelve Quaker brethren between 1667 and 1673. Nash was described as a cordwainer, or shoemaker, in both his will and on the inventory of his goods of November and December 1678 respectively.[53] Although Nash could only mark his will, his inability to sign was perhaps only the result of his impending death. He could probably read at least. Listed amongst various goods in his hall was 'a bible' and 'other bookes'. The total value of his goods was a modest, but comfortable, £82 10s 0d. Nash was a shoemaker of the middling variety.

Francis Bacon of Gamlingay, in Cambridgeshire, was presented to the ecclesiatical court of visitation in 1682 for absenting his parish church.[54] He was a member of the Bedford Open Baptist Church in 1691, as his name appears on a letter from the Gamlingay congregation written about that time.[55] He was a blacksmith of moderate status. In 1700, he left a messuage in Wrestlingworth, in Bedfordshire, to his son; and two messuages and three parcels of meadowland, in Gamlingay, to his wife.[56] His goods, appraised on 15 May 1700, were worth £96 16s 6d in total.[57] He kept a few animals to supplement the family income; including seven milk cows and sheep to the value of £10.

Isaac Delahoi [Delheyhoy] of Guyhirn, in the Isle of Ely, became a covenanted member of the Independent Church newly formed there in July

---

[51] Skinner issued an undated trade token describing himself as a mercer (see G.C. Williamson, *Trade Tokens Issued in the Seventeenth Century*, I (London, 1889), p. 79). However, some seventeenth-century mercers were 'virtually' grocers (see Trinder and Cox (eds.), *Yeomen and Colliers in Telford*, pp. 27–8).

[52] Parish register, Over, Cambs., 1641–1717, Cambs. RO P129/1/2 (unpaginated).

[53] Consistory of Ely, original will, 1678, CUL; Ely bonds and inventories, 1678, CUL.

[54] Episcopal visitation, 1682, Ely diocesan records B/2/66, fol. 40v, CUL.

[55] Tibbutt (ed.), *The Minutes of the First Independent Church . . . at Bedford*, p. 94.

[56] Archdeaconry of Ely, original will, 1700, CUL.

[57] Ely bonds and inventories, 1700, CUL.

1693.[58] He may have been the Isaac 'de la Haye' who acted as sponsor at the baptism of a child into the nearby Thorney Huguenot refugee church in March 1678/9.[59] Delahoi was described as a 'husbandman' on the inventory of his goods of February 1697/8.[60] This would appear to have been a fair assessment of his status. Amongst his livestock were five cows and four calves; a pig; two mares and two colts; two dozen hens and ducks; and six geese. He had £15 worth of oats in store, and a little hay. The whole of his goods were valued at a modest £57 2s 9d. Clearly, Delahoi was a husbandman of the lower 'middling sort'.

The 'meaner sort'

Although the poor and lowly sometimes left wills (and had inventories of their goods taken for probate purposes) they generally did so, for obvious reasons, to a much lesser extent than the more wealthy sections of society. Nevertheless, a good deal of evidence exists within testamentary material left by sectaries of all persuasions to show that the significant levels of poverty suggested by the pattern of hearth distribution was very real indeed.

William Easy of Littleport, in the Isle of Ely, was a one-time Baptist who turned Quaker in 1655.[61] He paid tax on a single hearth in 1674.[62] He made his will on 18 August 1678 and was described as a cordwainer, or shoemaker.[63] The total value of his meagre estate was only £12 2s 10d.[64] Included in this were 5,000 turves valued at £3. Clearly, Easy's heirs did not inherit much at all. He was a very poor man indeed. He scraped a living both making shoes and digging turves for fuel in the fen.

Mildred Badcock of Meldreth, a small village in southern Cambridgeshire, was recorded as being a member of the Cambridge Congregationalist Church in 1675, independent of any male of that surname from that parish.[65] She was in fact the wife of Richard Badcock of Meldreth, a poor labourer. Badcock made his will in 1680, but did not die until 1697.[66]

[58] K.A.C. Parsons (ed.), The Church Book of the Independent Church (now Pound Lane Baptist) Isleham 1693–1805, Cambridge Antiquarian Records Society, 6 (Cambridge, 1984), p. 160 (see above, p. 92 and n. 128).
[59] Henry Peet (ed.), Register of Baptisms of the French Protestant Refugees Settled at Thorney, Cambridgeshire, 1654–1727, Huguenot Record Society Publication, 17 (Aberdeen, 1903), p. 48.
[60] Ely bonds and inventories, 1699, CUL.
[61] Underhill (ed.), Records of the Churches of Christ, p. 146.
[62] Hearth Tax, Cambridgeshire, Lady Day 1674, PRO E179/244/23.
[63] Consistory of Ely, original will, 1679, CUL.
[64] Ely bonds and inventories, 1679, CUL.
[65] List of members of Cambridge Church of Christ, 26 April 1675, Bodleian Library, Oxford, Bodl. MS Rawl. D1480, fols. 123–6.
[66] Archdeaconry of Ely, original will, 1697, CUL.

He could only mark the document; even though he did not die until seventeen years later. He may have been worried into making the will through illness, of course, but, in all probability, he was illiterate (at least in the sense of being able to write). He left his wife Mildred a freehold cottage with ground in Meldreth. The total value of his goods, appraised on 25 May 1697, was a very meagre £4 10s 6d.[67] He left clothes and cash to the value of £1, and £3 10s 6d worth of miscellaneous goods. The humble cottage which Mildred shared with her husband contained only a single hearth in 1674.[68] Although the Badcocks came from within the taxpaying sector of society in 1674, they also came from that group of people who were never far removed from the poverty line. They lived at subsistence level, and always faced the prospect of sudden abject poverty.

In 1682, the widow Mary Cundy of Orwell, in Cambridgeshire, was presented to the church court for absenting national worship and joining a conventicle.[69] In 1686, the incumbent of Orwell, or his clerk, noted that Mary Cundy 'A Muggletonian' died excommunicate and was interred with 'the burial of an Asse' in a close adjoining the parish churchyard.[70] Widow Cundy was probably the mother of William Cundy of Orwell who died in 1676.[71] The poor widow received continuous relief at 1s per week between 1671 and 1686 and had her rent paid from 1676 until her death.[72] This suggests that she was living with William Cundy at the time of his death and could not afford to pay the rent thereafter. William Cundy was a poor carpenter. The total value of his goods, appraised on 26 August 1676, was a mere £11 19s 0d;[73] including timber and carpentry tools worth just 20s. The Cundy house appears to have contained just two ground-floor rooms and a single upstairs chamber. In 1674, it contained just a single hearth.[74]

The Quaker widow Anne Mott [Moate] of Fenstanton, in Huntingdonshire, occupied a one-hearth house in 1674, but was discharged from the Hearth Tax through poverty.[75] In 1681, Anne Moate 'a very poore woman of Fenstanton yt frequently takes collection' had two brass kettles, worth approximately 10s, distrained for the recusancy of her Quaker landlord

[67] Ely bonds and inventories, 1697, CUL.
[68] Hearth Tax, Cambridgshire, Lady Day 1674, PRO E179/244/23.
[69] Episcopal visitation, 1682, Ely diocesan records B/2/66, fol. 52v, CUL.
[70] Parish register, Orwell, Cambs., 1653–1806, Cambs. RO P127/1/2.
[71] She could not have been his wife as she was continually referred to as 'widow' in the Orwell overseers' accounts between 1672 (between the death of William Cundy) and her own death in 1686 (see overseers' accounts, Orwell, Cambs., 1664–1739, Cambs. RO P127/5/1, pp. 157–8).
[72] Ibid., pp. 157–8.
[73] Ely bonds and inventories, 1677, CUL.
[74] Hearth Tax, Cambridgeshire, Lady Day 1674, PRO E179/244/23.
[75] Hearth Tax, Huntingdonshire, Lady Day 1674, PRO E179/249/2.

Tobias Hardmeate.[76] On fourteen separate occasions between March 1673/4 and March 1684/5, the widow Anne Moate received a total of £3 0s 6d in poor relief. On 6 March 1683/4, it was agreed by the Huntingdon Quarterly Meeting that the widow Moate should be further assisted at the rate of 20s per annum for housing.[77]

The Quaker labourer William Bundey of Bluntisham, in Huntingdon-shire, made his will on 7 April 1694.[78] He made cash bequests to relatives of £32 in total. The value of his moveable estate, appraised on 17 April 1694, amounted to £54 13s 8d.[79] However, £42 10s 0d of this was owed to the deceased in debts. The value of Bundey's goods, therefore, was only £12 3s 8d. It is easy to see how families like the Bundeys, on the margin of poverty, could slip irretrievably below the poverty line.

Alice Harrison of the Huntingdon Quaker Meeting had slipped below this line by the mid-1670s. She received a recorded £1 10s 10d in poor relief between 1674 and 1680.[80] Of the 12s 6d she was awarded in December 1679, 5s was allocated for her immediate necessities; 5s to pay off her rent arrears; and the remainder to buy her a new pair of shoes. Alice Harrison's poverty came to an end in 1680/1. The Quarterly Meeting authorized that 12s be paid to William Starling 'yt he Layd out for [a] Coffin and burying Cloathes for her'.[81]

The Quaker shepherd Robert Chappel of Hemingford Grey, in Hun-tingdonshire, made his will on 13 November 1683.[82] Although being 'merry' and 'in good health', Chappel could only mark his will. This would suggest that he was illiterate. His good health and merriment, however, did not last long. He was dead by the following year. His goods were valued at only £9 9s 9d on 26 December 1684.[83]

Richard Macer was one of the original covenanted members of the Guyhirn Independent Church (which later became the Isleham Inde-pendent Church) in July 1693.[84] He came from Thetford, in the parish of Stretham, in Cambridgeshire, and, like several dissenters from that area, was a fisherman. His goods were worth a paltry £3 only in February 1701/

---

[76] Huntingdon Monthly Meeting sufferings book 1656–1793, Cambs. RO R59/25/1/2 (unpaginated).

[77] Huntingdon Quarterly Meeting minute book 1673–1699, Cambs. RO R59/21/1/2 (unpaginated).

[78] Archdeaconry of Huntingdon wills, probate register 25, pp. 308–9, Hunts. RO.

[79] Archdeaconry of Huntingdon inventories, 1694, Hunts. RO.

[80] Huntingdon Quarterly Meeting minute book 1673–1699, Cambs. RO R59/25/1/2 (unpaginated).

[81] Ibid., (unpaginated).

[82] Archdeaconry of Huntingdon wills, original will, 1684, Hunts. RO.

[83] Archdeaconry of Huntingdon inventories, 1684, Hunts. RO.

[84] Parsons (ed.), The Church Book of the Independent Church (now Pound Lane Baptist) Isleham 1693–1805, p. 160.

2.[85] His house appears to have consisted of two ground-floor rooms and a single upper chamber. Clearly, Macer was a very poor man indeed.

Quaker status: the great debate

The first serious study of Quaker social origins, over a wide geographical area, was completed by Alan Cole in the mid-1950s.[86] According to Professor Cole, first generation Quakers were drawn mainly from the 'urban and rural *petite bourgeoisie*'.[87] Cole found remarkably few members of the 'ruling class' and very little evidence that early Quakerism had a 'proletarian character'.[88] He found only one gentleman mentioned in Quaker marriage registers (his sole source of reference) before 1689, and an insignificant number of identifiable labourers. Instead, Cole's Quakers, in the main, were made up of tailors, shoemakers, weavers, woodworkers, leatherworkers, husbandmen, and such like – the rather dubiously named '*petite bourgeoisie*'.[89]

In 1969, Richard T. Vann challenged Professor Cole's findings. Based on his studies of early Quaker social origins in Buckinghamshire and Norfolk, Vann argued that it was the 'middle to upper bourgeoisie', rather than Cole's *petite bourgeoisie*, 'which was strikingly more prominent among the early Quakers'.[90] The 'stronghold' of early Quakerism, according to Vann, 'was among the substantial yeomen and traders ... and that poor husbandmen and artisans were numerically insignificant'.[91] Vann also found that labourers were under-represented and that the proportion of Quaker gentry 'was no lower than in the population at large'.[92] All this led Vann to the conclusion that early Quakers constituted a 'middle to upper', rather than a lower, 'bourgeoisie'.

Although Vann and Cole both included Buckinghamshire within their respective studies, they arrived at conflicting conclusions. Vann

---

[85] Ely bonds and inventories, 1701, CUL.
[86] W.A. Cole, 'The Quakers and Politics, 1652–1660' (Cambridge, PhD, 1955). The areas studied were Lancashire, Yorkshire, Gloucestershire and Wiltshire, London and Middlesex, Bristol, and Buckinghamshire.
[87] Cole, 'The Social Origins of the Early Friends', p. 117 (this article is an abbreviated version of Appendix A of the author's PhD thesis mentioned above).
[88] Ibid., pp. 116–17.
[89] It seems incongruous, to say the least, to talk of a 'rural' bourgeoisie. It is a contradiction in terms. Moreover, because of the nineteenth- and twentieth-century concepts of 'class' associated with the word 'bourgeois', it is considered much best avoided. In a pre-industrial society, in which social stratification was based upon deference rather than economic status *per se*, the use of such a term is clearly an anachronistic nonsense.
[90] Vann, 'Quakerism and the Social Structure in the Interregnum', p. 72.
[91] Ibid., p. 78.
[92] Ibid., p. 72.

accounted for this discrepancy by criticizing Cole for his total reliance on marriage registers as his only source of evidence.[93] Vann, on the other hand, had utilized a wide range of sources including registers, sufferings records, minute books, and testamentary records. Vann, however, had also resorted to the highly dangerous practice of attributing the status of 'yeoman' to all men who owned at least twenty acres of land or paid at least £4 per annum in tithes.[94]

In an attempt to clarify the situation, I decided to run a check on the occupational distribution of early Quakers belonging to the Upperside of Buckinghamshire Monthly Meeting.[95] The results are presented as Table 14. As the table shows, no gentlemen were mentioned in records pertaining to the Upperside of Buckinghamshire between 1655 and 1685. This does not mean, of course, that no gentlemen existed amongst early Friends. As Vann points out, there can be no doubt that the distinguished Buckinghamshire Friends Isaac Pennington, Thomas Ellwood, William Penn, and their like,

---

[93] Ibid., p. 76.

[94] R.T. Vann, *The Social Development of English Quakerism, 1655–1755* (Cambridge, Mass., 1969), p. 65. The practice of attributing the status of yeoman to any landholder of at least twenty acres is extremely ill-advised. As Margaret Spufford has shown, a significant decrease in the number of small landowners able to survive on half-yardland and yardland units in the clay-soil arable village of Orwell in south-west Cambridgeshire – combined with a corresponding increase in the number of larger landholdings during the first third of the seventeenth century – led to an economic polarization of the community that was not typical in the pastoral fen-edge village of Willingham in the north of the county. In Willingham, the small landholder's ability to engage in stock and dairy farming ensured the economic viability and survival of small landholdings (see Margaret Spufford, *Contrasting Communities*, pp. 19–119). It is not difficult to see, therefore, the extreme danger of classifying farmers, on a countywide basis, according to the size of their holding. A twenty-acre land-holder in the arable uplands might only deserve the title 'husbandman', whereas in pastoral or forest regions a similar sized holding could well have produced a prosperous yeoman. Furthermore, the practice of attributing yeoman status to any landowner liable to pay £4 a year or more in tithes can prove totally misleading. It is highly probable, for example, that a landowner would have farmed differing amounts of land, and thereby paid differing amounts of tithe, at different stages of his economic life-cycle. This could be dependent upon changing economic necessity, as well as the ability to cultivate in terms of age, health, and the ready availability of labour within the family unit. Consequently, under the £4 a year rule, a landowner could be judged a yeoman for the majority of his life by historians, and a husbandman for the latter part of it. For a typical example of the dangers involved, see my thesis: 'Economic and Social Status', p. 27.

[95] The Upperside of Buckinghamshire Monthly Meeting included members in south-western Hertfordshire. The principal Hertfordshire parishes were: Berkhamsted, Flaunden, Hemel Hempstead, King's Langley, Rickmansworth, Tring, and Watford. The Buckinghamshire parishes spread from Amersham northwards to Aylesbury, and southwards to the Berkshire border. See Map 7, p. 295, of this volume. In my re-examination of the economic status of early Friends I used exactly the same sources as Professor Vann, but confined my examination to the Upperside of Buckinghamshire and did not include the Lowerside Meetings as he did. The same sources were used for the compilation of Table 15, p. 356.

Table 14. *The occupational distribution of ninety first generation Quakers belonging to the Upperside of Buckinghamshire Monthly Meeting, 1655–85*[a]

Occupation	No.	%	Occupation	No.	%
Professional			Retail traders		
Physician	2		Salesman	4	
Chirurgeon	1		Butcher	2	
	3	3.3	Shoemaker	2	
			Mercer	2	
			Tailor	2	
			Glover	1	
			Ironmonger	1	
Agrarian			Shopkeeper	1	
Yeoman	8			15	16.7
Grazier	1		Craftsmen		
Farmer	1		Blacksmith	6	
Husbandman	20	(22.2)	Bodicemaker	2	
Labourer	11	(12.2)	Bricklayer	2	
	41	45.6	Carpenter	1	
Wholesale traders and			Clothworker	1	
large producers			Joiner	1	
Maltster	6		Lacemaker[b]	1	
Mealman	3		Hoopshaver	1	
Clothier	1		Turner	1	
Tanner	1		Wheelwright	1	
Miller	1		Weaver	1	
	12	13.3		18	20.0
			Others		
			Sawyer	1	1.1
			Total	90	100

[a] In cases where a particular occupation was held by ten or more individuals, the percentage of the whole is given in parentheses.
[b] The lacemaker is the only woman Quaker featured in this table.

were of gentry status.[96] But they were comparatively few (Vann could only name four), and peculiar to the Upperside Monthly Meeting.[97]

More importantly, it is extremely difficult to see how Vann could conclude that early Quakerism in Buckinghamshire was a 'stronghold' of substantial yeomen and wealthy wholesale traders. Only eight yeomen (8.9 per cent of the whole) are mentioned in first generation records. But Vann, of course, was willing to ascribe yeoman status to any twenty-acre landholders and £4 tithe payers (and the dangers of that practice have

[96] Vann, 'Quakerism and the Social Structure', pp. 79–81.
[97] No such string of 'obvious' gentry names are to be found amongst Friends in the Lowerside of Buckinghamshire or their brethren in Bedfordshire, Huntingdonshire, and Cambridgeshire in the early period of Quakerism.

already been noted). This no doubt accounts for the yeoman bias in Vann's calculations. Similarly, wholesale traders and large producers amount to only 13.3 per cent of the whole; not all of whom were 'prosperous'. The combined numbers of husbandmen and labourers, on the other hand, provide a substantial 34.4 per cent of the whole. Clearly, first generation Quakerism in Buckinghamshire, or at least in the Upperside part of it, was anything but a 'middle to upper bourgeoisie'. It was far more like the movement of small craftsmen and husbandmen depicted by Alan Cole. Indeed, husbandmen and craftsmen constitute 42.2 per cent of all the occupations listed in Table 14.

Both Cole and Vann, however, appear to have misrepresented the numbers of labourers in the early Quaker movement. According to Cole they were 'insignificant',[98] and for Vann they were 'substantially under-represented'.[99] According to my calculations, however, labourers constituted a significant 12.2 per cent of the whole. Even allowing for Vann's small proportion of gentlemen (who were most definitely there even if they did not feature in the records) early Quakerism in the Upperside of Buckinghamshire appears to have been a more plebeian movement than that suggested by either Vann or Cole. As Table 14 shows, it was a rural agrarian movement made up primarily of the lowest strata of agriculturalists – husbandmen and labourers – and a fair proportion of lowly craftsmen or artisans. It was a movement of the 'lower' and 'middling' sorts. A very substantial 54.4 per cent of the total was made up of husbandmen, labourers, and craftsmen.

The change in Quaker status through time

Richard T. Vann has stated, in reference to Buckinghamshire and Norfolk Friends, that 'later converts were of a lower social class and that the original gentry adherents – or more often, their children – tended to return to the established church'.[100] Consequently, the overall status of Quakers became lower as time progressed. Barry Reay, on the other hand, found that in Essex 'there may have been fewer gentry among early Quakers than Vann has suggested'.[101] T.A. Davies, like Vann, found that there was a gradual disappearance of the gentry in Colchester as Quakersim moved towards the eighteenth century. However, in Colchester, Davies also found that the 'proportion of wealthy adherents rose –

---

[98] Cole, 'The Social Origins of the Early Friends', p. 116.
[99] Vann, 'Quakerism and the Social Structure', p. 72.
[100] Ibid., p. 91.
[101] Barry Reay, 'The Social Origins of Early Quakerism', *Journal of Interdisciplinary History*, 11, 1 (1980), p. 61.

contrary to Vann's suggestion – but this was never to overtake the consistently high percentage of artisans in the movement'.[102] This trend was repeated in Essex as a whole. But for Davies, the change was 'certainly not large enough to warrant the conclusion that the social base of the movement had rapidly narrowed'.[103]

In Huntingdonshire, the reverse was true as far as the gradual disappearance of the gentry was concerned. There, in fact, gentlemen did not begin to appear in records until towards the end of the seventeenth century.[104] In other respects, though, the trend in Huntingdonshire appears to match that in Essex. The proportion of wealthy Friends, particularly wholesale traders, in Huntingdonshire also rose – but only very slightly.[105] However, there was also a counter-balancing increase in the proportion of craftsmen or artisans. In overall terms, therefore, Davies' description of Colchester in the later period is equally applicable to Huntingdonshire: 'the social composition did change, but not dramatically; on the whole there was a wider range of wealth among the Friends'.[106]

In Cambridgeshire, a similar picture emerges to that in Essex and Huntingdonshire. There, a decrease in the number of poor agriculturalists in the period 1695–1714 – coupled with an increase in the number of retailers – probably meant a slight increase in overall economic strength.[107] Wealthy Friends (gentlemen, substantial wholesalers, and yeomen) represented 25.5 per cent in the first generation and only 22.9 per cent in the early eighteenth century.[108] Although this indicates a slight reduction of wealth at the top of the scale, the rank-and-file had grown slightly more prosperous. In overall terms, therefore, collective economic strength had changed little.

It can be seen, then, that Vann's narrowing social and economic base is not apparent for Cambridgeshire, Huntingdonshire, and Essex. Nor is it for Warwickshire. According to Judith Jones Hurwich: 'Neither the hearth tax index nor the status index supports the hypothesis advanced by Vann: that the first generation of Quakers was dominated by gentlemen, substantial yeomen, and traders, and that the later recruits were consistently poorer.'[109] Alan Anderson, in his study of Lancashire Friends, however, found that 'Professor Vann's contention that the movement

---

[102] T.A. Davies, 'The Quakers in Essex 1655–1725' (Oxford, DPhil, 1986), p. 60.
[103] Ibid., p. 61.
[104] Stevenson, 'Economic and Social Status', pp. 65, 70.
[105] Ibid., pp. 71, 74.
[106] Davies, 'The Quakers in Essex', p. 60.
[107] Stevenson, 'Economic and Social Status', pp. 159, 160–1.
[108] Ibid., p. 161.
[109] Judith Jones Hurwich, 'Dissent and Catholicism in English Society: A Study of Warwickshire, 1660–1720', Journal of British Studies, 16, 1 (1976), p. 54.

experienced a discernible shift in the base of recruitment after the 1660's
... may have some substance.'[110]

In view of the fact that the only evidence of a downward trend in
Quaker wealth over time emanates from Vann (and only 'may' have
occurred in Anderson's Lancashire), I thought it necessary to examine
Quaker status over time in an area studied by Vann himself. Accordingly,
I have compared the occupational structure of early Friends in the
Upperside of Buckinghamshire between 1655 and 1685 with that of their
co-religionists in the period 1686–1700. The results are given as Table 15.
As the table indicates, Friends in the Upperside of Buckinghamshire did
not become poorer in the second generation. Quite the reverse; they
became a little better-off. The proportion of professionals increased from
3.3 per cent in the first generation to a slightly higher 3.7 per cent in the
second. Gentlemen do not begin to appear in records until the later
period (although a small proportion undoubtedly existed in the first).
More significantly, the proportion of yeomen increased in the later
period, from 8.9 per cent to a substantial 16.7 per cent, and the proportions of the poorer agriculturalists consequently decreased. All this represents an upward trend in collective wealth. Similarly, the proportion
of retailers increased from 16.7 per cent to 25.0 per cent over the two
periods. Also, the proportion of humble craftsmen or artisans became
reduced in the second period. In every occupational category except
wholesale traders and large producers, Friends became better off by the

Table 15. *A comparison of the occupational structure of Friends in the Upperside of
Buckinghamshire in the periods 1655–85 and 1686–1700*

Occupation	1655–85		1686–1700	
	No.	%	No.	%
Gentlemen	—		1	0.9
Professional	3	3.3	4	3.7
Agrarian, including	41	45.6	50	46.3
Yeomen	(8)	(8.9)	(18)	(16.7)
Husbandmen	(20)	(22.2)	(21)	(19.4)
Labourers	(11)	(12.2)	(10)	(9.2)
Wholesalers and large producers	12	13.3	11	10.2
Retail traders	15	16.7	27	25.0
Craftsmen	18	20.0	15	13.9
Others	1	1.1	—	
Totals	90	100	108	100

[110] Alan Anderson, 'The Social Origins of the Early Quakers', *Quaker History*, 68 (1979),
p. 39.

period 1686–1700 than they had been earlier. Clearly, Vann's contention that the social base of Quakerism became significantly more narrow as time progressed is not true for the Upperside of Buckinghamshire. Moreover, as the Upperside constituted a significant proportion of the area studied by Vann, it is extremely difficult to see how he could arrive at such a conclusion in the first place. His overemphasis of gentry adherents and his willingness to 'create' yeomen is no doubt to blame

Quite clearly, the social composition of first generation English Quakerism, and its degree of change over time, varied on a regional basis. Even if Vann did get it right for Norfolk and the part of Buckinghamshire not examined here, it was remiss of him to make broad generalizations based on evidence from only two counties. One thing is certain: the change in Quaker status did not conform to Vann's model in either Huntingdonshire, Cambridgeshire, Essex, Warwickshire, or even the Upperside of Buckinghamshire.

As we have seen, post-Restoration dissenters were drawn from a very wide cross-section of society at large. They included all of the major social categories and sub-groups, except for the nobility and the vagrant poor. The vast majority of dissenters, whatever their sectarian affiliation, lived and worked in the countryside.

All of the major sects attracted significant numbers of the 'meaner sort' Between 1671 and 1674, for example, a very weighty 38.1 per cent of sectaries, out of a total of 759 of all sectarian persuasions (in Bedfordshire, Huntingdonshire, and Cambridgeshire), were either exempt from the Hearth Tax for reasons of poverty or occupied humble houses containing just a single hearth; the traditional preserve of the poor and lowly. At the lowest end of the scale, the Bedford Open Baptist Church had a staggering 51.8 per cent of members in this poorest category.

But alongside poor widows, humble shepherds, labourers, husbandmen, and artisans – in nonconformist private meeting-houses and chapels alike – sat a goodly proportion of the 'middling' variety of mastercraftsmen and retailers; a fair proportion of wealthy yeomen farmers and wholesale traders; and a sprinkling of professional men and gentlefolk.

The wide social and economic base of post-Restoration dissent applied as much to Quakerism as it did to the other major sects. The Society of Friends were not a 'bourgeoisie' of any description; 'petite', 'middle to upper', or any other kind. Even in the Upperside of Buckinghamshire – an area studied by Alan Cole and Richard T. Vann – Friends included a significant proportion of farm labourers and husbandmen (34.4 per cent of known occupations between 1655 and 1685). First generation

Quakerism was a predominantly rural agrarian movement of the lower and middling variety of agriculturalists, rural craftsmen, and small retailers.

Moreover, the Quaker movement did not begin 'wealthy' and grow poorer as Richard Vann maintains. It was not an upper bourgeoisie with a progressively narrowing social base. Quite the reverse. First generation Quakerism began as the lower-to-middling rural agrarian movement outlined above, and remained much the same in terms of overall collective status. In Cambridgeshire and Huntingdonshire, as a whole, the proportion of wealthy Quakers (gentlemen, yeomen, and wholesalers) had actually increased slightly by the eighteenth century; although this rise was counter-balanced by an increase in the proportion of artisans. In Essex, too, as T.A. Davies discovered, the proportion of wealthy Quaker adherents also rose, contrary to Vann's model, but were still never to outweigh the consistently high artisan representation. Similarly, even in Vann's Buckinghamshire, a slight increase in overall Quaker wealth had occurred by 1700. In all of these counties, then, the proportion of wealthy Quakers had actually increased instead of declined. But in each of these counties the changes represented only a slight shift in emphasis. A moderate redistribution of wealth had occurred, with some status groups becoming slightly wealthier and others slightly poorer. In overall terms, however, Quaker collective status remained much the same. The Society of Friends was certainly not an early 'bourgeois' movement with a narrowing social base. Indeed, Quaker domestic hearth distribution and occupational structure have shown this not to have been the case.

Domestic hearth ownership and occupational structure, however, only tell part of the story of relative wealth and poverty in post-Restoration gathered church congregations. Some poor souls, who by right should have been discharged from the Hearth Tax, still found themselves included by overzealous or unsympathetic local officials. In 1667, for example, the 'poore widow' Susan Gunn of Haddenham, in the Isle of Ely, was: 'Rendered . . . to the Chimny man to be able to pay: when it is well knowen to severall of Hur honist nibours . . . she was not with in the compas of the Act.'[111] The economic plight of this unfortunate Quaker widow, and many like her, failed to get recognition, even amongst the

---

[111] Haddenham sufferings 1665–71, Cambs. RO R59/25/18/1. Further evidence that some people who should have been exempt from the tax were in fact included can be found in overseers of the poor accounts. The overseers of Gamlingay, in Cambridgeshire, paid the 'Chimley mony' for two widows between 1685 and 1687 (Cambs. RO P76/12/3, P76/12/6). Similarly, the overseers of Orwell, in Cambridgeshire, paid the hearth contribution of Robert Rownings, and then his widow, between 1674 and 1684 (Cambs. RO P127/5/1, pp. 163–81).

high percentages of parishioners traditionally discharged from the Hearth Tax through reasons of poverty.[112]

Moreover, the sudden impoverishment brought about by the premature death of a bread-winner, or an unexpected bout of sickness, as well as the more obvious harbingers of poverty such as creeping old age and infirmity, could bring abject poverty to otherwise sound petty craftsmen, small retail traders, and humble farmers. Such factors add a further dimension to the struggle for economic survival for which statistics of any description can never really do justice. It only helps a little to reflect that between 1673 and 1699, some sixty-one poor but 'faceless' Quakers were in receipt of relief from the Huntingdonshire Quarterly Meeting;[113] or that eighty indigent Friends received economic aid from benefactions specifically set up by members of the Huntingdonshire Monthly Meeting between 1696 and the early years of the following century.[114] I hope, therefore, that the inclusion of economic profiles on the poor and wealthy alike have given life and vitality to otherwise arid statistics, and faces to the faceless.

[112] As Paul Slack notes, the proportion of householders exempted from the Hearth Tax through poverty averaged between 30 and 40 per cent in Kent, Essex, Leicestershire, and Devon (see Paul Slack, *Poverty and Policy in Tudor and Stuart England* (London, 1988), p. 41).

[113] Huntingdonshire Quarterly Meeting minute book 1673–99, Cambs. RO R59/25/1/2 (unpaginated).

[114] Huntingdon Monthly Meeting book of benefactions 1677–1834, Cambs. RO R59/25/5/1, pp. 9–15.

CHAPTER 9

The social integration of post-Restoration dissenters, 1660–1725

BILL STEVENSON

Post-Restoration gathered congregations have often been portrayed as 'alternative societies'; as collectives of ostracized social misfits who neither sought nor gained acceptance within their local parish communities.[1] Clive Holmes, for example, has interpreted the highly cohesive nature of Quakers to have been a 'deliberate isolation from the world within their own closed community'.[2] Christopher Hill has claimed that the protestant Reformation initiated a breach in traditional English community relations which culminated in a transition from 'parish to sect'.[3]

Medieval English society has been described by Professor Hill as a 'federation of communities'.[4] Central to each parish community was regular collective worship and socialization in a unitary catholic church. But the protestant Reformation – and gathered church separation which followed in its wake – brought dramatic and irreversible change. According to Professor Hill:

> The old geographical communities, with their rough-and-ready but effective hierarchical subordination, their traditional ceremonies, their succession of popular seasonal festivals . . . were passing. The new communities of the sects which ultimately emerged were voluntary, electing and paying their own minister, relieving their own poor, imposing a more rigorous discipline on their members than the national Church could now do. Contract communities had succeeded status communities.[5]

---

[1] For a general discussion of the opinions of historians who have expressed such views concerning the Society of Friends, see T.A. Davies, 'The Quakers in Essex 1655–1725' (Oxford, DPhil, 1986), pp. 261–3. Dr Margaret Spufford once used such terms as 'alienation' and 'isolation' in reference to the social relations of dissenters in general (see *Contrasting Communities: English Villagers in the Sixteenth and Seventeenth Centuries* (Cambridge, 1979 edn), pp. 344–50. I am pleased to say that she has now revised her opinion.

[2] Clive Holmes, *Seventeenth-Century Lincolnshire* (Lincoln, 1980), p. 233.

[3] Christopher Hill, *Society and Puritanism in Pre-Revolutionary England* (London, 1964), p. 492.

[4] Ibid., p. 483.

[5] Ibid., p. 491.

The picture painted by Christopher Hill is that of a society undergoing radical transition. This transition from 'parish to sect' was but one of several complex causes which he assigns to the eventual collapse of traditional English community relations. If Hill's view is correct – and popular sectarian religion did in fact contribute to the dislocation and final disintegration of traditional community life – then, in terms of pure logic, members of sectarian groups themselves must necessarily have played a less active role in parochial affairs than did their conformist neighbours. However, as we shall see, dissenters were far more deeply integrated in day-to-day parish life than Professor Hill's thesis would suggest.

Sectarian cohesion

Seventeenth-century gathered congregations were highly cohesive social units. Of all sectarians, the Quakers were by far the most socially cohesive and unified as a group. This has the effect – superficially at least – of making them appear to have been the most remote from society in general. The Society of Friends instigated codes of conduct, deportment, and behaviour that were designed to differentiate their followers from the rest of the community. They refused to pay tithes[6] and church rates,[7] to swear oaths,[8] and to doff their hats to anyone.[9] They developed their own modes of speech,[10] and their own distinctive forms of dress.[11] All of these idiosyncratic forms of behaviour and 'peculiar' mannerisms served only to set them apart from other parishioners.

Both Baptists and Quakers were vigilant in their attempts to impose endogamy in marriage. The Midland Association of Particular Baptists, in October 1655, ruled it a 'very inconvenient and dangerous and uncomfortable thing for a churchmember to bee marryed to one who . . . Stand-

---

[6] Bruce G. Blackwood, 'Agrarian Unrest and the Early Lancashire Quakers', *Journal of the Friends' Historical Society*, 51, 2 (1966), pp. 72–6; Alfred W. Braithewaite, 'Early Tithe Prosecutions: Friends as Outlaws', *Journal of the Friends' Historical Society*, 49, 3 (1960), pp. 148–56; Eric J. Evans, '"Our Faithful Testimony": The Society of Friends and Tithe Payments, 1690–1730', *Journal of the Friends' Historical Society*, 52, 2 (1969), pp. 106–21; Barry Reay, 'Quaker Opposition to Tithes 1652–1660', *Past and Present*, 86 (1980), pp. 98–120.

[7] J. Besse, *A Collection of the Sufferings of the People Called Quakers*, I (London, 1753), pp. 1–2.

[8] Nicholas J. Morgan, 'Lancashire Quakers and the Oath, 1660–1722', *Journal of the Friends' Historical Society*, 54, 5 (1980), pp. 235–54.

[9] Arnold Lloyd, *Quaker Social History 1669–1738* (London, 1950), p. 80; John Sykes, *The Quakers: A New Look at their Place in Society* (London, 1958), pp. 58–61.

[10] Richard Baumann, 'Aspects of 17th Century Quaker Rhetoric', *Quarterly Journal of Speech*, 56, 1 (1970), pp. 67–74; Richard T. Vann, *The Social Development of English Quakerism 1655–1755* (Cambridge, Mass., 1969), pp. 190–1.

[11] Joan Kendall, 'The Development of a Distinctive Form of Quaker Dress', *Costume*, 19 (1985), pp. 58–74.

eth out against baptiseme and church communion'.[12] In October 1652, the Fenstanton General Baptists sent two of their brethren to admonish Anne Pharepoint of Earith, in Huntingdonshire, for 'taking a husband contrary to the mind of the congregation'.[13] Although Pharepoint ensured the delegation that she had married a man who did not 'hinder' her religion, she was informed: 'There is now none but the church and the world; if your husband were not of the church, he must be of the world, and so a stranger, and if a stranger, then he will turn your heart from the Lord.'[14] Pharepoint was excommunicated for her contravention of the group norm. The pages of the Fenstanton records are cluttered with similar disciplinary actions.

The Quakers were even more determined to confine the choice of marriage partners within the sect. Friends were required to propose their marriage plans openly at a public meeting; and young Friends needed the permission of both sets of parents before they received the meeting's approval.[15] It was agreed by the Bristol Men's Meeting, in January 1670, that those proposing intended marriages should withdraw from the hall afterwards 'so every friend may the more freely offer what he hath to say in the matter'.[16] Any breaches of the prescribed Quaker marriage procedure would invite the censure of the meeting. Clearly, any proposed marriage to a non-Quaker was doomed from the outset. If a Quaker married an outsider surreptitiously, then the offender faced the embarrassment of a public testimony concerning the evils of mixed marriage and probable disownment by the congregation. As Richard T. Vann has pointed out, such a rigorous insistence on endogamy in marriage must have served to isolate Friends as well as to deprive them of a useful source of converts.[17] However, as we will see, although Quakers and other sectaries may have been 'isolated' from the world in terms of marriage, they were far from isolated in other respects.

Both Quakers and Baptists hired their co-religionists as servants and apprentices; and Quakers employed their own as midwives and schoolmasters.[18] Although all such instances illustrate the highly cohesive nature

---

[12] B.R. White (ed.), *Association Records of the Particular Baptists of England, Wales and Ireland to 1660. Pt. 1 South Wales and the Midlands*, Baptist Historical Society (London, 1971), p. 23.

[13] E.B. Underhill (ed.), *Records of the Churches of Christ Gathered at Fenstanton, Warboys, and Hexham, 1644–1720*, Hanserd Knollys Society (London, 1854), p. 24.

[14] Ibid., p. 24.

[15] Vann, *Social Development*, pp. 183–8; Eric Josef Carlson, 'Marriage and the English Reformation' (Harvard, PhD, 1987), pp. 391–416.

[16] R. Mortimer (ed.), *Minute Book of the Men's Meeting of the Society of Friends in Bristol 1667–1686*, Bristol Record Society (Bristol, 1976), p. 29.

[17] Vann, *Social Development*, p. 187.

[18] William Stevenson, 'The Economic and Social Status of Protestant Sectarians in Huntingdonshire, Cambridgeshire and Bedfordshire (1650–1725)' (Cambridge, PhD, 1990), pp. 284–5, 312, 330–9.

of sectarian gathered congregations, in particular that of the Quakers, there is much evidence to suggest, as we shall see, that sectaries did not select their employees to the exclusion of society in general.

Popular attitudes towards sectarian nonconformists

Popular attitudes towards first generation sectarians were generally hostile, to say the least. Propagandist material in the form of polemic tracts; popular ballads, chapbooks, cheap printed images; plays; and verse[19] could all help to shape the cognitive stereotype of the dissenter in the minds of the population at large. Bishops and their agents; magistrates; elitist groups within the state church in general; and heresiographers in particular were understandably antagonistic towards any form of separatism. For them, the very fabric of society itself appeared to be under threat.

In the winter of 1646, the London Presbyterian minister and heresiographer Thomas Edwards issued a chill warning to the 'godly people' of England. He called it *Gangraena*. Rot and decay were his leading metaphors. For Edwards, the religious turmoil of 'his' particular present posed as great a threat to the successful maintenance of a stable social base as unrestrained popular violence does for so many in ours today. Edwards' primary objective was to make people 'afraid of forsaking the Publike Assemblies and joyning to Separated Churches where these monsters daily breed'.[20] The quest for a private pathway to salvation was to be avoided. As Edwards warned: 'we should not separate from this church and set up other churches, lest God let us fall from Independency to Anabaptism, and Antinomianism, and from Anabaptisme to be Seekers, and from Seekers to be Antiscripturalists, and Sceptiks, Yea, Blasphemers and Atheists'.[21] The imagined progression is clear: Anabaptism led to atheism which led to anarchy.

Contemporary concern regarding the safe preservation of public morality, in the face of the dangers of allowing freedom of worship, is perhaps nowhere better expressed than in the 'correspondence' section of *Gangraena*. An anonymous letter, from a 'person religious' warns of the practical moral dangers of seeking salvation outside of the state system. A bashful woman, we are told, about to undergo believers' baptism by total bodily immersion, 'having pulled off all her cloaths to the naked skin, ready to go into the water . . . covered her secret parts with both her

---

[19] T.M. Williams, 'Polemical Prints of the English Revolution 1640–1660' (London, PhD, 1987), pp. 123–36; Margaret Spufford, *Small Books and Pleasant Histories: Popular Fiction and its Readership in Seventeenth-Century England* (Cambridge, 1985), pp. 184, 220–1.
[20] Thomas Edwards, *Gangraena* I (London, 1646), p. 3.
[21] Ibid., II, p. 164.

hands'. The unprincipled 'dipper' – no better than a Peeping Tom in the correspondent's eyes – informed the embarrassed lady that it was 'an unseemly sight to see her hold her hands downward, it being an Ordinance of Jesus Christ, her hands with her heart should be lifted upwards towards heaven'.[22]

The attitudes of contemporary Church of England clergymen to first generation sectarians were naturally hostile. Anglican ministers were often so angered by separatist activities within their parishes that they recorded the births and deaths of sectaries within their parish registers with disgust. It was almost as if the minister concerned felt compelled to claim the right of jurisdiction over their *rites de passage* even though they had deserted him and his church. The register of St Benedict's parish, in Huntingdon, records the birth of the Quaker child Thomas Parker in 1696 with the caustic note: 'a new Renegade was born'.[23] The incumbent of the Cambridgeshire village of Over recorded the interments of twelve Quakers in the orchard of their co-religionist George Nash between 1667 and 1677.[24] In the Cambridgeshire village of Oakington, between 1680 and 1693, the minister recorded the burials of twelve Congregationalist 'Scismaticks' in their private burial ground.[25]

An incumbent could become even more vexed when sectaries buried their dead in 'his' churchyard without 'his' prior knowledge or permission. In August 1678, Silvester Burrowes of Over, in Cambridgeshire, was buried 'by his brethren & fanaticks in ye evening in ye churchyard without a Minister'.[26] Similarly, in May 1685, the daughter of John Woolman, of Over, 'a fanatick who had not had his child baptized', was buried 'unknown to me'.[27] However, by the early eighteenth century, in Haddenham in the Isle of Ely at least, clerical attitudes appear to have mellowed somewhat. In January 1715/16 and June 1716, respectively, the Quakers John Dobson and Nathaniel Purver were buried in the parish churchyard 'by the Quakers' at a charge of 10s each in mortuary fees.[28]

The Society of Friends was the most vilified of all the sects. Both elitist and plebeian groups alike heaped scorn upon the Quakers. Even other sectarian groups – particularly the Baptists – added further grist to the mill. This is perhaps not surprising considering the fact that Quaker proselytizing, in the early 1650s, lured many a Baptist into the Quaker fold.

[22] Ibid., (letters), p. 5.
[23] Parish register, St Benedict's, Huntingdon, 1603–91, vol. 4, Hunts. RO (new acquisition).
[24] Parish register, Over, Cambs., burials 1641–1717, Cambs. RO P129/1/2 (unpaginated)
[25] Parish register, Oakington, Cambs., burials 1561–1720, Cambs. RO P126/1/1 (unpaginated).
[26] Parish register, Cambs. RO P129/1/2 (unpaginated)
[27] Ibid., (unpaginated)
[28] Parish register, Haddenham, burials 1670–1740, Cambs. RO P82/1/2 (unpaginated).

There was a mass defection of Fenstanton Baptists to their Quaker rivals in Chatteris and in Littleport, in the Isle of Ely, in 1654 and 1655 respectively.[29] In 1653, the influential Bristol Baptist Dennis Hollister, whilst serving in London as a Bristol member of the 'Parliament of the Saints', had 'sucked in some Principles of this upstart Locust Doctrine'.[30] On his return, the defector Hollister took with him to the Quakers 'about 18 or nineteen members more, that rent away from ye church'.[31]

Early Quaker evangelists often received a rough hearing from town and village people alike. In 1655, at Colchester, in Essex, the evangelist James Parnell, whilst exhorting the people to repent, 'was met by a blind Zealot who struck him a violent Blow with a great Staff, saying. There, take that for Christ's Sake'.[32] The first Quaker evangelists to visit Cambridge in December 1653 were publicly whipped at the market cross 'so that their Flesh was miserably cut and torn'.[33] The fact that they were women appeared not to diminish their tormentor's zeal. Their crime had been to discourse religion with the scholars at Sidney Sussex College. Similarly, the two Quaker women evangelists who engaged Oxford students in religious debate, in 1654, were forced to a college pump where 'they pump'd Water upon their Necks, and into their Mouths, till they were almost dead'.[34]

Many of these instances of popular violence towards early Friends were perhaps triggered as much by simple xenophobic reactions to strangers interfering in local affairs as they were by outright hostility to Quakerism per se. It is not difficult to see how heated situations could arise when Quaker evangelists interrupted parish services, including burials, as they frequently did. The early Quaker practice of 'going naked as a sign' could also give rise to outbreaks of violent hostility. It is a truism that people do not like to be made aware of their shortcomings, real or imagined. Public indignation could run hot when such shortcomings were pointed out by outsiders, either through words or actions. The Quaker teacher Solomon Eccles must have presented a very strange sight indeed as he walked through London's Smithfield, in 1663, 'with his Body naked, and a Pan of Fire and Brimstone burning on his Head'. Eccles was exhorting the people to 'Repent, and remember Sodom'. But they sent him to Bridewell instead.[35]

---

[29] E.B. Underhill (ed.), *Records of the Churches at Fenstanton, Warboys, and Hexham, 1644–1720*, Hanserd Knollys Society (London, 1854), pp. 115, 141, 146.

[30] R. Hayden (ed.), *The Records of a Church of Christ in Bristol, 1640–1687*, Bristol Record Society (Bristol, 1974), p. 106.

[31] Ibid., p. 110.

[32] Besse, *Sufferings*, I, p. 190.

[33] Ibid., p. 85.

[34] Ibid., p. 562.

[35] Ibid., p. 393.

Even ordinary local Quaker folk, going about their daily business, were not safe from public abuse. In 1661, the Huntingdon Quaker shopkeeper Robert Raby and several other Friends assembled in his shop, had 'Dirtt and Mire cast upon them'.[36] Raby had offended by opening his shop on Christmas Day. He also made the mistake of leaving his windows open. In 1659, at Sawbridgeworth, in Hertfordshire, a 'Rabble' attacked local Friends at worship. The attackers threw 'Showers of stones, Dirt, rotten Eggs, human Dung and Urine' into the meeting-house.[37] To add insult to injury, the mob filled the Quakers' hats with dirt and put them back on their heads. In Cambridge, in the late 1650s, the Quaker widow Ann Cock disrupted a service in Sidney Sussex College chapel. She was ejected and ran a gauntlet of abuse from townsfolk as she made her way through the streets. A glover's daughters threw water upon her and a local tailor went one better in terms of abuse. He threw a 'piss-pot of Urine' at her.[38] In Suffolk, in 1655, an itinerant pedlar of Quaker books was 'hung up on a Butcher's Spirket' and given 'above twenty Stripes with a three corded whip, so that the Flesh and skin hung in Flakes torn in pieces on his Back'.[39]

Although numerous cases of public antagonism towards Quaker neighbours could be cited, public hostility was precipitated in many of them by actions considered to be 'normal' as far as Quakers were concerned, but which contravened the accepted order of things as far as the rest of the community was concerned. It is understandable that parishioners became upset when Quakers opened their shops on the Sabbath or on Christmas Day. Similarly, the interruption of the conforming parish at its worship was liable to provoke open rebuke upon Friends whether they were strangers or locals. The degree of abuse instigated by no cause other than a hatred and fear of Quakerism at the parish level is difficult to assess. Moreover, the degree of hostility incited through official channels is a further opaque area. In all probability, the majority of attacks on first generation Quakers by their neighbours were the result of the inability of Friends to temper their zeal to conform to the social mores and customs of their particular parish communities.

Magistrates often treated Quakers as if they were sub-human. In 1664, a Justice of the Peace was reported to have told the wife of the imprisoned Wisbech Quaker William Williams: 'If she wanted Food, she might take

---

[36] Huntingdon Monthly Meeting sufferings book 1656–1793, Cambs. RO R59/25/3/1 (unpaginated).

[37] Besse, *Sufferings*, I, p. 241.

[38] Edward Sammon et al., *A Discovery of the Education of the Schollars of Cambridge; by their Abominations and Wicked Practices Acted upon, and against, the Despised People, in Scorn Called Quakers* (London, 1659), pp. 3–4.

[39] Besse, *Sufferings*, I, pp. 657–8.

her Children, fry them for Stakes, and eat them.'[40] In 1659, the Cambridge-shire Quaker widow Morlin was accused of bewitching the Quaker apos-tate Mary Philips of Longstanton. According to Philips, she was trans-formed into a bay mare and ridden by two Quaker 'witches' to their ritual feast at Madingley Hall.[41] The likening of Friends to cannibals and satanists was the physical manifestation of a complex psychological reac-tion on the part of their accusers and abusers. It made such harsh persecu-tion appear justifiable. As Keith Thomas notes: 'The story of religious persecution in the early modern period makes it abundantly clear that, for those who committed acts of bloody atrocity, the dehumanization of their victims ... was often a necessary mental preliminary.'[42]

Even allowing for the highly propagandist nature of sufferings records, it is difficult not to conclude that first generation Quakers suffered gross humiliations from a very wide section of society indeed. According to Barry Reay: 'the general reaction towards the early Quakers was one of hostility and fear – at all levels of Society'.[43] But, as we shall see, there is another side to the story.

Sectarian integration within the community at large

Our knowledge of the highly cohesive nature of sectarian religion, coupled with the evidence of popular hostility shown towards sectaries, has led some historians to the reasonable conclusion that sectaries were not liked or respected; that they shunned society at large; that society shunned them; and that they could not possibly have shared much in the daily affairs of parish life.[44] Such conclusions, however, are far removed from the truth. If we accept Christopher Hill's thesis that the transition from 'parish to sect' was also a transition from a 'federation of communities' to a breakdown of traditional English community life, then such erroneous conclusions appear further attested. Recent research has shown, however, that sectarian groups, from the pre-Reformation period onwards, were far more involved in everyday community life than has previously thought to have been the case.

Derek Plumb has shown that Lollard heretics in the Thames valley, on the eve of the protestant Reformation, were deeply integrated within

[40] Ibid., p. 92.
[41] For differing accounts of this case, see anon., *Strange & Terrible Newes from Cambridge, Being a True Relation of the Quakers Bewitching of Mary Philips* (London, 1659); and James Blackley et al., *A Lying Wonder Discovered and the Strange and Terrible Newes from Cambridge Proved False* (London, 1659).
[42] Keith Thomas, *Man and the Natural World: Changing Attitudes in England 1500–1800* (London, 1984), p. 48.
[43] Barry Reay, *The Quakers and the English Revolution* (London, 1985), p. 63.
[44] For a discussion of such views, see Davies, 'The Quakers in Essex', p. 261.

their local parish communities. The Lollards of Hughenden, in the Upperside of Buckinghamshire, displayed a 'total involvement and commitment to parish life and to the parish church'.[45] The named Lollard Thomas Clerk of Hughenden, for example, was a churchwarden in 1496, around the time of his involvement with the heretical group.[46] Similarly, in 1505, John Mylsent of Amersham, in Buckinghamshire, was a Lollard and a churchwarden 'without seeing any contradiction between the two positions'.[47] In 1532, the named Lollard fishmonger John Seman of Newbury, in Berkshire, willed that his body be buried in the chancel of his parish church. He left money to the high altar and towards the rebuilding of the church.[48] The many further instances of community service and religious devotion provided by Dr Plumb all occurred at a time when the authorities were burning such people for their views.

Similarly, Christopher Marsh has shown that members of the Family of Love displayed high levels of social interaction with the community at large. Familists in and around the Cambridgeshire village of Balsham, in the south-east of the county, 'frequently left money to the poor people of their communities, and served regularly in local offices'.[49] Two questmen serving their parish in 1573 were arrested as Familists six years later.[50] Persecution by the state, however, does not necessarily signify persecution by fellow-villagers. As Dr Marsh points out, the fact that the majority of Balsham Familists remained in their villages until their deaths suggests that they were generally accepted by their neighbours.[51] Although members of the sect preferred their co-religionists as far as marriage and the witnessing of wills was concerned, 'they were by no means isolated within their communities'.[52]

How different, though, were seventeenth-century sectaries from Lollards and Familists? The short answer, of course, is that Baptists and Quakers, unlike their heretical predecessors, were outright separatists. Moreover, the Quakers were undoubtedly the most radical major sect yet to emerge. According to Barry Reay, popular hostility towards early Quaker radicalism was a major contributory factor in the conservative backlash which led to the restoration of the Stuart monarchy in 1660.[53]

---

[45] Derek Plumb, 'John Foxe and the Later Lollards of the Mid-Thames Valley' (Cambridge, PhD, 1987) p. 185.
[46] Ibid., p. 174.
[47] Ibid., p. 252.
[48] Ibid., p. 105.
[49] Christopher Marsh, ' "A Gracelesse, and Audacious Companie"? The Family of Love in the Parish of Balsham, 1550–1630', in W.J. Sheils and Diana Wood (eds.), Voluntary Religion, Studies in Church History, 23 (Oxford, 1986), p. 206.
[50] Ibid., p. 204.
[51] Ibid., p. 207.
[52] Ibid., p. 207.
[53] Reay, The Quakers and the English Revolution, p. 81.

Could it have been possible, then, for Quakers and Baptists to have been integrated members of society now that the so-called transition from 'parish to sect' was supposedly complete?

In his study of Quakerism in Essex, T.A. Davies has shown that a remarkable degree of social interaction existed between Quakers and their conformist neighbours.[54] The remainder of this essay will show that Essex was not a 'rogue' county in this respect. Indeed, both Quakers and Baptists, as well as other sectarian groups, enjoyed significant degrees of social acceptance in Bedfordshire, Buckinghamshire, Cambridgeshire, Hertfordshire, and Huntingdonshire. Moreover, the degree of social interaction displayed by Quakers in these counties will be shown to be even greater than Dr Davies found for Essex.

Quakers too (like Lollards and Familists) served as parish officers. The Huntingdon draper John Peacock was one of the Huntingdon Monthly Meeting's most steadfast supporters. He was also a parish constable for the year 1661–2. The Monthly Meeting was surprised that Peacock, being 'a constable yt yeare', had not been notified of the arrest of his co-religionist Robert Raby, a Huntingdon shopkeeper who had angered the authorities by opening his shop on the 'first day'.[55] The authorities must have been aware of Peacock's hankering for the Quakers. He was summoned to the church court in February 1663/4 in order to explain his continued non-payment of the church rate. His refusal to pay brought formal excommunication on 5 July 1664. In the excommunication paper read against Peacock from the pulpit of All Hallow's parish church, the congregation were exhorted that 'none should buy or sell with him'. In spite of a fear that the minister's words would ruin Peacock's trade, 'from that time it was better than Ever it had bene formerly'.[56] The inference, of course, is that Peacock had won the public's sympathy. Of more significance is the fact that the authorities had selected a prominent Quaker as a constable at a time of supposed intense animosity towards Friends.

In 1670, the Quaker yeoman Richard Cope of Chatteris, in the Isle of Ely, was distrained of four cows, worth £9, for non-payment of a £5 fine.[57] Cope, who was parish constable at the time, had refused to serve a distress warrant on a fellow-Quaker. The authorities must have been aware of Cope's Quakerism. The previous year he had been distrained of goods worth 30s for refusing to bear arms.[58] Yet he was still selected to serve as constable the following year.

---

[54] Davies, 'The Quakers in Essex', pp. 276–309.
[55] Huntingdon Monthly Meeting sufferings book 1656–1739, Cambs. RO R59/25/2/1 (unpaginated).
[56] Ibid., (unpaginated).
[57] Besse, *Sufferings*, I, p. 94.
[58] Ibid., p. 94.

In 1682, the Hertfordshire Quaker John Fisher 'upon an Information that he being Constable, had refused to act in breaking up a Dissenter's Meeting' was asked to swear the Oath of Allegiance.[59] Being a good Quaker, he refused. That same year, a John Fisher, labourer, of Wyddial, in Hertfordshire, appeared at the County Quarter Sessions for non-attendance at his parish church.[60] It appears unlikely that Fisher's religious opinions would have been a secret to the community in view of the fact that he was boycotting the parish church. Yet he was still chosen as a constable. Fisher was in trouble again two years later, in October 1684. The Quarter Sessions ordered that the trial of a group of Quakers, Fisher being named amongst them, be held over until the next sessions.[61]

The Quaker yeoman Edmund Cooke of Bow Brickhill, in Buckinghamshire, was confirmed as constable for his parish at the Epiphany Quarter Sessions, held at Wendover, on 12 January 1698/9.[62] In 1700 he was serving as overseer of the poor. Cooke experienced extreme difficulty that year in collecting the poor rate subscription from one of the churchwardens. The same churchwarden had demanded a payment from Cooke towards the repair of the parish church and for Communion bread and wine. As an absentee from the parish church, and a non-partaker of its Sacraments, Cooke refused to pay. The wily churchwarden simply kept back 8s 6d, which was his share of the poor rate, as Cooke's payment for the church rate.[63] That same year, a similar ploy was used by the churchwardens of Haddenham, in Buckinghamshire, against the Quaker overseer of the poor, Edmund Belson.[64] Also, in 1700, the Quaker constable Lazarus Percival of Green's Norton, in Northamptonshire, was tricked by a similar deceit. This time, though, the Quaker parish officer was tricked into paying a demand for tithes. An impropriator of tithes, who was having no success in getting Percival to pay his dues, simply stopped the amount out of the money he owed Percival for the constable's rate.[65]

Members of other sectarian groups also served their parishes. In 1669, it came to the notice of the Open Baptists at Bedford that one of their brethren, a Richard Deane of Bedford, had been in St Neots, in Huntingdonshire, soliciting charity 'for the supply of his outward wants'. According to Deane, his brethren at Bedford had advised him to 'goe abroad to

[59] Ibid., p. 252.
[60] William Le Hardy (ed.), *Hertfordshire County Records, Calendar to the Sessions Books, Sessions Minute Books and Other Sessions Records 1658–1700*, VI (Hertford, 1930), p. 363.
[61] Ibid., p. 384.
[62] Ibid., p. 191.
[63] Buckinghamshire Quarterly Meeting suffering register 1655–1793, Aylesbury Record Office, NQ/1/6/1, p. 77.
[64] Ibid., p. 78.
[65] Ibid., p. 78.

crave the liberality of the churches, and so began with them'.[66] The complaint had reached Bedford via Ralph Luke of Eynesbury, in Huntingdonshire, a member of the St Neots conventicle. Luke was also a parish officer of Eynesbury in 1674. His name appears on the Eynesbury Hearth Tax assessment of that year as 'constable'.[67]

In July 1670, a group of Buckinghamshire Quakers, meeting in a private house in Chalfont St Giles, were surprised and annoyed by the hypocrisy of Henry Reading, one of the parish constables. He had issued them with a warrant. Reading, they reflected, 'one of ye constables . . . himself bears ye name of a professour, & is said to frequent Presbiterian meetings in privat'.[68] If the Quakers knew of the Presbyterian constable's dual roles, then surely the authorities must have done. It appeared to be common knowledge. Once again we have an example of a sectary serving the community at the height of sectarian persecution under the Conventicle Act.

In July 1683, at the Midsummer Quarter Session at Buckingham, it was ruled that: 'Richard Tuckwell . . . be sworn petty constable of Aylesbury in place of Thomas Read who is discharched'.[69] The reason given for Read's replacement was that he was 'a dissenter from the Church of England and a frequenter of Conventicles, and, being a horse courser, is absent from the parish most part of his time, and therefore unfitt to serve'.[70] Read's frequent absence from the parish appears almost as important a reason for his disqualification as his unorthodox religious views. If not, why was it considered worthy of mention?

T.A. Davies found that Essex Quakers also held positions of responsibility at the parish level. They served as overseers of the poor, surveyors of the highways, vermin destroyers, and 'at the end of the [seventeenth] century' as constables.[71] However, as we have already seen, in Cambridgeshire, Hertfordshire, and Huntingdonshire, Friends were serving as constables from the early 1660s onwards. Furthermore, Davies found that it was 'unusual to discover Quakers holding office in rural areas'.[72] He suggests that the economic background of a parish may well have determined whether Quakers held office or not. Where Quakers were large employers, as in the Essex textile towns, their importance to the economic prosperity of the area may well have been reflected in their parti-

[66] H.G. Tibbutt (ed.), *The Minutes of the First Independent Church (now Bunyan Meeting) at Bedford 1656–1766*, Bedfordshire Historical Record Society, 55 (Luton, 1976), p. 63.
[67] Hearth Tax, Huntingdonshire, 1674, PRO E179/249/2.
[68] Miscellaneous loose papers, Aylesbury Record Office, NQ/1/61A.
[69] William Le Hardy (ed.), *County of Buckingham, Calendar to the Sessions Records*, I (1678–94) (Aylesbury, 1933), p. 128.
[70] Ibid., p. 128.
[71] Davies, 'The Quakers in Essex', p. 292.
[72] Ibid., p. 294.

cipation in office holding. However, no such urban/rural divide is evident in the counties I have studied. Indeed, rural Quakers appear to have held office as frequently as their urban brethren. This could be explained by the fact that none of my counties contained Quakers who were large-scale employers. Quakerism in my region was very much a rural agrarian movement.

The preponderance of urban Quaker parish officers over rural ones in Essex is in some ways curious. It would seem likely, for example, in small rural parishes, where the choice of suitable candidates may have been more limited than in the towns, that Quakers would have been forced to have served as officers quite often whether they liked it or not. Indeed, the question of Quaker willingness to serve versus pressure to do so from within a village itself needs to be held firmly in mind when considering office holding as evidence of social integration.[73] Having said this, in urban parishes such as Ramsey, in Huntingdonshire, where Quakers did serve their communities, but did not have any significant hold on the local economy as large-scale employers, it appears safe to assume that Quakers served the community because of a mutual desire on the part of the individual and the community that they should.

There is much evidence to suggest that by 1670, or so, public attitudes towards Quakers had softened considerably. Quaker records of sufferings, the very same source of accounts of public hostility towards Friends at the parish level in the early 1650s and 1660s, begin to record, increasingly, instances of public support and sympathy for Quakers from the 1670s onwards. Even allowing for the polemic and propagandist nature of sufferings records, the number and frequency of such references is striking.

In October 1670, the local magistrate William March and his men rode into the yard of the Quaker John Adams of Haddenham, in the Isle of Ely, in order to distrain his goods. Adams was at that time a prisoner of conscience in Cambridge castle, and his wife was not at home. The magistrate, therefore, commanded a neighbour, John Bushop (Bishop), a 'pore mane', to break open Adams' door. Bushop refused with 'tears

---

[73] My own research (as yet unpublished) on patterns of office holding, between 1660 and 1720, in the small rural parish of Millington-cum-Givendale, in south-east Yorkshire, has shown that parish officers, although drawn mainly from the ratepaying section of the community, often included the 'meaner sort' and even the illiterate. In a small parish such as Millington, with an estimated population of approximately 160 souls, a very wide cross-section of the community, by necessity, was drawn into parish office holding, even if for a brief period only.

tricklin dowen his Cheekes'.[74] He told the magistrate that he was 'Loath to wrong his peacabl nibours' and that he would 'borrow five shilling of tenn men' in order to pay Adams' fine. The magistrate called Bushop a 'logerheaded Blocke head' and commanded him yet again to break down the door. Bushop again refused. If the recorder's judgement regarding Bushop's poverty is reliable, then he was probably the John Bishop who lived in a house containing just a single hearth in 1674 and was exempt from paying any Hearth Tax accordingly.[75] Here we have a classic example of a poor parishioner standing his ground against a wealthy official in support of a Quaker. The magistrate William March lived in a house containing seven hearths in 1674. There is no evidence that Bushop was ever a Quaker. But he may have been of an independent frame of mind as far as matters of religion were concerned. One Ann Bushop of Hadden-ham was admitted to the Isleham Independent Church in May 1694.[76] She may well have been a relative of the Quaker sympathizer of 1670.

In April 1676, the parish officers of Fenstanton, in Huntingdonshire, were authorized to distrain the goods of the Quaker grocer Tobias Hard-meat as a result of his failure to pay a £10 fine. But the officers, 'being Convinced in their Consciences of ye Innocency of yr peacable Neigh-bour' refused to execute the warrant, 'but Rather chose to venture suf-ferings themselves'.[77] In January, 1683/4, the parish constable Richard Dickerson of Ramsey, in Huntingdonshire, himself paid a fine of £10 13s 4d in order to save the Quaker Samuel Nottingham from being distrained of cattle worth £16.[78] The name Dickerson, or any similar name, never appears as a Quaker name in any record between 1650 and 1700.

There are many similar instances of conformist parish officers in Bedfordshire, Hertfordshire, Cambridgeshire, and Huntingdonshire being unwilling to act against Quakers. T.A. Davies has noted a similar reluctance on the part of conformist parish officers in Essex to act against local Friends.[79] However, as Keith Wrightson points out, such a reaction could have been no more than a common-sense attempt on the part of parish officers to maintain a peaceful equilibrium within their parishes.[80]

---

[74] Haddenham Particular Meeting, sufferings 1665–71, Cambs. RO R59/25/18/1 (unpaginated).
[75] Hearth Tax, Cambridgeshire, Lady Day 1674, PRO E179/244/23.
[76] K.A.C. Parsons (ed.), *The Church Book of the Independent Church (now Pound Lane Baptist) Isleham 1693–1805*, Cambridge Antiquarian Records Society, 6 (Cambridge, 1984), p. 165.
[77] Huntingdon Monthly Meeting sufferings book 1656–1793, Cambs. RO R59/25/3/1 (unpaginated)
[78] Ibid., (unpaginated).
[79] Davies, 'The Quakers in Essex', pp. 303–7.
[80] Keith Wrightson, 'Two Concepts of Order: Justices, Constables and Jurymen in Seventeenth-Century England', in John Brewer and John Styles (eds.), *An Ungovernable People* (London, 1980), pp. 21–46 (esp. 21–2, 24, 29, 31, 44).

After all, a constable would have to continue to live amongst his neighbours after his term of office was complete. On the other hand, many conformist constables were no doubt friends and relatives of sectaries; or were simply sympathetic to their sufferings. In 1670, the Huntingdonshire Quaker John Ofley was fined 25s for attending a conventicle. Ofley's son, however, who was a constable at the time, but not a Friend, 'did not go thither to distraine'.[81]

Ordinary members of the public, who were not torn by a conflict between conscience and duty in the way that office holders may have been, and did not share the constable's vested interest in minimizing conflict within the parish, also helped to ease Quaker suffering. In 1670, 'two Straungers' to the Quakers paid the 10s fine imposed upon Elizabeth Deare for attending a conventicle.[82] The strangers were obviously non-Quakers. If they had been Friends, it would have been highly likely that the Monthly Meeting would have known them, even if they had been from a neighbouring county. There are many more instances of non-Quakers coming to the aid of respected Quaker friends and neighbours.[83]

A group of Quakers in Ramsey, in Huntingdonshire, were respected enough by the local conformist urban hierarchy to be entrusted in the joint provision of relief for the parish poor. Charles Hammond of Ramsey, who was never a Quaker, made the Quakers Richard Snazdell and John Peacock of Ramsey joint supervisors of his will dated 1 November 1691.[84] Hammond also left two lots of land to Peacock 'for the use and uses of ye poor of Ramsey'. Both the names of Charles Hammond and Richard Snazdell also appear on a bond of obligation signed by twelve trustees 'for the poor of the parish of Ramsey', dated 11 November 1676.[85] Amongst the other trustees were Silius Titus, lord of the manor of Ramsey, and other local gentry dignitaries. The Quaker yeoman Samuel Nottingham was also a trustee. Snazdell and Nottingham were the only two men to appear in Quaker records. The remaining ten were conformists. Charles Hammond's name also appears on a similar document dated 10–12 June 1693.[86] Hammond was cited as a serving churchwarden. He must have been a conformist. It would have been anathema for a Quaker to have served as a churchwarden. The Quakers Snazdell, Nottingham, and Peacock were also listed as trustees in the 1693 document. Clearly, Hammond had grown to trust such men over many years of dealing with

---

[81] Huntingdon Monthly Meeting sufferings book 1656–1793, Cambs. RO R59/25/3/1 (unpaginated).
[82] Ibid. (unpaginated).
[83] Stevenson, 'Economic and Social Status', pp. 305, 307–8.
[84] Archdeaconry of Huntingdon wills, probate register 25, pp. 324–5, Hunts. RO.
[85] Deeds and papers relating to property in Ramsey 1434–1867, Hunts. RO (James Sarjeant papers).
[86] Ibid., (unfoliated).

them for the mutual benefit of the parish poor. It is hardly surprising, therefore, that Hammond, a non-Quaker, should make the Quaker Peacock, a trusted and respected friend, the trustee for his personal contribution to the relief of the Ramsey poor. The fact that prominent Quakers should find this degree of acceptance amongst conformist dignitaries in 1676, a time of intense persecution under the Conventicle Act, speaks volumes on the subject of social integration.

The degree of an individual's esteem within the general community, or the lack of it, is perhaps no better measured than in the public reaction to his or her death. The Quaker Robert Falkner of Somersham, in Huntingdonshire, must have been a very well-respected man both in Quaker and conformist circles alike. On 11 June 1675, over 200 mourners were arrested at Falkner's funeral.[87] According to the Huntingdon Monthly Meeting, the funeral party was made up of 'severall friends & others'. Clearly, non-Quakers were present; and they must have been many in number. It would have required the attendance of almost every Quaker householder in the county to have equalled 200 mourners. The recorder of the meeting copied the official judicial records of the incident into the Sufferings Book. Twenty-seven Somersham residents were listed as attending the funeral. Of these, only one can be identified from Quaker records of all descriptions as being a definite Quaker. Clearly, the vast majority of the Somersham group were ordinary villagers paying their last respects to a respected neighbour. The fact that they risked the penalties of the Conventicle Act says much about the degree of respect the Quaker Falkner could command in the village. Moreover, the fact that many of the Huntingdon Quakers were fined for the Somersham residents' attendance, as well as their own, suggests that the authorities did not hold the villagers culpable under the provisions of the Conventicle Act and that they were not considered to be Quakers.

Many sectaries left cash bequests in their wills to the poor of their respective parishes as well as to the poor of their own particular sect. The Huntingdonshire Baptist yeoman Christopher Marriott, for example, in his will of 7 May 1669, left 20s 'unto the poore of Hemmingford Abbotts ... to be payd and distributed at my Buryall'.[88] He left a further 40s to his co-religionist Edmund Mayle to be shared amongst 'such poor brethren as he shall think meete'. In March 1693, the Quaker spinster Mary Seabourne of Bluntisham, in Huntingdonshire, left 40s to the poor of her parish.[89] She left a further 40s to the Quaker poor. She further stipulated that £5 should be 'bestowed att my funerall that poore and

[87] Huntingdon Monthly Meeting sufferings book 1656–1793, Cambs. RO R59/25/3/1 (unpaginated).
[88] Archdeaconry of Huntingdon wills, probate register 24, p. 306, Hunts. RO.
[89] Archdeaconry of Huntingdon wills, probate register 25, pp. 323–4, Hunts. RO.

friends may be refreshed'. Obviously, Seabourne expected confidently that people other than Quakers would be attending her funeral. Many other examples of sectarian benevolence to non-sectarians can be found throughout the period 1650–1725 in Huntingdonshire, Cambridgeshire, and Bedfordshire.[90] All these instances suggest that such men and women at no time saw themselves as being divorced or separated from the communities in which they lived.

There is a great deal of evidence, fragmentary though it may be, that dissenters of all persuasions were deeply involved in the day-to-day activities of parish social life. In July 1658, the Fenstanton Baptist John Blowes failed to attend a meeting specially designated for the election of a church deacon. It was noted that Blowes 'was not only absent from us, but that he was this day at a great foot-ball play, he being one of the principal appointers thereof'.[91] Even allowing for the propensity of such stern moralists to exaggerate the evils of the situation, a 'great foot-ball play' is suggestive of much more than a mere kick-about with the lads. It suggests a large-scale community event, perhaps involving a large number of villagers, and a great deal of organization on the part of Blowes.

Other Baptists were regularly in trouble with the elders of their churches for attending alehouses and fairs and other similar centres of public gathering. In June 1674, the Bedford Baptist sister Elizabeth Burntwood was reproved by the church for her 'immodest company keeping with carnal and light young fellows at Elstow faire'.[92] In 1663, the Huntingdonshire Baptist John Richardson of the Warboys church was withdrawn from Communion for 'frequenting alehouses in the company of vain men'.[93] It is obvious, of course, that the frequenting of such places as alehouses, fairs, and football matches required a good deal of social interaction with the community at large. Also, the fact that sectaries frequented alehouses with their non-sectarian friends suggests that they were accepted socially by the outside community.

The diary of the Presbyterian apprentice shopkeeper Roger Lowe of Ashton-in-Makerfield, in Lancashire, written between 1663 and 1674, displays evidence of a remarkable degree of social interaction with a wide cross-section of the community at large. Lowe was very devout: he also liked the company of young girls;[94] he liked music;[95] he enjoyed horse

---

[90] Stevenson, 'Economic and Social Status', pp. 310–11.
[91] Underhill (ed.), Fenstanton Records, pp. 243–4.
[92] Tibbutt (ed.), The Minutes of the First Independent Church . . . at Bedford, p. 77.
[93] Underhill (ed.), Fenstanton Records, p. 278.
[94] William L. Sachse (ed.), The Diary of Roger Lowe of Ashton-in-Makerfield, Lancashire 1663–74, (London, 1938), pp. 13, 14, 20, 21, 22, 23–4, 25, 26, 27, 28, 33, 34, 35, 36, 37, 41, 42, 43, 44, 45, 46, 48–9, 58, 61, 68, 69, 79, 84, 99.
[95] Ibid., pp. 16, 45, 94, 104.

racing;[96] he went bowling;[97] he engaged in betting;[98] he visited a cock-fight;[99] and he spent much of his time and money drinking with friends and customers in various local alehouses.[100] All such actions necessitate a great deal of social interaction and personal involvement with the general public.

Indeed, Roger Lowe was an extremely well-integrated and very useful member of society. He employed his literary talents in serving a wide cross-section of the community. He wrote letters for many people, including love letters;[101] he drew up bonds;[102] he cast accounts;[103] he instructed other people in the niceties of letter writing and the casting of accounts;[104] he drew up indentures,[105] and wills;[106] he assisted the parish constables by writing their presentments to the assizes, and in the gathering of the poll tax.[107] Clearly, Lowe was a party to many of the most intimate details of people's lives. He must, therefore, have been a trusted member of the community. It is unlikely that all the people he served would have been of the Presbyterian frame of mind; his circle of friends and aquaintances, both in a business and in a social sense, was far too wide.

Amongst all the entries in Lowe's amazing diary, one in particular helps to crystallize the general arguments put forward in this section. In February 1664, Lowe was 'envited amongst neighbours' to visit an alehouse for a farewell drink with a friend who was leaving the locality. A dispute over religion ensued between Lowe and John Potter, a neighbour. As Lowe puts it: 'he was for Episcopecie and I for Presbittery'.[108] Lowe and Potter did not speak to each other for two or three days following their heated row, but eventually Lowe went to Potter's house and 'all anger was removed'. Clearly, differences in religion did not prevent these two men from drinking together in saying farewell to a mutual neighbour. Neither did it prevent them from discussing those differences. It was probably only the mixing of alcohol with a large measure of godly zeal on both

---

[96] Ibid., pp. 27, 62.
[97] Ibid., pp. 28, 33, 86, 89, 103.
[98] Ibid., p. 36.
[99] Ibid., p. 105.
[100] Ibid., pp. 13, 14, 15, 16, 21, 26, 28, 34, 37, 41, 42, 45, 46, 47, 48, 51, 52, 53, 54, 56, 57, 58, 59, 60, 62, 63, 64, 65, 66, 67, 68, 70, 71, 72, 73, 74, 75, 76, 77, 78, 79, 80, 81, 82, 83, 84, 86, 88, 95, 97, 98, 100, 104, 106, 109, 110, 115, 116, 117, 120, 121.
[101] Ibid., pp. 15, 24, 28, 29, 42, 43, 46, 48, 51, 53, 55, 62, 63, 111.
[102] Ibid., pp. 21, 58, 72, 73, 87.
[103] Ibid., pp. 26, 62, 69, 76, 80, 86–7.
[104] Ibid., p. 53.
[105] Ibid., pp. 67, 87, 88, 120.
[106] Ibid., pp. 19, 61, 62.
[107] Ibid., pp. 69, 112.
[108] Ibid., p. 52.

their parts which caused their discourse to get out of control. Neither did such differences prevent Lowe and Potter from making up. Lowe also defended his religion against the attack of a 'papist'. The two disputants, however, were 'in love and peace in our discourse'.[109] Clearly, religious differences did not always bring social alienation.

An examination of the identities of the witnesses to wills in the Huntingdonshire village of Fenstanton, and the frequency with which they were required to perform such a service, provides a deep insight into the nature of social interaction at rural parish level. A total of 150 individuals bearing different names acted as witnesses to the wills of Fenstanton testators in one or more of the ninety-four wills proved in the court of the Archdeaconry of Huntingdon between the years 1661 and 1724. The frequency with which these names appear as witnesses is given in Table 16.

As the table shows, the witnessing of wills in Fenstanton was an activity which permeated the community. Out of all witnesses, 72 per cent (108/150) only acted in that capacity on a single occasion. This suggests that testators chose personal friends, relatives, and neighbours to act as witnesses and that a wide cross-section of the community participated in the witnessing of wills. However, to be asked to act in that capacity more than once was a rarity and presumably, therefore, an honour. Only 28 per cent of witnesses acted more than once. Of these, 21.3 per cent witnessed between two and four wills; and only 6.7 per cent witnessed more than five wills. Of the ten people to witness more than five or more

Table 16. *The frequency of appearance of 150 witnesses to 94 Fenstanton wills, proved 1661–1724*

No. of appearances as a witness	No. of individuals	
21	1	
15	1	
8	2	
7	2	(6.7%)
6	3	
5	1	
4	2	
3	11	(21.3%)
2	19	
1	108	(72.0%)
Total	150	(100%)

[109] Ibid., p. 64.

Table 17. The names of the witnesses of more than five wills made in Fenstanton, 1659–1722, proved in the archdeaconry court of Huntingdon, 1661–1724

No. of appearances	Name of witness	Range of dates	
		Will dates	Probate dates
21	Edmund Mayle	1659–97	1661–1708
15	Henry Cornwall	1707–22	1710–24
8	Andrew Arbrow	1657–71	1661–98
8	Robert Blemell	1684–1700	1684–1700
7	John Jellings[a]	1665–1721	1668–1721
7	John Lindsey[a]	1663–1707	1663–1723
6	Christopher Kay	1689–1706	1689–1705
6	John Martin[a]	1664–1719	1665–1721
6	John Woodward	1664–84	1665–84
5	Edward Jellings	1683–1721	1684–1724

[a] Denotes the extreme possibility of more than one individual sharing the same name.

wills, only two reached double figures. The indentities of this select group of witnesses can be seen in Table 17.

Edmund Mayle was by far the most prolific witnesser of wills in Fenstanton. He witnessed twenty-one wills between November 1659 and August 1697. It says much for the social integration of sectarian groups that Mayle was also one of the most active and prominent Baptists in the Fenstanton gathered church.

Edmund Mayle (Maile) appears regularly in the records of the Fenstanton Baptist Church between 1651 and 1687. He underwent believers' baptism in June 1645.[110] In May 1672, his house was licensed as a Baptist meeting-place, and at the same time he was licensed to be a teacher there.[111] On 5 June 1682, Mayle was presented to the archdeacon's court for chronic absenteeism from the Anglican Church.[112] Clearly, Mayle was a well-known and highly active Baptist at a time corresponding to the height of his activity as a witnesser of wills. Moreover, the majority of the twenty-one wills he witnessed were for non-Baptists; only seven of the testators were known members of the Baptist Church. The remaining fourteen never appear in Baptist records or in any other records as nonconformists. Mayle also acted as the scribe on nineteen of the twenty-one wills he witnessed. He was, therefore, also the chief scribe in the village. An examination of a selection of these wills puts the degree of social interaction exercised by Mayle into clear perspective.

[110] Underhill (ed.), Fenstanton Records, p. 251.
[111] George Lyon Turner (ed.), Original Records of Early Nonconformity under Persecution and Indulgence, I (London, 1911), p. 486.
[112] Archdeaconry of Huntingdon court records, Fenstanton, 1676–1872, 29/15, Hunts. RO.

On 20 October 1691, Mayle witnessed the will of Margaret Kilburne.[113] The name Kilburne never appears in any Baptist records. Mayle acted as a co-witness with Robert and Anne Blemell. The body of the will is written, unmistakably, in the cultured hand of Robert Blemell. Blemell was the Cambridge University educated Church of England rector of Fenstanton between 1678 and 1708.[114] Anne Blemell was presumably his wife. The fact that Margaret Kilburne chose Mayle and Blemell as witnesses, two men diametrically opposed in terms of religion, says a lot. The fact that each of them saw no incongruity in this choice, or at least were willing to act with the other in such a capacity, says even more. Mayle and Blemell were both highly respected men. Blemell was the third most popular choice of witness throughout the whole period under study. But Edmund Mayle outwitnessed them all.

On 18 October 1688, Mayle witnessed the will of the Fenstanton yeoman Edward Lindsey.[115] Lindsey never appears in Baptist records. The Anglican minister Robert Blemell acted as the scribe. Mayle's co-witnesses were Richard Harvey and Thomas Notte. Neither of these men were Baptists, and neither of their surnames were common to any other Baptist in the county.

In May 1684 and March 1684/5 respectively, Mayle witnessed the wills of John Martin, son of John Martin the elder,[116] and 'plain' John Martin.[117] He acted as the scribe on both occasions. One of these testators was probably the same John Martin who was listed as a member of the Fenstanton Baptist Church in 1676.[118] The other was probably a conformist. A 'John Martin' was one of the churchwardens who presented Mayle to the archdeacon's court in June 1682. Yet the churchwarden Martin, whichever of the two he was (and there is a good chance he was one of them), still required the services of Mayle as a witness and a scribe two years later. If the churchwarden was one of these testators, it says much for Mayle's forgiving nature. But, then again, Martin was perhaps only doing his duty in presenting Mayle in the same way that Mayle was simply exercising his function as the most sought-after scribe and witness in Fenstanton.

Between 1660 and 1685, Mayle also regularly appraised and listed the goods of deceased parishioners for probate purposes. For twenty-five

---

[113] Archdeaconry of Huntingdon wills, original will, 1691, Hunts. RO.
[114] W.M. Noble (ed.), 'Incumbents of the County of Huntingdon', *Transactions of the Cambridgeshire & Huntingdonshire Archaeological Society*, 3 (1914), p. 50.
[115] Archdeaconry of Huntingdon wills, original will, 1688, Hunts. RO.
[116] Ibid., 1685, Hunts. RO.
[117] Ibid., 1684, Hunts. RO.
[118] Underhill (ed.), *Fenstanton Records*, p. 256.

years at least, Mayle served both Baptists and conformists in this manner.[119]

Quakers too witnessed the wills of non-Quaker parishioners in Fenstanton. Christopher Kay, the Quaker schoolmaster from St Ives, witnessed the wills of six Fenstanton testators between March 1688/9 and August 1706.[120] It is little wonder that the highly literate Christopher Kay, who came from a family of Quaker schoolmasters, should be a popular choice when it came to the making of wills. Kay was the sixth most popular choice of witness between 1659–1722. Moreover, Kay acted as the scribe for all of the six wills he witnessed. None of the six testators who used Kay as a witness and scribe ever appears in the masses of Quaker records for this period. Obviously, Kay was in demand because of his literary talents. This demand was great enough for testators to go outside their own village, to the neighbouring town of St Ives, in order to secure his services. The fact that he was a Quaker appears to have made little difference. Christopher Kay also witnessed Quaker deeds,[121] and the wills of many known Quakers in Huntingdonshire. Like the Presbyterian diarist Roger Lowe, Kay appears to have been a very useful and well-integrated member of society.

Delanie Quarell witnessed two wills in Fenstanton in 1698 and 1703 respectively. The birth and death of Elizabeth Quarell, 'daughter of Delanie', was recorded by the St Ives Quaker Particular Meeting in October 1694 and November 1698 respectively.[122] Clearly, Delanie Quarell was a Quaker between these dates. In April 1698, several months before his daughter's death, Quarell acted as a witness to the will of John Allpress, labourer, of Fenstanton.[123] No person named Allpress ever appears in Quaker records. An Amy Allpress, though, was baptized into the Fenstanton Baptist Church in September 1655.[124] The testator John Allpress left £15 to his sister Amy following the decease of his unnamed mother. It is very likely, therefore, that the Baptist Amy Allpress was in some way related to the testator. The Quaker witness Delanie Quarell acted as a co-witness with the aforementioned Anglican rector of Fenstanton, Robert Blemell. We have, therefore, a fascinating example of a

[119] William Stevenson, 'Sectarian Cohesion and Social Integration, 1640–1725', in E.S. Leedham-Green (ed.), *Religious Dissent in East Anglia*, Cambridge Antiquarian Society (Cambridge, 1991), p. 81.
[120] Archdeaconry of Huntingdon, original wills: Thomas Bond (1689), William Sibley (1699); Anne Stokely (1702); John Kilbourn (1703); John Martin junior (1705); Elizabeth Bond (1706); Hunts. RO.
[121] Quaker deeds, St Ives, Cambs. RO R59/26/6/2.
[122] St Ives Particular Meeting, register of burials 1645–1753, PRO RG/6/1514.
[123] Archdeaconry of Huntingdon wills, probate register 25, pp. 562–3, Hunts. RO.
[124] Underhill (ed.), *Fenstanton Records*, p. 254.

Church of England minister and a serving Quaker witnessing the will of a testator with Baptist connections. It is extremely difficult, under such circumstances, to see Fenstanton as a community divided and torn by a supposed transition from 'parish to sect'.

The successful interpretation of evidence concerning will making and social integration is by no means problem-free. The exact reasons why a testator chose a particular witness or scribe in preference to another are often impossible to establish. Did a particular scribe, for example, appear more attractive than another because he charged a smaller fee, or perhaps no fee at all? The answers to such questions, of course, are destined to remain unknown. However, certain broad conclusions can be drawn from the evidence from Fenstanton. Firstly, a mutuality of religious views between testators, witnesses, and scribes was not the prime consideration. Indeed, T.A. Davies has shown that in Essex, between 1660 to 1700, 80 per cent of the witnesses to Quaker wills were non-Quakers.[125] Secondly, the high proportion of Fenstanton witnesses to act in such a capacity only once (72 per cent) suggests that testators selected witnesses from within their individual restricted circles of known and trusted friends, neighbours, servants, and relations, whatever their religion. When it came to the selection of a scribe, other factors came into play. Obviously, literary ability was a prime consideration. The level of fees may well have been another. However, it would seem probable that testators weighed up all considerations and made their choice from a select group of suitably qualified candidates whom they could trust. This trust would be based upon the ability to devise a will which was proficient in legal terms, and also upon a keen sense of discretion on the part of the scribe. Men such as Edmund Mayle would have been a party to some of the most intimate details of people's lives. Mayle must have been a trustworthy and well-respected man.

The question concerning Quaker aversion to the taking of oaths and the successful proving of their wills is another aspect central to the matter of sectarian social integration. Following the Affirmation Act of 1696, the problems surrounding the successful passage of Quaker wills through probate courts were considerably diminished by the acceptance of an affirmation instead of a sworn oath. However, Helen Forde has shown that Derbyshire Quakers, prior to the Affirmation Act, were resorting to a number of expedients in order to assure a smooth passage through probate. For example: testators were choosing non-Quakers as executors in order to circumvent the problem of oath-taking; Quaker executors sometimes chose non-Quaker substitutes, often the parish minister, to attend the court on their behalf (allowable in cases of infirmity); and

---

[125] Davies, 'The Quakers in Essex', p. 291.

Quaker executors could renounce their administrations in favour of non-Quakers.[126] Clearly, all such expedients required a great deal of co-operation between Friends and the population at large. Dr Forde even suggests that the courts may have accepted affirmations instead of oaths from Quaker executors before the Act of 1696, and that it was possible 'that the clergy turned a blind eye to the niceties of procedure where their Quaker parishioners were concerned'.[127]

Helen Forde's findings relating to Derbyshire appear further attested by those of T.A. Davies for Essex. In Essex, Quaker executors of Quaker wills totalled 75, 79, and 77 per cent of the whole for the 1670s, 1680s, and 1690s respectively. Yet Davies found no evidence to suggest that Quaker executors experienced any great difficulties in gaining administration of the estates under their charges. He concludes that: 'some kind of accommodation had been reached between Friends and the ecclesiastical authorities' regarding the taking of oaths.[128] Furthermore, the numerous Quaker wills I have examined suggest a similar degree of cooperation. Most Quaker executors gained administration within a very short time following the death of the testator. Indeed, 65.7 per cent of executors in Cambridgeshire gained administration within six months of the will being made.[129]

Helen Forde also maintains that 'negative evidence' suggests 'co-operation' if not 'collusion' between Friends and the state church as far as burial in woollen was concerned. Although negative evidence is no proof at all, Forde offers a powerful argument that Anglican officials were willing to connive with Friends in order to make the Quaker lot, as well as their own, an easier one. After all, as Forde points out, collusion between Friends and officials regarding the payment of tithes is well known.[130] Moreover, the fact that Friends permitted the interment of non-Quaker kin in their private burial grounds indicates a willingness on their part to minimize inter-familial friction across the religious divide.[131] Similarly, in September 1678, the Baptists of Amersham, in Buckinghamshire, allowed the burial of Thomas Boninder in their private graveyard. Boninder, a man 'that did not goe to such meetings in his life time', expressed a deathbed wish to be buried alongside Baptists.[132] The following month

---

[126] Helen Forde, 'Friends and Authority: A Consideration of Attitudes and Expedients with Particular Reference to Derbyshire', *Journal of the Friends' Historical Society*, 54, 3 (1978), pp. 117–18.
[127] Ibid., p. 118.
[128] Davies, 'The Quakers in Essex', p. 280.
[129] Stevenson, 'Sectarian Cohesion and Social Integration', p. 84.
[130] See Evans, ' "Our Faithful Testimony" '.
[131] Davies, 'The Quakers in Essex', pp. 287–8.
[132] W.T. Whitley (ed.), *The Church Books of Ford or Cuddington and Amersham in the County of Bucks.*, Baptist Historical Society (London, 1912), p. 213.

the congregation decided that: 'if any person desiered to Be Buried in the Buring place Excepting those which Belonge to the Congregation . . . thay shall paye the sum of 5 shilens'.[133] It would appear that the Baptists did not limit this privilege to the relatives of church members alone, but to any non-member whose executors were prepared to pay the fee. Once again, the overall impression left by such evidence is one of Christian neighbourliness and not of separatist introversion.

Furthermore, the transfer of manorial land between sectaries and conformists appears to have been lively. Although this is no proof of a mutual acceptance or toleration of differing religious views, the Huntingdon parish of Fenstanton, for example, appears to have operated in the same way as any 'normal' parish. Moreover, the aforementioned Baptist chief witnesser of wills Edmund Mayle sat as a juror for the Fenstanton Court Baron on 10 April 1661, and his co-religionist John Peverell sat on the jury of the Court Leet of the same date.[134] Similarly, the Baptist leader John Denne and his co-religionist William Woodward sat on the Fenstanton manorial jury of April 1663.[135] In January 1672/3, the Baptist John Lacy sat as a manorial juror.[136] Once again, the evidence appears to argue cooperation rather than conflict.

It may well be, of course, that a certain degree of social integration was inevitable in a small parish, such as Fenstanton, which contained a relatively high proportion of dissenters.[137] Otherwise, the parish could not have functioned on a day-to-day basis. The problem is, of course, that evidence regarding the social integration of dissenters in large parishes, containing a very small number of dissenters, is bound to be scarce whether dissenters were integrated or not. Yet, as we have seen, the evidence from relatively large urban parishes such as Ramsey, in Huntingdonshire, suggests that dissenters were by no means ostracized as far as parochial affairs were concerned. Dissenters did not form alternative societies.

Finally, there is a great deal of evidence to suggest that although sectaries often employed their co-religionists as servants, apprentices, and midwives, they did not always do so to the exclusion of the wider community. The young Yorkshire farm worker Josiah Langdale, for example, took up employment with a Quaker master at some time in the late 1680s or

---

[133] Ibid., p. 214.
[134] Fenstanton manorial court rolls 1656–61, Hunts. RO (no accession number).
[135] Ibid. 1663, Hunts. RO (no accession number).
[136] Ibid. 1672/3, Hunts. RO, 2272/205.
[137] The Compton Census of 1676 declared that Fenstanton contained 286 conformists and thirty-nine protestant dissenters (see Anne Whiteman (ed.), *The Compton Census of 1676; A Critical Edition*, Records of Social and Economic History, NS, 10 (Oxford, 1986), p. 319).

early 1690s.[138] Langdale's employer never pressurized him to become a Quaker; they 'had no discourse about Religion'.[139] Langdale did eventually become a Friend; but his conversion came through his observation of Quakers whilst on his master's business and not from any requirement on his master's part that he should.

There is much evidence to suggest that Quaker families employed conformist midwives and female attendants at the births of their offspring. The birth registers of Buckinghamshire Friends name twenty-nine individual midwives, and 222 women attendants, tending sixty-one different Quaker mothers between 1652 and 1707.[140] Of the twenty-nine midwives, only seven of them were known Quakers belonging to Buckinghamshire meetings; one was a celebrated Quaker midwife from a neighbouring county; seven of them shared surnames common to known Quakers within various Buckinghamshire meetings; and the remaining fourteen had surnames which never appear in any other Buckinghamshire Quaker records for the period. Of the 222 women attendants, ninety-six of them (43 per cent) bore surnames which never appear in Buckinghamshire Quaker records. Also, a non-Quaker midwife from Kendal, in Westmorland, served the same Quaker family in 1670/1 and 1674.[141] Obviously, there would have to be a great deal of mutual trust spanning the religious divide for such commissions to have taken place.[142]

Although seventeenth-century sectaries were members of highly cohesive tightly-knit groups, they were also widely involved in day-to-day parish life. They served their parishes as constables and overseers of the poor; they witnessed and wrote the wills of non-sectaries; they left money in their wills to the parish poor as well as to their poor brethren; they served on manorial juries; they acted as trustees alongside prominent conformist parishioners for the benefit of the parish poor; they socialized with non-sectaries in alehouses, at fairs, and at weddings; they were helped by non-sectaries when hounded by the authorities; they received the respect

[138] Josiah Langdale, *Some Account of the Birth, Education, Religious Exercises and Visitations of God to that Faithfull Servant and Minister of Jesus Christ . . . Josiah Langdale* (1723), Friends' House Library, MS Box 10, p. 6.

[139] *Ibid.*, p. 11.

[140] Leighton Monthly Meeting, register of births 1645–1774, PRO RG/6/1305; Buckinghamshire Quarterly Meeting, register of births 1654–1775, PRO RG/6/1367; Upperside of Bucks. Monthly Meeting, register of births 1656–1755, PRO RG/6/1406.

[141] Kendal midwife's diary, Cumbria Record Office, Crewdon papers, WD/Cr, pp. 15, 46.

[142] For a detailed discussion of midwives and sectarian social integration, see Stevenson, 'Economic and Social Status', pp. 330–9.

of the conforming community at their funerals; they hired conformists as servants, and as midwives and their attendants; they sometimes chose to be buried amongst conformists; they allowed conformists to be buried in their private burial grounds. All such actions point towards a much higher degree of social interaction and integration than the notion of 'alternative' sectarian societies would suggest.

Although public hostility towards early Friends appears to have arisen from most sections of society, public antagonism at the parish level appears to have diminished dramatically by the early 1670s. The reasons are twofold. First, once villagers and townsfolk alike had lived alongside Quakers for a decade or so, they came to tolerate them. They had become 'sensitized'. Once parishioners had seen that the men and women they trusted formerly had not been changed into ogres by their new religion, but remained trustworthy people, intense persecution at the parish level was mitigated. Secondly, from the 1670s onwards, Quakers appear to have been more willing themselves to propagate a closer relationship with the wider community. They began to allow the presence of non-Quaker relatives at their weddings and the burial of non-Quakers in their private burial grounds.[143] They also allowed non-Quakers at the births of their offspring. The reaction of the Church of England and the judiciary, however, remained hostile. Although magistrates tended to be extremely hostile towards sectaries (particularly towards Quakers), parish constables, bailiffs, and members of the general public grew sympathetic towards Quakers and attempted to minimize their sufferings.

By the turn of the seventeenth century, Quakerism had become quietist and was tolerated by all but its most ardent enemies. The less radical Baptists, especially those in the Huntingdonshire village of Fenstanton, appear to have enjoyed a remarkable degree of acceptance throughout the period. Christopher Hill's notion of a transition from 'parish to sect', and the concomitant breakdown of traditional English community life, is extremely difficult to accept in the light of such evidence.

Our view of the position of the nonconformist in society is conditioned by the types of sources we consult. Ecclesiastical and judicial sources are naturally hostile to dissenters; whilst spiritual autobiographies and parish records can sometimes provide an entirely conflicting view of the degree of acceptance enjoyed by sectaries within society as a whole. A good example of such a dichotomy of evidence is to be found in the case of the Muggletonian widow Mary Cundy of the Cambridgeshire village of Orwell. Although Widow Cundy was presented and excommunicated for her unorthodoxy in religion in 1682,[144] and was described as being

---

[143] Davies, 'The Quakers in Essex', pp. 287–8.
[144] CUL, Episcopal visitation, 1682, Ely diocesan records B/2/66, fol. 52v.

interred with the 'burial of an Asse' by the parish minister in 1686,[145] she was maintained by the parish, throughout her nonconformity, at the rate of 1s per week continuously between 1671 and 1686, and had her rent paid from 1676 until her death.[146] Clearly, the village as a whole appears to have had a much higher regard for the poor Widow Cundy than the harsh words of the incumbent would suggest.

If one single incident can express the degree of acceptance sectarians sometimes enjoyed within their local communities, then the case of Oliver Sansom expresses it best. In 1665, the Quaker Oliver Sansom of Boxford, near Newbury, in Berkshire, was told by his conformist neighbours that: 'if ever there should be a meeting at my House, if they had notice of it, they would come to it'.[147] Accordingly, on the occasion of the visit of a 'Ministring Friend' to Sansom's house, his neighbours were informed that a meeting was to take place. The Anglican incumbent, on receipt of information that an illegal conventicle was in progress: 'sent immediately for the Tythingman, who dwelt near, to come away forthwith, and break up the meeting. But neither he, nor the Constable, was at home; for they were both of them at my House, peacably assembled with many others in the Meeting.'[148] This amusing little tale does not depict a village divided by a transition from 'parish to sect', nor of sectaries being ostracized by the rest of society, but, instead, of parishioners living together in an environment of mutual peace and harmony. Far from shunning Sansom and his religion, his neighbours were interested in hearing more about it. Quite clearly, persecution by the church or state did not necessarily bring alienation at parish level. Unfortunately, some commentators have assumed, mistakenly, that it did. Although some conformists experienced an intense fear and mistrust of early dissenters, such feelings often changed quickly for the better. Running parallel with such negative attitudes, and eventually overtaking them, was a willingness by both sectaries and the public at large to accommodate each other for the common good. Cooperation, not conflict, became the order of the day.

---

[145] Parish register, Orwell, Cambs., 1653–1806. Cambs. RO P127/1/2.

[146] Orwell overseers' accounts 1664–1739, Cambs. RO P127/5/1, pp. 157–87.

[147] Oliver Sansom, *An Account of Many Remarkable Passages of the Life of Oliver Sansom* (London, 1710), p. 39.

[148] Ibid., p. 40.

CHAPTER 10

Critical conclusion
PATRICK COLLINSON

The World of Rural Dissenters is like one of those books of the English Renaissance which are about several things at once. One thinks of Sir Thomas Elyot's *The Boke Named the Gouerner* (1531), which discusses politics, the public role of the aristocracy, education, and the English lexicography, not necessarily in that order. The subject is dissenters, from Lollards to Quakers. But this is also a book about the importance of religion in the sixteenth and seventeenth centuries, with dissenting religion selected for study not so much for its own sake as for its relative accessibility. It is also about continuities and discontinuities in rural populations; about settled and itinerant ways of life; about community, the processes of getting on and falling out with people; about books, authors, book-pedlars, and above all readers, especially readers from the lower levels of society; and about the early 'proto-industrial' economy, more particularly of those woodland-pasture regions which encouraged both by-employment and dissent, together with the lines of communication which linked such regions to each other and to London.

Precious nuggets of particular information abound, such as the discovery that furniture making for the London market was probably the principal industry in parts of the Chiltern Hundreds of south Buckinghamshire: as we might have guessed from those great beech-woods which still run down to the Thames at Henley and Marlowe. We meet the Cambridgeshire village scribe whose goods at his death could not cover the cost of his modest debts, so that his widow was obliged to bid for her own child's cradle at auction; and Sister Sneesby, 'a deaf old fen woman' 'in a sad deplorable condition', who in her deafness was converted to Quakerism from Baptist principles by the printed word. In short, this volume is a kind of map of the exceptionally wide interests of its principal author, full of cartographical detail. It is also evidence of her happy gift of transmitting her particular enthusiasms and distinctive talents to her former pupils, and of rejoicing as well as collaborating in the fruits of their research.

In these concluding pages, I shall concentrate on the central theme of prural dissenters, while noting that three of the chapters, and these by no means the least interesting and rewarding, Eric Carlson on churchwardens, Tessa Watt on ephemeral religious literature, and Michael Frearson on the historical geography of the book trade, are somewhat artificially hitched to the dissenting bandwagon. Dr Carlson's essay, based on Cambridgeshire sources, was prompted (as Dr Spufford explains) by the need to discover how far dissenters stood in danger of prosecution, so providing the historian with evidence for their dissent which might otherwise pass unnoticed. It is useful for this purpose but otherwise stands as a notable free-standing essay on a neglected topic.* (The reader will not soon forget the Jacobean churchwarden whose offensive actions 'never went beyond urinating in several parts of the church'.) Dr Watt does not pretend that the trade in cheap 'godlies' was aimed especially at dissenters, or encouraged dissent. Ballads and chapbooks with a religious or moral flavour are evidence of a more diffuse moralism which Dr Watt happily characterizes as 'post-Reformation' but not always thoroughgoingly 'protestant', 'unspectacular orthodoxy'. Her work helps us to arrive at a balanced view of the convergent relations of religion and popular culture, correcting the excesses of some recent writing about Protestant England. Dr Frearson's study of communications is of fundamental importance if we are to understand the movements of dissenters and the propagation of dissenting ideas, nicely complementing the work of Ms Kate Peters on the comings and goings, meetings and partings, of early Quaker activists of both sexes, traced through their books as well as correspondence.[1] But the Frearson chapter is essential reading for anyone concerned with traffic in various kinds of literature, religious or otherwise, and the diffusion of all sorts of ideas in sixteenth- and seventeenth-century England. Equally, Margaret Spufford's enthralling and richly documented essay 'I bought me a primer' (the words of a Gloucestershire shepherd) has implications for the popular end of seventeenth-century culture in something like its entirety.

So we come to the subject of 'rural dissenters'. But was there such a thing as rural dissent? Dr Bill Stevenson can demonstrate that a majority of dissenters in his part of late seventeenth-century England lived in the countryside (like everyone else). But they went to market and had some of their places of meeting in the inns and, presently, the licensed meeting-

---

* Editor's note: Dr Carlson's essay was not originally intended to be 'free-standing'. It survives, with Dr Marsh's chapter on Balsham, as part of our second study area, centred on Haverhill. See Ch. 1, p. 11, Map 4, and Appendix A.

[1] I refer to Ms Peters' forthcoming Cambridge PhD thesis, 'Quaker Pamphlets and the Development of the Quaker Movement, 1652–1656'.

houses of market towns.† The multiple interactions of town and country, not their differences, are the proper study of early modern historians. It seems unlikely that 'rural dissent' had a peculiarly rural character and how it might have been characterized is in any case not a question addressed in this book. Except in Dr Spufford's heartfelt little essay on 'The importance of the Lord's Supper to dissenters', what dissenters preached and heard, how they prayed, how they sang, what they did with their dissent, are subjects beyond the scope of this volume.

But let that pass. *The World of Rural Dissenters* has four grand themes which, taken together, constitute a unified thesis embodying a major advance in our knowledge of what used to be called the English Nonconformist Tradition: not, to be sure, of its religious content but of its social construction. And yet there is a worm in this ripe apple, to which I shall return in concluding this Conclusion.

The first point concerns our perception of the social composition and profile of dissent, which will never be the same again. Gone are those contradictory notions, with their shallow polemical and ideological roots, which on the one hand connected nonconformity with the lowest of the low and on the other made it the possession of a burgeoning bourgeoisie, a monopoly of the industrious and thriving sort of people. Derek Plumb's findings for the Lollards of the Chiltern Hundreds in about 1520 are consistent with Bill Stevenson's for what the railways are beginning to call West Anglia, but also for the Quaker population of those same Chiltern Hundreds, in the late seventeenth century; and both are firmly grounded in sound statistics. Dissenters, whether Lollards or Quakers, display a cross-sectional profile not much out of line with society as a whole, lying for the most part between the seriously rich and the desperately poor, but if anything a small cut above the common norm. The Plumb and Stevenson chapters contain striking examples of dissenters of 'the better sort', exercising 'economic dominance within their communities'. This was more conspicuously the case with the Family of Love in the Cambridgeshire village of Balsham, the subject of Christopher Marsh's chapter, its leading lights constituting a social as well as religious elite, self-consciously so in both respects. Yet Dr Spufford herself continues to be

---

† Editor's note: when Professor Collinson wrote this, he had not seen Maps 2 and 7, firmly based on the market town of Amersham, and Map 4, showing part of the second area we attempted to study, based on the market town of Haverhill. These make it abundantly plain that we have always taken market towns as the natural meeting-places for dissenters, as for all rural people on necessary business in a money-rent economy. We had also stated that we assumed as a working axiom that the area from which a gathered church was drawn was likely to coincide with a marketing area (Ch. 1, p. 30) and Mrs Evans had discussed the point on pp. 289, 291–2.

strongly drawn towards the balancing evidence of the religious capacities of the female, elderly, and indigent elements in society.

It seems that almost anyone could be a dissenter. That the vast majority of people were not is a constant challenge to the explanatory powers of religious historians, to which arguments concerning occupational, or economic, or environmental determinism make an inadequate response. Whether family tradition, dissent in the blood, provides better, if still incomplete, answers is a large question posed rather than fully and satisfactorily answered in this book. If religious convictions are inherited, repeatedly over four or more generations, can we say that they remain convictions? This must be especially true of *dissenting* convictions. For someone from dissenting stock to convert back into the church establishment, or out of religion altogether, would be the true dissent. The early eighteenth-century high church fanatic Dr Sacheverell came from puritan stock.

The second discovery of the Spuffordians is of still greater moment. Even Dr Spufford herself used to think, along with most of us, that to be a dissenter in a uniformitarian and intolerant society was either to express a condition of alienation, or to depart into an alienating and unpopular inner exile. Dissenters were outsiders, occupying an alternative social space, detesting their neighbours and by them detested. Now we know that this was not at all how it was, at least not for the dissenting groups studied by Dr Plumb, Dr Marsh, and Dr Stevenson, from which I think that we may safely extrapolate. The survival, and often the material success, of dissenters is shown to have depended upon a benign double strategy of endogamous and exogamous integration. Heretics and nonconformists were not, for the most part, eccentric individuals but members of a disciplined and mutually supportive society, the hallmark of which was often that endogamy in the strict sense in which the Quakers would persist for three centuries. Dr Marsh calls this 'collective introversion'. When the elders of the Family of Love no longer insisted on marriage within the fellowship, the days of the Family were numbered.

But, on the other hand, Plumb, Marsh, and Stevenson uncover a contrary and consistent pattern of relatively harmonious participation in the world beyond the sect, which is to say, the wider community of the parish, neighbourhood, and district. Lollards, Familists, Baptists, and Quakers filled the niches in society appropriate to their station, performing such neighbourly offices as the witnessing of wills and attendance at funerals (with reciprocal attendance at their own burials), and shouldering the ordinary burdens of parochial and manorial office. The Family of Love was especially adept at eating its cake and having it, as Christopher Marsh demonstrates in his thick narrative of Familist Balsham, 'a picture of unimagined depth and subtlety'. For Familists this was not so much a matter of pragmatic convenience as of conscience. But the life strategies of many Roman Catholics were not so different. It is a pity that it was not possible to include in this collection a recent case-study of catholic cake-eating in the Cambridgeshire village of Linton,[2] for Linton was but a stone's throw from Balsham. As Professor Bossy long ago insisted, Catholics were also dissenters, in fact the first (post-Reformation) dissenters.[3] Such insights are encouraging for modern liberal ecumenists. In spite of what the law said, and of the starkly segrega-tionist advice offered in religious courtesy literature, whether recusant or puritan, it appears to have been live and let live for our religious ancestors, to a greater extent than conventional wisdom has allowed. None of the critical comments with which this Conclusion will end is intended to diminish the value of the first two of the 'grand themes'. Plumb–Marsh–Stevenson on the socially spectral character of dissent, and on endogamous and exogamous integration as the secret of survival and success, amounts to the most important research ever carried out on the subject.

Endogamous/exogamous is one paradox. Another, making the third plank in the Spuffordian platform, is that the continued strength of the dissenting tradition seems to have depended upon an equally strange and conflicting combination of geographical inwardness and out-wardness. Given the Chiltern Hundreds by Margaret Spufford, Nesta Evans found that she was researching what appears to have been the most static of all local communities in early modern England so far subjected to reconstitutive study. Hardly anyone ever moved away from this native heath, not even up to the point at which the 1990 telephone directory for the area was compiled. And an inordinately large proportion of these stay-at-homes are found to have been the highly indigenous sixteenth-century Lollards and seventeenth-century Quakers who turned the Chil-tern Hills into a kind of religious wildlife refuge. Dr Peter Spufford valid-ates Mrs Evans' findings with a magisterial, state-of-the-art survey of what is now known about the movement and non-movement of families and individuals in other parts of England.

Professor Jack Scarisbrick had some vague sense of the impenetrable ethnocentricity of the Chilterns when he suggested that the Lollardy of that region on the eve of the Reformation was typical of remote and barely Christian mountain country, 'upland semi-paganism'.[4] But Scaris-

[2] Andrzej Bida, 'Papists in an Elizabethan Parish: Linton, Cambridgeshire, c. 1560–c. 1600' (Cambridge, Diploma in Historical Studies Dissertation, 1992). The best account of non-recusant catholicism and of its perception and construction by both protestants and recusant catholics is Alexandra Walsham, Church Papists: Catholicism, Conformity and Confessional Polemic in Early Modern England (Woodbridge, 1993).
[3] John Bossy, The English Catholic Community 1570–1850 (London, 1975).
[4] J.J. Scarisbrick, The Reformation and the English People (Oxford, 1984), p. 6.

brick got the Chilterns, not to speak of the nature of its religious hetero-doxy, badly wrong. Not only were communications with nearby London excellent, with trading and other connections constantly active, but the region was traversed by long-distance trade routes from the west and north-west which left few places isolated from the outside world of the packhorse, cart, and barge by more than a few miles of sticky by-roads. Just as with two-way social integration, the south Buckinghamshire dis-senters seem to have enjoyed a double advantage. Fluids flowed in and out of this cask and yet were retained and matured within it. Developing the analogy, we might say that Buckinghamshire Quakers were a distilla-tion of generations of dissent, periodically topped up with new ideas from outside.

Or so *The World of Rural Dissenters* would have us believe, it being a sec-ondary concern of the book to make and justify the claim that there was a continuity of religious nonconformity in communities and blood-lines, a 'descent of dissent'. This was a sporting fox to hunt, with Plumb and Stevenson drawing the coverts and Nesta Evans whipping in the eager hounds of statistics. But was a continuity of dissent the consequence of the unusual level of social stability obtaining in the Chilterns and perhaps waiting to be discovered in other regions with a comparable religious history? Or its cause? Is the argument altogether free of circularity? What does it actually mean to speak, as I have now done, of 'the continued strength of the dissenting tradition'? Was there such a 'tradition'? If blood-lines can be established, as Nesta Evans has shown to some extent they can, connecting Lollard surnames with Quaker surnames, known ancestors with known descendants, what does that signify? This fox has not yet been killed, or hunted to its earth.

The descent of dissent is no new idea. It appealed long ago to noncon-formist historians like W.H. Summers, who in his studies of those same Chiltern Hundreds spoke of *Our Lollard Ancestors* as early Congregationalists, with some instinctive sense of those continuities which the researches of Mrs Evans have put beyond any doubt; and to historians in a Marxist tradition like Christopher Hill, who wrote an essay called 'From Lollards to Levellers'.[5] Margaret Spufford collects telling case-histories of godliness begetting godliness over the generations, but has had the ambition to place this phenomenon on a 'scientific' basis, to make it, in Nesta Evans' phrase, 'demonstrably true'. Strangely enough there is probably no histor-ian living who is more inclined to deny that religious history can ever be 'scientific' or 'demonstrable' than Margaret Spufford.

[5] W.H. Summers, *Our Lollard Ancestors* (London, 1904); W.H. Summers, *The Lollards of the Chiltern Hills: Glimpses of English Dissent in the Middle Ages* (London, 1906); Christopher Hill, 'From Lollards to Levellers', in *The Collected Essays of Christopher Hill*, vol. II: *Religion and Politics in Seventeenth-Century England* (Brighton, 1986), pp. 89–116.

No one would want artificially to separate the early sixteenth from the later seventeenth century as two unconnected religious continents. But what is supposed to have happened in the years in between, the years occupied by what I should still want to call the English Reformation, and claim as the greatest single watershed in English religious history?[6] There are three possibilities. (1) The Lollard tendency and its human networks were absorbed into the mainstream of the protestant Reformation, which in many parts of England was a partly puritan mainstream. For many decades there was little separatist dissent in England. The seventeenth-century sects which broke out of that mainstream were circumstantial in their origins and effectively, if not absolutely, novel. (2) There was a continuity of radical and at least semi-separatist dissent, an underground river undermining the protestant establishment and eventually resurfacing in the special conditions of the Interregnum and Restoration. Lollards, Anabaptists, Baptists, and Quakers were the 'same' people, differentiated only by generation. (3) Environment, not tradition, was all. Environments like the Chiltern Hills (and the Kentish Weald or High Suffolk), with their loose patterns of settlement, mixed economies and weak manorial and parochial control, were ever the natural home for dissent and other forms of insubordination. This model prefers horizontal to vertical accounts of religious history and these, outside the committed pages of denominational annalists, are the easier to sustain. However, these are far from mutually exclusive models and it remains possible that the truest account of rural dissenters will combine elements of all three.

Nesta Evans and Margaret Spufford lean to the second of our models. The verifiable circumstances, including the marked coincidence of Lollard and Quaker surnames and the appearance in their generations of known Lollards and Quakers within the same family stock, sometimes traceable through the female line, appear to work in their favour. But strictly speaking their findings are compatible with any of the three models. Unfortunately, the matter cannot be clinched if only because, as with a certain famous sweetmeat, this is a mint with a hole. The hole consists of almost everything that happened, religiously speaking, in the Chiltern Hundreds between the Elizabethan Settlement and the eve of the Civil War. Not, of course, that nothing happened; only that, given the extreme paucity of evidence, little of what did happen of relevant substance remains on record. We simply do not know enough about the religious dispositions of the three or four intervening generations, and

---

[6] Christopher Haigh, *English Reformations: Religion, Politics and Society under the Tudors* (Oxford, 1993), and my critical review, 'With a Small "r"', *Times Literary Supplement*, 22 October 1993.

must hope that someone, for the purpose of gaining a PhD, or merely of enlightening us all, will investigate those boxes of consistory court material at Lincoln to which Dr Spufford draws our attention, and which may yet supply at least some of our want of knowledge.

Speaking nationally, the hole, or shall we say gap, contains a long chronology of critically important interfaces: between late Lollardy and early protestantism, radical post-Lollard heresy ('Anabaptism') and magisterial predestinarian protestantism, conformity and nonconformity, separatist and semi-separatist forms of puritanism; late Henrician, Edwardian, Marian, Elizabethan, Jacobean waves, hitting the foreshore of any English region we care to mention, the Chilterns included.

From our knowledge of other regions, better served by the archives, Essex, west Suffolk, Kent, we may hazard a guess at what may have been going on in Buckinghamshire in the relatively hidden Elizabethan and Jacobean years: that is, apart from that conformity which Margaret Spufford (a shade too pessimistically) says has no history. I am thinking of sermons and gadding to sermons, sermon repetition in private house meetings, bible reading: in a word, 'godliness', accompanied by some friction between the ostentatiously godly and their opponents, leading to name-calling – 'puritans'. In all this there may have been little separatism as such.[7] (And yet The World of Rural Dissenters makes no mention of that line of radical dissent, a puritanism beyond puritanism, which ran from the East Anglian Brownists of the 1580s through the Barrowists and the 'Ancient Church' of Amsterdam of the 1590s into a complex delta of early seventeenth-century separatist and near-separatist experiments in England, Holland, and America.[8])

Given the strength of protestantism/puritanism in the ranks of the Buckinghamshire gentry, noted by Dr Spufford (this was Hampden and Milton country), this 'normal' puritan pattern is what we might expect to find in the Elizabethan Chilterns. Yet the absence of Buckinghamshire from such puritan manuscript collections as 'The Seconde Parte of a Register'[9] has always led me to suspect that this was not a reservoir of mainstream godliness. That could favour the Spuffordian thesis: sectarian dissent leap-frogging (or undercutting) the regular Reformation.

In the absence of late sixteenth- and early seventeenth-century evidence, somewhat desperate efforts are made in this volume to bridge the

---

[7] Contrary to Dr Spufford's report (n. 20 to Ch. 1, above) Dr R.J. Acheson who, before he began his research, expected to find a continuity of radical dissent in Kent, was unable to confirm it from the rich Kentish archives at his disposal. (R.J. Acheson, 'The Development of Religious Separatism in the Diocese of Canterbury, 1590–1660' (University of Kent at Canterbury, PhD, 1983).) See also R.J. Acheson, Radical Puritans in England 1550–1660 (London, 1989). And note Acheson's bounding dates.

[8] B.R. White, The English Separatist Tradition (Oxford, 1971).

[9] The Seconde Parte of a Register, ed. Albert Peel, 2 vols. (Cambridge, 1915).

gap. Derek Plumb calls his second chapter on the Lollards 'A gathered church?', but there are conceptual weaknesses in an essay which contains almost no evidence which would confirm that that was what Lollardy was. References to Lollard 'meetings' elsewhere in the volume, approximating these occasions to later dissenting 'meetings', do not involve any critical discussion of what Lollards did when they met. While to advance mid-sixteenth-century 'Anabaptists', as Nesta Evans does, following Michael Watts, looking towards later seventeenth-century Baptists, is to walk a rotten plank which will not reach that far. When, in 1636–7, Mrs Evans and Dr Spufford come across a rare reference to 'conventicles' at Wooburn and Chesham, they should not assume that that is necessarily our river, breaking out to the surface. 'Conventicle' is what the ecclesiastical authorities, especially in the 1630s, called the private house meeting for sermon repetition and the like, which in the perception of those who took part was nothing of the kind, if by conventicle is meant a break-away sect and counter-church.[10]

In the last resort, this splendid collection of essays, which is about so much more than rural dissenters, is unable to define dissent with sufficient precision to clarify its many imprecisions. Ecclesiology, whether of the theoretical or the practical, acted-out kind, is wholly absent. Is dissent taken to entail separation or patterns of religious behaviour short of separation? The authors, perhaps unconsciously following the rights of way laid down by the denominational historians, and located as they mostly are in the periods before the mainstream Reformation or after it, seem to think mainly in terms of a radical and separatist dissent. Presbyterians and Independents, let alone those many puritans who were neither, scarcely get a look in. This is strangely at odds with what Plumb, Marsh, and Stevenson have discovered about those rather consistent habits of external integration, semi-conformity, and semi-separatism. In the cases of the Baptists and Quakers, these strategies were combined with strict ecclesiastical separation. But with Presbyterians and Independents, not to speak of those many 'Old English Puritans' who resist such labelling, they point to a kind of religious voluntarism which contrived to remain in some sense and degree within the religious establishment. And so, as Dr Plumb and other recent historians of the subject have shown, with the later Lollards.

This suggests that there may be scope for further dialogue with historians who are at home in Elizabethan and early Stuart England. If the Spuffordians want to argue for a consistency and continuity of religious voluntarism, neither wholly in nor entirely out of the church, perhaps connected with particular regions, economies, occupations, and even tribes, I for one should have no grounds on which to disagree.

---

[10] Patrick Collinson, 'The English Conventicle', in W.J. Sheils and Diana Wood (eds.), *Voluntary Religion*, Studies in Church History, 23 (Oxford, 1986), pp. 223–59.

The impossibility of tracing dissent through time in thirty-six parishes on the Essex, Cambridgeshire, and Suffolk borders

NESTA EVANS

No one should again attempt the exercise of tracing radical religious continuity for the Essex, Cambridgeshire, and Suffolk borderland, which was our second study area, on which I spent three months. I took the area within a six-mile radius of the market town of Haverhill as our primary area of study, as we had focussed in the first place on the area within a six-mile radius of Amersham: our second area also included the market towns of Linton in Cambridgeshire, where the Familists marketed, and Clare in Suffolk. Foxe listed no less than eighty-one of the Essex Lollards at Birdbrook or Steeple Bumpstead, within six miles of Haverhill.

The first step, as for Buckinghamshire, was to collect and index all the names listed in 1524 and the 1670s for the parishes in the second area. The Hearth Taxes here are in much better condition than the Buckinghamshire ones, and have the added advantage of including the names of the exempt. The years used are 1674 for Cambridgeshire and Suffolk, and 1673 for Essex. This area contains thirty-six parishes, as against twenty-one in Buckinghamshire, and the total number of names is between a quarter and a third more. The parishes within six miles of Haverhill in 1524 produced 541 individual surnames (each counted only once), of which 215 reappeared in the Hearth Tax returns, that is 39.74 per cent; in Buckinghamshire the survival rate for the population at large was 29 per cent. This higher percentage for the second study area encouraged the hope that Lollard names would survive at least as well here as in Buckinghamshire.

However, only nine of the eighty-one Lollards or Lollard suspects named by Foxe appear in the 1524 Subsidy return for these two places. A search not only in all thirty-six parishes, but also in Essex parishes bordering the area, turned up only one more. Another was discovered in a manorial rental for Steeple Bumpstead. The names of six of the nine Lollard taxpayers, who had been identified in Birdbrook and Steeple Bumpstead in 1524, reappear in the Hearth Tax. The continuity of two-thirds of the family names of Lollards found in 1524 sounds impressive, but the number is far too small to be statistically significant.

Foxe leaves his readers with the impression that the Essex Lollards frequently moved around both within and outside the county, and he does not always firmly link them, as residents, to particular parishes. The existence of a Lollard conventicle at Birdbrook and Steeple Bumpstead is not in dispute, but the absence of members' names from the 1524 Subsidy suggests that it was a 'gathered church' drawing its adherents from a wide area. Most of the Lollards named by Foxe were tried as late as 1527–8 or 1533, but this can only partly explain why their names were not found in 1524. Their individual places of residence were apparently not usually noted by Foxe in this area, as they were in Buckinghamshire. It is not uncommon to find Essex Lollards named in more than one place. Since most of them were not taxpayers in 1524 in any of our thirty-six parishes, they seemed to have travelled considerable distances.

Unfortunately, no further identification of Lollards can be made in the two adjacent counties because there were no heresy trials at the relevant time in the dioceses of Ely and Norwich. Given the known propensity of Lollards to travel, the considerable number of late seventeenth-century dissenters in the area, and the presence of Familists in and around Linton and Balsham in the reign of Elizabeth I, it seems unbelievable that Lollardy did not spread into Cambridgeshire and Suffolk. However much the existence of Lollards may be suspected in these two counties, there is no way of proving their presence in the face of lack of activity, or at least of surviving records of any anti-Lollard action, by the Bishops of Norwich and Ely.[1]

The major weakness of the Haverhill area is that the Lollard base is too small and confined to too few parishes. In the late seventeenth century Quakers were the main dissenting group in the district. Lyon Turner lists only this sect in the Cambridgeshire parishes, Presbyterians and Quakers in Suffolk and nothing for the Essex parishes, except for Presbyterian teachers at Ridgewell and Stambourne. There seems no reason to doubt the accuracy of Lyon Turner's listings.

In other respects the records are inferior to those for Buckinghamshire. There is nothing to equal the Quaker minute books and Baptist church books for that county, and the visitation records are far less numerous and informative. Attempts to trace some of the Lollard families failed, largely because several of the parishes have registers which begin late, and there were not enough wills to supply the gaps. Irritatingly, there are much better nonconformist records further north in Cambridgeshire,

---

[1] Anne Hudson, *The Premature Reformation: Wycliffite Texts and Lollard History* (Oxford 1988), chapter 10.

and most of the Quakers listed in Essex visitation records lived to the south of the study area.

To sum up, this study failed to produce results to equal those from Buckinghamshire principally because too few Lollards were given parishes of origin by Foxe, and the other records were in many respects defective. In spite of this, it became apparent that there was considerable movement by Quakers across the county boundaries, indicating that a study area straddling two or more counties is not inherently unsuitable for this purpose. We do not think our failure in Essex invalidates our results in Buckinghamshire.

Bibliography

Original sources
1524 Subsidy return. Transcripts used for Essex and Suffolk.
Hearth Tax returns: 1674 for Cambridgeshire and Suffolk (transcripts) and 1673 for Essex.
Suff. RO (Bury St Edmunds) 909/11 Churchwardens' presentments, Clare Deanery, 1592.
Norfolk Record Office VIS2/1 Episcopal Visitation Book, 1593; VIS6/1 Episcopal Visitation Book, 1629; VIS7/3 Episcopal Visitation Book, 1677–8. (There are no archdeacons' Visitation Books for the Sudbury Archdeaconry before 1700, and no Norwich episcopal ones between 1629 and 1677.)
Visitation Books in Essex RO: D/AMV/7 Archdeaconry of Middlesex 1680–5; D/ACV/8 Archdeaconry of Colchester 1681–4.
Parish registers in Essex RO D/P331/1/1 Helions Bumpstead from 1558, TR168/2 Ashdon from 1558; in Cambs. RO transcripts of Shudy Camps from 1558, Castle Camps from 1563, Horseheath from 1558, Weston Colville from 1599, West Wickham from 1599, Linton from 1559; in Suff. RO (Bury St Edmunds) Cowlinge register from 1558, Withersfield from 1558.
Wills in Cambs. RO, Essex RO, and Suff. RO, and in PRO.
Essex Calendars of County Records: vol. XXII Quarter Sessions 1654–64; vol. XXIII 1665–71; vol. XXIV 1672–87; vol. XXV 1688–9. Essex RO Q/SO/2 Quarter Sessions Order Book No. 2, 1671–86.
Suff. RO (Bury St Edmunds) FK6501/1/1 Sudbury Quaker Monthly Meeting Book, 1666–1738.
Suff. RO (Bury St Edmunds) Haverhill Quaker Monthly Meeting register, on microfilm. Original in PRO.
Suff. RO (Bury St Edmunds) FK6501/4/11 a and b. Transcript of declarations of intention to marry made at Sudbury Quaker Monthly Meeting 1672–1738.
Microfilms in Essex RO of Quaker registers in PRO: Coggeshall and Witham Monthly Meetings, and Essex Quarterly Meeting up to 1700. Few relevant entries.

W.M. Palmer Collection (MSS) in CUL: B58 scandalous ministers, A12 ejected clergy, B25 episcopal returns for 1669, A56 notes on Linton nonconformists, B30 Linton Independent meeting-house.
MS list of Lollards compiled by, and in the possession of, Dr Derek Plumb.
MS list of Cambridgeshire Quakers compiled by, and in the possession of, Dr William Stevenson.

Printed sources
Besse, J., *A Collection of the Sufferings of the People Called Quakers*, I (London, 1753).
Foxe, John, *Actes and Monuments*, ed. Rev. Stephen R. Cattley, 8 vols. (London, 1837–41), IV, V, VII and VIII.
Strype, John, *Ecclesiastical Memorials* (Oxford, 1822), I, part II.
Turner, George Lyon (ed.), *Original Records of Early Nonconformity under Persecution and Indulgence* (London, 1911), I and II.

APPENDIX B

The parishes investigated for details of the genealogies of the nineteen families searched for in the Chilterns, and the genealogies of the Bartlet, Butterfield, Dell, Harding, Nash, Tredway, Gate, Nash and Child, Child of Coleshill, Randall, and West families

NESTA EVANS

The twenty-one Buckinghamshire parishes of the Quaker Upperside Meeting, covered by Map 7, are listed below. The dates are those of the start of their parish registers, and those of the asterisked places were searched when tracing the genealogies of dissenting families.

*Amersham (1561); Aylesbury (1564); *Beaconsfield (1631); *Bledlow (1592); Burnham (1561); *Chalfont St Giles (1584); *Chalfont St Peter (1539); *Chesham (1538); Denham (1584); *Farnham Royal (1635); High Wycombe (1674); *Hitcham (1559); *Hughenden (1559); Iver (1605); Gt Missenden (1678); *Lt Missenden (1559); *Monks Risborough (1587); *Penn (1563); *West Wycombe (1581); Weston Turville (1538); *Wooburn (1653).

As work on linking dissenters over a century and a half proceeded, it became clear that the registers of the following parishes would have to be searched:

Chenies (1592); Chesham Bois (1562); Hedgerley (1539); Gt Marlow (1592); Lt Marlow (1559); Princes Risborough (1561); Upton (1538).

Nineteen surnames known to have been borne by Lollards in the early sixteenth century, and by Baptists or Quakers in the post-Restoration period, were selected with the aim of proving positive genealogical links over a period of some 150 years. They were, in alphabetical order, Bartlet, Butterfield, Cock, Dell, Dorset, Fryer, Harding, Herne, Hickman, Hobbes, Hoare, Howse, Littlepage, Nash, Tracher, Tredway, Weedon, Widmore, and Woolman. Originally, Penn was included, but it was dropped after the discovery that the family of William Penn did not come from Buckinghamshire, and that the descendants of the Lollard Penns became Roman Catholic recusants. The constraints imposed by time and sources limited the number of successful linkages to six families in the male line, but there is no reason why further intensive work should not have increased this number.

Women were extremely important in the transmission of religious belief and dissent. A further two dissenting families have been traced through female lines, and the ancestry of Margaret West, who married into the non-comforming Tredway family, has also been followed back to the early sixteenth century. Finally, a somewhat tentative ancestry has been established for the Randall family, which although Lollard was not included in the original list of nineteen.

Four of the six male line families linked from Lollards to the late seventeenth century were Quaker, one Baptist and the sixth included adherents of both nonconforming churches. One of the two female lines ended in a Baptist, while the other produced both Quakers and Baptists.

The preponderance of Quakers in the successful linkages is due to the superior quality and better survival of this sect's records. Geographically the linked families are heavily weighted towards the Amersham area, but this is unsurprising as there were both Baptist and Quaker meeting-houses in the town, and a second Quaker meeting at Jordans, not far away. The hamlet of Coleshill, which was a detached portion of Hertfordshire although part of the parish of Amersham, seems to have been favoured as a place of residence for Quaker families. The survival of early registers for most of the parishes in this district is another reason for success in tracing dissenting families here.

Bartlet of Amersham and Chalfont St Giles

William I
A Lollard. Dead by 1522.

m. Katherine[1]
Died 1525 leaving a will. All her
children and their spouses named
as Lollards.

William II
A Lollard. Presumed to be the son
of Katherine.

m. ?
She was alive when her son John
made his will in 1545.

John[2]

m. ?
No wife is mentioned in John's will
made in 1545.

Nicholas
Nothing is known of him.

m. ?

Henry
He had eight children born
between 1596 and 1620. In 1620
and 1621 he was churchwarden of
Amersham, and in 1626 overseer of
the poor.

m. Katherine Mychell
Married on 11 February 1593–4 at
Amersham.

Joseph I[3]
Baptized on 29 October 1620 at
Amersham. He made his will in
1679, calling himself a blacksmith of
Chalfont St Giles.

m. Grace

Joseph II[4]
Blacksmith and Quaker.

m. Mary Russell
Married on 9 September 1673 at
Jordans.

Sources: Derek Plumb, 'John Foxe and the Later Lollards of the Mid-Thames Valley'
(Cambridge, PhD, 1987), list of Lollards, which gives details from the 1522 Musters and
the 1524 Lay Subsidy; Amersham parish register; wills of the Bartlet family: Katherine,
1525 Bucks. RO D/A/We/2/52, Isabel, 1547 Bucks. RO D/A/We/7/117, Margaret, 1558
Bucks. RO D/A/We/12/150, John, 1545 Bucks. RO D/A/We/6/40, Joseph, 1680 PRO
PROB 11/1680/92; 1662 Hearth Tax, PRO E179/80/350; digests of Quaker registers at
Friends House; M.M. Beatrice Saxon Snell (ed.), The Minute Book of the Monthly Meeting of
the Society of Friends for the Upperside of Buckinghamshire 1669–1690, Buckinghamshire Record
Society 1 (Aylesbury, 1937); Joseph Besse, A Collection of the Sufferings of the People Called
Quakers (London, 1753).

1 Katherine does not name her late husband in her will, but her eldest son was called William, and 'Old Father Bartlet' was named in the heresy trials, which ended in 1522, as father of Richard, Isabel Morwin, and Elizabeth Copland. These three were children of Katherine. In 1522 Katherine was assessed at 8s on land and £10 on goods; 1524 assessed at £8; in both years a widow. Her three sons, three daughters, two sons-in-law, and two daughters-in-law were all named as Lollards. Katherine bequeathed her soul to 'my maker and redeemer Jesus', and rather surprisingly made bequests to the high altar of Amersham church, Lincoln Cathedral, and the statue of St Katherine in the parish church. Her son Richard married Isabel, a named Lollard, who made her will as a widow of Amersham in 1547. Richard was alive in 1545 when he was overseer of his nephew John's will. Katherine's son Robert, who was probably dead when she made her will in 1525, married Margaret, a Lollard, who made her will as a widow of Wooburn Deyncourt in 1558. Some of the legatees and witnesses to her will were residents of Amersham.

2 In his will John named his sons Robert and Nicholas and two other young unnamed children. His son Robert married, but his wife's name is not known. Their two sons were Richard, baptized on 16 March 1566-7, and James, baptized on 6 February 1574-5.

3 Joseph's wife Grace is named in his will. He owned a cottage and a messuage in Chalfont St Giles. He left his son, Joseph II, the tools of his trade and mentions his granddaughter Mary. Joseph I committed his 'body to the earth to remain in hopes of a glorious resurrection'. He is listed under Chalfont St Giles in the Hearth Tax for 1662, but the number of his hearths is missing.

4 Joseph II's baptism has not been found, but he was probably born during the time when registers are defective. At his marriage he was called Joseph junior, and he, like his father, was a blacksmith. His marriage and the births of his two children come from Quaker records. Mary Russell was the daughter of William Russell, gentleman of Jordans in Chalfont St Giles, who lived in a four-hearth house in 1662. This was probably the farmhouse near the Quaker meeting-house at Jordans and now, much enlarged, used as a guest-house. Her marriage with Joseph Bartlet was first proposed to a Quaker meeting on 6 November 1672, but the couple were advised to wait because of 'some dissatisfaction of spirit' on the part of her father. Was this due to the social difference between the two families? Consent for this marriage was given at a meeting held on 5 March 1672-3. Joseph and Mary had two daughters, both born at Chalfont St Giles: Mary born on 25 August 1675 and Sarah born on 14 September 1676; she died on 16 September 1678. Mary's father is one of the small number of Buckinghamshire Friends whose names appear in the seventeenth-century Books of Sufferings as having 'suffered' for refusing to pay tithes. Besse records the fining of Friends who had met at William Russell's house at Jordans in July 1670.

Butterfield of Chenies and Flaunden

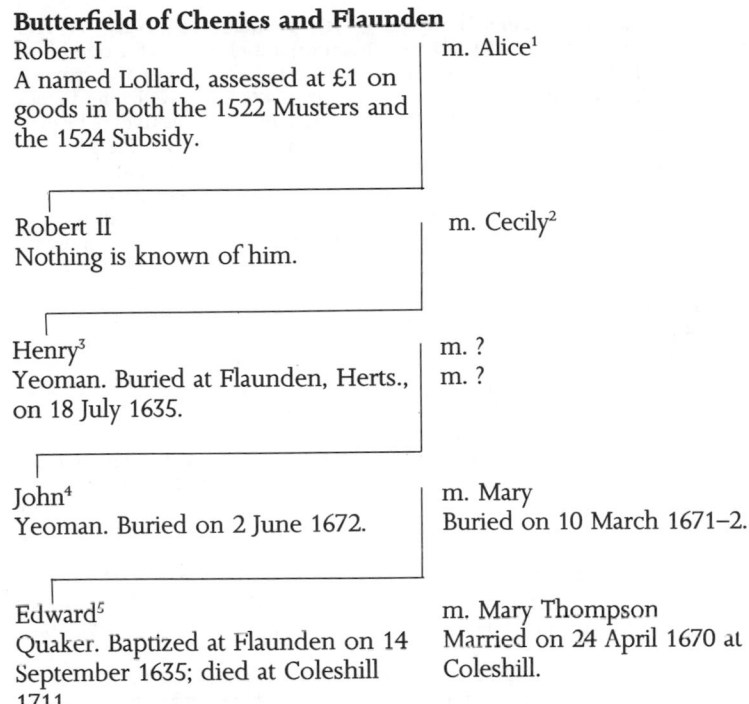

Robert I   m. Alice[1]
A named Lollard, assessed at £1 on
goods in both the 1522 Musters and
the 1524 Subsidy.

Robert II   m. Cecily[2]
Nothing is known of him.

Henry[3]   m. ?
Yeoman. Buried at Flaunden, Herts.,   m. ?
on 18 July 1635.

John[4]   m. Mary
Yeoman. Buried on 2 June 1672.   Buried on 10 March 1671–2.

Edward[5]   m. Mary Thompson
Quaker. Baptized at Flaunden on 14   Married on 24 April 1670 at
September 1635; died at Coleshill   Coleshill.
1711.

Sources: Plumb, 'Foxe and the Later Lollards', list of Lollards, which gives details from the 1522 Musters and the 1524 Lay Subsidy; wills and inventories of the Butterfield family: Alice, 1553 Bucks. RO D/A/We/8/6, Cecily, 1573 Bucks. RO D/A/Wf/7/228, Edmund, 1584 PRO PROB11 Watson 30, Henry, 1636 Herts. RO 10HW76, Henry, 1644 Herts. RO H23/124, John, 1672 Herts. RO 12HW18, Edward, 1713 Herts. RO 15HW23; bishops' transcripts for Flaunden in Herts. RO; digest of Quaker registers in Friends House; Snell (ed.), *Minute Book*; *Journal of Friends Historical Society*, 31 (1934), p. 82.

[1] There is no proof that Alice was Robert's wife, except that she had a son called Robert. She made her will in 1553, naming her sons Robert and John and the former's daughter Joan. Both her sons were married in 1553. She bequeathed her soul to God. When she made her will, she was a widow of Chalfont St Peter. The will of Thomas Butterfield of Chenies, made in 1540, was witnessed by Robert Butterfield.

[2] Cecily is assumed to have married Robert II as her eldest son was also named Robert. In her will she commended her soul to 'the lord God of truth who hath redeemed me'. She left 2d to Lincoln Cathedral, 12d to the repair of Chenies church, and 4d to the poor men's box. She mentions her daughter Joan, referred to in her mother-in-law Alice's will, and three married daughters, as well as her sons Robert, Francis, Edward, John, and Edmund. Also named are John's three sons: Henry, young John, and young Edward. Cecily's son Edmund of Chenies died childless, making his will in 1584. His brother Edward was his executor, and he also refers to his other brothers, Francis, John, and Robert, who had died by 1584. Edmund also mentioned his sister Joan, by now married, and two of his other sisters.

[3] Henry Butterfield, yeoman of Flaunden, was a widower when he made his will in 1635, and had moved the short distance from Chenies in Buckinghamshire to

Flaunden in the parish of Hemel Hempstead, Hertfordshire. Both places lie very near the county boundary. Henry must have been quite old in 1635 for one of his three daughters had seven children. His second daughter Grace had married Richard Read at Flaunden in 1625, so Henry probably made his move from Chenies before then. He made his will on 12 July 1635 and was buried at Flaunden six days later. He bequeathed his soul to God, and signed his will with a mark. His five sons were called Edward, John, Thomas, Walter, and Henry. When Thomas made his will in 1653, he was a tailor of Latimers in Chesham. He bequeathed his son Jeremy cottages in Chenies and Chesham, and one of the overseers of his will was his brother John of Flaunden. The Henry Butterfield of Flaunden, who died intestate in 1644, is probably the son of the elder Henry of Flaunden. Administration of his estate was granted to his widow Katherine. The total value of his probate inventory, made on 19 February 1643/4 is £179 14s 8d, of which £70 was due on bonds. His livestock and crops were valued at £67, and Henry lived in a four-roomed house: hall and chamber over, both heated, another chamber, and a buttery.

[4] According to the bishops' transcripts (no parish register survives for Flaunden at this period), John was buried on 2 June 1672, but his will, made in 1658, was proved on 27 May 1672 and his probate inventory drawn up on 1 May 1672. One must suspect an error here in the bishops' transcripts. When he made his will in 1658, he was in perfect health and memory. The religious preamble reads: 'I give my soul to God that gave it me and my body to be buried in certain hope of resurrection through the merits of Jesus Christ.' He had two sons, Edward and John. The former was executor of his father's will and was left a lately purchased freehold messuage with seven acres of land in Flaunden. The total value of John's probate inventory was £26 15s 8d, of which crops and livestock were worth £15 12s 0d. His house contained a heated hall with a chamber over it, kitchen, cellar, another chamber, and a loft over it.

[5] The marriage of Edward Butterfield with Mary Thompson is not recorded in either the Quaker register or the meeting minute book, but their marriage certificate was published in the *Journal of the Friends Historical Society* in 1934. It shows that Edward, son of John Butterfield, yeoman of Flaundon, married Mary, daughter of Philip Thompson, blacksmith of Flaundon, on 24 April 1670 at the house of Thomas Lane called Whelplie in Coleshill in the parish of Amersham. Coleshill was a hamlet of Amersham but a detached portion of Hertfordshire; this made it a safe place for Quakers and other dissenters. The witnesses to the wedding included William Nash and Henry Tredway. The latter is a known Quaker, and several members of the Nash family were either Baptists or Quakers. In 1672 the churchwardens of Flaunden presented Edward Butterfield and Mary Thompson as living together as man and wife, but 'never married', and that their children were not baptized. The Quaker register records the births of this couple's four children at Flaunden: Abraham in 1671, Isaac in 1676, Jacob in 1679, and Mary in 1681. By the time Edward made his will in 1711, he had moved to Coleshill and called himself a yeoman. Jacob is not mentioned in his father's will, so may have died, and Mary was married. Edward was able to sign his will, which was made on 28 April 1711; he refers to April as the month 'commonly called April'. The total value of his probate inventory was only £12 9s 2d, and lists no livestock nor crops, so he seems to have retired from farming. There were five rooms in his house: hall with chamber over, both heated, parlour with chamber over, and buttery. On the back of the inventory it says that Abraham Butterfield, his father's executor, swore according to the manner of the Quakers, 'tremuli' in Latin. Edward's second son Isaac married Anne Rutland in 1700, and they had a son John born in 1703. The Quaker minute book called Isaac a husbandman in 1705 and a yeoman in 1718. Edward himself is mentioned several times in the minute book of the Quaker Upperside Meeting. In April 1676 he was to inquire into an intention of marriage between a Flaunden man and a Watford woman. In May 1680 he inquired into an intention of marriage between a Flaunden couple. His name appears amongst those present at meetings in April 1682, August 1684, December 1685, March 1689, July 1689, and May 1690. Only a few names are listed at each meeting, presumably those of the most active members.

Dell of Chesham

Richard I[1]
Named as a Lollard. Assessed at £4
in goods in 1522 and at £2 in 1524.

m. Katherine
Still alive in 1551.

Henry[2]
Husbandman. He made his will in
1558.

m. ?

Thomas[3]
Labourer of Chartridge hamlet.
Buried on 1 October 1615 'senex'.

m. Jane Byrche
Of Chartridge in Chesham. Married
on 21 January 1564–5. Buried on 11
January 1600–1.

Richard II[4]
Labourer of Chartridge hamlet.
Baptized on 16 December 1565.

m. Mary Johnson
Married on 7 November 1605.

William[5]
Baptized on 3 April 1616.

m. Katherine

Richard III[6]
Quaker, husbandman/mealman.
Baptized on 10 February 1653–4
at Chesham

m. (1) Hannah Cock
(2) Mary Penn
(3) Sarah ? servant

Sources: Plumb, 'Foxe and the Later Lollards', list of Lollards, which gives details from
the 1522 Musters and the 1524 Lay Subsidy; Chesham parish register; 'Richard Bowle's
Book', transcribed by J.W. Garrett-Pegge, *Records of Buckinghamshire*, 9 (1909), pp. 329–48,
393–414; Bucks. RO D/A/V/2 Visitation of the Archdeaconry of Buckingham 1633–4;
wills of the Dell family: Richard, 1551 Bucks. RO D/A/We/154/89, William, 1551 Bucks.
RO D/A/We/154/89, Henry, 1558 Bucks. RO D/A/Wf/4/88, John, 1560 Bucks. RO D/A/
We/13/15.

[1] Richard and Katherine had five sons and two daughters. Two of the former made
their wills in 1551; neither mentioned wife or children, but did name their mother,
sisters, and brothers. The value of Richard's probate inventory appears at the end
of his will. It was £6 17s 11d. Both Richard and his brother William were living in
Chesham Woburn when their wills were drawn up. There is no will for their brother
Thomas, but the John Dell, servant to Richard Chamber of Great Missenden, who
made his will in 1560, could be a grandson of Richard and Katherine. Both Richard
and William refer to their brother, John the elder, and John of Great Missenden
mentions Thomas Dell of Chesham, who had in his hands a legacy left to him by
Thomas' late father.

² Henry's will is damaged. He bequeathed his soul to God, the Blessed Virgin Mary, and the holy company of heaven, the traditional pre-Reformation formula. No wife is mentioned in his will, and it names his sons Robert and Thomas and two daughters.

³ The Chesham parish register records the marriage of Thomas Dell to Jane Byrche and the baptisms of their nine children between December 1565 and March 1585. Seven of the entries in the register, between 1578 and 1606, describe Thomas as a labourer, and in 1589, 1601, and 1606 he was noted as a resident of Chartridge, one of the many hamlets of Chesham. Thomas did not contribute to the special rate for the repair of Chesham church in 1606, and was not given a seat in the church in the subsequent distribution of places. His third son William was a servant of a tanner of Chesham town, Robert Chase, when he died in 1601.

⁴ Richard was the eldest child of Thomas and Jane. The Chesham marriage register called him a labourer and a son of Thomas Dell of Chartridge. His wife Mary was a daughter of Nicholas Johnson. At the time of their marriage, both were servants to Robert Weedon, who was of Chartridge when the special church rate was levied in 1606. Richard, like his father, did not contribute to this rate. His six children were baptized between October 1606 and November 1619. Perhaps he was the Richard Dell senior presented in 1633 for not attending church.

⁵ William was the second son of Richard and Mary. His marriage has not been found, and his wife's name is known from the Chesham baptismal register. He is only known to have had one child, Richard. No William Dell paid Hearth Tax in Chesham in 1662, but one did in Chalfont St Peter. He is probably a different man of the same name. A William Dell of Chartridge in Chesham paid rates on eleven acres of land in 1671, and may have been the William under discussion here. The William Dell who paid rates on fifty acres in Ashridge in Chesham in 1650 is less likely to have been him. Everything else known about this family makes it very unlikely that any member of it would have farmed fifty acres.

⁶ Richard III is well documented in Quaker records. He was present at Quaker meetings held at Hunger Hill in April 1681, April and July 1682, April and July 1683, January, April, and December 1684. His marriages, the births, and deaths of his children, and the deaths of his wives are all recorded in the Quaker registers. In September 1684 an intention of marriage was recorded between Richard Dell and Hannah Cock, both of Chesham. Cock is a Lollard surname, and Baptist Cocks were buried at Amersham in the late seventeenth century. On 23 October 1684 Richard Dell, husbandman of Chesham, married Hannah Cock, spinster of Chesham, at Chesham. Their daughter Hannah was born at Chesham on 23 January 1685–6, and died on 12 April 1686. Her mother had died on 4 February 1685–6. Richard Dell was present at Quaker meetings at Hunger Hill in March and May 1685, July 1686, July and October 1687. An intention of marriage was recorded in June 1688 between Richard Dell, mealman of Chesham, and Mary Penn, spinster of Coleshill in Amersham. On 30 July 1688 this couple were married at Amersham. Richard was described as son of William and Katherine Dell of Chesham, and Mary as daughter of Thomas and Martha Penn of Adderbury, Oxfordshire. Adderbury lies just south of Banbury. Richard is again listed as present at meetings at Hunger Hill in July and October 1689. His daughters Mary and Martha were both born at Chesham, respectively on 22 November 1690 and 4 April 1692. Martha died on 27 June 1692, and her mother two days later. Richard was again described as a mealman of Chesham. Richard next appears in the Quaker minute book in August 1693 when it records the following: 'Richard Dell of Chesham hath lately fallen into a foul miscarriage . . . & brought great reproach & scandal upon Truth & Friends' because his maid servant was great with child by him. Friends had spoken to them and they were both penitent; they sent a paper to the meeting in which they condemned themselves. They had married; her name was Sarah. The paper was read out at Chesham monthly meeting in the presence of Richard and Sarah Dell.

Thomas Dell

Thomas Dell was a leading member of the Upperside Quaker Meeting in the Restoration period, but his ancestry can only be traced with certainty as far back as his grandfather. There is no reason why he should not be descended from a branch of the Chesham Dells; an example of a member of this family who moved is Henry of Beaconsfield, who mentioned his brothers Robert and Thomas in his will. Only four Dells are listed in the 1524 Lay Subsidy, all under Chesham. A possible, but doubtful, ancestry for Thomas' grandfather Richard is: Richard Dell of Chesham, who made his will in 1558, married Jane. They had two sons, Richard and James, who were both under age in 1558. James married Mary Alen of Tring on 1 October 1565 at Chesham; their son Richard was baptized at Chesham on 2 February 1575–6 and could possibly be the Richard Dell of Fulmer, who made his will in 1636.

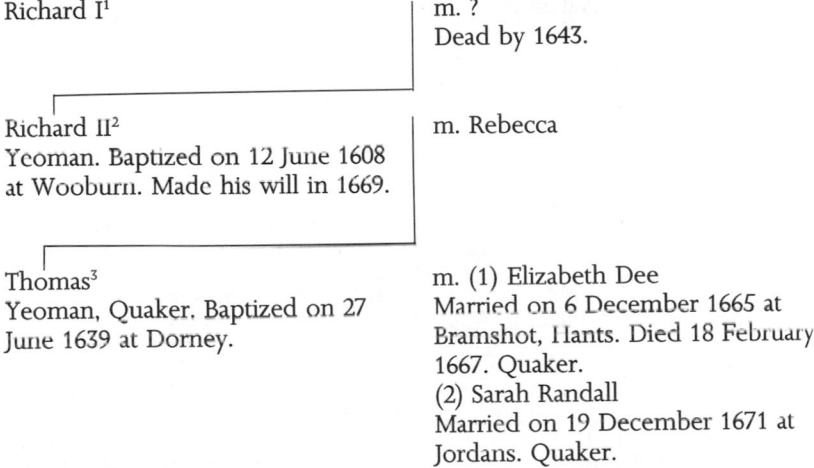

Richard I[1]   m. ?
                Dead by 1643.

Richard II[2]   m. Rebecca
Yeoman. Baptized on 12 June 1608
at Wooburn. Made his will in 1669.

Thomas[3]   m. (1) Elizabeth Dee
Yeoman, Quaker. Baptized on 27   Married on 6 December 1665 at
June 1639 at Dorney.   Bramshot, Hants. Died 18 February
                1667. Quaker.
                (2) Sarah Randall
                Married on 19 December 1671 at
                Jordans. Quaker.

Sources: Parish registers of Wooburn and Dorney; 1662 Hearth Tax return, PRO E179/ 80/350; Besse, *Sufferings*; Bucks. RO NQ1/1/1 Men's Minute Book, 1678–1761, of Buckinghamshire Quarterly Meeting (this includes a few births); Upperside Monthly Meeting Minute Book 1690–1713; Bucks. RO NQ1/6/1 Sufferings of Buckinghamshire Friends, 1655–1792; Snell (ed.), *Minute Book*; E.R.C. Brinkworth (ed.), *Episcopal Visitation Book for the Archdeaconry of Buckingham, 1662*, Buckinghamshire Records Society, 7 (1947); Episcopal Visitation, 1662; wills of Dell family: Richard, 1558 Bucks. RO D/A/We/11/ 134, Richard, 1636 Bucks. RO D/A/We/30/115, Thomas, 1645 PRO PROB 11 Twisse 40, John, 1646 PRO PROB 11 Twisse 40, Richard, 1669 Bucks. RO D/A/Wf/45/128.

[1] Richard Dell of Fulmer bequeathed his soul to God, trusting in Jesus Christ in whom he hoped to be saved. This preamble suggests that his beliefs were Calvinist. To his son Richard he left the lease of his house at Dorney wood with some land; his other son John was his executor. This will, made on 4 January 1635–6, was witnessed by Ralph and Thomas Dell. John Dell, yeoman of Dorney, made his will on 6 July 1643 and it was proved on 14 April 1646. His sister Mary, mentioned in their father's will, had by this date become the wife of Christopher Andrew. John

seems to have been unmarried, and the chief beneficiary of his will was his brother Richard's son Thomas, then under the age of eighteen. Bequests were also made to Thomas' sisters, Elizabeth, Rebecca, and Mary. Richard was the executor of his brother's will, and the overseers were Christopher Andrew and Henry Dell of Chippenham Court.

2 Although Richard II's father had left him the lease of a house and land in Dorney, he was a yeoman of Burnham when he made his will on 21 February 1668–9. In the 1662 Hearth Tax return he is listed under Hitcham. All these places are very close together. Richard gave his soul to God trusting through the merits of Jesus Christ to enjoy everlasting life. He asked to be buried in Wooburn churchyard. Richard and Rebecca had four daughters and three sons, the eldest girl was already married and the other three were bequeathed £120 each. Thomas, the eldest son, had already had his portion on his marriage. Son John was left £300 when he reached the age of twenty-one, and his brother Richard was left two messuages called Sheepcott and Mares with land in the parishes of Hitcham, Taplow, and Burnham. Richard Dell of Hitcham was presented at Quarter Session for not attending church at Michaelmas and Christmas in 1682 and 1683, and again at Easter 1684. Richard II's second daughter, Rebecca, was married at Jordans to John Gigger junior of Penn on 23 November 1671, less than four weeks before her brother Thomas' marriage. When this couple gave intention of their marriage earlier in 1671, she was of Beaconsfield, but by the time of her marriage she was living at Hitcham. Her father-in-law, John Gigger the elder, had his debts paid by his fellow-Quakers.

3 Thomas Dell was the chief legatee of his great uncle Thomas Dell, yeoman of Wooburn, who made his will on 20 February 1644–5. This man had brothers called William, Ralph and Richard and a nephew William, son of brother William. Other legatees included Arthur Nash of Chalfont St Peter, the testator's godson John Nash, and his kinsman Christopher Andrew and his wife Mary, who was a daughter of Richard Dell I. The executor of this will was Richard Dell II. Young Thomas, who was under seven years old when his great uncle's will was proved on 3 April 1646, was left land and tenements in Wooburn and Taplow. Like other members of his family he seems to have moved his residence more than once. The 1662 Hearth Tax lists two Thomas Dells at Burnham, one of whom lived in a four-hearth house. Both Thomas' marriages and the births of his children appear in a Quaker document which is partly a register, mainly of vital events at High Wycombe. On the sixth day of the twelth month 1665 Thomas Dell of Hitcham and Elizabeth Dee of Reading were married at Bramshot in Hampshire. The witnesses included the bride's father, William Dee, and John Raunce, a leading Quaker in High Wycombe. Just over a year later Thomas, son of Thomas and Elizabeth Dell, was born at Reading. In 1667 the Quaker register recorded that Elizabeth, wife of Thomas Dell of Hitcham, departed this life on the eighteenth day of the second month. Thomas Dell's second marriage, to Sarah Randall, took place at Jordans on 19 December 1671. Her ancestry, and that of her mother and stepfather can also be found in this appendix. The witnesses to this marriage included Henry and Margaret Tredway, Sarah's stepfather and mother, Richard and Thomas Tredway, Richard and Denise Dell and William Penn. Thomas was living at Hitcham at the time of his second marriage. The births of his five children by Sarah were all recorded in the Quaker register for the Upperside Meeting. The eldest, Richard, was born at Hitcham, and his four sisters at Upton. Sarah, the eldest daughter, was buried at Jordans in 1688, as was her mother who died on 4 August 1703. The Richard Dell, who witnessed the marriage of Thomas and Sarah, was presumably the brother of Thomas who was later presented for not attending church. Thomas' sister Rebecca was married at Jordans only a month before he was.

Under Burnham in the Episcopal Visitation of 1662: 'Thomas Dell in our parish doth suffer private meetinges in his house contrary to the lawe in that case provided to our knowledge.' Thomas and his family head the list of Quakers presented by the Burnham churchwardens in 1662. Thomas Dell also appears in Quaker records a number of times. His name appears in Besse on three occasions. In October 1660 he and two other Quakers were arrested at Maidenhead on their way to visit Friends in prison at Reading, and were themselves imprisoned. Possibly Thomas met his first wife or her father in this way. On 1 July 1665 he was arrested in Amersham, with several others, at the funeral of the Quaker Edward Perrot. In 1666 he was committed to prison for refusing to swear an oath. Finally in June 1683, twenty-two Friends including Thomas Dell were arrested at a meeting near Wooburn on the grounds that it was a riot. The same volume that contained the record of his first marriage, notes that in 1669 Thomas Dell was one of eight Quakers who signed an agreement at Weston Turvey in Buckinghamshire. On several occasions Thomas Dell is mentioned in the Men's Minute Book (1678–1761) of the Buckinghamshire Quarterly Meeting. In 1662 he was imprisoned for five months in Aylesbury gaol, with three others, for refusing to take an oath and to go to church. In 1663 he was imprisoned for nearly a year in the same gaol for his refusal to pay tithes to the rector of Burnham. After a year he was 'removed by the Priest to London'. In 1664 he was one of seven Quakers arrested at a house in Prestwood in Missenden and imprisoned. He was tried at the assizes and acquitted by the jury. In 1683 Thomas Dell, yeoman of Upton, was fined £20 for attending a meeting at Wooburn Heath in Headsworth parish. He was in prison when his goods were appraised at £20. His landlord said that if the goods were sold to him, he would pay the fine; this was done. There are sixty-four entries for Thomas Dell in the Upperside Monthly Meeting Minute Book for 1669–90. Most of them record his attendance at meetings; he was often appointed to inquire into proposed marriages. In 1685 he and Henry Child purchased 40s worth of hay for use at the stables where Friends attending meetings left their horses, and he carried out other financial transactions for the meeting. The second minute book covers 1690–1713. Thomas Dell senior attended meetings 1690 and 1691. In the latter year his son Thomas Dell junior of Upton declared his intention of marriage with Mary Eldershaw of Reading.

The Hardings of Amersham and Chesham show continuity of Lollard belief back to 1460s at least.

Thomas of Chesham
Held Lollard meetings at his house.
Assessed on £1 6s 8d land, and £32
goods in 1522 Musters and on £20
in 1524 Subsidy. Burnt as a Lollard
1532.
m. Isabel
Lollard teacher, abjured 1511.

John of Chesham
1524 Lay Subsidy. Will, made 1525,
named wife and two sons John and
Roger.

m. Florence

Roger I of Chesham and Amersham
Accused of heresy 1532. Assessed at
£30 in goods at Amersham in 1522
Musters, and at £20 at Chesham in
1524 Lay Subsidy. Inherited Thomas
Milsent's land at Amersham,
previously held, in 1541, by Simon
Harding. No evidence of marriage
or children.

Roger II[1]

m. (1) Isabel Harding
(2) ?

Jonas I[2]
Yeoman of Woodside in
Amersham. Overseer and
churchwarden. Baptized on 28
December 1583. Buried on 9
January 1645–6.

m. Anne Russell
Married on 10 May 1610 at
Amersham.

Jonas II[3]
Baptist. Overseer and
churchwarden. Baptized on 12
September 1613.

m. ?

Jonas III[4]
Baptist and overseer.

Sources: Plumb, 'Foxe and the Later Lollards', list of Lollards, which includes details of the 1522 Musters and the 1524 Lay Subsidy; Amersham parish register; Bucks. RO D/

A/V/10 Archdeaconry of Buckingham Visitation Book, 1673–84; W.T. Whitley (ed.), *The Church Books of Ford or Cuddington and Amersham in the County of Bucks.*, Baptist Historical Society (London, 1912); Bucks. RO PR4/4/1, PR4/5/2, PR4/12/2 churchwardens' and overseers of the poor's accounts for Amersham; John Wilson (ed.), *Buckinghamshire Contributions for Ireland 1642*, Buckinghamshire Records Society 21 (1983); Quarter Sessions records; Hearth Tax for 1662, PRO E179/80/350; wills of the Harding family: John, 1525 Bucks. RO D/A/We/154/20, Jonas, 1646 Bucks. RO D/A/We/224.

1 There is no proof of any link between Roger I and Roger II, except that they both have the same name. Roger II married Isabel Harding on 17 May 1576, and she was buried on 6 October 1578. His second marriage has not been found, and the Amersham baptism register only gives the names of fathers in the sixteenth century. Roger appears to have had at least two children by his first wife and six by his second.

2 In his will Jonas I described himself as Jonas the elder, yeoman, of Woodside in Amersham. He died on 6 January 1645–6, three days before he was buried. When he made his will, both his daughters were married: Christian, the elder, to James Grover of Amersham; and Elizabeth, the younger, to William Braig, 'minister of God's word' at Hartwell, which is just outside Aylesbury. The executors of this will were the testator's wife Anne and only son Jonas II, and the overseers were his brother Henry Harding and his 'loving friend and kinsman' William Russell the younger of Chalfont St Giles; the latter was his brother-in-law. William Braig witnessed his father-in-law's will. William Russell was perhaps the father of Mary Russell who married Joseph Bartlet II in 1673. In 1635 Andrew Harding, yeoman of Woodside in Amersham, made his cousin Jonas overseer of his will. This was probably Jonas I.

3 The marriage of Jonas II has not been found, but probably took place in the late 1640s when many registers are defective. His daughter Elizabeth was baptized on 23 February 1647–8, and his son Timothy on 31 August 1650. The baptism of Jonas III has also not been found, but the Amersham baptism register is defective in the 1640s and 1650s and the use of the name Jonas suggests that he is the son of Jonas II. In 1657 Henry Harding yeoman of Amersham bequeathed 'all my bees' to Timothy, son of Jonas Harding yeoman of Amersham. This Henry may be the brother of Jonas I, and thus Timothy's great uncle. Jonas II is listed in the 1662 Hearth Tax for Amersham, but the number of the hearths he was taxed on is missing. At the 1673 visitation he was presented for not being at Easter Communion; he was called a yeoman.

4 Neither baptism nor marriage have been found for Jonas III. Both he and his father were members of the Amersham Baptist congregation. In 1677 Jonas Harding and his two sons, presumably Timothy and Jonas, subscribed 7s towards the building of the meeting-house in the town. In 1682 'Brother Jonas Harding' was baptized, and from 1686 to 1693 Jonas Harding was one of the elders who signed accounts. In November 1687 Brother Jonas Harding's daughter was buried in the Baptist burial ground at Amersham. This entry is on a damaged page and the word daughter is doubtful. From 1697 to 1698 Jonas Harding was an elder. A Mary Harding was baptized in 1692. Widow Harding of Woodside was buried in 1707. Clearly both Jonas II and Jonas III were Baptists, but it is impossible to distinguish them in the church records. Later generations of this family remained Baptists and continued to use the name Jonas. The latest reference to a Jonas Harding in the Amersham Baptist Church book is in 1783. The surviving Upper Meeting Baptist chapel (now a private house) in Amersham was built in 1799 at the entire cost of John Harding, one of the trustees. The monuments in the burial ground included those of James Harding (1799), Jonas Harding (1804), Sarah and Caroline Harding (1830 and 1904), and John Harding (1803) and Sarah, his wife (1797). The Lollard Hardings of Chesham truly bred a radical line.

The Baptist Hardings in the Amersham churchwardens' and overseers' accounts.

Jonas Harding I
1612   Overseer of the poor.
1616   Churchwarden.
1628   Churchwarden.
1633   Overseer of the poor.
1640   Overseer of the poor.

Jonas Harding II
1647   Signed overseers' accounts.
1654   Signed overseers' accounts.
1655   Churchwarden.
1657   Overseer of the poor.
1662   Overseer of the poor.
1673   Overseer of the poor.
1676   Signed overseers' accounts for 1675.
1680   Overseer of the poor.
1680   In arrears for church rates: 8s 9d jointly with Widow Aldridge, and 1s 1½d on his own.
1682   To pay 2s 3d to a rate for the repair of the church. Living at Woodside.
1689   Contributed 3s to the relief of Irish protestants.

Jonas Harding III
1686   To pay 1s 9d church rate.
1687   Overseer of the poor.
1689   Contributed 2s 6d to the relief of Irish protestants.
1689   Among dissenters who took the Oath of Allegiance to William III and Mary II. Called a husbandman.
1690   Overseer of the poor. Jonas Harding junior.
1695   Jonas and Timothy Harding signed the overseers' accounts.
1696   Overseer of the poor.

The division between Jonas II and Jonas III is arbitrary. The elder man must still have been alive in 1690, when the Jonas who served as overseer was called 'junior'. By then Jonas II would have been seventy-seven years old.

The Harding family was deeply involved in running the affairs of the town of Amersham. The accounts of the overseers of the poor begin in 1611, and between then and 1700 there are thirty-five years when one or more members of the family served as churchwarden or overseer. For fourteen years between 1656 and 1680 a Harding was a parish officer. The Amersham overseers' accounts list the names of churchwardens as well as those of overseers.

Jonas Harding was churchwarden in 1655, but thereafter both he and his son only served as overseers of the poor. It is not unknown elsewhere for dissenters to be chosen as overseers. At Beccles in Suffolk in 1662 and 1668, four of the overseers were members of the Independent Church in the town.

Nash of Amersham: Quaker line

Thomas[1]   m. Joan
Lollard. Died 1521.

Richard[2]   m. Margaret
Of Woodrow in Amersham. Buried
on 8 January 1562–3. Assessed at £2
on goods in 1522 and £1 on land in
1524. An 'inhabitant within the
town' i.e. Amersham.

Edward   m. Sybil Foster
He had three sons and three   Married on 26 November 1580.
daughters.

William[3]   m. Susan Ives
Baptized on 28 April 1606. He had   Married on 19 August 1633.
three sons and three daughters.

John[4]   m. Elizabeth Ewer
Quaker. Baptized on 9 March 1633–4.   Married on 10 December 1660,
                                             Quaker.

Sources: Plumb, 'Foxe and the Later Lollards', list of Lollards, which gives details from the 1522 Musters and the 1524 Lay Subsidy; Amersham parish register; Hearth Tax returns 1662, PRO E179/80/350; Bucks. RO NQ2/3/1 Minutes of Upperside Quaker Women's Meeting 1677–1735; Bucks. RO PR4/4/4/1, PR4/5/2, PR4/12/2 churchwardens' and overseers of the poor's accounts for Amersham; Wilson (ed.), *Buckinghamshire Contributions for Ireland* 1642; wills of the Nash family: Thomas, 1521 Bucks. RO D/A/We/1/32, Richard, 1563 Bucks. RO D/A/We/1d/238.

[1] If Thomas is 'Mr Nash the elder', he and his wife were both named Lollards. He died in 1521, leaving two sons William and Richard, and three daughters Alice, Joan, and Isabel. The preamble of his will is in standard pre-Reformation form. Both his sons are listed in the 1522 Musters and the 1524 Lay Subsidy. William was assessed at £4 on goods in 1522 and had a good bill. He, like his brother, was an 'inhabitant within the town' of Amersham. The witnesses of Thomas' will included William Nash the elder and the younger.

[2] Richard, like his father, was a Lollard, and like his brother he had a bill in 1522 and was an 'inhabitant within the town'. He made his will in 1562, calling himself of Woodrow in Amersham and bequeathing his soul to God. He had three sons Robert, William, and Edward, and two daughters Sybil and Catherine. Other legatees were his grandchild Isabel, daughter of his son Robert, and Alice Dosset. Dosset is another Lollard name, and Alice could have been Richard's sister. The overseer of

this will was Walter Nash. Robert, the eldest son, may be the man of that name who hanged himself in 1587 or the Robert Nash buried on 11 October 1595. In either case he had three sons.

3 Like his father, William had three children of each sex. The youngest, Edward, was baptized on 19 January 1636–7 and buried on 8 March 1639–40. John, the eldest son, was baptized on 9 March 1633–4, and William on 7 April 1635. The latter married Susan Nash on 1 July 1660. She may be the daughter of John and Elizabeth Nash, baptized on 30 April 1660.

4 John paid Hearth Tax in 1662, but the number of his hearths is missing. On 6 December 1680 John Nash, maltster of Amersham, and Elizabeth Winch, spinster of Amersham, were married in a Quaker marriage at Amersham. There was more than one John Nash living in Restoration Amersham, so it is not easy to decide which this man is.

The following comes from the accounts of the Amersham overseers of the poor and churchwardens.

1680 John Nash assessed at 1s for church rates under 'town'.
1680 Another John Nash was a tanner.
1682 John Nash assessed at 1s 9d church rate for his malt house.
1689 John Nash senior contributed to the collections for the relief of Irish protestants, as did John junior, who was a tanner.
1691 John Nash maltster received 1s from John Child's gift.
1692 John Nash signed the overseers' accounts.
1695 The churchwardens paid John Nash senior's bill for 3s 9d.

From the above it can be deduced that John Nash maltster must be the man who made a Quaker marriage in 1680, while John senior and junior are presumably the father and son, with the former likely to be the John Nash baptized in 1634. The Upperside Women's Meeting inquired into this marriage, and their minutes show that John, maltster of Amersham, was the son of John Nash of Chalfont St Peter and was to marry Elizabeth, daughter of Joseph and Ann Winch of Amersham. At the Michaelmas Quarter Sessions in 1689, registrations of 'publick meeting houses for Religious Worship for the People called Quakers' included part of Joseph Winch's house in Amersham (Plate 7).

Nash of Amersham: Baptist line

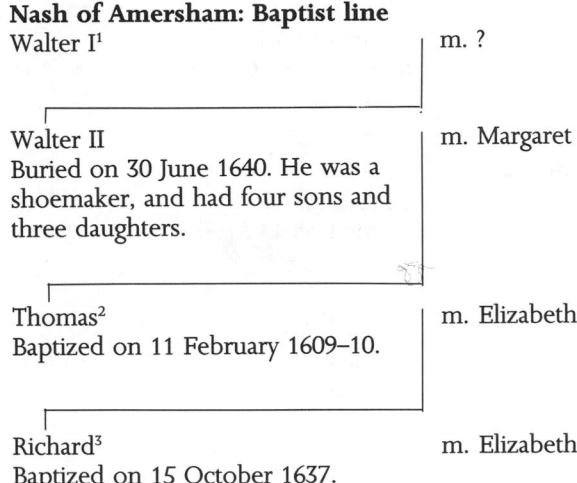

Walter I[1]   m. ?

Walter II   m. Margaret
Buried on 30 June 1640. He was a
shoemaker, and had four sons and
three daughters.

Thomas[2]   m. Elizabeth
Baptized on 11 February 1609–10.

Richard[3]   m. Elizabeth
Baptized on 15 October 1637.

Sources: Amersham parish register; wills of the Nash family; 1662 Hearth Tax returns, PRO E179/80/350; churchwardens' and overseers of the poor's accounts for Amersham; Wilson (ed.), *Buckinghamshire Contributions for Ireland 1642.*

[1] Richard Nash, the second generation in the Quaker Nash genealogy, appointed Walter Nash as overseer of his will, made in 1563. Thus it seems likely that there was a close relationship between the two men. It has not been possible to trace Walter I's ancestry. Two men called Walter Nash were born at Amersham in the early 1560s: Walter son of Walter baptized on 24 April 1561, and Walter son of Thomas baptized on 18 October 1563.

[2] Thomas had three sons, Thomas, Richard, and Walter, who was baptized on 26 January 1650–1 and married Alice Tappin in 1675. Walter contributed 1s to the relief of Irish protestants in 1689.

[3] Richard's marriage has not been found, but must have taken place in the late 1650s. His four children were all baptized on 27 March 1668, when the youngest was an infant. His two elder daughters were born in 1658 and 1663, and his only son Richard in 1660. Richard Nash of Amersham and his wife were Baptists in 1699, and could have been either Richard and Elizabeth, or their son Richard and his wife. Richard Nash paid Hearth Tax in 1662, but the number of his hearths is missing. He was assessed at 4.1½d for church rates under Woodrow in Amersham in 1680. He contributed 6d to the relief of Irish protestants in 1689. A Richard Nash signed, with a cross, the Amersham overseers' accounts in 1700. Some of these references may belong to the younger Richard.

The Tredway family

Henry I[1]
Of Hedgerly St Giles. Buried on 18 February 1558–9 at Hedgerly.

m. Agnes Pockley
Married on 10 February 1548–9 at Chesham.

Thomas[2]
Aged under twenty-one in 1559.

m. Alice Winley
Married on 14 April 1578 at Chalfont St Peter.

Henry II
Baptized on 1 January 1581–2.

m. Sarah Birch
Married on 19 November 1610 at Chesham.

Henry III[3]
Quaker. Baptized on 19 February 1624–5. Buried on 29 July 1700 at Jordans.

m. Margaret Randall
Née West as her second husband. Quaker.

Sources: Bucks. RO NQ2/3/1 Minutes of Upperside Women's Meeting 1677–1735; Bucks. RO NQ1/6/1 Sufferings of Buckinghamshire Quakers 1655–1792; Snell (ed.), Minute Book; Bucks. RO D/RA/2/65, 196–8, 294, deeds concerning Henry Tredway; wills of the Tredway family: Henry, 1559 Bucks. RO D/A/We/11/23, Henry, 1700 PRO PROB 11/ d56/119, Margaret, 1706 PRO PROB 11 Eedes 155.

[1] In his will, Henry Tredway of Hedgerly St Giles, mentions his mother, unnamed, his wife Agnes, his brother Edward, his son Thomas, and three daughters, Agnes, Joan, and Mary; all the children were under age. Henry said that he was patron of the church at Hedgerly St Giles; it is not clear what he meant by this. It is not possible to make a definite link between Henry, and the Tredways known from the Lay Subsidy and Musters and the Lollard trials of the early sixteenth century. The Lollard Tredways are Thomas of Chesham, his mother Agnes Ashford and Richard alias Ashford or Nash. Only George Tredway of Chesham is listed in the 1524 Lay Subsidy, but Walter and Thomas Tredway of Chesham join him in the 1522 Musters together with Edward of Amersham. Tredway is a fairly unusual surname in early sixteenth-century Buckinghamshire, so there must be a link between the above men and Henry who died in 1559. He mentions a brother Edward, so they were either both sons of Edward Tredway of Amersham, or of Walter and Joan Tredwaye of Amersham. Walter made his will in 1557 when his three sons, Harry, Edward, and Robert, all had children of their own. Two of the witnesses to his will bore the Christian name Harry, so Walter Tredway may have been in the habit of using Harry rather than Henry. The gentry Tredway family seems to be descended from Walter through his son Robert. There were also Tredways in Hertfordshire. Thomas of Rickmansworth made his will in 1486. His wife's name was Joan, and his three sons were called Walter, Richard, and John. Significantly he made a bequest to the church at Chalfont St Giles, not far from Amersham. There are wills for John and Richard Tredway of Rickmansworth, made respectively in 1503 and 1527, but not for Walter. There is thus a possibility that the Amersham Walter Tredway was the

son of Thomas of Rickmansworth. Whatever the relationships of these men, the names John, Richard, Thomas, and Walter constantly recur in the Tredway family.

2 Thomas and Alice had seven children, and either the eldest or the youngest could be the ancestor of Henry III. The descent from Henry II, Thomas's eldest son is set out above. His youngest son Richard was baptized on 24 February 1599–1600, and may have married twice. The Chalfont St Peter baptismal register does not always give the name of his wife. He seems to have had at least two. The name is not given for the eldest and youngest of his four sons, while Elizabeth was the mother of the second and Anne of the third. Henry, the eldest son, was baptized on 3 June 1632 and is the alternative candidate for the man who married Margaret Randall née West. It does not really much matter which of the two Henries was her husband, as they share a grandfather.

3 Whatever the parentage of Henry Tredway III, he is quite well documented. In 1687 Henry Tredway, yeoman of Upton, and his wife Margaret, late wife of Nicholas Randall, brickmaker of Hedgerley Dean in Farnham Royal, were parties to a lease and release concerning some land in Hedgerley Dean. The other parties to these deeds were Margaret's daughter Sarah, her husband Thomas Dell, yeoman of Upton, and John Nash, husbandman of Hedgerley Dean. Henry Tredway of Great Missenden was presented as a Quaker in 1670, and his wife Margaret, also of Great Missenden, in 1678. No Hearth Tax returns have survived for Great Missenden. In May 1668 Henry Tredway of Chalfont attended a Quaker meeting at Weston. That same year Henry Tredway of Hedgerly was fined 10s for not attending church and one of his cows worth £3 was seized. In July 1670 Henry Tredway was fined for attending a meeting at William Russell's house at Jordans; his horse worth £4 was seized. In the same year he was a witness to the Quaker marriage of Edward Butterfield and Mary Thompson. On 27 December 1699 he signed an appeal at Weston Turville for Friends in Newbury. When he was buried at Jordans in 1700 he was described as husbandman of Bulstrodes in Upton, as was his wife Margaret when she was buried there in 1706. She was called of Chalfont when she attended the Quaker Women's Meeting at Larkins Green in 1678. When her husband's will was proved, she affirmed; this will had been made twenty years before he died. Her own executrices, her granddaughters Rebecca and Mary Dell, also affirmed.

Gate of Chesham

Robert[1]   m. Joan
Of Whelpley Hill in Chesham.
Orthodox in religion. Buried on 8
August 1545.

Thomas[2]   m. Joan Dell
Of Tylers Hill. He had nine   Daughter of John, a Lollard. Married
children, and made his will in 1571.   on 6 November 1541.

Thomas   m. Bridget Ashbye
Labourer. Baptized 16 December   Married on 21 November 1568.
1548. He had four sons and a
daughter.

Martha[3]   m. Thomas Lewys
Baptized on 1 February 1578–9. She   Servant to Mr Ashfield. Married on
had five sons and one daughter.   7 May 1602.

Thomas Lewys   m. Elizabeth Harding
Baptized on 1 May 1603.   Married on 29 October 1629.

Elizabeth[4]
Baptist. Baptized on 29 September
1630. Buried on 29 December 1685.

Sources: Chesham parish register; Whitley (ed.), Church Books; wills of the Gate family:
Robert, 1545 Bucks. RO D/A/We/6/52, Thomas, 1571 Bucks. RO D/A/We/16/264.

---

[1] Robert Gate of Chesham made his will in 1545, and although he calls himself of
Chesham Woburn his will makes it clear that he is the Robert of Whelpley Hill
buried in August 1545. His will includes the value of his inventory, which was £30
13s 1d. Robert mentions his wife Joan, who was to have a chamber in his house at
Whelpley Hill for life, and his sons Richard, John, and Thomas. The last-named was
to have the land occupied by his father at Leyhill in Chesham. Robert's will shows
that he was engaged in mixed farming, as he bequeathed cows, sheep, and poultry,
and mentioned crops of wheat and barley. The religious views expressed in the
preamble to his will are orthodox, and he made bequests to the rood light in
Chesham church, and for a trentall of masses.

2 Thomas' father Robert Gate is listed in the 1524 Lay Subsidy under Chesham, as was his wife's father, John Dell. I am assuming that John was one of the five sons of Richard and Katherine Dell; Richard was a Lollard. Thomas Gate of Tylers Hill, which is in Botley hamlet in Chesham, made his will on 3 February 1570–1, leaving his soul to God. He left all his household stuff to his wife Joan, and the value of his probate inventory written at the foot of the will was £84 1s 4d. His eldest surviving son Thomas was bequeathed his father's house in Tylers Hill with its land. He also owned a house called Hodskins in Chesham, which was left to his son John. Thomas was also given carts, ploughs, harrows, and half his father's horses and harness, and was to occupy the family farm jointly with his mother during her life. Thomas' other two sons were bequeathed livestock, and their five sisters each received a cow and ten sheep. One of the overseers of this will was the testator's brother-in-law Henry Dell. By the time Thomas Gate made his will, his two eldest sons had probably died as they are not mentioned in his will. There is a gap in the Chesham burials from 1546 to 1548.

3 When Martha married Thomas Lewys, she was described as daughter of Thomas Gate, labourer of the town. Chesham, like Amersham, was divided into town and several hamlets. Her father had also been called a labourer at the time of her baptism. Martha and Thomas Lewys' eldest child, William, was baptized and buried on 24 May 1602, under three weeks after their wedding. They subsequently had three more sons and one daughter.

4 Elizabeth Lewys was the eldest of the three daughters of Thomas and Elizabeth. The Amersham Baptist church book records on 29 December 1685 the interment in the burial ground of Elizabeth Lewys. Burial entries in this volume describe most women as wife, widow, or daughter, so one can assume that Elizabeth was a spinster. No marriage for her has been found.

The Nash and Child families of Amersham

Thomas Nash[1]
Lollard. Died 1521. He had two
sons and three daughters.

m. Joan
Alive when husband made his will.

Richard[2]
Of Woodrow. Lollard. Buried on 8
January 1562–3. He had three sons
and two daughters.

m. Margaret

Robert
Buried on 11 October 1595. He had
three sons and two daughters.

m. ?
Before 1562.

Isabel[3]
Baptized on 12 April 1562. She had
four sons and one daughter.

m. William Child I
Married on 7 September 1584.

William Child II[4]
Eldest son of William I and Isabel.
Baptized on 20 February 1585–6.
Will 1645. Died at Penn 26 April
1645. Buried on 29 April 1645 at
Amersham. He had nine sons and
five daughters.

m. (1) Elizabeth
(2) Elizabeth Kender
Married on 18 November 1628 at
Amersham. Buried on 9 March
1638–9 at Amersham.

Giles
Eldest son of William II. Baptized
on 16 on December 1607.

Joseph Child
Third son of William I. Baptized on
24 January 1590/1. Buried on 12
October 1643. He had three sons
and four daughters.

m. Sarah Nash
Married on 22 November 1619.

William

Baptized on 8 October 1620.

m. Sarah
Before 1647 OR
Mary White
On 25 October 1657.

Giles[5]

m. Dorothy Loosely
Married on 17 October 1613 at
Amersham.

Sources: Plumb, 'Foxe and the Later Lollards', list of Lollards, which includes details of
the 1522 Musters and the 1524 Lay Subsidy; Amersham and Penn parish registers; 1662
Hearth Tax, PRO 179/80/350; digests of Quaker registers at Friends House; Whitley
(ed.), Church Books; wills of Child and Nash families: Thomas Nash, 1521 Bucks. RO D/
A/We/1/32, Richard Nash, 1563 Bucks. RO D/A/We/14/238, William Child, 1646 PRO
PROB 11 Twisse 1.

[1] If Thomas is Mr Nash the elder, he and his wife were Lollards. His daughter Alice
was also probably a Lollard. He made his will in 1521, naming his wife Joan, sons
William and Richard, and daughters Alice, Joan, and Isabel. Witnesses to this will
included William Nash the elder and the younger.
[2] Richard was of 'Woodrow in Amersham' when he made his will in 1562, and asked
to be buried in Amersham churchyard. He named his wife Margaret, sons Robert,
William, and Edward, and daughters Sybil and Catherine. Other legatees included
Isabel, daughter of his son Robert, and Alice Dosset. This is a Lollard name. His
son Robert was the executor of his father's will, and the overseer was Walter Nash.
[3] The youngest child of Isabel and William Child I was baptized at Amersham on 11
December 1595. Unfortunately, although the word son is clear, his name cannot
be read. If this name was Giles, it is just possible that he is the Giles Child who
married Dorothy Loosely on 17 October 1613. However, it is unlikely that a man,
below the level of the gentry, would have married so young.
[4] All of William II's fourteen children were baptized at Amersham, except two of the
three youngest who were baptized at Penn. When William made his will in 1645
he was living at Penn, where he had served as churchwarden in 1638. His wife
Elizabeth had been buried at Amersham on 9 March 1638–9. William II asked to
be buried in Amersham church near his wife and father, and the Amersham register
records the burial of William Child of Penn on 29 April 1645; he had died three
days earlier. He left £3 to the poor of Amersham and 20s to those of Penn. He
made bequests of land and houses, most of which he had bought, in Chesham,
Penn, and Amersham. His son James was left a house in Amersham, 'now occupied
by my brother Giles'. This is the ground for thinking that William I's youngest son
was called Giles. It seems possible that William II married twice. Giles, baptized on
16 October 1607 at Amersham, was his eldest child, and four more children were
baptized in 1615, 1619, 1623, and 1625. The second son Henry must have been

born between 1607 and 1615, as he was already married in 1645, but his baptism has not been found. After 1625 no more children of William II's were baptized until 1629, from which time they follow at fairly short intervals until 1638. No marriage has been found for William II before 1607, but on 18 November 1628 William Child married Elizabeth Kender at Amersham. This could well have been a second marriage for William II. William and Elizabeth Child's penultimate child was Elizabeth, baptized at Amersham on 26 February 1636-7. She cannot be the daughter Elizabeth, wife of Nathaniel Wingfield, mentioned in William II's will. All the children of William II are recorded in the baptismal registers of Amersham and Penn as having a mother named Elizabeth, so if William did marry twice, both his wives bore the same name.

5 Giles and Dorothy had eight children, all baptized at Amersham: Sarah in 1616, John in 1617 (buried 1620), Elizabeth in 1619, Anna in 1620, Mary in 1622, Susan in 1625 (buried 1641), Giles in 1626, and John in 1630.

Six Baptist and eight Quaker Childs are known from dissenting records. All except one lived in Amersham. The exception is Timothy, possibly the son of William II born in 1634 and who made his will in 1714. The number of Childs living in the study area makes it difficult to decide which were the known dissenters. They were particularly numerous in Amersham and Chesham. The Hearth Tax of 1662 records three Giles Childs and two Henry Childs, as well as William and three widows of that name in Amersham, and four Williams, a Thomas, and a Henry Child in Chesham. It is often not clear from the registers which William, for instance, is the father of a child being baptized.

Three men called Giles Child are known as dissenters in post-Restoration Amersham, perhaps the Hearth Tax payers. Giles Child, clothier of Amersham, married Elizabeth, daughter of Daniel and Elizabeth Baldwin of Bledlow, at Meadle on 2 August 1674; this was a Quaker marriage. Daniel was a fuller, who seems to have switched religious allegiance. He was recorded as a Quaker in 1659, as was his wife in 1660, but in 1669 he appears as a Baptist. The Episcopal Returns of 1669 incorrectly recorded him as a Presbyterian. Yet in 1674 he and his wife, together with two of their children, were witnesses at their daughter Elizabeth's Quaker marriage. Elizabeth, wife of Giles Child, was a Quaker in 1678, so this couple may have remained faithful to this sect. The Amersham Baptist church book records the burial of Giles Child senior in 1681, and of Giles junior in 1695; the elder of the two was married to Frances.

The other known Quaker Child couples are John and Sarah, and Henry and Anne. Both marriages and the births of their children are recorded in the Quaker registers. John Child, bricklayer of Amersham, married Sarah Parratt of Amersham on 15 February 1676-7, and the births of their three children Elizabeth, Edward, and Sarah took place in 1677, 1680, and 1683. Ann Child, perhaps Henry's wife, was present at the birth of Elizabeth. (For Henry, see Child of Coleshill.)

Child of Coleshill in Amersham

William[1]
Yeoman of Whelpleys, Coleshill.
Buried on 9 March 1606–7. He had
three sons and one daughter.

m. (1) ?
Buried on 5 December 1595.
(2) Joan
Buried on 22 February 1608–9.

John
Eldest son, of Deans Bottom Farm,
Amersham. He had three sons.

m. ?

Richard[2]
Second son. Yeoman of Porch
House, Coleshill. Baptized on 5
April 1600. Died 1658. He had five
sons and two daughters.

m. Mary?

Henry[3]
Second son. Yeoman and Quaker.
Baptized on 2 April 1632. He had
two daughters and one son by his
first wife. He had six daughters and
three sons by his second wife.

m. (1) Mistress Elizabeth Butler
Of Beaconsfield. Married on 15
March 1659–60 at Amersham.
(2) Anne
Daughter of Henry Ball of Coleshill,
both Quakers. Married on 12
February 1671/2.

Sources: Amersham parish registers; Quaker registers; wills of the Child family: William Child PRO PROB 11 Huddlestone 49, Joan Child Bucks. RO D/A/Wf/18/22, Richard Child senior PRO PROB 11 Wootton 480, Richard Child junior PRO PROB 11 Nabbs 31; John Chenevix Trench, 'The Houses of Coleshill: The Social Anatomy of a Seventeenth-Century Village', *Records of Buckinghamshire*, 25 (1983), pp. 61–109; information about the number of hearths in Coleshill houses comes from this article, not from the Hearth Tax, and is based on architectural evidence.

[1] When William was buried in 1607 he was described in the Amersham parish register as 'Old William of Coleshill'. He was thus certainly born before the Amersham parish register begins in 1561, and was probably a son or grandson of one of the five Childs living in Amersham in 1524. In his will, made on 16 September 1605, he bequeathed his soul to God by whom he hoped to be saved. His wife Joan was to live with his son Richard, who was the executor of the will and presumably lived at Whelpleys with his widowed mother. His other children were sons William and John, and a daughter Jane married to Christopher Clarke, who, with son John, was overseer of the will. William, made a bequest to his servant, Ralph Child, presumably a kinsman. William's widow, Joan, made her will on 16 February 1608/9, six days before her burial. She bequeathed her soul to God and Jesus Christ. Joan mentions four daughters not named in her husband's will, so this may indicate a

previous marriage for her. One of these daughters, another Joan, had married first George Russell and then Henry Tredway of Stockings. This farm was the home of the gentry Tredways and had six hearths in 1662; its land lay next to that of Whelpleys. After 1652 the Tredways let this farm to Henry Ball, the Quaker brother-in-law of Henry Child. William Child's farm, Whelpleys, took its name from a fourteenth-century owner and had four hearths. William's son Richard was baptized on 29 March 1573 and died childless, being buried on 9 January 1634–5. Whelpleys then passed to his nephew John, son of his elder brother John of Deans Farm. In 1670 the house appears to have been occupied by Thomas Lane, when Edward Butterfield married Mary Thompson there. See Butterfield genealogy.

2 Richard Child, yeoman of Coleshill, made his will on 11 May 1657, and it was proved on 22 June 1658. As no wife is mentioned, she must be presumed to have predeceased her husband. Her name may have been Mary, as six children of Richard and Mary Child were baptized at Amersham between 1630 and 1642. Two of these do not appear in Richard's will, while the baptisms of two of his sons have not been found. The Amersham parish register is defective in the 1640s and 1650s. Three of his five sons were left land or a house, and one of his daughters, Sarah, received £200. Richard, probably the third son, was left £140. This will was witnessed by William and Nathan Child; Nathan was the name of one of Richard's sons. James, the youngest son, was under sixteen years old when his father made his will. Richard junior made his own will in March 1660, calling himself son of Richard Child late of Coleshill in Amersham and now of St Michael's Cornhill in London. He was married, but apparently had no children. His four brothers and two sisters are all mentioned in his will, as well as two sisters-in-law. This Richard seems to have been in service, as he refers to a 'fellow servant'. The name of his sister Mary was not found in their father's will, but this is damaged and partly illegible. Richard senior called himself a yeoman in his will, but in the baptism register he appears as a husbandman in 1638 and agricola in 1640. Richard senior's home, Porch House, had been bought by his uncle Richard in 1626 and conveyed to him in 1627. This house had four hearths.

3 In his will Henry's brother Richard mentions his sister-in-law Elizabeth Child, and this confirms the name of Henry's first wife, whom he had married only five days before Richard made his will. His father-in-law was Henry Butler, the Presbyterian minister of Beaconsfield. When Mr Butler was ejected after the Restoration, he was given shelter in his son-in-law's cottage 'by Wickham Heathside' in Coleshill. This shows that the Five Mile Act was not always strictly enforced. This one-hearth cottage was known as Henry Child's cottage; Henry's father, Richard of Porch House, had bought the plot of land on which it stood before 1629 and it was probably built around 1640. Henry Child lived there for a time, but by 1661 had moved to Puddefats, a three-hearth house. Henry married into a Quaker family when he took Ann Ball as his second wife in 1672; both her parents, Henry and Sarah, were known Quakers. Amongst the witnesses to this wedding were Thomas and Margaret Child. The Quaker registers record the births of the nine children of Henry and Ann Child between 1672 and 1690. Their first daughter and eldest son, named Anne and Henry, must be assumed to have died, as another Anne and Henry were born later.

There are no known Child Lollards but some members of the family had married into Lollard families. On 27 November 1568 Emma Child married William Tredway, and on 4 February 1570–1 John Child married Elizabeth Tredway, both at Amersham.

The Randall family of Hedgerly

Andrew Randall of Rickmansworth, his wife, and his father are the only known Lollard members of the family. Seven Randalls were taxed here in 1524, but by the time of the Hearth Tax in 1672 there were none paying tax in the town. Only three Randalls are listed in the 1524 Lay Subidy for Buckinghamshire: John, Robert, and William, all of whom lived at Chalfont St Peter. In the late seventeenth century there were at least three Baptist Randalls, all members of the Amersham Baptist congregation; this does not necessarily imply that they lived in the town. Only two taxpaying Randalls were found in Buckinghamshire in the 1660s, but the Hearth Tax returns for this county are defective. In the late sixteenth and seventeeth centuries the family was living in several Buckinghamshire parishes: Chalfont St Peter, Chesham, Hedgerly, Great and Little Missenden and Chalfont St Giles.

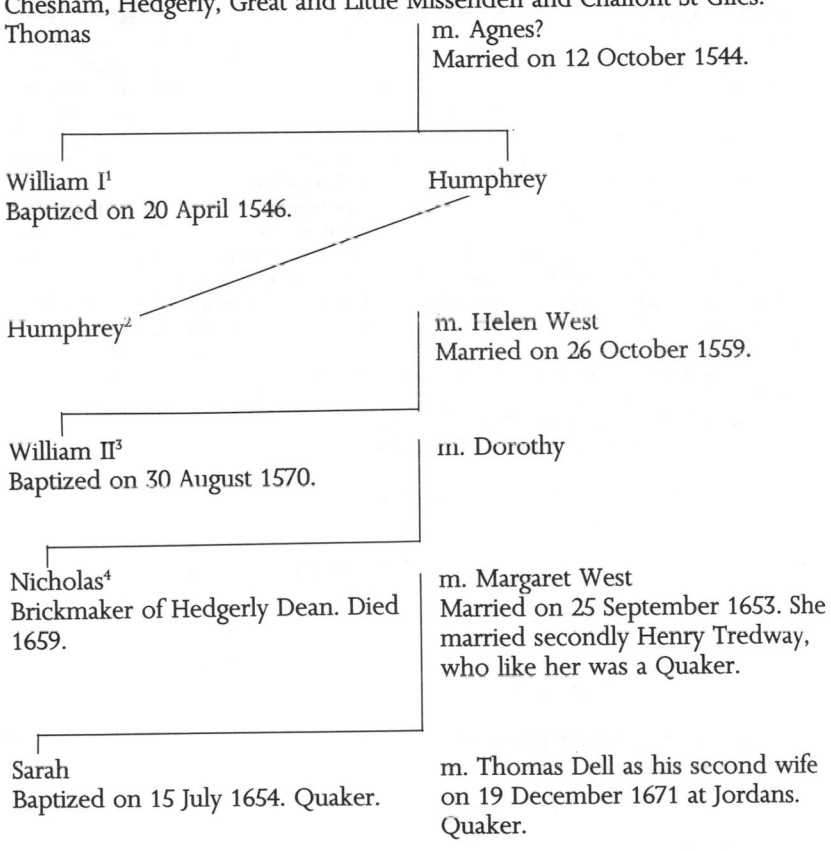

Thomas — m. Agnes? Married on 12 October 1544.

William I[1] Baptized on 20 April 1546. — Humphrey

Humphrey[2] — m. Helen West Married on 26 October 1559.

William II[3] Baptized on 30 August 1570. — m. Dorothy

Nicholas[4] Brickmaker of Hedgerly Dean. Died 1659. — m. Margaret West Married on 25 September 1653. She married secondly Henry Tredway, who like her was a Quaker.

Sarah Baptized on 15 July 1654. Quaker. — m. Thomas Dell as his second wife on 19 December 1671 at Jordans. Quaker.

Sources: Hedgerly and Chalfont St Peter parish registers; Whitley (ed.)., *Church Books*; wills of Randall family: Nicholas, 1613 Bucks. RO D/A/We/25/75, Nicholas, 1659 PRO PROB 11/1659/322.

1 The Hedgerly parish register is defective, and a number of sixteenth-century baptism entries do not name the parents. Amongst these missing entries are those of the parents of five Randall children baptized between 1560 and 1570. They were Thomas baptized 1560, Anthony baptized 1562, Agnes, George (no date for these two), and William baptized 1570. The last named could be a son of William I, or of Humphrey and Helen. No baptism has been found for Humphrey, but he could well be a brother of William I.

2 Alice, baptized on 6 January 1573–4, is the only child in the register whose parents are named as Humphrey and Helen. Between 1576 and 1594 a further eight Randall children were baptized at Hedgerly, all were children of Thomas, but was there only one Thomas Randall in Hedgerly during those eighteen years? The Thomas baptized in 1560 could have been the father of some of the later, although not of the earlier, children.

3 William and Dorothy Randall had the following children: Humphrey baptized 28 February 1601–2, buried 19 December 1653; John baptized 13 November 1603; William baptized 5 January 1605–6; Thomas baptized 20 March 1607–8; Helen baptized 25 April 1610; George baptized 2 April 1615. Humphrey is an uncommon Christian name, so giving this name to his first son suggests that William II was a son of Humphrey and Helen. The naming of his only daughter Helen also reinforces the likelihood of William's proposed parentage. It is not known when William II or Dorothy died, for there is a gap in the Hedgerly register from late 1654 to 1659.

4 In his will, made on 10 May and proved on 28 June 1659, Nicholas Randall mentioned his brother Thomas, his sister Ellen Cooper, and Deborah widow of his deceased brother George. The names Helen and Ellen are interchangeable at this date. It seems almost certain that the children of William II and Dorothy Randall baptized at Hedgerly are the brothers and sister of Nicholas. Another link is that William II, his son Humphrey, and Nicholas were all brickmakers.

Only one other Nicholas Randall is known. He was the son of Mathew of Chalfont St Peter and his wife Margaret, née Nicholas, and was baptized on 12 October 1560. He married twice, but none of his sons were given the name Nicholas. His children were all baptized at Amersham, where both his marriages also took place. When he made his will in 1607 he was living at Coleshill. No link has been found between this man and Nicholas Randall of Hedgerly.

An alternative ancestry for Sarah Randall is as follows:

William   m. Dorothy
Son of William I. Baptized 30 August 1570.

Nicholas   m. Margaret West
                                             Married on 25 September 1653.

Sarah   m. Thomas Dell
Baptized on 15 July 1654.   Married on 19 December 1671.

This alternative genealogy has one less generation than the other, and seems less probable than the first.

The ancestry of Margaret West

Thomas of Chesham[1] Taxed there in 1524. Will 1554.	m. ?
John[2] He had three sons, John, Richard, and Robert, and two daughters.	m. Margaret Deyne Married on 27 May 1564 at Amersham.
John[3] Baptized on 16 November 1567 at Amersham.	m. Joan Stanbrough Married on 23 November 1608 at Hedgerly.
Margaret[4] Baptized 17 January 1627–8. Died 1706.	m. (1) Nicholas Randall Married on 25 September 1653 at Hedgerly. (2) Henry Tredway
Sarah Randall Baptized on 15 July 1654.	m. Thomas Dell Married on 19 December 1671 at Jordans.

Sources: Amersham and Hedgerly parish registers; wills: Thomas West, 1554 Bucks. RO D/A/We/8/40, Nicholas Randall, 1659 PRO PROB 11/1659/322, Margaret Tredway, 1706 PRO PROB 11 Eedes 155.

[1] West is not a Lollard name, but the overseer of Thomas West's will was William Nash and this is a Lollard name.

[2] John's wife bore a Lollard maiden name. All their children were baptized at Little Missenden. John's second son Richard, who was baptized on 24 December 1570, married Cecily Bridges at Little Missenden on 10 June 1599. Their son was baptized there on 10 June 1599, so cannot be the John West who married Joan Stanbrough in 1608.

[3] John and Margaret West's eldest son was John, baptized on 16 November 1567. It is just possible that he is the man who married Joan Stanbrough in 1608, particularly if this was his second marriage. A gap of forty-one years between baptism and wedding seems too long for a first marriage, but too short to fit in another generation.

[4] Margaret and Nicholas Randall had only one child, Sarah, baptized at Hedgerly on 15 July 1654, before Nicholas died in 1659. Nicholas made his will on 10 May 1659 and it was proved on 28 June 1659. He called himself a brickmaker of 'Hugeley' Dean in Farnham Royal. He commended his soul to God 'hoping through Jesus Christ to have a blessed resurrection at the last day'. His daughter Sarah was left £100 to be paid when she reached the age of sixteen or on her marriage day, if that was earlier. Sarah Randall was only seventeen when she married Thomas Dell.

Nicholas mentioned his deceased brother George and his widow Deborah, living in Beaconsfield, as well as his brother Thomas and his sister Ellen Cooper. Margaret Randall was appointed sole executrix of her husband's will, and one of the witnesses was Robert Dell. The date of Margaret Randall's second marriage is not known, and she seems to have had no children by her second husband, Henry Tredway. See the Tredway family for more information about him. Margaret made her will on 31 December 1705 and it was proved on 4 July 1706; she was a widow. This will has no religious preamble. The overseer was Margaret's son-in-law Thomas Dell, and the executrices her granddaughters Rebecca and Mary Dell. When probate was granted they affirmed in the Quaker manner. Their brother Richard was also a legatee.

Index of contemporary names

General index

Abingdon, Berks., widows of, 65–6
Abington, Gt, Cambs.: churchwardens of, 185, 187, 188; nonconformists at, in 1676, 178
Abington, Lt, Cambs., churchwardens of, 185, 187
Affirmation Act of 1696, 382
Aldenham, Herts.: records of school at, 67; teaching reading in school at, 74
alehouses: ballads stuck up in, 253; locations of, in Chiltern Hundreds, 279
Allridge, Nick, 192
Amersham, Bucks., 14, 35, 325; Baptist burial ground at, 383; centre of Lollardy, 21, 107; centre of post-Restoration dissent, 21; entries in churchwardens' accounts for dissenting families, 414, 416; entries in overseers' accounts for dissenting families 414, 416; hamlets of, 289; incomers to, 276; Lollard 'gathered church' at, 6; Lollard groups at, 70, 160; Lollard influence in, 111; Lollard women's meeting at, 146–9; Lollards of, 29, 30, 120; market day of, 327; marriage between dissenters at, 301; nonconformists at, in 1676, 21; Quaker meeting-house at, 21, illustration of, 294; seventeenth-century settlement papers of, 327
Amersham area, reasons for choosing for study, 29–30
Amsterdam, 'Ancient Church' of, 395
Anabaptists, reported by churchwardens, 175
Anderson, Alan, 355
Andover, Wilts., conventicle at, 179
'Anticipation' of 1524, Lollard contributors to, 111

aphorisms, religious content of collections of, 265–6
apprentices, movement of, 310
Archer, Dr Ian, 192
Arden, Forest of, 47; metal industry in, 41
Arnheim, separatist congregation at, 25
Ashwell, Herts., teaching of children paid for by churchwardens, 75
Aubrey, John, 43, 44
autobiographers, spiritual, education of, 66–7
Autolycus, 237
Aylesbury, Bucks., dissenting petty constable at, 371

Babraham, Cambs., single churchwarden at, 185
ballad partners, 270; copyrights acquired by, 265; establishment of, 257; trade of, 81, 83; woodcuts used by, 253–4
ballad sellers: bad reputation of, 235; in city court records, 236; at major fairs, 236
ballads, 389; ABC, 75–6; anti-papist, titles of, 240–1; aphoristic, 241–2; continuing popularity of, 246–7; based on Old Testament stories, popular, 249–50; based on scripture stories, 242–3; best-selling, 84; didactic, 84–5; Familist, 66, 241–2; godly, 18, most popular, 66, picture of popular piety in, 251, varieties of, 240–3, written by Elizabethan puritans, 81, 83; illustrated, 251–5; as instruments of conversion, 271; moralizing, 241–2; parental advice, 269; popular religious, long survival of, 80, 244–5; popularity of, 240; practical advice in, 247; on protestant martyrdom, 269; protestant saints in, 251; Quaker attack on, 253; religious, decline in number of, 243–4;

444

sales appeal of, 251; on saving power
of faith, 242; specialization in trade in,
251; subject matter of, 66, 83–5; trade
in, connected with chapbook trade,
257; used by poor for libels, 81; used
by protestant reformers, 240–3; used
as decoration in cottages and
alehouses, 252–3, 254; used to present
protestant ideas, 264; wide market for,
80; written in Newgate by Anne
Askew, 83

Balsham, Cambs., 15, 390; balance of
power shift in, 220; Baptist meetings
at, 168; books hawked by pedlar at,
66, 236–7; centre of nonconformity
188; churchwardens of 186, 188, 200,
203; post-Restoration will preambles
used at, 203; Quaker meetings at 168;
violation of grave at, significance of,
208, 209, 221, 232–5; *see also* Familists,
of Balsham

Baptists: at alehouses and fairs, 376;
begging at St Neots, 370; evidence for
possible links with Lollards, 288;
excommunicated for exogamous
marriage, 362; General economic
status of, 334; insistence on
endogamous marriage by, 361–2;
involved in football match, 376; as
manorial jurors, 384; meetings in
south-east Cambs., 167–8; occupations
of, 337; Open, poverty of, 334, 336;
presented by Cambs. churchwardens,
178; social background of, 5; social
integration of, 20–1, 386; as witnesses
to non-dissenting wills, 379–80

bark for tanning, 62

Barrowists, 395

Bartlow, Cambs., single churchwarden
at, 185

Barton, Cambs., report by
churchwardens on non-collection of
fines, 172

Baxter, Richard, 26, 27, 68, 74, 176, 266;
book bought by father of, 255–6; book
sold to father of by chapman, 49;
comments on Quaker meetings at Bull
and Mouth Inn, 286; communion not
celebrated by at Bridgnorth, 91;
description of weavers reading by, 46;
home of visited by ballad seller, 235,
243; meditation for communicants
written by, 92; monthly communions
established by, 89

Beccles, Suff., women members of
Independent Church, 301

Bedford Open Baptist Church, 88;

poverty of members of, 76–7, 334,
336; wealthy member of, 345

Bedfordshire: composite mean hearth
ownership in, 336; nonconformists in,
5; Open Baptists in, 42;
post-Restoration dissenters in, 18–21;
surname survival in, 312, 313, 314

beds: made for London, in inventory of
Wendover joiner, 63; to let in Chiltern
Hundreds, location of, 280

beliefs: Calvinist orthodox, 10;
dissenting, lack of documentary
evidence for continuity of, in Bucks.,
304–5; orthodox, difficult to trace, 10;
of post-Restoration dissenters, 99;
religious, diffusion of, in rural society,
64, social spread of, 2–3, spectrum of,
7

believers, conforming, 7

Berkshire: Lollards in, 5; places where
Lollards found, 108

'better sort', dissenting, economic
profiles of, 342–5

Bible: seen as sole source of salvation by
Lollards, 107; stories from, in ballads,
242–3

Birdbrook, Essex, Lollards at, 167, 397,
398

Bledlow, Bucks., Presbyterian
conventicle at, 332

Book of Sports, 28

book trade, origins of small godly, 76, 78

books: affordability of, 256; carriers of,
135–6, 150, delivery to provincial
towns by London carriers, 238; cheap,
distribution network for, 69–70, 78,
238–9; godly, 259, 261–2, market for,
256; educational, 259, 261; Familist, in
library of George Fox, 289, possibly
sold in Balsham by pedlar, 236, 237;
godly, distributed by carriers, 285;
heretical, 57, distribution of, 237;
owners of, 47, 49, 51, 53, 57, 71, 106,
285; prices of, 256; published on
continent, 236; published for sale by
chapmen, 256; Quaker, distributed by
carriers, 237; Roman Catholic, sold by
travelling stationer, 237; sold by
chapmen, 70; stocked by Cambridge
bookseller in 1578, 258–9, 261–2;
stocked by Shrewsbury bookseller,
237; *see also* carriers

book-selling, by destitute vagrants, 65

Booth, Charles, 7–8

Boreham, Essex: high turnover of
surnames at, 314, 317; witchcraft
accusations at, 319